Canada: The War of the Conquest

Guy Frégault

Canada: the war of the conquest

Translated by MARGARET M. CAMERON

Toronto   Oxford University Press   1969

PUBLICATION OF THIS BOOK WAS ASSISTED BY
THE CANADA COUNCIL

The French-language edition of this book,
La Guerre de la conquête,
was published by Fides in 1955

Printed in Canada by
JOHN DEYELL LIMITED

Contents

List of Maps

Acknowledgements

The author wishes to express his gratitude to the following institutions, all of which allowed him to consult their collections and facilitated his research in every possible way: the Library of Congress, the New York Public Library, the Boston Public Library, the Widener and Houghton Libraries of Harvard University, the Massachusetts Historical Society, the Public Archives of Canada, the Bibliothèque Nationale du Québec, and the Library of the University of Montreal.

He wishes to thank the Social Science Research Council, which awarded him a study grant for the summer of 1953.

It is a pleasure to acknowledge here his special debt of gratitude to the companion of his scholarly explorations, Lilianne Rinfret-Frégault. Not only did she assist in the task of reading the texts upon which this study is based, but she typed the manuscript, revised it with great care, and made many valuable suggestions for improvements and corrections.

Preface

The war that resulted in the capitulation of Canada in 1760 and its cession to Great Britain three years later is the most important event in Canadian history. When the war broke out there were two Americas, one French and the other English. When it ended, with the defeat of Canada, the first of these Americas disappeared. This outcome meant more than an extension of the area marked in red on the map of the American continent. Less obvious results were, on the one hand, an upheaval whose extent has not yet been measured, and, on the other, a renaissance of which the tremendous repercussions continue to astound us.

The conquest of Canada heralds the second birth of British North America. In 1763 she was a young giant. Twenty years later she would change her name and claim her place among the nations. Her new name did not, however, change her origin. A British creation, the United States of America would continue to be an essentially British power. Henceforth there were two Englands, one whose centre was situated in northern Europe and the other which was to grow in size and importance until it came to be identified, more or less, with the New World. When the first of these two powers, limited by the conditions imposed by geography, conditions to which she owed her fortune, became too small to bear her hegemony alone, the second, after a period of phenomenal growth, took upon shoulders that had never bent under the weight of major defeat the heavy burden of world supremacy.

All this would be possible because the American question had been settled, once and for all, in the third quarter of the eighteenth century. A hundred years earlier, when Louis XIV was rising to power and when the Restoration had brought to an end England's first experiment in revolution, the history of the New World might have taken a different direction. At that time, if France had realized the value of the prize at stake, she could have assured her supremacy in America; but she allowed herself to be hopelessly outdistanced. In 1760 it was no longer possible for her to recover the ground she had lost; her last garrisons were disarmed and sent back to France, and New France gave place to a new England. Whereas the British world had added to its European base an immense field of action in America, the French world, shorn of its American wing and confined within its European boundaries, had no longer scope for those broad movements which were to be, henceforth, the requisite of real power.

The point of departure of England's victory is then to be found in successful colonization. If British civilization has exercised a lasting influence in America, it is because England created there a number of communities in her own image, if not exactly like her. But had not France done the same thing? France had done the same thing, but not to the same degree; and therein lay Canada's tragedy. Between Canada and the English colonies the great difference, as we have shown elsewhere,[1] was not one of kind but of numbers. All the basic elements of an English colony are to be found in Canada, but on a smaller scale. Nothing is more like a British settlement in America than a French community on the same continent. Similar preoccupations attended their birth and development, and in each case an essentially similar foundation supported a pyramid of interests. Each colony, French or English, had its own political framework, its economic organization, its social structure, and each was borne along on the current of its spiritual life. In each the civil administration was modelled—closely in the case of New France, more freely in that of British America—on a European model. Finally, each formed part of an empire which lived on it in some small degree and on which it lived.

Thus we see before us two communities, almost identical in formation. They also cherished similar aspirations, of which the most important was, for each, to bring the most desirable part of America within its own sphere of influence and exploitation. It would be a serious error to see in this ambition nothing more than unbridled lust. One block could not leave the other free to add to itself the richest and best situated parts of the continent without placing itself in a position of inferiority and fatally compromising its own destiny. The stake was opulence or poverty, freedom or servitude, life or death. The adversaries knew this, and said so. They recognized each other for what they were, irreconcilable enemies. Each, with terrible clarity of vision, perceived that its normal development must be built on the ruins of the other. The carnivorous beast has no choice; he must devour. For there could be no question of the victor's being satisfied with anything less than complete victory. This fact was not always clearly perceived in Europe, where the balance of power

[1] *La Société canadienne sous le régime français* (Ottawa, 1954).

made it impossible for any nation to entertain the hope of annihilating another; but in America the victor could not rest until he had exploited to the utmost the advantages placed in his hands by the fortunes of war. Hence it came about that Canada was not only defeated, but destroyed.

When the British in America, unlike many of their compatriots in the mother country, declared that the conquest of Canada was for them an imperative need, they were right, and the conquest resulted in a defeat at once military and political, economic, social, and cultural. The defeat was no more economic than cultural, no more social than political; it was all these at once and in the same degree. The disaster did not end with the substitution of one flag for another; it set in train a deep and complex transformation of which the immediate and visible evidences were the dismemberment of New France, the transfer of Canada to the British empire, and, with the royal proclamation of 7 October 1763, the birth of the 'Province of Quebec'.

Within the space of ten years a momentous change had been accomplished. In 1754 there was a Canada. In 1759 Canada still existed, reduced, crippled, but a living, united whole. In 1764 there were still Canadians, but there was no Canada, just as since 1713 there had been Acadians but no Acadia. The disintegration of the country might be compared with that of an army. An army is a body of combatants whose effectiveness depends upon a highly complex organization. The army can be beaten, decimated, without being disorganized. It can also be defeated without being exterminated. In the latter case, soldiers survive, but the army no longer exists. Such was the situation in which Canadians found themselves after the conquest.

To reduce the people of Canada to this pass had not been an easy task; the war that brought about the conquest was long and bitter, and the ardour that animated Canada's resistance throughout the struggle is some measure of the country's vitality and will to live, of its realization and acceptance of the need to resist the forces leagued together to destroy it. The people of Canada did not allow themselves to be conquered; their resistance was crushed by the weight of numbers. Should we sing the praises of those heroes? Their heroism would be a tempting theme for rhetorical effusions, but such effusions would not explain the fact. Canada did exactly what any other society would have done in a similar case. It resisted conquest with the same energy that every living organism displays in the face of death.

In its many aspects this conflict presents an almost inexhaustible field of study. Historians have already told the story of battles from which we may still draw lessons of strategy, if not of tactics. The conflict could still be considered with profit from the political angle, and it is our impression that its economic history remains to be written. We thought, however, that our attention might more usefully be turned in another direction. Although the history of a war must necessarily be 'military' history, our purpose has been less to recount battles than to define objectives, while at the same time keeping constantly in view the prime objective of the hostilities: the conquest. In the minds of the British Americans, who knew what they wanted, and of the most clear-sighted among the population of the mother country, there was no doubt as to the end to be attained: it was the elimination of Canada. This soon becomes apparent if one reads the declarations of leaders, observes the movement of public opinion, and follows the chain of logic linking the successive campaigns. Nor can one measure the import of the conquest without first examining both the motives and methods of those who achieved it and the reactions and subsequent destiny of those who suffered it. Thus it becomes evident that the object of our investigation is also that of the conflict we set out to examine.

Hence the title we have chosen for this volume: *Canada: The War of the Conquest*. But why this new designation? Were there not already enough names to identify this great fact of history? There were indeed enough, and too many, a sure sign that no one of them was quite the right one. The name 'Seven Years' War' corresponds reasonably well to the European phase of hostilities, but it is difficult to adjust it to the duel to the death in which New France and British America, with the support of their European seconds, were engaged. Some better name had to be found, if only because, in America, the Seven Years' War did not last seven years. Abbé Casgrain was conscious of the problem and suggested a solution with the phrase 'la guerre du Canada'. But there was more than one 'Canada War'. Professor Lawrence Henry Gipson's title, *The Great War for the Empire*, is an admirable choice—but only from the British point of view; and the same may be said of the sub-titles of the two volumes in which the eminent American historian relates the story of the war: *The Years of Defeat (1754-1758)* and *The Victorious Years (1758-1760)*. His years of defeat were years of victory for Canada, while his victorious years were those during which the defeat of Canada was consummated.

One last word. Notes have been added for the benefit of the historians —those curious, meticulous, and sometimes learned readers, who may like to see the texts that are the bases of the author's statements and to judge for themselves whether his conclusions are justified by documentary evidence. The notes, which have been kept as brief and succinct as possible, refer only to source material and to texts that may facilitate further investigation. They may be disregarded by readers for whom such questions have no interest.

Maps

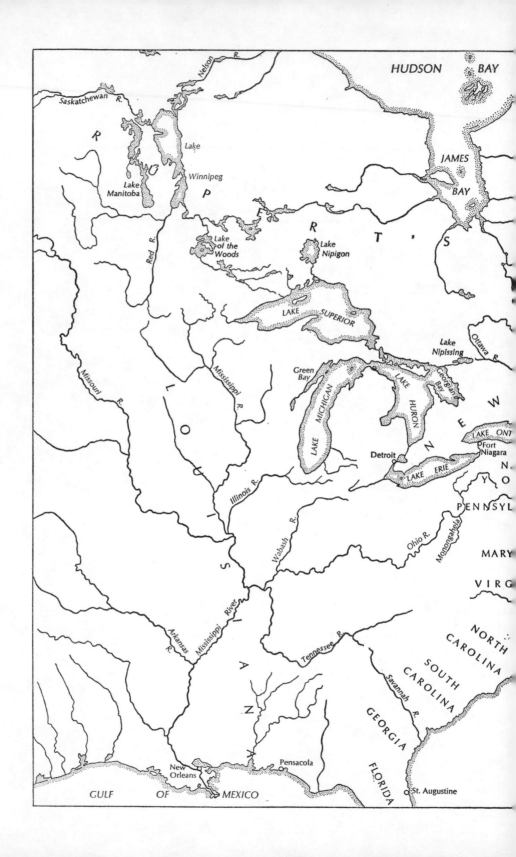

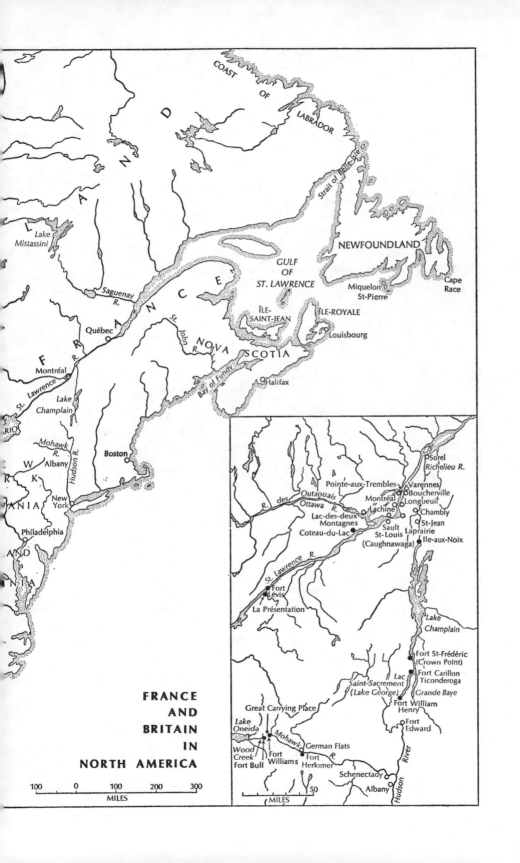

COAST OF LABRADOR

Strait of Belle Isle

NEWFOUNDLAND

Lake Mistassini

GULF OF ST. LAWRENCE

Saguenay R.

Cape Race

Miquelon St-Pierre

ÎLE-SAINT-JEAN

ILE-ROYALE

Québec

St. John R.

NOVA SCOTIA

Louisbourg

Montréal

St. Lawrence R.

Lake Champlain

Bay of Fundy

Halifax

RIO

Mohawk R.

Hudson R.

Albany

Boston

W

R K

ANIA

New York

Philadelphia

AND

N I A

FRANCE AND BRITAIN IN NORTH AMERICA

100   0   100   200   300
MILES

Sorel
Richelieu R.

Pointe-aux-Trembles

Varennes
Boucherville
Longueuil

R. des Outaouais
Ottawa R.

Montréal
Lachine

Chambly

Lac-des-deux Montagnes

St-Jean

Coteau-du-Lac

Sault St-Louis (Caughnawaga)

Laprairie
Ile-aux-Noix

St. Lawrence R.

Fort Lévis

La Présentation

Lake Champlain

Fort St-Frédéric (Crown Point)

Fort Carillon Ticonderoga

Lac Saint-Sacrement (Lake George)

Grande Baye

Great Carrying Place

Fort William Henry

Lake Oneida

Mohawk R.

German Flats

Fort Edward

Wood Creek
Fort Bull

Fort Williams

Fort Herkimer

Schenectady

Hudson River

Albany

50
MILES

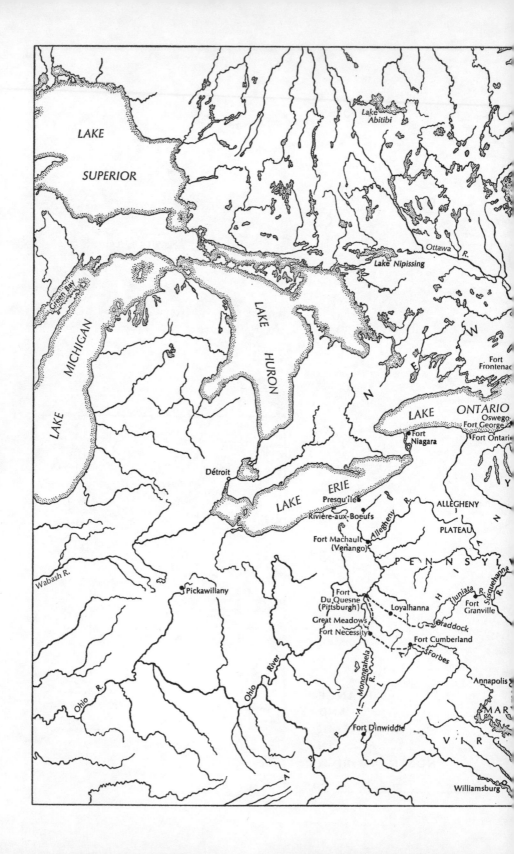

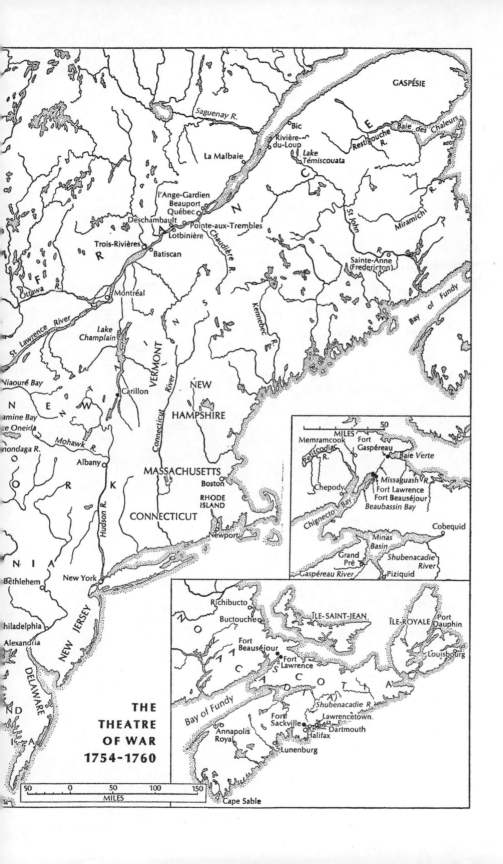

GASPÉSIE

Saguenay R.

Bic

Rivière-
du-Loup

*Lake
Témiscouata*

Baie des Chaleurs

Restigouche R.

La Malbaie

Miramichi

l'Ange-Gardien
Beauport
Québec
Deschambault
Pointe-aux-Trembles
Lotbinière

St. John R.

Trois-Rivières
Batiscan

Chaudière R.

Sainte-Anne
(Fredericton)

Ottawa R.

Montréal

Bay of Fundy

St. Lawrence River

*Lake
Champlain*

Kennebec R.

Niaouré Bay

Carillon

VERMONT

NEW
HAMPSHIRE

Connecticut River

amine Bay
ce Oneida

Mohawk R.

nondaga R.

Albany

MASSACHUSETTS

Boston

RHODE
ISLAND

CONNECTICUT

Newport

50
MILES

Memramcook
Fort
Gaspéreau

Baie Verte

Petitcodiac R.

Chepody

Missaguash R.
Fort Lawrence
Fort Beauséjour
Beaubassin Bay

Cobequid

Chignecto Bay

*Minas
Basin*

*Shubenacadie
River*

Grand
Pré

Piziquid

Gaspéreau River

Hudson R.

Bethlehem

New York

hiladelphia

Alexandria

NEW JERSEY

DELAWARE

ND

Richibucto

Buctouche

ÎLE-SAINT-JEAN

ÎLE-ROYALE
Port
Dauphin

Fort
Beauséjour
Fort
Lawrence

Louisbourg

Bay of Fundy

Shubenacadie R.

Fort
Sackville
Lawrencetown
Dartmouth
Halifax

Annapolis
Royal

Lunenburg

**THE
THEATRE
OF WAR
1754-1760**

50   0   50   100   150
MILES

Cape Sable

Part One

THE ADVERSARIES

Chapter I

Sentiments, Ideas, Facts

The War of the Conquest, which gave a new and decisive direction to the history of Canada and influenced to a marked degree the evolution of North America, is much better known in its results than in its causes. If the war had not taken place, or if it had had another ending, the nation-state called Canada would not now exist. The name, carried over from an earlier age, would probably survive, but the country itself would have neither the same inhabitants nor the same geography, neither the same economy, the same political and social structure, nor even the same cultural expression. Moreover, it is highly probable that the English colonies in America would not have won their independence at the time and in the way in which they did win it if Canada had not been defeated in 1760 and incorporated three years later into the British empire.

These consequences are so impressive in extent and importance that they have obscured the causes of the conflict from which they derive, and for this reason the consequences themselves are often understood only in a very general way. If one tries to measure their mass, one is faced with the difficulty of determining their substance—or rather their composition, for here nothing is simple. How can one define, except in the vaguest terms, repercussions whose first cause is not fully understood? It is clearly impossible to have a proper understanding of the situation resulting from the War of the Conquest if the causes of the conflict itself remain obscure. And those causes were in the men who were pitted against each other—Canadians and British Americans, French and English—with their ambitions and their resources, their fears and their pride, their ideas and their aspirations; in the men, or rather in the societies, since it was not individuals who confronted one another, but communities, for each of which it had become imperative to achieve a certain end, to maintain a certain position, to break a certain resistance, to assure its own development.

To seek causes in men is first of all to question and to listen. What have the men who lived through it to tell us of a gigantic conflict that steeped the world in blood through a period of almost ten years, at the full tide of the enlightenment and in an age that deemed itself realistic and, more than any preceding one, imbued with respect for reason? How did those men see the forces urging them into conflict? For they did not simply butcher one another without knowing what they were doing nor why they were doing it. Was the cause of the clash to be found in 'hereditary' hatreds? In irreconcilable conceptions of the person or—and this amounts to the same thing—of the state? They believed it was to be found in all these things, and in many others, those men who in many respects are so far from us, in many others so near, who speak a language very like ours, although they sometimes give to the words we use a sense very different from the one we attach to them—those men from whom no difference or opposition can separate us; for we meet on the common and fundamental ground of the will to live. In order to live they re-sorted, as we do, to time-honoured and violent means.

'It is in the blood of Englishmen to hate Frenchmen and to wish them ill.' These words, written twenty years before the fall of Canada, appear in a memoir that found its way into the office of France's minister of marine. 'And I confess,' continues the anonymous author, 'that in their case this sentiment has some foundation in reason. Enamoured as they are of their so-called liberty, they consider us the only nation powerful enough to cause them to lose it and in a position to do so . . . So they are constantly preoccupied with the need to undermine our power.'[1] The man is off to a bad start with his stereotyped and confusing image of Englishmen with hatred for Frenchmen in their blood. But the explanation he proposes goes much deeper. In order to apprehend its full significance, we have only to translate it into language that might be used by an author writing a similar memoir today. The argument would follow approximately the following lines: the English are attached to political ideas and institutions which, though obviously based in error, are more liberal than ours. Since we are, and they know that we are, the only state capable of endangering their liberty, their constant effort is to weaken us.

After the outbreak of war, the tone becomes more violent. In 1755 a French propagandist launched the following tirade: 'I am quite willing to concede this to England, that there is no nation comparable to her in anything related to the understanding of commerce; no nation so skilful in developing flourishing colonies; no nation that derives greater profit from its own products and from imported raw material; no nation that has carried the glory of its navigation into such distant seas. But, on the other hand, never was there a nation so self-interested, so greedy, so

[3]

ambitious, so ready to violate the law of nations when she considers such action necessary for the expansion of her trade.' Great Britain, 'a trading nation', subordinates everything to that which can bring in profits. Turned in upon herself, she holds herself aloof from, and above, the rest of mankind. Terence's *Homo sum* . . . awakens no echo in her sensibilities; for his maxim her people have substituted this egoistical formula: '*I am an Englishman, and for me anyone who is not English is as if he did not exist.*' Such an attitude betrays profound disdain for other men, and it is not surprising to see the English in Acadia 'distinguishing themselves by acts of hostility and depredation more worthy of a gang of bandits than of civilized men.' One can expect anything from a people 'that so despises other peoples that it is convinced there is no law of nations binding them to it and which it is bound to respect.' Grasping, materialistic, and unscrupulous, England seeks to raise herself on the ruins of the independence of the states of Europe. 'What a misfortune for Europe that there is an England, if to fulfil her high destiny, England must give the law to Europe!' If this predatory nation strives to bring down France, it is because France stands in the way of her ambitions. And the tragedy of Europe is also that of America, where the two rivals confront one another: 'The same fate that made them neighbours in the old world has chosen to bring them together in the new, in order to pit them constantly one against the other and to fan the undying hatred that has always divided them.'[2] If we disregard the hackneyed idea of 'eternal hatred' from which French thought seems powerless to free itself, we can retain the valid core of the author's analysis. For the English people domination was a means of expanding the national society they had created. In 1756 Louis xv, realizing that this was the mainspring of their policy in Europe and America, denounced 'that spirit of general domination which they would like to extend in the two worlds.'[3]

These declarations are all selected from one side of a dialogue in which the English also took part; what did they have to say? The first important engagement of the War of the Conquest took place in the Ohio country on 3 July 1754, when Coulon de Villiers drove Washington out of Fort Necessity after having subjected the defenders of this fortified camp to 'outrage and violence' and forced its commander to accept humiliating and 'insulting' terms of capitulation. England at once called Europe to witness that in their quarrel with the English the French were the aggressors, and that their aggression in this instance was obviously premeditated.[4] After this grave incident, the governor of South Carolina, James Glen, addressed the legislative assembly of the province. Anxious to restore the morale of his compatriots, badly shaken by this defeat, and to arouse in the colony's representatives an indignation equal to his own, the orator chose a patriotic theme for his discourse. 'If the subjects of an absolute prince' could show such courage in the service of 'their master . . . what spirit and zeal should inspire the sons of liberty' in the defence of their rights! For them it was a question of defending their constitution as well as their territory. 'We enjoy the happiest and most perfect frame of government in the world; it is the envy of all nations; the language of all nations is: *Who would not be a Briton?* By this constitution, this colony, from small beginnings, has, in a short space of time, become very considerable, and highly beneficial to Great Britain.' Such is the meaning of empire: union of ideals and community of interests. The governor goes on to evoke history: 'When our fathers came from thence to settle here, they brought with them the laws of the mother country as their birthright; and a glorious inheritance they are. They brought with them that inestimable jewel, the privilege of enacting laws for their good government, without which they could have made no progress; this privilege I hope we shall ever possess.'[5]

In English eyes, Frenchmen, victims of despotism and poverty, looked like barbarians, Goths and Vandals who, driven by hunger, invaded peaceful, ill-defended countries, and attacked populations dedicated to the arts of peace.[6] And what of Canadians? An English cleric, whose patriotic spirit impelled him to set himself up as a historian, grouped Canadians and Indians together as 'the true French savages.'[7] A political writer in New York agreed that Canadians were indeed true savages. 'They delight in blood; and in barbarity exceed, if possible, the very savages themselves.'[8]

The tone should not surprise readers who know what can be written in time of war or of armed peace, and it is perhaps idle to look for analogies between the troubled age we know through personal experience and that of the great conflict of two centuries ago. Each age has its own atmosphere. But it is wise to remember that the policy of nation-states has not changed in two centuries, and that in many of its aspects the conflict of which the War of the Conquest is the most important phase seems quite familiar to us. Hostilities were preceded, and for two years accompanied, by the generally stormy deliberations of an international commission, which settled nothing and which served no other purpose than to provide a tribune for the propaganda of the two great powers of the age, France and England. The diplomats pursued their negotiations while the war developed at sea and was the occasion of important movements of troops in America.[9] The French government represented the invasion of Menorca as a police operation carried out in reprisal for British 'acts of piracy'. A French minister considered a declaration of war a 'formality'.[10] In order to justify his country's capture of hundreds of French vessels before war was formally declared, an Englishman maintained that facts count for more than the gestures of protocol, and that the French had effectively declared war by attacking English settlements in America.[11] It took France a month to reply to England's declaration of war. The French correspondent of a Dutch periodical considered this attitude surprising but not inexplicable: 'This extraordinary procedure,' he wrote, '. . . is another example of the policy of our minister. Concentrating his whole attention on the task of overpowering his enemy, he does not pause for formalities that he considers vain.'[12]

We observe also that this was a world war, affecting the four continents then known. As it developed it revealed the extreme complexity of international relations. Isolation, as an intelligent observer remarked, became an illusion. 'The bonds of interest between states . . . form a sort of chain whose links are so firmly joined that no one state can be shaken without all the others immediately feeling the shock to a greater or lesser degree.' Atrocities perpetrated in the course of hostilities seemed to suggest that the world was once more plunged into the dark ages. 'Never, in truth, since the age of the Goths, the Huns, and the Vandals, were so many armies assembled at one time in one theatre of war, never did armies fight so bitterly, ravage countries with such fury or display such lack of humanity as they pillaged their unfortunate inhabitants.'[13] In America the war was no less cruel than in Europe. It was perhaps even more cruel. It brought about the massive deportation of a whole population with the expulsion of the Acadians. After the fall of Louisbourg, Amherst, instigated by political motives, ordered the destruction of the settlements on Île-Royale (Cape Breton). He realized the gravity of such an act, and his recommendation that the operation be carried out 'in a quiet way' betrays an uneasy conscience.[14] In England at least one critic spoke out against this almost 'sacrilegious' spirit of devastation, which he likened to the 'frenzy of the Goths'.[15] On the other side, Canadians and their native allies raided the English frontier settlements year after year, massacring, mutilating, and torturing men, women, and children. Bougainville and Montcalm were horrified by these raids; Bougainville made a point of dissociating himself from the Canadians and he was even artless enough to believe, apparently on the assurance of the gentlemen of the opposing army, that, when Canada was defeated, there would be 'two capitulations: one for the French troops and the other for the Canadians.'[16]

French and English accused one another of barbarism in accordance with the immemorial custom of civilized countries in time of war, and we can take at face value neither the praises that both nations sing of their own virtues nor their eloquent condemnation of the vices of their adversaries. Everything would be so simple if wars were fought between good and evil. A contemporary observer summed up the real situation very

[6]

neatly. When states have recourse to arms, he wrote, it is the usual thing for each to accuse the other 'of perfidy, craft and premeditated perjury.' But what do these eloquent declarations prove? That 'Every nation has the press at command in their own territories and the cause is bad indeed which cannot be defended in a paper war.'[17] Even when they wield a pen rather than a sword, the antagonists are concerned not so much to think as to defeat an adversary, not to understand but to fight. As a result their evidence, while it cannot be rejected as worthless, does not touch the essential facts of the case. It does not say that Frenchmen and Englishmen have in common a great many more ideas, traditions, and habits than they are willing to recognize. Although these two great peoples flatter themselves that they are quite different from each other, and emphasize—with a vanity more fitting in members of a primitive clan than in a modern nation—the elements that distinguish them and in which they recognize signs of indisputable superiority, the truth is that their resemblances are deeper, and incomparably more important, than the differences in behaviour and ideas in which they take so much pride. At the time of the War of the Conquest, France and England presented two more or less original expressions of one western civilization.

Both were nation-states. Local patriotisms had not been stifled in Britain any more than in France, but they had been checked. In this respect the role of Scottish leaders and Scottish troops in America provides a significant example. James Murray, who commanded the army of occupation in Quebec in 1759 and 1760 before his appointment as governor of the conquered province, was an assimilated Scot. Both Britain and France were nation-states and both were monarchies; different, certainly, since one presented itself as an absolute and the other as a constitutional monarchy. But without seeking to minimize it, we may ask wherein exactly this difference lay. After having lived for two centuries under an absolute monarchy and survived a certain number of political crises, England, in the course of her evolution, had reached a new formula for royal power, a formula better adapted to the development of her social structure and for this reason subtler, more effective, and more harmoniously tuned to her collective life than was the case with the French monarchy. In France the mechanism of the monarchy needed to be readjusted, simplified, and cleaned, so that its gears might mesh with those of the new force, the bourgeoisie, building up pressure in the very centre of French society. The British state had found its direction and was moving with its age; the French state, still imposing in its massive power, was behind the times. The deepest difference between the two monarchies, the difference that explains the growing dissimilarity between their institutions, is perhaps that one allowed itself to be outstripped by events, whereas the other kept up with them. It is worth noting that the space between the revolution of 1688 and the outbreak of the War of the Conquest was hardly more than two generations.

In the religious sphere both nations were traditionally Christian, although France had maintained her link with the Catholic church while England had long since brought her religion within the dimensions of her island. But differences in religion, important in the case of persons, who are endowed with conscience, do not affect states, which, for all practical purposes, have no conscience. Careful reflection leads one to conclude that for both states, faith meant faith in their own power. In the world of ideas and culture, minds on both sides of the Channel bore the mark of the scientific revolution which, since the end of the preceding century, had completely changed the intellectual perspectives of western nations and given them a common denominator of 'modernity'.[18] The intellectuals, English and French alike, who gave the age its tone, those who made a lasting contribution to European thought, were united in worship of reason, allegiance to 'humanitarian' ideals, and faith in progress.

Finally, the economic structure of the two countries was similar in essentials: both were capitalist countries, both were imbued with respect for 'trade'—a wide term embracing notably what we now call industry—and carried it on with a passion that sometimes came very close to ferocity. The elevation of trade was reflected in a corresponding rise in the status of the trading class, and representatives of the bourgeoisie were now to be found in every sphere of society: in government, on the bench, in the army, and of course among the aristocracy, where it was agreed that, as Madame de Sévigné had said, gold crowns were 'of good lineage', even when they constituted the dowry of a low-born daughter of trade. The middle class, already rich, was growing still richer as it met the need of the state for larger and larger supplies of money. England was ruled by the aristocracy of trade and finance in conjunction with the aristocracy of birth, to which it was linked by business interests and family ties. A reaction taking shape in France was to develop and to increase steadily in momentum as the old régime hastened to its fall. At the beginning of the War of the Conquest, an aristocrat of the old school, the chevalier d'Arc, denounced the omnipotence that money had achieved and at the same time the intrusion of commerce, the means by which money multiplies, into every sphere of society. Pronouncing roundly that the monarchy 'can have too much money', he declared war on personal wealth and on the luxury engendered by it. 'Is not trade the source whence luxury draws the venom it injects into the wounds it has itself inflicted, and renders them incurable?'[19] The vehemence of his reaction is proportionate to the importance of the place the bourgeoisie had assumed in French society.

[8]

This is not an attempt to portray a British France or a French England. It must be recognized, however, that these two nations had in common a basic civilization—the word connotes a living complex of spiritual forces and material elements—much broader than the differences in character that distinguished them. In any case, they undoubtedly nursed similar ambitions. In the war just beginning, there were no crusaders in either camp, either in Europe or in America.

On this side of the Atlantic it was a test of strength between colonies. And since colonial societies tend naturally to model themselves on those of their respective mother countries, the community of civilization apparent in the European peoples opposing one another was also reflected in the American adversaries. Canadians fought, not in order to be or to remain different from Anglo-Americans, but because they were resolved to be masters in their own country, masters of their economy, their political organization, their society; not in order to avoid becoming American (they were, though in their own way, just as American as their British neighbours), but in order to prevent the dismemberment of their economy, their political organization, their society. They were not defending touching and rather ridiculous 'inborn qualities', which the nineteenth century was naive enough to discover in them; they were fighting for existence. And since they were endowed with normal intelligence, they did not conceive the stupid notion—later to be conceived for them—of expecting from the enemy 'freedom to be themselves'. What they expected, and they expected it from victory, was freedom to be.[20]

The pursuit of the cause of the war through a crude analysis of the psychology of the peoples involved in it would then lead us into a blind alley. Such preoccupations can be left to astrologers and soothsayers strayed by mistake into the study of history. Nor is it particularly surprising, or even useful, to know that at the time each adversary painted his opponent as the personification of bad faith, despotism, cruelty, and materialism. The conflict was not primarily one of ideologies. Even when ideas and ideals were paraded, they were a screen for something quite simple. Here were two societies fighting to acquire what they could not acquire in any other way, and repelling what they could only repel by force. They were fighting to dominate and to avoid domination, partial or complete. At the time at which we have arrived, the economic aspect of the struggle had assumed paramount importance. One British observer admitted candidly that, in spite of the sincere desire for conciliation with which the courts of Versailles and St James's appeared to be imbued, the grave difficulties at the root of the rivalry between the French and British colonies were not susceptible of peaceful settlement; for 'this is a commercial dispute, which is not so easily determined as a political quarrel.'[21]

We must be careful, however, not to oversimplify the nature of the prize at stake. It is of course true that it contained economic elements, but it was not, and could not be, exclusively economic. It is only in books—and especially in mediocre books—that economic activity appears in isolation, divorced from the realities of life. Consider, for example, Virginia, New York, Canada: these are economic and at the same time political units, each forming an integral part of a great economic and political organism, the French or the British empire. The institutions of the empire, its needs, its markets, its credit, its industrial development and plant all affect the colony's economy, its prosperity, the direction of its growth, and its aggressiveness. And within each colony, population, wealth, power, and prestige are distributed in such a way as to give to that particular society its own peculiar structure and balance. Each colony has frontiers whose defence, easier or more difficult as the case may be, involves strategic considerations. Thus all elements are linked together: politics, economics, society, geography, government, business, social classes, parties, interest groups. Touch any one activity or function and all the others respond. Why? Because you have touched man, the human individual, at once provider and citizen, workman and fighter, who holds fast to ideas not entirely his own but fed by his experience. Consequently, although the war that was about to begin was not an ideological war, nor an economic conflict, nor a political quarrel, but all these at once, ideas too would fight.

Ideas would wave like flags over the opposing camps. The English took their stand under the banner of liberty. The king of France could make the following declaration: 'In my person alone resides the sovereign power, of which the essence is the spirit of counsel, wisdom and reason . . . to me alone belongs the legislative power, independent and entire . . . public order emanates from me; I am its supreme guardian . . .'[22] England would not have allowed George II to talk in this way. She despised France for bowing under such despotism. It is easy to discover the sources of her conception of liberty as it was defined by a London journalist. It sprang on the one hand from the popular philosophy of the day and on the other from the constitutional tradition of the nation. The tone of the article is very modern and rather conservative, reasonable and seductive: 'Our state or commonwealth, as I believe all others originally were, is founded on principles of liberty: no people were slaves from the beginning. Liberty is founded upon the equal balance of power in the body politic; for whatever the constitution of a state may be, the weaker part will always be oppressed by the over-powerful.'[23]

This doctrine was as familiar to British American as to the people of England. The theme presented in the London paper was developed in a New York periodical by an author whose clarity of expression matches his deep understanding of the theory: 'The British Government, in imitation of which the constitutions of our colonies are generally formed (*mutatis mutandis*), is neither a monarchy, or the arbitrary government of one man, like that of France; nor an aristocracy, or the government of the nobles, like that of Venice, nor a democracy, or the government of the populace, like that of Holland; but it is the quintessence of all these; it . . . adopts what is good from each of them without their respective inconveniences.'[24] Americans, like Englishmen, esteem themselves free, while Canadians are slaves by 'the nature of their government'.[25] The cult of liberty was as firmly established in British America as in Great Britain. A New York weekly exclaims over this special privilege vouchsafed to the British peoples: 'What is the glory of the British constitution more than that of the French but LIBERTY? . . . But if once LIBERTY is lost, there will be no difference between an English and a French government.'[26]

In France too propagandists sang the praises of liberty; but the word as used by French writers designated a reality of international politics rather than a constitutional principle. In 1755 a brochure published in Bâle in French and Italian expressed the views of the court of Versailles on the motives inspiring the conduct of Great Britain in America: 'It would be wilful blindness not to see that the first object of the English, in the troubles recently provoked, is to rid themselves of the obstacles that France can put in their way. After that will come, successively, the turn of Spain and of any other nations that have possessions in America and that refuse to bow their head under the yoke. It is by the destruction of liberty and independence in America that they propose to achieve their object of dictating the law to Europe.'[27]

It would have been child's play for Frenchmen to expose the threat to American 'liberty' inherent in British imperialism. If they had troubled to look, they would have found a rich source of arguments in the British press of the New World. In 1755 the *Maryland Gazette* pointed out one of the great advantages that the reduction of the French colonies would bring to the British empire. Having thus isolated Florida, the English would be in a position to 'oblige' the Spanish settlements in South America to open their ports without restriction to British trade. For, explains the author, 'if the Spaniards did not comply, we could march our . . . troops into Georgia after the conquest of Canada and Mississippi, and take St Augustine; then march them down across the peninsula of Cape-Florida to a place called Penicola [Pensacola].' Thus, Florida would become a sort of hostage in the hands of the English, in exchange for which Spain would have to allow British products to enter South America. This trade alone would bring England 'the balance of 2,000,000 pounds which the French now have of them yearly.'[28]

[11]

This fine plan was not entirely new. The year before, an English pamphlet had put forward a similar proposal for strangling the South American economy. The suggestion was to send an expeditionary force to southern Florida. Twenty-four hours' sailing would land the army in Cuba, and from there units could be detached to Puerto Rico and the Spanish part of Santo Domingo. Once these operations were completed, Spain could choose between complying, and then her possessions would be restored to her, and persisting in her refusal to grant the privileges demanded by England, and in that case she would find the passages out of the Caribbean blocked. Britain would exact rights of passage that alone would suffice to wipe out her national debt. However, it would be impossible to set to work on this brilliant policy without first 'driving the French out of the whole American continent'.[29] The most curious thing about this plan is that it was presented in all good faith. The same journalist was scandalized to see Canadians building forts in the valley of the Ohio. By establishing themselves solidly in this territory, he wrote, they showed forth the long-cherished intention to 'make themselves masters of all North America'.[30] But what right had he to protest, he who would have liked to see his compatriots conquer the northern continent and hold South America in fee as well? Obviously, to the pure all things are pure; nothing can be denied to the apostles of liberty.

Let us look at another example. During the summer of 1755 an American, in a veritable profession of faith, gave utterance to the sentiments that 'constrained' him to write: 'my duty to his Majesty, my love to Great Britain that gave birth to both my parents and with safety handed down my dear liberty; my natural affection to North America, my native land, and my zeal for the Protestant cause which I value as my life.' The occasion of this effusion? The writer's plea for the 'removal' of the Acadians! And the deportation of the Acadians was only one of the desires of this 'Cincinnatus', as he signed himself. He hoped also that 'the nation of England' would now 'strike a bold stroke, make themselves masters of all North America, drive all the French from every part of it, and destroy their navy and trade, and never suffer them any more to make any appearance at sea.'[31]

All this in the name of liberty? Strictly, it must be understood, in the name of that liberty which is the special heritage of every British subject, an element in his political culture, and one of the bases of what today we should call his nationalism. 'How many battles,' exclaims another American, 'have our ancestors fought, for the preservation of their liberties? What a number of years did our British forefathers oppose the tyranny of France?'[32] The English communities of the New World found examples of valiance and motives for pride no less in their own annals than in the history of the mother country. When Indian forays, organized by

[12]

Canadians, spread terror and desolation on the frontiers of the British provinces, a New York journalist recalled the heroic exploits of their forbears as he goaded his compatriots to action in the current crisis: 'Can we, the posterity of those noble heroes who for the sake of liberty trusted themselves to the licentious waves, endured almost innumerable hardships, fatigues and dangers in a howling wilderness, can we, I say, their posterity, remain in a scandalous inaction, while we see our country ransacked, wives killed, innocent children murdered, and aged parents destroyed . . . ?'[33]

Every man exalts the liberty that is suited to him. Because France had American colonies, she claimed for America freedom not to be wholly British. For Canadians the defence of that liberty was identical with the struggle for existence. As for the British, the political liberty of which they were the declared champions was the measure of their independence and the sign of their wealth, as well as the excuse for their ambitions, the mainspring of their societies, and the soul of their patriotism.

Fostered by this concept of liberty, an ardent patriotism was developing in the New World, a patriotism based in love of British America and hatred of the enemy, and capable of transporting to astounding heights of enthusiasm those who were moved by it. One such 'Philo-Americus', whose article appeared in the *New York Gazette*, gave expression to his feeling in an outburst of lyrical prose: 'If I forget thee, O English America, let my right hand forget her cunning; if I do not remember thee, let my tongue cleave to the roof of my mouth . . . Remember, O Lord, the children of France, who say of our land, raze it, raze it, even to the foundations thereof. O daughter of Canada, who art to be destroyed, happy shall he be that rewardeth thee as thou would'st serve us. Happy shall he be that taketh and dasheth thy little ones against the stones.'[34] It was only natural to execrate an enemy who had adopted systematically cruel methods of waging war, and each of the countless raids against British settlements added fuel to the fires of hatred. Three years after 'Philo-Americus', another patriotic citizen published a stirring call to arms: 'Rise then, my countrymen! . . . rise to secure to your posterity peace, freedom and a pure religion; rise to take vengeance on a perfidious nation for their breach of treaties, their detestable cruelties and their horrid murders.'[35]

French barbarity and Canadian savagery provided inexhaustible themes for the propaganda that soon crossed the ocean and spread throughout Europe. The following commentary on an Indian raid appears in a London dispatch to a Dutch periodical: 'Only a person entirely devoid of any feeling of humanity, could fail to shudder with horror . . .' Public opinion, added the writer, was rising with 'a kind of horror against the French.'[36] The English press reported 'shocking details of frightful

[13]

cruelties recently committed by Indians friendly to the French', cruelties of which the recital 'chills the reader with horror'.[37] Shocking and sensational these details were indeed. Did they not show that, far from treating their prisoners 'according to the rules of war and of humanity', French and Canadian troops handed them over as 'prey' to their savages who mutilated and slaughtered them 'in cold blood and long after the battle'?[38] According to one American weekly, the French were as ferocious, and even more ferocious, than the Indians. 'Satiating their cruel minds with . . . innocent blood', they strove 'to outdo even savages themselves in horrid cruelties.'[39] At the thought of such barbarity, every English subject veiled his face—even Lawrence, the artisan of the deportation of the Acadians. Four years after he had completed this task with such ruthless efficiency, the capitulation of Quebec was the occasion of a speech that, as governor of the province, Lawrence addressed to the legislature of Nova Scotia. He rejoiced at the fall of the Canadian capital, that 'barbarous metropolis', source of 'continual, unnatural and unpardonable wrongs' suffered by the 'good subjects' of the king in Nova Scotia, and he saw in the victory a promise that British troops would soon 'put a final period to those interruptions the enemy have too successfully thrown in the way of our progress in every part of this province, as well as to the monstrous cruelties they have hitherto exercised with impunity over the British American empire, in peace and in war, without distinction.'[40]

In reality, although French absolutism was open to criticism, and although the indignation aroused by the devastating Indian raids was understandable, the target on which the batteries of English public opinion were trained was neither political absolutism nor uncivilized war practices; it was France, and Canada, and everything French. Insular Englishmen, with more spite than wit, criticized French dancing-masters, French tailors, French hairdressers, and French cooks. One condemned all French historians, and those English historians silly enough to 'ape' them.[41] Another pronounced a solemn warning against a danger threatening English youth, and England herself. Too many young people were learning French! 'The French language, it is said, and the French fashions will, in time, pave the way to their universal monarchy. I do believe this; for every French schoolmaster and usher, at the very time he is by his profession teaching *miss* or *master* the language of that country is . . . syringing their ears with the glory, the brilliancy, the independency, the *Je ne sais quoi*, in short, of that flourishing kingdom . . . Thus do [the French] make us conquer ourselves! A much softer and surer way of carrying their point than by swords drawn, drums beating, and bayonets fixed.'[42]

Not only were French manners dangerously seductive; the French

[14]

themselves were depraved. French women were natural coquettes, frivolous and 'very free in their behaviour, [with] an air of ease and gracefulness peculiar to themselves.' They '[painted] their faces most extravagantly', but they were 'on the whole, vastly inferior, in point of beauty, to the English ladies.'[43] One may wonder what all this had to do with the war. Nothing whatever—although of course we must not forget Madame de Pompadour. It is curious, and interesting, to observe how much attention the English press devoted to the fascinating favourite. At the time of the Damiens affair, a Philadelphia paper reported a current rumour: 'It is said that the French King, touched with a remorse of conscience on his escape from death by the assassin D'Amien, has parted with the Marchioness of Pompadour.'[44] In 1758 the *London Magazine* published a biography of the Marquise. It appeared in instalments and it could have served as a model for later romantic serials. One episode digresses slightly from the main topic to describe the first meeting between the king and a fresh young beauty of fourteen who had been brought to his attention. 'Her extreme beauty, the freshness of her complexion . . . her infant graces, the air of sweet timidity natural to that age . . . that innocence he presumed and it is assured that he found in her, all conspired to excite desires' which 'one of his rank' could be sure of gratifying.[45] This sample suggests the tone of the story as it is presented: the king of France could properly be called a satyr! Less romantically inclined than the biographer of the *London Magazine*, Horace Walpole recorded in his memoirs a lampoon that stated in plain terms what Madame de Pompadour could be called. It had come to him, he said, from Versailles:

> *O France, le sexe femelle*
> *Fit toujours ton destin.*
> *Ton bonheur vint d'une Pucelle*
> *Ton malheur vient d'une catin.*[46]

English publicists used the excesses of Louis xv as a weapon against France; and what could be more natural in men whose own national conscience was clear? England's cause was just, and British Americans were sure that heaven was on their side. Canadians, it may be noted, were equally convinced that God was fighting for them. The annalist of the Quebec Ursulines saw in the victory of the Monongahela (9 July 1755) the hand of God appearing 'more visibly than ever before, to humble the pride of a new Holofernes in the person of General Braddock.'[47] On the other hand, for another Quebec sister, writing a little later, the war was 'one of the scourges of God's justice punishing our sins'. She grieved to hear 'how cruelly the Church was persecuted in France and the heights that irreligion had reached there.'[48] The following year, however, she

[15]

was comforted by a story brought back to Quebec by an English prisoner taken in Braddock's defeat. The English had seen 'a lady dressed in white hovering with outstretched arms above the French camp.' And, when they came back, continued the sister, 'our fighters, corroborating the story, said the English didn't know how to shoot and all their shots were wasted on air.'[49]

The New Englanders were quite as firm in their religious conviction as the nuns in Quebec. The Reverend Samuel Checkley of Boston compared his compatriots to 'the people of God under the Old Testament', surrounded by enemies seeking their destruction. He warned them not to presume on their own strength; 'God hath shown us the vanity of this in the inglorious defeat of our forces at the Ohio.' Johnson's victory over Dieskau on 8 September 1755 was the occasion of a reminder that 'the Canaanites were still in the land.'[50] A New York paper printed an extract from a text dating back to the time of Henry VIII: 'In resolving on a war, we are first directed by the Christian religion . . . to see . . . that we take up arms according to right and justice . . .'[51] In 1759, a week after the surrender of Quebec, an army chaplain, the Reverend Eli Dawson, chose the following text for his sermon to a congregation of soldiers: 'Therefore will I give thanks to thee, O Lord, among the heathen.'[52] For one Connecticut pastor the final capitulation of 8 September 1760 marked the triumph of good over the 'powers of darkness . . . the perfidious and cruel Canadians.'[53] The same event was hailed by a Cambridge minister as announcing the end of the reign of the Beast and the defeat of Antichrist in the New World: 'We may consider our French neighbours at Canada to be anti-christian: for they, in their professed principles of religion are of the Church of Rome, which we Protestants maintain to be Antichrist.' According to the minister, the outcome of the war demonstrated clearly where lay truth and where error. If the Canadians were defeated, it was because they had been judged and smitten by 'divine anger', whereas the wrath of the Eternal had never yet been 'put upon any of the Protestant provinces in this land.'[54] A British victory was the triumph of good and the chastisement of evil.

Although men and their ideas were engaged in the conflict—and by men we still mean societies—it does not follow that a mere enumeration of these ideas will reveal all the secrets of the conduct of those who professed them. The ideas had their value and their sense. But just as no man reveals all his value or all his significance if you fail to take into consideration what he thinks, so the thought of the societies pitted against one another in the War of the Conquest loses most of its meaning and interest if you detach it from the men who formulated it. Water taken from a spring and bottled is still water, but it is no longer a spring. If we try to follow that thought back to its source, or rather to its sources, we discover Americans forming communities and repeating the lessons they had learned in the schools of tradition and experience. The term 'American' is not to be restricted to the persons who are so designated in British and British-colonial publications. It includes also the inhabitants of the French colonies who, as Americans, have at least one point in common with their British neighbours. If the words and deeds of British and French colonists bear the mark of traditions differing in certain respects, similar experiences gave rise to practices that were much more closely related than the colonists' own protestations might lead one to believe. Moreover, these Americans, sprung from modern nations belonging to the same western civilization, were grouped in societies of closely related types, each with a clearly defined social hierarchy, a philosophy of capitalism—as capitalism was then understood—an influential bourgeoisie, which, in close association with the administrative powers, directed the country's economy. Thus when we speak of Americans we are referring to American communities, and we must not forget the elements in those communities that gave them their tone, those active minorities whose strength lay in their insatiable ambition, and whose members, with the perspicacity born of self-interest, were skilful enough to adjust their private interests to the dimensions and aspirations of the societies of which they formed a part. The result was that the community, sometimes after a longer or a shorter period of resistance, finally became the instrument of private interests by adopting them as its own.

Take, for example, the case of Virginia. When hostilities broke out in the Ohio valley, Canadians found themselves facing an army composed largely of Virginians. The 'Old Dominion' was taking the lead in the movement of settlement towards the west, and a hasty observer might conclude that the people of Virginia were attracted by the vast spaces beyond the Appalachians and their promise of a rich harvest of furs. But Virginia, a tobacco-growing province, quite literally had her back turned to the west. In 1755, tobacco made up two-thirds of her exports, whereas furs constituted two-thirds of Canada's exports. Virginia also exported cereals, meat, by-products of the forest and of her iron works; these products made up most of the other third of her export trade. Skins and furs accounted for six per cent of her sales. Why then should she want to fight the Canadians in the Ohio country? The population of Virginia, largely agricultural, could quite well do without the Ohio fur trade. It happened, however, that the small imperialist party, which held the reins of power in the colony, wanted to consolidate its own fur empire on the Ohio. For the members of this party it was by no means a matter of indifference that trade on the Ohio should become a Canadian monopoly; but a more urgent reason for wanting to appropriate the

[17]

western territories was that they hoped to realize rich profits from land speculation in the country about to be developed. Governor Dinwiddie— along with Governor Shirley of Massachusetts, who had more influence with the English government than any other man in America—was not merely under the influence of this party: he belonged to it. George Washington, who also belonged to it, was no mere tobacco merchant. Like the powerful group of interests with which he was associated, he dreamed of seeing the west opened up through Virginia—not through Pennsylvania, or Maryland, or the Carolinas, all favourably situated for access to the Ohio country and all animated by the same ambitions as Virginia. But the rich bourgeois of this last province would not profit from the economic penetration—the proper term is colonization—of the west by a neighbouring province. It happened that a war was quite compatible with the Virginians' plans; in the first place it would drive the Canadians away from the territory they coveted, and it would provide an opportunity for carrying out their plans partly at the mother country's expense. At the end of 1754 England decided to send an expeditionary force to America. General Braddock was appointed to command the army and was charged with the mission of dislodging the enemy from the Ohio. In order to achieve this objective, the English general would have to build a road, a task bristling with technical difficulties, extremely costly, and requiring a considerable labour force. Now a road was precisely the instrument of colonization the Virginia entrepreneurs needed, but it was beyond the limits even of their resources. So the military road must go through their province. What was their consternation, then, when Braddock gave the order to one of his divisions to advance towards the Ohio through Maryland! The Virginians besieged the general with representations, and when they had achieved the desired result of making him change his decision, Washington gave a sigh of satisfaction. His compatriots, he reported, had 'opened Braddock's eyes' and shown him that those ambitious Marylanders had imposed upon him.[55]

The Ohio Company was already in existence and played an important part at the beginning of the conflict. The idea of its foundation seems to have arisen as early as 1746; it was worked on during 1747, and the company was instituted the following year. It was not the result of hasty improvisation or the pressure of events. When the war began, the company was solidly established and its objectives were clearly defined. Among its members were Governor Dinwiddie, Governor Dobbs of North Carolina, and a few 'esquires' from Maryland, but the majority of its shares were held by Virginians. Two Washingtons, Augustine and Lawrence, figured among the latter,[56] and Lawrence Washington was at one time president of the company.[57] Powerful though it was, the Ohio Company was not without enemies, even in Virginia. The alluring prospect of western country waiting to be exploited inevitably inspired the creation of other enterprises with similar ambitions. At one time rival companies sprang up like mushrooms. Some of them had spokesmen in the legislative assembly, and even in the provincial council. The Ohio Company had to defend itself, and could only hold its own by keeping one step ahead of the others. In 1753 it decided on a master stroke and approached the British Parliament with the object of manoeuvring to absorb most of its competitors, but it had too many enemies and the attempt ended in failure.[58] Canada was aware of the existence and activity of the Ohio Company, and also, apparently, of some of its difficulties. This is the impression one gets from the reports of Pécaudy de Contrecoeur. On 16 April 1754, when this officer reached the forks of the Ohio with a strong Canadian expedition, he found a small British detachment engaged in building a fort there. He forced them to abandon the post and at once set his Canadians to work on a French fort, Fort Du Quesne. Pécaudy knew quite well that it was the Ohio Company he was evicting, but he affected to consider it an unimportant group of individuals, and in the declaration by which he summoned the British commander to leave the post, he insisted that the cause of this organization was not one with that of the British empire: 'I am assured, sir, that your enterprise was organized by a company of which the aim was to advance the interests of trade rather than to strive to maintain union and harmony between the crowns of England and France.'[59] France's minister of foreign affairs spoke in a similar vein. He instructed the duc de Mirepoix to make it clear to the court of St James's that the policy being pursued by Britain in America could 'favour only the greed of a few private traders.' And he added: 'It is in fact that which has given rise to the present dispute, for it was only after a few English traders moved in that direction that pretensions to the Ohio River were put forward in England.'[60]

The error of the secretary of state, and of Contrecoeur, lay in under-estimating the influence of those 'few private traders'. Not that the businessmen to whom Mirepoix referred were themselves powerful enough to determine British policy; but their aspirations, supported by a colonial government interested for various reasons in a movement of expansion towards the west, concorded with Great Britain's own views with regard to North America. The American colonies were starved for space, and they needed security. By fortifying her position in the mid-west, New France blocked their expansion and at the same time brought within range of her bases of operation the ill-defended British settlements in the interior; and that England would not tolerate. When he heard of the defeat suffered by Washington and his Virginians at Fort Necessity, the peaceable Duke of Newcastle assumed a threatening tone. The

French, he wrote to the British ambassador to the court of Versailles, had alarmed the American colonies. Their encroachments were becoming intolerable and would have to be arrested. Otherwise England would lose 'all America . . . and no war could be worse than the suffering of such insults.' In reality, continued Newcastle, the French claimed almost all North America, with the exception of a narrow strip of territory along the coast, and sought to confine the British settlements within this narrow strip. 'But that is what we must not, we will not suffer.'[61] Public opinion in England was no less attentive, no less clear-sighted or resolute than the government; it was even more so. The French, said one pamphlet in 1754, have built so many forts in America that they 'have stripped us of more than nine parts in ten of North America . . . and left us only a skirt of coast along the Atlantic shore, bounded on the north by the River St Lawrence and on the west by the Appalachian or Alliganey mountains which are nowhere above 280 miles distant from the coast, and in some parts not more than 120 . . . They have driven us, as it were into a corner and blocked us up.'[62] In this narrow space the British colonies could hardly breathe; they needed to spread beyond the Alleghenies and to have a free field in the Ohio valley. And why the Ohio country? In order to prevent the French from occupying it; for 'if the French had this country, they would in time be masters of all the British colonies.' They would link Canada and Louisiana, and control North America from the centre, 'one of the grand points which they have had in view ever since they entered the Mississippi and settled at New Orleans in 1699.'[63] One could not better define the objective of Pierre Le Moyne d'Iberville, the creator of New France, in founding Louisiana.[64] In a word, the English thought that to allow the Canadians to establish themselves in the Ohio country would be to surrender and to prepare the way for their empire in America.

What must be understood is that the imperialistic party that dominated Virginia was able to carry the province with it in a thrust towards the west because the western movement favoured at the same time the 'greed', to use the French minister's word, of a small group of colonial speculators and politicians and the high policy that the mother country hoped to impose on the New World. There might be cause for astonishment if the case of Virginia were an exceptional one; but it is on just such conjunctions of interests that empires are built.

This becomes evident if we consider what was happening in New England. There the colonists' eyes were turned not towards the interior but towards the north, towards Île-Royale, Nova Scotia, and the estuary of the St Lawrence. But although Massachusetts and the neighbouring provinces were not looking in the same direction as the more southerly colonies, they were moved by the same ambitions and by similar fears. The north-easterly corner of British America was the scene of intense activity. In 1749 Great Britain dipped into her enormous resources and a new town sprang up, or rather came ashore, on the coast of Nova Scotia. The founding of Halifax was an undertaking of great importance. Large sums were expended to bring in settlers, and the project was pursued with vigour and methodically organized.[65] What were the reasons for this sudden burst of energy? There were at least two. In the first place England felt the need to modify the ethnic composition of Nova Scotia's population, of which the great majority was still French.[66] In the second place she needed a strong naval base to protect the New England fisheries and to compensate in some degree for the restitution of Louisbourg to France.[67]

But, costly and well-organized though it was, the foundation of Halifax soon appeared as only a half-measure. On the Ohio it was not enough to build a barrier to stop the progress of the French; they had to be driven out of the country. And similarly, it was not enough to set up Halifax against Louisbourg; Nova Scotia had to be rid of all French influence. For, so reasoned Lawrence, the governor of Nova Scotia, and Shirley, the governor of Massachusetts, as long as France held the military port of Louisbourg and enjoyed the sympathy of the Acadians, it would be possible for her to land and maintain in that strategic zone an expeditionary force which, effecting a junction with a Canadian contingent, could attack New England, and even New York, in the rear. Nova Scotia, continued Lawrence, was the bastion of New England, but the bastion could not fulfil its function while the French continued to occupy their positions on the isthmus of Chignecto and the St John River, especially since these posts were links in a chain assuring uninterrupted communication between Canada and Louisbourg.[68] Taking a still broader view than that of his fellow governor, Shirley favoured a vast movement to sweep the French out of the country from the Atlantic seaboard to the Great Lakes. The destruction of French fortifications on the Acadian isthmus and the St John River, the reduction of Forts Saint-Frédéric on Lake Champlain and Niagara on Lake Ontario, the annihilation of the new posts in the Ohio valley, and the erection of English forts on the ruins of the French ones, which would be destroyed—these were, in his opinion, the only conditions on which British America could hope to free herself from a two-fold threat: the threat of a flank attack executed by a European army landed in Acadia, and that of an invasion from the rear by a force drawn from the military bases on the St Lawrence. Shirley's ultimate aim was the dismemberment of New France. He did not formally propose the conquest of Canada itself, but he made the significant

[21]

observation that the operations he had enumerated would, 'by putting His Majesty into possession of the principal passes into Canada, go half way towards the reduction of that whole country.'[69]

These strategical considerations lay well outside the normal preoccupations of the great mass of the people of New England, nine-tenths of whom were small farmers[70] whose horizons extended no farther than those of their local communities. Rather than the views of the population as a whole, they reflected the anxieties and appetites and calculations of a small group of active and intelligent politicians and leaders in the economic life of the country. For these latter, the empire was, among other things, a business, and war was a business enterprise. The House of Hancock, for example, whose development was stimulated by the conflict of 1744-8, continued to grow and flourish during the War of the Conquest on rich profits from contracts for war materials.[71] The expulsion of the Acadians even made it possible for Apthorp and Hancock to become contractors for deportation. Before that, these same associates had been called upon to furnish supplies for the army that, in the spring of 1755, was to capture the French forts on the isthmus of Chignecto. But at that time Shirley made them accept a new partner, his son-in-law, John Erving, who thus received his share of the very considerable profits.[72] Shirley's action in this case should not cause any great surprise. Two other governors, Dobbs and Dinwiddie, were members of the Ohio Company, and big business and politics always go hand in hand.

Similar conditions existed in New York, although there the situation was more confused. The north-westerly part of New York bordered on Canada, and there, as in Canada, the fur trade was an important element in the economy. There were two methods for profitable trading. The American trader could either offer stiff competition to his Canadian rival or combine forces with him in the easy and profitable business of smuggling. Many of the merchants preferred the latter method, which involved little risk and required little effort. The long expeditions into the wilds, negotiations with the Indians who provided the skins, all the hardest part of the hard life of the trader were the lot of the Canadian adventurer. The businessman in Albany simply sat on his doorstep awaiting the arrival of the voyageur, and fortune. Instead of going to the source of wealth, he let wealth come to him. His profits would have been greater, no doubt, if he had carried out the whole operation himself, but that would have demanded greater daring and more toil, and he was getting rich anyway. New Yorkers of wider vision tried to oppose this contraband trade. In 1720 the colonial assembly, prompted by Governor Burnet, had adopted legislation intended to put an end to it, but in 1726, as a result of pressure from the Albany merchants and the politicians who represented their interests, the law had been revoked.[73] For the 'Canada

[22]

trade' was the base upon which solid fortunes were built, fortunes that gave their possessors powerful political influence. The 'Canada Traders' constituted a veritable political party with several representatives in the legislative assembly.[74] The family of Lieutenant-Governor James De Lancey was linked with this group[75] in a pact that, like all such obscure influence peddling, was apparently reciprocal. De Lancey had managed to build up strong support for himself in the counties; it was said that he could play on local interests as skilfully as if he were playing an instrument. As a result he had the assembly at his mercy, and, through the assembly, he could dictate even the governor's line of conduct.[76] The war did not immediately put an end to the 'Canada trade'. Canadians continued to sell their furs in New York in order to avoid risking them on seas patrolled by British cruisers. They sold not only furs, but, among other things, some of the booty seized in countless raids on frontier settlements. One can well imagine the bitter resentment of visitors from Massachusetts who saw goods stolen from the villages of their own province in the hands of these shameless Albany profiteers.[77] Trading with the enemy ceased only when the merchants of Albany realized that they would gain more by filling British army contracts than by dealing with Canadians.[78]

The contraband trade, with voyageurs from Montreal acting as intermediaries, satisfied the petty ambitions of these unimaginative traffickers, but at the same time other merchants were planning and undertaking important commercial enterprises, of which the most profitable were those based on Fort Oswego on Lake Ontario. Governor Burnet had founded this post in 1727, as an answer to the Canadians who had just rebuilt Niagara at the other end of the same lake in order to have a post where furs could be collected as they came down from the west. Burnet had wanted to give the New York traders a similar advance post and thus make it possible for them to compete with Montreal for the western trade. Not all New Yorkers had understood his intention, and the Albany merchants had not followed his lead. The colonial assembly had doled out credits with such a parsimonious hand that the governor had made a personal contribution of six hundred pounds to help build the new post, a sum that was never entirely repaid.[79] The Canadians, more clear-sighted in this than their British neighbours, had immediately understood how serious this event was for them. A dangerous rival was establishing himself right in the middle of their trading empire. Montreal reacted promptly and significantly with the suggestion that a detachment of regulars and militiamen be sent to destroy Oswego. But that would have meant war; so they had to be satisfied with a vigorous trade offensive in which the first move was the construction of Fort Saint-Frédéric on Lake Champlain. If the foundation of Oswego had provoked resentment in

Montreal, the reaction of the Canadians was mild in comparison with the violent outburst of anger with which the New York merchants greeted the news that the Canadians, acting just in time to forestall the most aggressive of their competitors, were engaged in the construction of Fort Saint-Frédéric. Protests were not allowed to peter out in New York, but were transmitted to Versailles by the British ambassador.[80] Saint-Frédéric was a cause of special irritation, since it stood in the way of a movement of expansion in the Mohawk valley, where a group of speculators was planning to enlarge its sphere of operations to include the territory between the valley of the Hudson and Lake Champlain.[81]

While the Albany merchants continued to buy furs from Canadian voyageurs and sell them the trading goods without which the Montreal merchants would have had difficulty in maintaining their relations with the western tribes—and Canada would have been isolated from the western country[82]—other New Yorkers, taking advantage of the fact that the Indians preferred to take their furs to the British posts, where they were offered higher prices, traded directly with the interior. These traders developed highly successful companies. It is an axiom that trade follows the flag. But it is also true that the flag travels with trade, and the immense success of Oswego, reflecting a corresponding decline in the commercial value of Niagara,[83] was a trump card in the hand of British diplomacy. The post was a hotbed of intrigue against New France. In 1747 La Galissonière saw in Oswego 'a sure and permanent instrument, in the possession of our enemies, for corrupting our savages.' Eight years later this opinion was confirmed by Vaudreuil, who recognized in the British post 'the direct cause of all the troubles' with which the French empire in America was beset.[84] On the other hand, when Canada's understandably hostile policy proved an obstacle to their schemes, the most perspicacious of the British colonists, those who apprehended the full significance of the French moves, declared that in building Niagara and Saint-Frédéric the French were 'encroaching' on British territory. As time passed, this rivalry became more intense. By the middle of the eighteenth century it had heated to danger point an explosive mixture of political and economic elements.

In New York one man among many others personified this rivalry. William Johnson, soon to be created baronet and major-general, was inspired by dreams of grandeur. From his manor house, Mount Johnson, which Canadians apparently knew well,[85] this feudal lord of the forest reigned over a vast trading empire. His company maintained links with Oswego, whence it received great quantities of furs; with the West Indies, where it exchanged cargoes of flour for rum and sugar; with London and Manchester, where it took a varied assortment of manufactured products in exchange for furs.[86] Sir William was rich, he was becoming

[24]

famous, and he had still higher ambitions. Already the possessor of 200,000 acres, he was determined to establish, on the confines of Canada and New York, a vast and magnificent family domain such as those that the aristocrats of the mother country transmitted to elder sons from generation to generation.[87] His ambitions, like his fortune, were based on bales of furs; it would be vain to ask him why the war was being fought, and whether it was just to dislodge Canadians from Lake Ontario and Lake Champlain.

In short, all along the giant arc traced by New France from Ile-Royale to the mouth of the Mississippi, an arc encircling vast spaces broken by mountains, criss-crossed by rivers, and covered with forests interrupted only here and there by the clearings of scattered settlements—all along that dotted line through the heart of the continent, where every dot was a fort on the immense frontier of New France, the weight of British men, wealth, ambition was exerting an ever-increasing force. Either the line must give or the pressure decrease; either the Franco-Canadian arc must break or the British weight be reduced—unless, in Europe, the counterpoise of the powerful French infantry were brought to bear on decisions being made in London, the heart of the British empire, and were thus to restore the balance, which events in America threatened to upset. Until then, France's ability to restrict English penetration of the continent of America had been in direct proportion to the extent to which, with her enormous military resources, she had been able to affect England's interests on the continent of Europe. This was demonstrated in 1748 when she succeeded in having Louisbourg restored to her, although she had not gained a single victory in the New World. But she could no longer count on this means of triumphing over British America. Even if, under pressure from Versailles, England ordered her colonies to curb their ardour, she would not be obeyed. So reasoned the French minister of marine in 1752.[88] The drama was engaged in America; it was there that it would be played out.

For thirty years British America had been cramped for space in her old establishments. The movement towards the south and the west dated from 1726. About 1750 the human wave reached the crest of the mountains and began to flow slowly down the western slopes of the Appalachians. Ahead of the wave of settlement lay forbidden territory where Canadians, without founding permanent settlements, had established a sort of traders' colony protected by armed patrols. This was the land the British coveted, the land that businessmen in the colonies were prepared to occupy and exploit. The provincial assemblies, of which these men were sometimes members and which were always influenced by them to a certain degree, followed their lead, while the mother country gave full support to the colonies, whose interests were identical with her

[25]

own.[89] As Newcastle said, she would fight rather than allow the French to confine her American peoples to the territory east of the Alleghenies.

Space hunger is a social phenomenon whose repercussions vary with the strength, vigour, and structure of the societies that suffer from it. Those overpopulated countries that do not feel strong enough to extend their territory are faced with a choice between allowing their standard of living to fall as a result of an increase in population without a proportionate increase in productivity, and losing a part of their human resources through haphazard emigration. This group did not include the British communities in the New World. The British colonies were much stronger in numbers than New France, they were in full development, and their societies were so organized that they could gain in extent without any loss in strength. Not only did they feel able to 'take what was theirs wherever they found it', but they were spurred on to such action by the concordance or rather the fusion of important private and high public interests. These societies were dominated by oligarchies whose members could not have risen through them to the summit if they had not wielded both economic and political power. Consequently a war of conquest was not only a factor in the situation existing in America at that particular time; it was—and this was what made it inevitable—inherent in the social structure of America. The oligarchies would exploit, both for their own benefit and for that of the peoples upon whose shoulders they were borne, a very real need of land for colonization.

Were there then oligarchies in the land of the 'sons of liberty'? To be convinced that they did indeed exist, one has only to ask who governed the colonies. In Virginia it was the big planters, a group constituting only a small minority of the population. And what was true of the 'Old Dominion' was true of the southern states in general. In South Carolina a contemporary asked the question: who sits in the assembly? Artisans, workmen, small farmers? And the questioner himself provided the answer: no, the representatives are almost all, if not all, rich planters. The central provinces presented a comparable picture. In Pennsylvania only eight per cent of the rural population and two per cent of the population of Philadelphia were enfranchised. In New York the wealthy landed proprietors elected a certain number of legislators. New England had evolved considerably. The old aristocracy of learning and puritan virtue had made way for the aristocracy of money; businessmen and traders dominated the colonial assemblies and profited from the exalted position accorded to these representative bodies.[90]

If one examines them carefully there is really no contradiction here between facts and ideas. Thinking men realized that governing was the affair of 'gentlemen'. For gentlemen were, and were almost the only persons who could be, enlightened. The Reverend Jonathan Mayhew of

[26]

Boston found nothing to criticize in such a state of affairs. He considered it quite natural that the things of the mind should be reserved to 'those whom God has blessed at once with riches and with large sagacious minds.' The governor of Massachusetts, the historian Thomas Hutchinson, M.A. (Harvard), considered democratic government 'vicious' because a popular régime gave more importance to the numbers of men than to their value.[91] What becomes then of that liberty in whose name the leaders, alone endowed with knowledge, call the populace to arms? Here we must be careful. Liberty in this case was that British liberty of which it was said that 'it is to be considered that there is a public, as well as private liberty.'[92] And even 'private liberty' was a liberty of possessors. An essay published in 1754 advanced the theory that men group themselves in societies in order to protect their property. This is the end they seek in their pursuit of liberty; for 'liberty without property is like a man's having a good appetite without anything to satisfy it.'[93]

If this social situation could result in war, it was because the same situation existed in a very large measure in the adversary's society. Nothing was more like one North American colony than another North American colony; nothing more resembled the social structure of a British colony in America than that of a French colony in America. Not that Liberty— that glorious abstraction which inspired so many panegyrics in English —was invoked in Canada as a theme for oratorical development. This habit had not yet become a French one, and Canadians, therefore, were disinclined to adopt it—or so it seems. It would be well, however, to be quite sure on that point. His leaders kept repeating to the Canadian, even to the point of 'wearying' him, that he must fight to the end 'to maintain freedom for his religion and his possessions'.[94] When they spoke of freedom 'to possess', they were speaking a language that was current in French America as in the British colonies and that was equally well understood there. It was spoken on both sides of the frontier because in both places it corresponded to the same stage in political evolution and the same state of society.

In Canada, as in Virginia or New York or New England, an oligarchy held the reins of political and financial power, advanced its own interests and those of the community. At the moment when the war began, this little group gravitated about two men, the intendant, Bigot, and the governor, Du Quesne. And since, strictly speaking, the country was without representative bodies in the political domain, the dominant minority could neglect certain precautions that had to be observed by the oligarchs of the British colonies. It could limit more narrowly membership in its own group, and it was less hampered in its manipulation of the machinery of government. The presence of such a minority was not abnormal. Since comparable oligarchies existed in all the British provinces, its absence would have made Canada an exception among North American colonies.

There had always been an oligarchy in Canada. The social history of the colony is that of a succession of oligarchies and of the crises preceding and accompanying the transfer of power from one group to its successor. The operation, involving as it did the elimination of a dominating class in favour of a group of 'new men', was almost inevitably a painful one. One such change came about in 1645, when the fur aristocrats constituted themselves into the *Compagnie des Habitants*, which took over the economic activities of the country and which later, through membership in the councils instituted to advise the governor, inspired the political direction of the country as well.[95] Twenty years later Talon arrived with his plans for a 'great kingdom'. He shook up the administrative framework, enlarged it, became a part of it himself, and introduced into it a military aristocracy, which he favoured in every way to the detriment of the former team, whose members, after an initial effort of resistance, had to submit.[96] After Talon, in 1672, came Frontenac, and he, not content with enlarging the existing framework of administration, took violent means to break it. Although the extraordinary scenes the governor provoked in the sovereign council were ostensibly quarrels of precedence, their real cause was a conflict of interests, centred in mastery of the country's trade. It is worth remarking that Frontenac's enemies were men of affairs: Governor Perrot, Villeray, La Chesnaye (and with him Jolliet), Le Ber, Charles Le Moyne, and later the latter's son, that 'presumptuous youth' d'Iberville—and that his protégés were also traders: La Salle, to whom he conceded an empire (discovered by Jolliet), Moreau, Du Lhut, Cadillac.[97]

In the course of the eighteenth century, the same objective gave rise to similar political struggles. The death of Mgr de Saint-Vallier was the occasion of the quarrels that rocked Quebec in 1727 and 1728, but the adversaries who faced one another in the sovereign council were on the one hand the intendant, Dupuy, with the bourgeois members of the council, and on the other the governor, Beauharnois, nephew of a former intendant, Bégon,[98] and heir to some of his uncle's business enterprises, and the junior civil servants who were also brokers—those 'book-keepers and subordinates' who, bound to one another and to the governor by ties of family, or simply of interest, formed an association in order to speculate, with public funds, in manufactured goods required in the colony, furs, and government supplies.[99] A system so solidly established could not fail to last, and these men were still in the saddle twenty years later, in 1748, when Bigot arrived. The new intendant lost no time in ousting the men he found in the key positions and in placing himself and his own men in command of the country's great business interests. It soon became evident that he was an expert in the art of manipulating the 'crank'. He did not disdain to participate in the direction of a few trading posts (the most lucrative), but his chief interests were government food stores, army supplies, and transport for the service of the Crown. The value of operations that would have been profitable at any time was enhanced by the fact that in 1748 the country was still on a war footing and that this condition was to continue right up to the conquest. During this period the governors—La Jonquière from 1749 to 1752 and Du Quesne from 1752 to 1755—were active in the sphere reserved to them by virtue of their office: the administration of military posts and the organization of the fur trade.

The fur trade had of necessity political aspects, since it involved relations with the Indians, who supplied the furs, and with the British, competitors who also supplied a large proportion of the trading goods the Canadians bartered for pelts. There were two ways of understanding this triangular relationship. If, as the Canadian merchants thought, it was a matter of supreme importance not to be cut off from the west, they had to be careful to avoid engaging either British or Iroquois in a head-on encounter in that part of the country. For neither the British nor the Iroquois were hunters; they obtained their furs from the western tribes, which they strove to bring, and to hold, within their sphere of influence. The Canadians' task, then, was to win the western 'nations' from the English by sowing seeds of division among the tribes and by inspiring them with terror of Canadian arms. Shows of force designed to achieve this latter end—*quelques coups d'éclat,*[100] as Vaudreuil called them—brought into line a number of tribes that had shown an indiscreet preference for the advantageous terms of barter offered by the English. One such bold 'blow' was struck in the summer of 1752, when Langlade destroyed the village of Pickawillany in the Ohio valley. This policy of keeping a balance, remaining constantly on the alert but avoiding serious risks, was followed, by and large, under La Jonquière. After La Jonquière's sudden death, the affairs of the colony were for a few months in the hands of the governor of Montreal, the baron de Longueuil, a Canadian with a long tradition of trading and native diplomacy behind him. Longueuil tried to follow the method he knew to be effective, but he had counted without Bigot. The intendant resisted, intervened with appeals to the court denouncing the 'Canadian system', which consisted in 'not disturbing the Belle Rivière [Ohio] country, because of very special consideration and veneration for the Iroquois who live there.'[101] Disappointed ambition betrayed itself in the ironical tone of the brief.

[29]

The high functionary and civil servant wanted his consortium of interests to get its hands on the west. There was no end to the grand projects waiting to be carried out there.

Bigot was therefore delighted when Du Quesne arrived from France to take over the reins of government.[102] And the new governor did not suffer for want of ideas. The ministry in its instructions had armed him with admirable plans, and he soon conceived grandiose ones of his own. First, he tore the 'Canadian system' to shreds. As a matter of fact, the court was not favourable towards procedures elaborated in the colony. Then, in 1753, the governor lauched his spectacular campaign in the Ohio country. And whom did he choose to command the expedition? None other than Marin who, since 1749, had shared the Bay trade (Green Bay on Lake Michigan) with Bigot, La Jonquière, and Péan. In 1753 Péan was Marin's second-in-command, and Du Quesne described him as 'the mainspring of the expedition'. Now it so happened that this same Péan, already the possessor of big army contracts, was generally Bigot's factotum. The Canadian bourgeois could read the message quite clearly: with the help of the new governor, the intendant was driving them out of the west. They resisted, they protested, they blackened page after page with accusations directed against the governor and the intendant. These explosions, declared Du Quesne, were but the 'clamouring of bad citizens'. He allowed himself to be carried away in an outburst of noble anger against the 'infamous' jealousy of these 'pests' with their 'venomous pens'. Although he did not succeed in reducing to silence the partisans of the 'system' he was abolishing, the governor, as he said himself, could and did use the weapon of fear against recalcitrant citizens. But opposition continued to mount, the storm became more lowering. Echoes of the struggle reached France and gave rise to the conviction, in well-informed circles, that 'universal dissatisfaction' in the colony was on the point of exploding. One observer went so far as to suggest the possibility of 'some sort of revolution'. Du Quesne was recalled and Bigot ordered to return to France to defend himself against complaints lodged by the victims of his monopolies.

At Versailles, when the intendant appeared before a newly appointed minister of marine, he presented such a skilful defence that his journey became a 'triumph'. Reinstated in his post in 1755, he reconstituted around a nucleus made up of himself, Péan, and Cadet, a new staff, still more compact, better armed, and more rapacious than the one of which he had been the central figure in 1748. This was the 'Great Society'. The war, as it developed, required growing quantities of food and munitions and created a need for enormous transport operations. It complicated the country's finances and inflated credit, while increased armies demanded an expanded labour force. What a golden opportunity for the profiteers! This time the displaced oligarchy had to admit defeat. Its members had to be satisfied with positions of secondary importance under the great predators whose reign was now solidly established. Business had never been so flourishing; the powerful machine of government would continue to function until it was destroyed with defeat; and when it disappeared it would leave behind an odour of corruption and bitterness. In 1761 a Canadian citizen would write these words: 'You know that tyranny and greed caused the downfall of our country.'

No; the conquest was the cause of Canada's downfall. But perhaps responsibility for the conquest lay at the door of Bigot and his gang? Again, no; they were robbers, they were not traitors. How then could a contemporary, who appears to be a reasonable person, charge the Great Society with causing the loss of the colony? To answer that question, let us retrace our steps.

In 1753 Du Quesne sent 'an army' to occupy the Ohio country. By the spring of 1754 the French ministry of marine had heard, by way of England, that this display of force had 'caused a great stir in the English colonies, and particularly in Virginia.' Rouillé was worried: 'If we can believe this report,' he wrote to Du Quesne, 'the governor of this last colony has taken measures, and has even asked his neighbours for help, to march into the Belle Rivière country.'[103] The governor of New France acted promptly, and in mid-April Contrecoeur established Fort Du Quesne at the forks of the Ohio. A series of grave incidents followed. Jumonville was killed at the end of May; Villiers surprised and captured Fort Necessity at the beginning of July. Early in 1755 Du Quesne received a report from the French court: 'The events that took place last year in the Ohio country have aroused considerable discussion in Europe; and the expedition of the sieur de Villiers caused a special ferment in England.' When he wrote these words the minister knew that a resolute English government, with the full approval of opinion in that country, had dispatched two regiments to Virginia.[104] Feeling in Britain ran very high. 'A great quantity of papers,' wrote one Frenchman, 'has come off the presses and been circulated among the public to support the pretensions of the English nation. If violence of style is a quality of eloquence, one can say that eloquence was never more conspicuous than in these compositions.'[105]

Although undeclared, the war had already begun. The cause of the conflict is evident; neither Canada nor the British colonies wished to be ousted from the midwest. The French empire could not leave the English a clear field in the American hinterland, and the converse was true. It is comparatively easy to reach this conclusion today. But we must put ourselves in the place of the Canadian bourgeois who had recently been shut out of the field of big business by the Bigot-Du Quesne oligarchy. Up to

[31]

the time when Du Quesne abolished the 'Canadian system', Canadians had succeeded in exploiting their share of the midwest without any catastrophic results. They now saw themselves smitten by a war they had never desired, a war resulting from a policy they condemned as rash and inspired by sordid self-interest. The Canadian bourgeois observed both the scandalous profits being realized by their lucky rivals and the fatal imprudence of the latter's conduct. And they concluded—naturally— that the fate of Canada had been placed in jeopardy by a conflict provoked by 'tyranny and greed'. In the autumn of 1758, Montcalm echoed this opinion. His comment on the situation is worthy of special notice: 'Verrès [Bigot] arrived; in the course of building an immense fortune, he formed an association with a small number of persons, indispensable partners in the business of plundering. . . . Businessmen, excluded from the enjoyment of all privileges and sapped of their strength by all-powerful rivals with a monopoly of privilege, lamented and protested, but their weak, muffled voice could not make itself heard, and they were forced to submit to a law which would wipe out their enterprises. . . . Peculation cast aside its mask. Deals and contracts increased and multiplied, corruption knew no bounds. A single company monopolized domestic and foreign trade, devoured the whole substance of the country, made sport of human lives . . .' Up to this point, this was a fairly accurate description of the process by which Bigot's crew had taken the place of its predecessors in power. Montcalm went on: 'War came, and it was the Great Society whose criminal acts, perpetrated in its own selfish interests, provided the English with the pretext their ambitious schemes required in order to light the blaze.'[106]

Montcalm had not himself seen everything that he reported; he was writing of events that had preceded his arrival in Canada in 1756, and he could only repeat what he heard. It was a fact that a social upheaval had taken place in the colony on the eve of the War of the Conquest; one ruling class had supplanted another. When war broke out their accession to power and fortune was too recent not to count against these new men. They had not had time to take on a patina of respectability. Moreover, the war that provided the means by which they satisfied their appetites—the gluttonous appetites of parvenus—was to end in disaster, a tragic circumstance that showed up their misdoings in a sinister light. A similar situation arose in the English colonies during their period of reverses. There too the outbreak of war brought accusations of corruption. A letter in the New York Mercury of 5 January 1756 gave two reasons for Braddock's defeat: the idea itself was ill-conceived, and in the conduct of the campaign Braddock had been led 'to serve the interest of a private company at the expense of the welfare of the public.'[107]

Finally Canada's war profiteers brought discredit upon themselves by their attitude of complete cynicism. Not only was their rise to power too rapid; it was also too insolent, and it could be too easily explained. As the French engineer Desandrouins observed, if talent and industry were the only means to fortune, anyone could aspire to wealth. But no; the one requisite for success was 'indiscreet' patronage. 'Just have a relation or a friend among the members of the Great Company, and your fortune is made! Your ships will be equipped and sent to sea even if they are condemned as unseaworthy; they will be chartered in the king's service; valuable cargoes and the lives of brave men will be risked in them. If they are lost, your losses will be redeemed a hundredfold. Or you may be given contracts or sub-contracts with prodigious profits! . . . Or you may be sent to command a post; in which case riches will rain down upon you.'[108] How could one feel anything but scorn, and how could one fail to be fiercely jealous of these crass adventurers who arrived in Canada dressed in homespun and who, 'two or three years later, had acquired fortunes of 100,000 francs or 100,000 crowns'?[109] Another contemporary remarked bitterly that what 'discouraged' Canadians was the insulting prosperity of 'individuals who, sent from France to govern them, were much more eager to despoil them by diverting for their own profit funds destined to the colonies and their government.'[110] Even when hostilities were at their height, corrupt officials did not scruple to compete with the territorial army for the best militia units, which would be used 'to convoy goods to enrich diverse private individuals.'[111]

This group of executive officers, financiers, merchants, and middlemen is by no means anonymous. Some forty of their names can be found on the list of fifty-five accused—not all were guilty—summoned, between 1760 and 1763, to appear before a commission of the Paris Châtelet in connection with the famous Canada Affair. It would hardly be an exaggeration to identify this list with the financial and commercial directory of the colony at the time of its downfall. Bigot, Varin, Bréard, Cadet, Péan, Maurin, Corpron, Pénissault, Le Mercier, Boishébert, Noyan, Fayolle, La Barthe, Grasset de Saint-Sauveur, Deschenaux, Estèbe, Martel—these are the most important among the members of the oligarchy who, after the defeat, found themselves prisoners in the Bastille.[112] Among the forty thieves were senior and junior civil servants, officers and junior clerks, aristocrats and commoners. They had one common denominator: all were engaged in some way in trade. Many others aspired to be so engaged. Business activity in the colony had reached fever pitch. 'Everyone wants to engage in commerce,' wrote Montcalm in 1758; 'social classes are in a state of confusion.'[113] The government had great difficulty in finding candidates for the sovereign council; for young men, even those belonging to the best families, instead of preparing themselves for 'the judicature' were rushing into business.[114] Alluding to *La Noblesse commerçante*—a recent book in which the abbé Coyet had posed the question: was it permissible for noblemen to become businessmen?— Bougainville made the following comment: 'Everything that is happening in the colonies constitutes a criticism of aristocrats engaged in trade.'[115]

The great world traveller probably did not realize how true his words were when he wrote 'in the colonies', and not simply 'in Canada'. Obviously his generalization was valid for the French empire; but it was also valid, *mutatis mutandis*, for the British possessions in America. In many places, if not everywhere, the attentive observer could see the coalitions of economic and political interests at work; he could measure the influence of big business on government, and he could not fail to be aware of the involvement of government officials in important commercial enterprises. At the summit of every community, whatever its origin or political régime, was a group of active, ambitious, scheming men, who knew what they wanted and who brought all the weight of their powerful collective will to bear on the society they dominated. In French and British colonies these oligarchies performed a normal, and similar, function. They occupied the same position: the highest. And this was as true on one side of the Alleghenies as on the other.

The societies pitted against one another, with the same ultimate objectives, the same type of political structure, and similar methods of carrying on business, had still another common characteristic: they were colonial societies. And this fact was to have an important bearing on the conduct and tempo of the War of the Conquest. The English provinces maintained certain relationships with one another, and all were linked with the mother country, while Canada was linked with France. Within the framework of their own country, Americans—French and British— were very much alike. Were they very different when seen in the setting of the empires to which they belonged? That question—an interesting one— we shall now try to answer.

Chapter II

Colonials

To predict its outcome, one had only to compare the forces that the rival empires had at their disposal in the New World when the War of the Conquest began. The superiority of the British was overwhelming. According to calculations carried out by the Board of Trade and Plantations in the summer of 1755, the population of the English colonies on the American mainland was 1,042,000. This conservative estimate was based on statistics compiled by prudent civil servants, always inclined to choose the lowest among several possible figures. Thus, for example, they fixed the population of New York at 50,000, whereas a list drawn up in 1749 had given the province 70,000 inhabitants.[1] They took care to note that there were 100,000 foreigners, mostly Germans, living in the British communities. Significantly they estimated the population of Nova Scotia at 4,000, leaving in outer darkness the colony's 16,000 Acadians. The Acadians, to be sure, were anything but an element of strength for the British in America.[2] About the time when the Lords of Trade were drawing up their figures, an American newspaper published those that had appeared in the *London Magazine* a few months earlier, and in a pamphlet printed early in 1755. They counted 1,051,000 inhabitants in the British colonies. The British publications also included the information available to them on the French colonies in America. They fixed the total population of New France at 52,000, of whom 7,000 were settled in Louisiana and 45,000 in Canada, but this last figure is certainly too low. The Canadian census of 1754 lists 55,009 inhabitants,[3] and, although it appears to be very comprehensive, this enumeration itself is apparently incomplete, for another, carried out early in 1758, arrives at a still higher total. According to Montcalm, the reason for the discrepancy was not that the population had greatly increased during the interval, but that the census of 1754 had been 'badly made'.[4] In any case, it would be quite safe to estimate the population of British America, as the English themselves did, at twenty times that of Canada.[5]

How did it happen that, with such a decided advantage, the British did not win a speedy victory? That question was answered as early as 1755 when the *London Magazine* observed that the Canadians, who, although few in numbers, had good leaders, could give a great deal of trouble to adversaries superior in numerical strength but weakened by division. 'Union, situation, proper management of the Indians, superior knowledge of the country, and constant application to a purpose, will more than balance divided numbers, and will easily break a rope of sand.'[6] Even when this article appeared, the idea it expressed was not new. It had been circulating in America for some time. In February 1755 the *Boston News-Letter* drew a contrast between Canadians and British Americans. The latter were 'a numerous people, possessing a wide extended coast, rich in trade, and seated in a country where luxuriant nature sets forth her blessings with unlimited profusion', while the former, 'an inconsiderable handful', were 'shut up in barren wilds, strangers to the sweets of traffic, almost excluded from the world, and dependent on their enemies for their daily bread.' Who, asks the journalist, would not suppose that the British-American group would be able, not only to hold its own against the Canadians but 'to blot out their name from the face of the earth'? And yet, British frontier settlements were being terrorized by Canadians. 'Ought we not to blush that by our own negligence we thus give courage to our foes, and that their strength should consist in our weakness?'[7] Another anxious citizen, writing in the *New York Mercury*, had already observed that numbers were no guarantee of security. 'Perhaps we confide in our numbers. Vain confidence indeed! An omen of impending disaster!'[8] In December 1754 the same paper had announced on 'good authority' that the colonies were about to form a coalition. Each colony would provide a contingent for an army that, with help from the mother country, would clear the midwest of intruders. 'It is not doubted that we shall not only dispossess the French from the Ohio, but compel them to keep such limits as were prescribed to them by the Treaty of Utrecht.'[9] This was easily said; but it was not done, not immediately at least, nor for a long time.

There were several causes for the British Americans' failure to achieve the united action that was for them the only reasonable policy. The first of these was general and arose from the character of the people themselves. It was not easy for American provincials in the middle of the eighteenth century to apprehend the importance of the struggle in which French and British imperialism were engaged. Even now, when the historic consequences of that war of giants have been unfolding over a period of two hundred years, the mind must make a real effort in order to realize what was at stake. It must have been very difficult for colonials to establish relationships between their own aspirations, those of their

social group, those, often, of their party or faction, those of the developing province of which they were a part, those of the old country to
which they were bound by so many ties—and chiefly by the ties of
affection— and, finally, the aspirations of a British America, still strug-
gling to recognize itself but beginning, in spite of ignorance, habit, íntel-
lectual laziness, and provincial self-interest, to feel a confused sense of
solidarity. We must not forget that these men were colonials, nor that
the colonial mind is, by definition, limited. If they were to free themselves
from their narrow ideas, they would have to be led by the percipient
few, or constrained by events, to broaden their view.

Each of the American colonies, remarks a contemporary observer,
'is a distinct government wholly independent of the rest, pursuing its
own interest and subject to no general command.' These communities
act 'as if they thought themselves so many independent states . . . rather
than as provinces of the same empire.'[10] Curiously enough, the mother
country did not always discourage these provincial rivalries. English
politicians had even been known to encourage 'disunion among the
colonies', for fear that 'in an united state'[11] they might renounce their
British allegiance and organize their independence. Our observer considered such fears unreasonable. Even closely linked together, the
American colonies would never bring about such a revolution 'unless
they were driven to that extremity by usage which would make Britons
themselves impatient of subjection.' But it would be 'ridiculous . . . to
suppose any such danger at present or for many ages to come.' For the
Americans had no navy, whereas the formidable British navy could be
counted upon to keep the colonies in a proper attitude of respect.[12] So
the journalist concludes that the danger the colonies now face (early in
1755) 'will, in the end, prove a blessing instead of a curse', since it
will force them to oppose a common front to the invader.[13]

To cherish such illusions, the author of the foregoing comments must
have been singularly ill-informed. He could not have known what had
happened when the lieutenant-governor of New York apprised the legislative assembly of Marin's famous expedition. The immediate result of
the expedition was to be the erection of a French fort at Rivière-aux-
Boeufs (French Creek) in the Ohio country,[14] and these events had
taken place in 1753, a year before the establishment of Fort Du Quesne.
The assembly answered the governor in the following terms: 'It appears,
by papers your Honor has been pleased to communicate to us that the
French have built a fort at a place called French Creek, at a considerable
distance from the river Ohio, which may, but does not by any evidence
or information appear to be an invasion of any of his Majesty's colonies.'[15] Immediately after Washington's defeat at Fort Necessity, De
Lancey convened the assembly. Mindful, no doubt, of the rebuff he had

suffered the previous year, he pointed out to the members that the engagement had taken place 'on this side of the Ohio, within the undoubted limits of his Majesty's dominions', and that the French had built another fort (Du Quesne) at the forks of the Monongahela. 'It is evident,' continued the governor, 'and needs no argument to prove, how conducive it must be to his Majesty's service and the general welfare of the colonies' for the provinces to make common cause with Virginia, and to aid one another in case of invasion.[16] His eloquent appeal aroused little enthusiasm among the representatives, who voted a credit of five thousand pounds in aid of Virginia, but took no further steps.[17]

Five thousand pounds could, however, be considered a very respectable contribution to the war chest, and New York's attitude was more generous than that of some of the other colonies. To cite only one example, Maryland played an even less brilliant part. In 1754 the governor of this latter colony urged the provincial assembly to respond to Virginia's appeal for aid. The French, said the governor, were not Virginia's but the 'common' enemy, and the interests of all British America were at stake. He did not intend to labour the point 'lest . . . enlarging on the many obvious motives which must incite you to answer our neighbours' expectations should be construed to imply a suspicion.'[18] His disavowal of intention was, of course, purely rhetorical; far from concealing it, his words betrayed his fear that the people of Maryland might fail to answer the call. Six months later he tried once more to rouse them to action, and again without success.[19] In a document drawn up for the congress that met in Albany in June 1754, Franklin presented a picture of the provincial assemblies, 'one assembly waiting to see what another will do, being afraid to do more than its share, or desirous of doing less, or refusing to do anything because its country is not at present so much exposed as others or because another will reap more immediate advantage.'[20] The fact was that the British colonies, founded separately and at different times, with constitutions and economic frameworks that varied according to geographical and historical circumstances, knew little of one another and were steeped in jealousies born of fierce competition. The war revealed their lack of political maturity. Benjamin Franklin made valiant efforts to educate his fellow countrymen. His paper, the *Pennsylvania Gazette*, carried on a vigorous campaign to hasten the co-ordination of the different American groups. One article attributed the confidence of the French to the 'disunited state of the British colonies, and the extreme difficulty of bringing so many different Governments and Assemblies to agree in any speedy and effectual measures for their common defence and security.' On the other hand, continued the article, 'our enemies have the very great advantage of being under one direction, with one Council, and one Purse. Hence, and from the great distance of Britain, they presume that they may with impunity violate the most solemn treaties . . . kill, seize and imprison our traders, and confiscate their effects at pleasure (as they have done for several years past), murder and scalp our farmers, with their wives and children, and take an easy possession of such parts of the British territories as they find most convenient for them; which if they are permitted to do, must end in the destruction of the British interest, trade and plantations in America.' These reflections were accompanied by a drawing. A snake divided into eight segments symbolized the eight colonies, each identified by its initial letter: New England, New York, New Jersey, Pennsylvania, Maryland, Virginia, North and South Carolina. The legend, printed in large type, pointed the moral: 'Join or die.'[21]

Franklin played a leading part in the colonial congress that met in Albany on 19 June 1754. Delegates representing seven provinces had come together to lay the foundations of a new Indian policy and to prepare the way for a 'union' of the colonies.[22] The meetings were held during June and July, after Washington's too-easy victory over Jumonville and his humiliating defeat at Fort Necessity. In these circumstances the delegates, led by a few clear-sighted and far-sighted men, rose above petty provincial fears and concepts and drew up a sound plan of high policy for the provinces as a whole. Unfortunately the provincial assemblies either rejected it out of hand or allowed it to drop. It arrived in England at a somewhat inopportune moment, and the imperial government too gave it a very cool reception. While the political personalities assembled at Albany had been seeking, and finding, a 'plan of union', London had been the scene of a similar effort. On 14 June, the very day on which the colonial congress was to have held its first meetings, the secretary of state, Sir Thomas Robinson, asked the Board of Trade and Plantations to prepare a plan for co-operation among the colonies. The plan was ready on 9 August,[23] but the ministers rejected it as the provincial assemblies had rejected the Albany plan. Neither England nor British America was capable of initiating a policy of broad views. Franklin himself was to cherish bitter memories of the summary fashion in which his ideas were dismissed. In 1789, considering, and deploring, the political ruins the great British schism had brought in its train, the former delegate from Pennsylvania reflected that, if a union between the provinces had been realized their separation from the mother country, with all the damage entailed by it, would have been delayed, perhaps for a century.[24]

Meanwhile his paper kept up its campaign to persuade the colonies to unite and present a common front in the face of the French threat. In the issue of 5 September 1754 he reminded his compatriots that, although in America the French were fewer in number than the British, 'in Europe their numbers, their power, make the nations around them tremble. . . . It would be a small matter for the King of France to send ten or fifteen thousand men to America in order to accomplish so grand a design as adding an empire to his kingdom which is ten times as large as all his possessions in Europe.' Attributing to the French government a lucidity in complete contrast with its real lack of vision, Franklin went on to say that Versailles must certainly know that this was the time 'to strike an effectual blow.' The American colonies were isolated, their Indians were 'wavering' as a result of the recent reverse suffered by the Virginians. Still more serious, not only were the colonies reluctant to pool their resources, but they would 'neither exert their power separately by themselves, or in conjunction with one another.'[25]

Anxious voices made themselves heard elsewhere. Franklin's views were echoed in a letter published in the *Maryland Gazette*. The combined strength of the British provinces would suffice, said the author, to drive the French in Canada into the sea. But the British Americans, so vastly superior to the Canadians in numbers, were a 'disunited and distracted people', and therein lay their fatal weakness. Could it be that the British race had degenerated in the American environment? 'Have not the English, our mother country, as much inferior to the French in numbers, as we are superior to them here,[26] supported their liberty and religion, for ages, in spite of the utmost attempts of this ambitious nation? And do we, with impunity, suffer our repose to be disturbed, our trade ruined, and our inhabitants murdered or carried into captivity by a contemptible handful of that people and a few banditti, whom they have converted, as they glory, from among the heathen nations?'[27] The necessity for a 'general union of the colonies' was becoming more visible every day, declared the lieutenant-governor of New York. 'For in the present disjointed way in which the colonies act, and some will not act at all, nothing is or can be done' to defeat the French in their plan to make themselves masters of the continent and to monopolize the Indian trade.[28]

But these were voices crying in the wilderness. No single colony appeared to be able to see beyond its own immediate interests. If all finally agreed to do their share in the defence of the continent, each insisted upon doing its share in its own way, following a line of conduct that it had itself drawn up or that it had freely accepted.[29] Although they deplored the threat to Liberty, which they revered, they refused to sacrifice any of their own liberties. When they were driven to fight, it was in order to satisfy two imperious needs: the need to protect themselves against devastating frontier raids, and the need to expand towards the west. Whether the incentive to push beyond the mountains was the fur trade or overpopulation and the land speculation associated with it, each colony sought to attain its own specific objective, to meet its own needs, which might be identical with those of its sister colonies but which were never merged with them. Thus it came about that neighbouring provinces could institute, each for its own part, Indian policies not only different, but contrary, and even hostile, to one another, and that their great commercial enterprises could be pitted against one another in stubborn competition.[30] In such conditions it was only natural that their mutual distrust should result in disputes, or prevent them from taking effective action.

Early in 1755 the governor of South Carolina, James Glen, made an appeal to the colonial assembly. Perhaps because he feared that the string of patriotism would not respond, he also plucked that of personal interest; and as the prime concern of most peoples is peace, he concluded his message with a reminder that 'preparation for war is the most ready and effectual way of preserving peace.'[31] But his eloquence was wasted. Shirley reported a few weeks later that Carolina had made no move to contribute to the defence of British America. At the same time he reported that in Pennsylvania the politicians were engaged in an 'absurd' quarrel with the governor. With the enemy 'at their doors', the assembly had adjourned without even providing for the defence of its own territory. As for Virginia, 'rich and populous' Virginia, he did not even know whether she was taking measures to repair her defeat of 1754, a defeat that could itself be attributed directly to earlier improvidence in the matter of defence.[32]

The legislative assembly of Maryland met in February 1755. After having rejected unanimously the Albany plan for union because it tended manifestly to destroy the rights and liberties of his majesty's subjects residing in the province, it voted credits of ten thousand pounds for the prosecution of the war. Although by no means astronomical, ten thousand pounds was a very considerable sum; but the assembly framed the conditions of the appropriation in such a way that the legislative council could not fail to oppose it.[33] Thus the governor's hands were tied, and each party could attribute to its opponents responsibility for the impasse. Meanwhile Braddock was drawing up elaborate plans of campaign, to be co-ordinated with those that had already been worked out by Shirley and Lawrence. The effect of their vast combined move would be to drive the French simultaneously from Nova Scotia, the Ohio, and Lake Ontario. But towards the end of March, Shirley was still anxious: the generals' expert strategy could be compromised by southern apathy. The 'western provinces,' he wrote—and this term included the Carolinas, Virginia, Maryland, and Pennsylvania—had been the victims of continuous bloody raids throughout the winter, and they had previously suffered two reverses, one at the forks of the Ohio and the other at Fort

Necessity. One would have expected them to react vigorously, but they had recruited only a paltry total of 1,100 men to preserve the peace in their own provinces, and they had not provided a single recruit for Braddock's army. With the troops at his disposal, could Braddock march into the Ohio country without sacrificing the projected attack on Fort Niagara?[34] Shirley's fears were amply justified: the Lake Ontario project proved abortive and the Ohio expedition ended in disaster.

The governor of Maryland was in despair. His efforts to dazzle the province's assembly with visions of the advantages to be gained by the reduction of Fort Du Quesne met with no success.[35] But it was imperative for him to wrest from the members authorization to allocate funds for the organization of a few territorial units to patrol the vulnerable western frontier. More and more frequently along this frontier small defenceless settlements were the victims of savage raids launched from Fort Du Quesne, whose commander hoped by this means to slow down the advance of Braddock's army, and by keeping the British colonials busy at home to prevent them from attacking the French establishments.[36] Foiled in his attempts to procure the necessary credits, the governor appealed directly to the people, and proposed that a fund be raised by public subscription to recruit and maintain one or two companies of volunteers that he would post on the frontier at points particularly exposed to enemy raids. Roused to intense anger at this bold act, the assembly denounced it as unconstitutional and proclaimed its exclusive right to vote all monies placed at the disposal of the executive power. 'Certain of these patriots,' reported Sharpe, had recourse to every possible means in order to assure the failure of the subscription. And fail it did.[37]

On 9 July, the very day on which Braddock suffered his crushing defeat, Sharpe wrote to inform the ill-fated general that the legislature of Maryland still persisted in its refusal to grant him credits, although twenty-six settlers from frontier hamlets had recently been massacred or carried off as prisoners.[38] News of the Monongahela disaster did appear to shake the colony out of its apathy. In mid-August the *Gazette* announced that men were being signed up every day to go and attack the French on the Ohio.[39] But, unless it was published purely in the interests of propaganda, this announcement must have been inspired by excessive optimism, for at the end of September Maryland had enrolled a grand total of fifty recruits.[40] The province was unwilling to fight. According to Sharpe there were in the colony 46,225 Negroes and 107,963 whites, 26,000 of the latter fit for military duty. Even allowing for those who might claim exemption, there remained 16,500 eligible for service. But, quite apart from the fact that no more than two-thirds of these could be

adequately equipped from the supplies available, the assembly obstinate-
ly refused to authorize the governor to call out the militia.[41] Sharpe saw
only one possible solution to the problem: the imperial parliament would
have to intervene decisively, either to impose conscription on the American colonies or to dispatch five or six regiments to the New World. Experience had demonstrated that no spontaneous co-operation could be
expected from the colonies themselves.[42]

He might have been still less hopeful if he had been governor of
Pennsylvania, where he would have encountered the doctrinal pacifism
of the Quakers, and many other obstacles as well. For the Quakers were
not alone in their opposition to the governor's plans. Even when they
had retired from the political foreground and no longer dominated the
assembly, the latter body continued to oppose the financial policy of the
proprietors. On occasion it withheld the governor's salary, in reprisal or
in order to extort concessions from him, and it persisted in its quarrel
with Virginia over territorial claims.[43] The Quakers, however, had a
peculiar gift for sensational obstruction. Immediately after Braddock's
defeat, the assembly, where the Quakers were still predominant, sat,
imperturable in its wisdom, while a wave of terror swept through the
province and the people bombarded their legislators with petitions to organize the defence of the frontiers. The assembly made all sorts of
promises but spent its time in devising delaying tactics. And while the
people's representatives occupied themselves with speech-making, the
governor reported that Quaker preachers were delivering sermons on
peace, denouncing the 'sin' committed by those who wielded the sword,
and going from door to door encouraging the faithful to defend their
principles to the utmost. Some of their arguments were curious. They
declared, for instance, that Braddock's defeat was 'a just judgement upon
[the British] forces for attempting to disturb the French in their settlement.'[44] There were stories of scenes even more shocking than those
provoked by the Quakers. When it was rumoured in Philadelphia
that 'the Papists' had openly manifested their joy on learning of the
rout of Braddock's army, the authorities had great difficulty in restraining an indignant mob that threatened to demolish the Catholic church.
This was the sorry figure presented by the people of Pennsylvania, so
prone to boast of the speed with which, by bringing in foreigners from
Germany, they had built up the population of their province. In the eyes
of true British loyalists, such incidents revealed only too clearly the
absurdity of a colonization policy that had tried to do too much too
quickly.[45]

The truth is that in Pennsylvania the war appears to have provoked
a serious crisis. In November 1755, after a stormy session during

which he accused the assembly of having contributed by its ill will to Braddock's defeat,[46] the governor in despair declared that he was powerless to lead the province out of the impasse into which it had rushed, and that he could see nothing but calamity ahead. If Pennsylvania was not ravaged by French and Indian attacks, it would be torn by a civil war whose outcome no one could predict. Morris's meaning was quite clear: if the party controlling the legislature remained in power, no provision would be made for defence and Pennsylvania would perish; but the reigning party could be defeated only at the price of an equally dangerous revolution. A faithful servant of the mother country, Morris was filled with foreboding. The rebuffs he had suffered and his constant struggles with the assembly made him see everything in the most sombre light. A letter to Thomas Penn reveals his mood of frustration and pessimism: 'The people have lost all sense of obedience to Government and are countenanced by the Assembly who have their own scheme in view and make use of the people to gain their points . . .

'I must think that the Government at home have too long neglected the internal conduct of these colonies, and have suffered Assemblys to go such unwarrantable lengths in almost every one of them, that they have for some time thought themselves without superiors, and if they do not by some means or other give a check to that factious spirit that too generally reigns in these Provinces, they will soon find it more difficult to keep their own Colonys in order than they at present imagine.'[47]

In the northern provinces public and private morale, although much healthier than in the south, was not altogether without stresses and strains. At the end of 1755, in a letter to the Board of Trade, the governor of Nova Scotia, Charles Lawrence, confessed his fear lest persistent differences between the colonies and the disappointment resulting from the unhappy events of the campaign should present 'insurmountable difficulties' to any attempt aimed at enlisting their collaboration 'in another enterprise directed against the French.'[48] One of the 'persistent differences' to which Lawrence referred was the rivalry between Shirley and William Johnson. Johnson's animosity towards Shirley was skilfully fanned by De Lancey's party, with the result that a violent personal feud quickly degenerated into a quarrel between Massachusetts and New York. Johnson had two grievances: he accused Shirley of undermining his Indian policy and of depriving him of the means to dislodge the Canadians from Lake Champlain.[49] It was true that the governor of Massachusetts was removing units from the force that had been entrusted to Johnson and attaching them to the army that he was himself to lead against Niagara, and he was probably justified in taking this means of strengthening his own force. But unfortunately, even with the help of these reinforcements he accomplished nothing, whereas Johnson defeated Dieskau, and the people of Boston were apparently as much upset by the success of the New York expedition as by their own governor's failure. Finally the *New York Mercury* declared its resolve to 'stop the dirty mouth of New England defamation.' If Johnson's army had met with defeat, 'and it had a narrow escape, what then would have become of Oswego? What would have been the condition of the northern, as well as the southern colonies this winter? It is easy to answer, they must have been one field of desolation and blood.'[50]

The safety of Oswego was by no means assured, however, and the surrender of the fort (14 August 1756) embittered still further the quarrel between the two provinces. The New Yorkers, naturally, attributed the misfortune to Shirley. Shirley, they averred, had been guilty of a whole series of errors in 1755, and British America was now reaping the bitter fruits of his ineptitude. New Yorkers were not alone in this opinion; it was shared by the Philadelphia cartographer, Lewis Evans, who early in 1756 published an essay[51] demonstrating that 'the conduct of G . . . l Sh . . . y' had not been 'favourable to the conservation of Oswego.' New Yorkers had not always agreed with Evans's views, often very original,[52] but this time they seized with enthusiasm a whip that could be used to flog the governor of Massachusetts. It would be more correct to say the 'former' governor, for as a result of skilful manoeuvring the New York politicians had persuaded the Board of Trade to have Shirley recalled. Among the reasons for his disgrace, as set out by Lord Halifax, was his indiscreet encouragement of the 'paper war' against New York.[53] New York exulted. As it bade the discredited leader an ironic goodbye, the *Gazette* quoted the wish, expressed some months earlier by Evans, that Great Britain might reward Shirley's 'heroic deeds' as they deserved. This would be only just, 'especially should Os . . go, one of the most important posts the English ever had (or have) in North America, be now in the possession of the common enemy.'[54] Such insinuations were entirely without foundation, retorted a Boston weekly. Far from being due to any fault on Shirley's part, the fall of Oswego was directly attributable to his premature and unwarranted recall.[55] But New York remained unconvinced, and the *Gazette* continued to harp on the familiar theme: 'Certain . . . it is that we have lost one of the most important garrisons to England on this continent . . . and many poor and harmless persons on our frontiers will probably feel the dreadful effects of certain delays before the next campaign.'[56] Support for New York's opinion could be found in the London journals. First an English pamphlet and then the *London Magazine* wondered whether the government had been happily inspired in appointing a lawyer to succeed Braddock.[57] The *New York Gazette* was quick to pick up and exploit the suggestion thrown out by the English review. It agreed that

[45]

Braddock had shown himself to be an incompetent officer. The government had committed an error in appointing him, and a still more serious error in choosing to succeed him as commander-in-chief of the king's armies in America 'a man who had been worn out in the practice of the law as a barrister; who was by nature slow, diffident and inert; who had never seen siege or battle.'[58]

Lost amongst all this partisan clamour was an observation on a subject that the New York politicians would have been glad to see passed over in silence: the trade that was still being carried on with the enemy. 'It is a received truth,' wrote one reporter, 'that unless the French were supplied by us, both with provisions and war-like stores, they would never be able to annoy us.'[59] Corruption, panic, dissension, and incompetence had become so general that one pastor reached the grave conclusion that his compatriots had lost the high ideal, the guiding principle without which they could not hope to unite and to conquer. 'If the people of the frontiers were duly sensible of our inestimable privileges, and animated with the true spirit of protestantism, they would be as a wall of brass round these colonies.'[60] The difficulty was not that Americans were never willing to fight. At the very moment when the minister was making his profound observation Americans were fighting like lions on a colonial frontier—New Yorkers and New Englanders were exchanging rifle shots in a quarrel over ownership of a strip of territory on the confines of the two provinces.[61] In the light of such facts, one can sympathize with an American whose letter to a correspondent in England reveals a mood of profound discouragement. 'The people in England are not aware of the difficulties we meet with in carrying on the war here. Our enemies, rich and poor, are obliged to act against us. With us, our colonies, from envy and particular interests, draw against one another. In short, such is our situation, peace would seem necessary for the present in order to prepare ourselves for war.'[62]

The paradox persisted. The English in America, so vastly superior in numbers and in resources, were consistent losers in engagements with a weaker enemy. According to one American commentator, the only explanation for such a situation was divine intervention. Canadians were not alone in their unworthiness. British Americans too were 'a guilty obnoxious people', and as such deserving of reprobation. 'If civil societies are punished in this life because it is only in this life they subsist in that capacity . . . certainly Britain and its territories have reason to fear.'[63] A year later the *Pennsylvania Journal* commented on the situation. If, at the beginning of the 'disturbances', four colonies had been united and had furnished the contingents requested by the high command, the Franco-Canadian offensive could have been 'nipped in the very bud.' But years had passed, the power of the enemy had swelled with their successes, and the Americans must now seek not so much to triumph over their adversaries as to recover what they had lost.[64]

Reverses, however, did not reduce local rivalries. Rather they exasperated them. Towards the end of the campaign of 1756 the governor of Maryland informed the proprietors as to the action the assembly was likely to take. At most it would vote modest credits for the general commanding the king's forces in America. It was resolutely opposed to authorizing provincial units to serve outside the province, although as a matter of fact these units were recruited almost entirely from indentured servants who had nothing to lose by changing from their masters' to the king's service.[65] Sharpe's predictions proved to be only too well-founded. The lower house granted to Lord Loudoun, Shirley's successor, a modest sum of money from the public treasury. At the same time it stipulated that the Maryland troops would form a corps quite independent of the general command. The latter would have nothing to say as to the use that might be made of the force within the colony; and even beyond the borders of the province it would remain under the exclusive orders of Colonel Stanwix, who was himself responsible to the provincial government. Loudoun, who would have liked to include the Maryland contingent in his own general plan of campaign, fulminated against an act 'inconsistent in itself, and a direct infringement of the King's undoubted prerogative . . . of commanding all troops in his Dominions.' But what could the governor do? If he had rejected the legislators' conditions, they would have refused to vote the military credits, and Sharpe chose to accept less rather than be refused all.[66] He saw only one possible way out of an intolerable situation: a good militia law. The British Parliament would have to take it upon itself to impose such a law, however, for the men who held the power in the provincial assembly would never agree to adopt one. They declared themselves ready to recommend that the people of the province procure arms and learn to handle them, but they considered that to go farther would be to restrict unduly the liberty to which, as British citizens, they had an inviolable right.[67]

The people of Pennsylvania were no prompter than their neighbours to learn their lesson. Their pacifism was proof against the enemy's most violent attacks. In 1756 'some of the people called Quakers' presented a humble address, in which they deplored the fact that the conflict had made their country 'the theatre of bloodshed and rapine' and conceded that the Indian allies of the French were 'a barbarous enemy'. They deemed it unjust, nevertheless, to answer violence with violence, and, since 'all wars are attended with fatal consequences', they urged that further attempts be made, 'by pacific measures', to lead back to the paths of peace the Indians who were terrorizing the settlements on the western borders of the colony. The address concluded with the wish that 'the mind of the Governor be endued with that wisdom which the wisest of kings experienced to be "better than the weapons of war".'[68] Like his colleague in Maryland, Governor Denny would have liked to see the assembly establish the framework of a provincial militia. But he too reached the conclusion that on that point only the British Parliament could overcome the stubborn prejudices of the provincial legislature.[69] And he was obviously right. The people of Pennsylvania would change their attitude only if forced to do so by the supreme authority. In 1757 Lord Loudoun asked them for two hundred recruits, but this very reasonable request was refused, and Loudoun finally expressed the belief that the Pennsylvania assembly devoted all its attention to usurping the authority of the sovereign and thwarting every government initiative.[70]

Even in those colonies whose assemblies understood the need for collaboration with the British government in the great work of the empire, the people in general displayed little inclination to follow their leaders. Many, motivated by fear or personal interest, tried to evade military duty. Early in 1758 about a hundred men liable for such service in New England crossed over secretly to New York in order to avoid being called up. But they were pressed into service there and incorporated into New York units. And it served them right, wrote a journalist from New Haven. 'It is hoped that wherever these disloyal, cowardly deserters fly, they will in like manner be taken up.'[71] New Yorkers were no more patriotic themselves; in the course of an address to the assembly, Governor De Lancey confessed how deeply he had been mortified to learn that able-bodied men were fleeing from their homes in order to avoid conscription.[72] Young men in considerable numbers suddenly heard the call of the sea, and sailed away in privateers before they could be enrolled in the infantry.[73] Not only did they escape the risk of being scalped by so doing, but they were likely to improve their fortunes, for privateering was a profitable business and, since England was supreme at sea, it was attended by few dangers. One patriot, whose anger was aroused by tactics such as these, tried to shame his fellow countrymen by contrasting the courage of the Franco-Canadian troops with their own want of 'that noble and manly virtue', valour. 'We value ourselves upon high notions of freedom, to which we are justly entitled by our national constitution. They are born slaves, and fight under a false fictitious passion; not for liberty, but to gratify the ambitions of a tyrant; and yet must be allowed to have displayed such instances of courage and gallantry, in these latter days, as would add glory to the British name.'[74] In 1759 an irate Pennsylvanian upbraided his fellow officers, of whom a good half had resigned their commissions. And why had they done so? In order to become camp followers, to accompany the regiments as sutlers and pedlars![75] Such conduct might indeed make him blush, but we should lose our perspective if we attached too much importance to such individual, and almost inevitable, incidents. In a war occasional acts of cowardice count for as little as occasional feats of heroism. The essential factor is the direction given to the common effort by public powers interpreting the aspirations of the human groups that have chosen them as leaders.

Much more important than any of these isolated events is the action of the legislative assembly of Virginia which, towards the end of 1759, limited to four hundred the number of Virginians who might be dispatched by the governor to take part in military operations outside the colony.[76] It is entirely understandable that such a decision should have been made at that particular time. New France was breaking up, the Ohio country had been evacuated, Pittsburgh had replaced Fort Du Quesne. The Old Dominion had nothing more to gain from the war. Its objectives, which had always been limited ones, were attained; it could now afford to reduce its effort. In doing so, it was following the example set by several other provinces which throughout the war had manoeuvred to fight, and to spend, as little as possible while their citizens continued to make admirable speeches about liberty. The political immaturity already noticed appears here in its most ingenuous form. But what was Virginia exactly? What were the other British colonies, if not novices in the difficult art of governing themselves? It would be unreasonable to expect them to create the perfect government while they were still raw apprentices.

No, American governments were not political masterworks. While on the French side corruption firmly installed at the summit of the administration was a disturbing sign of a lowering of standards in public morality, on the British side contraband trade harmful to the interests of the empire was carried on in West Indian ports throughout the war, as actively in times of defeat as in days of triumph for British arms. Illicit trading reached such proportions—and herein lies the significance of the phenomenon—that its extent can only be accounted for by assuming the intervention of interested politicians, the collaboration of the judiciary power, and above all the complicity of public opinion. Clandestine exchange, which had been particularly active since 1746,[77] was generally carried on in the Dutch and Spanish islands, where French and British ships met. And commerce with the enemy was no picayune operation; during the war its extent was such that it reduced the effectivness of England's effort to blockade the French empire. The traders stopped at nothing in their determination to outwit the agents of the mother country.[78] One of their most shameless tricks consisted in chartering 'parliamentary' vessels. Ostensibly transports for prisoners of war due to be exchanged, these ships were actually used to carry cargoes of food, and even of war materials, to the enemy. Sharp, unscrupulous government officials carried on a remunerative business in 'parliamentary' commissions. There must even have been a certain amount of competition among the high officials authorized to sign such commissions, for the fee charged was comparatively modest. Governor Denny's price was apparently about a hundred pounds, a little more or a little less according to the fluctuations of the market.[79]

Some of these contraband supplies entered French territory through the port of Louisbourg. From Cape Breton some were taken to Montreal, and even to the French forts on the Ohio. In January 1755 the governor of Virginia made the following report to the secretary of state: 'I think it my duty to acquaint you that all the provisions the French have for conducting this unjust invasion on the Ohio is . . . by a supply from New York and Philadelphia. [Traders] carry large quantities of flour, bread, pork, beef, etc. to Lewisburg . . . where they sell it for rum, molasses, and sugar, the produce of [the French] islands.'[80] It is true that, towards the end of the summer, the *Maryland Gazette*, quoting a Halifax dispatch, reported near-famine conditions in Louisbourg, which was said to be feeling 'to a surprising degree' the effects of the rigorous measures adopted by several American capitals in a concerted drive to cut off the flow of supplies to Cape Breton.[81] But was the report inspired by wishful thinking? Or was it perhaps the rather obvious fabrication of illicit traders anxious to discourage investigators? One may well wonder, for seven months later, at the beginning of the campaign of 1756, the *New York Gazette* published a letter denouncing the 'abandoned' traffickers who had sold to Louisbourg, 'either directly or by way of the Dutch and French islands', everything necessary for the destruction of the British colonies. These facts were 'notoriously known', said the author of the letter, and only the fear of being called 'informer' restrained good citizens from publishing the names of offenders.[82]

The patriot might have had more serious reasons for restraining his zeal: the good citizen who raised his voice in protest would interfere with interests well organized and powerful enough to take severe reprisals, as a man called Spencer discovered in 1760 when he took it into his head to unmask the big profiteers in the contraband business. Not only did the editor to whom he offered his revelations refuse to publish them, but when the identity of the accuser was discovered, Spencer himself was attacked in the street, arrested on a false charge and incarcerated. He spent two years in prison without being brought to trial, the indiscreet victim of a conspiracy of merchants, judges, and directors of public opinion. No jury in any of the colonies would have liked to declare guilty a prisoner charged with trading with the French.[83]

Not all those guilty of illicit trading were Americans. During the summer of 1756 the governor of New York admitted that, no matter how anxious he might be to put an end to trading with the enemy, he would be powerless to do so as long as the king's subjects in the British Isles continued to set a bad example. The master of a colonial vessel had reported, on his return from a cruise in the West Indies, that he had seen five Irish ships, loaded with provisions, docking at the Dutch island of St Eustatius.[84] The only means of preventing the stream of British provisions from being unloaded in neutral ports and reshipped to French markets was to declare a general embargo, a measure that would cripple legitimate trade. No colonial government could resort to this means without first obtaining the consent of the assembly, and the assemblies were reluctant to adopt such legislation. In 1756, for example, the governor of New York persuaded the assembly to vote an embargo for three weeks. The embargo could be prolonged to a limit of three months—provided the neighbouring provinces passed similiar laws.[85] The colonies had no intention of being victims of their devotion to duty; none of them was prepared to sacrifice a profitable trade unless it was assured that the other provinces would not seize the opportunity to appropriate it.[86] Here, as elsewhere, provincial egoism would have had to be sacrificed for the common good of British America. This would have been possible if British America had had a political framework broad enough to embrace the motives and manifestations of activity in the country as a whole. A unified structure, the outward expression of a national consciousness, would have required the creation of a higher oligarchy powerful enough to curb the appetites of local oligarchies without sapping their vitality.

If the British colonies did not agree with one another, they also found it very difficult to work with the mother country. One is tempted to accept this situation as natural and to see in it a foreshadowing of the revolution. But this is a superficial and mistaken impression. Twenty years were to pass between the beginning of the War of the Conquest and the outbreak of the Revolutionary War; and during the twenty years that separate the Treaty of Paris and the Treaty of Versailles, events in the history of America were to move at an accelerated pace. When this period of transition began, institutions destined to die still presented the appearance of vigorous life, while those that were to be were still little more than a promise. The British provinces were more closely linked to the mother country than to one another; hence the important part England was to play in the defeat of Canada. Although they were incontestably superior in strength to their adversaries, the British communities were obviously incapable of organizing their human and natural resources to win the victory that was necessary for the fulfilment of their destiny. Britain had to procure this victory for them. The framework of the British empire was still solid, while that of the American nation had not yet been built. But although it was still firm, the British framework was narrow and ill-adapted to the surging life of ambitious communities and expanding populations. Moreover, it had been conceived for an old, improvised empire; whereas from the war, which stimulated productivity, fore-shadowed territorial changes, and underlined the need for political reor-ganization, only a new empire could emerge. Relations between a nation and her colonies, involving as they do relations between colonials and citizens of the mother country, are always rich in misunderstandings. The colonial is often over-sensitive, the European too sure of his own superiority, and conflicting interests can result in savage battles. Colonial opinion was severe in its judgement of peculation on the part of agents of the imperial government, and certainly no royal appointee came to America to admire the scenery. Franklin remarked in 1754 that gov-ernors 'often came to the colonies merely to make fortunes.'[87] This seems highly probable, and the same thing could be said of the rival empire. A French official in Canada defined a colony as 'a country to which one goes only to grow rich.'[88]

Not only were personal relations between provincials and high officials of the mother country subject to strain, but governing an American col-ony was a task of peculiar difficulty. As Loudoun observed, a governor arrived imbued with a sense of his dignity. But the provincial assembly watched his every step. Among its members were men of experience, skilled in parliamentary tactics, quick to discern the slighest intrusion on the part of the executive power on the prerogatives of the representative body, ready to trip up the king's representative at the first opportunity. Once down, the governor could never recover. It would be impossible for him to retrieve that first false step or to win a point against the assembly.[89] Conscious of their power and determined to increase it, colonial assemblies appeared to be taking advantage of difficulties created for the mother country in every part of the world by the war to wrest constitutional victories from her.[90]

Sometimes the political objectives of the colonials were linked with religious convictions. At one time the Quakers were the dominant force in both the New Jersey and Pennsylvania assemblies. Loudoun predicted that, as long as that was the case, the assemblies would oppose every government measure and maintain that spirit of independence so deeply rooted in all the people of America, but more particularly in the Qua-kers.[91] And in fact Pennsylvania continued to be ungovernable as long as the Quakers gave the tone, a heated one, to the lower house. The Quakers professed pacifism where the enemy was concerned but they were not moved by the same feeling in their relations with their governor. On one occasion a message from the governor informed the members of the assembly that he had 'little hope of good . . . for the defence and protection of this unfortunate country' so long as they continued 'in such a temper of mind.' He regretted that at a time when every citizen ought to be 'consulting and acting for the public good, [they] should delight to introduce new and unnecessary disputes, and turn the attention of the people from things of the last importance for their future safety.' The rebuke provoked a storm of anger and the house adjourned in protest, but not before the members had composed their answer to the governor. It concluded with these words: 'If our constituents disapprove our conduct, a few days will give them an opportunity of changing us by a new election; and could the Governor be as soon and as easily changed, Pennsylvania would, we apprehend, deserve much less the character he gave it of an *unfortunate country*.'[92] The legislative council, the upper house of any colony, was likely to be involved in the struggle between the assembly and the governor. The councillors, appointed by the English authorities and typically loyalist and conservative, tended to support the governor against the people's representatives.[93] So the council was the *bête noire* of the lower house, notably in Pennsylvania, where the governor accused the assembly of treating the council 'with the greatest ingratitude' and representing its members as 'enemies of the community'.[94]

Relations were quite as strained in the military sphere as in the field of government. Generally speaking, British Americans accused officers in the regular British army of assuming the airs of oriental potentates, while English officers complained of the conceit and incompetence of their provincial colleagues.[95] When regulars and colonial units took part in the same expedition, it was understood that British captains and subalterns would take precedence over American officers of the same rank. But what of field officers? Would colonial field officers have command over regular captains and subalterns? Certainly, in theory—but as the governor of New York confessed to Lord Halifax, the problem was 'knotty and difficult', for 'the captains of the regulars will think it hard to be commanded by field officers of provincials, and the field officers of the regulars will likewise think so in having them on an equal foot.'[96] It is understandable that, in circumstances such as these, American commanders preferred to be charged with separate missions and to restrict as much as possible their association with British army units. In 1756 Major-General Winslow of Massachusetts tried to avoid an interview with Loudoun, and it was only after receiving a peremptory order from the commander-in-chief that he reported at general headquarters.[97] Franklin realized perfectly why the force Winslow was to lead against Fort Frédéric preferred to act without English support. The Americans were afraid that the regulars would claim all the credit if the expedition was successful, and that in the event of failure responsibility for the defeat would be imputed to the colonials. 'They say,' wrote Franklin to Sir Everard

Fawkener, 'that last year [1755], at Nova Scotia, 2,000 New England men, and not more than 200 Regulars, were joined in the taking Beauséjour; yet it could not be discovered by the account sent home by Governor Lawrence, and published in the *London Gazette*, that there was a single New England man concerned in the affair.'[98]

In the eyes of British leaders such modest estimates of the colonial contribution to the war effort in America seemed quite justified. Their indignation was aroused when some of the provinces refused to fight, and they regarded as presumptuous the claim of those that did provide fighting men to participate in the planning of the campaign in which they would be engaged, or to play their own part in the common task. Exasperated by these constant claims and by the disputes provoked by the provincial assemblies, Lord Loudoun soon worked out his own plan of procedure: he would make whatever use he could of the provincial governments, but he would try to prevent their interference in military matters and he would make of the regular army corps under his command a military machine that need not depend on their uncertain aid.[99] His attitude betrayed his disdain for colonial troops and his lack of confidence in them. Other British military leaders expressed their feelings more bluntly. Wolfe, for example, wrote to Lord Sackville in 1758 that 'the Americans are in general the dirtiest most contemptible cowardly dogs that you can conceive. There is no depending on 'em in action. They fall down dead in their own dirt and desert by battalions, officers and all. Such rascals as those are rather an encumbrance than any strength to an army.'[100]

On the other hand the professional soldiers, with all their air of superiority, did not greatly impress the Americans, and it must be admitted that the English generals were not of a stature to command admiration. They were at best undistinguished and at worst completely incompetent, and the record of the first commander-in-chief of the British forces in North America—Braddock—was not likely to create a favourable impression of the ability of English officers in general. On 9 July 1755 the force of regulars under his command was routed three leagues from Fort Du Quesne by an enemy inferior in numbers and in armament. 'Few generals,' said a contemporary historian, 'have been so severely censured for any defeat as General Braddock for this.' He was 'universally loaded' with a 'torrent of blame'.[101] If in some quarters opinion veered slightly in his favour,[102] expressions of approbation were timid and fleeting. People accused the general of rashness, arrogance, 'shameless negligence', and chose to see in him the prime cause of the disaster.[103] He had, they said, no aptitude for command and no experience; he had never seen a battlefield.[104] 'Respected by his officers, he was hated by the men who, since he took command, had been harassed with unnecessary duties.[105] A long and significant list of the causes of the disaster in which he perished could be compiled from contemporary journals: Braddock's obstinacy, his excessive severity, his lack of respect for the opinions of his junior officers, 'his contemptuous attitude towards the provincials.'[106] In 1758 an article in the *New York Gazette* recalled his 'inhumanity towards his men', his temerity, his pride, and especially the conceit that had led him to despise 'the counsel of those [who knew] the American wilderness and its savage inhabitants.'[107] A few weeks earlier a Boston weekly had published a letter from London warmly applauding the furious attack that Pitt, speaking in the House of Commons, had directed against officers of the naval and military forces. The Great Commoner had stigmatized their 'want of application to geography, the different arts of war and military discipline, their insolence to their inferior officers and tyranny over the common men', and he had insinuated that these 'little fribbles, perfumed and scented *petits maîtres*' owed their commissions to influence rather than to merit. The correspondent, who quite evidently concurred in Pitt's judgement, pronounced the speech 'the finest oration that ever was made in an English senate.'[108]

The Americans did not restrict their blame to Braddock and his junior officers; they included the whole British army in their sweeping condemnation. This absurd judgement was the natural reaction to a systematic campaign, carried on by the staff officers of the defeated army, to divert attention from their own incompetence by attributing the disaster to the cowardice of their men.[109] The young George Washington allowed himself to be manoeuvred by skilful superiors into making his contribution to this disgraceful argument *pro domo*. The regular soldiers, he reported, 'were immediately struck with such a deadly panic that nothing but confusion and disobedience of orders prevailed among them.' While 'the officers in general behaved with incomparable bravery' and 'the Virginian companies behaved like men and died like soldiers . . . the dastardly behaviour of the English soldiers exposed all those who were inclined to do their duty to almost certain death.' Their cowardice was the immediate cause of the carnage by which that dreadful day was marked.[110] Some provincial governors immediately adopted this version of the engagement. Dinwiddie attributed the 'dismal defeat' of 9 July and 'the death of the general and so many brave officers entirely . . . to the dastardly spirit of the private men.'[111] In New York, De Lancey instructed Johnson to persuade the Iroquois to think, 'as the truth is, that the success of the French was entirely owing to the European troops being unaccustomed to and unacquainted with wood fighting.'[112] By a curious coincidence a Boston newspaper reported some two weeks later that when Johnson informed his Indians of Braddock's defeat, they betrayed no emotion but observed on the contrary that 'they were not at all surprised to hear it, as they were men who had crossed the Great

Water and were unacquainted with the arts of war among the Americans.'[113]

A debate was carried on in the British press as to whether the Monongahela defeat should be attributed to cowardice on the part of the troopers or to undisciplined, negligent, and incompetent officers. Was the conduct of the latter indeed above reproach? How much weight should be given to the testimony of the Virginian who claimed that the cause of the rout was the soldiers' dislike of their officers? The London *Monitor* demanded an inquiry on these points, for if the troopers' complaints were justified it would be useless to send other units to America. The results would continue to be disastrous unless the government made sure the troops went into battle under 'such commanders as [would] treat them like free-born subjects of Britain.'[114] Walpole considered that everyone had been wrong. The ministry had been ill-advised in its choice of a commander. Braddock, 'though remiss himself', exacted from others 'the utmost rigour of duty.' He was 'desperate in his fortune, brutal in his behaviour, obstinate in his sentiments, intrepid and capable.' The government had made a second mistake in placing an ill-chosen general in command of inferior troops, 'drafts of the most worthless in some Irish regiments, and disgusted anew by this species of banishment' to service in the New World. But the capital error, in Walpole's opinion, had been to entrust a mission such as the capture of Fort Du Quesne to Europeans. Provincials, less well trained but more accustomed to Indian methods of warfare, would have succeeded where English troops were bound to fail.[115] This interpretation of the facts and this attribution of responsibility were to be widely accepted by future historians. Meanwhile they were very flattering for colonial vanity, and the colonials gloated.

If by accusing their men of cowardice the English officers had hoped to protect their own honour, their hopes were deceived. They succeeded in discrediting their troops, but in doing so they helped to inflate the self-esteem of the colonials without enhancing their own reputation. The *New York Gazette* of 25 August 1755 contained a letter in which an American reproduced a conversation he had had with an English officer who had been drilling a company of colonial recruits on the parade ground at Albany. 'When the men retired,' wrote the author of the letter, 'I told the captain we exercised our men that were to fight against the French and the Indians in a different manner.'

> *'Pray, sir,' said the captain, 'how is that?'*
> *'Only to load quick and hit the mark, that is our whole exercise.'*
> *'What! do you take aim at the enemy,' said he?*
> *'Yes, good aim or not fire,' said I.*

'So, if an officer appears,' said he, 'twenty shall aim at him . . . abso-lute murder!'[116]

The story probably amused more than one reader, but the letter was not written merely to amuse. American critics did not limit themselves to poking fun at British officers. The *Boston News-Letter* (14 August 1755) must have taken a special pleasure in publishing a letter from a New Yorker who, while he had no admiration for the regulars, held the New England troops in the highest esteem: 'We put no confidence in any other troops but yours and it is generally lamented that the British regulars were not put into garrisons and New England irregulars sent to the Ohio.' It was because the provincials were fighting for a principle that their labours were crowned with success.[117] The theme was developed the following week in the same paper. 'New Englanders . . . of all others, are best qualified for American wars. They fight, not, like regulars, for pay; but from the highest and most powerful motives—to revenge the blood of their nearest friends or relations or to redeem them from the miseries of a captive state.'[118] Here the writer betrays his own feeling and that of many colonials: the English soldiers were mercenaries, a sort of 'foreign garrison'.[119] The Monongahela disaster was only the first in a series of humiliating setbacks. The loss of Oswego in 1756, followed the next year by that of Fort William Henry and the failure of Lord Loudoun's plan to attack Louisbourg, led a New York observer to draw the following bitter conclusion: 'The more we are strengthened by land forces from Great Britain, the more we lose ground against the French, whose number of regular troops is, according to the best information we can get here, inferior to ours.'[120] Contemporary historians expressed the same opinion,[121] and it would be difficult to say whose contempt was greater, that of the English for American troops or that of the Americans for British officers and soldiers.

This unedifying and inharmonious chorus of recrimination is understandable when one considers the long series of military reverses that were its immediate cause. But the quarrels provoked by circumstances sprang from a bed of soil already sown with the seeds of permanent misunderstanding. British Americans, true to the pattern of thinking of all colonials, especially in the hour of danger, were inclined to believe that England was not sufficiently mindful of their affairs. Towards the end of 1756 a New Yorker complained that the colonies 'had been too long neglected by the mother country.'[122] Two years earlier Franklin had already reminded England that the colonies were helping to enrich her, for although they did not themselves pay taxes directly to the imperial treasury the taxes paid by British producers and merchants were passed on to colonials in the higher prices paid for imported goods. Moreover, while the old country was free to restrict imports, the colonies were not permitted to regulate the entry of British goods, so that 'our whole wealth centres finally among the merchants and inhabitants of Great Britain, and if we make them richer, and enable them better to pay their taxes, it is nearly the same thing as being taxed ourselves and equally beneficial to the crown.'[123] From this premise he concluded that America had every right to demand protection from the mother country.

Although Franklin's argument still appeared rather academic, it must have provoked questions in the minds of some of his readers. Were not Americans over-conscious of the usefulness of colonies to Great Britain? Were they not too complacent in their conviction that they were making an essential contribution to the prosperity of the mother country? But the feelings that might have provoked such questions were not simply a form of colonial vanity. They were more probably a defence reaction to the detachment with which a considerable body of English public opinion viewed overseas possessions. 'The partisans of the ministry damn the plantations,' wrote Horace Walpole in 1755, 'and ask if we are to involve ourselves in a war for them.'[124] The idea was sufficiently widespread to be considered dangerous. A letter in the *London Magazine* of March 1755 protested vigorously against it: 'A most pernicious, narrow, selfish spirit is with great industry propagated at present, that our plantations and colonies in America may, and ought to, defend themselves and that we ought not to engage in a war on their account.'[125] Fifteen months later a writer in the same magazine, after calling forcible attention to the very considerable contribution of the American colonies to Britain's prosperity, added an indignant commentary: 'And yet there is a set of people now here who grudge every expense we are put to for the support of our colonies either in time of war or in time of peace. In time of peace, they cry, our colonies do not stand in need of any support from us; and in time of war, they say, we ought to oblige our colonies to defend themselves. It is to be hoped that such narrow-minded politicians have at present no influence upon our councils.'[126] Very often the motive of the 'narrow-minded politicians' who sought to measure the aid granted to America was fear lest excessive generosity prove both useless and dangerous. In April 1755 a correspondent reported from London that 'some persons have been apprehensive that our colonies and plantations in America might in time shake off their dependence upon us and set up for themselves.'[127] A few months later another London observer defined the essential terms of the colonial problem: 'The Americans are doubtless too thirsty after power; and perhaps we are too suspicious of its uses. . . . Could we not upon mature consideration find some method of arming them with power without alluring them by the specious bait of independence?'[128]

[58]

To speak of American independence in 1755 was to give proof of singular powers either of percipience or of imagination. As one English journalist observed, the hostilities developing in the New World must inevitably strengthen the bond between Great Britain and her colonies by awakening the latter to the realization that 'without the fleets and the forces of their mother country, they would soon be deprived of their possessions.'[129] It was quite true that the events of the sombre years between 1754 and 1758 would make Americans appreciate the advantages of belonging to the British empire. But in 1758 the tide turned. Louisbourg, Fort Frontenac, and Fort Du Quesne fell one after the other. The Franco-Canadian forces no longer threatened the northern and western frontiers of British America. At that point an American journalist brought up the question of independence, and it is important to understand the circumstances that led him to consider it. The fall of Fort Du Quesne, he wrote, placing at the disposal of British America the country the fort had been built to defend, gave her access to new sources of wealth and power. There were Britons who thought 'the British plantations . . . already grown too large', but the idea that the extent and vitality of the colonies could constitute a danger for the mother country must be ranked among 'the greatest of vulgar errors'. In reality the American provinces were small and poor. From New Hampshire to Carolina the land suitable for farming was 'not equal in quantity to half the arable land in England.' Massachusetts, which had been erected into a bugbear, was 'not as large as Yorkshire.' Moreover, the colonies had no thought of separating from the mother country, to which they were attached by ties of blood and friendship. To break with the old country they would first have to unite, and that was a condition they would not fulfil. Each colony had its own government, and no one of them would be allowed to assume a position of leadership. These were 'unsurmountable obstacles' to their ever uniting, to the prejudice of England, to forward any ambitious views of their own. It was true however, and here the author pointed a severe warning, that Great Britain might herself drive her colonies to take desperate measures. She could do so by subjecting them to 'repeated and continued ill usage' or by 'sacrificing them to the ambition and intrigues of domestic and foreign enemies.' Politicians confident in their own judgement asserted that the existence of a strong hostile community on their borders was the best guarantee of the colonies' loyalty to the mother country. Nothing could be farther from the truth! On the contrary, that was exactly the situation that might provoke 'an attempt of independence'. And for that reason, continues the author, 'it becomes those who would regard the future interests of Britain and its colonies to suppress the growth of the French, and not the English, in America.' The conclusion to be drawn from these

[59]

grave considerations was that it would be a mistake for Britain, impelled by an unfounded fear that the natural resources of the Ohio country would increase unduly the wealth and population of her colonies, to restore the territory to France. Rather she should hold it and make it the base of a new establishment, at the same time taking precautions 'against the scandalous engrossing of the land by private persons or public companies.'[130]

Thus when the conflict began, relations between the mother country and the British colonies were by no means idyllic; when it ended they had deteriorated still further. The breakdown in understanding was evidence that within the framework of the empire individual communities had developed to the point where each had its own distinctive views and where solid political units had become sufficiently differentiated for each to strive towards its own peculiar objectives, while all more or less consciously pursued a common aim. And this evolution, or rather this moment in the evolution of an empire, could be observed in the French world as well as in the British.

It is true that the divisions that poisoned relations between the British colonies did not exist in New France. One reason for this was that the political organization of the two groups was quite different. British America was not organized as one political unit; its colonies were all on the same footing, whereas there was a recognized hierarchy of colonies in New France. Canada, the seat of the 'general' government of New France, took precedence over all other French colonies. The question of union was discussed by the British colonies in 1754; there was no occasion for any such discussion in the case of New France. Moreover, Canada's geographical position, her development, and the size of her population in comparison with that of the other establishments made it inevitable that she should hold first place. Canada intervened directly in Acadian policies, and between 1749 and 1758 it was Canada that supported the short-lived 'French Acadia'. Canada made a modest but significant contribution to the defence of Île-Royale. She could not have done more; it would have taken squadrons to save Louisbourg, and only France had squadrons. As for Louisiana, a country destined, as La Galissonière said, to grow 'in Canada's shadow', it was not invaded, and hence was in a position to give some help in men and supplies. And yet rivalries did spring up in France's American empire, and in the natural course of events Canada and Louisiana found themselves pitted against one another. Both colonies were interested in the fur trade; each of the oligarchies that held the reins of large-scale trading operations tried to trespass on territory the other regarded as its preserve. Echoes of claims and counter-claims reached the seats of government, and until the war put an end to them such disputes were a frequent cause of friction between Quebec and New Orleans.[131]

In the case of Canada, however, as in that of the British empire, the war embittered relations, always delicate,[132] between colonials and native Frenchmen. Professional soldiers from England did not consider colonials competent to give an opinion on military questions; Montcalm's attitude towards Canadians was no less disdainful. 'Bourgeois, financiers, merchants, officers, bishops, curés, Jesuits: they all plan, hold forth, talk, retract, make pronouncements on the art of war. Every one of them is a Turenne or a Villars.' Their 'prejudices' and 'stupidity' would, in the general's opinion, be the cause of great misfortune to the country.[133] With only a few exceptions, Canadian officers were written off by the commander-in-chief in a warning to Lévis: 'Remember,' he wrote, 'that Mercier [Le Mercier] is a weakling and an ignoramus, Saint-Luc a garrulous braggart, Montigny admirable, but a looter, Villiers and Léry good, Langy excellent, Marin brave but stupid; the rest are not worth mentioning, not even Rigaud, my senior lieutenant-general.'[134]

The British forces in America were made up of three elements: European regulars, provincial units, and militia. In this respect the situation in Canada was very similar. After 1755 infantry battalions were dispatched to Canada by the ministry of war; these were the 'land troops', commanded successively by Dieskau, Montcalm, and Lévis. Their staff and junior officers were also French. The land troops were expected to remain for the duration of the war. The country's permanent garrisons were made up of a varying number of *compagnies franches de la marine*, for which the men were recruited in France and the officers in Canada. They were commonly known as *troupes de la colonie*, but the term was ambiguous, since the troopers were French. The officers, however, did belong 'to the colony', Canada was either their native or their adopted country. The militia companies were raised in the various parishes of Canada. As a general rule their own officers—the 'militia captains'—played a secondary role, and on military expeditions militia units were commanded by 'colonial' officers. The rivalry between land officers and colonial officers was intense. Major-General Montreuil was distressed to have to report that 'Officers of colonial troops do not like officers of the land forces.'[135] The governor, Pierre de Rigaud de Vaudreuil, was supreme commander of all the troops: land forces, colonial troops, and militia.[136] He was a Canadian and a former colonial officer, and he would have liked to reorganize the colonial troops on the lines of French battalions. His intention, obviously, was to constitute a Canadian staff similar to Montcalm's, and thus to procure for Canadian officers ranks identical with those of the French officers. But the ministry of marine, upon which he depended, refused to carry out the change he

[61]

had proposed.[137] Like British provincial officers in a similar situation, Canadian officers hated to fight under the orders of French officers. It was 'unpleasant' for them, said Le Mercier (Montcalm's 'weakling'), to be commanded by men who, although they were their seniors in rank, were very much their juniors in experience.[138] This feeling, in which the governor sympathized most heartily, was something more than a manifestation of *esprit de corps*. Without exaggeration it could be called a national spirit, and Montcalm recognized it as such when he accused Vaudreuil of always being 'partial, in favour of the Canadians and against the French.'[139]

The French officers' estimate of the worth of Canadian fighters was no higher than that of English officers fighting with colonial troops. Desandrouins maintained a certain discretion when he stated that 'the Canadians have lost their old warlike spirit';[140] but one of his fellow officers let himself be completely carried away in an angry tirade against the militiamen serving under him. He evoked the memory of their ancestors, criminals who should have been broken on the wheel, but who had been deported to Canada instead. 'The scoundrels have inherited all the traits of their gallows-bird ancestors; I am sure it would take a second redemption, reserved just for them, to wipe out the stain of this second original sin.'[141] The idea recurs frequently in the writings of French observers. A friend of Montcalm made use of it to belittle Vaudreuil in the eyes of the French court. Even if the governor were endowed with every talent, 'he would still be marked by one inborn defect, he is a Canadian.'[142] When an artillery officer, Pontleroy, felt that he was being persecuted by the Canadians, he inverted the terms of the comparison. 'Allow me to tell you, monseigneur,' he wrote to the minister of marine, 'for the people of this country, I am marked with the original sin of being French.'[143]

The British colonists accused Braddock of 'inhumanity' and brutality. Reliable witnesses deplored the fact that Dieskau commanded his troops 'in the German fashion'.[144] Vaudreuil affirmed that Montcalm was a harsh commander for Canadians,[145] and the minister of marine advised the general to have some 'consideration for them'. He also directed him to see that his French officers corrected the painful impression they had created in the colony by 'treating militiamen too harshly on several occasions'.[146] After his victory, Montcalm was accused of allowing his regulars to rob the civilian population. These reports, which come from a number of different sources and are in general agreement with each other, are very convincing.[147] One could pursue still further this parallel between happenings in the two empires. A few months after William Pitt's speech stigmatizing the incompetence and frivolity of British officers, a Parisian writing in the *Mercure de La Haye* denounced French officers in terms reminiscent of Pitt's speech: 'Instead of studying their duties, preparing themselves for them, seeking to forward the good and the interests of their country . . . we see, to the shame of our nation, that most of the senior officers have sought only to enrich themselves with spoils from the devastation and ruin of the enemy country. . . . Thus is the Bastille provided with occupants.'[148] One may suppose that if there had been any newspapers in Canada such an article would have been welcomed by them, and that some journalist would have been tempted to establish a relationship between the scandals that brought officers to the Bastille and the singular conduct of land officers in Canada. The behaviour of the latter must have been notorious to justify Bougainville's report on their life: 'I confess that until now some officers have lived as they would have lived in a period of peace and of great abundance, playing for enormous stakes and eating choice food, and that, in short, luxury, good cheer, an easy life, appear to be the main preoccupation of men who should be concerned only with glory. But alas! I ask myself in the bitterness of my heart, what has become of the desire for glory, of delicacy of feeling, emulation, honour? Our soul is degraded . . .'[149]

Just as the Americans were convinced of their own superiority over the British when the field of battle was in the New World, so Canadian officers, with Vaudreuil in the lead, deemed their own tactics much more valid than those of the officers commanding the land forces.[150] Montcalm was beside himself with indignation; in his opinion colonial methods had had their day, and now war was established 'on a European footing, with planned campaigns, armies, artillery, sieges, battles. . . . What a revolution!'[151] Vaudreuil considered himself better able than a Frenchman to elaborate the strategy suited to American conditions; specifically he considered himself better fitted than anyone else to handle the Indians, whose friendship was so precious. That too was a delusion, said the French general, who boasted of having won an ascendancy over the minds of the Indians that astonished the governor himself. 'He was born in Canada, and he and his friends have claimed systematically that his name was enough to win the confidence of the Indian nations. Today I think I might be equally sure of mine.'[152] But what shocked Montcalm most profoundly was Vaudreuil's failure to adopt the 'European system of tactics' and his persistence in consulting Canadian advisers, 'ignorant empirics', instead of relying upon the 'senior officers sent out to him by the Court.' Montcalm's opinion flattered the vanity of his compatriots, and the chief grievance of the court against Vaudreuil was his Canadianism.[153] Montcalm regarded the regulars—officers and soldiers—under his command as 'troops expatriated and exiled, so to speak.'[154] His second-in-command and successor, Lévis, made no secret of the fact that his motive in coming to America had been to win promotion.[155] Just as

[63]

English units in the eyes of British colonials, so were French professional soldiers, in the eyes of Canadians, 'mercenaries'. It was natural that this should be so, and yet Montcalm felt offended for himself and for his officers. He gave vent to his feeling in a bitterly sarcastic rendering of the Canadian image of the members of his staff: 'Hessian officers dispatched by the King to defend the colony, and in whom, since they are foreigners, one cannot have confidence.'[156] For Vaudreuil this was no subject for light irony, and his tone was serious, even grave, as he undertook to 'point out the difference between troops who are dependent upon the colony, whose property, family and fortunes are there, and expatriates whose one ambition is to get back to their families without having brought dishonour upon themselves, and for whom any harm suffered by the colony, even its total loss, is a matter of small concern.'[157]

British Americans thought they had some reason to accuse England of neglecting the colonies. What would their reaction have been if the mother country had threatened to abandon them altogether, as the minister charged with responsibility for the French colonies did in mid-July 1755, at the very moment when invading armies were in action against New France at four different points. The secretary of state, Machault, wanted to bring about a reduction in expenditures for Canada. He could not be satisfied with small economies; they must be important, even spectacular, and it was in these circumstances that he made the following declaration: 'In spite of the protection with which the King has until now honoured this colony, protection that His Majesty is now manifesting in efforts to provide for its safety, he would soon be obliged to abandon it, if expenses connected with it could not be reduced.' The minister meant to make his meaning quite plain. The governor and the intendant, to whom the dispatch was addressed, must not suppose that he had not measured his words. He had given careful thought to all the implications of his warning: 'For, I repeat, the efforts His Majesty is now making for the colony would be the last, and nothing could prevent him from abandoning it, if he had not evidence that you are giving effective attention to the reduction of expenses.'[158] In 1759 Berryer carried out the threat made four years earlier by Machault.

To complete this parallel between Franco-Canadian and Anglo-American relations, we must ask whether any French subjects had envisaged the possibility of eventual separation, except by abandonment, between Canada and France. In a moment of irritation at the resistance that Frenchmen met in Canadian society, Bougainville commented bitterly on the situation: 'We seem to belong to another, even an enemy, nation.'[159] This striking but hasty judgement is doubtless symptomatic, but it betrays impatience rather than understanding. Much more significant is a comment made in France, again by Bougainville, early in 1759.

Bougainville had been dispatched to the court with a mission to obtain reinforcements for New France, and he had found that the mother country was not favourably inclined towards the idea. For there were some persons there, reported Bougainville, who considered that it was not important 'for France to keep Canada.' One of their main arguments was that 'when once Canada was well established, it would pass through many phases', and in that case, asked astute observers of the political scene, 'would it not be natural that kingdoms and republics should be formed there and should separate from France?' The interest of the question lies in the fact that it was posed in 1759. And Bougainville's answer is no less significant: 'It is true that in the course of time those vast territories may be divided into Kingdoms and republics, and the same thing is true of New England.'[160]

These last words should be marked. To observers of the age whose intelligence is not clouded by an absurd tradition of historical interpretation divorced from reality, the perspectives in French America are similar to those in British America. What else should we expect? Here were societies that had lived through, and were living through, the same collective experiences. They were colonial societies and they had the same attitudes towards their respective mother countries. They belonged to the same age and they cherished the same basic aspirations. From those conditions there resulted similar sentiments, often expressed in the same words by Canadian and British colonists. Basically that means that they were all Americans, Canadians as well as British. And nothing is more like an American than another American.

Part Two

THE VICTORIOUS
RESISTANCE

Chapter III

The Clash
1754-5

Early in the summer of 1754 the American papers had news of considerable importance to report. A dispatch from Annapolis, dated 13 June, informed readers that on 27 May a young major, George Washington, had set out from Great Meadows in the upper Ohio valley to intercept a small Canadian detachment whose presence in the neighbourhood had been reported by Indians. The British, after marching all night, had surprised the 'French' camp on the morning of 28 May. The dispatch went on to say that the French had opened fire and that answering volleys had killed seven or eight men and put the rest to flight. The Virginian major was supported by an Indian chief, the Half-King, and he with his band of warriors first cut off the fugitives' retreat and then killed and scalped the Canadian commander. This was the version of the encounter presented in the press: an ordinary frontier incident not even worthy of front-page honours.[1] At first public opinion seemed to attach little importance to it; a handful of 'Frenchmen' had dared to challenge the legitimate proprietors on a corner of British territory, and had met their master in the person of an obscure provincial officer who had punished them as they deserved—those Frenchmen didn't know how to fight anyway. Such was the general tone of the reaction provoked by the incident.[2]

Washington was almost the only person to become at all excited. 'I heard the bullets whistle,' he wrote in his account of the engagement, 'and believe me there is something charming in the sound.' Those who read the young braggart's words just shrugged their shoulders. He would learn to 'blush for his rodomontade.'[3]

Would the skirmish lead to further action? It would have been rash to make any such prediction, since the French minister of marine, who was better placed than anyone else to measure the importance of the event, refused to see in it any indication of ' a rupture on the part of the English'.[4]

However, on 28 June the commander of Fort Du Quesne placed Jumonville's brother, Louis Coulon de Villiers, in command of a corps of five hundred men charged with the mission of avenging the 'assassination' of the ill-fated officer and driving the aggressors from the domains of the king of France. On 3 July, after a march of sixty-five miles, the expedition reached Fort Necessity where Washington was entrenched. The Virginian was quite unready to put up any effective defence: half his men were drunk and the whistle of bullets was far from amusing. Washington had to admit defeat and sign a dishonourable capitulation acknowledging in two separate articles that he had 'assassinated' Jumonville. But perhaps the most troubling feature of the adventure was the presence among Villiers's fighters of a large number of Indians: Shawnees, Wolves, and even Iroquois—all tribes that the British looked upon as allies. Washington's men recognized among the group individuals with whom they had traded and called them by name, but alas they were met with the 'worst insults the Indian dialects can express'. This was no trivial incident, but an engagement between important bodies of troops. The press was full of it; some papers even published 'supplements' and several printed the terms of the capitulation of 3 July, including the words 'assassin' and 'assassination'.[5]

In fact the battle that had just been fought was the first scene of a drama of which the last would be played out on 8 September 1760 under the walls of Montreal. Not that the capture of Fort Necessity was the cause of the War of the Conquest. Rather it was the incident that marked the beginning of its crucial phase. As early as 1744 Vaudreuil had recommended the erection of a French fort on the Ohio. His aim was to make a start on commercial colonization in the region and to attract its native population into the French sphere of influence.[6] In 1747 La Galissonière spoke of 'preventing the English from establishing themselves on the Ohio', where they could 'interrupt our communication with the Mississippi.'[7] He returned to the subject in 1749,[8] when the English were already solidly established on the Belle Rivière. In November 1749, on his return to Montreal after a tour of the principal Indian villages on the Ohio, Céloron de Blainville painted a very discouraging picture: 'All I can say is that the tribes in those regions are very ill-disposed towards the French and completely attached to the English.'[9] He wondered by what road they might be led back to their former allegiance. What road? There remained only one, the war path or, as Vaudreuil put it, that of 'coups d'éclat' (raids). In 1752 one such raid struck the

Miami village of Pickawillany on the Roche River. The destruction of this British trading and diplomatic centre spread terror among the tribes and shook the foundations of trading alliances built up by Virginians and Pennsylvanians in the heart of the continent.[10] In mid-October Governor Du Quesne wrote 'in strictest confidence' to inform Pécaudy de Contrecoeur, the commander at Fort Niagara, of a proposed plan of campaign. A contingent made up of 2,000 Franco-Canadians and 200 Indians would leave Montreal the following spring. Their mission was to seize and hold the Ohio country 'whose loss is imminent unless [we] act with all possible speed.'[11] The governor's plan has very much the appearance of a full-scale offensive. He speaks of 'taking' the Ohio country and to the question 'why?' he gives the conclusive answer: 'The King wants it, and that is reason enough to act.'[12] 'The King' meant 'the State'. The state wanted the Ohio because its possession was essential to the existence of New France and the development of Canada: or rather, the territorial integrity of New France, the American frame in which Canada was set, required that the Ohio valley be closed to British expansion. But English settlers had already advanced into the Ohio valley and colonies were developing there at a rapid rate. In view of the lead already established by the adversary, Canadians had no choice: they had to take the offensive. If the 'Canadian system' had been adopted, they would have followed the indirect strategy of 'Indian wars'. With the victory of the French system in the person of Du Quesne, they were committed to a policy of overt attack. In 1753, then, Canada embarked on important military operations. Between the middle of April and the end of June a whole army embarked at Lachine. The troops were to proceed to the Niagara portage and thence to Lake Erie. They would build forts at Presqu'île on the south shore of the lake and on the Rivière aux Boeufs, and they would leave a third garrison at the Indian village of Venango at the confluence of the Rivière aux Boeufs and the Ohio. Even as the expedition was getting under way a British officer at Oswego gave an accurate measure of its importance: he predicted that the Canadians would drive his colonial cousins out of the midwest and turn against them the tribes that until then had encouraged English penetration into the Ohio country.[13]

Now this was something the British Americans could not allow. So it happened that in December 1753 Washington appeared at the fort on the Rivière aux Boeufs with a letter summoning the Canadian commander, Le Gardeur de Saint-Pierre, to evacuate 'peaceably' a post within 'the western part of the colony of Virginia'.[14] He took back to Williamsburg a polite but vigorous refusal addressed to his chief[15] and a high opinion of French strength in the Ohio valley. His report soon made conversation in the province. The French—so it was said—had thrown up two forts in the Ohio country, each with a garrison of five hundred men, and a large force of Canadians was assembled not far to the rear, ready at the first alert to come to the aid of these posts.[16] Faced with the *fait accompli*, the British empire had only one alternative: to accept it or to fight. To accept it? Dinwiddie's commission to Washington proved that Virginia at least rebelled against any such possibility, and opinion in the mother country was no less adamant in opposing the idea. In the autumn of 1753 the *London Evening Post* described the situation: 'The British dominions . . . on the continent in America, have they not been invaded by the French?' But the limits of the colonies overseas had been fixed by treaties. Let France observe the international conventions to which she had herself subscribed! 'Surely' the English would not be so 'tame' as to give way to their rivals, especially since they were well aware that to give way meant to be driven back east of the Alleghenies, to agree to being hemmed in between the mountains and the sea, to abandon the interior to Canada, to compromise the future irreparably.[17]

In May 1754 a colonial officer went down the Monongahela to within a short distance of the point where the Franco-Canadians, after having driven out the Virginians, were laying the foundations of Fort Du Quesne. He reported that in the course of his journey he had been given a 'particular' description of the Ohio, its tributaries, and its basin, and he was full of praise for this 'inviting' country, its waterways, its woods, its soil. 'In my opinion,' he concluded, 'to possess it would be a greater acquisition to France than the conquest of all Flanders.'[18] And to ensure her possession of the country was precisely what France meant to do. In the written summons that was entrusted to Jumonville at the 'camp at Fort Du Quesne' on 23 May 1754 and that he was ordered to present to the commander of any British troops he might meet in the course of his mission, Contrecoeur gave final warning to the English to evacuate 'the territory of the King [his] master.' Henceforth the French were determined to 'constrain them to do so by all effective means for the honour of the King's arms.' They repudiated all responsibility 'in the event of any act of hostility.'[19] Soon after the capitulation of Fort Necessity, the governor of Maryland declared that 'the designs of the French must now be evident to everyone.'[20] They could not but result in war, and through the month of July it was rumoured that the two powers had indeed declared war on one another. In New England the rumour was so persistent that panic-stricken fishermen deserted the fishing grounds and took shelter in their home ports. In an effort to reassure them the governor of Massachusetts directed newspapers to announce that 'strict inquiry' had shown the report to be 'without foundation'.[21]

Was the news false or merely premature? The question might well be asked. Towards the end of August a band of Indians from Bécancour raided the village of Horeck, northwest of Albany, burning houses and bringing back scalps and prisoners. The object of this raid and of others like it, reflected De Lancey, could only be to spread panic in the provinces in order to put them on the defensive and thus prevent them from sending help to Virginia.[22] For Virginia needed help from the neighbouring provinces to repair the damage she had suffered from the erection of Fort Du Quesne and even more from the painful incident at Fort Necessity.[23] If this was the Canadians' goal, they were not long in attaining it. Anxious for the security of Albany, the New York legislature had the town's fortifications repaired and mobilized the militia from neighbouring areas to defend the capital in case of an eventual alarm.[24] In mid-December De Lancey reported to the British government: his earlier fears were by no means allayed; the northern frontier of his province was threatened with invasion. The hour was grave and desperate ills required heroic remedies. The government should send a regiment to New York. It should also create and build up a line of defence comprising four forts, of which one, half-way between Niagara and Oswego, would be at the same time an advance bastion and a base of operations against Canadian roads and forts on Lake Ontario.[25] But De Lancey did not allow himself to be carried away by ambitious schemes: for the moment it would seem wiser to make ready to repulse the enemy and not to indulge in grandiose plans for conquest. On 30 December Governor Morris of Pennsylvania apprised the New York assembly of news that had reached him: 'a body of 6,000 soldiers of the best troops of France' had just arrived at Fort Du Quesne.[26] Two weeks earlier a letter from Pennsylvania had warned that the French were encamped only 250 miles from Philadelphia. The writer predicted a 'bloody campaign' for the summer of 1755.[27]

Another journalist foresaw 'fearful calamities'. If, he reasoned, the French were building forts within the limits of Great Britain's American domains, it was in order to create a wide fortified corridor between Louisiana and Canada. Such permanent communication would in time make them masters of the continent 'from Cape Breton to the Gulf of Mexico'. And just watch their manoeuvres! Not satisfied with upsetting the relations existing between the British and the Indians, they were making use of the latter to harry the British provinces while they themselves perpetrated acts of the bitterest hostility towards any British subjects who might be exposed to their cruelty. The colonists must stiffen their resistance, defend themselves. Against the redoubled attacks of the Franco-Canadians? Yes, of course. But more especially they must head off the consequence of successful acts of aggression: French preponderance on the continent.[28] The governor of North Carolina, Arthur Dobbs (it will be remembered that he was a director of the Ohio Company), gave forcible expression to the same views. By allowing the French time to execute the plans upon which they had embarked, the British colonies would invite the inevitable loss of their liberties, their property, and their religion. In other words they would be inviting the destruction of the political, economic, social, and cultural structures of their various communities. 'How miserable must be the condition then of all our colonies when confined within the mountains, deprived of all the inland trade of the continent'—exposed on the landward side to the intolerable pressure of Indian raids on their frontiers, and on the seaward side to still more dreadful pressure from the French navy and French privateers infesting their sea-lanes and attacking their coasts. 'In this situation we must submit to be slaves of France, become their hewers of wood and drawers of water, supporting them with most enormous taxes.'[29] The governor's analysis of the situation is a penetrating one, his expression blunt. What Dobbs did not say was that once the predominance of Britain was established, history would familiarize Canadians with the situation he had foreseen; their fate, after their defeat, is an indication of what the condition of Anglo-Americans might have been if they had been defeated.

All this does not mean that the English colonies were in serious danger of falling into the hands of the Canadians. Population statistics sufficed to prove how unlikely such an eventuality was. They did have reason to fear, however, that a monopoly of inland colonization on the part of their adversaries and the counterweight of territorial balance might hinder their growth and retard their development. Clearly the prospects opening up before them differed widely according as they were in a position to exploit the whole continent or were forced to abandon three-quarters of it to New France. A similar idea was advanced a short time later by Henry McCulloh, a London merchant who had visited North Carolina where he had interests and where for some time he occupied an important post. The Treaty of Utrecht, remarked McCulloh, had opened up a vast field of expansion to the British provinces when it had given them the Iroquois country, including the five great lakes and the 'territories thereunto belonging; but by neglecting to form a system in American affairs all the advantages which might have arisen . . . by wise and proper regulations were lost.'[30] In other words, it was impossible to reconcile the vital interests of Canada and the natural aspirations of British North America.

Exceptions are always more striking than constant factors. They surprise; they invite attention by the very fact that they are unusual; and that is why historians often have an unfortunate tendency to throw a brighter light on them than on other facts. Thus historians emphasize the attempt of Canada and New York to conclude a treaty of neutrality at the beginning of the War of the Spanish Succession, or they linger over the illicit trade that went on in wartime between Albany and Montreal. But these are exceptions; they have their importance, but they must not make us forget the rule. The rule is that from the end of the seventeenth century the English colonies wanted war with New France because they wanted the spoils of war. They coveted her trade routes, her soil, her resources, her furs, her fisheries; and time merely whetted their desire.[31]

Hence the deep respect of the English for the Treaty of Utrecht. It had given them everything except lower Louisiana and Canada—but these exceptions were more important than they had appeared in 1713. Canada had neither the climate nor the wealth nor the future of the mid-west, but it had the men to keep the midwest within the political and economic framework of New France—it had the men to shut the British Americans out of the promised land. Shirley had recognized this fact and in 1745 had recommended the conquest of Canada.[32] At the time he had been a voice crying in the wilderness, but nine years later (16 September 1754) an article in the *New York Mercury* echoed his cry. One could foresee, 'without the spirit of prophecy', that there would never be 'a lasting peace in North America' without the annihilation of the enemy. The time had therefore come to 'take the advice a Roman senator used so often to inculcate upon his countrymen . . . *Delenda est Carthago.*'[33]

However, British America was more prolific in Catos than in Scipios. More eager for war than for combat, richer in legislators than in generals, she could not undertake to subdue New France without the help of the mother country—without the concerted action of British diplomacy, the British army, and the British navy. But the British government did not want to take possession of Canada, and public opinion, though more easily roused than the Newcastle cabinet, was still very slow in reaching a consensus. It did not become unanimous on this point until 1763. Absorbed by domestic and European problems, private citizens and politicians had little attention to spare for such speculations as the acquisition of new territory in North America at the expense of the French empire.[34] Besides, in its initial phases the conflict developed too gradually to spark general enthusiasm, and the frankly mercantile image that it presented at the beginning limited its interest to the 'world of trade', that is to an active but somewhat unattractive minority only recently promoted to a position of importance in the nation.[35] We must also bear in mind the views generally held by English statesmen of the age. Their predecessors, the men who had imposed the Treaty of Utrecht on France, had kept their sights trained on the sweep of British trade and conditions that would ensure the maintenance of British supremacy at sea; they had bent their main effort on wresting from defeated enemies a maximum of concessions in Europe.[36] Not that they had hesitated to carve pieces off the New World. But what had they taken? Acadia, Newfoundland with its fisheries, Hudson Bay with its furs. And they had stipulated that in the lake country as elsewhere all the Indian tribes should 'enjoy full liberty of going and coming on account of trade.'[37] They had negotiated less as strategists than as traders, as if they could have assured to themselves the exploitation of the midwest without ousting the Canadians and as if they could have ousted the Canadians from the midwest without destroying Canada. The English politicians of 1754 were no more 'tempted by the idea of empire' than were those of 1713. Neither they nor their business-men advisers cherished dreams of colouring the map of America in red. They attached little value to Canada and still less to the territories west of the settled part of the country. In the early months of 1755 the English government was disposed to conclude with the court of France an agree-ment that would have resulted in the creation of a neutral zone in the heart of the continent, between the Wabash and the eastern part of the present state of Ohio. (But Lord Halifax would have none of it; nor would Rouillé in Versailles. And would the American colonies have accepted it? It foreshadowed fairly accurately the zoning of the royal proclamation of 1763.) And that was not all. The fears inspired by the immense cost of a great modern war inclined the minister towards a policy of economy—that is, a defensive policy. It seems established that before the crisis of the summer of 1754, Newcastle and his colleagues would have liked to limit the action of the mother country to two well-defined objectives: financing the building and maintenance of a fort at the forks of the Ohio and encouraging a union of the colonies that would have made it possible for them to resist Canadian offensives.[38]

In October 1754, anxious to counteract the bad impression created by an 'indiscretion' of the war office—for the war office had not remained entirely inactive—Newcastle wrote to Albemarle, the British ambassador in France, that 'nothing was farther from the thought' of the cabinet than to plunge the nation into war.[39] Yet at the same time the same Newcastle was protesting vigorously at the 'annual' dispatch of troops from France to Louisiana and Canada (although the minister of marine had done no more than fill vacancies and maintain garrisons at their normal strength). He accused France of violating the peace by invading the domains of George II and driving the English out of their forts (allusions to Fort Du Quesne and Fort Necessity), of pirating their trade with the Indians and dividing the continent by a chain of fortified posts 'from Canada to the ocean along the Mississippi'.[40] Deny as he might any desire for war, Newcastle could not so easily disown the desire of the British empire for the centre of America—territory of which ownership was an imminent cause of war. The peace-loving Newcastle was, as we know, the man who would declare that it was better to accept combat than to allow the American provinces to be restricted to the point where they would form a mere strip along the Atlantic coast. In short, careful examination reveals only a shade of difference between the minister's real thought and the one expressed by a contributor to the *Westminster Journal* of 5 October 1755. According to the latter, rupture with France appeared 'inevitable' unless the French withdrew into Canada, made ample reparation for damage they had caused to American subjects of his Majesty, and abandoned all their claims to Acadia.[41]

With the Canadians confined to the St Lawrence valley, New France would be no more than a memory or an unfulfilled ambition, and that was in reality what the people of Britain had desired confusedly ever since 1713. What was the goal envisaged by the authors of the American clauses of the Treaty of Utrecht? Expansion of the economic and territorial bases of the British provinces, an expansion that would have rendered illusory any idea of a Canada linked with Louisiana. An English journalist writing in 1755 observed that ever since 1712 the aim of French policy in America had been precisely the creation of a link between Canada and Louisiana.[42] Some years later the historian Entick declared that the French project of usurpation had become manifest in 1720, when they had begun to realize it systematically, 'in defiance of the Treaty of Utrecht' and of the 'solemn concessions' granted in it by France in favour of Great Britain.[43] Were all such observations made after the event? By no means. It was a fact that in 1720 a report of the Board of Trade and Plantations called the attention of the government to the 'great industry' displayed by the French as they pursued the task of opening communication between the St Lawrence and the Mississippi valley, and bringing the Indian tribes under their dependency—in a word, of constituting for themselves 'an universal empire in America'.[44] Another historian observed that the British public first became gravely disturbed about the schemes of the French when it learned that the Canadians had succeeded in winning over the Iroquois tribes 'recognized in the Treaty of Utrecht as the allies of Great Britain'.[45] These ideas, current among the people of England, were also those of the government. In a letter of 16 January 1755 the duc de Mirepoix reported to Rouillé observations that had been made in the course of an official conversation by the British secretary of state, Sir Thomas Robinson. Sir Thomas had said to him that Great Britain held indisputable title to possession of the Ohio valley, since the Iroquois inhabitants of the country were her 'allies and subjects'. Moreover, since these tribes had since 1713 destroyed the other natives who also lived there, and had taken possession of the whole country and subsequently sold it to the English, these last were now its legitimate masters and the French had 'no right to molest them there'.[46]

[76]

In other words, the British people could not accept the existence of New France. In their eyes New France was the incarnation of the French will to 'universal empire in America'. Louis xv, said the *Westminister Journal* of 21 September 1754, was reviving the old dream of Louis xiv to extend his empire from the mouth of the Mississippi to the shores of Hudson Bay.[47] This can be translated: France did not mean to give up the centre of the continent. The international convention of 1713 had left her Canada (and also Louisiana, which hardly counted; it had at that time a population of barely two hundred). The English had not thought it essential to take Canada, because the articles of the treaty sufficed to ensure the security and the economic development of their colonies. What more could they ask for? What more could the British of 1754 ask for? Furs? They would get the best furs in the world from Hudson Bay. Territory? They had enough already. It was really not in their interest to seek war. They would have liked nothing better than to put an end in one way or another to the minor incidents that disturbed their distant colonies—but on one condition, said an English diplomatic memorandum: '. . . on condition that first all possessions in America be re-established on the footing prescribed in the Treaty of Utrecht and confirmed in the Treaty of Aix-la-Chapelle.'[48] France protested that these were exorbitant claims. The king could not allow them 'without admitting the English into the midst of his domain and then making it possible for them to possess themselves subsequently of Louisiana or Canada.'[49] Canadians therefore penetrated deep into the Ohio country and drove out the British with rifle fire. In 1713 Louis xiv had eaten sour grapes; now his children's teeth were set on edge. The people of Canada were so placed that they had to assume the villain's role. The British empire, on the other hand, could play the hero: it was acting in self-defence.

In September 1754 a dispatch from London made the point that the American provinces could not defend themselves without help. It was the duty of the mother country to come to their aid and she would have to send two or three regiments to Virginia.[50] And why should she hesitate to do so? France was doing much more. Another dispatch asserted that there were already 11,000 French soldiers in Canada as well as 'several very able engineers' and a 'formidable' force of Indians of proven fidelity. 'Common talk was that they intended opening an uninterrupted communication betwixt Canada and the Mississippi by building a strong chain of forts at the back of our settlements.'[51] Could it be just by chance that the government decided at that time to send two regiments to America? They were to be infantry units, each 500 strong, and colonial recruits would bring them up to a strength of 700 each. Two colonial regiments of 1,000 men each would also be raised.[52] The mission of these troops, as set out in a memorandum that passed through the hands of the Duke of Cumberland, was to 'recover territories belonging to the colonies and subjects' of George II, to dislodge the French who, 'most unjustly and contrary to solemn treaties subsisting between the two Crowns of Great Britain and France', had raised fortifications in them, and 'to secure for the future His Majesty's subjects and allies in the just possession of their respective lands and territories.'[53] On 24 September 1754 the government appointed General Edward Braddock to command the proposed expedition.[54]

To decide to send an expeditionary force, to appoint a general to command it—these were grave acts, but they were in certain respects no more than half measures. In reality these provisions added little to British America's existing resources. Although glorified with the title of commander-in-chief and furnished with ambitious instructions, Braddock was still almost a general without an army. All told, his troops amounted to seven regiments: the 40th (Hopson), the 45th (Warburton), the 47th (Lascelles), the 44th (Halkett), the 48th (Dunbar), the 50th (Shirley), and the 51st (Pepperrell). Of these the first three constituted the permanent garrison of Nova Scotia and were being assigned to a task beyond their strength. The last two, provincial units, had been disbanded in 1748 and would have to be reconstituted. The two new elements, the 44th and the 48th, mustered 500 men each; the human resources of the colonies would have to be called upon in order to complete their roster.[55] The British government was sending 1,000 men to America; it was not refusing aid to the colonies, but it was limiting its aid to a strict minimum.

The modest size of the contingent is evidence of a strange confusion in British thinking. On the one hand the country's leaders and the most enlightened elements of public opinion had a general understanding of the value of America. They knew that France must be prevented from interfering with the development of British establishments in the New World. One observer presented his view of the situation in a letter reprinted in the *New York Gazette* of 16 June 1755: 'It is my settled conviction that were the French permitted to conquer Flanders, this nation would not suffer so much by that enlargement of France as [by] permitting that nation to possess the ports of Nova Scotia and New England, with the regions behind the British colonies lying between the Mississippi and Canada rivers.'[56] It would be difficult to state more emphatically the importance of Britain's American frontier. Great Britain attached enormous importance to assuring her hegemony in the New World. Her desire to maintain, at any price, uncontested superiority made it imperative that Nova Scotia should embrace an immense territory and that nothing should threaten the security and normal growth of her establishments in the interior; and this in turn implied, in her eyes, that she should possess Lake Champlain, Lake Ontario, and the Ohio valley. The British empire would be satisfied, it would be relieved of anxiety, only when its security on the American continent had become absolutely inviolable; and this unconfessed objective would be achieved only when the Canadians had been driven back to the St Lawrence. Britain felt obscurely that mastery in America was indivisible. Since her mastery was questioned, she meant to maintain and strengthen it.

On the other hand, the official attitude of the government was clearly defensive, and on the whole public opinion was no more desirous for a war of conquest than were the country's leaders. It was against the 'encroachments' and the 'unjust acquisitions' of France that ministers and public inveighed in all good faith. It was obvious that, shorn of the territory acquired by these 'encroachments', New France would no longer be viable and that once removed from the frame of New France, Canada would sink into insignificance. It was obvious that merely by defending the position established in 1713 England could hold America at her mercy. It was obvious that England's supreme desire was to prevent French America from reducing British America to the condition to which Britain meant to reduce French America. And because all these things went without saying, the British did not say them. It would have been better for them, however, if the true objectives of the war—the ones they achieved—had been made explicit at the beginning. British action would then have appeared less confused.

In spite of the general tenor of opinion there were observers in England clear-sighted enough to go straight to the core of the debate in which the two great imperial powers were engaged, and to offer salutary warnings. The author of a pamphlet published in 1754 frankly recommended a general offensive against French America and presented a detailed plan of attack. According to the plan six thousand English regulars would be dispatched to America, 14,000 colonial troops would be raised, and a fleet would lay siege to Quebec. He estimated that it would take seven months to conquer Canada and destroy the French posts in the west. He had also calculated the cost: according to his estimate it would cost the kingdom less than 800,000 pounds to bring this decisive undertaking to a successful conclusion. The sum was 'a trifle' in comparison with the subsidies that England poured into foreign courts 'on the pretext of maintaining the balance of power in Europe.' He was confident that the balance in Europe would be held by the power possessing the continent of North America. His reasoning was admirably logical and his views admirably clear, but the action he envisaged presupposed that Great Britain disentangle herself from the doctrine of defence in which she was beginning to flounder, that she perceive clearly the end that, without daring to admit it to herself, she was pursuing—to despoil France of her empire in America—and that she adopt the most direct and rapid means to

[79]

achieve that end. She should concentrate her effort not on driving the French back within the limits of their boundaries but on driving them out of America. For to force them back into their territories would cost ten times more than would the successful conclusion of the operation the author of the pamphlet proposed. And it must not be forgotten that during all this time—while England strove to keep the Canadians confined within Canada—English trade with America would continue to decline.[57]

The British, said another propagandist, could choose between two methods for foiling the ambitious schemes of the French Americans: they could either sweep them by force of arms out of the territories attributed to England by the Treaty of Utrecht or establish themselves and build forts in the regions they claimed. 'If the first course be pursued,' he continued, 'we cannot do better than follow the rules of their own scheme, that is to take their capital Quebec and finish the war at once. Preparatory to which, the proper way would be to sweep all the country south of the St Lawrence clear of the French and demolish their settlements! That is the surest and most effectual method, and what will put the nation at least expense.'[58]

The views expressed were not often so clear. Not that the English journals were backward in commenting on the situation in America. Some articles were so violent in tone that the French minister of marine lodged a complaint with the British ambassador at Versailles, but he was snubbed with the answer that the British press was free.[59] Sometimes there was more rhyme than reason in the contributions. The *Westminster Journal*, for instance, printed the following couplet:

The brave should fight; but for the fops of France,
'Tis theirs to cook, to taylorize and dance.[60]

Such trifles should not be taken too seriously, but thoughts expressed in some of the other articles are worthy of notice. A contributor to the *Gentleman's Magazine*, starting from the premise that England's naval power was 'as yet, superior to that of France', concluded that there appeared to be 'no necessity for pocketing insults and tamely bearing encroachments or staving off a war by tedious negotiations.' England could still find money to carry on a sea war. 'And such a war we may wage with the French till they have not one ship of war or merchantman left, provided we begin in time.'[61] The idea underlying these words was that the destruction of the French fleet would entail the loss of France's trade and of her colonies. Then England would fear neither commercial competition nor imperial rivalry. What was an empire in the eyes of most Englishmen? A colossal trade organization serving national power. Inspired by this idea, a contributor to the *Westminster Journal* poured forth his feelings in lyrical prose: 'How powerful, how august, how magnificent, how rich has England become by the produce of her American plantations! And shall she not exert all her power, all her authority, all her wealth in support of such desirable possessions?'[62] Another writer took up the theme. For England, to lose her American colonies would be to lose her trade, and to lose her trade would be to be delivered into the hands of France; for the independence of nations depends on wealth as well as on power.[63] Imbued with the same idea, the *Daily Advertiser* proposed that England wage economic war with Canada: the best means of subduing that country would be to cut it off from the fur trade. Deprived of this vital commerce, the country would collapse.[64] (The people of Canada knew this only too well; that was why they were so determined to keep New France, the territorial foundation of their economy.) Looking back on this period, the *St James Chronicle* of 1761 would recall England's motives for engaging in the war: 'We began to wage war in order to maintain our possessions and to prevent the ruin of our North American trade.'[65]

This purely economic conception of the empire was, however, narrow. The mercantilist formula of which it was a reflection itself appeared too limited and too fragile to contain the extraordinary destiny of the British empire. The businessmen whose doctrine informed government policy and public reaction to it were right when they saw in the colonies a fabulous market for British trade; but they were wrong in seeing only that. What was being created on the new continent was in reality a second Britain, one that could come to the aid of the first, and that could one day—a less attractive possibility—succeed it. The situation presented opportunities for enormous expansion and for terrible misunderstandings—misunderstandings that were not long in coming to light. In the decade following the elimination of Canada, British America would manifest a less traditional and more intelligent form of imperialism than the one put forward by a body of influential opinion in the mother country; and conservative thinkers would resist these new ideas in the name of the same mercantilist principles that had led the powerful merchant class to force the mother country to go to the aid of her overseas provinces. England's leaders realized that the immediate crisis must be resolved; they could not be expected to take the long view. An America weakened by a rival French Canada would be no more than a limited market; they must hasten to conjure away this peril. And since a French irruption into Flanders would in their opinion have less serious consequences for British finance and trade than a sudden contraction in the New World's purchasing power, the feeling gained ground that England should stifle her worries about Europe, relegate to second place the Hanoverian preoccupations of her monarch, and direct her policies towards America.

[81]

It is difficult, however, to escape the impression of a certain disproportion between the upsurge of national feeling in the British people and the action in which it found expression. 'The expedition for Virginia goes on with great vigour,' announced a London dispatch of 1 December 1754; 'numbers of troops being already embarked: and the remainder will go on board the beginning of next week; so that it is to be hoped we shall in time be able to secure our valuable possessions in America.' There follows an allusion to the colonial offensive that had resulted in the capture of Louisbourg in 1745: 'The natives there act with great spirit, a specimen of which we experienced in the taking of Cape Breton.'[66] What did the English mean to do? To attack or to defend? They were assuming an attitude too aggressive for mere defence, but the force they were mobilizing was quite inadequate for serious offensive action. With deep-seated reasons for wanting to fight and plausible pretexts for starting a war, they chose to parade the latter though the former were uppermost in their minds.

They were playing a dangerous game, as the year 1755 was to prove. The discrepancy between what the English wanted and what they professed to want was evident in the uncertainty of public opinion and in an irritating lack of harmony between public opinion and government. The British empire wanted war. 'The topic of discourse now,' wrote a Liverpool correspondent in mid-February 1755, 'is war with France; both sides seem to make preparations with the greatest expedition.'[67] Europe was becoming alarmed; her fears were betrayed in the reassuring tone adopted by the *Mercure de La Haye*. Everything, reasoned the *Mercure*, presaged the outbreak of war in 1754. But 1754 passed without catastrophe: 'What has become of you, all you fearful and chimerical conjectures invented by prophets who seemed to see the world in arms and the flames of war on the point of breaking out in Europe? . . . Imagination brought you to birth, truth has destroyed you.' Everything would be arranged, the governments of Louis xv and George ii would reach an 'accommodation'.[68] A month later, with a perceptible tremor, the same review assured its readers that 'flattering hopes' for peace were gaining strength: 'Things are very far from being forced to the point where open rupture becomes absolutely inevitable.'[69]

Such statements roused the English to fury. The government made all haste to equip his majesty's ships, and press gangs became doubly zealous in their efforts to man them. But they could not satisfy public opinion, which found them too slow to act. It condemned 'the unaccountable supineness and inattention of our men in power', accusing them of doing nothing to prevent the conquest of the American colonies, 'or, which will be near equal to it, their destruction by being made the theatre of war

[82]

and desolation.'[70] Pamphlets published in London pointed to the 'wisdom' of France's colonial policy. By remaining constantly vigilant, France had succeeded in making her colonies not only strong enough themselves but 'formidable' to the neighbouring British provinces. In contrast, Great Britain had neglected her empire, and her inaction had had two equally unfortunate consequences: on the one hand the transatlantic provinces were exposed to attack by communities less populous but better organized than theirs, and on the other the British people were in danger of losing sight of the 'relations of interdependence' that must bind the colonies to the mother country. Such a situation bore in it the seeds of future conflicts of interest within the empire itself.[71]

In March the *Mercure de La Haye* threw off its mask of optimism and published a letter from London whose tone reflected the angry impatience of the people of England: France had still not given them satisfaction in the New World, and they insisted again and more vehemently that conditions must revert to those that ought to obtain 'by virtue of diverse treaties'. As it appeared unlikely that the French would accept this ultimatum, 'the decision must be made by force of arms.'[72] About the same time a writer in the *Daily Advertiser* stated his opinion: 'I presume there is not a man of common sense or competent knowledge in all the British territories, but is convinced that peace with France is inconsistent with the honour and interest of Great Britain.' It was high time to act, and the action proposed was that a large body of British troops should be landed in New York and dispatched to Albany. The objective of the campaign would be the capture of the 'fortified places . . . upon Canada River', an affair of 'three or four months'.[73]

Not everyone, however, was in favour of a land attack. Many of those who offered suggestions would have preferred a war at sea. 'The ocean is our element,' said one journalist. France, a continental power, could defeat England on land. But why give her the choice of arms? She must be attacked at sea.[74] When, in late summer 1755, the government authorized the pursuit of French ships on the high seas, England went wild with joy. From London came the story that the ghost of Oliver Cromwell had appeared at Whitehall and that it was 'from his advice that the resolution had been taken to seize all the French ships that our men of war can meet with and keep them as hostages till . . . every article of the Treaty of Utrecht be complied with.'[75]

The proposed strategy, surprising though it might at first appear, really did not require any supernatural explanation. Colonial war calls for sea war. Command of the sea meant command of the North American continent, and hegemony in the New World depended upon naval supremacy. All were part of one whole. 'By pretending to make the Appalachian mountains the natural boundaries of the British dominions in

America,' the French would exclude the British 'from a tract of land about 500 miles in length and about the same breadth in Carolina alone.' If their project were successfully carried out, 'they would keep all the Indian tribes under subjection . . . make themselves masters of the fur trade . . . and in a little time drive us clean off the continent of North America. Then adieu to our island colonies, and indeed to all our commerce!' France's navy and merchant marine would increase in proportion to her trade, British 'floating castles' would disappear from the seas, 'and instead of true religion, liberty and plenty, superstition and tyranny, hunger and nakedness, chains and wooden shoes, would be the portion of Britons.' Their future was at stake, the future of their trade and of the whole British empire. The 'opulence and grandeur' of the nation, her dignity in the world, were subject to her volume of trade, for it was as a result of her wealth, itself the product of her economic activity, that England had been 'enabled to humble the proud tyrants of the earth . . . and set nations free.'[76]

The traditional mercantilist doctrine added weight to this argument. According to an estimate that appeared in the *New York Gazette* of 16 June 1755, the colonies bought one-third of Britain's manufactured goods, and 30,000 seamen were employed in the transportation of all this wealth. If England were to lose this outlet and France were to create a similar one for her goods, the former would gradually sink into decadence while the latter would be exalted. The struggle was already engaged between the two great colonial powers; the prize was world supremacy. Obviously such a conflict was not susceptible of peaceful settlement, and compromise could only postpone the inevitable test of strength. 'Let the power and riches of this nation be vigorously employed' and France would be abased not only in America, but throughout the world.[77] Newspapers never wearied of publishing these arguments. They harped on the relationship between the security of the mother country and her fleet, between her navy and her trade, between her trade and the extraordinary American market. 'Whoever holds possession of our colonies in America will keep the sovereignty of the Atlantic Ocean through which the homeward-bound trade of the East and West Indies usually passes.'[78] No price was too high to pay for supremacy at sea, and it was the business of the navy to assure it: 'We must be masters at sea, all nations must pay honour to our flag.'[79] All 'local views', as well as the 'particular and private interests of a few single persons'—could this be an allusion to the European domain of George II?—must give way to this grandiose plan. The general good of the colonies and the aspirations of the kingdom demanded it.[80] The *Daily Advertiser* saluted the union of sword, buckler, and trident: Mars, Minerva, and Neptune had joined the fleet to serve the genius of Great Britain and to bear its thunder, its terror, and its vengeance to the ends of the earth.[81]

It seems obvious that if France really was developing her colonial policy with all the 'wisdom' attributed to her by the London journalists, England would take steps to parry the blows aimed at her; but there was no agreement among the British on measures to be taken. Early in 1755 it was common knowledge that France was arming an important fleet. All Europe had its eyes turned towards Brest. In February the *Mercure de La Haye* noted that such unusual activity in France's great naval base had caused many people to conceive 'the idea of a rupture and war . . . in the American colonies' between France and England.[82] French shipbuilding and ship launching are all to the good, answered the *London Magazine*; the more ships they launch the more there will be for England to scatter, capture, sink. France presents no threat to England at sea; only her armies are to be feared. For Great Britain the essential thing is not to let herself be caught by French schemes for trapping her into a continental war.[83]

Other observers maintained that Louis xv did not want war and would do little for Canada, too weak to defend herself. A letter from Paris, published in New York at the end of March 1755, echoed misgivings which, if the writer could be believed, were current in French political circles. According to the report, people were saying that if she were attacked, New France could not defend herself without powerful help from Europe. To maintain military positions between Louisiana and Canada was no small task, one that Canada could certainly not carry out alone. And even assuming that Canada could succeed in such an undertaking, what would France gain thereby? The object of colonies is to bring rich lands under cultivation, to create populous settlements, and to give to the mother country the fruits of the colonists' industry. The English in America are numerically strong enough to carry out this fine program. But the Canadians 'by attempting to do it too soon will never be able to do it at all.'[84] Thus anticolonial sentiment in France encouraged the confidence of British Americans. The *Virginia Gazette* declared that the court of France had never been in such difficulties. England's vigorous policy placed France on the horns of a dilemma: if she declared war she would meet certain defeat; if she failed to do so she would be an object of contempt 'and the little states of Algiers, Tripoli and Tunis [might] be expected to insult her next.'[85]

Was war then inevitable? On reflection it seemed impossible to doubt that it was. But a purely colonial confrontation might develop without provoking a world conflict. Hostilities might be carried out in America without turning Europe into a battlefield. That was the opinion of a writer in the *London Magazine*, an opinion based, so he said, on letters from Paris.[86] A period of extreme tension could be foreseen for the immediate future; one false step might provoke a rupture between the great powers. The risk was so much the greater since in reality it was less a question of rectifying frontiers between colonies than of transferring the whole of North America to the British empire. 'If the French were drove out of that continent,' wrote one ardent English patriot, 'how many more ships and hands employed! how much more of manufactured goods might be yearly sent into that country! and how many thousands more of our manufacturers and poorer sort of people might then be employed.'[87] In reality the possibility of a war confined to North America could only be entertained by the British; world forces were so balanced that they had the upper hand in America, while France with her massive population dominated Europe. In a war limited to the colonies France was bound to lose, whereas it was possible for her to save her colonies—at least it was natural that she should think this was the case—by winning a war in Europe. In other words, it was equally vain to suppose that France would remain passive in Europe while England prepared to humble her in America and to imagine that England would remain inactive at sea at a time when France was disposed to challenge her claim to hegemony in America. From such a situation there could be but one issue: armed conflict. And that conflict would be world wide.

The English people understood this in a confused sort of way. Statesmen and diplomats, slower to anger than the general public—or more mindful of international proprieties—affirmed that the measures being taken were strictly defensive. But their protestations did not deceive the French court. Early in 1755 the minister of marine informed Du Quesne that British troops were being sent to Virginia, and he added the following warning: 'And you may expect them to act, for even supposing they have in fact orders to remain on the defensive, the claims made by the British, however unjust they may be, will serve as a pretext to make any action they may take in the disputed territory appear as purely defensive.'[88] Six months later Du Quesne's successor was also warned to be on his guard against the 'excessive and . . . unjust claims of the English.' The minister instructed Vaudreuil to conduct himself with the British 'in such a way that he could not appear the aggressor', and to 'limit himself to taking all possible measures in order to be ready to meet force with force.' He added, however, that if the enemy attacked resolutely, the governor should not restrict himself to defensive action. Answering attack with attack, he should launch military operations that would redound to the greatest glory of the king's arms.[89] The English would have their war since that was what public opinion demanded. But it would be a longer and bloodier war than they had foreseen.

British Americans lived through the first half of 1755 in a state of bliss. The heady wine of victory was ready, waiting to be poured out for them. They were sure of a speedy triumph, not so much because of their superior numbers as because they could now count on support from the old country. England was beginning to send them men and, still better, she was preparing to bring her powerful navy into play. The *New York Mercury* of 5 May reported that, 'to the honour and glory of the Ministry', England was making preparations for a parade of naval strength 'only . . . paralleled by that in Queen Elizabeth's and Cromwell's time.' These preparations would be carried forward unless France gave positive proof of her 'intention to preserve peace with the court of Great Britain.' Moreover, in the event of a rupture, England would immediately bring into action a fleet of 150 men of war.[90] The Americans themselves realized they needed this help; for 'the same thirst for dominion and the unbounded extension of territory for which the European French are so remarkable [appeared] equally conspicuous in the Canadians', who were resolved to obtain for themselves a predominant position on the continent. Although few in number, they exposed British Americans to dangers 'too great to think of without horror.' As a nation they had sacrificed liberty to strength, and 'their indefatigable pains in training up their people with a particular eye to war [furnished] them with almost as many soldiers as men.' It therefore behoved Americans to be grateful for preparations being made by Britain to arm for the combat, the more so as these preparations presented 'a fresh demonstration of the watchful and parental protection of our most gracious sovereign.'[91]

The colonists were quite right in assuming that they could count upon Great Britain. On 25 March 1755 George II conveyed to the Lords and Commons a message that created a great stir in France. The message stated that the 'present situation' made it necessary to increase the king's land and sea forces in order to maintain peace in Europe and the just rights and possessions of the Crown in America. The next day the Commons in a wave of enthusiasm voted credits of a million pounds sterling, thus making it possible to recruit 5,000 men for the army and 20,000 for the navy.[92] It was understandable that the lion's share should fall to the navy: two months earlier the government had charged it with a very important assignment to be carried out in the waters off the coast of America. In January the secretary of state, Sir Thomas Robinson, had informed the colonial governments that the mother country intended to dispatch a squadron to America. He asked them to communicate to the commanding officer, Vice-Admiral Boscawen, any information they might be able to gather on movements of French ships carrying war materials.[93] While reinforcing her own American defences, England meant to prevent help from reaching New France.

The empire was indivisible; a threat to any part of it was a danger for all, and Britons knew instinctively that damage to any of its members would weaken the whole. The council of Virginia, answering an address by the governor, spoke of the need to ensure the security of the empire, a thought that 'must warm the patriot's breast.' As council members they knew full well that there is more than one patriotism; and they recognized the need for their fellow citizens to rise above local loyalties. They must consider 'the great and important business of the Ohio . . . in a national light, not as Virginians but as Britons.' For men imbued with this spirit and engaged in the glorious cause of 'King and . . . country',[94] there were no insurmountable obstacles. The British world was one. In his address, Governor Dinwiddie had exhorted the people's representatives to be true to their British origins: 'Continue . . . to distinguish yourselves the sons of Britons, and convince the world that the heroic martial spirit of your progenitors (famed over the universe) still animates their children in the remotest regions.'[95] A European review, the *Mercure de La Haye*, quoted the words of a citizen of Massachusetts rejoicing at the British government's decision to send aid to the colonies and thus prevent France from reigning supreme in America and the West Indies: 'for the moment when France succeeded in realizing such a design would mark the beginning of the ruin and decadence of Great Britain.'[96]

In London, Newcastle went on with the business of rearming the country, but without abandoning hopes for negotiation. Meanwhile a war party was formed within the government itself. The object of its manoeuvres was to hasten the outbreak of hostilities. Its leader, the Duke of Cumberland, was supported by Henry Fox and Granville, and soon by Pitt, but in the spring of 1755 Cumberland played the leading role. In the words of the Prussian ambassador, he was 'one of those who inflame the nation most', and he, more than any other man, was responsible for preventing the consummation of a reasonable understanding with France.[97] The absence of the king, who could not be distracted even by a national crisis from visiting his beloved Hanover, favoured Cumberland's plan to intercept the squadron the French government was preparing to send to New France with six battalions comprising 3,000 men. Secrets of military preparations were no better guarded in France than in England, and by the end of January the former intendant, Hocquart, knew of the court's decision to send out 3,000 troops to maintain France in just possession of her territories. With the wisdom of long American experience, Hocquart wondered how European soldiers, 'accustomed to eating bread in well-supplied camps, clothed and shod for well-travelled roads, cared for, if they fell ill, in the towns and villages through which they passed', would stand the 'infinitely greater hardships' that awaited them in the New World, 'lacking in all these resources.'[98] In mid-February Machault informed Du Quesne that Du Bois de la Motte would command the fleet destined for America and that two of the six battalions being transported would be landed at Louisbourg.[99] On 10

April a dispatch from Brest, which later appeared in an American paper, announced that the embarkation had begun. A 'prodigious concourse' of people had come to Brest to see the fleet, 'one of the finest . . . fitted out here since the reign of Louis XIV.'[100]

At first sight the fleet did indeed appear to be an imposing one, counting as it did no less than fourteen ships of the line and four frigates.[101] But only three were 'armed for war'—that is, equipped with all their guns. The others had been stripped of most of their guns and equipped 'as transports' in order to make room for companies of soldiers and munitions. The minister of marine had adopted this expedient in order to ensure a rapid crossing for the troops, warships being faster than ordinary cargo boats. By so doing he gained time, but at the expense of safety. Tension between England and France was mounting—war might break out at any moment—and France was exposing twenty of her ships of war, most of them practically unarmed, to the possibility of a fatal encounter with the enemy. What a temptation for England! By capturing the fleet she could break her rival in a single engagement. So it is hardly surprising to learn that she chose not to let such an opportunity slip.[102] The squadron, which was to have sailed from Brest towards the middle of April, did not reach open sea until 3 May, one week after Boscawen had sailed from Plymouth in command of a fleet comprising eleven ships of the line and one frigate. On 8 May a second squadron, eight ships and one frigate under Rear-Admiral Holburne, received orders to join Boscawen's fleet.[103] Boscawen had received 'secret orders' charging him to patrol the sea routes from France and to 'do his best' to seize French ships of war and transports carrying men or war materials. 'In case of resistance,' ran the orders, 'you will use all means at your disposal to capture and destroy them.'[104] On the morning of 6 June, as they were approaching Newfoundland, Du Bois de la Motte sighted a group of some ten sails, and as he had been separated by fog from about the same number of his own ships he signalled them to approach. There was no reply. Since French ships would have answered their commander's signal at once, La Motte knew they must be English. The fog closed in again, hiding the enemy's movements, and the admiral seized the opportunity to slip away, glad to have been able to avoid an encounter. 'We should have been at a great disadvantage,' he confessed later, 'since we should have been at most three warships armed for battle against at least ten ships more heavily armed.' While some of the English ships engaged the ships that were equipped with guns, the transports would have fallen an easy prey to the others.[105] As well as big ships and entire battalions of soldiers, the British would have captured Vaudreuil, the newly appointed governor of New France, and Dieskau, the commanding officer of the land forces.

[89]

The next day, 7 June, towards seven o'clock in the evening, three other French ships that had become separated from their consorts were southeast of Newfoundland, off Cape Race. They were the *Alcide*, captained by Toussaint Hocquart and armed for war, and two big ships equipped as transports, the *Lys* and the *Dauphin Royal*. The *Lys* would normally have carried sixty-four guns and the *Dauphin* seventy-four. Before nightfall they sighted in the distance the ships that La Motte had avoided the day before. The morning of 8 June the two groups were three leagues apart. Hocquart recalled later that there was almost no wind and 'the sea was as smooth as glass.' At eleven o'clock the French and British ships were close enough to speak one another. From the movements of the British Hocquart surmised that they were preparing to attack. But, he related later, 'we had to wait for [the English] to open hostilities since when we left Europe war had not been declared and I knew the serious consequences of appearing to be the aggressor; the enemy could accuse me of having started the war and thereby made me appear as in the wrong in the eyes of all Europe.' In order to find out exactly what the situation was, the captain of the *Alcide* gave orders and the question: 'Are we at peace or at war?' was shouted out three times in English. 'We can't hear,' replied the *Dunkirk*, the closest of the British ships. Thereupon Hocquart himself seized the megaphone and repeated the question: 'Are we at peace or at war?' and Captain Richard Howe replied in good French: 'At peace, at peace.' To justify the duplicity of the English on this occasion the claim has been made, by the traitor Pichon and later by others, that this reply was obviously ironical.[106] But it was no time for pleasantry, and Hocquart concluded bitterly that Howe had resorted to the trick in order to attack him to better advantage. Scarcely had the word 'peace' died away when the *Dunkirk* opened fire on the *Alcide* with a broadside. Each gun was loaded with two cannon-balls and all sorts of small shot. Four other English ships followed in the wake of the *Dunkirk* and pounded the French ship, whose rudder had been shot away in the first volley. The *Alcide* held out for one hour—one report said eight hours—but with her rigging shot away and eighty men dead, she was finally obliged to lower her flag. At the same time the *Lys*, caught between two fires and unable to defend herself, had to surrender in her turn. The *Dauphin Royal*, perhaps the best sailer in the French navy, was able, thanks to her 'greater speed', to elude pursuit and to reach Louisbourg with news of the loss of her two consorts, 'an event that revealed the whole English plan.'[107]

News of the surprise attack was not long in reaching France. The court knew of it as early as 17 July, a week before the disaster was reported in Quebec. The minister of marine was surprised, for there was 'still no war declared.'[108] The government informed Parisians of the attack with 'the laconic simplicity that always marks the announcement of bad news here.'[109] Louis XV made impressive gestures: he ordered his ambassador in London, the duc de Mirepoix, to return to France without taking leave and, significantly, he broke off relations with Hanover.[110] These dramatic gestures were also fraught with meaning. They opened up before the English people not only the prospect of war at sea, but the much less attractive prospect of a conflict that would affect their interests on the continent of Europe.

If France was so soon informed of the capture of the *Alcide*, it was because the news had made a great stir in England and provoked an explosion of popular enthusiasm. A dispatch from London to the *Mercure de La Haye* reported that news of the naval engagement had 'caused much joy among the people, who saw in the British victory a happy augury for others that might, that surely would, follow.'[111] The source of all this enthusiasm was not so much the capture of two warships as the prospect for England of the naval war that she had desired. Publicists continued to insist that this act of aggression and others that followed it were merely the fruit of a vigorous political defensive, and that they should be regarded as no more than spirited reprisals; but such specious arguments convinced no one.[112] The American colonies were fully aware of the significance of the act. A Boston contributor to the *Maryland Gazette* made the following comment: 'This action, no doubt, will bring on a general war. It is reported Admiral Hawke is gone to the West Indies with the same orders from our good King.'[113] In Halifax, Lawrence rejoiced at Boscawen's success and also at the recent feat of arms of his own lieutenants at Beauséjour.[114] The admiral's easy victory had preceded by one week the still easier British triumph in Acadia. When the capture of Fort Beauséjour was made known in Halifax, transports of joy swelled the bosoms of all those who were not 'indifferent about the prosperity of [their] country and the inestimable blessings of a free government and the Protestant religion.'[115] They looked forward confidently to further victories. Admiral Holburne's squadron was at times within range of Louisbourg's batteries, but 'monsieur' did not dare to open fire. 'He remembers,' sneered a Halifax man, 'that it is a time of peace.' Optimism was at its height in Nova Scotia, New York, and Maryland.[116] The future—the near future—looked bright. ''Tis privately talked here,' said a letter from Halifax, 'that Louisbourg will be in the possession of England between this and the first day of December next.' Naval officers were betting heavily on the date of surrender of the fortress.[117]

While Boscawen was acclaimed by the people in England and in the colonies, members of the government were more pensive. When they had authorized the vice-admiral to 'capture and destroy' La Motte's squadron, they had expected to be able to take advantage of the fact that some twenty ships were not equipped for battle. They had hoped to dispossess France of twenty big combat units and by winning the first battle to win the war. The ambassador of the king of Prussia to Versailles was immediately aware that this was their strategy. The English, he wrote to his government in the spring of 1755, would not fail to defeat the French fleet on its way to New France, and in this defeat he foresaw an epoch-making event. It would signal 'the destruction of the French navy, which would take many years to recover from the blow.'[118] But far from destroying the enemy's naval forces, Boscawen had not even impaired them, while at the same time he had placed the British government in a situation quite as difficult as if he had really harmed France; La Motte had returned to France with his mission accomplished and without having suffered any serious loss. After reading the report— a very vague one—from the victor of 8 June to Lord Anson, the chancellor, Hardwicke, remarked to Lord Newcastle: 'We have done too much or too little.' He also confessed his anxiety to the First Lord of the Admiralty: 'It gives me much concern that so little has been done since anything has been done at all. *Voilà* the war begun!'[119] Meanwhile Dieskau in Quebec wondered at the failure of the *Alcide* and the *Lys* to appear. 'I do not think however,' he wrote at the end of June, 'that they have fallen into the hands of the English; we cannot suppose that they would want to break the peace in order to capture two ships.'[120]

Even among the general public, once the first glow of enthusiasm had passed, observers in England began to recover their sense of proportion. A London journal warned its readers against excessive optimism; it would be a mistake, it insisted, to laugh at the efforts of the French government to increase the strength of their navy. Englishmen might allow themselves to indulge in the hope that the British fleet could capture French ships as fast as French shipyards could build them, but French resources would make it possible for her to continue that game indefinitely, and in the end the adversaries were likely to find themselves in a situation all too familiar to parties at the end of a lawsuit: the loser is stripped naked while the winner has nothing left but his shirt.[121] Another journalist discharged his political spleen in typical British fashion by attacking the government. According to him the government had been guilty of 'negligence' in leaving the sea open to the French and allowing their ships to sail where they would, even within sight of British men of war. Britain treated French ships too 'tenderly'. The enemy had been allowed full latitude to increase the strength of their navy, while England had lost a whole year of precious time that had been used by the French to ravage the defenceless frontiers of Virginia and Pennsylvania.[122]

Suddenly hostilities broke out at sea, and at the same time leaders in New France were dismayed at the speed with which the land fighting was spreading. Vaudreuil, who had landed in Quebec on 23 June, learned early in July of the capture of Fort Beauséjour on the isthmus of Chignecto. He also knew that preparations were being made in Albany for an offensive against Lake Champlain, and the British were giving him still further cause for concern by increasing the small navy they maintained on Lake Ontario, thus threatening Niagara. He confided his worries to the minister of foreign affairs: 'The colony is being attacked on every side, and by forces stronger than any it has ever had to withstand.' He had been officially posted before leaving France on 'the state of negotiations with the British court.' How could he have expected to be faced with a war both 'general' and 'hard-fought'? Even his predecessor, with whom he had conferred on his arrival in Quebec, had greeted him with the assurance that he need not worry, since events were expected to follow their normal course.[123] He, Du Quesne, had taken certain 'precautions', of which the inadequacy now became painfully evident.[124] The fact was that the country was quite unprepared for defence against an attack.[125]

Stunned, swamped by events, Du Quesne cried treason. Early in July he revealed to Puyzieulx that he had only recently been informed that the plans carried out by the enemy conformed to instructions given the previous year in 'letters from [Sir Thomas] Robinson, Secretary of State' to the governors of the British colonies, and communicated by them to the provincial assemblies. 'It is most unfortunate,' he complained, 'that negotiations provided them with a mask behind which to conceal their schemes.' He had hoped to leave the colony 'if not completely calm, at least with only a few frontier districts to defend'; instead, he had to hand over to his successor a colony that was being 'attacked in the heart of its oldest establishments.'[126] Bigot, although he had been more farsighted than his colleague, was almost equally surprised. True, he had warned the ministers during his recent journey to Versailles that the real objective of the British was to 'capture Canada', but, as he admitted, when he left France he did not think the enemy would proceed at once to launch attacks such as those to which New France was now exposed; 'for they are falling upon us from every side, they have plunged us into war without even declaring war.'[127]

The offensive of which 'French Acadia' was the victim was only one of four that Braddock had been planning for months. When he had disembarked in Virginia in mid-February he had found preparations already far advanced for the campaign organized by Shirley and Lawrence against the Canadian positions on the isthmus of Chignecto; they had only to be approved by the commander-in-chief. But when plans were being formulated for simultaneous attacks on the Ohio, Lake Ontario, and Lake Champlain fronts, his was the deciding voice. He was to have general supervision of the three operations, and he would take personal command in the Ohio theatre. Shirley and Lawrence respectively would direct the Lake Ontario and Lake Champlain campaigns. Shirley was not convinced that this was sound strategy. Instead of dividing the British units between the Ohio and Lake Ontario, he would have preferred, if his counsel could have prevailed, to see the forces united for the attack on Niagara. His plan would also have allowed for the possibility of a later attack on Fort Du Quesne. Familiar as he was with the geography of New France, Shirley knew that by establishing their occupation of Lake Ontario, the British would cut the lines of communication between Montreal and the Ohio posts, and that the latter, if isolated, would fall automatically. On that point Johnson was in agreement—but not Braddock.[128] On 19 April Braddock wrote to inform the British government of the plan he was about to execute: as he did not wish to weaken Shirley's army, he had had to reduce the strength of the force he was to command in the attack on the Ohio forts, but he could not help flattering himself that his plan would meet with success.[129] He had drawn up an exact timetable of the movements of his troops: departure from Alexandria (Virginia), 20 April; Alleghenies crossed, beginning of May; victory at Fort Du Quesne, June.[130] Who could stop him? Certainly not the force of 1,200 or less that, if one could believe the report of a Montreal trader, the Canadian government had sent to the Ohio.[131] The British were undoubtedly strong; the only shadow in the picture was the manifest incompetence of their commander-in-chief. But what did that matter since he was supported by able subordinates? One of the latter, however, expressed grave doubts as to whether their positive qualities could make up for his deficiencies. In his opinion it was nonsense to suppose that Braddock's subordinates could counterbalance his incapacity.[132] Braddock himself, naturally, had no doubts whatever concerning either his talents or his future triumph. His one fear, he admitted, was that the Franco-Canadians might blow up the fort before abandoning it and before his forces had reached it. That would be a nuisance, because he would have to rebuild it if he were to carry out his plan to man it with a garrison of colonials from Maryland and Virginia.[133] The governor of Virginia, no less optimistic than the commander-in-chief, expressed the hope towards the end of June that Braddock's next dispatch would be dated from Fort Du Quesne.[134]

June passed and Braddock still had not reached the Ohio. His army, heavily encumbered with elaborate supplies of every kind, moved slowly. A long line of wagons was followed by great flocks of sheep to feed the troops and by a heavy train of artillery—far more than they needed, as a

French observer remarked after the event, to lay siege to the Ohio forts.[135] Unwilling to take the slightest risk, Braddock had burdened himself with siege artillery and even with heavy naval guns from the *Norwich*, a warship moored at Alexandria. No one believed he could transport pieces whose weight was proportionate to their great fire-power through forests and across mountains, over a terrain without roads and broken by water courses.[136] He did succeed in doing so, but at the price of superhuman effort and loss of mobility; his monstrous war machine did move forward inch by inch towards the French fort. Contrecoeur was quite sure that if the enemy were allowed to get within firing distance of the fort, they could pound it to rubble. Accordingly, all his efforts, from the beginning of June onward, were directed towards checking the advance of the British force. He sent out detachment after detachment, all charged with the mission of harassing the enemy, but the British column maintained its order and continued to move relentlessly forward. He sent raiding parties to ravage and burn the frontier settlements of Maryland and Virginia, but Braddock left the settlers to their fate.[137] Nothing could distract him from his objective, and on 8 July he was within six leagues of the fort.

The next morning Contrecoeur decided that the moment had come for desperate measures: he would send 'everyone that could be sent out of the fort' to block the enemy's path. He formed a detachment of 72 marines, 146 Canadians, and 637 Indians under the command of Liénard de Beaujeu. But the Indians, observing that Beaujeu had confessed and performed his devotions in preparation for his departure,[138] took fright: 'What, father!' they asked. 'Do you mean to die and to sacrifice us?' Beaujeu answered their fears with a taunting challenge: 'Will you allow your father to act alone? I am sure to defeat them.'[139] His confidence proved infectious, and by eight o'clock the little troop was on its way to stop the enemy at the passage of the Monongahela.[140] But they were too late; the tortoise had won the race. Before the first Franco-Canadians had reached the river they found themselves face to face with the enemy's advance units—to the great surprise of both parties. Beaujeu charged first, 'with great daring but without any plan', as Dumas later observed. Shaken for a moment by the impetuous attack, the front ranks of the British quickly re-formed and fired three volleys. Beaujeu fell, a victim of the third volley, and even as he took over command of the force Dumas realized that the situation was extremely grave. The enemy had already got a small cannon into action, the Canadians were faltering, and the Indians were ready to give way. There was not a moment to lose if he was to take full advantage of a favourable terrain. A narrow road bordered on both sides by dense forests led up from the shores of the Monongahela to the higher ground where the two forces had met.

[95]

Knowing that he could count on his regulars, Dumas deployed them in the road. Their first volley riddled the ranks of the British vanguard, advancing to charge and confident that the battle was already won. The survivors fell back in disorder, hampering the movements of the main body of troops attempting to come to their aid. At sight of the enemy retreating the Indians took heart, as did the Canadians, although many of the latter were badly shaken. They were 'unfortunately only children . . . The best had been left at the Ohio to transport provisions.' However, under good leadership they took courage as their officers deployed them and the Indians on both sides of the road among the trees and on the height that Braddock did not think of occupying until it was too late.

The combat then entered its second phase. Before the English had time to re-form their ranks they found themselves caught between two fires, with no room to manoeuvre. The fixed formations in which they had been drilled in Europe were of no use to men pitted against an invisible enemy. After the engagement many of the British soldiers admitted that they had not seen a single adversary during the whole day. Under cover of the forest Canadians and Indians were free to fire on a vulnerable mass—defenceless, disorganized, blind. In the slaughter 'whole ranks fell at once.' The soldiers stood fixed, dazed with the horror of the carnage, powerless to act. Infuriated at being stopped within three leagues of Fort Du Quesne, Braddock galloped up and down the road, whipping his men back into their ranks with the flat of his sword. He tried to disperse small detachments through the wood to encircle the enemy, but his staff was melting away; officers fell before the general's orders could be delivered, more and more soldiers were deaf to commands. How, in any case, could regulars hope to catch Indians and militiamen in a forest? 'You might as well send a cow in pursuit of a hare as one of our soldiers loaded as they are against naked Indians or Canadians in their shirts.'[141] But still Braddock persisted. Five horses were shot under him before he fell, mortally wounded. The five-hour nightmare ended with the complete rout of his army.

Losses on the English side were staggering. Braddock had divided his army, and of some 1,500 combatants that he led into battle, 977— almost two-thirds of the men and three-quarters of the officers—were killed or wounded,[142] while Beaujeu's detachment lost only twenty-three dead and sixteen wounded.[143] These figures are evidence that the affair was a massacre rather than a battle. The victors captured thirteen pieces of artillery, a large number of rifles, quantities of munitions, and about a hundred oxen and four or five hundred horses.[144] At the news of this almost incredible exploit all Canada thrilled with pride and exultation. Marine officers counted it an honour to tell at court the story of 'what happened on that day, so glorious for Canadians.'[145] Among the spoils of war were Braddock's papers. The under-secretary of the provincial council of New York, one of the first to express concern at this loss, was dismayed, as he had every reason to be, for with Braddock's papers all the British plans were in the hands of the enemy.[146]

Vaudreuil was only too pleased to 'unravel' the documents. He found among them a good plan of Fort Du Quesne, secret instructions from the British government to Braddock, a very revealing letter from the Duke of Cumberland, and several letters from Braddock—to Newcastle, Halifax, Vice-Admiral Keppel. A letter to Robinson, dated 19 April, was full of explicit details of the projected campaign against Niagara. Braddock explained that he had appointed Shirley to command the expedition because it was 'the most important of all'. The same document also contained detailed information on the expedition against Saint-Frédéric, an operation that would engage 4,400 men under the command of Colonel Johnson. Vaudreuil sent the whole packet to Versailles, confident that he was providing the court with material for scandal in diplomatic circles. For his part he saw in the papers 'most authentic proof of extensive plans, for long the principal occupation of the court of Great Britain, to surprise this colony and invade it at a time when, on the faith of the most respectable treaties of peace, it should be safe from any insult.' Shedding a new light on local colonial policy, the letter revealed to Vaudreuil the close connection between British American aggression and orders from the 'British court'. Far from acting independently, the colonials had merely followed directives from London; and Vaudreuil concluded that Washington had brought about the 'assassination' of M. de Jumonville with the knowledge and consent of the British ministers. He recalled the shelling and capture of Beauséjour, the capture of the *Alcide* and the *Lys*, the blockade of Louisbourg, and the violence suffered by the Acadians, who were now being threatened with 'death and slavery' because they refused to take up arms against Canadians. These, said Vaudreuil, were not unrelated incidents, but parts of a plan conceived by the British empire for the destruction of New France.[147] The story of Braddock's abortive campaign and Vaudreuil's commentary on it spread quickly through France. The *Mercure* published a full account of the battle of 9 July, pointing up evidence that the British offensive was premeditated. How right the court had been, said the article, to send troops to Canada. It repeated and approved Vaudreuil's opinion. These grand-scale campaigns, 'authorized and fomented by the government of England at a time when it was assuring France of its peaceful dispositions and when it would have liked to lull her with empty negotiations . . . are proof of their design to take possession of Canada.' If the English ever succeeded in carrying out their plan, 'nothing henceforth could check their greed.'[148]

The Monongahela affair struck fear into British American hearts. Three weeks after the disaster the lieutenant-governor of Pennsylvania presented to his provincial assembly the 'sad report' of the defeat: the general killed, most of his officers dead or wounded, almost all the artillery in the hands of the enemy, the remnant of the army in retreat. 'This unfortunate and unexpected change in our affairs will deeply affect every one of his Majesty's colonies, but none of them in so sensible a manner as this province, which having no militia is thereby left exposed to the cruel incursions of the French and their barbarous Indians, who delight in shedding human blood.'[149] Five days later Dinwiddie repeated the message to the legislature of Virginia.[150] An article in the *Boston News-Letter* commented bitterly on the fiasco and its consequences: 'How much innocent blood may be inhumanly sacrificed to the cowardice of the British soldiers in that action before the winter be passed no man can tell, though we have the highest reason to fear the worst.' It was now essential to renew the offensive, if only 'to retrieve the glory of the British arms.'[151] So the governor of Virginia proposed that Colonel Dunbar, Braddock's successor on the Ohio front, should resume the expedition against Fort Du Quesne. He reasoned that the season was not far advanced, they could count on at least four months for their campaign, the western army still numbered at least 1,600 men, and Virginia would gladly provide 400 recruits.[152] Shortly before the middle of August Shirley, who was now commander-in-chief and who shared Dinwiddie's views, dispatched to Dunbar the order to resume his march towards Forts Du Quesne and Presqu'île with the surviving British troops, reinforced by provincials from Virginia and Maryland.[153]

But neither Dunbar nor his troops could face the idea of fighting. Their defeat was too recent; it had been too terrible. After the defeat of 9 July the panic-stricken fugitives had paused in their flight only when they had effected a junction with the second division of the army. Then, as if the enemy had been right on their heels, they destroyed what remained of their heavy equipment in order to hasten their flight to Fort Cumberland and thence to the interior of Pennsylvania.[154] On 29 July Governor Morris received an astonishing communication from Dunbar: the colonel wished to establish winter quarters immediately in Philadelphia. The governor could hardly believe his eyes. 'Winter quarters in July!'[155] He would have been less surprised if he had known the true situation of the army of the west. Anyone who thought it could still keep the field, wrote one of its officers, knew nothing of its condition. The army had lost all its baggage, the soldiers had 'scarcely a shoe or hose among them', some were even 'without breeches'.[156] Washington, who had returned to Mount Vernon, gave a similar report. There could be no question, he wrote, of attacking Fort Du Quesne without artillery, and the British had not a single one of the pieces they had transported so painfully across the mountains; most of the guns had fallen into the hands of the Canadians, and in his haste to escape Dunbar had had the rest destroyed.[157]

And yet, a few days after routing Braddock's army, Contrecoeur had admitted that if the enemy had returned to the attack with the thousand fresh troops they had in reserve the defenders of the fort would perhaps have been 'seriously embarrassed'.[158] The English, who would have been very much surprised to hear this admission, decided to postpone their attack to the following year. Early in September a superior officer in the British army calculated that 'next year's campaign . . . if the attempts upon Niagara and Crown Point succeed as those have already done upon Fort Beauséjour and St John's, will put us in a position to attack Montreal and Quebec and afterwards to go up the river and attack Fort Du Quesne.'[159]

The expeditions against Niagara and Saint-Frédéric continued then to be a vital element in British strategy. Less than a month after the 'fatal' defeat of 9 July, De Lancey addressed the members of the New York council and assembly. They must, he declared, 'abate the pride of the French, curb the insolence of their Indians', and re-establish British positions in America. 'We have the means, under God, in our power. Let us then with unanimity, spirit, and resolution exert those means He has put into our hands, in the defence of our religion from popery, our persons from slavery, and our property from arbitrary power. The safety and being of the British Colonies are near a crisis.'[160]

The governor spoke eloquently, and he was ready to follow up words with deeds. Immediately after addressing the colony's representatives, he wrote to London to propose three possible plans for action to the British government. The first was a very ambitious one: a fleet would sail up the St Lawrence with an army and lay siege to Quebec. Only the mother country could provide a squadron and an expeditionary force equal to this task; the utmost the colonies could do would be to create a diversion by attacking Montreal by land. His second plan was more modest and better adapted to the colonies' resources. It could be carried out in three stages. First an assault on Saint-Frédéric and the capture of the fort would put an end to Canadian-inspired Indian raids on New York's frontier settlements. Once in command of Lake Champlain, the invaders would build a fleet of light vessels in which they would slip down to Saint-Jean and Chambly. And finally, from Chambly they would march on Montreal. The third plan was more elaborate; it required fewer troops than the second, but it involved a very considerable extension of the British lines of communication. One detachment would be sent to

Oswego with the immediate objective of taking Niagara. If Niagara were captured, they could leave the Ohio forts to crumble slowly away, since their maintenance would present insurmountable difficulties for Canada. Or, if they wanted speedier results, the British could push on immediately to Fort Presqu'île. Fort Du Quesne could not hope to hold out for long after Presqu'île was captured. Such an expedition, less costly and less risky than a direct attack on Fort Du Quesne, would have another advantage: the blow would strike a vital part. To capture Du Quesne would be to 'cut off a toe', whereas to divide New France at the latitude of Lake Ontario would be to amputate 'a whole limb'. But that was not all: Oswego offered two great possibilities. With Oswego as a base of operations, one could either launch an attack such as the one De Lancey had outlined, or strike to the east. In the latter case, the first objective would be Fort Frontenac, and from there the British army would go down the St Lawrence and attack Montreal. This operation could even be combined with the Lake Champlain offensive of the second plan.[161] The three plans, carefully thought out, anticipate the campaigns of 1759 and 1760. They could hardly fail to impress the people of New York. The invasion routes marked out by the lieutenant-governor were at the same time trade routes. The roads the army engineers would build would help to direct to Albany trade that now flowed towards Montreal. In James De Lancey the entrepreneurs of the Ohio Company had an apt pupil.

The novelty of these plans lay in their coherence, which in turn was due to the sureness with which the governor put his finger on the objective being pursued by British America in the war. When he spoke of preserving religion and liberty, protecting property, establishing security, what did he mean? That the culture and material civilization of the British communities must triumph in America. The very existence of Canada compromised the development of that civilization and of the culture that was fed by it. It was therefore essential to throttle Canada —to reduce her to a state of impotence, and not merely to limit her 'encroachments'. De Lancey was not alone in such thinking. His words were echoed in the colonial press. The *New York Mercury* (18 August 1755) clamoured for immediate action. The danger became constantly greater with delay. 'Now we can attack them in what they call their own country, and convert their produce to the support of our armies . . . but should they make a descent on different parts of the continent, we should all be in confusion and dismay—all thrown into terror and alarm.'[162] In other words, with one victory the war would be half won by one side or the other.

Vaudreuil in Canada saw as clearly as De Lancey in New York the fundamental prize at stake. Soon after their inception in the spring of

1755, he was informed of New York's efforts to launch two expeditions which, if successful, would put the British in Saint-Frédéric, half-way to Montreal, and in Niagara, half-way to the Ohio. He knew, 'through trustworthy Indians in various villages' who spied for the Canadians, that the British were preparing to send four thousand men to Oswego with the aim of 'capturing Niagara and Fort Frontenac', and his intelligence service had also informed him that an army was being assembled at a big camp near Albany 'to march against Fort Saint-Frédéric and then to advance on our settlements.'[163] Colonists who had settled around the military post of Fort Saint-Frédéric in 1741 had been dispersed five years later by the fortunes of war. Undaunted, they had begun to come back in 1749,[164] and now, threatened once again by an invading army, they would be forced to abandon their farms and retreat towards the interior.[165] But the governor, convinced that Lake Ontario was in greater danger than Lake Champlain, decided to direct his main effort towards Niagara and to limit to a small force the aid sent to Fort Saint-Frédéric. 'The preservation of Niagara,' he explained, 'is what concerns us most. If our enemies were masters there and if at the same time they held Chouaguen [Oswego], the upper country would be lost to us, and we should have no communication with the Ohio.'[166] Vaudreuil was also convinced that if an English army reached the point of attacking the post, Niagara was theirs. The fort was in disrepair, its garrison 'composed of thirty men without rifles.' It was therefore imperative to prevent the enemy from investing the fort. And how was that to be accomplished? By taking Oswego. To capture Oswego was to eliminate the English from Lake Ontario, to make it impossible for them to attack Niagara and Frontenac, to ruin their system of Indian alliances, and finally to rob them of their best trading post. Then 'the prodigious quantity of beaver skins that went to the English [would revert] to the French trade.' Vaudreuil planned an expedition involving more than 4,000 men: 2,000 regulars, 1,800 Canadians, and a few hundred Indians. Starting on 12 July, they would proceed in small detachments towards Frontenac, where they would regroup before advancing to attack the English fort. Dieskau, who was to command the operation, was confident of its success, provided he was well supplied with 'food and munitions'.[167]

At the beginning of August the governor was busy translating his plan into action, 'speeding up' preparations for the Oswego campaign. He visited the Indian villages of Sault-Saint-Louis and the Lac des Deux Montagnes, and when he gave 'the war cry' the Indians promised 'not to spare the English.' If it had not been for contrary winds that had delayed the arrival of boats from Quebec, the heavy equipment of the last division of the force would already be on its way to Lake Ontario.[168] But

[101]

in the second week of August alarming news reached Montreal: it was reported from Saint-Jean that a considerable army, under Johnson's orders, was on its way to attack Saint-Frédéric. Unless it were stopped at once it could take the fort, and to allow that to happen would be to abandon to the ravages of the enemy the whole southern part of the colony, right up to Montreal. Vaudreuil immediately called to arms 'all men in the government of Montreal who were fit to serve.' The harvest could wait; 350 harvesters would be summoned from the governments of Trois-Rivières and Quebec to cut the wheat. The last detachment on its way to Frontenac would be recalled to Montreal. Dieskau would lead a force of about 3,000 men against the enemy: 1,500 regulars, 1,000 militia, and some five or six hundred Indians. The troops would leave Montreal in 'brigades' between 10 and 20 August. By the first of September the units were encamped at Carillon.[169] Bigot was confident of a decisive victory, comparable to the triumph at the Monongahela. It would be 'too bad', he thought, if the English succeeded in avoiding a confrontation, for they would certainly be defeated.[170]

Johnson had been preparing for this encounter for months. The plan approved by general headquarters allowed him 5,000 men, but recruiting was proving more difficult than had been expected. Shirley was taking men from the Lake Champlain force to swell his own ranks; illness and—even more—desertions were decimating the colonial troops. On 18 August, Johnson had only 2,932 men, but he was counting on the New Hampshire contingent to increase the number to 3,200.[171] The British, who had been so confident of victory on the Ohio, were now apprehensive of disaster on Lake Champlain. Governor Banyar implored the leader of the expedition not to repeat Braddock's blunders, and to beware of ambushes.[172] In his opinion the important thing was, not to defeat the Franco-Canadians, but to restrict their expansion in northern New York. 'Whatever obstacles you may encounter,' he wrote to Johnson, 'and whatever the enemy's strength may be, I am confident that you will reach Ticonderoga, which seems to me a very suitable place for a fort . . . which should be built in the French fashion.'[173] Others saw the colonials charged with the duty of redeeming at Saint-Frédéric the English defeat on the Monongahela, and more especially of erasing the memory of that defeat from the minds of the Indians, now disposed to favour the French.[174]

One can readily understand that in such conditions Johnson exercised the greatest prudence in carrying out his movements. On 8 August he set out from Albany to join Colonel Phineas Lyman at the 'great carrying place' on the Hudson, fourteen miles from Lake George. He intended to build a fort there so that 'in case they were repulsed (which God forbid) it might serve as a place of retreat.'[175] This was Fort Edward, called Lydius by the Canadians from the name of a trader of dubious reputation who had his headquarters there.[176] When he arrived at Lyman's Camp, Johnson realized that a surprise attack on Saint-Frédéric was out of the question. Reports from diverse observers agreed that the enemy's movements showed they were fully informed on the movements of his army and were hastening preparations to meet it. The road between Montreal and Saint-Jean swarmed with wagons loaded with munitions. At Saint-Jean supplies were transferred to two small vessels that shuttled between Saint-Jean and Saint-Frédéric. One could see by the movements of the Canadians that they meant to occupy Ticonderoga, where a favourable terrain would make it possible for them to resist forces greatly superior to their own.[177] How could the British meet this new situation? They could redouble their precautions: build another fort at the end of Lake Saint-Sacrement to stem a possible advance and to serve as a base of operations against the enemy's positions. Accordingly, in the last days of August, Johnson pushed on with the greater part of his troops to the shores of the lake, which he renamed Lake George, and established a camp on what was to be the site of Fort William Henry.[178]

On 3 September Dieskau questioned a British prisoner who had just been brought in by a patrol. He thought he understood that construction at Fort Edward was by no means completed, and that the main body of the army had withdrawn to Albany leaving about 500 men in camp. They were expecting 2,400 men at the Great Carrying Place, but these were to proceed under Johnson's command to Lake Saint-Sacrement where another fort was to be built. In short there were now in the enemy camp only 500 colonial troops. It was a wonderful chance for the Franco-Canadians to cut them to pieces. So Dieskau decided on the spot to change 'the defensive into an offensive.' He formed an élite corps of 1,500 combatants: 600 militia, 200 regulars, and the rest Indians, confident that with this force he would 'overwhelm the enemy's camp.' The detachment embarked on the fourth and sailed to Grande Baye (South Bay), where the boats were beached. At sunset, 7 September, they had reached the shore of the Hudson some two miles from Fort Edward. Meanwhile, during the afternoon of the same day, Johnson's scouts had reported the movements of the French troops to the camp at William Henry. The British commander sent a dispatch-rider to warn the Hudson fort of imminent attack; but the messenger was intercepted by Indians, his letter was delivered to Dieskau, and Dieskau decided to launch an immediate surprise attack.

His Indians, however, were in complete disagreement with this decision. They were reluctant to attack any fort, even one that was only half-built. Terrified at the idea of facing cannon fire, they refused to march, and the general, faced with this refusal, unwisely divided his forces. Since his contingent of white fighters was not strong enough to allow him to disregard objections and attack Fort Edward without the Indians, he decided to direct his attack on camp William Henry, less solidly fortified and with fewer guns than the fort—or so it was thought. At the time—he was to express a different opinion later—he appeared to have no serious regrets about retracing his steps: it would just be a matter of coming back to the Hudson after using the Lake Saint-Sacrement diversion to show his allies how easy it was for him to beat Englishmen. The enemy had perhaps a stronger force at the camp than at the fort, but that was of little consequence: 'The more there are of them, the more we shall kill.' At daybreak, 8 September, the detachment turned away from the Hudson. The troops advanced in three columns: the French in the centre, on a 'most beautiful road' built by English engineers; the Canadians and Indians on either side, 'in the woods and on the mountains . . . which made the march extraordinarily fatiguing for them.'

Meanwhile Johnson was becoming more and more anxious. Fort Edward must be relieved. If the French succeeded in establishing themselves there, the Lake George force would be isolated from Albany, and retreat would be impossible. On the morning of the eighth, as the enemy was advancing to attack, Johnson, with the consent of his officers, decided to send one thousand men under the command of Ephraim Williams, an officer from Massachusetts, to the aid of the fort. The Franco-Canadians realized before the British did that the armies were approaching one another, and Dieskau resolved to catch these provincial troops in the same trap that had shattered Braddock's regulars. Accordingly he ordered his Indians to take to the forest and harass the British from the rear; the Canadians would attack on the flank, while he would be ready with his regulars for the frontal assault in the road. But either by accident or from excess of zeal, the Indians opened fire before the enemy had become fully engaged in the ambush. Williams was killed, but his men fell back before they could be surrounded. Panic—as Johnson's aide, Peter Wraxall, admitted—spread rapidly through the whole body of troops and they fled in disorder towards the camp. 'The enemy,' continued Wraxall, 'pursued and kept firing upon the nearest fugitives. Our people ran into camp with all the marks of horror and fear in their countenances, exaggerating the number of the enemy; this infected the troops in camp.' Fortunately, as Johnson reported in his letter to Sir Charles Hardy, 'the enemy did not pursue vigorously, or our slaughter would have been greater, and perhaps our panic fatal.' Reasons were not lacking to explain the pursuers' comparative lack of vigour. They had been on the march since morning, and Canadians and Indians alike were exhausted. Dieskau and his regulars came within sight of the camp, hot on the heels of the fugitives and closely followed by small groups of 'panting' militiamen. The Indians, 'angered at having lost a few men', had retaliated by 'massacring thirty or forty prisoners, British and Indian, after first disembowelling the Indian chiefs.' If Dieskau's force had been at full strength, he would have invaded the camp, with disastrous results for its defenders, although every means had been taken to secure its naturally strong position in wooded marshy land. The fort was surrounded by a wall of upturned boats, carts, and big tree trunks, and Johnson had mounted several pieces of artillery. 'Amazed' by the cannon, the Indians refused to fight, but the regulars carried out the general's commands while the Canadians deployed on the right of the French column, climbing up into trees and establishing themselves on slopes from which they could overlook the enemy's breastworks. The encounter could not but end in a stalemate; the Franco-Canadians could no more dislodge the British than the British could annihilate them. Brisk fighting continued for five or six hours before the attackers withdrew, chastened but still strong enough to discourage pursuit. 'I don't know,' confessed Wraxall, 'but what a pursuit might have been dangerous to us. The day was declining—the rout of the enemy was not certain —the country all a wood—our men greatly fatigued, provided neither with bayonets or swords, undisciplined, and not very high-spirited.' His report to De Lancey added the significant comment: 'Our cannon and breastwork saved us.' Clearly the British had no desire to relinquish this double advantage.

One fact especially gave the battle of 8 September the appearance of a British victory: although seriously wounded, Dieskau turned a deaf ear to Montreuil's entreaties that his men be allowed to carry him to the rear, and he was taken prisoner on the field of battle. Meanwhile a third engagement was about to take place. The Canadians, retreating from William Henry, returned to the theatre of their victory of the morning with the intention of recovering the baggage they had left there. But a few hours earlier the commander of Fort Edward, informed in his turn of the presence of the enemy in the region, had sent 250 men under Captain McGinnis to join Johnson at William Henry. McGinnis, coming upon the Canadian equipment, had taken possession of it and remained on the spot to await its owners. When 300 militia and Indians appeared, it was an easy task for his fresh troops to surprise and scatter them. A valiant officer, the baron de Longueuil, was killed in the engagement.[179]

The failure of the expedition, according to Montreuil, could be laid to the fact that instead of re-forming his army after defeating Williams, Dieskau had chosen to launch an immediate attack against '3,000 entrenched defenders with a force of 1,500 men extenuated with fatigue, no longer in any sort of battle order, and whose ardour was spent.'[180]

Vaudreuil considered that Dieskau had shown bad generalship: he had contravened the orders of his commander-in-chief and divided his forces. Consequently he had confronted Johnson with 'less than a third of his army'. If he had led his whole body of troops against them he would have 'massacred the English'. His rashness and insubordination had cost him the victory.[181] It was natural, wrote a Quebec Ursuline, to expect 'a man of such great experience' as Dieskau to triumph, but 'since they do not fight in this country as they do in France, things turned out very differently!' And after comparing the losses suffered by the two armies, she concluded that neither side could claim a victory.[182] Her opinion on this point was confirmed by that of Peter Wraxall: 'I believe . . . the number of our slain and wounded were not greatly inferior to the enemy's.'[183] In fact British casualties were slightly higher than those of the Franco-Canadians, who counted between 100 and 120 killed and 133 wounded. When Dieskau reported that 'the regular forces bore the brunt of the enemy's fire and almost all perished in the battle',[184] he was exaggerating. In all, the French regulars lost seventy-eight officers and men, and of these twenty-seven were killed.[185] The British counted 191 dead, sixty-two missing, and about a hundred wounded; the newspapers carried reports that most of the wounded succumbed because the Canadians had used poisoned bullets.[186] It was also widely reported in the British colonies that Dieskau's army had lost seven or eight hundred men, perhaps as many as a thousand, but this absurd claim was rectified later in a pamphlet published in New York. Enemy losses, said the author, 'less than ours', amounted to no more than 200 killed and wounded. The earlier distortion of the truth was the work of zealous partisans anxious, for political reasons, to exalt their hero at the expense of Shirley and to make people believe the New World had brought forth 'a kind of second Marlborough'.[187]

For the most part British colonial bosoms swelled with pride. The victory they delighted to celebrate—and to magnify—was a triumph for colonials. When the French commander finally gave the order to retreat he did so, said one American, because he saw quite clearly that he was not dealing with a Braddock.[188] Walpole confided a similar comment to his *Memoirs*: 'What enhanced the glory of the Americans was taking prisoner the baron de Dieskau, the French general, an able *élève* of Marshal Saxe, lately dispatched from France to command in chief, while the English commander was a colonel Johnson, of Irish extraction, settled in the West Indies and totally a stranger to European discipline.'[189] Not all Americans, however, acclaimed Johnson as their saviour. Hardy was convinced that if after 8 September Johnson had attempted to take Saint-Frédéric he would have run the risk of seeing his whole army destroyed at Carillon, and he confided his opinion to Lord Halifax: 'In

[106]

short, my Lord, I shall tell your Lordship what I should not care to say publicly, that, after the battle and the defeat of the baron Dieskau, I firmly believe that the army did not care to put themselves in the way of such another bout.'[190] There is in fact every indication that the provincials at William Henry were far from feeling secure. Not only were they afraid to venture outside their camp until the following day, but the first detachment that was sent out 'became alarmed, went back . . . and came out shortly afterwards.'[191]

Late in October the *New York Gazette*, after first observing that Johnson had been preparing since the spring to lay siege to Saint-Frédéric and that he was still far from his objective, asked some pertinent questions: 'What have we been doing all these eight months past? Did our people go only to eat and drink, or with an expectation not to fight? Did they think Crown Point would come to them . . . or did they expect the walls of that fort would fall to the ground at the terror of their name as the walls of Jericho did at the sound of horns? if they did they ought to have surrounded them first.'[192] To his own question as to what had been the result of this campaign another observer gave the ironical answer: 'The erection of a wooden fort.'[193] It was not Shirley's intention that Johnson's activities should stop there, and he urged him to push on at least to Ticonderoga. 'If,' he wrote, 'Crown Point is inaccessible to the army now with you through the route you have taken to it, it will probably be more so to double the number of troops the next year.' In that case Fort William Henry would be 'of little or no utility' either as a base of attack against the French or as protection for the Hudson valley.[194]

While the British strutted and quarreled among themselves, Vaudreuil ordered Lotbinière to build a fort at Ticonderoga. This would be Fort Carillon. In the eyes of the governor nothing could be more urgent than this task 'of infinite consequence'. Bigot might protest with all his might that it was 'impossible to support such expense'; this was the reasoning of a man who had never wielded a sword, and Vaudreuil brushed it aside: 'I have ordered that work be begun without a moment's delay.'[195] Thus would Lake Champlain be snatched from the English.

And Lake Ontario? Vaudreuil was still more preoccupied with the fate of Niagara than with that of Saint-Frédéric. On 26 July, wishing to encourage Dunbar to resume the offensive on the Ohio, Dinwiddie assured him that Shirley was on the way to Niagara, that in fact the fort was probably already under siege.[196] This had indeed been Shirley's intention, but, as the *New York Mercury* was soon to remind its readers, there's many a slip . . . Shirley, said the *Mercury*, was undoubtedly an able officer, but he had under his orders no more than 2,500 men, principally 'raw recruits unacquainted with any kind of war, [who might]

ere long repeat the scandalous behaviour of the regulars upon the Ohio.'
And was it not also to be feared that while the New England provincials
were engaged in capturing Niagara the French veterans stationed at
Frontenac would occupy Oswego and cut off Shirley's retreat?[197] The
attention of press and public was focussed on Shirley's advance, on the
co-ordinating movements of the different sections of his army, and on the
progress of his preparations for the campaign.[198] Early in October the
Maryland Gazette announced that the governor of Massachusetts had
embarked with his troops and everything that was required for a regular
siege. The only question was where he would strike: at Frontenac or at
Niagara?[199] He would strike neither at Frontenac nor at Niagara; it was
too late. Vaudreuil had lost no time. He had retained at Niagara all the
Canadians and Indians returning from Fort Du Quesne now that the
Ohio was no longer under threat from the British, and by this means had
increased to 1,200 the strength of the garrison defending the important
Lake Ontario fort. It appeared unlikely then 'that the body of troops at
Chouaguen would stir.'[200] But the governor did not rely on this pre-
sumption; he also sent to Niagara the Guyenne battalion and colonial
troops, he dispatched Pouchot to the post with orders to strengthen its
fortifications, and he had the heavy artillery captured at the Monongahela hauled up and mounted for action. At the same time he posted an
infantry regiment in Fort Frontenac just in case the English should conceive the idea of attacking this first base of supply for all the posts in the
upper country.[201]

While Canadian defence posts on Lake Ontario grew progressively
stronger, the British commander saw his strength melting away. Sickness
and desertions wrought such havoc that by 8 September he had no more
than 1,400 men at Oswego; and since at least 400 would have to be left
to garrison the fort, the contingent he would lead against Niagara would
be only about 1,000 strong.[202] In the course of the 400-mile journey from
Albany he had lost almost half his men, and he was now in a helpless
situation. A letter of 12 September addressed to Johnson reflected his
discouragement: ever since his departure from Albany he had been
dogged by disappointments, of which the most serious were 'the want of
wagons and desertions of bateau men'.[203] On 27 September he agreed
that the campaign would have to be abandoned. He knew that the French
reinforcements at Frontenac would suffice to capture Oswego while
British troops were engaged in the siege of Niagara, and that Niagara's
chances for victorious resistance were greatly strengthened by the fact
that the British were no longer exerting pressure on Fort Du Quesne. In
these circumstances it was preferable to postpone the campaign to the
following year.[204] Late in October Boston learned by a dispatch from

Oswego that 'Major General Shirley had laid aside the intended expedition to Frontenac and Niagara.' The Boston correspondent of the *New York Gazette*, reporting to his paper, confessed himself 'not a little startled at this advice'. 'We presume not,' he went on, 'to pry into the secret reasons of this conduct but are obliged to suppose from the acknowledged wisdom and resolution of those who framed and conducted the expedition and the great charge to the crown with which it has been attended that they are very substantial ones.' The same correspondent had also been informed of another 'startling' decision. An express from the camp at Lake George had brought news that the forces there 'were not likely immediately to proceed to Crown Point.' The people of Boston had been 'thrown into great consternation—And it is to be hoped,' concluded the journalist, 'that the several colonies concerned in this most important and expensive expedition will make the reasons of this *strange* delay the matter of a most serious enquiry.'[205]

Articles such as this one expressed the anger of the general public. Military leaders too were exasperated by the setback, but they seemed to find a certain compensation in working out new plans for 1756. Shirley himself proposed a very ambitious scheme to the members of a council of war assembled in New York on 12 December 1755: that 5,000 men be assembled at Oswego, of which 4,000 would be detached to capture Frontenac and La Présentation; that Niagara, Presqu'île, and the Ohio fort be captured; that 3,000 men be sent against Fort Du Quesne to carry out the mission in which Braddock had failed; that a second force of 6,000 be sent to Lake Champlain; and finally that, in order to create a diversion, 2,000 men be sent to attack Quebec by way of the Kennebec and the Chaudière.[206] Johnson would have preferred to revive his earlier plan to organize an expedition in collaboration with a British fleet, which would sail up the St Lawrence as far as Quebec. Then, said Johnson, if 'our operations chime together I cannot doubt but we might next year be masters of Canada, put an end to the French power this way and be masters of the invaluable fur trade etc.'[207]

A correspondent writing from England explained that he wanted to dispel a certain misunderstanding that had crept into the discussions. 'Had the French been content with the north side of the River St Lawrence . . . the New England people would have wished them happiness and never . . . coveted a foot of their possessions', but the country on the south side of the river was so very 'agreeable, especially when you come about the lakes that Monsieur' coveted it. 'If the New England people have at all threatened to drive the French out of Canada, it must be meant only of what they have of late falsely called so; that is their settlements upon the Lake Ontario and Erie and at Crown Point etc. . . .

for while they are there settled the people of New England, New York, Pennsylvania, Virginia, etc. must expect nothing but eternal encroachments and not one day of certain peace.'[208]

The problem was badly posed. Of course the British Americans did not want the parishes, the seigneuries, the towns, of the colony on the St Lawrence; but they did want what kept those towns and parishes and seigneuries alive in their world. They did not seek to destroy Canada by force, but they were resolved to deprive her of the territorial (and economic) base without which she would fall in ruins. They could only achieve this end by dismembering New France, and the first great campaign of the war had already shown them that if New France were to be disrupted, Canada must first be destroyed. What La Galissonière had said in 1749 of Louisiana was equally true of all New France: 'It could be maintained only in the shadow of Canada's strength.'[209] Britain could dispel that 'shadow' only by destroying the powerful body by which it was cast.

To sum up: Canada was the mainstay of French America. And what drove the people of Canada, rooted in a country so difficult of access as the St Lawrence valley, to spend themselves in the effort to maintain this immense empire? Was it caprice? Megalomania? We know that it was neither. If, in order to hold together, this huge domain needed Canada, it was equally true that in order to survive Canada needed the rest of French America: Louisiana and the Ohio valley—the strategic link between Louisiana and Canada. Vaudreuil, the Canadian who best understood the structure of New France, explained this to the government of the mother country: 'France could not do without the Ohio, which is Canada's natural and only direct means of communication with Louisiana.' The slightest concession made by the king to Great Britain in the Ohio country 'would completely cut off communication between the two colonies whose maintenance depends upon mutual aid.' It must never be forgotten that if the lines of communication were cut, the first clash between the two powers would result in the loss to France of all the upper country. The Ohio valley must be held. 'Otherwise,' wrote Vaudreuil, '[Canada] will be continually at war, even in time of peace; we have had sufficiently striking experience of that, for since the last war [1744-8] we have been constantly occupied . . . thwarting the ambitious views and schemes of the English.'[210]

So the terms of the problem become clear, with Canada on the British as well as the French side of the equation. Canada was manifestly the prize at stake. But Canada was almost invulnerable: her approaches were defended by natural obstacles and redoubtable armies. Only England could bring about her conquest; only England possessed the means to strike at Canada's heart—Quebec—because she alone had the weapon, her fleet, that could achieve that end. In these circumstances, the publication of a list of Britain's naval units in the *New York Mercury* of 22 December 1755 appears particularly significant.[211] Was it an appeal? One should at least see in it the expression of a hope.

Chapter IV

The Year of Chouaguen

1756

At the end of 1755 Britons had every reason to feel that fate had betrayed them. Of the campaigns they had envisaged as victorious forays, all but one—the Acadian expedition—had failed. Du Bois de la Motte's fleet had eluded Boscawen, the march on the Ohio had ended in disaster, the thrust against Lake Ontario had proved abortive, Johnson had not succeeded in capturing Crown Point. When she was planning her great offensive, one of Great Britain's trump cards had been the possibility of a surprise attack; now she had lost that precious advantage. She had not, however, given it up without a struggle. As soon as the disappointing results of Boscawen's mission became known, the British government conceived another bold scheme. This time England would attack and capture any ship flying the French flag on any of the seven seas. In July Vice-Admiral Hawke was authorized to scour the seas and to carry out this program. For England was still pursuing the same ends: to force France to bow to her even before war had been declared, to reduce the French navy to impotence, to disorganize her trade, and as a result to provoke an economic crisis and demoralize the nation.[1]

Early in October a dispatch from London announced that 110 ships of a value of 400,000 pounds sterling had been brought into British ports.[2] Towards the end of the same month another London correspondent was pleased to observe that the number of prizes was now 'almost 170', and that the merchants in France were 'most ruined, owing to so many ships we have taken, and so valuable.'[3] A news item from Paris confirmed the claim: 'The English gain this considerable advantage over us every day, and if this went on we should finally be ruined.' 'More than 250 ships' had already been lost to the enemy.[4] In the spring of 1756 another Parisian struck the same mournful note: 'It means the ruin and downfall of our trade, which will perhaps never recover from the almost immeasurable losses resulting from the capture of several hundred of our merchant vessels . . . taken from us by the English in every part of the world.' The number and importance of bankruptcies increased drastically. One case cited in Marseille involved a sum of seven million francs.[5]

A British historian writing soon after the end of the war expressed great satisfaction at the success of this strange policy. Specifically England's gains from it up to Christmas 1755 had amounted to 300 French merchantmen and 8,000 sailors captured. The order authorizing the captures was ascribed to Fox and 'nothing could be better timed, after negotiations were found fruitless.'[6] This was the reflection of a victor saved by victory from the consequences of his acts of aggression. The opinion expressed by Lord Waldegrave at the time and recorded in his memoirs was quite different. He felt that England should either have declared war on France or refrained from attacking her ships, 'whereas, on the contrary, without previous notice, we at once commence hostilities; Hawke, in pursuance of orders, seizes every trading vessel which has the misfortune to meet him; whereby a foundation is laid for much dispute and cavilling, perhaps also for a considerable retribution if the war should prove unprosperous; and in the meantime we are called robbers and pirates.'[7] This last term appears in a note of 21 December 1755 from the government of France to the secretary of state. After emphasizing the gravity of the 'offensive orders' given to Braddock and Boscawen, Rouillé went on to speak of the 'acts of piracy committed over a period of several months against the ships and trade of the subjects of his Majesty, in defiance of the law of nations, the faith of treaties, established custom among civilized peoples, and the respect they owe one another.'[8] What shocked the English still more than the haughty tone of the protest was the fact that when Fox answered it he wrote in French, whereas no member of the British cabinet should have so little regard for his country's honour 'as to speak to the French court in any other language but plain English.'[9]

One can readily understand such reactions on the part of British opinion. In spite of the raids perpetrated by Boscawen and Hawke, Great Britain was faring little better on the sea—her element—than in the New World. In the first place, the French navy did not suffer any serious damage from the English attacks, and in the second place, although French trade did suffer severely it did not founder. Not only could the English not prevent neutrals from trading into French ports; so profitable was the business of supplying France—and especially French colonies—that the state could not prevent even British shipowners from taking a share of the spoils.[10] And finally, French sea power

[113]

was not to be despised. Immediately after the peace of Aix-la-Chapelle, Maurepas had drawn up an elaborate program of shipbuilding that would, over a period of ten years, provide 110 ships of the line and 55 frigates. He had not progressed very far in the accomplishment of this program when the marquise de Pompadour succeeded in procuring his disgrace, but in spite of difficulties the number of French ships of war had more than doubled between 1749 and 1755. When hostilities began, the ministry of marine had at its disposal almost seventy big ships and a good number of lighter vessels.[11] In June 1756 it was reported in England that the enemy could bring 110 ships and frigates into action.[12]

Of course the British navy was still much more powerful than the enemy's fleet. In 1755 an Englishman could throw out his chest and boast of his country's naval strength: 148 ships carrying from 50 to 100 guns each, 103 frigates, and 80 smaller craft—sloops, bombards, and fireships—in all 336 units manned by 42,000 sailors.[13] But its relative inferiority notwithstanding, one historian remarked that during the first years of the war the French navy had the secret of doing a good job and foiling the schemes of the British admiralty. While formidable British squadrons were at sea in all kinds of weather, keeping watch on the enemy's movements in the Bay of Biscay and the Mediterranean, the French formations bided their time in the sheltered harbours of Brest and Toulon, where they ran no risk of storms and where they could renew their supplies most economically. Then one fine night they would slip out of harbour, and once on the high seas they were safe until they reached America and the possibility of concealment in a favourable fog. Their mission accomplished, they regained their bases of operation— stealthily, as they had left them. When luck favoured them their losses were not too severe,[14] and in order to repair them French shipbuilders redoubled their efforts. In November 1756 it was reported that the royal shops at Brest were working 'more vigorously than ever'; it was expected that in the spring they would be producing armaments quite as much to be dreaded by the English as those produced during the reign of Louis xiv.[15] In the task of building her ships and keeping them constantly in repair, England spared neither effort nor gold, and in this way she preserved and increased her superiority, but France's naval arm was also a serviceable one. Following a skilful line of defensive strategy based on prudence and care to avoid any conclusive engagement, the French navy came very close to reducing the enormous British fleet to impotence.[16] It was not until 1758, after years of an exhausting war of attrition, that the British navy developed more effective tactics and succeeded in interrupting communications between France and her American colonies.[17]

When this feat was finally accomplished, the success was attributed to Pitt; and it was true that the idol of the empire had realized, even before he came to power, how immensely important it was to subordinate the war in Europe to the colonial war, to harmonize the economic appetites and the political ambitions of the nation, to co-ordinate effectively the means at her command, and more especially to exploit boldly and fully England's margin of superiority at sea. Pitt must be given credit for seeing this picture clearly; but it must also be remembered that he had the benefit of favourable circumstances in at least two instances: he was able to take advantage of the admirals' new and improved strategy, and also to gather the fruits of the unrelenting efforts of his predecessors. For they had not laboured in vain. Between 1752 and 1756, 54 vessels had been added to the navy's strength; and in 1756, a year of extraordinary activity, the number of ships fitted for service had increased from 87 in April to 125 in August.[18] In the heat of war fever the British people accused the ministers of not providing them with spectacular victories, of failing to define the ends they were pursuing. They forgot that the government had made one first great effort to win the war by surprise in America and at sea, that since war had not been declared it must sometimes refrain from speech even when it did not hesitate to act, and that it was manifestly unjust to accuse the men in power of failure to act.

Meanwhile France was stiffening her resistance. The British public had counted too soon on the disintegration of her naval and colonial strength. While the British people clamoured for victories, the European situation worsened. 'What aggravates our difficulties,' confessed a London journalist, 'is that the French try to persuade anyone who will listen that for them war in Europe is inescapable, especially since we have begun to hunt down their ships in these seas.'[19] The more perspicacious observers had long since foreseen the possibility of an extension of the war unless 'the famous admirals Anson, Hawke, and Boscawen' made a short end of French naval resistance.[20] On the other hand public opinion was, understandably, loath to see the country engaged in 'the labyrinth of continental politics'. There was a widespread feeling in the country that the 'maxims' on which England's action was based should be different from those that governed the policy of other European powers. 'Our proper strength,' it was said, 'is maritime and should chiefly be exerted at sea. Trade is our natural employment, in which the French, who are our inveterate enemies, greatly rival us. We can by a sea war support our commerce and cramp theirs.' To give up this advantage, to pour out good money to buy the friendship of petty German princes, still worse to sacrifice British lives on European battlefields, would be to play France's game by allowing her to choose the terrain on which battles were to be fought.[21] These were simple—over-simple—ideas. They were for that reason very popular, and they were embodied in the person of William Pitt. Did Britain desire to rule the waves? Let her then concentrate her attention on her navy. Did she feel that in order to remain rich and to become still richer she needed America? Let her then make war there. But what if France were disposed to retaliate by an offensive against Hanover? Well, that could not be helped; Hanover could be recovered later when more serious business had been disposed of. But George II could not subscribe to such a doctrine. He would like to ensure German support in Europe by means of subsidies. When in May 1756 the Commons were asked to vote one million pounds for war expenses, Pitt rose in the House to denounce the irresponsible policy of a government that had incited Britain to provoke a declaration of war by France before the country was prepared for defence and that, once war was declared, had slept. Parliament had already voted funds, which had been 'diverted' for the benefit of Hanover.[22] People whose memory was not too short then remembered suddenly that Mr Pitt had had a great deal of experience in American affairs during his term of service as paymaster-general of the forces. They remembered too that when everyone else had expected great things from Braddock's expedition, he had pointed out that the plan was too limited in scope.[23] Those in a position to mould public opinion were with Pitt. The *London Magazine* of January 1756 contained an allegorical engraving rich in mythological allusions and accompanied by the following legend: 'The Right Honorable Mr Pitt (represented under the figure of Perseus) flies swiftly to the relief of Britannia who, under the guise of Andromeda, is chained to the continent, figured by a rock; and by cutting her bonds in twain frees her from the distress brought upon her by unnatural connections, and delivers her from the fell monster of corruption by whom she is near being devoured.'[24]

No amount of rhetoric could alter the fact that England was moored to the continent. It was impossible for her to forget Europe and to look only towards the sea and her colonies. Nor did Europe allow herself to be forgotten. In the courts of Europe, French diplomats allowed it to be understood that Louix XV was quietly preparing to invade England or Ireland. On 23 March a message from the king called the attention of Parliament to the unwonted activity in French ports.[25] A month earlier the *Mercure de La Haye* had warned its readers that war was imminent: 'War, which is approaching by giant strides, is preparing tragic scenes for our eyes. At Brest more than 6,000 men are at work night and day building and outfitting ships of war. The Toulon squadron comprises twelve ships of the line and six frigates, while six other vessels are being armed and will be ready in a fortnight. The marquis de La Galissonière will command this fleet.'[26] These preparations gave rise to much com-

[116]

ment. Could they mean a threat to the soil of Britain? England was certainly not invulnerable; the *London Magazine* recalled that since the time of William the Conqueror she had been invaded twenty-three times, three times successfully.[27] The maréchal de Belle-Isle drew up elaborately detailed plans for the invasion: crossing of the Channel by the Brest and Toulon fleets; diversions on the coasts of Scotland and Ireland; in the Mediterranean, a secondary operation directed against Minorca; on the other side of the Atlantic, the threat of an attack on Halifax. On the north coast of France he massed 118 infantry battalions and twenty-eight squadrons, a force stronger than the whole British army. The thought sent a shudder through those who did not realize how completely Britain's safety was secured by her traditional strategy. The sea immobilized the powerful French regiments; or rather, the famous 'Western Squadron' barred the enemy's naval divisions from access to the Channel, while frigates and sloops kept troop transports prisoners in their home ports.[28] But disaster could strike quickly and, in an age of sail, ships could not be concentrated merely at a word of command, so that in certain conditions the defensive value even of the most powerful fleet in the world was subject to chance.[29] But Pitt was not unduly disturbed. Neither in 1756, nor in the following year when the threat of invasion was repeated, did he experience the slightest apprehension; a brief study of the disposition of the French forces convinced him that an invasion was an impossibility.[30]

Those who shared Pitt's confidence on this point had other fears. They wondered whether the government, preoccupied with European questions, might be tempted to accept something less than complete success in the New World, and, in order to have a free hand in Germany, might conclude a hurried agreement, which in exchange for unimportant concessions from France would confirm Canada's preponderance in the vital region of the Great Lakes.[31] If that were to happen, the English public would not have its war; and, as the Duke of Cumberland realized, it wanted war more than ever. In December 1755 Cumberland, supported by the 'voice of the people', persuaded the cabinet to authorize the recruitment of ten new battalions of infantry. It was in his apartments that, one month later, the decision was made to distribute 120,000 pounds among the four provinces of New England and to raise the number of troops serving in America, regulars and colonials, to 13,400 men.[32] In mid-January Machault wrote to the governor general of New France: 'Although war has not yet been declared, the English must be expected to exert further efforts and to strive for better success than they had last year in the execution of their plans against Canada.'[33]

The English were obviously determined to fight, and they were prepared to fight with money as well as with soldiers. The nation wanted conquests and was willing to pay for them. The national debt would double, rising from 72 million pounds in 1755 to 147 million in 1763.[34] But, as a perceptive observer remarked in 1755, most of this money would remain in England or be spent in America. Contracts for equipping the navy would give work to a large number of Britons, and enrich some. Everyone would benefit: the farmer, the carpenter, the shoemaker, the weaver, and most of all, the entrepreneur and the big merchant. What a stimulus this sudden increase in consumption would be to industry, finance, and trade! This shrewd economist summed up his argument in the following conclusion: 'Whatever we disperse is among our own countrymen, and after circulating a little and thereby answering many excellent purposes in our colonies at length finds its way back to Great Britain.'[35] Businessmen in the colonies seized upon these attractive arguments. They were eager for war. Since 1750 they had been suffering from a serious depression, the result of a sudden contraction in business after the peace of Aix-la-Chapelle. The good years of the last international conflict had left nostalgic memories. Now markets were dull, money rare, credit paralysed. In July 1755 the mere rumour of general hostilities caused a temporary rise in prices. When in the following summer a state of war was declared, New York merchants expressed the hope that the conflict would be as 'fortunate for this place' as the preceding one had been.[36]

England declared war on France on 17 May 1756. She took this action in answer to the attack on Menorca, launched, said the French government, in reprisal for British 'acts of piracy'. The declaration of war was a formality and the terms in which the instrument was couched followed a familiar ritual: 'The unjustifiable proceedings of the French in the West Indies and North America, since the conclusion of the Treaty of Aix-la-Chapelle, and the usurpations and incroachments made by them upon our territories and the settlements of our subjects in those parts, particularly in our province of Nova Scotia, have been so notorious and so frequent that they cannot but be looked upon as sufficient evidence of a formed design and resolution in that court to pursue invariably such measures as should most effectually promote their ambitious views, without any regard to the most solemn treaties and engagements.'[37]

These were high-sounding words, but the public wanted acts. After all, hostilities were entering their second year, and the newspapers demanded that the government put more vigour into the war effort. The *Monitor* condemned in advance any treaty 'worded in a dark and ambiguous manner'. Now that the war had become official it must produce important results; otherwise the people would regard it as a Noah's mantle cast over political corruption. What had been done, asked the newspaper, with the credits voted for aid to America? They had been used to raise corps of foreign mercenaries, to pay a big subsidy to the king of Prussia in order 'to keep him in good humour', to maintain a regular army in England, to arm squadrons that did little fighting, and to distribute pensions to favourites.[38] If the war had an objective, it was to take America. It would be a waste of time and trouble to try to achieve that objective in Europe. Public opinion required of the politicians that they make straight for their goal.[39]

But what was happening in America? America presented an astounding spectacle. The well-populated English colonies could do no more than maintain a painful defensive while they were harassed everywhere without respite by Canadians and their Indian allies. Shirley was still fussing over his plans, of which the latest included, among other operations, a renewal of the attack on Fort Du Quesne. But neither Pennsylvania nor Maryland nor Virginia was willing to take part in any such adventure. All the provinces south of New York were concerned with building a chain of fortified posts along their western frontiers.[40] That effort required all their money, their troops, and their energies. British America appeared to be backed up against a wall. The autumn and winter of 1755-6 were terrible. The southern settlements suffered countless raids. A Pennsylvania man saw these raids as a full-scale invasion by means of which the enemy had made themselves masters of 'almost all the country between the Ohio and the Susquehanna rivers', while thousands of colonists had had to flee from the western settlements and take refuge in 'the interior'.[41] Indians who but lately had been friendly to the British had now joined the ranks of New France's allies. Anxious to prove their zeal and fidelity to a power of which they were themselves terrified, they committed massacres 'in all the country extending from Carolina to New York.'[42]

In the newspapers tragic stories of Indian forays were repeated with monotonous regularity: here, more than a hundred settlers were killed and the roads filled with 'women and children fleeing for their lives';[43] there, at the news that the Indians had burned all the houses for fifteen leagues around, a whole village emptied of its people, an example followed by others in the neighbouring hamlets.[44] Incendiary raids were driving the people from the country that should have been protected by Fort Cumberland.[45] 'In the five counties of Cumberland, York, Lancaster, Berks and Northampton that make up more than half the territory of Pennsylvania, nothing is to be seen but scenes of disorder and desolation.'[46] From every side came stories of 'villages laid in ashes, men, women, and children cruelly mangled and massacred.'[47] Cries for help were sent out from Bethlehem in Pennsylvania and from Augusta county in Virginia.[48] Scenes of horror were enacted in the 'old colony' and fearful 'butcheries' were reported from Maryland.[49] Two counties in New York, Ulster and Orange, suffered bloody raids.[50]

Repercussions from these incursions were felt far from the settlements that were their immediate victims. The influx of several thousand colonists from western Pennsylvania into the eastern towns created a delicate provisioning problem. The crops that had been planted would not be harvested, and besides the refugees had to be fed. Pessimists cried famine.[51] At the same time Virginia, instead of raising the units of an expedition to be sent to attack Fort Du Quesne, had to recruit 1,500 men to protect her own frontier.[52] But all these considerations were merged in the atmosphere of terror that spread throughout the British territories. The English learned the meaning of the words 'the horrors of war'. It was reported in Philadelphia that a planter from Cumberland county had been 'killed and mangled in so horrid and cruel a manner that a regard for decency forbids describing it.'[53] Lieutenant Brooks from Connecticut, surprised two miles from Fort Edward, had 'his mouth cut open and tongue cut out, his entrails taken out of his body and afterwards crammed into his mouth.'[54]

Atrocities were part of a system. Vaudreuil said he attached special importance to the organization of Indian raids because 'there is no surer way to sicken the people of the English colonies of war and to make them desire the return of peace.' He is delighted to note that in this terrible game 'the English have lost a hundred heads to our one.'[55] This tactic made it possible for Indians numbering rather more than two thousand—Wolves, Shawnees, Illinois, Miamis, Ottawas—and perhaps a thousand Franco-Canadians to make the British provinces tremble and to reduce them almost all, except New England, to impotence.[56] 'Pennsylvania and Virginia,' wrote Montcalm, 'are truly desolate.' Letters found on the bodies of officers described the state of alarm that possessed the people of these provinces, who were, in Montcalm's words, 'not warriors'.[57] One of the letters stated that after their victory over Braddock the Canadians inspired such terror that they could have taken 'all Maryland and Virginia simply by going there.' The 'greatly vaunted' Colonel Washington would certainly not have stopped them: 'He is really only an Indian trader about twenty-five years old who had never seen service.'[58]

During the first months of 1756, British America was demoralized. The southern provinces appeared to be licking their wounds: Virginia was trying to provide herself with a protective shield; Maryland, whose frontiers were covered by the neighbouring provinces, was doing nothing; Pennsylvania feared for her farming settlements in the west and could think only of their defence.[59] A journalist writing in the *Virginia Gazette* reflected on the vanity of numerical strength, of which the British empire in the New World had just given such a striking demonstration. He evoked the proud resistance of the 'little states of Greece' that had 'stood their ground against all the power of the vast Persian Empire, mortified the insolence of Xerxes, and defeated the most numerous army that ever was raised upon earth.' Greeks against barbarians, Franco-Canadians against British: the implied comparison was not flattering to British pride, but, continued the journalist, 'these instances are sufficient to mortify our confidence in our numbers.' Strength is not merely a question of mass. 'It is courage, my countrymen, it is courage and good conduct, hardiness, resolution and unanimity, which determine the fate of nations.'[60] The governor of New York, writing in the same vein, deplored the disunion that created conditions in which 'a perfidious and vigilant enemy, though small in number . . . put us poor disunited millions in defiance, committing by means of their Indians the most unheard-of barbarities, and laying waste our lands without opposition.'[61] The massacres and ravages perpetrated by the French 'should fire [their victims] with a suitable spirit of resentment', but alas they merely awoke 'gloomy apprehensions'.[62] A New York correspondent gave the following lucid outline of the principles governing Canadian policy. The Canadian colonists had established themselves in a 'cold and arid country', too far from the ocean for them to carry on foreign trade with profit. Consequently they had been led to concentrate their attention on the fur trade and to extend their activities to the midwest, where they had come into collision with several of the British provinces. If Britain had not come to the aid of her colonies, there was every reason to fear that the latter might have fallen victim to the greed and ambition of their 'perfidious enemies'. Now the British empire was trying to prevent France from subjugating America and dictating her law to the world, and the French were reacting with the ferocity of 'so many beasts robbed of their young'.[63]

But what aid was England prepared to send to her colonies? In mid-January the French government was not convinced that she meant to send them any more men; she would probably provide only financial aid in the form of subsidies for recruiting and maintaining territorial troops. Information reaching the court had, however, warned that the enemy would not remain inactive: 'It is claimed that they are considering an operation against the town of Quebec itself and that preparations for the expedition are going forward in Boston and in Halifax.'[64] Five weeks later the French minister of marine, whose intelligence service was apparently excellent, warned the governor of New France that Britain would send America not only funds but soldiers 'under the command of Lord Loudon [Loudoun] who is to replace General Braddock.'[65] The appointment of the new commander-in-chief became official on 17 March.[66] Lord Loudoun was one of the sixteen Scottish peers, an intimate of the Duke of Argyll and a friend of Fox and Lord Halifax.[67] He had been wanting for several years to serve in America, and he had been spoken of in 1752 as a possible governor of New York. Later Benjamin Franklin in caustic mood likened him to 'King George on the signposts, always on horseback but never advancing.'[68] His ship did not reach Sandy Hook until 22 July, and he made his entry into New York at three o'clock in the morning, in a hurry as usual, because as usual he was late. The *New York Mercury* reported that 'as his Excellency came up so early in the morning, the City Regiment could not be drawn out to receive him, as was intended.'[69] It was to be the fate of the unhappy general to be always out of breath, always striving vainly to make up for lost time.

Since Great Britain was increasing the strength of her regular forces in the New World, France could not afford to do otherwise. Vaudreuil had asked for two infantry battalions; the court complied with his request. He had also asked for ten marine companies: 500 men. The minister sent him 450, enough to raise from 50 to 65 the number of men in each of the thirty companies already serving in the colony. The governor would also have liked some heavy artillery; Machault sent artillerymen and promised that guns would follow in 1757.[70] The French government also proposed to send to Canada a general officer and a staff to command the land forces. M. de la Morlière was mentioned for the commander's post,[71] but in March it was known that the appointment was to go to the marquis de Montcalm.[72] Some months earlier Vaudreuil had written to Machault that a battalion commander was not 'necessary',[73] and the minister had answered: 'Although the King's confidence in you is all that you could desire, and although he has a high opinion of the officers in Canada, he nevertheless considers it necessary to replace messieurs Dieskau and Rostaing in the command of troops being sent to the colony. The officers he has chosen for this mission are M. de Montcalm, maréchal de camp, and the chevalier de Lévis, brigadier; to them he has added the chevalier de Bourlamaque as third in command.'[74] Montcalm was to exercise 'only the same powers' as those held by M. de Dieskau. His role would be limited to 'executing and causing to be executed . . . orders he received from the governor.'[75] The minister of war also made a point of reassuring Vaudreuil: the governor would have every reason to 'be satisfied with [Montcalm's] discretion. . . . You will find him disposed to co-operate with you in every way for the good of the King's service.'[76] These tributes did not solve the problem. No one was satisfied: neither Vaudreuil, whose recommendation had been disregarded, nor Montcalm, who considered himself most unfortunate in being assigned the ambiguous role of 'a kind of general, although quite subordinate to the Governor General who has naturally the decisive and preponderating vote.'[77] In a letter to his wife Montcalm described the situation in which he found himself before he supplanted his colleague: 'I am a subordinate general-in-chief, passing on orders, meddling with nothing, or on certain occasions with everything, esteemed, respected, loved, envied, hated, haughty, amenable, difficult, friendly, polished, pious, courteous etc.—and deeply desirous of peace.'[78]

The antagonism between Montcalm and Vaudreuil was significant. Was it a conflict of character, the lively temperament of the southerner opposed to the slower Canadian disposition? Was it the inevitable discord between the 'amateur' clad in supreme authority and the career soldier forced, by an unfortunate turn of circumstance, to occupy second place? Or was it a still more tragic rivalry between the pretentious incompetence of a governor and the talents of a persecuted general, 'perhaps the most competent field officer of the war'?[79] The conflict has been the subject of much debate. But the division that split the high command was more than a personal quarrel. It involved societies—and what it is that causes societies to be created and to arm themselves to endure.

Like all backward-looking imperialists, Montcalm brought his own little group from the mother country to the colony where his mission called him. He established himself in the centre of a French clique—a closed group. He regarded as deserters Frenchmen who on occasion shared Vaudreuil's opinions. He scoffed at the bishop, monseigneur Pontbriand, who did not give the 'land armies' a place of honour in his mandates. 'Which is hardly surprising,' he continued, 'since the said prelate (a man incidentally of great piety and irreproachable morals), although born in France, has all the prejudices of a Canadian. He orders prayers to be said for the recovery of our Governor from illness.'[80] When Captain Pouchot of the Béarn regiment spoke with deference of Vaudreuil (who thought well of him), Montcalm lost all confidence in his junior and poured irony on his 'Canadian arguments'.[81] Lévis was on good terms with the governor and could have had still closer relations with him had not prudence restrained him. 'I am not anxious,' he confided to Mirepoix, 'to be more in his confidence than I am, because M. de Montcalm would be jealous.' If Lévis agreed with Vaudreuil against Montcalm, the latter complained of the 'obstinacy' of his second-in-command, whose opinion, agreeing with the governor's, prevailed over that of 'the army'.[82] The governor was always wrong, and the general's petty recriminations betray the man. Lévis was not tempted to stoop to such tactics since he had no desire to make his career in Canada. He had come there to seek advancement as an officer. Montcalm, however, had his sights fixed on the office of governor general.[83]

Vaudreuil was defending himself, and also the Canadian oligarchy of which he was the most typical representative. In this connection the arguments he put forward when he was trying to obtain the post of governor of Montreal for his younger brother Rigaud are particularly significant. Rigaud had been governor of Trois-Rivières since 1749, and when, with the death of the baron de Longueuil in 1755, the post of governor of Montreal became vacant he should normally have succeeded to it. But the court made no move to fill the vacancy, and in April 1756 Machault explained to Vaudreuil why he had not recommended the appointment of Rigaud. It was because, in the event of a governor general's sudden death, the governor of Montreal acted in his stead, and the minister did not think that Rigaud was the man to direct the affairs of the colony if such an emergency should arise. 'The proper fulfilment of all the duties of that office requires a breadth of talents and intelligence that is not the natural portion of every man and that no amount of good will can procure.'[84] But, answered Vaudreuil, if you exclude Rigaud the post will go to a French candidate. It would be 'regrettable' if Canadians were excluded from district governorships, 'for these are the only prospects open to them and the highest reward for their services after they have advanced through the military grades.' The 'colonists'—that is the colonial bourgeoisie—would share Rigaud's disappointment. They could not fail to see their horizons narrowing, they would feel that they were being restricted to subaltern positions, and their 'sensitiveness' to this treatment 'might perhaps temper their zeal.'[85] Since Rigaud could not hope for further promotion, Vaudreuil asked that he be granted an honourable retirement 'in consideration of his services' and those of his father and brothers.[86] For the Vaudreuil family had lived and still lived on the empire. It had served the empire in France, in the West Indies, in Louisiana, in Canada. The governor general showed no hostility towards the mother country. Like his father and brothers, he was her agent. Like them he was an imperialist, but his imperialism, rooted in the Canadian community, did not create a little France around him: it created a Canada. Vaudreuil was working to reinforce the social structure and the political armature of Canada. If a Frenchman sought to weaken them, he opposed that Frenchman. The position he adopted was not exceptional but normal. It was that of all great colonials. The governor knew, as they do, that empires are not built on air, that they are based in groups of communities, each of which has its own internal dynamic. His destiny and that of the people he represented were one with the destiny of Canada.

At the end of their unsuccessful campaign of 1755, Vaudreuil foresaw that the enemy would renew their attacks on Saint-Frédéric, Niagara, and

Fort Du Quesne, and immediately began to lay plans for the campaign of 1756. Preparations would be made to contain the enemy on Lake Champlain and on the Ohio, while he himself would direct an offensive against the central front, where he would lay siege to Oswego and thus preserve Niagara from attack.[87] In February 1756 his strategy, which had not changed, had a firmer foundation on which to rest: Saint-Frédéric was now covered by the fortifications beginning to rise at Carillon, and Pouchot had made of Niagara a fort to be respected, with a garrison of three hundred men who had wintered there. The governor felt reassured. 'I am confident,' he wrote to Bigot, 'that the English will make no progress and that they will suffer losses',[88] and Bigot shared his optimism. By mid-April an auxiliary troop was on its way to the Ohio, and Canada's modest armies were ready to move towards Lake Champlain and Lake Ontario. The English had spent the winter trying to woo Indian allies. But the tribes of the upper country, impressed by the French victory on the Monongahela, repulsed their advances. Even the Iroquois refused to be involved with the British; they were disposed, on the contrary, to send a large delegation to Montreal.[89]

While the Canadians regrouped their forces, the British provinces made desperate efforts to carry out at least a part of the ambitious program they had drawn up for themselves. It would seem natural for them to aim at destroying Fort Du Quesne, the base of the raids that had terrorized their western settlements. But the southern colonies were not prepared to contribute to an expedition against the Ohio forts. The plans for a double offensive against Saint-Frédéric and Niagara presented a possible alternative. But the central and northern provinces did not feel strong enough to launch two attacks at the same time, and when Shirley, the promoter of the Lake Ontario offensive, fell into disfavour, his project was abandoned. There remained only the plan to capture Saint-Frédéric, and the Anglo-Americans embarked on preparations to carry it out. As the campaign was being set in motion the colonial press expressed high hopes for its success, as it had done for that of the previous year. Early in July the papers had the satisfaction of announcing that 6,775 provincial troops, under Winslow's command, were spread out between Half Moon camp, ten miles above Albany, and Fort William Henry.[90] A later dispatch from the army revealed that all the provincial units, now more than 7,000 men, were massed around Fort Edward and Fort William Henry. Behind them were 2,000 regulars maintaining communication with Albany and ready to come to the support of the colonials in case of need. New York expected great things of the united force of the two armies: 'A unity between them will render the possession of Crown Point inevitably ours if not Canada into the bargain.'[91]

The governor of New Hampshire, Benning Wentworth, did not share this fine assurance. He reflected that since last year a new obstacle had arisen to bar the path of the invading army. The enemy were 'strongly entrenched and fortified' at 'Carolong'.[92] Even though Winslow was ready to lead the attack and though his regulars were eager to follow him, the march on Crown Point promised to be an arduous one. The regulars, more mobile than the provincial troops, would have to take the lead in the offensive; but the Americans were afraid that if they had to share the honours of victory there might be nothing left for them. Meanwhile, while Winslow was bogged down at William Henry, Vaudreuil had sent a force—three regiments of regulars and a contingent made up of 800 Canadians and Indians—to bar the invaders' route at Carillon. When he learned from prisoners that the English were starving their Lake Ontario force in order to concentrate all their strength at Lake George, the governor sent a fourth battalion to Lake Champlain, as well as another contingent of militia and troops from the colony. Montcalm and Lévis were also sent to Carillon, and Montcalm's presence there was reported to the English in the latter part of June. This was exactly what Vaudreuil had hoped for; he wanted to make them believe that he was meditating an attack on William Henry. During July and August barely a week went by without one or two 'parties', often fairly large ones, being sent out to 'annoy the enemy' and to probe their defences; and these parties always brought back with them information, prisoners, and scalps.[93] Early in September Montcalm expressed surprise that 'Lord Loudoun, with very superior numbers', had not dared to draw out 'an army that had never counted more than 3,500 men at most.'[94] But the British were in no condition to press forward. In August they had 1,500 men on the sick list; they were losing about ten every day, and as they buried more and more soldiers, the health of the army deteriorated steadily. Never had camps been so ill kept. Kitchens, latrines, cemetery, slaughter-house were huddled together pell-mell. The filth was revolting, the air fetid. The odour was, in the words of an English order, 'enough to cause an epidemic.'[95] An epidemic of smallpox did break out and spread to Albany. Soon, wrote Wentworth, they would have to think of sending the troops into winter quarters with none of their designs accomplished.[96] Once again the campaign had failed.

Montcalm did not stay long at Carillon. He left Montreal on 29 June; and when he returned on 19 July, he was very much surprised to find that during his absence Vaudreuil had 'given a great many orders' designed to put the finishing touches on preparations for an attack on Oswego. The general had suspected that the governor was 'rather anxious' to dislodge the English from Lake Ontario, but he had not taken the proposed expedition very seriously. He had arranged things in such a way as to leave two of his own men, first Bougainville and later Doreil, 'to press him in connection with diverse arrangements', but now he considered that Vaudreuil was going much too fast. In his eyes the undertaking appeared 'full of obstacles to be surmounted', and he had left for Carillon, as he said, uncertain and unconvinced on the subject of the Oswego expedition.[97] Bougainville, as a loyal follower, had echoed his chief and told Bourlamaque on 29 June that 'M. de Montcalm [might] remain at Carillon throughout the campaign.'[98]

This stratagem took no cognizance of the governor's passionate will to destroy Oswego. Chouaguen, as the Canadians called it, had installed British competition on the greatest of the western trading routes; the fort had also given the enemy a base for Indian diplomacy in the very centre of the network of tribal alliances that New France had created with such effort. The annihilation of Chouaguen was the most Canadian of the objectives at which the colony might aim. In the autumn of 1755 Vaudreuil had begun to assemble and store in Fort Frontenac provisions for '4,000 or 5,000 men who will be employed in the siege of Chouaguen next spring.'[99] On 26 February 1756 he had dispatched from Lachine a force of some 400 men under the orders of Lieutenant Chaussegros de Léry. Their mission was to seize the fortified storage depots that the English had built at the ends of the great portage on the way from Schenectady to Oswego, a task so arduous in mid-winter that, in the words of one chronicler, 'it was manifestly impossible' to accomplish it successfully. On 27 March the little army succeeded in capturing Fort Bull, the post nearest to Chouaguen, and on 7 April news of the capture reached Montreal. This daring foray had resulted in the following gains: the Canadians had blown up a British fort, destroyed enormous stocks of provisions and powder, burnt a whole flotilla of enemy craft; and if they took only three or four prisoners it was because 'M. de Léry was no longer master of his men, who killed everyone they encountered.'[100] The raid caused a sensation in the British colonies.[101] If they still wanted to attack Frontenac and Niagara they would first have to rebuild their depot and reassemble their stocks of munitions, and that would give Canada time to reorganize her defences on Lake Ontario.

But Vaudreuil was less concerned to repel the British than to make it impossible for them to repel him: 'I am taking every means in my power to prevent the union of the enemy's forces at Chouaguen . . . My aim is to maintain a blockade of the position until it is reduced.'[102] He sent orders to the commanding officer at Niagara to 'keep sending out parties to strike in the neighbourhood of Chouaguen.'[103] One witness, observing that as spring advanced preparations were being speeded up in Montreal, concluded that 'everything seemed to be going well for Canada.'[104] The governor of New York shared this opinion: he had immediately recognized Vaudreuil's strategy. An increase in the number of Indian attacks on the water routes convinced him that 'the plan of the French was to harass convoys of provisions on their way to Oswego.'[105] Most of the raiding bands came from Niagara and Toronto, and they were relentless.[106] From April onward the fort at Oswego was progressively isolated from other British settlements. Canadians and Indians attacked and scalped workers, and captured soldiers right under the walls of the fort. Firing went on constantly in the surrounding woods, and on 24 May Indians surged into the 'town' itself.[107]

The governor did not stop at small raiding parties in his effort to paralyse the defence of Oswego. On 19 May, Coulon de Villiers left Montreal with a force of six hundred men and orders to cut the enemy's communication. On 5 June Villiers established his base of operations at Niaouré Bay (Sackets Harbor), and on 16 June he was before Chouaguen. His troops, deployed in front of the British positions, maintained their fire for several hours. The garrison replied with its artillery, but did not risk a sortie. The fourteen or fifteen soldiers killed or captured had been surprised outside the fort by the Canadian troop. When Villiers withdrew in good order, the British did not even attempt to harass his retreat, and Vaudreuil interpreted their inactivity, correctly, as evidence of demoralization.[108] A letter from the fort, dated 12 June, contains this revealing statement: 'Oswego is still a part of the British Dominions.'[109] An Albany correspondent was equally aware of the wretched conditions existing at the fort: 'If we still hold it, it is only because of the enemy's lack of skill and capacity.'[110] At the end of June, although the approaches to the fort were becoming progressively less safe,[111] Bradstreet and his boatmen succeeded in bringing in a big convoy of supplies from Albany. Having been informed of the movements of the convoy too late to intercept it, Villiers took counsel with his officers. 'We decided together,' he wrote in his diary, 'that the boats that went down had to come up again.' Acting on this assumption, they intercepted them on the Onondaga River 3 July. The battle went on for three hours with much complicated manoeuvring, and both sides claimed the victory. Villiers thought he had killed five hundred English, 'and what is quite certain is that we had forty prisoners.' The British, although they admitted to having had forty killed or wounded, boasted of having inflicted a 'defeat' on the Franco-Canadians. The latter, however, had lost only one officer, two militiamen, and two regulars 'who were taken prisoners as they were pillaging.'[112] What conclusion can one draw from such contradictory claims? Attacked by surprise, Bradstreet came off worst; but he had provisioned Oswego, and his troop, although it suffered heavy losses, was not cut to pieces. On his arrival in Albany on 10 July, he was in a position to give Major-General Abercromby, who was acting as commander-in-chief in the absence of Loudoun, exact details of the situation of the

British garrison on Lake Ontario and the dangers to which it was exposed. Abercromby was disturbed by his report, and with good reason. He ordered a regiment to hold itself in readiness to hasten to the aid of the fort. But troops could not be ordered to march without supplies for the journey, and Shirley's supply officers had made no provision for emergencies. The depot at Schenectady was empty, and without wagons it was impossible to have supplies sent from Albany.[113] So Oswego would not be relieved.

Meanwhile successive reinforcements were added to the troops in Villiers's camp, and when Rigaud arrived, on 27 July, he took command of 1,200 men. There were also three infantry regiments at Frontenac; and, finally, four Canadian ships patrolled Lake Ontario between Frontenac and Niagara. On 30 July they captured a British schooner.[114] These comparatively impressive numbers did not, however, restore Montcalm's confidence; and when he landed at Frontenac on 29 July he was still undecided on the question of an offensive against Chouaguen. A letter written to Lévis on 30 July implied that he would perhaps take no action at Oswego, and another, dated four days later, again expressed his misgivings and indicated his immediate plan: 'I do not want it to be said that I embarked on a siege only to raise it later or that I exposed my artillery to unnecessary risks. I am leaving the day after tomorrow in the evening or early the following day with four field pieces, ammunition for two thousand men, and less king than pirate, I am going to see with my own two eyes what is to be done, and work at preparing a road.'[115] Lévis, who was at Carillon, continued until mid-August to receive letters from his chief expressing 'no certainty as to the success of the siege of Chouaguen.'[116] Fortunately the other officers on the expedition had enough influence with the general to persuade him not to leave his cannon, mortars, and howitzers at Frontenac. Great fire power would be needed for the reduction of the three forts defending Oswego. The advance was to be made in three stages: first Niaouré Bay, already in Canadian hands, then Anse aux Cabanes, three leagues from Oswego, and finally another creek that Le Mercier had discovered a mile and a half from the fort. According to the engineer Desandrouins, from there to the British fortifications the road 'presented no difficulties.'[117]

Montcalm, however, saw difficulties everywhere. Even after reaching Niaouré, he still hesitated. He insisted that it would be 'more prudent' to leave the artillery there; he did not want 'to endanger the King's arms.' At the last lap he started all over again: the creek was too small, it would be risky for the guns, how could the army be speedily re-embarked 'if we were worsted'? He argued, raised every possible objection, and almost succeeded in working up a general state of consternation. It was Le Mercier who finally produced the decisive argument: action. When in obedience to his orders four cannon were landed and 'disposed on the shore', the ease with which the operation was completed restored the general's sense of security. 'On that occasion,' wrote Desandrouins, 'Le Mercier rendered a signal service. It was recognized, at least later on, that the position was a good one.'[118] They were now only half a league from Oswego, but how were they to get there? Rigaud volunteered to lead an advance force to lay siege to the fort. The general agreed but gave him only 550 Canadians, keeping the other 1,200 to prepare a road for the cannon. He did not intend to spare the militia: he had decided that if the supply convoys should be interrupted the Canadians would have to 'make a sort of porridge with flour, and the French soldier to be satisfied with a smaller ration of bread and a larger one of peas.'[119]

When at dawn, 11 August, Rigaud's units took up their position before Fort Ontario, the English were already beaten. For months they had scarcely dared to venture outside their breastworks to observe the movements of the Franco-Canadians by whom they were harassed, and they had not been informed of Rigaud's approach until the day preceding his arrival. Rigaud stationed his men on a rise overlooking the fort; some climbed into trees or hid in the brush, and for two days their deadly accurate fire kept the defenders imprisoned within the fort. On the morning of the 12th Mercer, the commander, sent scouts to urge the New York regiments to come to their aid, but the messengers were captured by Indians and their messages delivered to Montcalm.[120] The same evening the road was completed between the French camp and the fort, a trench was dug, the cannon arrived, a battery was mounted. The next day, while his artillerymen rained bombs, cannon-balls, and grenades on the French line, Mercer called his officers together in a council of war. All agreed that the fort would become untenable as soon as Montcalm's battery opened fire, and by a majority of votes the council decided that it would be better to withdraw the garrison immediately to the two forts that had been constructed on the other side of the river rather than allow the men to be blown to pieces by the enemy's projectiles. A heavy artillery barrage covered the retreat. At five o'clock in the evening silence fell on the fortress: it had been evacuated.[121]

Montcalm then realized that the morale of the British had been broken and that their resistance might 'lack vigour'. He must not give them time to recover. Accordingly in the night of 13-14 August he had a second battery mounted in great haste; it would batter the walls of Fort George. Towards five o'clock on the previous afternoon he had also ordered Rigaud to cross the river with almost all his force of Canadians and Indians and to deploy them behind the two positions still held by the English. By daybreak the besiegers had mounted nine cannon on their side of the river, and they opened fire with devastating results. Fort

George had no parapets on the water side, which would normally be protected by Fort Ontario. In front the men were exposed 'right down to their feet', while the main defences of the fort rose useless behind them. The trenches offered the only possible shelter and they took refuge in them.[122] About eight o'clock the sun disappeared, a storm broke out, and the ground was soaked with rain. In his haste to mount his battery Montcalm had neglected to provide platforms, and with each shot the guns sank deeper into the mud; the projectiles fell too high, too low, or short of the target. The guns of the fort did not suffer the same disadvantage, and their superiority in this respect soon began to tell: one of the French pieces was put out of action and the others were threatened with the same fate. The defenders took courage; Mercer prepared to make a sortie. At nine o'clock he was on the point of giving the order when he was killed by a stray bullet. About the same time Rigaud's troop, which had begun to cross the river at dawn,[123] came up behind the British posts, and Mercer's successor in the command, Lieutenant-Colonel Littlehales, felt himself caught in a trap. Impelled by 'the fear of falling into the hands of the Indians', he decided to surrender. At ten o'clock he raised the white flag, and at noon he had signed the capitulation.[124]

The English soldiers laid down their arms and became prisoners of war, to remain captive until they were exchanged for a corresponding number of French combatants. Officers, soldiers, and other occupants of the fort were allowed to keep only their 'baggage and clothes'.[125] British America lost between 1,500 and 1,600 soldiers. Not many were killed, about forty-five according to Vaudreuil's estimate—'12 in action and the others in the woods by our Indians as they were running away.'[126] For the Indians gave no quarter. 'I do not speak,' observed Desandrouins, 'of the horrors and acts of cruelty perpetrated by the savages. The idea that people in France have of them is quite right in this respect. It is dreadful to make war with such people, especially when they are drunk. In that condition nothing can check their fury.'[127] In spite of the massacre of fugitives, Chouaguen was not on the whole a bloody victory. As well as the forts, which they demolished, the Franco-Canadians captured six vessels and a great quantity of artillery—55 cannon, 14 mortars, 5 howitzers, 47 stone-throwers—which went to strengthen the defences of Frontenac, Montreal, and Niagara. French and Canadians accused one another of pillaging the great stores of ammunition that were taken.[128] When the siege was over, Montcalm bragged of victory. An inspired chronicle of the operation presents the following somewhat curious conclusion: 'This was one of the most surprising undertakings of the war. We arrived before Chouaguen with 1,300 regulars and an equal number of militia. Our artillery was quite inferior to that of the English; they were in a position to hinder our landing; the transport of provisions would have been difficult and uncertain if the siege had been a long one: all these obstacles were surmounted by the talents and energy of the general and the indefatigable zeal of the troops.'[129] Montcalm also wrote his own report to the minister of war: 'This is perhaps the first time that 3,000 men with less powerful artillery have besieged 1,800 who could be reinforced promptly by 2,000 more.' He goes on to apologize for his 'audacity'. 'My conduct in this whole affair and the manner in which I made use of 1,800 men are so completely at variance with the ordinary rules that the audacity displayed in this undertaking must appear as temerity in European eyes; and I beg you monseigneur to grant me this one favour: to assure his Majesty that if he ever wishes, as I hope he may do, to employ me in his armies, I shall conduct myself according to different principles.' Montcalm would like the court to know to whom the credit for this extraordinary success should be given. He admits that he made use of Canadians, but he took care not to employ them 'in operations that might be exposed to enemy fire'; in that he did not repeat the error of 'the unhappy Monsieur de Dieskau', defeated in 1755 because he had taken too seriously 'the self-flattering talk of the Canadians who consider themselves on every point the first nation in the world.' 'And my respected Governor General,' continued the letter, 'was born in the country. He married a Canadian and he is surrounded with relations on every side.' This was one way to discredit Vaudreuil, whose post Montcalm coveted. But it occurred to him that to give the impression that the people of Canada did not like him would not be a good way to recommend himself. So he was careful to state that he got on well with the common people although the leaders in the colonial community would have liked to be rid of him: 'the Canadians are well pleased with me, the officers esteem and respect me and wish they could do without the French and their general, and so do I.'[130]

Montcalm would have liked people to forget the reluctance to march against Oswego that he had manifested ever since the beginning of the campaign. But in Canada everyone understood, as Bigot did, that 'if M. de Vaudreuil had not been firm in the order he had given to lay siege to it, the English would still be in possession of [the fort].'[131] Vaudreuil was more keenly aware of this fact than anyone, and he did not allow the court to remain in ignorance of it. He was glad, he told the minister of marine, that he had been adamant in his determination to carry out his plan in spite of 'the opposition so persistently presented and the inconsidered reflections made upon it by [Montcalm's coterie].' If it had not been for the Canadian officers, for Le Mercier and especially for Rigaud, the only result of all the careful preparations for the expedition would have been a vain parade and a fruitless diversion, 'without any possibility of repairing such a blunder.'[132] What would the consequences have been? The British, who were on the point of establishing for themselves naval superiority on the Great Lakes,[133] would 'that very autumn' have commanded the waters of Lake Ontario. In the spring of 1757 New York, with one month less winter than Canada, could have massed its forces at Chouaguen before the Canadians had time to interfere, taken Frontenac and Niagara, and, unchallenged master of the lake, destroyed the Ohio forts, captured Detroit, and conquered the upper country. The Indian tribes would have been as eager to embrace the British cause as they now were to ally themselves with the Franco-Canadians. If New France was saved from such a fate, it was because the governor had stuck to his idea and refused to be dissuaded from it. It was also because the Canadians, always in the van, had, by the boldness and speed of their movements, rendered abortive the enemy's measures for defence. Vaudreuil recognized that 'the land forces had comported themselves with characteristic zeal', but he did not minimize, as Montcalm would have liked to do, the part—in Vaudreuil's eyes the decisive part—played by Canadians in this French victory.[134] The governor was not alone in his opinion; the whole country shared it. A note written by Bougainville expresses his indignation that this should be so: 'The Indians and Canadians [have] taken Chouaguen unaided . . . [an] easy operation in the opinion of the Canadian people, the marquis de Vaudreuil, and the Bishop, who, so he said, could have captured it with his clergy; doubtless in the same way that Joshua took Jericho, by marching twice around the walls.'[135]

Hostilities were not confined to Lake Ontario. While Franco-Canadian troops were engaged in the Oswego operation, the British still appeared to be threatening the Canadian positions on Lake Champlain. So immediately after the spectacular victory at Oswego, Vaudreuil dispatched the victors from Chouaguen to Carillon. At the same time he wondered whether, when they were united on the southern frontier, the French regiments and the colonial troops could not 'do something better' than await the arrival of the English.[136] If the enemy's situation did not prohibit such action, he would have liked Montcalm and Lévis to take the offensive.[137] When asked for his opinion, Lévis answered that a forward movement seemed to him 'very difficult considering the position occupied by the enemy.'[138] The governor did not press the point, and the rest of the season was devoted to strengthening the fortifications at Carillon.[139] But the army was not inactive. In mid-September a detachment of seven hundred Canadians and Indians, raiding in the immediate vicinity of Fort William Henry, spread panic among the British. Loudoun thought the fort was in danger and sent reinforcements up the Hudson.[140] The raids continued until the troops began to move into winter quarters in the first half of November.[141]

The military operations carried out in northern New York were typical of the military art perfected in Europe towards the middle of the eighteenth century. They were like a game of chess. Generals manocuvred to occupy positions, capture supply depots, cut lines of communication, reduce fortresses. They avoided pitched battles. With the armaments available at the time, such battles had to be fought in a theatre of limited dimensions—the expression 'field' of battle still had some meaning—where volleys were terribly costly to victors as well as to vanquished. This would be seen on the battlefields of Quebec in 1759 and 1760.[142] At Oswego, after six months of patient campaigning, during which he had put into practice a strategy of bold manoeuvres aimed at successive small gains, Vaudreuil had to his credit two forts with their garrisons almost intact and a very important strategic region. At the same time Lévis's elaborate manoeuvres on Lake Champlain contained the British armies on the Hudson and on Lake George.

Meanwhile the Canadians had other opportunities for practising the methods of warfare learned in the course of the century and a half of conflict that constituted their history. Mingling with their Indian allies, they kept the western frontiers of the central and southern colonies under constant pressure. Defenders in the forts could not relax their vigilance for a moment. Their every movement was watched by an enemy ready to pounce at the slightest opportunity. The British were prisoners in their own posts, and it was not unusual for soldiers to be massacred right under their walls.[143] Forts that had been built to protect the country around them served rather to shelter settlers obliged to seek refuge in them.[144] On 30 July Villiers's detachment fell upon one of these block-houses, Fort Granville in Pennsylvania, twenty miles from the mouth of the Juniata. The post had a garrison of seventy-five men, but the commander had sent fifty of them to answer an appeal for help from a nearby settlement. When Villiers withdrew, Fort Granville was only a heap of ashes with, in the midst of them, a pole bearing a while flag.[145] Panic spread throughout the neighbourhood. The whole county was emptied of its population, which became one more army of 'beggars'.[146]

From Fort Dinwiddie in Virginia it was reported that forty persons had been killed or captured in less than a week: 'each minute' brought news of murder or fire.[147] In October the Maryland assembly adopted desperate measures: it offered a premium of fifty pounds to anyone delivering an Indian scalp to a magistrate.[148] In Virginia a society was formed under the patronage of the governor. Its members, 250 or 300 volunteers, proposed to carry out reprisals against Indian villages, a dangerous game as the Virginians attacking Logstown discovered. Their retreat was cut off by Normandville and a small group of Canadians; a large number of them were captured, and the others scattered through the woods.[149]

Early in August a letter from Vaudreuil related the feats of ten war parties that Dumas, the commander of Fort Du Quesne, had sent to strike at the English. Dumas had reported that for a week he had 'done nothing but receive scalps', and that these constant raids had rendered Virginia impotent 'not only to venture on any expedition outside the province, but even to make any effort to protect herself.'[150] The following month the governor praised the work of thirteen more of his parties, led by officers bearing such names as Du Buisson, Repentigny, Belestre —some of the proudest in Canada. Now, however, Vaudreuil complained that this sort of war was becoming 'difficult'; the enemy fled too far and the raiders had to 'journey 100 miles over frightful roads to track them down.' But track them they did, and attacks were of 'frequent or rather daily occurrence'.[151] The last dispatches to leave Fort Du Quesne in the autumn of 1756 contained stories of eleven raiding parties, and some fifty scalps were delivered in Montreal along with the news.[152] Ohio exploits were repeated at Niagara where Pougeot, the commander of the fort, in his turn received presents of English scalps, among them 'thirty-eight in one sack' from the Iroquois.[153]

As the campaign was drawing towards its close, the engineer Desandrouins summed up its results: 'We hear on every side that the English colonies are in the greatest possible distress; the immense taxes they have been obliged to pay to maintain forces much greater than ours, far from placing them up to now in a position to undertake action against us, have not even saved them from all the horror of a cruel war or from the loss of the Port Mahon of North America, I mean Chouaguen.'[154] The comparison between the fall of Minorca (which had capitulated on 28 June) and that of Oswego suggested itself quite spontaneously to a man writing from Canada. It was also drawn in Europe. Walpole asserts in his memoirs that the English considered the loss of the Lake Ontario fort ten times more serious than that of the citadel of Port Mahon.[155] In the opinion of another Briton, 'it was of as much or greater importance to maintain this post on the continent of North America to overawe the wavering and hostile Indians, to protect our allies, to cover our settlements, and to chastise our enemies as to preserve Fort St Philip's [Minorca] in Europe.'[156] French propagandists exploited to the full the success of French arms at Oswego. The Mercure de France published a full account of the campaign, and it was given wide publicity in Holland and in all the courts of Europe. The French ambassador in Naples had the story translated and circulated in Italian.[157]

While in France news of the victory was received with pleasure, in Canada it spread joy throughout the country. 'Chouaguen is taken,' wrote one Montrealer on 18 August, the very day when Villiers made his triumphal entry into the town, preceded by the 'five beautiful flags' taken from the defenders of Oswego. 'Chouaguen is taken'—Canadians had been waiting for thirty years to hear those words, and the writer scarcely needed to add that they inspired 'very deep and very general joy.'[158] The flags were distributed among the churches of Montreal, Trois-Rivières, and Quebec, and when they received them the members of the clergy prepared to unite in thanks to God 'with the warrior defenders of the country.'[159] In Quebec on 20 August, the bishop took part in a solemn religious procession 'the most magnificent that could be.' The procession paused at several churches, and at each of them two chevaliers de Saint-Louis 'abased' the enemy standards 'on the steps of the sanctuary.' On 17 September there was a second procession: the sacrament was carried through the streets of the capital with 'the three reliquaries of St Paul, St Flavian, and Ste Félicité'.[160] For Canada, 1756 was indeed the year of Chouaguen.

It was also the year of Oswego for the British colonies. With the news of the fall of Oswego a wave of terror broke over them and engulfed them. Fear spread through the civilian population and infected the army. On 4 August Lord Loudoun had ordered the 44th regiment, under General Wood, to Lake Ontario. They left Albany on 12 August and six days later, at the Palatine village of German Flats, they received the news of the surrender of the fort. Webb was panic-stricken. Fearing that Montcalm might penetrate deep into New York by Wood Creek and the portage on the Mohawk, and acting without instructions from his commander-in-chief, he ordered a dam of tree trunks to be thrown up across the creek. He then destroyed Fort Bull, which was being rebuilt by Major Craven, at one end of the portage, and Fort William, which Léry had not been able to reach in the spring, at the other. When a month later these measures were reported to Bougainville, he refused to believe that any officer could have given such extraordinary orders.[161] When Loudoun heard what had been done, he was furious: Webb's panic was quite inexcusable. However, the commander-in-chief instructed Winslow not to undertake any action against Carillon: it was wise to keep the colonial troops available in case the Franco-Canadians might attempt to penetrate the province from the west.[162] New York really feared an invasion. The Indians, observing this dreadful apprehension, realized how dangerous partnership with the British had become, and even the Iroquois hastened to disengage themselves from their traditional alliance.[163] The English stood alone to face an enemy fired with the ardour of victory and conquest.

After the disastrous campaign of 1756 and in anticipation of that of the following year, Loudoun wrote to Lord Cumberland that in his opinion the only possible way to defeat the enemy was to capture Quebec; the fall of New France would follow inevitably.[164] This idea was repeated in the American press as it took stock of the situation. 'Oswego is lost,' lamented one New Yorker, 'lost perhaps forever', and with Oswego the Lake Ontario fleet and the fur trade that had been for so long an object of the nation's solicitude and the mainstay of the frontier town of Albany. The root cause of these disasters lay in the weakness arising from divisions among the provinces, which were now almost exhausted, their finances ruined by costly but unsuccessful military operations. Would they then sink in despair—or persist in their efforts? In any case, one sure conclusion could be drawn: so far the colonies had wasted their strength trying to lop off the branches when the tree should have been attacked at the root. It was Canada, Canada that must be destroyed. '*Delenda est Carthago*,' admonished the writer. Otherwise the fate of the colonies was sealed.[165] Three months later the *New York Gazette* reminded its readers that they had only to look at the map to see that it was no more difficult to attack Quebec than Crown Point or Fort Du Quesne. And, continued the journalist, 'nothing is more certain than that when the head is lopped off, the inferior members will fall of course; why then is not this effectual step attempted?'[166]

The British colonies suffered defeat in 1756. Montcalm proclaimed the campaign 'the most brilliant . . . that has ever been fought on this continent.'[167] Unlike Canada, however, British America could continue to lose battles for years on end without losing the war. The numerical strength of her population did not save her from reverses and every kind of suffering; it did save her from defeat. Oswego fell, the western frontiers were ablaze, but in the big towns of the colonies life went on. In September 1756, some two weeks after the fall of Oswego, a brilliant ceremony took place at King's College, New York. Fine speeches were delivered in English and young gentlemen defended theses in Latin.[168] The victors, on the other hand, were living in conditions of austerity, almost of destitution. The series of Canadian victories continued in 1757, but at the beginning of the summer 'lack of provisions' forced the Quebec Seminary to take the unusual step of sending its students home, and the grammar classes did not reopen in October. Only students at the Grand Seminary resumed their studies, for the institution could not feed any more.[169] Thus with the year of Chouaguen began the last school year of the French régime during which the seminary functioned regularly. Lost among manifestations of general rejoicing, this sign of distress is nonetheless significant; and as early as the autumn of 1756 Lévis understood that, in spite of the success of Franco-Canadian arms, peace was 'to be desired.'[170]

Canada was like a hornets' nest under attack. She defended herself fiercely. She won battles. But if the war lasted, was she rich enough in human resources to triumph in the end?

[137]

NOTE

What precisely was the role of Rigaud in the swiftly moving dénouement of the siege of Oswego? Thomas Chapais minimizes it (*Le Marquis de Montcalm*, 132-4). As he does nothing more than follow step by step 'a long and interesting essay in M. de Kerallain's book on *La Jeunesse de Bougainville*, pp. 44, 45', it is wiser to ignore the words of the pupil, however diligent he may be, and go straight to the master, Kerallain, whose lesson has been so faithfully repeated. Kerallain considers that Rigaud's crossing of the river was of 'no importance', and he quotes Bougainville's journal: '14 August . . . Order given to M. de Rigaud to go with the Canadians and Indians to cross the river three-quarters of a league from here, and to harass the enemy. I was detached to cross the river with him and to summon the enemy to surrender at noon.' If, reasons the author, Bougainville was dispatched towards Fort George at the same time as Rigaud, the movement cannot have taken place until after nine o'clock in the morning—that is, after Mercer's death had caused the enemy's resistance to collapse.

Certain texts, however, are at variance with Kerallain. Pouchot, an eyewitness, reports that Rigaud's militiamen forded the river 'at daybreak'. Another eyewitness, Desandrouins, places the manoeuvre at four o'clock in the morning (Gabriel, 58). In a letter to Machault dated 3 September 1756, Bigot invokes the evidence of British officers taken prisoner at Oswego: 'They would have held out longer in Chouaguen, so they assured me, if the Canadians and Indians had not crossed the river; they saw them advancing with such ardour, although they were in the water up to their chests, that they feared they might be caught and killed in their entrenchments, which were being bombarded from behind by our artillery.' The *Mercure de France* for December 1756 (pp. 221-3) published a 'Relation de ce qui s'est passé cette année en Canada avec le journal historique du siège des forts de Chouagen ou Oswego, commencé le 11 août 1756 et fini le 14 par la prise de ces forts'. This is what this report says: 'The 14th, at daybreak, the marquis de Montcalm ordered the sieur de Rigaud to cross to the other side of the river on foot with the Canadians and Indians, and to go into the woods to disturb communications at Fort George, where the enemy appeared to be carrying out important movements. The sieur de Rigaud executed the order immediately . . . At nine o'clock the besiegers had nine pieces of artillery mounted and ready to fire; and although until then the fire of the besieged troops had been superior, they hoisted the white flag at ten o'clock. The sieur de Rigaud sent to the marquis de Montcalm two officers whom the commander of the fort had dispatched to him with an offer to capitulate. The speed of our operations in a terrain that the enemy had considered impassable, the rapid mounting of our batteries, the idea that these manoeuvres gave of the number of French troops engaged, the death of Colonel Mercer, the commander of Chouaguen, and more than anything else the bold manoeuvre of the sieur de Rigaud and fear of the Canadians and Indians, who were already firing on the fort, without any doubt made the English decide not to prolong their defence' (pp. 232 f.).

The author of this 'Relation' was the king's historiographer, Jean-Pierre de Bougainville, the brother of Montcalm's aide-de-camp. After reading it the aide could not resist the desire to correct his brother, and he wrote to him on 3 July 1757: *'The sieur de Rigaud sent to the marquis two officers*, etc. The officers came directly to our battery, where M. de Montcalm was, and did not even see M. de Rigaud. I know, for I was sent to make the famous crossing with the latter and at a given signal to summon the English to surrender. It was during this interval that they showed the white flag. So you see you were mistaken in writing further on, *and, more than anything else, the bold manoeuvre of the sieur de Rigaud.* The English officers had already reached our trenches when this manoeuvre was executed' (Kerallain, 45). Moreover, Montcalm informed Lévis on 17 August: 'Finally M. de Rigaud's contingent, after a delay of twelve hours, following the order he had received to that effect, forded the river above me to invest the fort on the other side' (Casgrain, 6:34). And that is not all. On their return to English territory after spending some time in Quebec, members of the English garrison captured at Oswego reported that on 14 August 'about 9 o'clock [in the] morning 2,500 of the enemy passed over the river in three columns, from the east to the west side of the river, in order to fall on us on that side. Lieutenant-Colonel Mercer on being informed that the enemy were passing the river and not knowing their numbers ordered Colonel Schuyler with 500 men to oppose them. Which would accordingly have been carried into execution, and consequently those 500 men being [*sic*] cut off had not Colonel Mercer been killed by a cannon-ball a few minutes after' ('State of facts relating to the loss of Oswego collected from the information of some gentlemen lately arrived from Quebec who were made prisoners at Oswego', *Coll. de MSS*, 4:63). Finally Malartic, after noting in his diary (pp. 73 f.) the death of Mercer at nine o'clock, continued: 'At the same hour M. de Rigaud crossed the river with a body of Canadians and all our Indians. A quarter of an hour later the fort showed the white flag. Firing ceased on both sides.'

There are then four pieces of evidence: Bougainville's diary, his remarks to his brother in 1757, Montcalm's letter to Lévis, and the report based on the recollections of British prisoners. From these documents Kerallain drew the following conclusions: 'Rigaud had probably received the order to cross the river at dawn; but whether from negligence or some other cause, its execution was inordinately delayed; however, several officers who knew the order had been given must have thought it was executed immediately. In fact the crossing was not effected until between nine and ten o'clock . . . Colonel Mercer, informed of the Canadians' movement, was preparing to send Colonel Schuyler to oppose it when he was killed, which disorganized the defence.' After a rapid consultation with his fellow officers, Littlehales decided to surrender 'and sent two officers directly to Montcalm, while Rigaud, Bougainville and the Canadians forded the river unopposed. Thus Bougainville could think that Rigaud's move was quite fruitless, whereas the English themselves—the men at least if not the officers of the garrison—admitted that it had aroused their fears, without distinguishing very clearly whether this impression had been produced before or after the event.' In short, if we accept this hypothesis, it must be assumed that Rigaud's troops had not yet reached the western shore of the river when the British made their decision to open negotiations for surrender. In that case the manoeuvre carried out by the Canadians and Indians would not have affected the outcome.

Only Bougainville makes this affirmation. The evidence of Malartic, though sketchy, implies that the defenders of the fort hoisted the white flag immediately after Rigaud had crossed the river. The author of the 'State of facts' places the death of Mercer immediately after the Canadians' advance. Kerallain tries to explain that the British commander had been 'warned' of this movement. How else could he be warned of it than by seeing it being executed? On the subject of Montcalm's assertion, it is worth noting that, after Kerallain, Chapais, who is not usually afraid to quote at length, transcribed only three lines of Montcalm's letter to Lévis: 'Finally, M. de Rigaud's contingent, after a delay of twelve hours, following the order he had received to that effect, forded the river above me to invest the fort on the other side. The enemy took fright and asked to capitulate; the cannon fire had just killed the two commanding officers' (Casgrain, 6:34). This text, it is true, remains ambiguous: why did the enemy take fright? Was it because Rigaud had arrived 'to invest the fort'? In order to interpret these statements clearly, we must compare them with the corresponding passages in Montcalm's *Journal*. What does the *Journal* say? 'Practically all the Indians and Canadians had crossed the river at daybreak six hundred fathoms from the fort, under the orders of M. de Rigaud, to complete the investment of the enemy. This manoeuvre was carried out in a brilliant and decisive manner, no one being stopped by the high water. The marquis de Montcalm had kept 100 Canadians in order to be able to have the Béarn battalion and a few pieces of artillery ferried over by the lake early in the night [14-15

August] to unite with M. de Rigaud in a combined attack on Fort George . . . But the speed of our operations in a terrain that they had considered impassable, the manoeuvre of the group that had crossed the river, made them think, according to what the captured officers told us, that we must be 6,000 strong. Colonel Mercer had just been killed. The fear of falling into the hands of our Indians—all these reasons caused the lieutenant-colonel of Pepperrell's regiment, M. Littlehales, who had been in command since Mercer's death, to send and ask us to grant a capitulation. They raised the white flag at ten o'clock' (Casgrain, 7:98). In a letter of 28 August addressed to the minister of war (*AG*, 3417, no 208), Montcalm makes it clear that Rigaud had completed his man-oeuvre before the English made their decision to surrender. After mentioning the sudden death of Mercer, he adds that even if he had not been killed, the fall of the fort 'would have been delayed by no more than a day or two.' And why? 'You will see by the diary that I had had the Canadians and Indians cross to the other side of the river, and that by the morning of the 14th I had a battery of nine cannon mounted.' Thus Montcalm's letter confirms the account in his diary and the diary clarifies the obscure passage in Lévis's famous letter: the enemy 'took fright' because Rigaud had crossed the river.

One question remains to be answered: what did the general mean when he wrote 'after a delay of twelve hours'? The following is Chapais's gloss: 'The order had probably been given during the evening [of the 13th], and if it was not executed until about nine o'clock the following morning, that would make about twelve hours' delay.' But how can that explanation be reconciled with the evidence of Montcalm's *Journal*: 'Practically all the Indians and Canadians had crossed the river at day-break'? If he had not been dazzled by Kerallain's word-juggling, Chapais would have realized that it was at five o'clock on the evening of the 13th that Montcalm had given Rigaud the order to cross to the west bank; was it not at that very hour that the French had become aware of the evacuation of Fort Ontario by the English? Thus Rigaud would have made the crossing about five o'clock in the morning, 'at daybreak', 14 August, about twelve hours after the withdrawal of the British garrison: Montcalm could very naturally have worked out his double plan of investment and bombardment immediately after being informed of the enemy's retreat.

Montcalm, Pouchot, and Desandrouins agree then in stating that Rigaud executed his manoeuvre at daybreak. It is also certain that the Canadian force had begun its operation before Mercer's death (*NYCD*, 7:127; Mackellar's journal, Pargellis: *Military Affairs in America*, 212). But at what time had the operation started? A colonial newspaper gives the following report: 'About eight o'clock [in the morning of 14 August] we discovered the enemy crossing the river about a mile above us in three columns and have reason to believe they had passed over five or six hundred the night before. Colonel Mercer immediately gave orders for a party to oppose them, but before his orders could be executed he was cut in two by a cannon shot. At ten o'clock we discovered the enemy filing off to surround us' (*Boston Gazette*, 23 May 1757). This text leads to another point that is not without importance. If, as Montcalm's diary says, Rigaud had with him 'practically all the Indians and Canadians', his contingent was more than 1,500 strong. It would have required a considerable time for such a large number of men to wade across the river, and the crossing may quite possibly have been made in groups. It would be entirely normal for it to begin at the end of the night—or 'at daybreak'—and to be still going on about eight o'clock in the morning. The defenders might understandably have the impression that five or six hundred Canadians had reached the west bank 'the previous night'. An English historian, writing a few years later, attributed the rapid surrender of Oswego not so much to the effectiveness of the French bombardment as to 'a bold action of a body of 2,500 [*sic*] Canadians and savages who swam over the river in the night between the 13th and the 14th and cut off the communication between the two forts [George and Oswego]' (Entick, 1:477).

These diverse sources are in agreement on another point. As we have seen, during the morning of the 14th a sudden storm reduced the precision and the effect of the French bombardment. The British were about to gain the advantage in the artillery duel when they offered to capitulate. As Desandrouins remarked: 'The English, one must agree, have very little understanding of war; they surrendered at the very moment when we were being knocked out by their artillery' (Letter of 28 August 1756, *AG*, 3417, no 209). Why did they surrender when things were going so well for them? Obviously because the Canadian-Indian operation inspired them with terror.

Chapais did not have at his disposal all the documents from which we have quoted. Those he did see, however, should have put him on guard against errors such as the one in this passage: 'There is a great diversity in the statements as to the hour at which M. de Rigaud crossed the river and the influence of this operation on the final outcome of the siege.' When compared with one another the affirmations to which the author alludes do not reveal such a 'great diversity' as he thinks: a little methodical reflection establishes this fact. And the 'influence' of Rigaud's march on the hasty surrender of Oswego is self-evident. It is to be regretted that Chapais, although he was not himself moved by the passion that inspired Kerallain, allowed himself to be taken in by the French apologist whose one aim was to exalt Bougainville.

Chapter V

British Reverses
1757

If at the end of the campaign of 1756 any Canadian had paused to measure the possible consequences of defeat for himself and his country, he would almost certainly have been taxed with pessimism by some reasonable compatriot. Everything was going well. For two years New France had been winning victories and repulsing the assaults of the English, while the English, with all their impressive demonstrations of strength, had attained none of their objectives, with the single exception of Acadia, and even there they were finding it very difficult to exploit their success. Moreover they had suffered a disastrous defeat on Lake Ontario and their frontier settlements were constantly ravaged—not a day passed for them without losses in men and prestige. A Quebec merchant gave the following report on the situation in a letter to a friend in the Islands: 'The English on this continent are in dire distress, the poor devils don't know which saint to turn to, for as you know they are not acquainted with many. It is estimated that since last year we have killed 4,000 of their men without counting those they lose every day by destitution and desertions.'[1] The British fared no better in Europe than in America. The fall of Menorca and Byng's retreat from an encounter with the French squadron under La Galissonière had dealt a severe blow to British pride. The empire shuddered in indignation and shame.[2] A poet represented Britain lying 'pensive beneath an oak's extensive shade.' She had 'cast away' her arms in anger, and she was tortured by an agonizing question:

> *Why with reproach do now my fleets*
> *Inglorious run away?*
> *Why, tho' superior leave to France,*
> *The Empire of the sea?*[3]

Yet the British navy had not lost its position of supremacy. At the moment when these despondent verses were being written the admiralty had at its disposal 125 ships of the line, 79 frigates, and 126 other war vessels, while vigorous recruiting maintained a strength of 50,000 sailors.[4] Moreover the royal navy was supported by a very active auxiliary fleet: the shipowners of New York, Philadelphia, Antigua, and Jamaica 'spread the ocean' with their privateers and in the autumn of 1756 had 'already reaped the wished advantages from their public spirit.'[5] French trade suffered; Dutch newspapers informed all Europe of bankruptcies affecting highly respected and important business houses, failures that brought in their train a 'decline in industry' and the collapse of credit.[6] In the autumn of 1757 a dispatch from London noted that because of the increasing insecurity of sea transport, insurance rates in France had risen to 75 per cent and constituted 'a clog sufficient alone to ruin' the country's maritime trade.[7]

This was, however, only one side of the medal. Although inferior to that of the enemy, the French navy was still in the fight. Warships were sunk or captured from time to time, but France's naval shipyards, working at high pressure, more than made up for war losses: in a few weeks at the end of 1756 five new warships and one frigate were launched in Toulon alone.[8] Considering the great size of the British merchant marine, there was nothing surprising in the ease with which French privateers— as rapacious as their adversaries—took prizes, nor in the number of prizes they took. It was true the English had gained a head start in this respect during the months preceding the declaration of war, but the French seemed well on the way to overtaking them. In July 1757 it was estimated that they had captured 637 merchantmen, while they had lost to the British 681 merchantmen and 91 privateers.[9] At the end of 1757 Great Britain drew up a balance sheet for the year: she had lost 581 units large and small and taken 364.[10] March had been a particularly disastrous month for her: of 21 vessels outward bound from South Carolina, almost all with cargoes of indigo, 19 had fallen into the hands of the enemy.[11] Even the 'little shipowners' of Louisbourg had their privateers that came into harbour laden with booty. Montcalm reported in the spring of 1757 that they had brought in prizes worth 250,000 livres, and this was a modest estimate. An official list drawn up in October of the same year named 39 enemy ships, of a value of 806,776 livres, taken over a period of fifteen months.[12] One can well imagine the feelings of astonishment and dismay inspired in England by France's fine showing at sea, but there was nothing really mysterious in the phenomenon. As French strategists conceived it, for France sea war was necessarily a war of attrition. Only time and new methods would give England the decisive advantage. In the last months of 1758 a London observer, wise after the event, wrote that 'the French, with their practice of sending small squadrons to sea [were] losing their whole navy by bits.' Why were they not bolder? he asked. 'With all the war vessels they have lost in the last two years they could have formed a fleet that would have caused us serious anxiety.'[13] But the 'small squadrons' had formed a fleet, and an aggressive one. Its elements were scattered, and although the enemy could gnaw at it he had not been offered a chance to gobble it up in one glorious engagement.

The power of the nation soon to triumph over France did not lie in her navy alone. It was also manifest in the cold anger, the obstinate resolve, the profound sense of empire that inspired Britain's ruling class and the British people. On the occasion of the opening of Parliament in 1756 the city of London—the nerve-centre of British finance, politics, and public opinion—delivered significant instructions to its representatives: 'The cruelties suffered and losses sustained by our fellow subjects in North America,' said the message, 'have long called for redress.' Up to that time attempts to support the colonists had been so mismanaged, the moment for sending help so ill-chosen, that these gestures had 'only served to render the British name contemptible.' It was a matter of the utmost importance to 'detect' all those who, by 'treachery or misconduct', had contributed to 'those great distresses'. The king had given assurance that justice would be done on those persons who had been 'wanting in their duty to him and their country.'[14]

The first effect of the national resentment that was to culminate in the execution of the ill-fated Admiral Byng was to hasten the fall of Newcastle and the formation of Pitt's first ministry. Newcastle and the professional politicians in his group—Pitt inherited several of them—could have carried out most of the reforms accompished by the famous prime minister. In many respects he continued the work begun by them and he changed his own course accordingly. It is nonetheless true that he expressed better than any other individual the new tendencies of British imperialism: he could lead the movement and direct it towards specific objectives. His views were those of the Englishmen and Americans for whom the real target in the war was the total destruction of the colonial and maritime power of France. To the question: how could this objective be attained? Pitt answered: by the conquest of Canada. In his eyes to possess Canada was to make British America safe and to promote its normal expansion, an expansion necessary to England, whose greatness depended upon trade and whose trade required a broadened American base.[15] These were simple, coherent ideas. They were also effective, because they expressed the fundamental ambitions of those who strove to increase at the same time Great Britain's wealth and her political power. The speech from the throne delivered at the opening of

[145]

Parliament in 1756 contained a declaration that must have given great satisfaction to Britons concerned with affairs in the New World: 'The succour and preservation of America cannot but constitute a main object of my attention and solicitude; and the growing dangers to which our colonies may stand exposed from our late losses in those parts demand resolutions of vigour and dispatch.' The royal message then went on to emphasize the need to ensure the defence of the British Isles and to remove grounds for discontent in the nation.[16] In its answering address the House of Commons mentioned 'with pain' the reverses suffered in the Mediterranean and in America, and approved in advance the dispatch of 'speedy succour' to Britain's 'invaluable possessions' on the new continent.[17] About the same time the American papers published dispatches from London offering the hope that the situation might soon be rectified. They gave assurance that the government was considering 'new methods' for protecting the colonies from Franco-Canadian raids, for it was 'computed that the loss of the said settlements would be far more detrimental to the trade of Great Britain than both Gibraltar and Minorca.'[18] Another paper announced that the new ministers had 're-solved to make America their chief object of military attention', and that orders had been given in preparation for the next campaign.[19]

Pitt was out of favour with the king, who could forgive him neither his prolix eloquence nor—especially—his earlier hostility towards Hanover. As the prime minister struggled in the midst of untold difficulties to maintain himself in power and to postpone the inevitable fall of his ministry—it was to fall early in April—powerful economic interests combined to bring pressure on the king in favour of the American empire. On 1 January 1757 'the merchants of the city of London interested in, and trading to, the British colonies of Virginia and Maryland' presented a 'petition and remonstrance' that revealed how close were the relations between economic activity and colonial policy. These merchants did not conceal the fact that they had personal interests to defend. America's present misfortunes made them fearful of 'fatal consequences for themselves' as well as for 'the most essential trade of this kingdom.' They had therefore every reason to implore his majesty's 'further protection to these colonies adequate to the imminent danger to which they [were] exposed.'[20]

Public opinion was on their side. In January 1757 the influential *London Magazine* reminded its readers that before the fall of Oswego, New York had exported great quantities of furs, and that the same province had begun 'to make and export large quantities of pig iron.'[21] An article in the February issue of the same periodical sang the praises of Pennsylvania. What fertile soil! What a perfect climate! Statistics for the port of Philadelphia were evidence of the flourishing state of the province's agriculture and trade.[22] Next on the honour roll came the Carolinas. Customs records showed that their products, like those of Pennsylvania, were a fruitful source of exchange helping to maintain Britain's favourable trade balance. The prosperity of active colonies was reflected in the mother country in increased wealth for her merchants and better living for her 'poor industrious people'.[23] Such propaganda repeated month after month could not fail to have its effect.

The wave of imperialist enthusiasm sweeping Britain was swelled by statements of exports, shipping schedules, employment curves. The extension and the stubborn violence of a conflict now developing on a world scale were not to be attributed, as a Dutch observer thought, to the excessive 'haste . . . the lack of reflection . . . and the natural impetuosity of the English nation.'[24] They were the results of careful calculation on the part of a society mindful not to lose sight of the goals it was pursuing and led by circumstances to gamble with war as a means to attain them. England's aim was to attract the wealth of continents to her islands and, in order to achieve that end, to open America's vast spaces to colonization—to Britain's powers of political organization and economic exploitation.

Decisive action in America was a necessary element in this policy. On 23 December 1756 the Duke of Cumberland transmitted to Lord Loudoun a plan of operations, in which the most important element was an expedition to the St Lawrence with the capture of Quebec as its objective.[25] The project was in complete agreement with the views of the commander-in-chief, who one month earlier had drawn up a plan of campaign designed to bring about a radical change in the nature of the war. It was imperative, he wrote, to pass from the defensive—which extended frontiers and the enemy's situation made it impossible to maintain without great expenditures and very heavy losses—to the offensive, specifically to an attack on Quebec by way of the St Lawrence River. The general saw three advantages in this strategy: it would place him in a position to press hostilities to a successful conclusion; it would make the northern colonies secure in the possession of the whole of their territory and procure for them the possibility of extending their new establishments; and finally it would give England all the northern fur trade, of which such an important part had been hers and which she had almost completely lost.[26]

Pitt was inclined to share this opinion, but he feared, so it seemed, that it might be rash to attack the capital of Canada before first reducing Louisbourg. Accordingly on 22 December he instructed the general to begin by driving France from her bastion on Île-Royale. At the same time he announced the dispatch of a powerful squadron and 8,000 men.

With the regiments already stationed in the colonies, this expeditionary force would give Loudoun some 17,000 regulars, a force that Pitt considered strong enough to capture Louisbourg in a brief operation before it made its main attack on Quebec.[27] Although obviously disconcerted, the commander-in-chief nevertheless expressed himself as pleased that the minister's plans coincided 'in large measure' with the projects he had himself formed. After all, Quebec was still the objective of the campaign; the Louisbourg expedition was merely a preliminary operation. Working on this general plan, he proposed to take the following measures: to assemble in New York an army of 5,500 regulars, to proceed with it to Halifax where he would effect a junction with the 8,000 men that Pitt had promised him, to attack the fortress on Île-Royale, and then to advance on the capital of New France. He would leave behind only the essential garrisons and just enough men to mount guard on the Lake George front and on the Hudson, in all 1,700 regulars and 6,000 provincial troops from New England and New York.[28]

The plan was a good one but difficult to execute, since its success depended upon diverse factors and complicated movements. In order to command American waters, the British fleet must appear early in the season, the junction between the British and American army corps must be carried out promptly, the conquest of Île-Royale must be accomplished speedily so that the threat of invasion would immobilize Franco-Canadian strength on the St Lawrence. Otherwise, with the whole British offensive force massed at one point on the coast of British America, it would be only too easy for Canada to strike a blow elsewhere. And was not the road to Quebec already long enough without adding a detour to include Louisbourg? These arguments were perhaps brought forward in government circles in England, where the plan to attack Quebec directly had its supporters. However that may be, the cabinet revoked Pitt's decision and allowed Loudoun to choose whether he should direct his first attack against the capital of Île-Royale or the capital of Canada. Now that his hands were free the general announced that he would make his final decision in Halifax, when the British reinforcements had arrived and he had consulted the commander of the squadron, Vice-Admiral Holburne.[29]

Meanwhile the press kept up a running fire of comment. New York hailed the rumour that a 'bold push' was to be made.[30] Boston recorded the opinion of officers in America that a major operation in the St Lawrence would make the British 'masters of Quebec and, in consequence, of all Canada; whereas the present manner of carrying on the war among thick woods, where a single Indian can fire his piece without discovery, may linger on without effect for many years.'[31] Thus the public was prepared for a decisive battle.

The French government, for its part, was following British preparations very closely. Moras, the minister of marine, was very well informed.[32] Before the end of February he warned Vaudreuil that seven regiments of British regulars and two battalions of Scottish highlanders were about to embark for America. He knew too that the troops would be escorted by a powerful squadron of fifteen or sixteen warships. He did not know the precise point in French America at which the attack of these powerful forces would be directed—the British did not know that themselves—but he concluded that it must be either Louisbourg or Quebec. Basing her own plans on the enemy's movements, France prepared to send important reinforcements to Canada, and to Louisbourg a considerable naval force that 'could also serve for the defence of Quebec if the enemy undertook to attack it.'[33] When, early in April, he learned that they planned to 'attack Canada by sea at the same time as they attacked it by land', the minister added two battalions of the Berry regiment to the troops he had promised the colony. He did not, however, make any change in the measures already taken to ensure a solid naval defence for Île-Royale,[34] a decision he had no cause to regret.

The rest of the story is well known: British troop transports delayed for months in European waters by adverse winds; a slow crossing both for them and for the war fleet, which could not move faster than its convoy, while Loudoun waited with feverish impatience in New York; Loudoun's desperate decision to risk exposing his transports to a disastrous encounter with a French squadron and to proceed with his army and its very inadequate naval escort to Nova Scotia;[35] and finally, on 30 June, his arrival in Halifax, followed on 10 July by that of Holburne. Meanwhile, as precious time ebbed away, three groups of French ships were converging on Île-Royale: Beauffremont's came into port on 31 May, Revest's on 19 June, and Du Bois de la Motte's the following day. This last officer, who assumed direction of naval operations, had under his command eighteen warships and five frigates. He immediately dispatched a brigantine to Brest with the good news of the junction of the three squadrons at Louisbourg.[36]

Vaudreuil reported in triumph that Louisbourg was saved and Quebec 'out of danger.' He predicted correctly that 'the great British preparations' would be fruitless. Their fleet would 'probably not leave Halifax.'[37] And what would Du Bois de la Motte do? He was an old sailor, laden with honours and experience—too much experience perhaps. Fifty-nine years of service weighed heavily on his prudent calculations. He could have headed Loudoun off, and attacked him on his way to Halifax. Then he could have waited for Holburne's fleet, impeded by heavily laden transports, and attacked it with a superior force. He appears to have entertained the idea. But why face the hazards of battle? Had he not attained his goal, which was to make the fortress of Île-Royale inaccessible

to the enemy? So his ships stayed in harbour, where an epidemic decimated his crews.[38]

While the massed guns of the French fleet remained silent under the
walls of Louisbourg, Loudoun in Nova Scotia discussed plans with his
colleagues and, excellent administrator that he was, administered the
affairs of his squadron and his army. Eighteen warships, a dozen frigates,
and almost two hundred transports were lined up in Halifax harbour—a
splendid fleet, so well equipped and manned that one might think nothing could resist its 'floating fortresses'. On land a formidable camp,
scrupulously clean, occupied a height whose surface was levelled 'as
smooth as a floor'. The general put some of his soldiers to work preparing the ground for a large garden to supply fresh vegetables for the sick
—and the wounded, if his troops ever went into battle.[39] Meanwhile they
were being prepared for what would be for many of them their baptism
of fire. 'All those things which might have thrown them into confusion
in the assault by their novelty were rendered familiar' by remarkably
realistic war games. One group defended entrenchments while another
attacked, repulsed sorties, took prisoners, and the mock battle 'afforded
much mirth to a numerous crowd of spectators.'[40] But all this careful
preparation was wasted. Not that the commander-in-chief abandoned
his project willingly. On 2 August his troops were embarked: 11,288
men, exclusive of artillerymen, marines, and rangers. They were packed
tightly in the ships as a large number of transports had to be reserved
for fascines, gabions, flatboats, and all the equipment required for the
siege—the siege of Louisbourg, of course.[41] But at the last moment, faced
with the probability of disaster, Loudoun had to abandon the idea.
Moreover, a very dangerous situation in New York now required his
presence there.

If, as Loudoun had expected, important engagements had taken place
on Île-Royale and especially at Quebec, all the other fronts would have
remained quiet, and the seven or eight thousand men he had left on
guard at Lake George and on the Hudson would have sufficed to contain offensive movements that, according to this hypothesis, could not
have been anything more than diversions of no great importance. He
had, however, been held in check, and Vaudreuil had seized the opportunity to move against northern New York. As a matter of fact, his
preparations had begun several months earlier. At the close of the
campaign of 1756 he had fixed as his next objectives the capture of
Fort William Henry, at the end of Lake George, and Fort Edward
('Lydius'), five or six leagues away, on the Hudson. The task would not
be an easy one, first because in the case of posts of such great strategic
importance the enemy must be expected to maintain a stubborn defence, and secondly because Montcalm, still surprised and mystified by

his victory at Oswego, had as early as 1 November 1756 concluded that it would be 'difficult' to besiege Fort William Henry, 'impossible' to besiege Fort Edward.[42] But Vaudreuil no doubt expected that the new strategy that had brought such signal success at Oswego would be equally successful elsewhere.

Just as he had launched a preliminary expedition against Fort Bull in order to isolate Oswego, so now, early in 1757, his first objective was to reduce the strength of Fort William Henry. He had a special reason for wanting to do so: he feared that the enemy was preparing to use the fort as a base for a thrust against the defences of Carillon and Saint-Frédéric—the outermost defences of Montreal.[43] Under the command of his brother Rigaud, a detachment of 1,500 men left Saint-Jean in the third week in February, came within sight of Fort William Henry on 17 March, and withdrew six days later. They had burned more than 300 boats, four large barks, two galleys, two sheds full of war equipment and lumber, a hospital, two provision depots, a mill, and a group of houses 'forming a sort of lower town below the fort.'[44] Rigaud had fulfilled his mission. The British would boast that they had prevented the Franco-Canadians from capturing their fort.[45] The Canadians on the other hand claimed 'complete success'. They had attained a major objective: as a result of the expedition Fort George was cut off.[46] Vaudreuil exulted. 'This event,' he reported, 'changes the colony's situation, making it, one might say, as favourable as it was previously critical.'[47]

Not as favourable as you may think, retorted Montcalm who, still grumbling, refused to take seriously the 'burn' inflicted on the enemy on Lake George. For he had his own plan, which differed from the governor's. It was 'to create a diversion by the Chouaguen River to ravage Corlaer [Schenectady]'—an idea he was to oppose heatedly when Vaudreuil proposed it in 1758—to continue to build up the fortifications of Carillon and Niagara, to strengthen 'little Fort Saint-Jean', in short to do as little as possible.[48] However, in spite of his lack of enthusiasm for the scheme, he did allow himself to be goaded by the governor into leading an expedition against the New York frontier where, as might have been foreseen, his invading army swallowed up Fort William Henry in a single mouthful (9 August 1757). General Webb, the military commander of the region, who had his headquarters at Fort Edward, was the British counterpart of Montcalm: he allowed the fort to be captured since, as he explained, he did not consider it 'prudent' to attempt to relieve it with only 1,600 men fit to bear arms.[49] Between the victorious army and the rich valley of the Hudson, only Fort Edward remained, and the fort sheltered a weak commander.

A general alarm was sounded throughout the British colonies. In Pennsylvania it was feared that the French would penetrate deep into

New York.[50] Fort Edward must fall, wrote the governor of Maryland to the governor of Pennsylvania, unless the militia of the northern provinces could be assembled there without delay. Prisoners taken at William Henry must surely have revealed the precariousness of Webb's situation; the enemy must know he could not hold out for long against a resolute attack.[51] So obsessed was he by the threat to Ford Edward that, two days after writing to Denny, Sharpe passed on to Governor Dinwiddie of Virginia a report that Montcalm had laid siege to the fort on 10 August.[52] Dinwiddie in turn transmitted the story to the governor of South Carolina, adding the information that the fort had had to surrender to superior numbers.[53] 'I am in pain for New York,' he confessed, 'I fear the enemy may be at Albany by this time . . . Pray God protect us and I hope they sent expresses to Lord Loudoun who probably may send reinforcements of ships and men.'[54]

Webb had indeed appealed to the commander-in-chief, who was in despair. Loudoun was certain that William Henry was lost even before the news was confirmed. As for Fort Edward, he supposed that it too would be abandoned by Webb, whose one idea was to retreat. 'Where he intends to make his stand,' wrote Loudoun, 'is more than I can judge from what he says.'[55] Two days later, assuming that Fort Edward had suffered the same fate as Fort William Henry, Loudoun declared that every effort must be made to save Albany.[56] Every possible effort? Yes and no. This is what the general meant: they must organize their defensive with a view to retarding the Franco-Canadian advance, but they must be careful not to expose the American militia in a decisive engagement, for if they lost one battle it would be impossible to make them face the enemy again. His orders were therefore to blow up all bridges, pile up roadblocks, destroy boats that might fall into the enemy's hands, limit action to skirmishes in the easily defended Mohawk valley.[57] Loudoun trembled, and Holburne too.[58] The British were badly frightened.

Luckily for them they were more frightened than hurt; for Montcalm simply decided to stop at Fort William Henry. Vaudreuil insisted that he should push forward, but only succeeded in making him furiously angry. Montcalm refused to march. On 11 August Webb sent Loudoun a message that would allay his worst anxieties: he had 'reason to believe' that Montcalm would not press his advantage 'and it will be happy for the province if they should not do so.'[59] Governor Sharpe, informed of what had happened, just could not understand Montcalm's decision. 'What was the reason that Mr Montcalm declined to attack Fort Edward we know not. Some are inclined to think that he was afraid Quebec would be attacked in his absence, others that he was apprehensive of being opposed by a vast army of militia but that he will return again and reduce that place also so soon as the militia shall leave the frontiers.'[60] No, Montcalm would not repair his error. His friends Bougainville and Desandrouins later tried to defend an indefensible decision.[61] Bigot, however, reported the claim advanced by 'several senior army officers . . . that if the general [Montcalm] had gone [to Fort Edward], the militia, far from putting up a defence, would have decamped, and I would be of the same opinion.'[62] According to Vaudreuil, if Lévis had been in command he would have attacked and captured the Hudson River fort, 'but,' added Vaudreuil, 'as he was M. de Montcalm's subordinate, he could not be guided by his own zeal, and I know positively that M. de Montcalm always considered every move he [Lévis] proposed very difficult, even though it was most appropriate.'[63] The governor was inconsolable.[64] Without realizing it, Montcalm had shaken New York's western front and could have broken through it. 'New York, New Jersey and Connecticut lay unprotected before him'; it was a stroke of luck for these provinces that he chose to withdraw 'tamely' to Carillon.[65] There was every indication that 'the approach of the French would have been the signal for a British retreat.'[66] 'Fort Edward, if attacked . . . must fall and Montcalm would have the way open to Albany and New York itself.'[67] No wonder Loudoun and his comrades in arms were in a cold sweat.

The shiver of fear was followed by a shudder of horror. The morning of 10 August was marked by the 'massacre' of a part of the garrison of Fort William Henry by the Indians attached to the French army. It is not our intention to examine the details of this episode, which lies outside the scope of our subject. It raised a clamour of indignation. An American witness with a sinister sense of humour described in his diary how the Indian doctors proceeded to cure the sick and the wounded with their tomahawks. They then took possession of swords, watches, hats, and coats. They even tore the shirts from the backs of officers and soldiers before finally scalping their owners.[68] The press was quick to seize on the incident and show up in the harshest light the events of that dreadful day. 'The throats of most, if not all, the women were cut, their bellies ripped open, their bowels taken out and thrown upon the faces of their dead and dying bodies; and 'tis said . . . that the children were taken by the heels and their brains beat out against the trees and stones, and not one of them saved.'[69] Did any more horrible crime ever cry for vengeance? asked the *New York Gazette*. 'Will it not be strictly just and absolutely necessary from henceforward that we . . . make some severe examples of our inhuman enemies when they fall into our hands?'[70] The *Pennsylvania Gazette* took up the cry: 'To what a pitch of perfidy and cruelty is the French nation arrived! . . . Is it the *Most Christian King*

[153]

that could give such orders? or could the most savage nations ever exceed such French barbarities?'[71] Later, when the first passion of indignation had passed, the *New York Mercury* was honest enough to admit that the massacre had been less general than had first been supposed. 'But,' continued the article, 'that the Indians destroyed all the sick and wounded is beyond dispute.'[72] Loudoun was beside himself. He attributed responsibility for these brutalities directly to the French court. Before leaving for America he had seen in London the papers Vaudreuil brought back with him after his term as governor of Louisiana. The French spy, Pichon, had obtained them for him after many adventures.[73] In a letter written a few days after the massacre Loudoun recalled certain passages in these documents. Vaudreuil had expressed there the maxim that the best time to attack the English was peacetime. He had related with some complacency the tale of the 'barbarities' perpetrated against the British in the Mississippi valley between the two wars— with the approval of France's ministers! 'This maxim,' concluded Loudoun, 'was followed at the taking of Oswego . . . and it has now again been repeated at Fort William Henry under Montcalm's own eye.'[74]

The excessive reaction of the British in this instance can be readily understood. The massacre of Fort William Henry was one more atrocity —a spectacular one—in a long series of atrocities. Bands of Indians, sometimes led by Canadian officers, had spread terror and destruction along the British frontiers. The colonies built forts, but efforts to protect their pioneer settlements were wasted.[75] A Virginia correspondent made the bitter comment that a few hundred Indians had 'kept three populous provinces in play, ravaged and depopulated whole countries, butchered and captivated hundreds of families . . . and that almost with impunity, in spite of all our forts and garrisons.'[76] Vaudreuil tried to strike at all the colonies in this way. One day he reported to the court that in giving orders for Indian raids he had not made an exception of New Jersey,[77] and a few days later a cry of pain was heard in New Jersey.[78] Nova Scotia was not immune, nor far-away Newfoundland.[79] Mutilated bodies were found every day in the country districts of Virginia, inspiring poets to lament for the victims.[80] This war of sudden surprise attacks was organized systematically by the Canadian government. Its principal base of operations, Fort Du Quesne, was a 'monstrous depot for scalps',[81] and Fort Niagara had a similar function in the Iroquois country, for bands of young Iroquois, Senecas especially, joined in the festival of blood. This was something, reported Montcalm, 'that we shouldn't have dared to hope for a year ago.'[82]

The provinces hardest hit were Pennsylvania and New York. One has only to glance at a newspaper to come upon stories of massacre and capture. The people of Pennsylvania seemed incapable either of defending themselves or of running away.[83] After listing a number of war parties, returned with prisoners and scalps from the Quaker province, Vaudreuil reported that some of the colonists, 'no longer able to keep up the war', had tried to save themselves from death at the hands of the Indians by declaring that 'they had never done them any harm, that they were so tired of the cruel war being waged against them that they could not but sue them for peace, and that they intended to make the same plea to the French.'[84] A letter intercepted in Pennsylvania reflected the same terror of the Indians, even the 'neutral' tribes, for all without exception prowled 'like bears on the frontiers' to 'assassinate, kill, and capture defenceless families.' The north was no less vulnerable than the southern provinces. 'I think,' said the author of the same letter, 'that if the French have a stronger army, as I think they have, they can without much trouble capture the province of New York.'[85]

Montcalm did not take New York, but behind the main front small detachments were constantly in action. Vaudreuil employed them to ravage the settlements on the Mohawk and the Hudson. Missisaugas, Wolves, and Iroquois raided as far as four days' journey from New York. They caused 'great damage to the enemy'. The prisoners and scalps they brought back were so much evidence that their mission had been 'perfectly' successful.[86] French reports were confirmed by those of British colonists. A letter from Ulster county reported the 'dreadful effects' of an Indian war: 'Nothing has yet been done to succour us; the frontier settlers are all coming in, having abandoned their little habitations, to preserve their lives.'[87]

The most important episode of this guerrilla war was the destruction of German Flats, a village on the north side of the Mohawk founded by industrious farmers and traders from the Palatinate. Acting on vague rumours that the 'Palatines' were 'very dissatisfied with the British government', and that they maintained regular relations with some of the Dutch settlers—'Flemings'—who were themselves so impatient of British domination that they were said to have 'come to blows with the troops from Old England' in New York, Vaudreuil had tried to win them over to the French cause, to get them to 'shake off the yoke of the Englishman's government'.[88] When his overtures were rebuffed, he conceived the idea of teaching them by experience that such a policy could only 'contribute to their ruin'.[89] Their village was well guarded: almost opposite, on the south shore, rose Fort Herkimer (which the Canadians called Kouari), occupied by 200 British regulars. Preceded by several small parties, which spread out through the region,[90] 300 men led by Ensign Picoté de Belestre took an oblique line from Famine Bay on Lake Ontario to Lake Oneida, then advanced along the Mohawk, marking as they went five forts—among them Fort Bull—abandoned by the enemy. About a mile from Fort Herkimer, Belestre veered off towards German Flats. On 13 November at three o'clock in the morning his men surrounded the sleeping village, which had been lulled into a sense of security by the protection of five blockhouses. The attack was almost unopposed. Resistance was confined to one quarter and was brief. There were probably about 300 Palatines, of whom 150 gave themselves up to the invaders and 32 were scalped. Several were drowned in an attempt to cross to Fort Herkimer. The commander did not dare to make a sortie for fear his post would be captured if the garrison were reduced. Pillaging was 'rich' and went on for two days. The loot included coined money worth more than 100,000 livres; one Indian took back gold pieces worth 30,000 livres. China, silver, trading goods—everything that could be carried was taken away. The rest was destroyed. The losses inflicted on the enemy were enormous.[91] When Loudoun learned of the disaster it was too late for him to take effective action. He dispatched Lord Howe in pursuit of Belestre, but by that time he was already far away, leaving in his wake such desolation that at first it was thought to be the work of 800 men.[92] The Palatines were severely 'punished'.[93] Their crime invites reflection. What precisely was their crime? It consisted in opting for the British after having been invited to join the French empire. It was not very different from the crime of the Acadians. In theory, when North America came under the domination of one empire, such conflicts over questions of assimilation would not arise.

For that condition to come about, one of the two empires would have to defeat the other. At the end of 1757, a year marked for her by so many reverses and disappointments, it was the British empire that envisaged the possibility of defeat. Pitt admitted that 'the state of the nation [was] indeed a perilous one, and fitter for meditation than discourse.' Horace Walpole, bitterly ironical, suggested that it was 'time for England to slip her own cables and float away into some unknown ocean.' Lord Chesterfield thought the winter of 1757-8 would bring peace, 'a bad one for us, no doubt, and yet perhaps better than we shall get the year after.'[94] Public opinion was completely exasperated. The downfall and ruin of nations, said an article in the *London Magazine*, are generally preceded by military defeat, the capture of towns, the devastation of territories. It will have been Great Britain's unique fate to perish without losing her fleets or her armies. And why? Because neither her fleet nor her army had fought; because, in spite of their exceptional talents, British admirals and generals had been 'so prodigiously unlucky'! So the waters of the seas and American soil were red with the blood of the brave fallen in the Ohio valley, at Oswego, at Fort William

[156]

Henry, before Minorca, and elsewhere.[95] The cost of living had doubled, said the *London Sentinel* about the same time. The misery of the people was increasing and would become worse. 'Every mail acquaints us with some new triumph of the enemy, the country is saddled with a debt of eighty millions, the interest of which we can hardly defray . . . oppressed with taxes almost insupportable.' The future promised to be still blacker than the present, and Britain was threatened with every plague that could be visited upon a nation doomed to destruction.[96] In contrast, France seemed insolently fortunate. The news from Germany and America was so good that people hesitated to believe it, 'for our warriors, and our journalists after them, are accused of emphasizing a little too much, and sometimes even of exaggerating, our slightest gains.'[97]

The historian Entick painted a sombre picture of England, in 'real distress, without an ally but who required powerful aid . . . engaged in a war with the most formidable enemy in Europe' and making no headway, 'without any system in its councils', and with a court careless of the nation's peril and attentive only to 'who could get and keep the best places.'[98] That was before Pitt's return to power at the end of June 1757, when the country was living in terror of an invasion.[99] Pitt did not believe the French would invade British soil, and he was right,[100] but the moment was nonetheless critical. The country had been at war officially for a year, 'a year of the most dishonour to the Crown, of the most detriment to the subject, and of the most disgrace to the nation that ever blemished the annals of Great Britain.'[101] This opinion was expressed in the *New York Gazette*. An article from a London paper, addressed to the People of England and reprinted in Boston, sounded the same note: '[Never were] the circumstances of the nation . . . at a more dangerous crisis than at present; when were your future honour or dishonour, prosperity or adversity, freedom or slavery in a more critical suspense, [when did they] hang in a more doubtful scale than at this time?'[102]

What exactly did these jeremiads mean? That England was indeed in grave danger, that the crisis was approaching, and that no one could say how it would be resolved. We know what Pitt represented: the empire; that is, briefly, the attractive idea that uncontested mastery of the seas and the possession of America were the essential ingredients of British prosperity and power. The Great Commoner had the nation behind him, but that did not mean necessarily that he had the support of Parliament, and the king did not like him. If Pitt embodied the empire, the group of favourites and politicians who on 5 April 1757 brought about his fall represented Europe. Pitt or the king, the Hanoverian: the empire or Europe, the sea or foreign countries, American dividends or subsidies to Europe's petty kings. This is not a true picture; its lines are too grossly simplified. In reality there was something—more than a little —of the politician in Pitt; his adversaries were more deeply tinged with imperialism than we like to think. But opinion takes no account of shadings, it sees only contrasting colours.

The *London Magazine* (1759) gives 1755 as the date of formation of the 'British party'. This group, which today would probably be called 'the nationalist party', was reluctant to see the country engaged in a continental war, sure to be very costly and probably disappointing in its results. They wanted Great Britain to concentrate her efforts in those places where she already enjoyed the advantage in materiel and organization: at sea and in the colonies. If this was her choice, so argued the members of this group, England could without undue effort continue the war until France, bled white and with her ships blockaded in her ports, would be 'compelled . . . to submit to reasonable terms of peace.'[103] The *Monitor* defined the course that Britain should take: 'Let England pursue her own interest in America; let her exert her naval power on the coasts of old France, and there is not the least doubt of seeing the day that their trade and navigation will be brought so low as not to enable them to maintain [their] mighty armies . . .' That would be the best means for Britain to give effective aid to her European allies. In case the allusion had not been sufficiently transparent, the article was signed: 'A Hanoverian'.[104] An article reprinted in the *New York Gazette* did not mince words either; it claimed that if the sums paid to mercenaries for the protection of Hanover had been spent on the British navy, it could have protected British trade and at the same time ruined that of the enemy and destroyed their fighting ships.[105] In short, Britons seemed to be wondering if England, by failing to make the most of her natural advantages, was not on the way to losing the war.

It was no mere coincidence that the American newspapers reprinted these articles; the debate was vital for the New World. The colonies were the first to suffer from the defects and uncertainties of Britain's strategy. Moreover, firm enlightened direction was a necessity for them. And what was happening? In June, before Hardy and Loudoun embarked for Halifax, Governor Morris of Pennsylvania reviewed briefly the situation in British America. He observed that military preparations generally were proceeding 'as slowly as the enemy could desire.' In the south the colonies were still without defences, the legislative assemblies as determined as ever to take no action, and 'in Pennsylvania the Indians [were] scalping as fast as ever.' The north presented almost as sorry a figure as the south. 'New Jersey,' wrote Morris, 'has still the honour to be governed by Mr Belcher, who can neither stand, nor speak, nor write. The very little understanding that he once had is now quite annihilated, and the public affairs . . . are performed by his wife and a few canting

New England parsons that are always about him.' The British authorities had been aware of the situation for years, but had made no attempt to remedy it: 'It is owing to such . . . ministerial inattention and disregard of the colonies that the French get the better of us everywhere with one twentieth of the people that we have.' New Jersey had set the pattern that was about to be followed in New York. Hardy was resuming his service in the navy, and the province would 'in little time be in the hands of . . . De Lancey.'[106] Another witness reported that things were going so badly for the English that in a few years they would have neither people nor colonies in the northern part of America. The poor starving colony of Canada was victorious wherever it attacked.[107]

Great Britain's manifest impotence in the New World struck terror into the hearts of those Britons—and they were no small number—who were clear-sighted enough to recognize the stakes for which the war was being fought. In August 1757 one of them, Thomas Pownall, the governor of Massachusetts expressed the feeling of the group. 'The war,' said Pownall, 'is no longer about a boundary, whether the French usurpation shall extend to this or that mountain, this or that river; but whether the French shall wrest from British hands the power of trade, whether they shall drive us out of this continent.' Hegemony in the New World, on which hung the fate of the two empires, was an infinitely complex question, of which no single aspect could be understood except in relation to the whole. 'If our colonies are ruined, where is our naval power? If our fleets become inferior, where is our dominion? And if our naval dominion is lost, Great Britain is no longer a free government and the British colonies no more a free people.'[108] In London the loss with which Britain was threatened was measured by the gains the enemy wished to achieve: 'It is certain that the growth of the British colonies has long been the grand object of French envy.'[109] At that moment in the history of the British empire—and this was equally true of the French empire—all parts of the whole were interdependent: the loss of her colonies would reduce the status of the mother country, and as the power of the mother country declined, her overseas settlements would fall apart.

It is easy to imagine the distress and rage of men so well prepared to foresee the repercussions of British defeats in America. Lord Chesterfield, abandoning his gentlemanly tone and precepts, launched a vicious attack on Loudoun. That 'disgustingly avaricious character' actually thought that 'a victory would be disadvantageous to him', and must therefore bear much of the responsibility for the humiliating Louisbourg fiasco.[110] 'We talk much,' wrote a disillusioned collaborator in the *London Chronicle*, 'of driving the French out of their encroachments; but it does not seem to be so easily done. We have been three whole years in only going to attack them, and have not yet been able to do that. They gain ground upon us everywhere; while we seem to do nothing but sit still and look on. Our strength and dependence seems to be our numbers in North America. This is the only advantage we have over our enemy, of which, however, we seem to make no use to counterbalance the many advantages they have over us.'[111] The editor of the London *Monitor* declared himself completely nonplussed. England had dispatched the most powerful fleet and army that had ever been sent to America and English colonies had once again been subjected to the cruelties of roving enemy bands. 'It is better not to proceed than to be obliged to return without being able to act.' But what else can be expected 'so long as a ministry has not the discernment to detect and avoid those men in public offices and contracts who have got great fortunes by deceiving their masters, ruining their measures, and plundering the nation'?[112]

What observers of the scene could not forgive was that instead of exploiting the massive superiority of his armies and the power of his 'prodigious fleet', Loudoun had concentrated his troops at a point where there was no fighting and had left only a small force at the place where the fighting actually took place.[113] The truth was that the general had chosen to stake everything on one play and had lost. There was a certain irony in the situation that some observers were quick to seize upon. Lord Hardwicke addressed a sarcastic query on the subject to Newcastle: 'According to these gentlemen's accounts, what a country are we throwing away all this blood and treasure about? It is unapproachable either in summer, autumn, or winter.'[114] November brought the ultimate humiliation. When Du Bois de la Motte arrived back from Louisbourg with his squadron intact the *London Magazine* reported the event: 'M. Du bois de la Motte's squadron arrived safe at Brest with a great number of British prisoners taken in America on board as we have no French prisoners there to give in exchange.'[115] This fact was in itself eloquent proof of victory on the one side and of defeat on the other.

Canada, however, was only moderately triumphant. In spite of his inclination towards boasting optimism, Vaudreuil realized that the attack on Louisbourg and Quebec, although it had proved abortive in 1757, had only been postponed. The ships wintering in Halifax left him in no doubt that 'the enemy would resume their undertaking early next spring.' If France wanted to ensure that the effort would again be 'in vain', she must again be ahead of the English at Louisbourg, and she must also send large quantities of provisions to New France.[116] It was not without reason that the governor made this last request. In October Canada had known conditions of 'severe famine', the result of a very poor harvest and the loss to the enemy of 'a great quantity of ships'.

[160]

Bigot had instituted a ration of four ounces of flour a day. And famine was not the only calamity to strike the country: the battalions sent from France, riddled with illness when they landed in Quebec, spread an epidemic throughout a population already weakened by insufficient nourishment. An Ursuline described the plight of Quebec: 'Three plagues have descended on our country, pestilence, famine, and war; but famine is the worst of all.'[117]

The situation in Canada was all the more tragic since the English were aware of it and meant to exploit it. In 1758 when he embarked for Louisbourg—and, he hoped, for Quebec—Amherst had among his papers a memorandum on Canada compiled in October of the previous year. The document, based on a wealth of information and carefully composed, contained a description of the colony and brief suggestions for a plan of campaign. Canadians, declared the author, were now so tired of the war that they appeared 'ripe for revolt'; many of them wished the English would deliver them from their 'misery' and hoped to obtain a 'mild' government from their conquerors. Harvests had failed both in 1756 and 1757, and all the ships bringing food to Canada had been captured. At the same time, so little of the land was under cultivation, the climate was so severe, and the farmers so much occupied with the king's service that it had been manifest ever since the beginning of hostilities that the country could not produce enough food to keep an army of six thousand men in the field. That, incidentally, was why the French were always so late in starting their military operations: they had to await the arrival of provisions from the mother country. (All this was true except—as the invaders would learn to their sorrow—the report on the spirit of the Canadian people. But is it not an enduring delusion of British conquerors to imagine that any people deprived of the benefits of British liberty must consider itself oppressed and would therefore welcome them?) This exhausted colony, continued the memorandum, could be subdued in two operations: a concerted attack by land and water on Quebec and an overland expedition against Montreal. The power of resistance of Canada's one fortress, Quebec, lay more in its natural defences than in its fortifications. Built high on a rock, it could withstand a naval bombardment. Therefore the town could not be reduced by a fleet acting alone; it would have to be subjected to a 'regular' siege. But a siege would present special difficulties, since the landing troops could choose neither the tactics to be adopted nor the terrain they were to occupy. The only possible landing place lay between the St Charles River and the falls of Montmorency, a space where field defences could easily be thrown up. The wall surrounding Montreal offered little protection. Moreover, since Montreal was the centre of the fur trade, the essential element in the country's economy, and since the surrounding farm lands, the richest in the colony, made it Canada's granary, it followed that Canada itself would fall with the fall of Montreal. The only difficulty was to get there! To sum up, it was not so much the strength of her fortifications as the difficulty of getting at them that constituted Canada's strength. This was what had been learned from three campaigns that otherwise had brought meagre results.[118]

The English, although exasperated by this series of setbacks, hung on doggedly and bided their time. When, at the end of November, Governor Pownall of Massachusetts addressed the assembly, he did not ask his compatriots to resume the offensive against New France immediately: 'I advise you to save your strength, to collect your force, to treasure up your money till God by the course of his Providence shall call us forth one and all to wreck his vengeance on the breakers of peace, the violators of faith, the enemies of liberty, the French in Canada. When that good time shall come we know that one and all we are willing, one and all we are able to destroy them.'[119]

Early in December, England, speaking with the voice of her king, engaged her 'utmost efforts . . . for the recovery and protection of the possessions and rights' of the British Crown and 'British subjects in America'.[120] At the moment when chiefs of state in Great Britain and in America were addressing these messages to their people, these were the forces the two empires had assembled in the New World in preparation for the supreme struggle: in Canada 6,800 regulars, in British America 23,000.[121] The numerical disproportion between the two populations was many times greater. With such overwhelming superiority, wrote a young officer fated to a great destiny, James Wolfe, England should be sure of conquering Canada in two campaigns.[122] It took three, and on the thread of that third campaign hung the fate of the Canadian people.

Although England and her colonies had repeatedly suffered defeat at the hands of Canada, Canada herself was on the brink of disaster. If her enemies could once reorganize their forces they would destroy her; and if Canadians wanted to know how it would be done, they had only to look eastward. Acadia was being dismembered right at their doors. In the autumn of 1757, although there were still Acadians, Acadia had ceased to exist. If Canadians wanted to see what defeat was, history was even then painting its horrid portrait in eastern New France.

Part Three

A DEFEAT

Chapter VI

The
Deportation of the Acadians
1755-62

The immense interest of the events that took place in Acadia at the time of the War of the Conquest lies in the fact that in their main outlines they constitute a prototype of those that might result from a French defeat in Canada. There is no end to the comparisons to be established between the two colonies. In both territories a French experiment in colonization was carried out, in both the process of colonization was slow and limited in scope, slower and more limited in Acadia than in Canada; hence both—the first still more than the second—present opportunities for measuring the consequences for a colony of insufficient numbers of settlers. Moreover, here were two American colonies that were objects of envy to colonies of a rival power whose rapid development was compromised, not so much by the wealth, power, or intrinsic value of the French colonies (these were limited by the scope of France's colonial policy) as by their strategic value. The war came and both colonies fell, Acadia first and then Canada. They fell—that is to say, they were defeated. In the perspective of two centuries of history, they are seen to have followed analogous courses: alike in that they led to the same result, different in that Acadia was impelled at a greater speed towards the end of the road. The distinction to be drawn is then a distinction of degree: Acadia, smaller and weaker, sooner conquered and sooner destroyed—by a process so literally radical that it could not have been applied in Canada—rushed more rapidly than her sister colony to her inevitable fate.

Let it be stated once more: it is impossible to understand what happened in America in the middle of the eighteenth century without going back to the Treaty of Utrecht. The treaty should have sealed Canada's fate and reduced it to a small agricultural country, destined to economic decline and consequently to social disintegration. Yet Canada, because it remained attached to the French empire, was able to subsist for almost half a century longer. On the other hand, in 1713 Acadia became a British conquest. It was not the first time that England had seized a European colony in America; in the preceding century she had built New York on a Dutch foundation. But in that case New York's Dutch population, surrounded on every side by the mass of British colonists, could not possibly fail to be absorbed. The Acadians were in a very different situation. Settled to the east of New England on a sort of offshoot from the continent, they were in a better situation to resist assimilation, since on the one hand England was extremely slow in developing her new province and on the other the important military and commercial port of Louisbourg, by maintaining the presence of France in the immediate vicinity of her lost colony, acted as a counterpoise to British influence.

A generation of Acadians bridged the years between 1713 and 1744, thanks to this balance of forces. The balance was delicate and the equilibrium far from stable, as the War of the Austrian Succession would show. In 1745 the Anglo-Americans captured Louisbourg. In 1746 the French government charged the duc d'Anville with the mission of recovering Acadia and Île-Royale. It would be an 'easy' task, predicted the minister of marine, for the inhabitants of the colony had 'never ceased to wish to return to the rule of His Majesty.' All the inhabitants? The court could not be too sure, and d'Anville was instructed accordingly: 'If there are any whose fidelity cannot in his opinion be counted upon, he will make them leave the colony, and will send them either to Old England or to one of the colonies of that nation, according to the facilities at his disposal.' As for the others, those who were to remain, he would administer to them the 'oath of allegiance to His Majesty.'[1] Oaths of allegiance, expulsion: these were, in Acadia, the instruments of imperialism—whether French or British.

The peace of Aix-la-Chapelle left unchanged the positions of the two European powers in the northeastern corner of America. Louisbourg was restored to France, and England remained in Acadia. But the war had revealed the essential vulnerability of Île-Royale: easily isolated, it could be as easily captured. How could the defences of America be reinforced at this vital point? The ideal solution for France would be to re-establish herself in Acadia, thus forging the last link in the chain of fortified positions she had thrown across the continent between Louisbourg and New Orleans. But that was manifestly impossible; she would have to be satisfied with less. She must then restrict Acadia to the peninsula: keep the English from crossing the isthmus of Chignecto and cut them off from access to the territory they claimed farther west. For, explained La Galissonière, 'if we abandon to England that territory with its more than eighty leagues of coastline . . . we shall have to give up all overland communication between Canada and Île-Royale, and every means of sending aid to the former or of recovering the latter.'[2]

The English, for their part, were haunted by the nightmare of Quebec communicating with Louisbourg by way of western Acadia. 'For,' it was reasoned in London, 'if that nation should obtain more than their right in this part of America, they may, with the contiguous colony of Cape Breton . . . be rendered more powerful in America than all the other acquisitions she had hitherto made there can possibly do.'[3] The question could hardly be better posed, but it was posed at least as well in France. Taxed with coveting more than territory in Acadia, the French turned the charge against their accusers. The true 'object' of the English, they said, was not the lands of western Acadia, 'for the most part ungrateful, sterile, and empty of trade.' No; the English wanted to extend their territory in the direction of Canada. In order to get possession of Canada? Again, no: but 'to prepare the way to universal empire in America and to the wealth of which America is the most abundant source.'[4]

This was the crux of the debate. Shirley had already defined its terms in less general, more precise, language. He was speaking of Nova Scotia, and by Nova Scotia he understood, as the English always did, more than the peninsula: 'That province, which is the key of all the eastern colonies upon the northern continent . . . abounds with . . . safe and commodious harbours . . . and hath a fertile soil.' In the hands of the French, it could support a large expeditionary force sent directly from Europe. If France should undertake such an operation, what would the consequences be? 'The *immediate* loss of most of the eastern parts of New England and the whole province of New Hampshire.' Moreover, with such a broad base of operations France could, in the long run, so tighten her hold on America that she might perhaps 'accomplish the reduction of every one' of the British colonies.[5] In short, in Acadia, as on Lake Ontario and in the Ohio valley, rival strategies confronted one another.

A study of France's carefully articulated movements in Acadia after the conclusion of the Treaty of Aix-la-Chapelle reveals four components of her strategy:[6] to block the isthmus of Chignecto; to constitute, next door to Nova Scotia, a 'French Acadia' peopled with emigrants from the English province; to send Indians (and Acadians) to raid British settlements;

and to make use of French missionaries to foment unrest among the Acadians in Nova Scotia.

In the autumn of 1749 La Jonquière assigned to the chevalier de La Corne the duty of blocking the isthmus. In the spring of 1750, and again late in the summer, La Corne's men encountered a British detachment under the command of Charles Lawrence. The first time the rival forces challenged one another and the second time shots were exchanged. To command the isthmus of Chignecto, linking the peninsula to the continent, was to hold Nova Scotia by the throat. It also meant possession of a communication route between Cape Breton and western Acadia: this narrow strip of land between Baie Verte and Beaubassin Bay, an arm of Chignecto Bay which itself opened on the Bay of Fundy, was scored with rivers and could be crossed by boat with a portage of less than two leagues. It was the route taken to reach the St John River, where Boishébert had established a post, and, on the other side, Île-Saint-Jean (Prince Edward Island) and Île-Royale. More than that, this important network was linked with Canada by the road Bigot had just opened between Lake Temiscouata and the Rivière du Loup, a road that reduced the time of the journey from Quebec to Chignecto to ten or twelve days and from the St John River to the capital of New France to a week. On the isthmus the adversaries hastened to choose their positions and entrench themselves: the English on the ruins of the Acadian village of Beaubassin, where they built Fort Lawrence, and the French opposite them on the hill at Beauséjour and at Gaspéreau, on the Baie Verte side.

Beauséjour soon became a focal point for French colonization. The mission of La Corne and Father Le Loutre was to persuade Acadians to emigrate to the country about the fort and farther west. The migration did not come about spontaneously, but required active stimulation. From the beginning La Jonquière predicted that things would not go 'altogether without difficulty', since the inhabitants considered themselves as 'belonging to the English.' Their view can be readily understood when it is remembered that a whole generation of Acadians had been born under English rule. In this respect facts amply justified La Jonquière's apprehensions. In order to persuade many of the Acadians who did migrate to 'French' territory, Le Loutre had to resort to hard-hitting and fiery arguments—the tomahawks and incendiary torches of his terrible Micmacs. What happened in the region of Beauséjour was repeated in the St John valley: a few Acadians chose to move there, but most were 'too much attached to their possessions to leave them.'[7]

The Indians appear to have played a very important part in this 'transplantation'. Acadians more than once declared to British officials that this was the case; they would stay quietly on their farms, and in order to do so would bow to English demands, if they did not fear that as a result of their obedience they would be molested by the Indian allies of the French.[8] In the summer of 1754, some of the farmers who had moved to 'French' Acadia actually initiated negotiations with a view to returning to their old homes, but when they were told they must take the oath of allegiance, they abandoned the idea, for 'unless they were assured that they should remain neuter . . . it would be impossible for them ever to think of returning as they would every day run the risk of having their throats cut and their cattle destroyed'—obviously by Le Loutre's Indians.[9] One might be tempted to question the value of such evidence, coming as it does from an English source; but it agrees with Bigot's statement of the case. 'The Indians,' said the intendant, 'being at war with the English, also aided in the transplantation of Acadians to French territory. They even forced them to break off all relations with [the English].'[10] And by whom were the Indians incited to such acts? By Canada's colonial administrators, who boasted of what they had done.[11] It goes without saying that the Indians also raided the English establishments in Nova Scotia. The restoration of Louisbourg to France gave the signal for the raids, and Governor Cornwallis knew quite well by whom they were organized. 'He fulminates against us,' jeered Bigot.[12] La Jonquière, for his part, made the raids serve a double purpose. He ordered the Indians to include in their parties 'a few Acadians dressed and painted like Indians', in order to compromise the white population still more deeply and thus provoke violent repression by the English. This, in La Jonquière's opinion, would help considerably 'to attract Acadian families to our territory.'[13]

As frontier incidents and Indian raids became more numerous, unrest increased in Acadia. The English returned to their old idea of requiring an unrestricted oath of allegiance. No sooner had the demand been made than a message reached the hands of the English governor: the Acadians refused to engage themselves 'to bear arms . . . even if the province were attacked'; in other words, they would not protect the interests of England against France. They repeated these declarations in letters addressed to the governments of France and of Canada, whose protection they sought. In these documents and others like them it is easy to detect the hand of agents of French policy. Their authors were not all unlettered. A plea signed by 125 farmers from Port Royal, emphasizing the fact that the Acadians had 'stood fast here without aid', cited a man of letters as authority: 'You have only to read Father Charlevoix's History.'

In reaction to Acadian resistance, the British became more grimly determined not to relax their hold on the province. On his arrival in Nova Scotia in 1749, Cornwallis had indignantly denounced the neglect from which the colony had suffered up to that time: '[Nova Scotia] has been called an English province for thirty-four years and I don't believe that the King has one true subject without the fort of Annapolis. I cannot trace the least glimpse of an English government.' The management of affairs with respect both to the Acadians and the British garrisons had been 'scandalous'.[14] Now that Cornwallis was there he would try to make up for the time lost by his predecessors and for their failure to colonize the country. He had brought with him a specific plan inspired by one that had been drawn up by the great imperialist, William Shirley.

The War of the Austrian Succession had opened Shirley's eyes. After the campaigns of 1746 and 1747, during which the Canadian invasion of Nova Scotia territory had met little effective opposition, the governor of Massachusetts had pointed out the need for energetic action. At the same time he recommended certain measures designed to parry immediate threats to British territory and to achieve far-reaching results. These were his proposals: to land 2,000 provincial troops from New England and dislodge the enemy's detachments from the isthmus of Chignecto, to deport to Massachusetts and the neighbouring colonies Acadians from the isthmus who had sympathized too openly with the French invaders, and to distribute the farms of which they would be dispossessed among the families of provincials called to service in the region. He hoped that with the help of time, business associations, and marriages, the nucleus of British settlers would absorb the Acadians grouped around this strategic centre, and that in this way New England would in three or four generations digest the conquered Acadians.[15]

Although the proposals formed a coherent plan, they proved premature, for it appeared that neither the British government nor opinion in Britain was ready to adopt the idea of expulsion even of certain groups of the 'neutral French', as the Acadians were called. Not that public opinion rejected this solution out of hand; on the contrary, the London Magazine of April 1749 examined it seriously. In the author's opinion it would be 'not perhaps so unjust as unpolitic.' In the first place it would be 'an unpopular transaction and against the faith of treaties', and secondly, 'as a country is reckoned wealthy in proportion' to the number of its people, Nova Scotia would be impoverished by the departure from the province of such a large number of its inhabitants.[16] As for the imperial government, there is nothing to indicate that at that time it envisaged the possibility of deportation.

The government had another plan: to destroy the ethnic and religious homogeneity of the province, not by expelling its inhabitants but rather by introducing large numbers of Protestants (British and foreign).[17] There was no question of proselytizing; but it so happened that the most active French agents were the missionaries, so that by modifying the religious personality of the province, England would make it less vulnerable to their propaganda. Where would the new colonies be planted? Shirley had designated the Chignecto region, London chose Chebucto, and it is easy to find reasons for the choice. Chebucto Bay, where the duc d'Anville had moored his fleet in 1746, offered a splendid harbour. As Bigot had said, 'All the King of England's ships could anchor there.' The object of the British government in creating a naval base at Halifax —a mission that fell to the new governor, Cornwallis—was obviously to establish Britain in a strategic position from which she could strike quickly and capture Louisbourg. At the same time the base would strengthen Britain's hold on Nova Scotia. Bigot saw the picture at a glance. 'If that establishment proves successful,' he wrote, 'we can abandon Acadia.'[18]

But was this certain? Undoubtedly Halifax had advantages, of which the greatest was that it provided an excellent starting-point for an offensive; but this meant that the British navy could exploit all its possibilities only in time of war. Moreover, although this military port protected Nova Scotia on the seaward side, on the landward side it was itself cut off from Annapolis, which up to that time had been the pivot of the English occupation; and since it was also separated by sea from New England, its power of resistance to an invading force would be in direct proportion to the strength of the naval units anchored beneath the guns of its citadel. Finally—and this point was particularly important—Halifax, a military stronghold, was ill-adapted, by reason of its position in the province, to stimulate the intermingling of ethnic elements so essential to Britain's plans for colonization. There were almost no Acadians on the eastern shore on which the new settlement was being built. How then could it be expected that the groups of British settlers, imported at great expense, would be able to carry out Shirley's project of absorbing the stubborn remnants of the French population? English and German immigrants could of course be settled there on unoccupied land, but this would result in the creation of another British colony, not in the heart of Acadia but on its outskirts.

In any case, although Shirley's original plan was better suited to the necessities of colony-building, its effective development would have taken time, and time was short. When the Lords of Trade answered La Galissonière's aggressive imperialism with a specific act of colonization, the founding of Halifax, the agents of French policy undertook to organize counter-action of the same nature. In a statement of his plans, Father Le Loutre shows that he was aware of the intentions of his adversaries: 'I shall therefore set out for Acadia and do my utmost to assemble my savages . . . My plan is to engage the Indians to get the English to say they will not allow new settlements to be established in Acadia and to assert that it' must remain as it was before the war . . .'[19] But Le Loutre also knew what he wanted himself. As soon as La Corne's posts were planted on the isthmus of Chignecto, the fiery missionary wrote to the court asking it to guarantee to Acadians 'freedom to leave Acadia and the means to establish themselves on French land.' The 'French land' to which he referred included the St John valley and the territory of which La Corne, acting on orders from La Jonquière, had just taken possession. Father Le Loutre went on to develop his idea: 'The Acadians will defend with their lives the land they have occupied, they will work hard to cultivate the soil, and they will build up a flourishing trade . . .' What was this if not a plan for colonization? And the motive underlying this project of settlement and economic development? To serve the French empire. The colonists of New Acadia would be an invaluable asset: 'They will supply Île-Royale with provisions of all sorts, and in time of war can provide more than 1,000 men to bear arms either in defence of Louisbourg or in the reconquest of Acadia. In such an event you will see Acadians marching against the English and fighting like heroes against the enemy of the state.'[20]

A conflict was about to take place between rival movements of colonization. But whereas the British settlements in eastern Nova Scotia were still at the stage of interesting experiments, 'French Acadia', carved out of the territory extending west of the Missaguash, was making rapid progress. In 1754 the British had already founded Halifax and Dartmouth, the German colony of Lunenburg, and Fort Sackville; they had also laid the foundations of Lawrencetown on a concession of 20,000 acres of land twelve miles from Halifax.[21] As for the French, in August of the same year, when Lawrence, recently promoted to the rank of lieutenant-governor, received the report of an intelligence agent on the isthmus of Chignecto and the St John River, he gave a cry of alarm. The post on the St John hardly gave cause for anxiety: three miserable little guns, less than twenty Franco-Canadian soldiers, and rather more than 150 Indians. But Beauséjour was growing. The fort, although not very large, seemed solid; it bristled with guns, and it was occupied by sixty-six officers and soldiers of the regular army, as well as 400 Indians. More than that—within forty-eight hours the French could assemble there a force of 1,400 or 1,500 Acadian combatants drawn from Baie Verte, Île-Saint-Jean, Chepody, Petitcodiac, Memramcook, etc.[22] Events were to prove that this last estimate was scarcely exaggerated. For the moment the Acadian situation might be summed up in the following manner: on the east coast, in an isolated region, British colonization was just getting off to a new start; in the west, in territory over which soldiers from Canada mounted guard, a 'French Acadia' was rapidly taking shape. Between these two poles of attraction a people waited—hesitant, torn between material well-being and 'French' loyalty.

In order to uproot the Acadians from the soil to which they were attached, the French had recourse to a new tactic: to deprive them of spiritual direction and at the same time to show them that the way to obtain such guidance was to leave the peninsula. This was the policy that Father L'Isle-Dieu, the vicar-general of the bishop of Quebec in France, explained to monseigneur de Pontbriand: 'I am informed from Louis-bourg and Acadia that the French Acadians who are still on the peninsula under English domination earnestly beseech you, monseigneur, to send them priests . . . but it is my duty to make known to you the spirit of the court and its views on that subject . . . It appeared to me that they were much more zealous to supply priests to those who had left the peninsula, with the idea that priests sent to serve those who were still there would simply keep them there. M. Le Loutre made the same observation to the court and it has no doubt been communicated to you.'[23] Three months after writing this letter, the vicar-general returned to the subject. The task of getting Acadians to emigrate was already difficult enough without the court's sending them missionaries and thus providing them with one more reason for not moving. Their reluctance to emigrate was inspired 'by natural cupidity and by their desire to keep their little holdings in that peninsula that is all the more difficult to leave since they have spent so much time and toil in its cultivation and it is now better prepared to bring them returns for the effort they have spent.'[24]

Obviously France held most of the high trump cards. She appeared to have things her own way in northeastern North America, and England seemed at a loss to know what course to adopt. In the spring of 1754 Lawrence placed this question before the Lords of Trade: how could the British authorities give rulings in disputes arising between Acadians—who were naturally addicted to lawsuits—on the subject of their lands? To pronounce judgements would be to recognize tacitly the legal title of these farmers to their concessions. But on the other hand they could not hold such title without first swearing unreservedly the oath of allegiance that England required of them. However, the insecurity resulting from the application of this policy might drive them to emigrate and thus add to the strength of 'French Acadia'. But on the other hand, to confirm them in possession of their property before they had taken the oath might encourage them to persist in their resistance. How could the dilemma be resolved? Their lordships left the question open.[25]

In 1749 a contributor to the *London Magazine* had suggested a possible solution for the Acadian problem: 'I see no reason,' he wrote, 'why they may not be put under the restraint of such laws as may reduce them into a proper obedience and the condition of hewers of wood and drawers of water under the natural subjects of the mother country.'[26] Although he spoke bluntly—and perhaps for that reason—the political journalist judged rightly. The normal relations between conquerors and conquered are those of masters and slaves. A conquered people is fated to become a people of 'hewers of wood and drawers of water'—on one condition, however, and that was the only point the author of the article neglected: that the conquest is really a defeat. Acadia had been conquered forty years earlier; she was still not defeated. She had still to be broken.

How was this result to be achieved? By translating hard thinking into decisive action. The architect of Acadia's defeat was Charles Lawrence, a man of clear vision and relentless determination. A letter of August 1754 from Lawrence to the Board of Trade dealt with the Acadian problem. The various functions he had exercised in the province during the last five years, he wrote, had kept him in constant touch with the French inhabitants, and he knew them. Up to that time it had been thought that they could be won over by the 'mildness of English government'. What an error that had been! Far from becoming reconciled to their conquerors, they had continued to cherish their 'partiality' for France; and now a large number of them had gone to work for the French at Beauséjour. Lawrence had forbidden them to go, and in order to dissuade them had offered them employment himself, but to no avail. It was a long time since they had brought any produce to the British markets, although they supplied the French regularly. And not only did they provide labour and food for the French settlements, they also acted as spies for the commanders of their posts. England should not allow herself to be deluded; the situation would not change so long as the Acadians had 'incendiary priests' among them and so long as they had not sworn the oath of allegiance, which they would only do under compulsion. What could be done then? Could colonies of British settlers be planted in the parts of the province occupied by Acadians? But 'as they possess the best and largest tracts of land in the province it cannot be settled with any effect while they remain in this situation, and though I would be very far from attempting such a step without Your Lordships' approbation, yet I cannot help being of opinion that it would be much better, if they refuse the oaths, that they were away.' This was what the lieutenant-governor had been leading up to. The exodus of the French population would have only one disadvantage: Lawrence admitted that they might take up arms and join forces with the Indians to harry the British colonists, but he was inclined to minimize this risk: 'Indeed I believe that a large part of the inhabitants would submit to any terms rather than take up arms on either side. But that is only my conjecture and not singly to be depended upon in so critical a circumstance.' The whole question could not be resolved at once, but it would be well to begin by building a fort on the Shubenacadie River as an obstacle to communication between the French and the Acadians. The British must also patrol the Bay of Fundy to prevent skippers from Boston and Louisbourg from provisioning French Acadia.[27] The letter as a whole throws a great deal of light on the curious situation that existed in Nova Scotia —a British province whose population was in large part foreign and refractory to assimilation.

It was now London's turn to speak. Faced with the facts, the Board of Trade realized their gravity; the 'lenity' of British rule had not succeeded in 'weaning' the Acadians from France. The population in general looked upon the French and the English just as they had done before the conquest. The fact was, however, that after the Treaty of Utrecht the Acadians could continue to live in the province only on condition that they become subjects of Great Britain, and in order to acquire this status they must take the oaths required by the British authorities. It was therefore most important to consider to what extent they could be treated as British subjects if they refused to take the oaths, and whether refusal to do so would not cancel their titles to their property. Their lordships did not undertake to rule on this question, but they hoped the lieutenant-governor would submit it to the chief justice of the colony, whose opinion could serve as a basis for measures that might be taken at some future date with respect to the inhabitants in general. The Lords of Trade were unwilling to commit themselves, but their statements sufficed to authorize the principle of massive deportation: if the Acadians had not the status of British subjects they had no right to the land they were cultivating, for it was British land; and if they had no right to the land, it would not be illegal to dislodge them from it. It would require only the decision of a colonial magistrate to give this reasoning the force of law.

This was the situation as it concerned Acadians in general; a particular case was presented by the farmers from the Chignecto region who had gone over to Beauséjour. It would be quite in order, if this were the opinion of the chief justice, to concede their abandoned lands to British settlers: an English settlement in that strategic zone could not fail to be helpful 'if it was possible to establish one in the present state of affairs.' But the question was: was it possible? On the one hand Shirley reported to Lord Halifax that there were in New England a large number of persons ready to emigrate to the region of the isthmus. But on the other hand, it was the opinion of the Lords of Trade that it would be absurd to embark on a plan for an English settlement in that region unless the French forts at Beauséjour and Baie Verte were destroyed, the Indians dispersed, and the French obliged to seek refuge in the arid island of Cape Breton, on Île-Saint-Jean, or in Canada. Even when taken alone, the statement of the Lords of Trade is a very important one; it has added significance when read in conjunction with that of the chief justice. England first established her right to deport the whole population of Acadia and then affirmed that no methodical plan of colonization could be undertaken until 'French Acadia' had been eliminated. The two parts of the argument were interdependent.

The Board of Trade did not stop there; it developed a policy for Nova Scotia in the contexts of international policy and North American policy in general. In the first field, tension between the two great European powers was mounting; and in the second Britain had reached the decision to resort to force of arms and to send troops to the New World. On 24 September 1754 Braddock was appointed to command the expeditionary force, and the war party at once began to plan the campaigns that would be undertaken in 1755. Lawrence was ordered to hold himself in readiness for any eventuality and to see that the batteries of the fort at Halifax were mounted with all possible speed. The moment was critical, wrote their lordships, and his majesty was preparing to maintain the just rights of his empire: 'every governor in America should be particularly attentive to the security and defence of the colony under his command.'[28] The importance of the message need not be emphasized: it foreshadowed the fate of a whole people.

Even before receiving advice Lawrence, impatient to act, had set about the task that seemed to him most pressing: the capture of Beauséjour, the nerve-centre of 'French Acadia'. We have already observed how deeply disturbed he was by the growth of the French settlements, and they were making constant progress. It was true the French had not attempted any further 'encroachments' for some time, but according to Lawrence there were two reasons for this. In the first place they were busy consolidating their positions and strengthening their defence works at Beauséjour and Gaspereau; they had just completed a very good road between the two forts and they were continuing to do their utmost to attract the Acadians to their side. And in the second place they were so deeply involved elsewhere on the continent that they had to go slowly in the northeast. This, wrote Lawrence to Shirley early in November 1754, was a situation of which they must take advantage.[29] At the same time he informed him that he had conceived a plan for displacing the French from Chignecto and the St John River. But he could not carry out his plan without help from New England. He needed troops and he asked for 2,000 men. He would like to have them in the field in the spring of 1755, before the arrival of the warships that France sent out every summer to Île-Royale. Lawrence's plan rested upon one fundamental consideration: the need to act quickly in order to take advantage of the delicate situation in Acadia and the extreme complexity of French policy in America. 'Your Excellency must undoubtedly be sensible,' he wrote to Shirley, 'what an advantage we shall gain upon the French by attacking them first, more especially as their chief dependence is the Indians and our deserted French inhabitants, who most probably will leave them when they find they are not able to keep their ground and who would infallibly assist them if they should begin with us.' Moreover, all eyes were on the Ohio. This was the time, then, to launch an attack on Beauséjour; besides, this action would benefit the whole of British America: it would create a diversion and force the enemy to divide his forces. Lawrence sent his message by Colonel Monckton, whom he proposed to place in command of the expedition.[30]

While Lawrence was organizing his campaign for 1755 in conjunction with Shirley, the British government was putting the last touches on the vast plan of operations that would, so it was thought, dismember New France in one season and drive the French back to the St Lawrence. Less than three weeks separate Lawrence's letter to Shirley and the 'Secret Instructions' of the British ministry to Braddock. The latter, as we know, was commissioned to sweep the French from the Ohio valley, Lake Ontario, and Lake Champlain. He also received—this was the eighth item in his instructions—orders to 'destroy the French fort of Beauséjour, which will allow us to recover our province of Nova Scotia', and with regard to that subject to communicate with the lieutenant-governor of Nova Scotia, who also had plans.[31] There was thus perfect agreement between the British government and that of Nova Scotia. There were not two Acadian policies, Lawrence's and that of the Board of Trade and Plantations; there was only one policy, but it was being worked out in London and Halifax simultaneously. London and Halifax were in agreement on the principles and also on the means of applying them. Before giving his instructions to Braddock, the secretary of state, Sir Thomas Robinson, had seen a letter from the Board of Trade emphasizing the importance of the French settlements and forts on the St John River, at Beauséjour, and on Baie Verte. The letter contained a quotation from Lawrence's dispatch of 1 August.[32] The Lords of Trade underlined the 'fatal consequences' of the enemy's 'encroachments'. The colony, they continued, could not make any progress, as Colonel Lawrence had 'pertinently' observed, so long as it continued to be threatened by the natives, and this scourge would continue 'so long as the French remained in possession of the north shore of the Bay of Fundy.'[33]

It was only in mid-January, after receiving Shirley's reply, that Lawrence reported to the Board of Trade on the steps he had taken. He also informed them that a fort on the Shubenacadie was no longer a sufficient guarantee of security for the province. He had 'discovered' that no really efficacious measures for protection could be taken until the French forts west of the Missaguash had been 'absolutely extirpated.' The enemy, he repeated, must be driven out before they had time to unite their forces. But he had been worried. He wondered whether he might not be reproached with having involved himself too deeply with Shirley before asking for the approval of the Lords of Trade. Fortunately he was reassured by a recent letter from Sir Thomas Robinson, recommending that he proceed with his plans after first making sure of Shirley's co-operation. Shirley was quite in agreement, and everything would be ready in the spring. He had already acted upon the instructions he had received concerning the Acadian inhabitants. 'According to Your Lordships' orders, I have communicated to the Chief Justice the point of law concerning the right of the French inhabitants. He has it now under consideration and I will transmit his report to Your Lordships by the next opportunity.'[34] In very truth everything would be ready.

The lieutenant-governor now needed only the explicit approval of the Board of Trade and Plantations, and he had not long to wait for that. Early in May the Lords of Trade assured him that he could count on their 'aid and support' in any 'just and necessary measures' he might decide to take in order to promote 'the well-being and security' of Nova Scotia. The general statement was followed by a specific directive. Beauséjour and Gaspereau were having a 'harmful effect' on the development of the colony; they were causing uneasiness in the neighbouring provinces. There could therefore be no doubt as to the 'appropriateness and utility' of the attack for which preparations were being made. The Lords of Trade wished luck to the officers directing the operation. They hoped that success in this campaign might be the forerunner of victory in any future operations his Majesty might find it necessary to undertake to defend his just rights and protect his subjects. These were not merely fine words. They were the expression of a deep conviction, and they were borne out by tangible evidence: the dispatch of a warship and transports loaded with arms and provisions.[35] The expedition against Beauséjour would mark the turning-point in the history of the defeat of Acadia. It is obvious that the decision to undertake the expedition was Lawrence's; but it is equally obvious that his decision merely anticipated the desire of the imperial government.

While this exchange of correspondence was going on, events in New England had not stood still. Shirley was feverishly busy in Boston, and at the end of March 1755 he was able to announce that preparations for the campaign were already well advanced. He was urging them forward with all speed because he wanted to start out himself for Alexandria in Virginia, where the governors were to meet Braddock and to try to co-ordinate the action of the different British colonies against New France.[36] The Beauséjour offensive would of course be discussed at the meeting. Braddock studied the plans drawn up by Lawrence and Shirley, and confirmed the appointment of Monckton as commander of the expedition.[37]

The rest would be an affair of three weeks. On 26 May a convoy of more than thirty sails, escorted by three frigates, sailed out of Boston Bay; the next day it reached Annapolis and effected a junction with another squadron from Halifax. The combined fleets then proceeded to Fort Lawrence, which they reached on 2 June. Two days later 2,000 provincials and 250 British regulars were encamped on the 'very fine road' linking Beauséjour and Gaspéreau, and the following day they were one mile from Beauséjour. On 8 June they entrenched themselves on a height half a mile from the fort, and on 14 June their mortars opened fire. Beauséjour surrendered on 17 June, and Gaspéreau the following day.[38] It was an episode of modest dimensions even for American military history; but it resulted in an immense strategic advantage for the English. It was the end of 'French Acadia'.[39]

What was the reason for this sudden collapse? Was it due to cowardice on the part of the commander of Fort Beauséjour, Louis Du Pont du Chambon de Vergor? At the news of the British advance, Vergor had sent messages to all the Acadians he could reach, some 1,200 or 1,500, to hasten to the defence of the isthmus, and they came in great numbers. However, conscious of the seriousness of the adventure in which they were engaged, they demanded from the commander a written order requiring them, on pain of death, to bear arms. Thus if they fell into the hands of the enemy they had proof that they had served against their will. It was a bad sign. With the bombardment of 14 June the Acadians began to show signs of demoralization; the next day, panic-stricken, they wanted to leave the fort before it was invested. The final blow fell on 16 June when a big bomb demolished a casemate, killing all its occupants. Vergor had to open negotiations for surrender. It had been a foregone conclusion from the moment when a corps of 450 Acadians and Indians, entrenched in an advanced post on the shore of the Missaguash River, capitulated after resisting British pressure for an hour.[40] It is worth noticing that Vergor made use of all his equipment and ammunition. His guns poured fire on the invaders, one of whom reported that 'nothing was to be heard but the roaring of cannon and the noise of men.'[41] He could not use his men as effectively, for they lacked the will to fight. When Beauséjour surrendered there were only 150 regulars and 300 Acadians in the fort, some of them wounded. The others had disappeared. They had not dared to persist in their resistance, for fear of compromising themselves irretrievably and risking the penalty for high treason—the hangman's rope.

Drucourt, the governor of Île-Royale, judged that the resistance offered by Vergor had been 'proportionate to his situation', while Villeray could not even think of defending Gaspéreau. The post was no more than a storage depot. He might be reproached for surrendering the post instead of burning it, but Drucourt considered his conduct in this respect due to 'a lack of intelligence rather than of courage.'[42] Machault, who would have liked to make an example of them at the very beginning of the war, ordered the two men to appear before a court martial and recommended severity,[43] but both were vindicated.[44] Boishébert placed responsibility for the defeat elsewhere. Speaking of the deportation and its accompanying atrocities, he said of Acadians in general: 'Let us hope that the ill-treatment they are experiencing will make them realize how much it is to their advantage to be subject to us; they would be much more to be pitied if they had not behaved like real cowards when M. de Vergor was attacked.'[45] This was a hasty judgement. The truth was that 'French Acadia' fell apart at the first shock, and for this reason: it had never been a solid structure. It was an artificial creation. Born of fear, it perished by fear.

Predictably one article of the capitulation of 16 June concerned the Acadians. It stipulated that, as they had been 'forced to take up arms on pain of death', they would be 'pardoned'.[46] The victors subscribed to this condition. However, as early as 28 June Lawrence, reporting to the Board of Trade that the Acadians serving under Vergor had given up their arms, informed them as to the instructions he had given to Monckton: 'I have given him orders to drive them out of the country at all events.' However, if their services were needed to build barracks for the British troops, he might 'first make them do all the service in their power.'[47] A few months later, in answer to an inquiry from the Board, Lawrence explained the reasons underlying his orders to Monckton. The word 'pardoned' in the fourth article of the terms of capitulation meant simply that French inhabitants captured armed in the fort would not be put to death. Monckton had never understood that the article meant more than that, for before he set out Lawrence had advised him that any Acadians found among the French were to be expelled from the country. Moreover, Monckton had done well to let these men believe that they would be pardoned; they must not be reduced to despair nor driven to seek refuge in Canada.[48] This was the language of a politician. The idea could have been expressed more clearly and more simply: if they had given the Acadians to believe they would be 'pardoned', it was in order not to inspire them with the courage of despair, in order to prevent them from escaping and to have the benefit of their labour before taking extreme measures against them.

The little new 'French' Acadia had been cut off at the root. Boishébert still had a few bands of guerrillas with him, but after burning his post on the St John River, he retreated with them towards the interior.[49] But what of the real Acadia, the Acadians' Acadia? Its fate was decided in July 1755.

Lawrence began by working on a representative group of Acadians— delegates who had come to Halifax from Minas Basin. They were summoned by the lieutenant-governor to appear on 3 July before the provincial council, which considered, article by article, an 'arrogant' memorandum presented the previous month to the military commander of their district. The council then invited them to swear allegiance to George II. The delegates hesitated and asked permission to go and consult the people they represented. The councillors replied that each person must decide for himself, and gave the delegates twenty-four hours to consider the matter.[50] The next day the Acadians again appeared before Lawrence and his colleagues. Had they modified their attitude? No; they still insisted upon being exempted from bearing arms against the French. The council was ready with its answer: they could no longer be regarded as British subjects, and they would be detained on George's Island until they could be deported to France. Two weeks later Lawrence reported that the prisoners had expressed an ardent desire to take the oath, and that they had been informed that permission to do so would not be granted until the council had received a report on the attitude of the rest of the inhabitants.[51]

Thus, with little commotion, the 'great displacement' began. There still remained one formality to be completed, but it entailed only a short delay. The Board of Trade and Plantations, it will be remembered, had advised the lieutenant-governor to ask the chief justice for a definition of the Acadians' right to tenure of their land. The judge was Jonathan Belcher, a Boston man who had been appointed to his post in Halifax in the autumn of 1754. Not that these details have any importance: any other judge would have played the same part. Since the question had been submitted to the chief justice, two decisions—to deport the inhabitants of French Acadia and to deport the delegates from Minas Basin— had intervened in rapid succession. After that the judge could not fail to pronounce a sentence of deportation, and it is difficult to regard the trial conducted by him as anything but a 'judicial stage setting'.[52] Even if it is true, as Lawrence states, that the question was already under consideration in January 1755,[53] the judge's conclusion was not delivered until 28 July, when he presented his report to the provincial council.[54] Although his judgement had been anticipated, the report itself is of the greatest interest. It is made up in large part of vain recriminations, but from this welter emerges the fundamental motive of the expulsion of the Acadians: grim determination to build a British colony, a colony that would replace one previously existing and that would be built on its ruins by exploiting a defeat to the utmost.

What does Belcher say in his report? 'The question now depending before the Governor and Council, as to the residence or removal of the French Inhabitants from the Province of Nova Scotia, is of the highest moment to the honour of the Crown, and the settlement of the colony, and as such a juncture as the present may never occur for considering this question to any effect, I esteem it my duty to offer my reasons against receiving any of the French Inhabitants to take the oaths, and for their not being permitted to remain in the province.' The judge then drew up a list of these considerations: 1—Since 1713 the Acadians had appeared 'in no other light than that of rebels to His Majesty.' 2—Acquiescence in their continued presence would violate the king's instructions to Cornwallis and in the judge's 'humble apprehension' would 'incur the displeasure of the Crown and the parliament.' 3—It would also 'defeat the intent of the expedition to Beauséjour.' 4—It would 'put a total stop to the progress of the settlement' for which the mother country had incurred 'vast expense.' 5—The Acadians would unquestionably 'return to their perfidy and treacheries' after the departure of the British fleet and the New England troops, and at that time 'the province [would] be in no condition to drive them out of their possessions.'

Belcher develops these five points one by one. His brief history of the Acadian 'rebellions' would have only the interest of a curiosity if it did not point up the fact that ever since the founding of Halifax the Acadians had incited the Indians to harry the infant settlement, and that they had consistently served as provisioners and intelligence agents for the French troops in the region. As a result the British colonists had had to shut themselves up in their fortified posts and had not been able to farm the land granted to them. That was why half the colonists brought into the province at great expense had left it to settle 'in other plantations where they could get their bread without risking their lives.'

From an analysis of Cornwallis's instructions, the judge concludes that it would be 'observing them to the letter' to expel the Acadians, a conclusion that would carry little weight if Belcher had been alone in accepting it. But the Lords of Trade and the British government had seen the judge's report,[55] and by failing to disavow it had tacitly approved his interpretation of the ends pursued by England since 1749.

The fall of Beauséjour, continued Belcher, should have been followed by the collapse of Acadian resistance. But 'even in the presence of the admirals [Boscawen and Mostyn]' they had refused to take the required oaths. 'And if this be their language while the fleet and the troops are with us, I know not what will be their style and the event of their insolence and hostilities when they are gone.' This reflection is related to the judge's fifth point: they must profit by the presence of the expeditionary force from New England to carry out an expulsion that the colony could not undertake with its own limited resources.

The fourth item in the report completed the first. The government could not allow the Acadians to remain in the country 'without retarding the progress of colonization and perhaps compromising it completely.' Here the factor of demography, a vital one in any colonial development, came into play. Belcher calculated that there were some 8,000 Acadians in the province and only about 3,000 English. These were not exact figures, but proportionally they appeared to represent the gap in numbers between the two populations. The comparative failure of the settlements on the eastern coast had shown the English how difficult it would be to achieve equality with the French population. It would be all the more difficult since the numerical superiority of the French might 'disquiet' British colonists already settled in Nova Scotia and discourage others from joining them. The Acadians must therefore be expelled.

It was then a question of empire-building, and we have seen how the question presented itself. To sum up. British America had to have Nova Scotia as an anchor because the geographical structure of the continent required it. If Britain's empire in America allowed France to come back to Acadia, or rather if it did not drive her out, it would be handing over an enormous bridgehead to a rival empire and abandoning to it an uninterrupted chain of communication between Louisbourg and New Orleans. In such conditions all the British colonies would be under constant pressure on their flank and their rear, and their normal development would thus be impeded. Moreover, long and painful experience had shown that if British power were to take root and spread in Nova Scotia, it must first supplant what was left of the French colony. Unless Britain resigned herself to creating a colony parallel to the well-established French settlement—which had naturally sent down its roots in the regions most favourable to the growth of a vigorous community—a colony that would be costly to build, that would be viable only after a long period of time (that might indeed never be viable), it was imperative for her to uproot Acadia from the land that gave it being. Then, but only then, would Britain be able to create an English country. Lauvrière betrays a certain naiveté when, after reproaching Belcher with being nothing more than a colony builder, he adds this disdainful comment: 'Thus the pecuniary interest is always uppermost in this nation of tradesmen.'[56] But the whole history of America at that time is a history of colonial rivalries, and all colonizers are alike. The dreadful episode of the dispersal of the Acadians could only be conceived in the context of a war of empire-builders: to be precise, although here further clarification appears superfluous, of empire-builders who came into conflict for this very reason—that they were bent on achieving the same objective at the same time.

The document in which Belcher outlined the principles of British policy was dated 28 July 1755. The same day the Nova Scotia council reached its decision; or rather, since its role was a more modest one than that of the chief justice, it reached the following conclusion: 'As it had before been determined to send all the French inhabitants out of the province if they refused to take the oaths, nothing now remained to be considered but what measures should be taken to send them away and where they should be sent to.' Lawrence, the councillors, and Admirals Boscawen and Mostyn, who sat with them, recommended unanimously that the Acadians be 'distributed amongst the several colonies on the continent.' Their dispersal was designed 'to prevent as much as possible their attempting to return and molest the settlers that may be set down on their lands.'[57] Displacement, dispersal, replacement: these are three steps in the operation begun in 1755, and it must be emphasized that they are equally important.

This fact emerges from the explanations set forth in Lawrence's letter of 18 October to the Board of Trade. Since the attitude of the French inhabitants had made it necessary to force them to leave the country, the provincial council 'immediately took into consideration what might be the speediest, cheapest and safest method of giving this necessary resolution its intended effect.'[58] Sending Acadians to Île-Royale or to Canada would be tantamount to giving militiamen to French colonies, so it had been decided to disperse them among the British colonies, from Georgia to New England. Lawrence emphasized the point that the operation would be carried out with the strictest economy. The livestock belonging to the displaced farmers—he passed more lightly over this point—had been handed over to those British inhabitants who could feed the animals during the winter. But this was only the first step; they must now bring into Nova Scotia the settlers who would inherit the farms of the Acadians. One of the 'favourable' results of his policy foreseen by the lieutenant-governor was that the immigrants would make it possible for the colony to supply its own needs, and also those of the British garrisons stationed there. Another was that the confiscation would provide 'a large quantity of fertile soil' ready to give an immediate yield. The Board of Trade received the letter on 18 November and took it under consideration a week later.

The sequel is not without interest. The Lords of Trade were apprised of the deportation on 25 November. The following day they recommended to the king that Lawrence be appointed 'Governor-in-chief' of Nova Scotia, 'he appearing to us to be every way qualified for and highly deserving of that station.'[59] On 18 December the ministry acceded to their request.[60] Lawrence's commission was dispatched on 25 March 1756 and was accompanied by this message from the ministers: 'We have laid that part of your letter which related to the removal of the French inhabitants and the steps you took in the execution of this measure before His Majesty's secretary of state, and as you represent it to have been indispensably necessary for the security and protection of the province in the present critical situation of our affairs we doubt not but that your conduct herein will meet with His Majesty's approbation.'[61] After Lawrence's promotion, how could anyone have doubted it? The deportation met with approval in London's political circles; how would it be received by the American governments? In announcing the news to his fellow governors, Lawrence repeated the explanation he had given to his superiors: it had become necessary to get rid of 'a set of people who would forever have been an obstruction to the intention of settling this colony.' The measure was 'indispensably necessary to the security of this colony, upon whose preservation from French encroachments the prosperity of North America is esteemed in great measure dependent.'[62] The lieutenant-governor of Massachusetts immediately pronounced the expulsion 'a wise precaution'.[63] Everywhere else there were signs of a certain embarrassment. In Pennsylvania, Morris simply presented Lawrence's letter to the council and summarized it for the legislative assembly.[64] He did not know what to do with the exiles that Nova Scotia had sent him, and left them cooped up in the ships that had brought them to Philadelphia until the doctors warned him of the danger of an epidemic.[65] Dinwiddie was 'surprised' to see Acadians appearing in Virginia and wondered where he could put them. All the land in the main part of the colony was taken up, and there could be no question of requisitioning land for them. They could not be sent to settle on the frontiers, where they would join forces with the bands of Indians and Canadians already spreading death and destruction along the border. It is not surprising then that the governor had great difficulty in persuading the majority of his council to open the doors of the colony even a crack to the exiles.[66] Dinwiddie finally sent all the Acadians he had on his hands to England, thus invoking the displeasure of the imperial government.[67] More than a thousand Acadians landed in South Carolina in 1755 and the early months of 1756, but about half of them were allowed to disappear. Some went to England and some to France;[68] and France, too, found them a burden.[69]

Lawrence, however, was triumphant; in December 1755 he had expressed great satisfaction at the progress of the happy though costly operation of 'extirpating those perfidious wretches, the French neutrals', and had seen a brilliant future opening up for Nova Scotia.[70] In April 1756 he was pleased to announce to their lordships that the different provinces had welcomed the French inhabitants that had been sent to them.[71] But this time his pleasure was short-lived; for groups of Acadians, especially in Georgia and South Carolina, were organizing their escape while authorities turned a blind eye or encouraged their initiative; it was even said that some local governments provided them with boats. The governor of Nova Scotia became alarmed and urged his fellow governors to do everything in their power to thwart such 'pernicious designs'. The return of the exiles would be 'fatal' to British interests 'in this part of the world.'[72]

It was to be expected that governments would see the dispersal of the Acadians in the perspective of public interests served or harmed by it. For governments it was a matter of policy. But was public opinion aroused? General Winslow inscribed in his diary the following message read to the people of Grand Pré on 5 September 1755 along with the king's order for their deportation: 'The part of duty I am now upon is what though necessary is very disagreeable to my natural make and temper as I know it must be grievous to you who are of the same species.'[73] This official platitude is one of the rare expressions of human compassion for the victims of the expulsion recorded in America at the time of the event. The following dispatch from Halifax, dated 7 August 1755, was published in New York and elsewhere: 'We are now upon a great and noble scheme of sending the neutral French out of this province . . . If we effect their expulsion, it will be one of the greatest things that ever the English did in America; for by all accounts that part of the country they possess is as good land as any in the world. In case therefore we could get some good English farmers in their room, this province would abound with all kinds of provisions.'[74] Generally the newspapers printed without comment news items concerning the expulsion. Suceeding steps in the operation were followed in the press. We shall disperse 3,000 inhabitants, said one paper;[75] three weeks from now, said another, they will all have been deported;[76] still others announced the arrival of 'neutral French' or of 'so-called neutral French'.[77] The Reverend Nathaniel Appleton, preaching in Boston in October

1760, referred to the expulsion of the Acadians and asserted that their presence in Nova Scotia would have been 'an obstacle to any British settlement in that province.'[78]

When the fall of Beauséjour was announced in Great Britain, the *London Magazine* predicted that it would now be possible to 'reduce' the ten or fifteen thousand Acadians 'to become subjects of the crown of England.'[79] Opinion in the mother country does not appear to have been prepared in any way for the dispersal, but it provoked no adverse reaction. Early in 1756 an English correspondent of the *Mercure de La Haye* sent his review a letter from Halifax, a first-hand report on events: soldiers serving in Nova Scotia are busy putting Acadians on board ships for the British colonies; the better to 'extirpate' them—the expression appears frequently in English reports—the British 'have burned and destroyed their houses, barns, farms and villages; their farm animals have been driven into the woods where anyone who likes can take possession of them. Thus one of the most beautiful countries in the world is now ravaged and empty.'[80] In 1760 the *London Magazine* published a series of articles on the history of the war. It mentioned in passing the expulsion begun in 1755, and offered the following explanation for it: 'As they were all bigoted papists, it was therefore deemed impossible to expect any fidelity from them whilst they remained so near their countrymen in Canada and Cape Breton.'[81] In the chronicle that he published immediately after the war, the Reverend John Entick described Lawrence's activities: 'General Lawrence did not only pursue those dangerous inhabitants with fire and sword, laying the country waste, burning their dwellings, and driving off their stock; but he thought it expedient for his Majesty's service to transport the French neutrals.' The measure itself he considered 'very commendable', but the execution 'not quite so prudent', since some 7,000 Acadians were dispersed 'in that rigorous season of winter, almost naked and without money or effects to help themselves.' The governor's most serious error, however, lay in not sending them far enough away.[82]

Neither in England nor in America was the British conscience uneasy. It is to be noticed, however, that the question was more clearly defined in America than in England. Public opinion in Britain does not appear to have touched the main aspect of the policy pursued in Nova Scotia, the idea of empire-building. The policy in this case was followed systematically for years, and it would be a gross error to see in the expulsion the result of a sudden access of violence—a monstrous fit of bad temper on the part of Lawrence and his colleagues, and foreign to the British government. No; the dispersal continued into 1762 and was neither incidental nor accidental. It cannot be described otherwise than as the fruit of a policy, a deliberate policy initiated before July 1755 and developed over a period of seven or eight years, a policy of which the mother country could not have been ignorant and which, as we know, she had approved and adopted; a policy, however, that was not specifically British, a policy of conquest, of empire-building that nine years earlier France had been prepared to apply in so far as her needs required that she do so.

Six or seven thousand Acadians were rounded up in the great sweep of the summer and autumn of 1755.[83] While they were taken away others succeeded in escaping from their settlements before the arrival of the British detachments sent to capture them. In this way a whole village, Cobequid, migrated to Île-Saint-Jean, where in the last months of 1755 and the early months of 1756 the number of refugees rose to about 2,000.[84] If as it is generally believed there were about 16,000 Acadians in Nova Scotia, including those that over a period of six or seven years had gone over to 'French' Acadia, we realize that Lawrence's operation, extensive though it was, was only partially successful. But we must be careful to avoid an error into which it is very easy to fall. Although it is true that the task of the government was not yet completed in 1756, it is also true that Acadia had been dealt a death blow the year before. All that remained to do was to hasten the end. What interest then, one may ask, can there be in following the rest of the story, even in brief outline? There is this interest: a study of the dispersal will help us to define the objectives and methods of British colonization, as well as the scope and significance of the Acadian defeat.

The Acadians of French origin still in Nova Scotia after 1755 were a cause of grave anxiety to Lawrence and his superiors. When the two battalions of provincials that had campaigned at Beauséjour and carried out the deportation were sent back to New England, the governor complained to the secretary of state. The Lords of Trade declared that his complaint was quite justified, and regretted that he had been deprived of the means to execute his excellent plan and complete his work by removing the French from their settlements on the St John River. They were still more distressed because there was now no hope of converting the soldiers into settlers and establishing them on the land evacuated by the French. It should not be very difficult, they considered, to attract from the neighbouring provinces farmers in need of cleared land, but they must not delay. Each day reduced the value of the farms and made the task of resettling the colony more difficult.[85]

This was true, perhaps even more so than the Board of Trade realized. The country was becoming dangerous. It was reported in New England that some of the outlawed Acadians had escaped deportation and hidden in the woods. Bitter, desperate, 'more barbarous than the Indians', they prowled about in small groups and had already scalped several English settlers.[86] Vaudreuil followed these events with the greatest attention. The preceding autumn he had repeated the stories of atrocities that came to him from Nova Scotia: British soldiers were said to have whipped two Acadian women to death and to have cruelly beaten several others. He had encouraged Boishébert, who from his headquarters on the St John River led bold raids against the enemy, to 'avenge these cruel acts' by delivering his prisoners into the hands of the Indians.[87] In the summer of 1756 he was pleased to be able to make the following report to the court: the English had had a boat burned in Gaspereau River and twenty men killed on the Missaguash; the Indians had struck at Port Royal, Baie Verte, and in the neghbourhood of Fort Cumberland (Beauséjour); the enemy were at a standstill, they dared not stir out of their forts; Boishébert was welcoming refugees who were strengthening his forces; he had had 600 men with him during the winter of 1755-6.[88] The young officer was doing wonders. He was accomplishing his double mission to perfection: reorganizing Acadian resistance and preserving a foothold for France in Acadian territory in anticipation of the treaty that would one day bring hostilities to an end.[89]

Meanwhile Lawrence was champing with impatience. Yes, he answered the Lords of Trade, he was doing his utmost to resume the work of colonization and to resettle the villages that had been emptied of their French inhabitants. But the New England farmers he counted upon had not come. A colonization company had been created in New York, but it had had to abandon its plans for want of colonists. The reason for this failure was quite simple: no one would settle in a country where one ran the risk of having his throat cut at any moment by implacable enemies familiar with a terrain that offered them an inaccessible retreat after they had committed the barbarous acts dictated to them by vengeance and cruelty. Before the colony could be resettled, troops would have to be sent in to clear it completely of its former inhabitants, and especially to stamp out the hotbed of resistance on the St John River. How could farmers survive in country so infested with guerrillas that detachments of British soldiers were sometimes attacked on the way from one post to another? In such conditions it was useless to try to encourage immigration. It was no mere chance that not a single British settlement had been established since Lawrencetown, founded before the expulsion.[90] As time went on the situation grew worse and even Lawrencetown had to be abandoned. Only the garrison remained, with a few farmers who dared not venture into the country for fear of being ambushed by Acadian guerrillas.[91]

Lovely Acadia, the promised land, resisted the covetous invaders.

Although nominally its possessors, the British occupied no more than a few strongholds, and hostile raiding parties sometimes struck right under the guns of the forts.[92] It was true that colonists could settle in the immediate neighbourhood of Halifax, but, as John Knox remarked, this country was 'entirely rude and not worth cultivating.' In Halifax itself, the townspeople eked out a precarious living from the sale of clothes, household goods, and liquor, but these sources of livelihood would disappear with the departure of the military and naval contingents brought there by the war.[93] And yet Lawrence could not forget that there would be room for 20,000 families in the districts of Cobequid, Minas, Piziquid, Port Royal, if only they could be settled there without risking their lives. 'Rich individuals from New England' were to send fifty families to Cape Sable, but alas 'there were still neutrals and Indians at large in that part of the country.'[94] It would take two years for the English to round them up and take them prisoner.[95] A few scattered fragments of the Acadian people still survived. In March 1758 a band of some forty 'friends of Beaubière [Boishébert]' appeared near Fort Cumberland; they boarded the English boats lying at anchor, disabled and looted them, killed the sailors who were on board, and disappeared.[96]

Thus between 1755 and 1758 British settlement remained at a standstill. This situation could not but persist so long as Louisbourg and Île-Saint-Jean—the latter full of refugees from Nova Scotia—remained in French hands. If the English had been less unlucky, Louisbourg would have fallen into their hands in 1757. The following year London drew up its plans for invasion with greater care, and the Lords of Trade had no doubts as to the outcome of the campaign. The capture of Louisbourg, they wrote to Lawrence on 7 February, would remove one obstacle to the settlement of the colony. They instructed him to extend to all the American colonies the propaganda that until then he had limited to New England. 'We have already said so much to you,' they reminded him, 'upon the important point of settling the vacated lands and you seem so fully sensible of the great advantages which would follow from it that it is not necessary for us to say much further upon it at present.'[97]

At the end of July, as might be expected, Île-Royale capitulated. From Louisbourg Lord Rollo was sent to Île-Saint-Jean to carry out the task of deporting the population, which he estimated at 4,100 inhabitants,[98] grouped in five main settlements. Lord Rollo was horrified to find British scalps in the house of the local commander, Villejouin; the Acadians on the island had adopted the 'inhuman practice' of collecting English scalps in Nova Scotia and selling them to French officers.[99] So the expulsion was resumed with even greater determination. In his haste to pile all these people into the boats at his disposal Rollo broke up families. After reporting the fact, Villejouin added this comment: 'The treatment to which they are subjected by the British . . . does not inspire any of the inhabitants with the desire to remain under their rule.'[100] Even so, the victors could not work fast enough to achieve their object. While they were emptying the bigger settlements, hundreds of islanders from the small remote villages fled to the north shore where they were embarked on four French ships to be transported to Miramichi or Quebec. The invaders nonetheless succeeded in capturing 3,500 Acadians whom they sent to Europe—and under what conditions! They were piled into wretched little boats so unseaworthy that some of them did not survive the crossing.[101] The events of 1755 inflicted a mortal wound on Acadia; those of 1758 finally killed her.

In the spring of 1758 Lawrence and his council had intensified their effort to encourage the resettlement of Nova Scotia.[102] On 12 October, after the end of the campaign, the governor issued a proclamation to be circulated throughout British America. Now that British victories had brought about the reduction of Louisbourg and driven out the enemy who had 'formerly disturbed and harassed the province of Nova Scotia and much hampered its development', a favourable opportunity presented itself for occupying the lands taken from the Acadians. A tempting description of the country accompanied the invitation.[103] The agents of the province set to work first in Connecticut, Rhode Island, and Massachusetts, and their propaganda bore fruit. New England farmers had more than one motive for migrating to the northern province: good land was becoming scarce; the burden of taxes was becoming heavier and heavier as a result of a very considerable war effort; and they were being offered fertile soil—free land already cleared and irrigated by generations of peasants. Lawrence still had cause to lament, however. The fall of Louisbourg had not brought about the dispersal of the bands of Acadians prowling through Nova Scotia; these were still powerful enough, according to him, to terrorize the promising British settlements that he was anxious to establish.[104] After the surrender of Île-Royale, the British had made one attempt to drive the French out of the St John River country, but the operation had not been entirely successful.[105] Moses Hazen, an officer from Massachusetts, made a second attempt in a more favourable season. In mid-winter (February 1759), he marched up the St John River as far as Sainte-Anne (Fredericton) and burnt 147 houses, two churches, barns, and stables. His object obviously was to expose those who escaped fire and sword to death from cold and hunger. Then, having accomplished his task, Hazen returned to his garrison duties, taking with him six scalps and a few prisoners.[106]

Even such radical measures as these did not suffice to suppress the Acadians, and in September 1759 Lawrence complained that they had become more vexatious than ever. From highway robbery they had turned to piracy; armed shallops cruising along the coast had captured more than fifteen British vessels, and at the same time small bands of Acadians kept striking at various points in the province, killing colonists in isolated settlements.[107] This letter was written two days after the fall of Quebec, and the following year all Canada succumbed. When Lawrence died in the night of 18-19 October 1760,[108] the policy of which he was the chief architect had still not been crowned with complete success, for not all the Acadians had disappeared. Six months later Belcher gave some figures. There were, he said, still 280 families of French origin in northeastern Nova Scotia, almost 1,600 souls all told. Their chief occupation was piracy. From time to time some of them came and gave themselves up to British officers, but never willingly. Only hunger or terror could force them to adopt such a course. Among those who submitted were a few former inhabitants of the Beaubassin country who had not given up all hope of one day recovering possession of their farms. These, reported Belcher, were the most dangerous; they constituted a real threat to the security of the colony, and it was not without reason that, in spite of Vaudreuil's insistence,[109] they had been excluded in the terms of Canada's capitulation in September 1760. How was he to dispose of them?[110]

The question was purely rhetorical. Belcher had known the anwer for five years. He would expel them by force of arms. Towards the end of 1761 he sent Captain Frederick McKenzie with two small war vessels to surprise the Acadians on the Restigouche. McKenzie found about 800, of whom he transported 335 to Halifax. Belcher declared that these defeated men could not be reinstated as inhabitants of Nova Scotia since, like their compatriots, they would be a danger to the province.[111] The danger was growing less every day, however, especially since the conquest of Île-Royale and Canada. Time was working against the Acadians, who could no longer hope for aid from outside the province. In the spring of 1759 the Cape Sable group—some 150 persons—had offered to negotiate with the authorities and had surrendered at the discretion of the latter. They were confined on George's Island and later transported to England.[112] Others, driven to desperation, would follow this first example. In November 1759 when two hundred Acadians from the St John settlement surrendered, Lawrence and his council decided to treat them as prisoners of war. They would be detained in Halifax and transported to Great Britain.[113] Two delegations presented themselves at Fort Cumberland almost at the same time. The first represented 190 Acadians from Petitcodiac and Memramcook, the second 700 from Miramichi, Richibucto, and Buctouche. The commander realized what had impelled them to take this step; 'since their Canada [was] taken from them', they were in desperate straits, and in fact had come to beg. The provincial council decided to distribute 'so much provisions as shall appear absolutely necessary for their sustenance.' They would be disposed of in the spring when navigation was open and they could be assembled by boat.[114] Other similar delegations followed the first ones. In March 1760 Lawrence estimated that 1,200 outlaws from the Chignecto region had given themselves up to the commander of Fort Cumberland. What was to be done with them? They must be deported, decided the council. 'Such a measure . . . seemed to be absolutely necessary to facilitate' the exploitation of their lands by the Americans who were coming to take them and who 'otherwise would be liable to be obstructed in their progress by the incursions of these French inhabitants.'[115]

In fact the Americans began to arrive before the small groups of Acadians scattered through Nova Scotia had completely disappeared. Immigration into the province did not come about spontaneously, but by the end of 1758 Hancock's advertising campaign in Massachusetts had begun to bear fruit. Lawrence's agent in Boston was besieged with requests for information; and in the early days of 1759 Lawrence himself, anxious to take advantage of this wave of interest, issued a proclamation settting the conditions that would govern the entry of New England colonists into Nova Scotia. Townships of 100,000 acres would be created in which each colonist would be granted a concession of 1,000 acres. Rents, fixed at one shilling for fifty acres, would be payable only at the end of a ten-year period. The proclamation pointed out that these were remarkably low charges for lands that had been 'cultivated for more than a hundred years past never failing of crops nor needing to be manured.' And this was not all. Nova Scotians would pay no personal tax. The political status of the province would be similar to that of New England, with freedom of conscience for all—except Catholics. Grants would be made without payment of any fee. What more could one ask? The assurance of peace perhaps? Well, the government would create posts to protect settled townships.[116] Prospective immigrants were being offered a great deal—too much, protested the Lords of Trade, who could not understand why the governor was preparing to give Acadian farms away free and apparently ignoring the fact that they were much more valuable than uncleared land.[117] Even before the rebuke reached him, Lawrence had written to submit his defence. He had had to act quickly, but he could now present the completely convincing argument: success. The number of settlers promised was so great that they would occupy six or eight more townships than he had dared to expect. Soon there would not be a single Acadian farm that had not been reoccupied. Moreover, British colonists would soon be settled all along the coast from Halifax to Cape Sable.[118] The Board of Trade understood the situation at once and agreed that Lawrence was right. They informed the king that his 'zealous governor' had succeeded in bringing Nova Scotia to the notice of America. Thirteen townships of 100,000 acres each would shortly be peopled with immigrants. The province gave promise of growing up quickly. In a few years it would have ceased to be a burden to the mother country. Its products would support an active export trade, profitable to Great Britain and to the rest of the empire.[119] Beginning in 1759 the Americans arrived—too many of them in some places for the Acadian farms they were to occupy,[120] but the governor continued to advertise for settlers.[121]

Although the population of the province was soon to increase at a rapid rate, Lawrence's resettlement project had first to overcome certain difficulties: very natural apprehensions and unforeseeable ill luck. In the autumn of 1759 a tidal wave destroyed the aboiteaux—gates of the dikes built by Acadians to protect their fields from the Bay of Fundy's high tides. This disastrous accident flooded the land with salt water, and for three years it produced no crops.[122] Still more serious, the American farmers did not know how to repair the damage. The government had to call in the Acadian prisoners to rebuild the aboiteaux. Belcher explained that they had no choice, since nothing must be allowed to hinder 'the progress of those settlements which are so much the object of the public regard and the attention of his Majesty's ministry.'[123] The new settlers were naturally alarmed at the news of Lévis's victory at Sainte-Foy in April 1760, but they were relieved to hear a few weeks later that the Canadians had been forced to raise the siege of Quebec.[124] They continued, however, to be beset by a nagging anxiety as several hundred Acadians clung persistently to their native soil. In reality, these expatriates in their own country were a nuisance rather than a grave danger to the colony. But there was the future to think of. As James Murray confessed to Belcher, it would hardly be wise to allow these dispossessed families to start new lives in old Acadia, since 'the very spot must renew to them in all succeeding generations the miseries the present one has endured and will perhaps alienate forever their affection from its government however just and equitable it may be.'[125] But this was no more than a worry, a passing worry as Lawrence had realized. In the spring of 1760 he had inferred quite clearly in a letter to the Board that prospects for his scheme were opening up,[126] and two months later he reported that the settlements were making good progress.[127] He was right. It was true that agriculture did not flourish in the eastern part of the province, but that had always been the case: the soil was poor. However, the fishing was excellent and shipbuilding was making rapid progress. On the other hand farming was being carried on with increased vigour on Acadian land that had been taken up by immigrants from Massachusetts, Rhode Island, New York, and Connecticut. After the autumn of 1761 it could be said that the British settlers were no longer camping in the colony; they were there to stay.[128] Nova Scotia had succeeded Acadia.

The scattered remnants of the French colony were gradually reduced still further. In 1762 Belcher reported that he had 950 inhabitants of French origin on his hands. His one desire was to get rid of them; but Amherst, whose advice he asked, did not share this desire. The commander-in-chief inclined 'towards letting them remain in the province under proper regulations and restrictions.' They would contribute to the general prosperity and, considering the situation to which they were reduced, they could 'hardly be mad enough to attempt anything against the establishment of the province.' For those living near the western frontier, in the vicinity of Canada, he favoured Murray's plan of deportation to the French colony.[129] But Belcher refused to listen to Amherst, and shipped off all the Acadians within reach to Boston.[130] However, the legislative assembly of Massachusetts, which had no intention of being guided by the whim of the governor of a neighbouring province, sent them back to Halifax.[131] The opinion expressed by the Board of Trade and Plantations when the matter was brought to its attention appeared to be that of the general public: while it might have been 'expedient' to deport the Acadians during the war, when they were in a position to act in liaison with the enemy threatening the colony from outside, now that the cessation of hostilities had eliminated that danger it was no longer 'either necessary or politic' to disperse them. On the other hand, if allowed to remain 'they might by a proper disposition promote the interest of the colony and be made useful members of society.'[132]

Belcher, who in 1755 had seen clearly that the Acadians would be refractory to assimilation as long as they formed the majority of the population, was not intelligent enough to realize that seven years later, in 1762, the situation was completely changed. The Acadians were now no more than the residuum of a society that had ceased to exist, and it would have benefited the province to assimilate this inoffensive minority. Amherst and the Lords of Trade, as intelligent colonizers, understood this; but Montague Wilmot, who in 1764 succeeded Lawrence and Belcher as governor, shared their desire to see the former French colonists as far away from Nova Scotia as possible—in the West Indies, for instance.[133] So he took no effective measures to prevent a group of 500 from crossing over to the island of St Pierre.[134] When 600 others set out at their own expense for the French West Indies, he expressed his satisfaction in a letter to Lord Halifax: 'Thus, my lord, we are in the way of being relieved from these people who have been the bane of the province and the terror of the settlements.' The imperial government could rest assured that France would gain nothing by admitting them to the islands, for 'the climate is mortal to the natives of the northern countries.'[135]

Nova Scotia rejected the Acadians like so many foreign particles, and henceforth they would be foreigners everywhere. This was as true of those who landed in France as of the others. On 26 August 1768, Praslin, France's minister of marine, brought up the urgent question of establishing the 400 or 500 Acadian families, some 2,400 souls, that for several years had lived scattered throughout the provinces bordering on the sea. The state supported them more or less, but the allowance granted them, six sous a day for adults and three for children, was obviously not enough for them to live on, 'especially since bread was so dear.' They might be told to work, and they would be only too glad to do so. But, as Praslin went on to explain, the intendants could scarcely find enough work for the natives to whom they were naturally inclined to give the preference; so that the Acadians, whose enduring loyalty had impelled them to abandon their property and expatriate themselves in order to live as subjects of the king, were now 'abandoned to the most pitiful want and despair.'[136]

Want and despair, these are the normal consequences of defeat.

History does not often present so clear an example of the way in which a society can be reduced to fragments. Not that such cases are rare: all societies are built on the ruins of other human creations. Every replacement presupposes a displacement. The displacement can come about, however, without changing the territorial environment of the victims. In such a case we see the defeated group, deprived of resources and direction, being absorbed over a longer or shorter period of time by the victorious group, which owes its victory to superiority in equipment and power of organization. At the same time a new economy takes shape, an economy to which the separate members of the former system, no longer held together, adhere. When a strong social structure develops, the defeated group, after living for a time as its parasite, finally merges with it. The defeat is not achieved without crises, but it is complicated by so many episodes and stretches over so many generations that it becomes impossible to recognize it except in its very diverse consequences—and these in turn may present aspects so misleading that only through thorough, persevering analysis can one penetrate to the fundamental explanation: displacement, assimilation, replacement of one nation by another. In other words, the defeat of an organized human group may come about through transformation, and this is what happens most often. In exceptional cases it is achieved by eradication, and that is what happened in Acadia. We have observed that the men responsible for the dispersal of the Acadians frequently pronounced the word 'extirpate'. They themselves were aware that quite literally they were uprooting a population from its soil. What was their motive? Did they do it for pleasure? No, for we know that it gave them no pleasure.

Why then did they act as they did? In order that Nova Scotia might play its part in the British empire. It would have been absurd to pretend that it could play that part when, in the words of an English pamphlet of 1755, three-quarters of the territory of the province was occupied by the French[137] and three-quarters of its population was not even British by allegiance. It had to become an English colony and, considering the circumstances existing at the time, to do so without delay. But there can be no colony without colonists, and there was an obstacle in the way of British colonization: Acadia had already been settled by the French. England's first manoeuvres were directed towards absorbing the French population, but she had neither the space nor the time required to bring this operation to a successful conclusion. She therefore took the only way open to her: she destroyed Acadia. There could be no colony without colonization, and no colonization without colonizers. The colonizers were Lawrence and Belcher, the Nova Scotia council, the Board of Trade and Plantations, Apthorp and Hancock, Shirley's son-in-law Erving, Baker and his agent Saul, and still others: politicians, merchants, men who were at the same time merchants and politicians, some with ideas, others with ambitions, many impelled by greed; in short, a group of typical empire builders.

That is all that need be said of them, and we could stop there. Or rather we could if historians had not already brought up, each for his own reasons—to denounce or to attempt to thrust back into the shadows that had allowed them such free play[138]—the passions uncovered by a study of the expulsion. It seems to us that historians have erred, not in trying to throw light on the question—one of absorbing interest—but in presenting it as they have. It has been said that from the beginning of the first phase of the deportation, in 1755, there was a 'scramble for the spoils'.[139] Le Jeune, after summing up the grievances already listed in Lauvrière's *Tragédie d'un peuple*, concentrates his attack on Lawrence: 'His own private looting operation took two months. He deputed a Huguenot horse dealer, Moses des Derniers from Jersey, to procure six of the best stallions for him; he founded Lawrencetown on 20,000 acres of land and supplied the settlement generously with cattle that had been seized.'[140] This brief statement has at least one merit: it separates one precise accusation from the deluge of words in which it was engulfed and in so doing reduces it to its real proportions. Who could possibly imagine that the famous governor of Nova Scotia expelled the Acadians in

[196]

order to obtain six horses for himself and to distribute animals among the inhabitants of the village he had founded? Playing up 'the scramble for the spoils' in order to have the honour of shouting 'thief' may make effective propaganda; it does not make good history. It allows the incidental to assume the guise of the essential. It is possible that Lawrence gave evidence of greed, and there were certainly some rogues among his associates. But is that the important point? We think not. What matters is that Lawrence was the architect of a plan—undoubtedly a cruel plan—of colonization. It should also be remembered that every war has its 'merchants of death', and every society, especially when it is being equipped for some special task, its profiteers. Nova Scotia was at war and it was engaged in a movement of intensive settlement. The expulsion of the Acadians was an episode in that war and that movement. How could it be exempt from shady transactions? To suppose that it could would be to imagine that Lawrence and his collaborators were little saints. They were only little men.

British citizens have an institution designed to contain within reasonable limits abuses committed by those who govern them. It is called representative government. In his first allusion to this system, Lawrence underlined the 'numberless inconveniences' that would result from its introduction into Nova Scotia. The letter of 12 January 1755 in which this reference appears was the first in an exchange of letters on the subject that went on for several years between the governor and the Lords of Trade. A letter of 7 May 1756 instructed Lawrence to have the question studied immediately by the chief justice, but results from this method of procedure were less prompt than in the case of the deportation. Lawrence transmitted Belcher's report but added his own commentary: a legislative assembly would be a tool in the hands of the merchants, since there were not enough big landholders to counterpoise the merchants' electoral influence, and the merchants might 'sometimes have views and interests incompatible' with the 'well-being' of a province so vulnerable to the threat of French invasion as Nova Scotia. These considerations did not convince the Board of Trade, which continued to press for the creation of a legislative body. At the end of 1757 Lawrence, who was apparently running out of arguments, was reduced to pleading that the 'most substantial of our inhabitants' had presented memorials begging him not to allow an assembly to be instituted before the end of the war. One might judge from his story that the partisans of a lower house were all agitators impelled by personal interest, or slanderers determined to discredit the government because it had refused them the 'places and employments' they sought. This time their lordships lost patience and ordered their subordinate to have a legislature elected without delay, and Lawrence complied, though unwillingly. He hoped he would not find in the electors' representatives 'a disposition to obstruct his Majesty's service or to dispute the royal prerogative'—in other words the governor's policy.[141]

Taken out of context, Lawrence's reservations would not be significant; he was not the only governor in America to see little merit in elected assemblies. But at the very moment when he was evading recommendations from his superiors and obviously manoeuvring to gain time, grave suspicions were being cast upon him and his associates. It was pointed out to the Board of Trade that a few officials in the colony had 'every latitude to perpetrate fraud and succumb to corruption.' Each of these officials presented his accounts to the governor, who countersigned them without the advice, consent, or even knowledge, of the council. Favourites had been given enormous herds of cattle seized from the Acadians, and it was suggested that an inquiry might be made into the disposal of the cattle, valued at 20,000 pounds. It was also observed that although the British government had voted important sums of money for the fortifications of Halifax, the capital's defences were still deplorably weak. It was even suggested that the men responsible for guiding Nova Scotia's affairs might perhaps 'be glad to see this important colony annexed to the Crown of France that they might never be called upon to answer for the misapplication of the nation's money.'[142] (Here we are once more reminded how closely colonies resemble one another; the remark we have just quoted has a close parallel in the one that Montcalm made a few months later about Canada's high officials: 'It appears that they are all in haste to make their fortunes before the loss of the colony, which some perhaps desire as an impenetrable shroud for their conduct.'[143]) One would think they were commanding a garrison rather than governing a colony, said another report. The public purse seemed to serve only military officers, the governor, and a few creatures of the governor 'such as Mr Saul (Mr Baker's agent) who is very officious, and by his advice endeavours to prevent the Inhabitants enjoying their civil rights, or any benefit from the government; who accepts of all contracts and employments for himself and friends; and who, in the space of seven years, from being an under clerk to Mr Baker, has got a fortune computed at twenty thousand pounds sterling.' (Here we have another parallel, between Saul's career and that of Joseph Cadet, a butcher who became a commissary-general and whose rapid promotion made it possible for him 'suddenly to exchange his butcher knife for a sword.')[144] After such revelations it is quite easy to understand why Lawrence was reluctant to have his activities discussed in an assembly, the more so since the author of the report, a freeholder of the province, saw himself and his fellow subjects as 'the slaves of Nova Scotia, the creatures of military governors whose will is our law, and whose person is our god.'[145]

The chief event of Lawrence's term of office, the capture of Beauséjour with the subsequent expulsion of the inhabitants of the district, cost the British government almost 100,000 pounds. And to whom were the profitable contracts for supplies awarded? To Apthorp, Hancock, and Erving, whose share was 77,080 pounds, and to William Baker and Thomas Saul, who received respectively 11,500 and 10,000 pounds.[146] These contracts did not include the provisions supplied to Acadians from the isthmus during their captivity and their journey. As Lawrence had explained to Monckton, the provincial council had begun by confiscating 'their whole stock of cattle and corn', which was to be 'applied towards a reimbursement of the expense the government will be at in transporting them out of the country.' The 832 barrels of flour found at Fort Beauséjour would 'victual the whole of the French inhabitants on their passage to their place of destination.' The governor even anticipated that there would be some flour left over; it was earmarked for the settlers in Lunenburg.[147] The deportation contractors did not do badly, and in this particular deal they took the lion's share of the profits. Apthorp and Hancock were hard bargainers—Cornwallis had been unable to meet their unreasonable conditions[148]—but although for a governor of Nova Scotia they were important personages, when seen through the eyes of a governor of Massachusetts they were men of lesser stature. Shirley assured Lawrence of his 'kindness' for them both, but at the same time reminded him discreetly that they had not been appointed by the Board of Trade. 'I have a daughter,' he continued no less discreetly, 'lately married to a merchant here who is a young man of extreme good character . . . eldest son to a merchant of the largest fortune of anyone in Boston.' For this young man, John Erving, Shirley requested a share of one-third of the profits from contracts awarded in connection with the campaign of 1755, and 'upon future occasions likewise.' The father-in-law did not think that this agreement 'would be disagreeable to Lord Halifax.' This was how it happened that Erving's name was added to those of Apthorp and Hancock.[149]

What became of the Acadians' stock, their only liquid asset? That mystery at once gave rise to speculation and cried out for an explanation. Obviously the cattle was not distributed to British colonists since, as was shown by a deposition made before the Board of Trade on 18 June 1760, the requests of farmers who asked for stock were rejected, and the farmers who had driven stock onto their own farms were obliged to give it up. It was also reported that Saul had had several thousand barrels of salt pork packed. Was this pork destined perhaps for the Lunenburg settlers who were being fed by the government? No, for the government was spending vast sums to import supplies from New England for the German settlers.

It was only natural then that the suspicion of jobbery should fall upon Nova Scotia's officials. There appeared to be some basis for the 'opinion that there had been collusion in this affair between the governor and Mr Saul.'[150] To satisfy their curiosity, the Lords of Trade made discreet inquiries. They discovered that the contractor Baker and his agent Saul had sold a 'considerable part' of the stock to the state, and that it had been used to feed the Nova Scotia garrisons; the partners had also sold some of the meat to his majesty's ships. So, since the Acadians' animals had been confiscated by the province, the contractors must have bought from the province the meat they had supplied to the army and navy, and these operations would appear in the colony's accounts. The Lords made inquiries of their colleagues in the treasury department, who replied that no credit corresponding to any such sale was recorded in the accounts for 1756, 1757, or 1758.[151] Thus wily manipulators had sold to the state stock that already belonged to it by right of confiscation.

The interest of this story of misappropriation lies in the light it throws on one aspect—a very minor one—of a typical colonial government. The episode is significant because it is true to a pattern, the pattern of peculation, looting, and pilfering that underlies all colony-building, whether in French or British America, or elsewhere. Just as it would be silly to suppose that states plant colonies in order to create opportunities for profiteers to amass fortunes, it would be proof of serious lack of judgement to claim that the British empire organized the dispersion of the Acadians in order to satisfy the rapacity of a handful of merchants and politicians. In Acadia there was looting and there was deportation: the deportation created an opportunity for looting, the looting was not the cause of the deportation.

Since she had been conquered, Acadia was doomed to destruction. The combination of circumstances we have observed determined the manner of her destruction: the deportation of her population. In other circumstances—at another time, in another place—the same society might have come to its end in some other way. A colonial community linked by force to an alien empire, it could only be freed, assimilated, or broken. Liberation was impossible. France did try to reconquer a part of Acadia, but the operation—badly planned, late in starting, and undertaken with inadequate means—ended in disaster. Acadia's fate was sealed, whether she was uprooted by the conqueror or she remained to rot slowly in British soil—which would have come to the same thing in the end.

To Canadians threatened with conquest and its inevitable consequences, the example of Acadia was an object lesson in the meaning of defeat.

Part Four

THE DISINTEGRATION
OF THE RESISTANCE

Chapter VII

The Turn of the Tide

1758

After 1757 England and her colonies seem to make a fresh start towards their goal of conquest in America. At first sight one is struck by the contrast between the period of defeat suffered by the English after 1755 and the victorious era that opened for them in 1758. If, however, one penetrates beyond this superficial impression, one observes that the solution of continuity between the two phases of the War of the Conquest is more apparent than real. Not that one should attach any great importance to the rare British successes of the first period of the war or to the sporadic French victories of the second. But on the one hand the new concept of empire that gave its full significance to the conquest was hardly more popular in 1758 than it had been at the beginning of hostilities—this would become evident in the violence of the imperial debate of 1760—and on the other hand the ultimate causes of the series of victories starting with the fall of Louisbourg had begun to act long before France's American fortresses succumbed one after another to the victors' power. British naval supremacy, after being contested for three years, was established without question; intense economic activity made it possible to finance an extremely costly war, and Britain's heavy industry was geared to provide strategists and combatants with the instruments of victory. The War of the Conquest was to be a modern war: it would not be limited to the battlefield, but would be fought and won in the offices of financiers and tax collectors, in banks and business houses, in ports and naval shipyards, in iron works and armament factories, on farms and in meat-curing plants. It was because the British empire had produced and had engaged in trade that it was able to send regiments of well-fed infantrymen into the front lines, to support them with powerful artillery, and finally to prevail over the rival empire.

Nevertheless, when people felt that 1758 marked the end of an epoch and the dawn of a new day their feeling had some foundation in fact. A political historian, writing some five years later, recalled the dark days of 1757 when the empire 'was shrinking' and Britons of all ranks, beset by fear of invasion, were so downhearted that they would have been glad to accept any peace that guaranteed them life and liberty. Who would have thought then that British possessions were to swell to the dimensions they would assume in 1763?[1] But by the middle of 1758 there was a distinct feeling that the tide was turning. 'When,' asked a London journalist loftily, 'did Britain ever appear more terrible to her foes, more respectable to all nations than in the year 1758?' Her navy was stronger than ever; she could defend her possessions in every quarter of the globe. 'Our men, money and ships under faithful and wise counsellors who prefer the interest of Britain to all other considerations are a match for the whole world.'[2] It should be noted that in the opinion of this observer the important factor in the sudden change was a change of orientation in British policy. The new policy, embodied in Pitt, subordinated everything—that is, European strategy as a whole—to the interests of Great Britain. As Pitt reminded Newcastle in the midst of the Christmas festivities of 1757, it was in America that 'England and Europe would be fought for.'[3]

The essential character of this period appears in its whirlwind start. Pitt gave the war an impetus that he managed to maintain throughout his ministry. The price was high, but he paid it. In order to restrict France's freedom of movement in Europe, he hastened to sign a treaty with the king of Prussia, who undertook to keep 55,000 men under arms and who received in return an annual subsidy of 670,000 pounds sterling, almost seventeen million French livres. Britain's budget, which in 1756 had been ten and a half million pounds, had almost doubled in 1760.[4] By a stroke of genius Pitt had realized, in spite of the understandable wailings of English taxpayers, that Britain's financial resources were infinitely greater than had been supposed, and he used those resources to procure a victory that would bring rich rewards to the nation. He poured out money for the war almost without counting the cost. When, in 1761, a critic taxed the government with having spent four million pounds for the conquest of Canada,[5] his estimate was fairly accurate. The sum, a fantastic one for the time, was the equivalent of two billion French livres. In comparison the total of Canada's budget for the years between 1755 and 1760 was 115,556,767 livres.[6]

To the money spent by the mother country must be added the sums spent by various English colonies for the reduction of New France. The amounts varied from province to province and from year to year at the whim of provincial assemblies, and in the period before 1758 this financial instability was reflected in the halting progress of the war. In a determined effort to eliminate the elements of risk and unpredictability from colonial aid, Pitt continued and improved upon a policy already initiated by his predecessor. He promised not only to remit to colonial governments the costs of arms, munitions, and provisions supplied to regiments raised in the provinces, but to reimburse them in part for recruiting expenses and for soldiers' pay. In these latter cases compensation would be granted 'according as the active vigour and strenuous efforts of the respective provinces [should] justly appear to merit.'[7] The pledges made by Newcastle and Pitt were scrupulously honoured by the mother country and the sums promised were paid as promptly as the deliberate processes of parliamentary machinery allowed. Seven chests of gold and silver pieces unloaded in the port of Boston in January 1759 had been dispatched by the mother country to repay expenses incurred by Massachusetts for the campaign of 1756.[8]

Pitt's system, which not unnaturally was accepted with enthusiam by most of the colonies, brought swift and remarkable results. In 1758 it put 21,000 combatants into the blue uniform of the provincial troops, although it cost Great Britain 200,000 pounds and it was estimated that in the same year and for the same price she could have kept 27,000 regulars under arms for five months, or some 10,000 for twelve months. Although provincial troops were less well trained for battle than regulars, they cost more to maintain. The explanation of this phenomenon lay in the fact that the provincial governments were prepared to be magnificently generous at the expense of the British government. Their recruits received much higher pay than that of British soldiers, as well as enlistment gratuities of as much as eight pounds sterling. This was equivalent to 200 French livres. At that time no militiaman or regular soldier in Canada would have been given such a gratuity. If it were granted to an officer, it would be as a reward for distinguished service—or because he enjoyed the favour of a protector. One result of Pitt's arrangements was that money easily acquired was put into circulation in the colonies. Provincial assemblies seized the opportunity to send stiff bills to the imperial government, and the payments made it possible for them to put their financial houses in order. The case of Connecticut is particularly interesting in this respect. Of all the colonies it put forth the most considerable war effort, and it derived the greatest benefit from Pitt's system. Connecticut was able to keep its taxes at a very moderate level throughout the war, to settle almost all its war debts before 1763, and at the same time to accumulate in London banks credits that sufficed to defray its government expenses for several years after the war.[9]

But that was not all. Most of the provisions for the British expeditionary force were bought in the colonies and colonial trade reaped the profit. In November 1758 the Reverend Jonathan Mayhew, D.D. testified that 1758 had been a fat year. From her abundant crops Massachusetts had sold quantities of provisions to his majesty's ships and troops. 'By this means we have not only been enabled to help forward the military operation and common cause in which we have a very particular interest, but considerable wealth has been brought into the country, I may properly say into the community.'[10] The eloquent divine allowed it to be inferred that the country people had been especially favoured, but on this point he was perhaps under an illusion. If one can judge by the agricultural crisis that followed the war, the farmers of British North America contracted heavy debts during the period of hostilities. Poor harvests in the years immediately following, and contracting export markets, made it difficult to settle these debts. The result was a period of depression and uncertainty in all the northern colonies.[11] These economic difficulties might perhaps be interpreted as the consequence of a sudden excessive enlargement of the bases of credit during the war, the outward symbol of the economic euphoria evoked by Dr Mayhew. According to this hypothesis, the whole community felt the effects of an acceleration in the economy created by a sudden injection of British capital, but those who profited most from it were on the one hand the governments and on the other the contractors for war supplies, entrepreneurs, merchants—always the same aristocracy of money—while the farmers had contracted obligations that were too heavy for them. In any case the British colonies, unlike Canada, did not suffer from insufficient supplies of food during the war. If at the end of hostilities their economy was somewhat disturbed, it is quite possible that it was suffering from over-prosperity. In any case the disorder could not be compared to the bankruptcy that at the same time reduced Canada's economy to a state of ruin from which it never recovered. Pitt's financial policy, taken as a whole, showed itself to be both bold and wise: bold because he took the risk of burdening Britain with heavy taxes and doubled the national debt, but wise too in that he did not hesitate to pay the price of victory. It should be recognized that the extent of the results he achieved was less surprising than the means by which he achieved them. One further observation remains to be made. Pitt did not hesitate to dip into Britain's wealth. He subordinated all other considerations to one end—the conquest of Canada—and in this he was understood and followed with enthusiasm. An echo of his thought can be found in the message of Governor Denny to the legislative assembly of Pennsylvania after the fall of Fort Du Quesne. The expulsion of the French from the Ohio had been a costly operation, but the consequences that would have resulted from their continued presence there must be weighed and considered. By appropriating and fortifying the interior of his majesty's colonies, the French were laying the foundations of slavery for the king's American subjects and opening a communication route between their establishments in Canada and those in the Mississippi valley. When these facts were taken into consideration, no true friend of liberty could think the conquest too dearly bought.[12] Journalists in England were proud to report the 'general zeal and enthusiasm' with which the people not only submitted to but almost solicited 'grievous impositions', inspired as they were by the knowledge that the British forces abroad were displaying great 'ardour and intrepidity'—in other words that they were gaining victories.[13]

Britain's immense outlay of funds brought about a considerable expansion of her military potential. The prodigies accomplished by the British navy during 1758 must be recognized as the fruit of long patience and of the advantage in equipment that Britain was careful to maintain and increase. The capture of Louisbourg, the most decisive victory of the year and the one that really marked the turning-point of the war, was accomplished at sea rather than under the walls of the French fortress. The organization of that campaign was a masterpiece of naval strategy, but a masterpiece that could not have been achieved without naval supremacy. What the French found difficult to understand was that in spite of the exploits of their ships, individual victories of which they had every right to feel proud did not reduce the steady rate of enemy reinforcement. In the spring of 1758 the *Mercure de France* published figures drawn from 'English Gazettes'. According to the report, between 29 October 1757 and 10 January the following year France had captured 152 English ships, and England 100 French ones. 'Thus, according to their account, our prizes exceed theirs by about sixty vessels.'[14] Not that the naval strategy of the French was open to criticism; considering their resources it was the only one that offered any chance of putting off the day of final reckoning. That day was approaching, however, faster than they realized; and they had almost reached it in 1758. An article in the *London Magazine* for August 1758 gave the following summary of the state of the French navy: of her 89 ships of the line France had lost 19 and of 69 frigates also 19—in all, a quarter of her naval strength.[15] These figures are impressive in themselves, but their full significance can be measured only in the context of military operations in the New World. In 1758, when it tried to repeat its exploit of the previous year and cut off invading ships from access to Louisbourg, it failed miserably. On that occasion the navy's real weakness was manifest.

It was also manifest in France's inability to protect her lines of navigation. Although the losses of the British merchant marine were heavier than those suffered by its rival, they were less crippling, since they affected a smaller proportion of its global tonnage, and that was what counted in the long run. George II had good reason to emphasize, as he did in a message delivered at the opening of Parliament on 23 November 1758, the fact 'that the commerce of his subjects, the source of [their] wealth [had], by the vigilant protection received from his Majesty's fleet, flourished in a manner not to be paralleled during such trouble.'[16] A few weeks earlier the ambassador of France in Saint Petersburg had presented the same situation from a very different angle. Addressing himself to the neutral nations whose hostility had been aroused by the capture of their ships at sea—French cargoes were often carried in ships flying a neutral nation's flag—the diplomat called the attention of Europe to the excessive naval power of the English. For a century, he declared, they had striven to turn the world against France on the pretext of maintaining the balance of forces on the continent, and during all that time 'they were incessantly labouring (and have unhappily but too well succeeded) to destroy the balance of power by sea, without which, however, that upon land cannot subsist. This is a thing to which other nations should give the most serious attention as it threatens no less than the entire destruction of their navigation and the usurpation of all commerce by the English.'[17]

Galvanized by Pitt's devouring ambition and with enormous means at its disposal, the British government decided to strike a great blow. It was invited, encouraged, urged to do so in programs for action and plans of campaign that poured in from every quarter and from a great variety of persons. In December 1757 a merchant, Denis de Berdt, submitted to the minister a proposal for a landing on the St Lawrence and a march on Quebec, with detailed suggestions for making the most effective use of a fleet, British regiments, and colonial units. Next William Bollan, the agent for Massachusetts in London, recommended that Quebec be besieged, and transmitted information according to which the city was short of food. The Lord Mayor of London, Sir Theodore Janssen, sent Pitt a plan, drawn up in 1744, for the capture of Louisbourg. The prime minister received other similar proposals and information from the governor of Massachusetts, the agent for Virginia in London, and spokesmen for Pennsylvania.[18]

A good deal of this pressure on the British government came from the colonies, and there was joy in America at the news that the objective of the forthcoming campaign was nothing less than the reduction of Canada. The announcement was made in a proclamation by the governor of Massachusetts: 'His Majesty, feeling for the miseries that his people of these his dominions daily suffer from the ravages and massacres of a perfidious and savage enemy, and sensible of the very dangerous and urgent crisis to which this country is reduced, has determined to make a general invasion of Canada and to carry the war into the heart of the enemy country.'[19] At last the moment had come, said a Boston correspondent for the New York Gazette, 'to retrieve the errors' so far committed in the conduct of the war. 'We have endeavoured, at an immense charge, only to lop the branches without laying the axe to the foot of the tree.' But conditions henceforth were to be radically different; instead of wasting time in endless detours they would make straight for the goal, confident of success. 'We have the fairest prospects . . . of destroying at a blow that power that has so long harassed us and threatened our destruction. *Delenda est Carthago*, Canada must be destroyed, is the voice of the Sovereign: let it be propagated along our coast; let it penetrate our woods . . . let it echo from our hills and vales and rouse the sons of New England to arms.'[20] A news dispatch from Boston described the spirit of enthusiasm that reigned in Massachusetts. It was hard to say which had shown the greater 'alacrity'—the government of the colony in authorizing the levy of a large body of provincial troops or the people in offering to serve in it. 'All seem to be sensible of the necessity of making a vigorous push in order totally to subdue those who aim at nothing less than totally extirpating us.' New life had been injected into the 'old New England spirit' by 'the uninterrupted attention of the mother country to her American interest.'[21]

The colonies had reason to be touched by the zealous 'attention' of the mother country. Not content with assuming a heavy burden of debt in order to finance the American war, she herself dispatched to the theatre of conflict unprecedented numbers of men and quantities of war materials. Pitt meant to engage 50,000 soldiers—as well as some 20,000 sailors—in the struggle. Fourteen thousand regulars and 600 rangers were destined to the siege of Louisbourg; 20,000 provincials and 9,500 regulars to an expedition against Montreal by way of Lake Champlain and the Richelieu; and finally 6,000 combatants, of whom 5,000 were American, to an attack on Fort Du Quesne.[22] 'We shall have (if accident don't prevent it),' wrote Wolfe as he was about to sail for Louisbourg, 'a great force this year in America, and the country has a right to expect some powerful efforts proportionate to the armaments.'[23] The way in which the troops were distributed shows which of the three objectives stood first in Pitt's mind: it was Louisbourg. Although the army charged with the conquest of Île-Royale was less strong numerically than the one that was to attack the advance posts and the city of Montreal, it was made up almost entirely of regulars, while the support it would receive from the 'shock power' of the fleet operating in American waters would more than double both its strength and its effectiveness. This, the most powerful of the expeditionary forces, was charged with a double mission: if it could capture Louisbourg, the fortress guarding the entrance to the St Lawrence, early enough in the season, its second objective was Quebec itself.[24]

In order to give greater impetus to the campaigns he was planning, Pitt reorganized the military staff in America completely. He put himself at the head of the whole operation. Without assuming the title of minister of war he took over direction of the army, the navy, and war diplomacy, and welded these three elements into a single powerful precision instrument. Since for all practical purposes Britain's supremacy at sea was established, he did not waste time in chasing French ships; instead Britain's wide margin of superiority would permit the fleet to co-operate closely in the activities of the regiments it transported to strategic points. This was the key to what Pitt called his 'system'. To use his own apt and striking metaphor, in his eyes the army and navy were the blade and the handle of a single weapon.[25] The officers he had chosen would act under him. Loudoun, whom he considered incompetent, was replaced by General James Abercromby, but the new commander-in-chief was allowed little latitude. Five new brigadier-generals were also appointed: John Stanwix, John Forbes, Lord Howe, Governor Charles Lawrence, and Edward Whitmore.[26] The last two were attached to the expedition against Louisbourg, in which two other officers were also given new commissions: Brigadier-General James Wolfe and Major-General Jeffrey Amherst. Amherst and Boscawen jointly were to direct operations against Île-Royale.[27]

Pitt's plan was then to launch a triple offensive—against Louisbourg (and Quebec), Montreal, and Fort Du Quesne. The plan, though a bold one, was not fundamentally original. It was the plan that Loudoun had proposed to the British government after the failure of his campaign. For Loudoun Quebec was still the 'great object' at which an offensive should be aimed. The conquest of Quebec would bring immediate peace to all the northern British colonies. But in order to win a victory at Quebec, it was essential to blockade Île-Royale and to cut off access to the St Lawrence, including access by the Strait of Belle-Isle, as soon as navigation opened. As for Louisbourg, it would be madness for a fleet to try to force entrance to the port once it was occupied by a French squadron. Such an operation would entail great losses even if there were no French ships guarding the harbour (and this was a lesson that Boscawen would not forget). The first attack should be made by land, and the fleet should come into action only when the fortress was ready to fall under the land attack.[28]

This was no more than a general outline, but early in 1758 Loudoun drew up a plan of specific measures he proposed to carry out. He was now the most experienced British officer in America, and even in the whole empire. He had organized excellent auxiliary services for his expeditionary forces: transport, commissariat, engineers, artillery. He had made his regular troops independent of the hesitancies and whims of local governments. He had learned that, in the conditions in which war was waged in the New World, it was not numbers that counted but

[209]

quality, and that a small well-equipped professional army, ready and able to come into action at the right place and the right moment, was much more useful than great masses of fighters slow to move and difficult to handle.[29] He had come to understand what others had realized at the end of the previous campaign—that what made Canada such a redoubtable adversary was its great distances, the vast spaces that provided natural ambushes for its fighters. Distance was the enemy that had to be mastered and, if possible, turned against the French; and the movements of troops projected by Loudoun were co-ordinated with this capital consideration in mind. In the east, just as ships were to spend the winter in Halifax in order to close the entrance to the St Lawrence and to cut off access to Louisbourg, so six regiments would remain in Nova Scotia ready to join forces with 8,000 provincials from New England and to land in Île-Royale at the earliest possible moment. Reinforcements could also be brought in from Great Britain if the occasion arose. In the centre the commander-in-chief would take command of a force of twelve battalions stationed in New York. Their mission was to capture Forts Carillon and Saint-Frédéric very early in May, before river navigation was completely open and while it was difficult for relief to reach the forts. The way would thus be open to Montreal. At the same time Bradstreet, with a body of specially trained men, would attack Fort Frontenac, while in the west Stanwix, with two regiments of regulars and provincials from the southern colonies, would set out early in the season for Fort Du Quesne. They would expect to arrive there before the middle of June and before reinforcements from Montreal could reach the Ohio valley. This time Canadian resistance would be broken.[30]

There was then little or no difference in substance between Loudoun's plan and Pitt's. But what a world of difference in the means of execution! Instead of making provincial troops from New England travel hundreds of miles to northern New York, the general would have sent them to Louisbourg, where they would have been naturally inclined to do their best. Rather than burden the Lake Champlain army with exhausted colonials—Abercromby's British regiments could hardly move 'without stepping on provincials who were not fitted for their job'[31]—Loudoun would have pressed forward with a highly mobile force capable of great fire-power. He would certainly not have allowed useless troop movements to delay the expedition against Fort Du Quesne and to compromise its success. Comparing Loudoun's orders and Pitt's, Major James Robertson pointed out how much the British had lost by 'laying aside' the plan drawn up by the former commander-in-chief—a plan 'calculated to improve every advantage that climate, situation, and numbers could give us over the enemy—and by adopting another, made without any knowledge of these advantages, which, by a misapplication of our force, made even numbers and expense destructive to our scheme.'[32] Robertson was not alone in his opinion. It was impossible to imagine, said the governor of Maryland in a letter to his brother, how deeply America regretted the loss of Lord Loudoun.[33]

In short, then, nothing could be more admirable than Pitt's energy and activity, nothing better suited to the permanent interests of England and of the empire, no strategy more firmly founded than his. But the statesman was not the brilliant tactician he imagined, and overconfidence in his own judgement was to limit the gains from the extraordinary war machine he had set in motion. If it had not been for that element of human weakness, Wolfe's forecast would have been realized and two campaigns would have sealed Canada's fate.

For Canada was in dire distress. After a dreadful winter the people had almost nothing left to eat. An official reporting in the spring presented a pitiful picture of conditions: 'Labourers, artisans, and journeymen are no longer capable of work. They are so weak they can scarcely stand.'[34] The intendant 'has put us on a ration,' wrote a sister from Quebec; and the daily ration, two ounces of bread, was a meagre one. Moreover, the weather was so bad that they could not count on a normal crop. It rained without ceasing, it was so cold that houses had to be heated in the middle of June, and of course there was nothing growing on the farms. When French ships appeared at Quebec on 19 May, they were greeted with explosions of joy. 'People climbed up on the roofs and chimneys to assure themselves the news was true and to announce it to everybody.' Other ships followed, and they continued to arrive throughout the summer and into September. That did not mean, however, that there was an abundance of food. Bigot fixed the bread ration at four ounces a day in order, as he wrote at the end of June, 'to supply the upper country where all these gentlemen and the troops are going to attack the enemy.'[35] The common people still lacked the necessities of life, and it was reported towards the end of the year that a number of persons had died of hunger.[36]

How can we explain the persistence of famine conditions in spite of real efforts on the part of France to relieve them? The fraudulent manipulations of the Great Society certainly did not improve the situation.[37] We should be exaggerating their importance however if we regarded them as the chief cause of the lack of food. The consequences of France's inferiority at sea were much more far-reaching. A large number of the ships laden with food for Quebec were seized by the enemy,[38] a loss that was not unforeseen. In August Moras informed Bigot that some 60,000 quintals of flour as well as other foodstuffs had left the ports of France for Canada. 'Supposing,' he added, 'that only two-thirds of the cargoes reach Quebec, you will still receive 36,000 quintals of flour.'[39] Such a conjecture was in itself a confession of impotence.

Here was one important cause of Canada's distress, but we still have not gone to the heart of the problem. In 1758 Canada's economic activity had been geared to war for almost fifteen years. For almost fifteen years the production, distribution, and consumption of goods and services had been affected by the conflict. Moreover, the framework of the Canadian economy had always been fragile and its human resources inadequate, while at the same time its military organization was developed largely from its own population. What happened then? The increase in consumption resulting from hostilities was further accentuated by the arrival of considerable numbers of French soldiers. Moreover the geographical structure of New France—her great extent in relation to her population —and the absolute need to defend her distant frontiers in time of war, combined to give first priority to the factor of distribution. Since geographical conditions made the transport of men, military supplies, and food very difficult, this too caused a heavy drain on Canada's manpower and resources. And where would the men come from? From the Canadian population, whose numbers were already inadequate and whose reserves were by no means inexhaustible.

Four or five thousand men, according to one report, were sent each year to the distant posts and 'employed by the convoys transporting food for a handful of men stationed in these little forts.' These transport workers could have made 'so many warriors' instead of 'scouring the waterways and consuming the colony's food to no purpose.'[40] The estimate of four or five thousand seems high, but that is not the essential point; what the author of these remarks did not understand was that it was impossible to maintain the western forts without an extensive and complicated supply system, and that it was equally impossible to hold Canada without maintaining its great ring of posts. It was a fact, however, that the service took large numbers of men and wore them out. For instance, when Vaudreuil heard of Braddock's march on the Ohio in the summer of 1755 he trembled for Fort Du Quesne: he was afraid the fort might be captured 'because the troops and militia charged with its defence were busy transporting food and munitions.' And if in the party that Contrecoeur sent out to stop Braddock there were only 250 white soldiers with 650 Indians, it was because some of the men, 'having crippled themselves hauling supplies and munitions to Rivière aux Boeufs', were immobilized in the fort.[41] In 1758 Bigot reported that '3,000 of the best men' had been assigned to transport service,[42] and it is to be noted that this meant a loss in quality as well as in quantity to Canadian military strength.[43] It must also be noted that these men were taken away from agriculture, and that in consequence production was reduced at the very time that consumption increased.

If these conditions had been temporary the balance could have been restored, but the situation grew worse from year to year. Consignments of supplies from the mother country did not suffice to fill the widening gap between what the colony produced and what it consumed. Even if the navy succeeded in renewing Canada's food supplies, it would be providing a palliative and not a solution of the fundamental problem created by the war—the problem of subsistence. By midsummer 1758 Bigot knew that the problem was insoluble. Vaudreuil and Montcalm, he warned the court, would ask for still more men, and they would certainly need them. And yet, however careful the king's government might be to provision these troops, their arrival in the colony would be the cause 'of still greater misery.' The mother country must understand, continued the intendant, that even if the harvest was good and Cadet, the colony's commissary-general, had still more food sent out from Europe, famine would reign as long as the war lasted. 'Canada is too exhausted,' he explained, 'for it to be otherwise.'[44]

Canada's military effort was paralysed by famine, and there were good grounds for Loudoun's conjecture that the country's outer defences would not withstand a series of attacks launched early in the season. In May Montcalm gave a brief outline of the situation: 'I fear nothing may be accomplished in this campaign . . . The colony may perish for want of bread.' The only thing that could be done was to send some of the regulars to Carillon: 'Lack of provisions precludes any further action.'[45] Even this movement of troops was dictated by famine rather than by strategic considerations. 'I had a little store of provisions,' reported Vaudreuil, 'preciously hoarded, at Carillon.'[46] If he sent troops there, it was because 'there was nothing to give them' in the interior of the colony.[47] Soldiers dispatched to Carillon were so many mouths that for the time being the Quebec region would not have to feed. Helpless, the governor bemoaned his fate and the 'harsh necessity' that forced him to dip into this stock:[48] 'In the circumstances in which I find myself, especially in respect to provisions, I cannot consider any but defensive action; I cannot even flatter myself we can keep the body of troops I am entrusting to M. Montcalm in Carillon for more than two months unless we are fortunate enough to receive help as abundant as what reaches us may, we fear, be meagre.'[49] When Montcalm set out for Lake Champlain, it was not with the hope that he was embarking on a fruitful campaign. He knew that his little army could not be mustered there until between 5 and 8 July, late enough to allow the enemy to be there first with a stronger force. 'Provisioning,' he wrote, 'made it impossible for us to do otherwise. And that is really a great misfortune.'[50]

It was not that Vaudreuil had failed to make plans. Fearing that the English might be ready to open the campaign a month sooner than the Franco-Canadians, he was preparing to mislead them 'by a bold manoeuvre.' By allowing them to suppose from Montcalm's advance to Carillon that the offensive against Fort Edward was being resumed, he would draw the bulk of the British forces to Lake George and at the same time he would send Lévis to Lake Ontario with a body of picked troops. Their mission would be to skirt round the British army in New York, to penetrate into the Mohawk valley, and to push on as far as Schenectady. This strategy was aimed at several objectives: to create 'indecision' among the English by upsetting the disposition of their forces; to prevent them from re-establishing themselves on Lake Ontario, where it was to be feared that they might rebuild Fort Oswego from its ruins; to make sure of collaboration from the Indians, who required before striking that the Canadians should show their strength; and finally, to have advance units in the west if it were necessary to defend the Ohio valley. If Fort Du Quesne were threatened, Lévis's force could go to its relief. And that was not all. Anticipating a British offensive against Louisbourg, the governor had sent Boishébert off across the frozen wastes to Miramichi; the brilliant young officer was under orders to recruit a detachment of Acadians and Indians to strengthen the garrison of Île-Royale. They would constitute a mobile unit of fighters familiar with the country.[51]

Vaudreuil's plan had more than mere boldness to recommend it: the English were to carry the war to the very points that his provisions would have covered—Louisbourg, Carillon, Lake Ontario, and Fort Du Quesne. Even Montcalm, who said he knew 'Vaudreuil by heart on the campaign', had to admit that 'his general system' was good. He added, however: 'Our shortcoming will be in the details.'[52] No, in this case the plan as a whole would be wrecked not in its details but by penury of means to carry it out: Canada suffered not only from famine, as we have already seen, but from lack of arms and munitions of war. Without the booty from the battlefield of the Monongahela in 1755 and the stores captured at Oswego and Fort William Henry, 'I should not have had enough,' confessed the governor, 'either to attack or to defend myself.'[53] But the one incurable lack was lack of men. Montcalm recognized this fatal weakness when he compared the British forces with those at his disposal: the disparity was enormous.[54] Always a provident politician he meant to make this disparity serve his personal interest. He asked his friend Bourlamaque, who had a military almanac in his pack, to consult it and make up a list of the British regiments serving in America. His intention, he explained to Bourlamaque, was to send the list to France. 'Compared with [our] little handful of men (4800 regulars) it will frighten courtiers and townsmen alike, and it will always serve to enhance the general's glory or to mitigate blame.'[55]

Even though the Canadian government had plans (that would eventually have to be adjusted to the colony's means), the French government had to have plans of its own. In March a dispatch from Paris to the *Mercure de La Haye* reported that although the English had built up the greatest force of arms for America since the beginning of the war, the court appeared 'to be counting on the measures already taken to put Île-Royale and [France's] other possessions in that region in a good state of defence.'[56] Even though the minister of marine, writing to Vaudreuil in August, advised him not to limit himself 'merely to defensive action',[57] he did not seem anxious to launch an assault on the British positions in America himself. The most he seemed to hope for from the 'measures' he was taking was a repetition of the events of 1757 on Île-Royale. Apparently convinced, as Montcalm was, that the enemy would repeat the strategy of the previous year and direct the weight of its main force against Louisbourg,[58] convinced too that the fate of that fortress might decide the issue of the conflict,[59] he made a great effort to build up a strong naval force in Louisbourg harbour. But the French ports and the American coast were being watched, so it was impossible to send the units of a powerful squadron out of any one French port at one time. The ships that would first convoy men and war materials to Île-Royale and then defend the island would have to sail in several divisions. Circumstances dictated that there would be six such divisions.

The first group of ships, from the Mediterranean fleet, left Toulon under the command of Admiral La Clue. Having failed in its attempt to get through the Strait of Gibraltar, closely guarded by Vice-Admiral Osborn, it was forced to take refuge in the Spanish port of Cartagena. The minister ordered a fleet to be sent to its aid under the command of the marquis Du Quesne, the former governor of New France and now a rear-admiral. Du Quesne was not to go to Louisbourg, but to sail with La Clue some distance beyond Gibraltar and then come back to cruise in the Mediterranean. His flagship, *Foudroyant*, the most powerful ship in the French navy, would be accompanied by two other warships and a frigate. The fleet sailed from Toulon on 16 February; on 28 February, before the junction had been effected with La Clue's ships, it encountered an English squadron commanded by Vice-Admiral Osborn. The *Foudroyant* was put out of action by the *Monmouth*, a ship of inferior tonnage and armament, the fleet was captured, and Du Quesne and his officers were taken as prisoners to England. They landed at Spithead on 20 April. La Clue seized the first opportunity to regain Toulon, where his ships were dismantled.[60] Meanwhile the marquis des Gouttes set sail from Rochefort with the *Prudent* (seventy-four guns), three frigates, and two transports, and after endless difficulties reached Louisbourg towards the end of April. The crew of the *Prudent* was 'in a very sad state', with only a hundred seamen in good health. Although he was sailing 'in sight of seven enemy ships', Des Gouttes, now in command of the naval forces, just managed to make port with the *Prudent* and one other ship. These were followed later by two more.[61] Before Des Gouttes's arrival a warship, stripped of its guns and equipped as a merchantman, had slipped into harbour with a cargo of provisions to relieve the shortage of food in the fortress.[62] Still another ship, the *Magnifique*, had left France early in February and on 31 March was within sight of Île-Royale, but the entrance to Louisbourg was blocked by ice and efforts to force a passage proved fruitless. Finally, as the captain later reported, 'the surgeon-general assured us that if we were delayed two days in the ice not one of our sick would be saved.' The ship had perforce to return to its home port where it dropped anchor early in May. There hundred and forty-two men had been buried at sea during the voyage.[63]

In mid-March the French government commissioned Beaussier de Lisle to take a group of four warships (three of them serving as transports) and one frigate from Brest to Louisbourg. It was admitted that La Clue's mission had failed and the little fleet would compensate in part for the failure. Beaussier was lucky; on 5 April he escaped from Hawke, who arrived too late to intercept him at Brest, and on 28 April he sailed into Louisbourg, scarcely more elated at his success than were 'the inhabitants, who sang a *Te Deum* the day after [his] arrival.' He had eluded the vigilance of Hardy, whose squadron of nine ships appeared some twenty hours after the French ships' safe entrance into harbour.[64]

Without this relief it would have been idle to consider plans for resisting invasion, but the relief was not sufficient to ensure that the island would be saved. The minister of marine was well aware of this fact, and on 2 May a second expedition sailed out of Rochefort harbour. Its four ships, under the command of Du Chaffault de Besné, carried a battalion of reinforcements for the garrison. Four weeks later, when the fleet reached Île-Royale, the commander learned that ten British ships were blockading Louisbourg; he continued on to Port Dauphin where he landed his troops. On 10 June he sailed for Quebec, and he continued to patrol the St Lawrence until 10 September.[65] If Du Chaffault's fleet had reached Louisbourg, said Des Gouttes, the reinforcements he brought in 'men and naval strength' would have 'made the enemy's plans futile'; the English might even have been 'beaten'.[66]

Earlier a small fleet—one warship-transport, the *Bizarre*, and two fully armed frigates, the *Echo* and the *Aréthuse*, the latter commanded by the famous Vauquelin—had succeeded in reaching Cape Breton. The two frigates anchored below the fort of Louisbourg on 29 and 30 May while the *Bizarre* sailed on to the St Lawrence, where it joined Du Chaffault's division. On the way back to France, after separating from Du Chaffault's ships, it took several prizes, of which the most valuable was a frigate of 24 guns.[67]

So far the court had sent ships, troops, munitions, and food to Île-Royale. It had also decided, in March, to send a commander. The comte de Blénac, lieutenant-general in the naval forces, was accordingly appointed commander of the land and sea troops in Louisbourg and was given detailed instructions for the defence of Île-Royale and of Canada. But it was only on 10 May that the *Formidable*, with Blénac on board, and the *Raisonnable* sailed from Brest. On 13 May they were sighted by four enemy ships which, after chasing them for three days, came within striking distance. The *Raisonnable* succumbed to the ensuing attack and the *Formidable* escaped in the fog only to fall in with two English ships on 6 June off the coast of Île-Royale. Once again, however, the fog was Blénac's salvation. Three weeks later he was back in Brest, 'very glad', as he confessed, to have saved the king's ship.[68]

France had made a truly remarkable effort. The warships the minister of marine tried to send to the relief of Louisbourg reached the impressive total of twenty-three, although twelve of the ships were used as transports. Seven warships, two of them fully armed, came into port, as well as three frigates (one a frigate-transport) and diverse cargo vessels.[69] Of the ships that did not reach Louisbourg some, as we have seen, accomplished a part of their mission. The garrison was reinforced by two battalions and reasonably well supplied with provisions. At the time of the capitulation, the forces in Louisbourg counted more than 2,000 officers and men of the land troops and 1,000 marines, as well as 2,600 seamen and 400 militiamen.[70]

To sum up. Under the impelling influence of Pitt, in whose eyes supremacy in the New World was the prime objective of the war, the British government had brought powerful forces into play in its efforts to conquer America. To face these forces France and Canada had organized a defensive at once bold and ingenious, a defensive designed to obtain the best possible results from the elements still available to them. The main front, as both sides realized, was in Cape Breton. France, wrote Montcalm to the minister of war, must send a squadron to save Île-Royale.[71] The naval forces that France tried to send to the island were much stronger than those that actually reached it. The latter did not suffice to save Louisbourg, but they did save Quebec, and with Quebec Canada.

The English had begun to prepare for the Louisbourg expedition in the last weeks of 1757. The war fleet commanded by Boscawen counted forty-one units, twenty-one of sixty guns or more. Its fire power was formidable: the ships carried in all more than 1,900 guns. General Amherst had under his orders an expeditionary force of 13,200 officers and men. This force added to the squadron's 14,968 sailors made up a total of more than 28,000 men.[72] Thus the strength in men of the attackers would be about five times that of the defenders.

In order to be first in the field Pitt sent the squadron out early: Boscawen sailed from Plymouth on 23 February. Moreover, in order to make sure the warships would not be held back on the high seas, the minister made the decision, less rash than it at first appears, not to require the warships to convoy the transports. In spite of this bold measure, Boscawen did not reach Halifax until 9 May, too late to prevent all the French ships from entering Louisbourg harbour. It was true that Hardy had been cruising in those waters since the first of April with the ships that had wintered in Halifax but, as an English officer remarked, one cannot count very much on such blockades.[73] Wolfe could not get over his astonishment at the length of the crossing. 'From Christopher Columbus's time to our days,' he wrote, 'there perhaps has never been a more extraordinary voyage. The continued opposition of contrary winds, calms, or currents baffled all our skill and wore out all our patience. A fleet of men of war, well manned, unencumbered with transports, commanded by an officer of the first reputation, has been eleven weeks in its passage.'[74] However, when he wrote to his father on 20 May he still expected the operation to be a brief one. The army would start to move in four or five days and once the landing was completed the 'business' would be half done. 'I hope it will be all done,' he added, 'before you receive this letter.'[75] Actually the landing was not completed until 8 June.[76]

Wolfe was right: the fate of the fortress was sealed by the successful landing. And yet, it held out for seven weeks before capitulating on 26 July. To what can this long resistance be attributed? To the French ships that had succeeded in entering the harbour. 'Louisbourg is so situated (as you must have heard),' wrote a British officer, 'that if the enemy got five men of war into the harbour, before we got before it, the enterprise would miscarry.'[77] In reality the situation was not quite so simple as this officer thought. Given the disproportion between the land forces confronting one another, the fall of the fort was inevitable. The only question now was how long it would hold out, but it was a question of major importance. Without its naval defences the fort would have been subjected to simultaneous attacks by land and sea, and there is little doubt that it would have surrendered before the end of June. And after that? After that Amherst and Boscawen would still have had enough time to reduce Quebec to the same fate as Louisbourg. Hence time became the prime factor in the campaign, a fact whose importance was fully appreciated by Drucourt: 'It was a matter of deferring our fate as long as possible,' he wrote. 'Thus I said: *if the French ships leave on 10 June . . . the admiral will enter immediately after that.* And in that case we would have been taken before the end of this month, and that would have given the attacking generals the advantage of using July and August to strengthen their forces in Canada and to take their ships up the river while the season was favourable to them.'[78] The marquis des Gouttes, who could not understand Drucourt's reasoning, kept pressing him to 'save' the fleet by allowing it to leave the harbour, and at his request the governor called a council of war to consider this grave question. The council, by a majority of votes, approved the opinion of Drucourt and Franquet: the defence must be 'prolonged' even if this entailed the sacrifice of the ships, since these had been sent out by the king precisely 'for the defence of the fort.'[79] Clearly the English were anxious to establish themselves in Louisbourg quickly and to push on to Quebec; and no less clearly the only obstacle preventing Boscawen from coming to the support of Amherst was the presence of Des Gouttes's ships.[80] 'The ships of war,' wrote the British officer whom we have already quoted, 'did much mischief, and retarded the siege greatly, keeping a constant and terrible fire on our works.'[81] The squadron was sacrificed. Vauquelin's *Aréthuse* had been dispatched to carry messages to the mother country, but France lost eleven other warships—eight sunk, three captured—as well as the fortress of Louisbourg.[82]

But Quebec was saved. As Amherst confessed to Wolfe, he had hoped to pursue his operation against the capital of Canada immediately after the capture of Louisbourg; ' 'Tis the best thing we could do if practicable.' However the defeat suffered by Abercromby in the bloody battle at Carillon forced the general to replace this with a less ambitious plan: to send five or six regiments to New York and other troops to the St John River where some Acadians were still maintaining their resistance, and to dispatch two or three battalions to ravage Canadian settlements on the lower St Lawrence.[83] Wolfe was beside himself with impatience. In his opinion the evacuation of 'that cursed French garrison' from Louisbourg —the garrison troops had a bad reputation; one French officer was accused of making an immoral attempt on a Scottish soldier[84]—was wasting precious time; he would have liked to fly to the help of Abercromby (abandoned, he was sure, by the Americans); he would have liked a 'war of destruction' in the gulf of St Lawrence. 'I cannot look coolly,' he confessed, 'upon the bloody inroads of those hell-hounds the Canadians; and if nothing further is to be done I must desire leave to quit the army.'[85] These were the words of an angry and impatient young man. Amherst and Boscawen did precisely what their young colleague considered beyond his power: they kept the use of their reason. After having considered together 'the present situation of affairs in America' and studied orders from England concerning combined movements to be carried out after the fall of Louisbourg, they reached the conclusion that although it would be preferable to take the whole army to Quebec, that plan could not be realized, and they would have to be satisfied with sending two or three battalions to destroy the small French settlements on the lower St Lawrence and as far up the river 'as the season allowed.'[86]

This latter operation, which had been allowed for, was entrusted to Wolfe.[87] The English fleet—thirty-three sails including nine warships—appeared in sight of the Gaspé coast early in September. The destruction of fishing villages was pursued systematically. Vaudreuil reported that the attacking parties had orders to 'carry off even bits of old iron and to burn all the houses and generally everything they could not carry away.' They treated any prisoners they took 'very well' and tried to persuade the Canadians they would lose nothing by a change of allegiance. 'With [the British] they would no longer be reduced to four ounces of bread a day.'[88] As none of his adversaries could offer any resistance, Wolfe regretted that he had not been able to add to the reputation of the king's arms; but he took some satisfaction in having taken 140 prisoners and so disorganizing the Canadian fisheries that 'it would be impossible to take a single quintal of cod' as long as the war lasted, and the colony would thus be deprived of an important source of food.[89] It was a far cry however from these modest feats to a victorious campaign against Quebec.

Another factor besides the lateness of the season had affected the decisions made by Amherst and Boscawen after 26 July. This was the defeat suffered by Abercromby on 8 July at Carillon. The battle was remarkable for several reasons. First, the heavy British thrust on Lake Champlain had come as a surprise, although Vaudreuil had got wind of it in time to send Lévis with 300 French soldiers to join Montcalm, as well as a Canadian detachment that arrived while the battle was in progress. Then, instead of holding the forward portage post, which was comparatively easy to defend, Montcalm had withdrawn his troops and chosen a very strange position in which to make his stand: bad in that it was open to attack on its flanks or from the rear but good against a frontal attack, although the French commander, who had had time to do so, had neglected to provide it with guns.[90] If, observed one of Montcalm's officers, the English 'had had a skilful and enterprising general, it would have been difficult for us to extricate ourselves from that pass.'[91] According to Wolfe, the situation of the fort at Carillon and the numerical superiority of the attacking army—'which could bear to be weakened by detachments'—should have made it possible for Abercromby to oblige 'the marquis de Montcalm to lay down his arms.' Even if it were true that Abercromby might attempt to renew the assault, Wolfe could not 'flatter himself that the attack would be successful.' This conviction arose 'not from any high idea of the marquis de Montcalm's abilities but from the very poor opinion of our own.'[92]

Abercromby's performance was assuredly not brilliant, but was he on this occasion so completely inept as has been thought? He is charged with two offenses: having been repulsed although he was in command of a large army, and having ordered his men to attack without first studying the enemy's position. Pitt had planned for an army of 7,000 regulars and 20,000 provincials, but Wolfe had foreseen in the spring that this latter number would have to be cut in half and that the remaining 10,000 provincials would be 'not good for much.'[93] The prediction was justified in both respects: with his 6,367 regulars[94] Abercromby had only 9,024 provincial troops under his orders and, if one may judge by the losses suffered by the two groups, the provincials certainly did not accomplish very much. Their losses were 86 killed, 240 wounded, 8 missing, while the corresponding figures for the regulars were 464, 1,115, and 19.[95] One might almost say that the battle was fought between 7,000 English regulars and 3,500 men protected by a barricade of tree trunks.[96] The French lost 106 men killed and 266 wounded.[97] The second charge against Abercromby remains: he had to retreat because he attacked the French position from the front, the only direction from which an attack could fail. The explanation of his decision is a simple one. He gave the order for a frontal attack because he thought he had no choice. He had been informed by prisoners that the enemy had 6,000 men ('5,000 and some hundreds' according to Vaudreuil's account);[98] that orders for the Mohawk expedition had been countermanded, thus freeing Lévis and his 5,000 men to come to the help of Montcalm; and that the entrenchments defending the French fort were being made stronger every hour. Hence the precipitate decision to launch an assault.[99] It was a grave mistake; Montcalm would commit a similar error on 13 September 1759.

Notwithstanding reports circulated at the time and repeated later, the victory at Carillon was in no sense a 'miracle'.[100] The only foundation for such a belief lay in the extravagant figures supplied to the public by the victorious general and his friends. In their accounts they gave the enemy 20,000, 25,000, even 27,000 men, and they inflicted upon them losses proportionate to what Doreil called 'the supernatural valour of the French troops': 3,000 killed—without counting the wounded—or according to another report 3,000 killed and wounded.[101] It would not have been difficult to verify these figures: Lévis knew 'the enemy had had

500 men killed at the fort and 1,000 or 1,100 wounded',[102] and Canadian officers were not so guileless as to accept the French estimates. Desandrouins was scandalized when his Canadian colleagues questioned reports on 'the numbers of the enemy and the number of dead, which they claimed was not more than 400.'[103] The gap between 400 and 550—the exact number of British dead—is a good deal narrower than between 550 and 3,000. The defeat of 8 July stopped Abercromby's advance on Montreal.[104] It forced the British to adopt a defensive position on Lake George[105] and created consternation in their camp. They considered the possibility of reorganizing for a counter-attack on Carillon, but by mid-October this project had been abandoned.[106]

While Montcalm awaited a renewed attack, Abercromby was complying with a request from Lieutenant-Colonel Bradstreet, who wanted to lead an expedition against Fort Frontenac. The expedition would follow in the opposite direction a part of the route that Lévis would have taken if he had been able to carry out Vaudreuil's first instructions. Abercromby transferred 3,600 men to Bradstreet's army,[107] but because of the arduous nature of the journey—a distance of 430 miles with 84 miles of portages—desertions were so numerous that the force was reduced to 3,339 at the Great Carrying Place and to 3,092 at the end of the journey.[108] The army reached Frontenac on 26 August, one month to the day after the fall of Louisbourg, and the fort surrendered the following day. The defenders had been taken completely by surprise: no one expected the English in that quarter. In April Montcalm had observed 'nothing very interesting' on the Lake Ontario front, merely problems of Indian diplomacy.[109] In mid-July he knew that 5,000 enemy troops with artillery were marching towards the Mohawk—perhaps, he thought, to be ready to oppose any renewal of 'the secret expedition' that Vaudreuil had planned against them, perhaps too with the intention of re-establishing themselves at Oswego.[110] His misjudgements did not prevent him from playing the prophet after the event and writing to the court (1 September): 'News has just reached me that the English are at Frontenac. I had been afraid of that for a long time.'[111] Vaudreuil for his part had some 'grounds for a feeling of reassurance': he had sent Longueuil with 300 men into the Iroquois country, and information gathered by the party seemed to indicate that the enemy's immediate aim was to rebuild Fort Bull, or even Oswego. But when Bradstreet's force was embarked on Lake Ontario, messages of warning were brought to the commander at Fort Frontenac by Indian scouts who had been kept on the alert. News of Bradstreet's advance did not reach Montreal until 26 August, too late to prevent the fall of Fort Frontenac, but the governor at once dispatched a considerable relief force in the hope that it might at least be possible to save Niagara.[112] Niagara was the key to all the upper country, and Bradstreet might well advance on it. When they arrived at Fort Edward the British prisoners who had been exchanged for the French garrison at Frontenac, and who knew how weak the Canadians really were at Niagara, declared that it was 'a most unlucky thing' that Bradstreet had not pressed on there.[113]

In Wolfe's opinion Bradstreet was a 'most extraordinary man' and the capture of Frontenac a 'master stroke'.[114] He might better have said a hit-and-run raid. For Bradstreet beat a hasty retreat after burning the fort and the French ships in the port. The fort offered the enemy enormous quantities of booty: 800,000 pounds of furs and trading goods, and a great store of food and powder. All this was shared equally among the combatants. The commander's delicacy in refusing to take anything for himself was remarked upon.[115] Montcalm was in despair at the loss of Fort Frontenac. The colony would be 'cut in two.'[116] No; the colony would be weakened by the loss of Frontenac, but there was still Niagara. Two Canadian officers returning in mid-October reported various signs of the haste of Bradstreet's departure: several buildings were still standing inside the walls and the fort itself could easily be repaired. Six guns of medium calibre had been found in it intact.[117] What made this a serious defeat was not the loss of a position—the enemy had not occupied the fort—but the loss of food and munitions stored there for transport to the upper country and the destruction of the Canadian fleet on the Great Lakes. If after the victory at Carillon Vaudreuil had disregarded the sneers of Montcalm and revived his plan of an attack on the Mohawk, Bradstreet would never have been able to strike on Lake Ontario.[118]

Farther south Forbes, with an army of 7,000 men including 2,000 Virginians, was advancing inch by inch towards Fort Du Quesne.[119] The prospects for the campaign were not good and at the end of June Montcalm did not think the English would 'attack the Ohio.'[120] They did attack it, however, although with signal lack of success at their first attempt. Major James Grant, who had been sent ahead with 838 picked men, advanced rapidly to within reach of his objective, but in an encounter that took place on 14 September his detachment fled in disorder after losing 300 men.[121] Grant himself fell into the hands of the enemy. The engagement, judged by Montcalm a 'very fine and brilliant action',[122] taught the enemy that the Canadians on the Ohio still knew how to defend themselves.[123] They even tried to prove they could take offensive action. On 12 October, 440 Canadians and 130 Indians made a raid lasting four hours on the important advance post of Loyalhanna, some forty miles east of Fort Du Quesne. The aim of the raid was to seize the enemy's pack horses in order to retard, and if possible to stop, their advance, but it was a desperate attempt: the defenders of Fort Du

Quesne had reached the end of their tether. The following week the commander, Ligneris, calculated that he had supplies only 'for eighteen days
and 1,200 men.' When he was assured that in spite of the raid of 12
October the English were still assembling, he realized there was only one
course for him to take: to scatter his soldiers between Detroit and the
Illinois country, send his Canadians back to their villages, keep a garrison of 200 regulars, and await events. He reported to Vaudreuil in a
letter of 23 October: 'I am in the saddest situation one could imagine.'[124]

On the other side, Forbes judged himself to be 'in the greatest distress.'
He was making no progress and he feared that if he could not soon reach
the French fort he might be blocked in the mountains for the winter, for he
knew quite well that he could not think of recrossing the Alleghenies with
his heavy siege artillery.[125] On 16 November a council of the colonels
and engineers attached to the expedition reached the same conclusion.[126]
On 25 November, however, the English gained entrance to 'that nest
of robbers', as Bouquet termed the fort, 'that had cost so much blood.'[127]
Informed of Ligneris's terrible difficulties, Forbes had resolved to try
one last thrust with 2,500 picked men and a train of light artillery.[128] At
his approach the Canadian commander loaded his guns and ammunition
into boats to be dispatched to the Illinois country, blew up the fort,
and withdrew with 100 men to Fort Machault.[129] The dismay provoked
by a reverse that must have been foreseen as a normal possibility was
heightened by the fact that people in Canada were under the impression
the Ohio had been saved. On 25 November, the very day that Forbes
stepped from his litter on the soil of Fort Du Quesne, a Canadian officer
just back from the Ohio reported all quiet on the continent: 'The English
will make no further attempt this year on our forts.'[130] The same story
was repeated in Paris in January 1759,[131] but on the preceding 28
November an Englishman writing to a correspondent in New York had
dated his letter from 'Pittsburgh (formerly Fort Du Quesne)'.[132]

The British had experienced a similar misadventure some months earlier.
In August a letter from London to a European periodical had brought
'news that General Abercrombie . . . had been fortunate enough to beat
the French army sent out to oppose him.'[133] The following month, however, the correspondent had had to confess that the people of London
had been too quick to accept an unfounded rumour: 'Instead of beating,
our troops were beaten.'[134] Public opinion turned solidly against Abercromby. Governor Sharpe enumerated the errors attributed to the defeated general,[135] and the press added to the list.[136] Naturally Abercromby
was relieved of his command, and when he embarked for England in
mid-January 1759 no ceremony marked his departure.[137] He was replaced—no less naturally—by Amherst, the hero of the Louisbourg

victory.[138] Amherst was fêted and extolled. The commander-in-chief of
the British army conveyed messages of congratulation to him from 'the
principal corporations' of England.[139] The explanation of this explosion
of joy was that the British government had always attached great importance to Île-Royale. 'The English minister hopes for great things
from this expedition,' wrote the Spanish ambassador from London in
February 1758, and he repeated in May that the British placed all their
hopes on its success:[140] 'A minister of His Britannic Majesty has said that
the outcome of this operation will decide whether the British dictate
peace terms or submit to them.'[141] When news of the fall of the fortress
reached Pitt, he sent a letter by mounted messenger to his wife so that
she might be among the first to hear it. Her answering letter was an
effusion of joy. 'No words can thank you enough, my angel,' she wrote,
'for having forwarded the messenger of this news to me, but a thousand
kisses shall express my gratitude when I am blessed with the happiness
of receiving you in this joyful place, made so by you, my glorious love.'[142]
A New York poet celebrated the victory in a poem to be sung to the air
of *God Save the King*:

> *Amherst and Boscawen*
> *And all their British men,*
> *Like heroes shone:*
> *Thanks to Patriot Pitt,*
> *Whose penetrating wit*
> *And wisdom judged it fit*
> *To set them on.*[143]

Church bells in Boston rang for almost an entire day,[144] while Newport
(Rhode Island) celebrated with elaborate fireworks: 'The inhabitants . . .
were agreeably entertained with several beautiful figures, representing
Britannia holding the emblem of peace and war and trampling the standard of France under her feet, Mercury descending and approaching
Britannia with the welcome message of the surrender of Louisbourg.
The arms of Great Britain in miniature and underneath Fame pointing
towards the illustrious guardian of our American liberties, the Honourable William Pitt, esq. . . .' Also represented were 'a French minister
and his lady looking over his shoulders, with a most dejected aspect, expressing the present distressed circumstances of France.'[145] In Halifax
the victory was toasted with copious libations: it was reported that on that
occasion 60,000 gallons of rum were drunk.[146] The Lord Mayor and
aldermen of London addressed a message of congratulation to the
king,[147] and the king declared a day of public thanksgiving.[148] On 6
August the flags captured at Louisbourg were deposited with great pomp
in St Paul's cathedral.[149] The British empire had good cause to rejoice,

and its people to dwell complacently on the 'prodigious consequences' of the acquisition of Louisbourg for 'a trading and maritime nation such as ours.'[150] France no longer held a single port on the Atlantic coast; the capture of Louisbourg had restored to the British 'uninterrupted possession of American waters.'[151] In actual fact British navigation and commerce soon began to reap the fruits of victory: insurance rates on cargoes for America, which had been 30 per cent before the capture of Cape Breton, fell to 12 per cent.[152]

There was less rejoicing over the secondary operation at Fort Frontenac. The feeling of the court is reflected in the comment of the Spanish ambassador: 'The capture of Crown Point or the post at Ticonderoga would no doubt have been more important.'[153] New England seemed better able to appreciate the long-term results of this victory. The governor of Massachusetts considered that the defeat of the French fleet on Lake Ontario assured to Great Britain 'the dominion of the Lakes, which sooner or later must be the dominion of America.'[154]

The destruction of Fort Du Quesne was quite another matter. Again the Spanish ambassador reported to Madrid from London: 'That expedition is regarded here as of the greatest importance.'[155] A Boston journalist poured out his feelings in the *News-Letter* of 28 December. 'Blessed be God, the long looked for day is arrived that has now fixed us on the banks of the Ohio . . . in the finest and most fertile country of America lying in the happiest climate in the universe.' Possession of Fort Du Quesne 'lays open to His Majesty's subjects a vein of treasure which if rightly managed may prove richer than the mines of Mexico, the trade with the various nations of western Indians.' Gain for the empire meant loss for France, who could no longer hope to forge her 'chain of communication between Canada and Louisiana, a chain that threatened this continent with slavery.'[156] A speech delivered by the governor of Massachusetts about the same time was couched in similar terms.[157]

The British had an impressive balance of victories for 1758, not only in America but in Africa, where Senegal and Gorée succumbed, and in Europe where Cherbourg suffered a disastrous raid. The British took delight in counting up their conquests.[158] But was there nothing to be entered on the debit side of the ledger? True, conceded the Reverend Jonathan Mayhew of Boston, the enemy had stopped a large army at Carillon; true, 'with the assistance of their good friends and brethren the savages' they had 'cut the throats of some men and great numbers of poor women and children'; but they had 'made no descents on our coasts . . . made a conquest of no place . . . obtained no considerable victory.'[159] The value of the British victories was enhanced by the fact that they were decisive both economically and strategically. The capture of Louisbourg opened the way to Quebec and at the same time gave the

English the Atlantic fisheries, while the British flag flying above Fort Du Quesne announced that it was to be the base of a new trade development. Or at least that was what the London merchants understood and what they said in the messages of thanks they presented to Pitt.[160]

Fortune had smiled on the British empire, and the British people were resolved to bring the task they had undertaken to a successful conclusion. British Americans, said Governor Pownall of Massachusetts, must not allow themselves to be discouraged by the failure of the expedition against Carillon. 'We have received a check which has somewhat delayed matters, and no wonder that we should at the post which the enemy defends as their very gates. But we have put our hand again to the plough and if we do not look back it must go over the very foundation of the enemy's country.'[161] These were no vain words. England's strength, mustered for the colonial war, was increasing daily. Although the British navy had never been more formidable, it was reported in December that, in order to widen its margin of superiority, the government had ordered ten ships from various private shipbuilders and others were being built in the naval shipyards.[162] Pitt was determined to continue the war until the French were 'dispossessed of all Canada', and he tried to make the king share his conviction that 'the war in America would be the deciding factor.' He wanted Great Britain to take Canada, and to hold it when the terms of peace were fixed. It was a country that would 'increase her power and her land and sea trade.' It would also indemnify the nation 'for the considerable expenses . . . incurred for this war.'[163]

The full force of Britain's dynamic power can be measured only in relation to Canada's desperate condition and the attitude of France towards her colony.

New France was breaking up. 'Canada is now surrounded on every side,'[164] wrote Montcalm. Vaudreuil echoed his words: 'I must expect to be attacked from every side,'[165] and Bigot in turn repeated them: 'We are hemmed in on every side.'[166] 'Without the peace we need Canada is lost,' said Montcalm on 1 September 1758.[167] 'Peace appears to me an absolute necessity,' declared Vaudreuil the following day.[168] The two leaders had not consulted together before making these statements: one was at Carillon and the other in Montreal. The enemy might come from any direction. Where could armies be found to stop them? 'You know what the total forces of the colony are,' wrote Vaudreuil to the minister of marine, 'subdivide them, monseigneur . . .'[169] The country, open to invasion, was also weakened by a famine that was growing more severe every day and for which there was no remedy.[170] After receiving the news of the fall of Louisbourg, the court had advised

Canada's administrators that they must expect to receive even smaller quantities of supplies from France than the preceding year: 'You know the losses to which we have been exposed this year, even in less critical circumstances, to transport the supplies that reached the colony.'[171]

In this crucial situation Montcalm and Vaudreuil were opposed on the question of the strategy to be followed in Canada. Montcalm stood for a defensive policy. From the beginning of the campaign it was understood that in order to avoid open disagreement with the governor Bourlamaque 'could talk of sieges and expeditions whenever he considered it advisable to do so but that in reality he would be concerned with our defences.'[172] In September, when he drew up a memorandum that began by defining principles, Montcalm's tone was more serious. As he saw the situation, 'small measures, small ideas' had become 'dangerous'; military ideas until then held in honour in Canada—'principles native to the soil'—were now 'errors'. What then did Montcalm recommend? 'Radical measures, measures that would be decisive.' These were the 'radical measures' he proposed: to incorporate fifteen Canadian militiamen into each company of 'land' troops; to form marine companies of equal numbers of militia and regulars; to re-establish the French fleet on Lake Ontario and to create one on Lake Champlain; and to start immediately to strengthen Quebec's fortifications.[173] Another idea expressed more than once in Montcalm's diary was that of abandoning the far posts. As early as 1757, for example, he would have recommended 'blowing up Fort Du Quesne, regarding Niagara as the barrier in that part of the country and thus drawing [the colony's] defences in towards the centre.'[174] Basically, Montcalm's two ideas were to incorporate the Canadians into the French troops and thus bring them directly under his command, and to reduce the perimeter to be defended. Vaudreuil could not accept the first of these ideas, in which he saw nothing but a 'desire . . . to dominate the colonials.'[175] As for the defence of the west, Vaudreuil's plan was certainly to 're-establish' the fleet on Lake Ontario and to hold Niagara, but it was also to refortify Frontenac and prevent the enemy from getting a footing again at Oswego. His objective was to maintain communication between Niagara and Montreal; for if Niagara were isolated, 'limited, for defence, to its garrison . . . it could not fail to be taken if the English besieged it.'[176] The governor defined his position quite clearly in a letter to the minister of marine: 'It is in the true and fundamental interest of the colony that I devote my main effort to defending the soil of our frontiers foot by foot against the enemy, whereas M. de Montcalm and the land troops seek only to preserve their reputation and would like to return to France without having suffered a single defeat.'[177]

Whatever the system of defence adopted, Canada could not do without help from France. In order to obtain this help Vaudreuil dispatched Brevet-Major Péan to Versailles. He also authorized Bougainville and Doreil, the messengers favoured by Montcalm, to set out on the same errand. In France, Péan made no impression on Berryer, who refused to listen to him, while Bougainville had some success. Not that the sheaf of memoranda he deposited with the ministers of marine and war persuaded the government to send any considerable reinforcements to Canada, but he was well received, Berryer lent a sympathetic ear to his stories against Vaudreuil, he obtained promotions and decorations for himself, for Montcalm, and for Montcalm's protégés, and, still more important, he succeeded in having the French general placed in command over the Canadian governor.[178] One can picture the new commander-in-chief strutting about the following spring when Bougainville came back from France laden with favours, letters of praise, and congratulations. Montcalm had become the darling of the court, his victory at Carillon was lauded to the skies, archbishops and bishops— on orders from the king—spread the news in their pastoral letters that 'with 4,000 Frenchmen' he had 'defeated 20,000 men.'[179] Best of all, he alone 'was named' in the news (in other words, Vaudreuil was not mentioned). He felt famous and powerful: 'I may not look like the man of the hour in Canada, but that is what I look like in Paris.' He had assumed the role of dispenser of the king's favours: 'You have only to tell me, sir, what you want me to ask for.' In a word, 'the ambassadors', Doreil and Bougainville, had 'done well.'[180]

They had done well for Montcalm but obtained nothing for Canada. When Bougainville arrived in Paris, 20 December 1758, the minister of marine had apparently already laid down the line of conduct he meant to pursue with respect to the far-off colony. Berryer would present his views to the king's council and they would be adopted at the historical meeting of 28 December. The deliberations of the council are reported in a document bearing that date.[181] The council first noted that in order to provide the help Canada required, it would have to dispose 'for that one object of the whole united strength of the king's navy.' That, they reflected, would mean 'risking his Majesty's entire navy without any certainty of success' and leaving the coasts of France exposed to British raids.

What measures could be taken then? The council could order Vaudreuil to remain on the defensive, to continue to resist the enemy as long as it was possible to do so, but 'to limit his defence strictly to the territory that in his judgement could be held with the troops available to him.' That meant: to evacuate the Ohio country, the Ontario and even the Lake Champlain forts, to mass his military strength on the St Lawrence—if one can use the word 'mass' in this context—and to await the invader there. Up to that time British pressure had been directed against the periphery of New France and had been opposed not only by forts and garrisons, but by natural obstacles, including vast tracts of country where troops were constantly exposed to the danger of ambushes. The new strategy would make it possible for the enemy to advance straight into the heart of the country—a great improvement!

There was always the danger, as the report went on to observe, that the enemy, 'meeting no opposition either on the Ohio or on Lake Ontario or Lake Champlain', might invade Canada with an army so superior in numbers that resistance would be impossible. In that event, would it not be wise to indicate to Vaudreuil when and how he should capitulate—of course after having been 'reduced to the utmost extremity'? The instructions to be followed in such a situation would be unequivocal: 'It does not appear that we should suggest in any way to M. de Vaudreuil conditions of surrender in case he were reduced to the last extremity and forced to capitulate, for in such a case the colony could only submit to the law of the victor.'

The order, then, would be to fight to the finish. And the reason for this order? Could it be the hope of defeating the English? Obviously not. But here considerations of 'general policy' come into play. The day would come when France would be negotiating terms of peace with Great Britain, and it would be easier to obtain the restitution of Canada if France still had 'a foothold' there. Moreover, if the peace terms forced Louis xv to give up the colony he would obtain better conditions for France if he were abandoning to the enemy a country still partially occupied, rather than one that had been evacuated. That meant that in the situation being envisaged Canada would have suffered and fought 'to the last extremity' in order to allow France to obtain better terms for herself from a victorious England. In other words, the king's council wanted Canada to persist in its hopeless resistance so that even though the game was lost the diplomats representing France at the peace conference would still hold a trump card that would make it possible for them to keep their losses to a minimum.

These vitally important decisions were to be implemented in the acts, or rather the lack of action, implied in them. In February the minister of marine informed the governor that the court would not send a single warship to the colony; the people of Canada must compensate for the loss of reinforcements that would not be forthcoming by redoubling their own effort. Vaudreuil must call up 'all men fit to bear arms' and leave 'to old men, women, and children the task of carrying on work on the land.'[182] The minister of war instructed Montcalm: 'You must limit your plan of defence to the most vital points and those that are nearest so that, gathered together within a smaller area, you may always be

[230]

in a position to communicate with one another and to help and support one another.'[183] Belle-Isle knew that since Canada was without means of defence the British would seize the opportunity to strike a telling blow. Nevertheless he wrote to Montcalm: 'The memory of what you did last year leads his Majesty to hope that once again you will find means to foil their plans.'[184] Had not the general performed a 'miracle' at Carillon?

Such an attitude of detachment—and here the word must be understood both literally and figuratively—can only be explained by the spirit of anticolonialism then reigning in France. And of all the colonies, Canada was perhaps the object of the most unfavourable publicity. We can disregard Voltaire's comments as those of a man of letters. What was said in the office of the minister of marine—the minister charged with responsibility for the colonies—is more directly relevant. The following reflections appeared, with others, in a memorandum 'delivered by M. de Beaucat' to Berryer: Canada produced only about a million and a half worth of furs a year. What little timber it furnished was 'very oily'; the mother country had to send help to the colony when the crops failed; it was buried in snow for six months of the year; it was infinitely less useful to the navy than Santo-Domingo—'And that,' concluded the memorandum, 'is the prize that has cost France so many men and so much money.'[185]

About the same time a high official of the ministry of marine drew up his own memorandum on the colonies. Its author, the marquis de Capellis, claimed some knowledge of 'the interests of maritime trade.' The chief interest of the ideas he set forth lies in their lack of originality: they could be found in many an article penned by an English journalist. He conceded that Canada possessed immense territory, 'but allow me to remind you that the wealth of princes lies not in the soil of their countries but in the number of their subjects.' A colony 'of modest area' producing exotic foods is to be preferred to 'immense empty spaces'. Moreover a colony that produces only what is produced in the mother country is worthless; in such a case it would be better for the farmer 'to cultivate a field in the kingdom itself than in the New World.' That is why, in his thinking, the Antilles took precedence over Canada. It was true that America was rich in fishing grounds—training grounds for sailors—but it was Newfoundland, not Canada, that attracted fishermen. Hence it followed that Newfoundland and half Santo-Domingo were 'much more valuable' than Canada's vast spaces. The truth was that Canada had actually retarded France's colonial development. For the last ten years the greater share of the funds allotted to the ministry of marine had gone to maintain Canada. Why not abandon the country to England? 'It would be one more cause acting to hasten her ruin by favouring the defection of her colonies in North America; they will soon be richer than Old England and will undoubtedly shake off the yoke of the mother country.'[186]

A former collaborator of La Galissonière, the marquis de Silhouette, who could see nothing more in this complicated reasoning than a search for 'motives with which . . . to colour the abandonment' of Canada, gave evidence of uncommon lucidity in his analysis of the problem confronting the French government: 'The struggle in which England and France are now engaged,' he explained, 'is for preponderance in America.' The attention Britain had devoted to this phase of the conflict, her energetic efforts and the expense she had incurred, proved that in her eyes the 'American system' was superior to the European. And she had good reasons for her opinion. This modern concept was the antithesis of the 'Gothic system', according to which France could 'do without colonies' and needed 'only farm-hands and soldiers.' Look at Russia, said Silhouette. 'There is no dearth of soldiers in Russia—nor of farm-hands, since she exports wheat; and yet Russia receives subsidies from foreign powers, so true is it that the dignity, greatness, and power of a state require something more.' A great modern state needs colonies because it must have wealth in order to supply its necessities, because trade brings wealth, and because the volume of a country's trade is in direct proportion to the dimensions of its colonial base. And, to return to Canada, its great value lies in the fact that it is the keystone of French America. If Canada falls, with it will fall the other 'French colonies, which England will be able to take over without any difficulty once the obstacles, fear of Canada and resistance by Canada, have been removed.'[187]

Capellis represented little France, and Silhouette France the world power. The former reasoned from an outdated notion of the nation-state, the latter from the modern concept. The two schools of thought existed in England too. But there William Pitt, who embodied the idea of England the world power, was in the saddle, stronger than ever with the prestige of the victories of which he was the architect.

Chapter VIII

The Year of Quebec
1759

Such was the course of events: . . . Those who do not go beyond the superficial details of the story can hardly fail to count ours among the disasters to be attributed to fortune; this will not be the case of those who, inspired by an enlightened zeal for the good of the state, penetrate beneath the surface to discover the true causes . . . 'Extrait d'un Journal tenu à l'armée que commandait feu M. de Montcalm, Lieutenant-Général', 1759, *AC*, c 11A, 104:255.

At the end of 1758 French colonial policy was crumbling. If France was striving to find some elegant pretext for abandoning Canada, it was because she knew she was outclassed at sea. That was the fundamental cause of her attitude. It was noted in 1759 that for some time every ship entering a French port had slipped in stealthily. When reinforcements were sent to the colonies still held by France the convoys always sailed at night in order to elude the vigilance of British cruisers. Meanwhile British squadrons 'insulted' the coasts of France at will, burned towns and forts, captured ships right under the guns of fortresses or forced them to run aground on rocky shores. As a consequence France's sea trade was no longer merely 'disrupted', it was 'annihilated'.[1] The country was short of ships, and still more short of sailors. To cite only one case: in mid-December 1758 eight warships and several frigates were moored in the roadstead at Brest, unable to sail for want of crews.[2]

To crown its misfortunes the French navy lacked direction. The secretary of state charged with the important ministry of marine should have been an organizer and a policy-maker. Nicolas Berryer was a policeman who devoted most of his energies to overseeing his subordinates and tracking down 'abuses'. He also applied himself 'especially' to the task of procuring funds for the services he directed and 'preventing any of those funds from being misappropriated as had unfortunately happened too often.' Some French subjects flattered themselves that the minister's concern for such matters would give the navy 'a new form'.[3] In Berryer's hands the navy was soon in very poor form, while he kept an eye on transport charges[4] and an ear open to informers' tales, which he said he was 'glad . . . to receive.' There was no dearth of intriguers who knew his weakness and wanted posts, and who cultivated his good graces by supplying notes for his dossiers.[5] At the same time Berryer himself was busy uncovering scandals. He charged an underling with the task of going through all the Canadian correspondence from 1751 onward in order, as he said, that he might be informed on certain 'affairs relating to the administration' of the colony.[6] The truth was that in anticipation of the loss of New France he was looking for a scapegoat and preparing in advance his case against Bigot.

It was quite true that the 'administration' in Canada needed to be subjected to careful study. But apart from the fact that it was then very late to initiate such a study, the colony had other more urgent needs. Above all it needed soldiers. The minister assigned exactly 356 soldiers for service in Canada, and what soldiers! Thirty deserted before the contingent reached its port of embarkation and of the others forty-two had scabies and three were epileptics.[7] Canada was crying out not only for defenders but for food and munitions; but, although the king was 'perfectly aware' of the situation, Berryer decided to reduce the fleet of transports for Quebec to two frigates equipped as merchantmen and 'four private vessels' loaded with war materials and trading goods. The state did not even assume the risk in case the cargoes were lost. Expenses for the fleet (including the two frigates) would be borne by a syndicate of shipowners who would try to recover their investment by privateering. A convoy with such a history could not be expected to travel far, and this one did not. So much for munitions. As for revictualling the colony, that was a problem for the commissary, Cadet, and his agents in the mother country; it was for them to renew Canada's food supply. The commissariat was no concern of the minister, who washed his hands of any responsibility in the matter. To the governor and the intendant he explained that the war, the risks of a long sea crossing, and the necessity for keeping the naval forces of his majesty united made it impossible for him 'to risk a part of those forces in order to send . . . reinforcements that might not arrive and that could be more usefully employed in . . . expeditions promising prompter and more decisive results.'[8] The excuse he offered Montcalm for sending such inadequate help was that he was prevented by 'circumstances' from doing more 'at a time when the

[234]

strength of the navy was being concentrated so that all sectors might be relieved by one decisive operation.'[9]

It is a most remarkable fact, considering the difficulties and risks involved in an offensive against Quebec and the extreme importance of the objective, that France, although fully informed as to Pitt's intentions,[10] made not the slightest attempt to thwart them.[11] The reason for France's failure to act on the American front was the plan for a 'decisive operation' to which Berryer had alluded. This plan—for an invasion of England—had been favoured at the beginning of the war and revived later with the object of alarming the enemy. It now reappeared once again, and this time it was promoted by Choiseul and adopted. The operation was to be combined with a propaganda campaign designed to influence the opinion of neutral powers. Its objective was not the conquest of the British Isles but, as the minister of marine had said, 'to relieve all parts' of the French empire by striking at the head of the rival empire. What Choiseul and his colleagues hoped to do was to create panic in the enemy camp, to provoke a financial crisis by means of a direct threat to London and England's great seaports. Louis xv would take advantage of the crisis to dictate a treaty whose terms would include the restitution of her colonies to France.[12] In short, since France could not curb Britain's advances in America, she sought to stop her in Europe. Pitt was endeavouring to sap the bases of French greatness by planting a buttress for the British empire—that is for the British economy—in the soil of the New World. After allowing Pitt to choose the field of battle and leaving him in command of it, Choiseul hoped to save everything by deploying his forces in another theatre.

One is astounded at the ignorance and lack of foresight inherent in that extraordinary project. Ignorance first of all of the British empire. That empire was an organic whole, as much alive on its far-flung frontiers as at its centre. Great Britain was not only London, it was not only Britain, but also British America. By the beginning of 1759 the British colonies had mutilated New France. The conquest of Canada, which was to complete the work of destruction, was essentially an American idea; and although advanced British opinion adopted it as a political program, it nonetheless remained American in its conception. It was, moreover, in a certain sense an idea that would be imposed on the mother country by America; for, as facts were to demonstrate quite clearly, the conquest of Canada had two phases: the armed phase, which ended in 1760, was followed by the diplomatic phase, which did not end until 1763. Great Britain—inspired by America—played the leading role in the armed conflict, but it was the idea of empire, an American concept, that proved to be the determining factor in the consummation of the conquest by the cession of New France. In other terms: Pitt could defeat France in

America, whereas Choiseul could not defeat British America in Europe.

One realizes that ignorance was compounded by lack of forethought when one examines the tactics by means of which the French ministers meant to execute their imperfect strategy. Their plan envisaged the concentration in the ports of Normandy and Flanders of two expeditionary forces, 50,000 men in all, one commanded by Soubise and the other by Chevert. These troops would be loaded into a fleet of flat boats, being built with all speed, that would make straight for the coast of England while another body of 20,000 men, in ninety transports convoyed by six ships of the line, would be sent to create a diversion in Scotland and a secondary division would be sent to Ireland to carry out a raid designed to distract attention from the principal offensive. The armies of Soubise and Chevert would be supported by the French squadrons. These would sail from their home ports on the Mediterranean or the Atlantic coast and would assemble at Brest, whence they would be sent out to sweep the Channel and open a passage for the boats carrying troops.[13] It was not long before this plan was bruited abroad.[14] Understandably the people of England were anxious, and Newcastle was panic-stricken. But Pitt kept his head and refused to change his plans for attacking France's American positions. He knew that the enemy could not effect a landing in England;[15] that could be prevented by taking care not to allow the Toulon fleet to effect a junction with the Brest squadron nor the Brest squadron to assemble in the Channel.[16] Moreover, the plan for the proposed operation was based on the false assumption that ships of war could be equated with units in a land army, and transports with baggage and artillery trains. This false analogy vitiated the entire direction of the operation. And finally, how could it be conceived that French fleets that did not measure up to those of the enemy when they had only to fight could reduce those same fleets to impotence when they themselves were hampered by a whole flotilla of small landing craft?[17]

In any case rumours of invasion found credence elsewhere than in England and were echoed even in the forests of America. In the autumn of 1759 a group of Mohawks, emissaries of the English, went to persuade Father Piquet's Indians at La Présentation to abandon the Franco-Canadian cause. They assured them that the Anglo-Americans 'would soon eat the remainder of the French in Canada and all the Indians that adhered to them.' 'Brethren you are deceived,' answered Canada's allies, 'the English cannot eat up the French. . . . Our father Onontio has told us that the English . . . like a thief have stolen Louisbourg and Quebec from the great king while his back was turned and he was looking another way; but now he has turned his face and sees what the English have done he is going into their country with a thousand canoes and all his warriors', resolved to regain possession of his territory as he did 'about ten summers ago' at the peace of Aix-la-Chapelle.[18] While these words were being exchanged the French attempt to invade England had suffered its first setback. The Toulon fleet, commanded by the same La Clue whose expedition against Louisbourg had proved abortive the previous year, succeeded in leading his ships through the Strait of Gibraltar, but only to be defeated on 17 and 18 August by Brodrick and Boscawen off Lagos on the coast of Portugal. As for the Brest fleet, Hawke pounded it to pieces south of Belle-Isle on 25 November. These two disasters cost France some thirty warships and as many frigates, and marked the end of the French navy.

As may be imagined, France's desperate attempt to invade England did not prevent the latter from continuing to perfect her plans for a methodical advance in America. Pitt exposed his intention to Amherst at the end of December 1758. He had decided to attack Quebec. The operation would be entrusted to James Wolfe, who would lead an army of 20,000 men. Amherst himself would direct an expedition that would proceed, either by Lake Champlain and the Richelieu or by the rapids of the St Lawrence, to Montreal and even to Quebec. The ideal would be for him to effect a junction there with Wolfe. This immense pincer movement would be complemented by a thrust on Lake Ontario, where they must rebuild Oswego and capture Niagara in order to 'cut off the communication between Canada and the French settlements to the south'. The general plan would be completed by measures taken with the object of consolidating the British hold on the Ohio valley.[19] Six weeks later the prime minister added a further recommendation. The attacks so far projected affected only Canada and its dependencies, but Louisiana must not be left undisturbed. Since operations on the northern front would of necessity be suspended at the end of autumn, it would be a good idea for the commander-in-chief to co-operate with Vice-Admiral Saunders, in command of the naval force, in a joint attack by land and water against the French settlements on the Mississippi and the Mobile. Such an operation would counteract the influence of the enemy over the southern tribes and 'secure the future safety and tranquillity of his majesty's possessions on that side.'[20] Pitt was thinking of the future and of the peace treaty of which the future still held the secret.

Urgent preoccupations soon brought the prime minister back to more immediate considerations. On 10 March he wrote to Amherst of an anxiety that was worrying him: what if the Canadians had launched a winter attack on Fort Edward, where provisions and equipment for the Richelieu campaign were stored? That would be enough to put an end to the operation of the king's troops in that sector before it had well begun. Great care must therefore be taken to protect Fort Edward. He heartily approved a proposal—put forward by the general himself—that

Amherst 'attempt with the utmost vigour the reduction of Canada.' Whether the French colony were invaded by way of the Richelieu or the St Lawrence rapids, or by both these routes simultaneously 'in order to divide the enemy . . . an irruption once effectually made in whatever part it be, Canada must necessarily fall and with it the French power in North America.'[21] Pitt's objective, which was well known, aroused the British public to enthusiasm. A merchant returning in April to Charleston, South Carolina, reported his impressions of England: 'Mr Pitt reigned the unrivalled darling of the people . . . America and its interest he continues to have as much at heart as ever; and they expect the operations of next summer will, with God's favour, put it out of the power of any of our enemies to disturb us in the possession of the northern continent.'[22] Pownall spoke in the same sense to the legislature of Massachusetts; the British government gave unstintingly to win victory for the cause of its colonies, and the whole nation stood behind the government. The campaign about to begin would be a decisive one.[23] This is no time for pleasure, exhorted a poet, 'when thee and I and all should take up arms.'[24]

The British world was expecting great things. Was it not justified in nourishing the highest hopes after its victories of 1758? As the finishing touch to the last issue of the year, the editor of the *London Magazine* inserted another of those allegorical engravings requiring a paragraph of explanation: 'Time turning a terrestrial globe and pointing to Louisbourg. He shows it to history, who leans on his shoulder writing the great events that have happened. Britannia appears on the other side, well pleased with the labours of History. She is led by Concord, who points upward to the figure of Victory, intimating that Britain will be always successful.'[25] The preface to the volume for the year contained the editor's comment on the months just past: 'At sea we have nothing that dares venture to oppose us, and in America . . . we are masters of the key to the principal French settlement in that part of the world.' It was then not unreasonable 'to hope that before the end of next year we shall be able to destroy that nest of French vipers in Canada.'[26] His optimism had not diminished when a few weeks later he reviewed the successes and failures of the struggle against France and Spain in which Britain had been engaged for the last twenty years.[27]

Meanwhile the European periodicals kept their readers informed on the progress of preparations being made in England's ports for naval expeditions against New France and the French West Indies.[28] At first the French press tried to reassure its readers,[29] but the tone changed with confirmation of the news that twenty warships and sixty transports had sailed from England for New York and the St Lawrence.[30] Preparations were also going forward in the American colonies, where Amherst was making ready for the campaign that would begin as soon as the season was far enough advanced. Although cautious by nature, the commander-in-chief felt confident. 'Il me semble nous avons beau jeu,' he wrote to Ligonier in his halting French.[31] He did not doubt that Quebec would fall. He considered difficulties of navigation in the St Lawrence 'more imaginary than real.' No doubt all the troops, including the militia, assembled to defend Quebec would constitute a 'respectable' army; but if the Canadian forces were massed around Quebec, Montreal would be left unprotected and the fall of one or other of the two cities would be followed by the collapse of the whole country. Thus the conquest of Canada was certain, and the victorious general might be either Amherst or Wolfe.[32] In February Montcalm was anxiously calculating the strength of the enemy forces already in America; he estimated that there were 23,600 regulars and about the same number of provincials as the previous year.[33] The British colonics, however, required some persuading to provide the number of troops requested by Amherst. Massachusetts, the most zealous of all the provinces, agreed to raise 6,500 men; but at the same time it was pointed out that the colony was bearing much more than its share of the common burden and that it had been doing so 'patiently' for years.[34] However such symptoms of incipient war-weariness did not prevent the colonial governments from raising some 21,000 men.[35]

Abandoned by France who, instead of sending them direct aid, had launched on an adventure that would cost her her navy, and threatened by an enemy who now enjoyed the enormous advantage of a springboard for his attacks nearer the heart of the country, the people of Canada had to gather all their forces to meet the invader in desperate combat. But how could weak and exhausted men face fresh troops that were also stronger in numbers? The colony was drained dry. 'Suffering here has reached an extreme point,' wrote Montcalm. 'Peace, or all will go ill. 1759 will be worse than 1758. I do not know what we shall do.'[36] Malartic echoed his words,[37] and a military commissary, Bernier, wrote in the same vein.[38] Famine kept Canada's little army immobilized and Montcalm repeated what he had written a year earlier in a similar situation: 'Lacking provisions, it will be very difficult for us to overcome the enemy in the field.'[39]

In fact the picture was much darker even than in the previous year. In 1758 the king's government had itself undertaken the task of reprovisioning Canada. In 1759 it left this duty to private enterprise. Would private enterprise accept the challenge? It was only too anxious to do so, for though the risks were great, the profits promised to be still greater. Basing their demands on the need to relieve the 'suffering' among the people of the colony and the need to feed the troops, the merchants exacted exorbitant prices from the agents of the commissary-general, Cadet. Commercial houses in Bordeaux carried on a cut-throat campaign to obtain contracts for supplies. Abraham Gradis, for example, was a former partner of Bigot. Some years previously he had decided that the risks of sea transport were too great and had prudently stopped shipping cargoes to Quebec before incurring any loss. The activity of his fellow citizens, who were also his competitors, revived his ambition, and we find him once more engaged in a complicated combination of manoeuvres, the object of which was to carve off a big slice of the Canadian market for himself. Shipowners, following the example set by the merchants, demanded as much as 800 or 1,000 livres a cask in transport charges. The profit was juicy, but what matter? The colony would have something to eat. During the last two weeks in March a convoy of eighteen ships under the command of the famous lieutenant-commander, Kanon—'one of the best of our naval officers'[40]—sailed out of the Gironde and set a course for the St Lawrence. Sixteen of the ships anchored at Quebec on 18 May. Bougainville, returning from France on board the *Chézine*, had preceded them by six days, and other units continued to arrive during the following week.[41] They were ahead of the English.

Kanon's fleet rescued the colony from a desperate situation, but it could not provide abundance. It unloaded the equivalent of eighty days' provisions for the regular army 'at the rate of half a pound of flour and half a pound of pork per head', which, as Bigot observed, was much less than 'the proper ration'. Canada's officials received roughly one-third of the amount they had asked for.[42] The commissary might perhaps have succeeded in doing a little more, reported Lévis, 'but he was hampered by the paucity of means furnished by the minister who considered anything sent to that country as useless.'[43] On his return to France Kanon reported to the minister of marine that Canada's leaders complained of 'the scanty help' they received from the government.[44] Since supplies from France were inadequate, Vaudreuil had to resort to all sorts of expedients in order to provide food for the army. In July and August he sent La Naudière to the government of Trois-Rivières to requisition cattle. His orders were drastic: to take all the oxen except the number needed to draw one plough for every two farms and all the cows that were not 'indispensible'. The governor reminded his emissary of the need for tact and 'gentleness'. It must be made clear to the farmers that the decision had been forced upon the governor and that it had been made in order to maintain an army between them and the English. 'Besides,' Vaudreuil assured him, 'I do not mean to deprive them of the animals I am asking for, but to replace . . . them with the ones we shall requisition in the Montreal district.'[45] The Montreal farmers were rich!

[240]

As in the previous spring, famine was to dictate the first movement of troops, although the operation also figured in a plan of action adopted by Vaudreuil after long and acrimonious discussions with Montcalm. Late in April and early in May 2,500 men were moved to Carillon.[46] The general's fundamental strategy was still the same: to shorten the colony's lines of defence. A letter of 27 February once more recommended it to the governor. The enemy, explained Montcalm, disposed of at least 50,000 men who could converge on the St Lawrence from every side, while Vaudreuil had 'neither the forces nor the means to oppose them.' The Franco-Canadians would therefore have to shorten their lines, hold the most important frontiers, 'and leave the rest to fortune and very small forces.' That meant, in practice, that they would have to withdraw the Ohio garrisons to Presqu'île on the south shore of Lake Erie and eventually to Niagara, to withdraw the partisans operating in Acadia, concentrate their effort on 'preserving the central body of this unhappy colony', and not concern themselves with maintaining garrisons in outlying territories with the idea of holding the latter when peace came to be negotiated.[47]

Vaudreuil shared Montcalm's conviction that a massive attack on all fronts was imminent, but his conception of resistance was quite different from that of the general. He was opposed to the idea of evacuating the Ohio country without fighting; he wanted 'to maintain a diversion there that with a small force would keep a considerable number of the enemy busy', and he was resolved to act on the same principle in Acadia. He conceded that defences at the extremities of the colony must continue to be flexible, but the case of the Lake Ontario forts, where he meant to stand firm to the end, was different. In his opinion a strong post should be built at the head of the St Lawrence rapids near La Présentation, while at the end of the lake Niagara would require reinforcements. 'We must not sacrifice too strong a garrison' at Niagara, argued Montcalm. We should, countered Vaudreuil, make that fort the focal point of our resistance in the west. All the Ohio forces would fall back on it in case of a decisive English advance. In the central region, although he considered that Carillon was most seriously threatened, Montcalm would have liked to station 'the smallest possible garrison' so that it could be easily evacuated. He would have adopted the same tactics in the case of Saint-Frédéric and based his defence on 'good positions' at the head of the Richelieu, near Saint-Jean. The governor, on the contrary, would have preferred to hold Carillon and entrench himself at Saint-Frédéric: 'Unless the English advance on Quebec, I shall not allow Saint-Frédéric to be besieged without opposing the enemy with the strongest force available to me.' As for Quebec, although they must 'play for luck' there,

Montcalm would choose to 'take certain general measures' in advance: close the town, establish batteries, draw up a plan of battle, prepare fireships. These were precisely the measures that were being taken, replied Vaudreuil. He had charged Pontleroy with the duty of 'closing the town', artillery officers would 'work unceasingly at the batteries', constant watch was being kept on the St Lawrence above 'Saint-Barnabé and La Malbaie.'[48]

The governor's decisions were incorporated in a plan drawn up on 1 April. In the Ohio sector Ligneris would remain at Fort Machault to maintain Canada's ascendancy over the Indians of the valley, cover Lake Erie, worry the enemy, and prevent them from marching 'unless with an army.' The defence of Niagara would be assured by the troops at Machault, which would be sent to relieve the fort if it were besieged, by the tribes that were being assembled by the governor's orders at Toronto, and especially by Pouchot, who was about to oversee the finishing touches in the construction of two corvettes at La Présentation and who from there would go on to Niagara with 500 combatants. 'If it had not been for the shortage of food,' wrote Vaudreuil, 'I should have sent a larger number, but of all our enemies famine is the most to be feared.' Vaudreuil intended to send Carillon a first detachment of 2,500 men, including two battalions of regulars. As soon as he had word that the English were on the march or as soon as he knew there were supply ships in the river, this first division would be followed by the regulars stationed in the Montreal and Trois-Rivières districts and by the marine companies. The governor conceded that these movements would leave Quebec exposed, but that could not be avoided. 'I do not suppose,' he reasoned, 'that the English will attempt to march on Quebec, but even if I were convinced that they would, I should not alter my plan for the distribution of our soldiers.' These were his reasons: if the English were allowed to occupy Carillon and Saint-Frédéric, it would be essential to have a 'considerable body' of troops above Saint-Jean to prevent them from advancing by the Richelieu to Montreal, whereas if the two Lake Champlain forts were held until the enemy appeared in the St Lawrence, the main body of troops could be brought back from the lake to Quebec while the small force remaining would hold up the invasion 'successively' at Carillon and Saint-Frédéric. That, said Vaudreuil, 'would give us time to have one or two battles' before Quebec. A single victory would throw the British army on the St Lawrence back into the river, the fleet would sail away, and the French forces would go back to stop the enemy's advance at the head of the Richelieu. In a word, the same professional soldiers would defend both Montreal and Quebec. Around the capital they would have the support of all the country's militia, which Vaudreuil would have assembled there ready for the decisive encounter at the first news of the approach of the British fleet.[49] As the governor repeated early in May, he was not 'losing sight of the defence of Quebec.' In all the parishes along the shores of the St Lawrence below Quebec militia companies were ready to march at the first order, rafts had been built, everything was prepared 'to make our enemies fail.'[50] In his eyes the problem was to save the capital without risking the loss of Montreal.

Conscious that the country was threatened on every side and anxious to take advantage of established strategic positions, Vaudreuil had worked out plans for a balanced defence of which one virtue was that they took into account both the military and political aspects of the situation. He knew that Montcalm was critical of his ideas and it irritated him.[51] Although it may be noted that the two men were not opposed to one another on every point—both recognized the need to 'count on luck' on the Quebec front—they clashed on the basic principles of defence. Who was right? Vaudreuil with his theory of extended lines of defence that could be contracted when the need arose, or Montcalm with his idea of fixed lines and a restricted perimeter? In the light of the experience of recent years and considering the transport problems facing invaders, it was by no means certain that Montcalm's method was the better one.[52] If to these military considerations one adds the fact that Canada, cut off from its dependent territories to the east and west, was torn from the economic frame that assured its continued survival and hence became almost valueless, was it not natural that Canadian policy should aim at preserving, as far as that was possible, the territorial integrity of the country? Montcalm objected that it was useless to cling to the Ohio with the idea of holding it at the peace since, according to him, the European diplomats would create a neutral zone in the Ohio valley. As for Acadia, he was quite sure that the small band of partisans 'wandering in disorder through that part of the country' would not suffice to persuade the governments of the mother countries to fix boundaries to suit the interests of Canada.[53] But after all what did he know about it? What was certain in any case was that even if France won the war, Canada, without Acadia—and certainly Canada without the midwest—would fall automatically. Lévis had come very close to the truth in a statement on the Ohio frontier made at the end of the campaign of 1757: 'We must . . . maintain ourselves there at whatever cost. In the present conjuncture, the salvation of the colony [Canada] and of Louisiana depend upon it.'[54]

As events turned out, Vaudreuil was not given an opportunity to test his strategy in 1759. Bougainville had won over the court, and the minister had placed Montcalm in supreme command. The new commander-in-chief made no change in plans for the western front already adopted before the return of his 'ambassador', but the Richelieu and Quebec campaigns were organized according to his own views.

We have already observed that important naval manoeuvres had played a primary role in the capture of Louisbourg, and the long battle for Quebec that went on throughout the summer of 1759 was essentially of the same nature. It would be impossible to exaggerate the importance of the part played by the British navy in that operation. The fleet commanded by Vice-Admiral Philip Durell had spent the winter in America —as Hardy's had done in 1758—in order to block the estuary of the St Lawrence and intercept relief ships from France. Even this powerful squadron of fourteen warships did not succeed in stopping the French fleet of frigates and transports commanded by Lieutenant Kanon, but it followed them closely and on 22 May came to anchor opposite Bic. Some of the ships then continued on up the river and the fleet was spread out between Bic and the Île-aux-Coudres as it awaited the arrival of Saunders and Wolfe. On 18 June Saunders reached Bic with twenty-two warships and 119 transports, and others followed.[55] On 21 June Montcalm reported that the enemy's fleet had 'been increased by 132 sails',[56] and about the same time its strength was estimated at 164 units.[57] When on 23 June it sailed through the dangerous Île d'Orléans traverse, the components of the armada were counted: twenty-nine ships of the line, twelve frigates and corvettes, two bomb vessels, eighty transports, fifty or sixty smaller craft.[58] It carried some 9,000 soldiers and 30,000 sailors. England was attacking Quebec not so much with an army as with a powerful war fleet and a substantial landing force.[59] Thirty-seven thousand men, equipped with enormous quantities of war material, would be engaged in the operation.

And yet that formidable war machine functioned badly and in relation to its strength gave very poor results. In Wolfe's hands it seemed heavy, slow, awkward. Not that he was too careful of it; on the contrary he pushed it about, forced it, mishandled it. It creaked and balked and came very close to breaking down completely—while the obstacle it might have crushed stood and faced it for months, and finally fell of itself.

Wolfe was a man of violent character. He set out for Quebec breathing fire: 'I own it would give me pleasure,' he wrote, 'to see the Canadian vermin sacked and pillaged and justly repaid their unheard-of cruelty.'[60] From the beginning of the siege he tried to terrorize the Canadian population. He warned them that if, inspired by 'misplaced obstinacy and imprudent valour', they resisted the troops, they must expect to suffer 'the utmost in cruelty that war could offer'; they could imagine the excesses that might result from soldiers' 'unbridled fury'.[61] He carried out his threat so thoroughly that it might have been thought his chief objective was the destruction of the small rural communities of the Quebec government. Orders were given for fires to be set and 'the sides of the river began immediately to present a most dismal appearance of fire and smoke.'[62] 'If we can't beat them, we shall ruin their country,' boasted an English officer.[63] The training Wolfe gave his men in devastating the countryside and ravaging farms created a problem for Murray, who confessed that 'the plundering kind of war which had been carried on this last campaign had so debauched the soldiers that there was no putting a stop to these [disorders] without very severe punishment.'[64] The British gained little from atrocities that only served to strengthen the courage of the Canadians. The victorious enemy, predicted Vaudreuil, 'would completely exterminate everything Canadian' and make of the St Lawrence valley another Acadia.[65] The comparison was truer than at first sight appears.

In response to Vaudreuil's orders to militia captains in the villages, the country people flocked into Quebec. The governor had been quite right to count on the rural population, among whom competition in loyalty was so keen that lads of twelve years of age came to the camp at Beauport to volunteer. French officers made sure the Canadian recruits did not idle; all the 'fatigues' fell to their lots, all 'the most arduous tasks.'[66] 'Half these militiamen are old men or children,' observed Montcalm. They would not make very good soldiers, but they did 'more than could be hoped for.'[67] Wolfe too was astonished: 'Old people of seventy years and boys of fifteen fire at our detachments and kill or wound our men from the edge of the woods. . . . Very little quarter is given on either side.'[68] The English were startled to see this extraordinary army rising out of the ground. 'Almost the whole force of Canada,' according to Governor Sharpe of Maryland, was assembled to defend the capital. 'And therefore,' he added, 'many people look upon the entire reduction of that city this campaign as an event by no means certain.'[69] Before long 15,000 combatants had gathered around their flags to defend Quebec. This legion of the people included an especially significant and moving contingent of 150 Acadians.[70]

The people of Canada were defending their country. By this we must understand that—like any organized human group in the same situation —they were risking their lives not, as conventional declamations suggest, in order to prevent the violation of some stretch of land or water, but in order to remain an organized human group, a society constituted for the purpose of fostering a certain collective life—the communal life that is the condition of individual well-being and self-realization for its members. For some it was a conscious motive, for most a spontaneous feeling. The following are typical examples.

François Daine was a rich bourgeois, a public official who had served the government for forty-four years. In the autumn, after the fall of Quebec and when he saw the inevitable defeat approaching, he asked that if the colony should become an English one, he might be allowed to go to France and complete his career as an administrator.[71] His case was a simple one: there was literally no place in a British community for a member of the aristocracy of politics and finance. After all he could hardly take up farming! The second case is that of Mother Marie-Agathe Le Clerc de Sainte-Marguerite, an Ursuline of forty years' standing who died before the English took over Quebec. An entry in the old Ursuline 'Récit' tells of the circumstances of her death: 'She died gladly, Our Lord having granted her the grace she had prayed for without ceasing and taken her from the world before the loss of the colony.'[72] The prayer was the expression of a natural and spontaneous feeling, obviously shared by the sister who recorded it. The attitude of the official, on the other hand, was dictated by reason. Daine was not alone in thinking as he did; and when everything was over large numbers of persons, reacting in the same way, migrated to the country, where, if they must live outside Canada, it would be least difficult for them to start a new life. The sisters' patriotism, though inspired by loftier motives, was no more profound than that of the government official. The latter knew there was no place for him in the British world. When the land that bore him gave way beneath him, he clutched at another, Canada's mother country. The Ursulines, on the other hand, once assured that the religious life would be possible in Canada, adapted themselves to a British society; after all they no longer belonged, as the rich bourgeois did, to this world. There remained the common people, the workers and fighters. The Canadian people continued to evolve within its political framework as long as the framework lasted. When that gave way the group too began to fall apart.

The forces confronting one another were on the one side a magnificent instrument of conquest and on the other a people mobilized for war (in so far as a people could be mobilized in the middle of the eighteenth century). The manifest inferiority of the Franco-Canadian force was counterbalanced to a certain degree by the nature of the theatre where the action would take place. Both above and below Quebec the left bank of the St Lawrence was extremely difficult of access. Below the town the natural defences were further strengthened by a line of entrenchments on which work had begun during the last week of May, and that stretched from the falls of Montmorency to the town and almost a league up the right bank of the St Charles River. As Vaudreuil had foreseen, they had had a whole month to work on these defences before the arrival of the English, who established their first bridgehead at the upper end of the Île d'Orléans on 27 June.[73] The same day Wolfe examined Montcalm's positions from this vantage point and took note both of their natural strength and of the works constructed by the defenders in their effort to make them 'impenetrable'.[74]

Three days later Monckton landed 3,000 men at Pointe-Lévis. The landing was opposed only by a handful of Canadians led by the seigneur of Beaumont, Jean Charest, who returned to the camp at Beauport a few hours later with some thirty scalps. They had fought well but they could do no more than bait the enemy, who could have been driven back to their boats by a well-organized full-scale resistance. Montcalm, however, preferred to make no move. 'There was some murmuring . . . in the army at this inaction', and there was good reason for it. The heights of Lévis were not without importance. Not only would it be easy to defend them, but English batteries mounted there could pound Quebec. An attempt to stop Monckton could have been made almost without risk, since if the attempt failed the troops who had made it had a safe retreat in the neighbouring woods where, as everyone knew, 'Canadians and Indians have . . . a great advantage over regulars.' Why then did Montcalm allow the English to establish themselves calmly right opposite Quebec? Because he thought the only real threat was to Beauport. Beauport, below the capital, was the pivot of his defence system; and he was afraid that if he left Beauport exposed in order to prevent the enemy from getting a footing at Pointe-Lévis, he would be opening a passage for them along the north shore and risking the loss of Quebec in a single battle. Moreover, he was convinced that Wolfe's army was 20,000 strong, and it took some time for him to be 'disabused' of this notion 'in spite of the most palpable proof.'[75]

He was still not disabused when Wolfe made a second landing. It was carried out during the night of 18-19 July below the Montmorency Falls and to the left of the French lines, and again it was unopposed. This second camp, it is true, was much less important than the first one; but it offered an excellent opportunity, if Montcalm had chosen to take it, for disabling one wing of the army of invasion. Wolfe was guilty of grave imprudence. He himself led the first division of his force to l'Ange-Gardien, and Townshend was to join him with the second. But when Townshend stepped ashore in inky darkness there was no one to guide him to the post where he was to meet his commander. A large part of the equipment lay strewn along the river bank, and Townshend shuddered with apprehension. In the confusion a small band of Indians could have destroyed the baggage and sown panic among the men.[76] The suggestion was in fact made to Vaudreuil: would it not be a good idea to force the English back to the river before they had time to entrench themselves? But the governor, bound by the orders he had received from the court, could make no decision. He could, and did, call a council of war, but the conclusion arrived at was that it was not possible to attack the invading force. The comment of one observer reveals this council as the very model of a deliberative assembly: 'The truth is that M. de Montcalm

References.

1 Small Vessels with Artillery Stores.
2 Sea Horse.
3 Leostoff.
4 Squirrel.
5 Transports with Troops ready for
 Landing after the First Batallion had
 gained the Heights.
6 Buoys that deceived the Enemy and
 to which the Boats moor'd that protected the Fleet from the Rafts of Fire.

British M

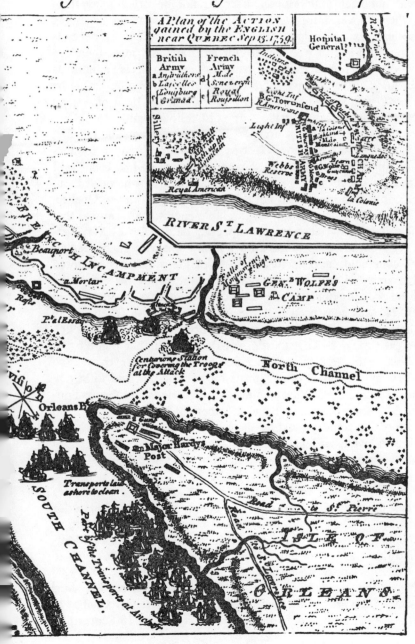

RER ST. LAWRENCE, *from the* Falls *of*
tions of the SIEGE of QUEBEC. 1763.

A Plan of the ACTION
gained by the ENGLISH
near QUEBEC Sep.13.1759.

British Army	French Army
a Anstruthers	Mde
b Lascelles	d Sennezergi
Louisburg	e Royal
Grenad.	Rousillon

Indians

Light Inf
B.G. Townsend
R. Americans

Light Inf

Hospital General

R. St. Charles

Webbs Reserve

Royal American

La Colonie

RIVER ST. LAWRENCE

Beauport ENCAMPMENT

a Mortar

Pt. al Esson

Falls of Montmorenci High

GENL. WOLFE'S CAMP

Centurions Station for Covering the Troops at the Attack

North Channel

Orleans B.

Majr. Hardys Post

Transports laid ashore to clean.

Road to St. Pierre

Part of the Transports at Anchor

SOUTH CHANNEL

ISLE OF

ORLEANS

was not in favour of an attack, and it may be said that having talked privately to the officers before the council he had so to speak disposed them to represent such a course as impracticable.'[77]

These two episodes are typical of the Quebec campaign as a whole. Wolfe could not keep still; Montcalm could not be pried away from Beauport where he was 'intrenched up to the chin.'[78] From the beginning he had espoused one principle: 'The salvation of the colony depends essentially on the issue of one battle. Our constant aim must therefore be not to divide our forces.'[79] But he would avoid that decisive battle as long as he could. 'The Marquis of Montcalm,' wrote Wolfe, 'is at the head of a great number of bad soldiers and I am at the head of a small number of good ones . . . but the wary old fellow avoids an action, doubtful of the behaviour of his army.'[80] Deep down Montcalm felt that he was engaged in a lost cause. It was a situation familiar to him. Throughout almost the whole of his career in Europe he had been fated to participate in events that, through no fault of his own, turned out badly.[81] His apprehensions could not fail to accompany him to Quebec, where he was pitted against a truly formidable enemy. One can see that from the first days of the siege he was expecting defeat. On 31 May, acting on advice from the court[82] and after consultation with his colleagues of the high command, he ordered that most of the provisions be stored at Trois-Rivières and only enough retained in the capital to supply the army and the civilian population for six weeks. Six weeks seemed to him an eternity. He was convinced that the town would have fallen before that and he would have liked to adopt the 'principle that only enough for a fortnight should be kept there.' Not daring to 'flatter himself that he would be able to check the enemy's first movement', he even went so far as to draw up an outline of proposals for capitulation and to have a copy made for Ramezay.[83] What was even more serious was the assumption, which Montcalm shared with the members of his immediate circle, that the fate of the country must be dictated by that of the capital. His emissary, Bougainville, had made this quite clear in Paris: 'Once Quebec is taken we must capitulate for the country at the same time as for the capital city.'[84] Immediately after the battle of 13 September 'diverse officers of the land forces' were heard to say 'out loud in the presence of the soldiers' that there remained no other course than to 'capitulate for the whole colony.' When at the same critical moment Vaudreuil sent, as duty commanded, to ask the advice of the commander-in-chief, Montcalm replied that there were only three possible courses from which to choose: to counter-attack, to retreat, or 'to surrender for the colony.'[85] It was also at this juncture that he addressed to Townshend a short letter of which these are the first words: 'Forced to surrender Quebec to your arms . . .'[86] The surrender that was to be signed on 18 September, and that even then was premature and by no means inevitable, was still five days away.

The capture of Quebec could entail the collapse of the whole colony, but only if one condition were met: only if Wolfe manoeuvred in such a way as to entrap the army assembled east of the town, for that army included the greater part of the country's armed forces. With their overwhelming naval superiority the enemy had a free hand on the river. At the same time the capital could defend itself only so long as it could maintain communication with its sources of supply—the stores of provisions at Trois-Rivières and the crops from the Montreal district. When the English made their appearance towards the end of June, they found the Canadians in arms below Quebec. They could have made a feint against the town and by landing twenty miles above the capital closed a trap on the army that Montcalm had fixed at Beauport. Why they did not do so is, as has been justly said, 'a mystery'.[87] A victory won in those conditions would have delivered an army into their hands instead of a town in ruins. But rather than attempt that operation, Wolfe first established himself on the south shore of the St Lawrence. When he did decide to cross to the north shore he chose a landing place below the town at the far end of the Franco-Canadian line; and when, on 31 July, he launched an attack, his troops were repulsed by Lévis with heavy losses. He then spent the month of August doing nothing.

For from the military point of view, sacking and burning villages may be counted as nothing, and the heavy bombardment to which Quebec was subjected was not much more effective. Certainly the population did suffer. The first British projectiles, which fell on the city in the evening of 12 July, filled them with 'terror'. A witness has left a picture of 'large numbers of women with their children near the citadel, weeping, lamenting, and praying . . . gathering in groups to recite rosaries.'[88] For two months the bombardment went on: bombs, cannon-balls, shells, firebombs fell on the town. Montcalm might have repeated the words he had used twenty-five years earlier to describe Philipsburg, pulverized by French artillery. Quebec now was '*en cannelle*'.[89] A British dispatch dated 10 August reported that Quebec was in ruins: 'We have expended three times the ammunition already as we did the whole siege of Louisbourg.'[90] Another news item, sent to Boston after the siege, described conditions in the town: 535 houses had been burned and those that had escaped had had their walls and roofs damaged by cannon-balls. Malartic confirmed the enemy's estimate of damage: 'Not a single house without a hole in it.'[91] The fate of the neighbouring hamlets, as described in an English chronicle of events, was no better than that of the capital: 'Masters of a great part of their country, [we] burned upwards of 1,400 of their farmhouses . . . This has . . . hurt the enemy greatly, and will take a long time, half a century, to recover.'[92] Pontbriand reported that the farms were wiped out: 'the poor farmer' and his family, returning to their concession, were reduced to 'living in a hut, like Indians.'[93] Bigot's comment was brief: 'M. Wolfe is cruel.'[94] And as one English officer realized, his cruelty was gratuitous. 'We frequently set their town on fire . . . but I can't learn that we hurt their batteries, and therefore individuals suffer more than the common cause, and indeed I fear the campaign will end so.'[95]

Everything pointed to the same conclusion: Wolfe was accomplishing nothing. In a letter of 6 September Townshend confided to his wife his opinion that Wolfe's tactics were no better than his health, which was bad. Until the end of August, he added, the general had not consulted his senior officers.[96] He was referring to the fact that a few days before the letter was written, Wolfe had submitted to him, as well as to Monckton and Murray, three different plans of attack against Beauport. The officers, judging them at their true value, rejected all three and recommended instead the plan dictated by every consideration of common sense: to 'carry the operations above the town.' They then presented their reasons in simple and rational terms: 'If we can establish ourselves on the north shore the marquis de Montcalm must fight us on our own terms, we are between him and his provisions, and between him and the army opposing General Amherst [on the Richelieu]. If he gives battle and we defeat him, Quebec and probably all Canada will be our own, which is beyond any advantage we can expect by the Beauport side.'[97] Although weariness appeared to be influencing him in that direction, Wolfe refused to take the advice of his subordinates. His inclination was rather to adopt the fantastic idea of an immediate direct assault on the lower town. It took all the authority of Patrick Mackellar, the best British engineer of the war, to dissuade him from this rash course of action.[98] Only after further discussion with his officers in the first days of September did Wolfe finally decide to initiate an operation above Quebec.[99] On 3 September the British army evacuated the position east of Montmorency that it had occupied for two months. Montcalm allowed it to leave, as it had arrived, without hindrance. A British officer with a sense of humour acknowledged the 'generosity' shown by the French general in this 'particular and critical juncture.'[100] In the French camp many persons judged this generosity 'severely'—many, but not all, for the marquis had his train of flatterers who continued to repeat that he had 'conducted himself like a consummate general.' As to that, 'the reader can judge,' said a laconic chronicler.[101] On 9 September Wolfe announced that he would be guided by the 'unanimous' opinion of his officers, although it was obvious that he expected no good to come of such a course. He wrote in despondent vein to the secretary of state for the department of the North: 'My constitution is entirely ruined without the consolation of having done any considerable service to the state or without any prospect of it.'[102] When it became known in London, Wolfe's pessimistic view of the situation at Quebec created fears of an imminent British reverse.[103] Was Wolfe then going to follow his officers' advice and give orders for a landing at Pointe-aux-Trembles? No; on 10 September it was decided that the troops would land at the Foulon,[104] and Vice-Admiral Holmes doubtless weighed the words of the comment he wrote a week later: 'This alteration of the plan of operation was not, I believe, approved by many beside himself.'[105]

The thirteenth of September should be known as the day of errors. Wolfe owed his qualified success to the fact that Montcalm made as many mistakes as did his adversary. As Murray later admitted, the British victory came as a surprise: 'The fact is we were surprised into a victory which cost the conquered very little indeed.'[106] Wolfe's troops did not have to land at l'Anse au Foulon; the idea that it was the only possible landing place is pure legend.[107] Murray never forgave Wolfe his 'desertion of the sensible, well-concerted enterprise to land at the Pointe-aux-Trembles where without opposition, with his whole army and artillery, he might have taken post and entrenched himself betwixt the enemy and their provisions [for] the almost impossible, though successful attempt, thanks to Providence, at the Foulon.'[108] The general had taken the crazy risk of challenging a stronger enemy without assuring an avenue of retreat for his own forces; if he had lost the battle, his army would have been annihilated. And in that mad adventure he risked the lives of 4,800 men.[109] Most surprising of all is the fact that he took the risk in the full consciousness of what he was doing. These are the words he addressed to his troops before the battle: 'I have led you up to these steep and dangerous rocks, only solicitous to show you the foe within your reach. The impossibility of a retreat makes no difference in the situation of men resolved to conquer or die.'[110] Vaudreuil judged the situation accurately: 'Although the enemy had forestalled us, his position was very critical.'[111]

Fortunately for Wolfe, Montcalm played the same sort of game. His fixed idea was to prevent access to Beauport. When Vaudreuil expressed the fear that the English might take advantage of a dark night to land at l'Anse des Mères—near the Foulon—he received the insolently noble reply: 'Only God, sir, can do the impossible . . . and we cannot believe the enemy have wings that would allow them in one night to cross water, land, climb rugged slopes, and scale walls; especially since for this last operation ladders are required.'[112] When the governor pressed his point, he was told to send 100 militiamen to l'Anse des Mères: 'I assure you that 100 men posted there would give us time:

we could wait for daylight and march there by our right.'[113] Send more men? There were 'far too many' there already; a simple observation party was all that was required. 'By day we shall see the enemy coming . . . and they will not attempt an impassable road by night.' The point of danger lay between Beauport and the St Charles River. '[We must be sure] that Wolfe's object is not, by causing us to worry about our right and left flanks, to get us out of position and launch his own assault on the part of the line between Beauport and the St Charles River. So let us not be misled into overdoing our defence.'[114] An entry in Malartic's *Journal* for 2 September reveals his doubt that the English would ever attack at Beauport: 'It is not clear that they are aiming at that point, and we are not giving enough thought to others.'[115] The same day Montcalm wrote to Bourlamaque: 'I believe Wolfe will be like a man in a gaming house, first playing the left side of the board [Montmorency], then the right [Pointe-aux-Trembles], then placing his final bet between the two [Beauport].'[116] He was quite lost; as he confessed a few days later he could not make out the enemy's manoeuvres.[117] He was still convinced on one point, however: Vaudreuil should not get excited. 'The governor,' he explained, 'is more apprehensive than I for our right'[118]— the Foulon was on the right. Two days after the foregoing words were written, a French deserter informed the invaders that Montcalm thought the 'flower' of the British army was still below the town and that he could not be 'prevailed upon to quit his position' at Beauport.[119] He mistook the feints being carried out by the British ships for the main operation and the main movement for a feint.[120]

The morning of 13 September saw the English troops drawn up in order of battle near the capital. But 5,000 soldiers could not cross the river and land without making any noise, and in fact about one o'clock in the morning 'a great noise of barges' had been heard. There was no need to ask where they were going; where else than Beauport would they go? So the regiments were called out to line the entrenchments of Beauport. About three o'clock Quebec gave 'the signal agreed upon to indicate that something had passed.' The warning was shrugged off. Those people in the town were a nuisance with their signals! At daybreak, as all was 'quiet' in the Beauport sector, the soldiers could be sent off to get their sleep. This was about to be done when a Canadian appeared, completely out of breath and showing 'every sign of absolute terror.' He had a wild tale to tell: the English had surprised the Foulon post and had an army deployed on the heights. Really! 'We knew so well how difficult it would be to penetrate our lines at that point—if it was defended—that we did not believe a word of the man's story; we thought he had been driven out of his senses by fear.'[121] When finally

[254]

their eyes were opened to the facts, they had to come out from behind their useless entrenchments and make all haste to meet the enemy on an open field.

Montcalm marched out some 3,500 men from the camp and lined them up between Quebec and the 'thin red line'[122] of the British army. All was not lost if the game were played well. Bougainville was behind the invading army with his corps of picked troops. Vaudreuil was bringing up reinforcements. The town was defended by a garrison and by cannon. By waiting two or three hours Montcalm would have had at his command almost 10,000 men with strong artillery support. Co-ordinating his movements with Bougainville's he could have caught Wolfe between two fires and cut his lines to pieces. Instead, about ten o'clock he appeared before his troops mounted on a spirited horse and with his unsheathed sword in his hand. 'Thinking he could win the victory alone',[123] he gave the order to advance and his army rushed forward in a blind, disorderly charge. The British regiments responded to their orders with mechanical precision, and fifteen minutes later everything was over. The French battalions, gripped by 'a terror without equal', scattered in hopeless disorder.[124] But only the regulars were completely routed; the Canadians, trained to turn suddenly 'in the manner of the ancient Parthians' and attack the foremost units of a pursuing force, slowed down the British considerably and prevented the victors from entering the city on the heels of the fleeing regulars. One militia regiment, covered by the woods to the west of the Saint-Jean gate, raked the ranks of a highland regiment with devastating effect. Holmes attributed most of the British losses to this 'hidden rascally fire'.[125]

What might have been a great victory thus became a defeat for which in our own day a writer has offered the following explanation: 'The gods turned right about; after having flown in the face of probability and almost saved the French cause, they were led by an equally unpredictable whim to ruin it in a single swift encounter.'[126] To such lunatic conclusions does facile writing entice us. What gods were these? Given the conditions in which the battle was engaged, there was nothing unpredictable in its outcome. 'Would to God,' exclaimed Foligné, 'that he [Montcalm] had awaited the arrival of M. Bougainville . . . It is the opinion of everybody that not a single Englishman would have got back to his boat.' He was right, and most of his contemporaries shared his opinion. 'Never,' wrote one of them, 'was a situation more favourable, never were so many errors committed in one day.'[127] Even one of the general's defenders added his word: 'Although I looked upon M. de Montcalm as too brilliant for me to dare to offer him advice, I did however take the liberty of saying to him, before he had given the order for battle, that considering the limited number of his troops he was not in a position to attack the enemy.'[128] Montcalm's haste on this occasion is reminiscent of Abercromby's at Carillon fifteen months earlier. How can it be explained? By the fear that Wolfe might be given a chance to 'entrench himself',[129] a fear for which, as was noted at the time, there was 'no semblance of foundation.'[130] Lévis made the same observation in May 1760, when he laid siege to Quebec. The terrain occupied by the British army was not suitable for entrenchments.[131] Moreover, an army could not establish respectable positions in two or three hours. This was particularly true in this instance when the soldiers, constantly harried by 1,500 irregulars, had to keep lying down to avoid their deadly fire.[132] Lévis was the best soldier of the French army in America. What opinion did he express? Speaking in measured terms, he vouched for his superior officer's good 'intentions', and reported Montcalm's belief that he could 'do no better.' That was in an official letter.[133] A private letter added significant advice to a friend: 'Since there is some truth in all the arguments that are being repeated, the only answer I can give you is to show things as much as possible from the good side.'[134] This is obviously what he did himself; but history is not bound to imitate him, and the best workers in the historical field have felt obliged to point out the 'strange' nature of the costly errors committed by the defeated general.[135]

Even when the battle was over the list of errors was not complete. Wolfe's victory was no more than a partial success, since the English had captured neither the gates of Quebec nor the army defending the city. The Franco-Canadians had lost a battle but they were not vanquished. The greater part of their army, including Bougainville's élite corps, had not even taken part in the combat. The last thing that should have been expected was to see these troops, still fresh, run like hares before the English—who made no move until 18 September. And yet that is what happened. Not that it was Vaudreuil's wish. He called a council of war, which met in the afternoon of 13 September, and proposed that they attack Townshend's army at dawn the following day. But none of the colonels would follow him. The French officers had only one desire: to withdraw beyond the Jacques-Cartier River, thirty-two miles above the town.[136] The governor no longer had any authority. By 'remarks . . . spread abroad not altogether unintentionally', Montcalm had caused him to lose 'the confidence of the soldiers, the people, and even the savages.'[137] Faced with the opposition of the colonels, Vaudreuil realized that he could not 'compromise the colony' by leading them into battle against their will.[138] He followed the army to avoid being forced to sign a general surrender, but he recalled Lévis from the Montreal front, and Lévis, taking over the command that had been Montcalm's, ordered the troops to return to Quebec so that an effort might be made to save the capital. The attempt, which would probably have succeeded, was fore-stalled by Ramezay's surrender on 18 September.[139] This precipitate act was a godsend for the enemy, as Townshend was the first to recognize. In an order for the day he directed the soldiers' attention to the fact that the 'early submission' of the capital had 'spared the troops much fatigue and perhaps illness.'[140] A month later a news dispatch from London con-ceded that the victory of 13 September was by no means decisive. When Ramezay offered to surrender, continued the journalist, 'we had not yet mounted a single battery and our trench works were hardly begun.'[141] The official French version of the capitulation published in Paris tended to minimize the scope of the disaster: 'The English hold no more than the ruins of Quebec; only four houses remain standing in the town.'[142]

This version of the situation might be defended if the fall of the capital were an isolated event. Wolfe, as we know, had a chance to break Cana-dian resistance on the St Lawrence; he let it pass. On the other hand, when Montcalm was offered an altogether unhoped-for opportunity to destroy the splendid British war machine, he did not grasp it. But these were, after all, only episodes in the drama of 1759. There were many others: some military, the most important of quite a different order.

The Lake Ontario and Lake Champlain campaigns were being carried on at the same time as the Quebec one, and were not without their effect upon it. The Lake Ontario front was divided into two sectors, of which the western one seemed likely at one time to be extended to the Ohio. In the spring Bouquet had doubts about the 'new fort of Pittsburgh'; it was neither big enough nor strong enough to withstand the artillery that the Canadians could bring down from Fort Machault, and it was surrounded by tribes whose hostility towards the English was being suc-cessfully fostered by French diplomacy.[143] An Indian raid in the neigh-bourhood of Loyalhanna gave further cause for worry.[144] But Amherst decided that Pittsburgh must be defended against the attack that was even then being contemplated by the Canadians.[145] Early in July Ligneris was at Fort Machault with 700 whites and 400 Indians. These were joined, between 9 and 11 July, by 500 more Indians. Judging that his expeditionary force was now ready to move down the Rivière aux Boeufs, Ligneris called a grand council on 13 July and urged the Indians to follow his troops the next day. The council was still deliberating when couriers arrived with a message from Pouchot: Niagara had been under siege since 6 July and Pouchot asked Ligneris to bring up his forces to relieve it.[146] So the order was given to set out at once for Niagara. The British offensive on Lake Ontario had helped to save Pittsburgh.[147]

The French could not say as much of the relief expedition commanded by Ligneris. On 24 July the contingent was cut to pieces by Johnson's troops, and the following day Niagara changed hands.[148] When the 640 soldiers making up the garrison arrived as prisoners in New York, one witness of their arrival was surprised to see them looking so well: 'The officers and men in general . . . don't appear as if they had fed for some time on horse-flesh.'[149] But the defending troops had not spared themselves, and the English conceded that they had fought 'bravely'.[150] Pouchot and his men had held out for three weeks against an extremely violent bombardment that destroyed one of the bastions, opened a large breach in the wall, and decimated the garrison. The value of the stake may be judged by the force of the attack and the energy with which it was resisted. For Canada, the loss of Niagara meant the loss not only of all the upper country but of one of the bulwarks of Montreal. It is therefore easy to conceive the 'sensation' created in the colony by this disaster.[151] To reinforce the defences of the upper St Lawrence was a matter of the utmost urgency. The general staff decided to dispatch Lévis with 800 men to that theatre. Lévis left Quebec in all haste during the night of 9 August and, travelling 'like a cat on hot coals',[152] reached Montreal the evening of 11 August.[153] The defence of the capital was weakened by his departure: it has been conjectured that if Montcalm had had Lévis at his side during the early days of September, events might have taken a very different turn.[154] For New York, on the contrary, planting the British flag at Niagara meant acquiring two inseparable elements of power: an immense trading territory and a vast network of Indian alliances. Johnson considered Niagara infinitely more important than Oswego. In Oswego the English could count on trade with the Iroquois and on their fidelity; in Niagara the French reigned over the great western tribes, compared to which the six nations were a mere handful of men. People talked of the Oswego trade; it was nothing in comparison with the trade that was carried on at Niagara. How had the first of these trading posts been built up? In great part by illicit exchanges with Canadian middlemen. These latter bartered with the Indians they attracted to Niagara goods they had themselves procured in Oswego, so it was they who realized the big profits. This was the gist of Johnson's report to the Board of Trade; these were his reasons for recommending so warmly that their objective be the conquest of Niagara rather than the reconstruction of Oswego.[155]

Amherst considered that both objectives should be retained. Economic and strategic motives pointed to the capture of Niagara, military considerations of immediate urgency demanded that Oswego be rebuilt. While Johnson and Prideaux besieged Niagara—Prideaux was killed during the siege—Haldimand got a footing at Oswego. La Corne set out with a force from the rapids in an attempt to dislodge him, but was himself repulsed. Now the whole of Lake Ontario was in the hands of the

English.[156] The back of New France was broken. The post at La Présentation was the only obstacle blocking the enemy's path from the outlet of the lake to Montreal. La Corne, who was in command of the post, considered the position a poor one to defend and its defence force no better as fighters. If the enemy advanced on the post he could only 'withdraw to Côteau du lac', and since Côteau was 'the entrance to the first habitations in the colony, the post was regarded as lost if the enemy reached it.'[157] This was the situation that dictated Lévis's mission to that point on the frontier. The situation was rendered still more critical by the fact that the Franco-Canadians had to rely almost entirely on their own resources, since their most dependable allies had become detached from them early in July: 'Our settlement [Indians],' mourned Rigaud, 'seem no longer willing to rise to the bait.'[158] Lévis quickly realized that La Présentation could not withstand a determined British attack. Towards the end of August he set about building a fort to bear his name at Île-aux-Galops, below Father Picquet's mission, and the precaution was by no means excessive. On three different occasions Gage, who had been in command of the Oswego campaign since the death of Prideaux, was ordered by Amherst to drive the Canadians away from the rapids and to establish himself there. To the annoyance of the commander-in-chief,[159] Gage objected each time that he had neither the men nor the time to undertake an expedition of such scope.

Meanwhile what did Amherst himself do? Matching prudence with deliberate action, he captured two ruined forts on Lake Champlain. Ahead of him, quite close but always out of reach, was Bourlamaque with an ill-disciplined army whose effectiveness was still further diminished by the fact that it was fighting a retreating action. To keep his corps of 3,000 men intact and to keep it between Amherst and Montreal —such was the task with which Bourlamaque had been charged by Montcalm. His orders were to withdraw slowly, not to allow his forces to suffer any loss, to abandon Carillon and Saint-Frédéric successively as each of these forts was threatened with encirclement, and to fall back on Île-aux-Noix. There, entrenched in positions that could be easily defended, he must call on all his resources to block the English advance, for once they had passed this post 'there was nothing that could stop the enemy and prevent them from penetrating into the interior of the government of Montreal.'[160] Executing this plan, Bourlamaque evacuated Carillon when Amherst appeared; the rear-guard that he had left in the fort lit the fuses to blow it up and withdrew in the evening of 27 July. The movement was carried out 'in such disorder that twenty soldiers were left behind, prevented by drunkenness from following the troops.'[161] On 31 July Saint-Frédéric was blown up in its turn. The fort that since 1731 had been 'the terror of the northern colonies'[162] fell, without striking a blow, into the

British empire. Amherst was a builder. He repaired Carillon (now Ticonderoga) with care. Beside the dismantled walls of Saint-Frédéric he built Crown Point. Since the Canadans had a navy on Lake Champlain, he built a better one. While these tasks were being performed time passed, and when the British commander was ready to make his assault on the defences of Île-aux-Noix the season was so far advanced that he scarcely had time to sound them out. Astonished at having held off an army three times as strong as his own, Bourlamaque wondered how his adversary would 'save his head', for he had conducted 'a stupid campaign'.[163]

Not only did Amherst save his head; he was promoted and showered with praise.[164] The governor of Massachusetts expressed 'the country's gratitude' to him; the commander-in-chief had assured the future of Americans and set the British empire in America on a firm and lasting base.[165] It was a fact that the autumn of 1759 saw the history of the New World launched on a course that would not be changed. The future would no doubt be more complicated than was foreseen, but the essential foundation was laid. America would be British—not necessarily English, but necessarily not French. Canada must give up her hold on the continent. Before the campaign was over, British colonization was spreading out into the territories that British arms had opened to it. Amherst's decision to build a strong fort at Crown Point was not dictated by military necessity alone. He assured the lieutenant-governor of New York that the fort would effectively protect the whole surrounding country. At the same time he suggested that settlers who had been driven from their holdings by fear of the Indians should be urged to return to settlements they had abandoned, and even to found new townships.[166] The reason for his bitter regret that Gage's offensive had for the moment stopped short of La Présentation was that the threat presented by a Canadian post so close to the north shore of the Mohawk made it impossible for New Yorkers to settle there without risk. They would be able to do so eventually, however, and meanwhile they gave evidence of the vitality of their colonizing spirit by flocking to the country between Fort Edward and Lake George.[167]

Amherst's victories, though unspectacular, were important, the more so since they formed links in a chain of triumphs. When Britons spoke of these triumphs, the word 'marvellous' came spontaneously to their lips. For them 1759 was an *annus mirabilis*, as bulletins followed one another announcing victory in all parts of the world. From America came dispatches reporting in turn the capture of Guadeloupe, Marie-Galante, Carillon, Niagara, Quebec; from India news of the defence of Madras and the capture of Surat; from Europe the story of the 'Marathon of Minden' that saved Hanover.[168] An orator in New London quoted scripture: 'This was the Lord's doing, and it is marvellous in our eyes.'[169] A journalist in London hailed the feats of the year just ended: 'We have now finished the happy and wonderful year 1759—a year as glorious as ever appeared, even in the glorious annals of this nation . . . for the glory of Great Britain may now be justly said to extend from the southern to the northern pole—from the rising to the setting sun.'[170] Fortune 'accompanies our generals,' said Washington.[171] This was the comment of a soldier in whom the great statesman had not yet been revealed. A Boston minister, Samuel Cooper, was more far-seeing. For him these victories were not simply feats of arms; they gave promise that the enemy of British American 'liberties' and 'development' would be removed. His imagination conjured up scenes of happiness founded on the hope of a stable and lasting peace on this good earth—of growing towns and expanding trade, of British settlements, freed from any fear of attack, spreading out on every side and transforming deserts into fertile fields.[172] The minister was right: the victory was a victory for British colonization.

Songs of victory echoed throughout the British empire. Britons rejoiced at the fall of Niagara,[173] but it was the capture of Quebec that carried them to the heights of enthusiasm and to the most extravagant expressions of joy. The case of the young Scottish officer who in September 1759 made the following admission in a letter to Bougainville was certainly an isolated one: 'Mon cher confrère, Je suis du même opinion que Volontaire [sic] dans Candide que nous faisons la guerre pour quelques arpents de neige dans ce pays.'[174] French culture had obviously left its mark on him; he was quite out of tune with the feelings of the British court and people. The Russian ambassador to the court of St James's was at a loss for words 'to describe the joy and general enthusiasm' inspired by the capture of Quebec. He added, doubtless echoing what was being said around him, that 'it would decide once and for all the American question that has been the cause and origin of this bloody war.'[175] Cannon in Hyde Park and at the Tower of London gave the signal for bonfires and fireworks; the whole United Kingdom followed the example set by its capital city,[176] and the king declared 29 November a day of thanksgiving.[177] One London journalist felt overwhelmed by 'so stupendous a blessing of Providence' as the conquest of Quebec; it would take time for him to become accustomed to the idea.[178] In a speech couched in a style even more grandiloquent than was his wont, Pitt lamented the death of the victorious young general at the height of his glory. The prime minister, wrote Walpole, 'speaking in a low and plaintive voice, pronounced a kind of funeral oration.' The speech, although it suggested that Mr Pitt had done more for Great Britain than any orator for Rome, 'was perhaps the worst harangue he ever uttered',[179] but it created the Wolfe legend. The people of England were transported with admiration and enthusiasm. 'Carthage may boast of her Hannibal,' proclaimed the *Monitor*, 'and Rome may decree triumphs to her Scipio, but true courage never appeared more glorious than in the death of the British Wolfe.'[180] 'Who,' asked another admirer, 'wrote, like Caesar, from before Quebec? —Who, like Epaminondas, died in glory? . . . Who bequeathed Canada as a triumphant legacy?—Proclaim—'Twas WOLFE.'[181] Wolfe would forever be named *'The Conqueror of Canada'*.[182] Rejoicing was at least as fervent in the colonies as in the mother country. In Boston 'the general joy which appeared on this occasion was perhaps as great as ever known.'[183] New Yorkers, for whom 'the consequences of such a victory' were happy 'in an especial manner', were delirious with joy.[184] Once again the words of Samuel Cooper speaking from the pulpit struck a deeper note: 'God has heard our prayers and those of our progenitors— We behold the day which they desired to see, but saw it not—We have received a salvation from Heaven greater perhaps than any since the foundation of the country—The power of Canada is broken.'[185]

At the end of 1759 Canada was no more than a shadow of itself. The deluge had passed, leaving in its wake only a broken stump of country along the St Lawrence between the rapids and the Jacques-Cartier River. Although the 'residue' of military forces holding out inside a circle of ruins could still surprise the victors, in the field of imperial strategy France and Britain judged correctly when they wrote off Canada as a French colony.[186] Its final destruction, as Amherst concluded after a conversation with Major Grant in New York, could not be delayed more than a few months. Grant was more familiar with conditions in Canada than any other Englishman in America. Taken prisoner in 1758 near Fort Du Quesne, he had had occasion to observe the enemy at first hand and to talk frequently to their officers. At the request of his commander-in-chief he wrote a report on what he had learned. The Canadians, according to this report, were all 'heartily tired' of the war. Those for whom the war had been an opportunity to amass great fortunes had hastened to place their money in safety in France. The common people were 'harassed', and extremely reluctant to go on fighting without pay and almost without rations. Their leaders encouraged them with 'the hopes of peace in the spring', and if peace did not come soon most of the population would 'wish to fall into the hands of the English.' The government was still strong enough to keep the people under arms, but if they were disappointed in their hopes of an early peace and the arrival of a French fleet, Canadian resistance would suddenly crumble.[187] Amherst drew the conclusion that 'from the present posts his majesty's army is now in possession of, [even] if no stroke was to be made, Canada must fall or the inhabitants starve.'[188]

Grant's report was a good one as far as it went, but it did not go quite far enough, in that it was too narrowly limited to the military aspect of the situation. Even so, it presented a terrifying picture. Lévis counted up the fighting men he would have under his orders when the campaign was resumed in the spring of 1760: a maximum of 3,600 regulars with little or no equipment; the militia from the governments of Montreal and Trois-Rivières, and it would be 'difficult to muster them'; about a thousand Indians, provided France sent out a squadron, for 'otherwise we shall be lucky if they are not against us.' It was absolutely essential that supplies be sent from the mother country. Without supplies, the general foresaw that Canada would be forced 'by want' to surrender.[189] This gloomy prospect did not differ from the one that Amherst had evoked. With only 3,600 regulars the high command had to rely more than ever on the militia, and the militiamen were at the end of their tether. Those who had returned to their homes after the 'Quebec affair' and who were called back to the colours 'reported sick.'[190] In most cases, as Vaudreuil recognized, this was not a pretext to avoid military service: 'There are now in all the parishes more sick than well.'[191] The commander of Fort Lévis at the rapids saw his garrison melting away. Although he took great care to grant leave only to those who were 'really ill', he had to allow a large number of his men to go: 'only a small number of troopers', but 'many' Canadians, because the latter, ill-clothed and underfed, 'were more subject to illness' than the regulars.[192]

The morale of the Canadian people was more seriously impaired even than their health. The main action of the tragedy of the conquest took place in the minds of the people. The first blow to their spirit of resistance came from the attitude of France and the French people. The mother country had abandoned Canada in her hour of danger, and British propaganda hastened to make the most of this tactical error. France, proclaimed Wolfe, 'unable to support her peoples, abandons their cause in the moment of crisis.'[193] Still more serious, statements similar to Wolfe's had been current in Canada for years. One such complaint was made as early as 1752: 'It appears that the king is not much concerned for this colony.'[194] The reflection was repeated in stronger terms early in 1761: 'The court is very ill-disposed towards Canada.'[195] Bitter disillusionment did not, however, prevent the people of Canada from rallying from every part of the country to the defence of Quebec.

However, some weeks after the battle of 13 September a British dispatch reported that 'the poor remains of the French army (about ten thousand Canadians)' had retired to the Jacques-Cartier River, but that 'the Canadians [were] deserting in great numbers every day and coming in to surrender themselves and taking the oath of allegiance to his

Britannic Majesty.'[196] The form of the oath was explicit: 'Je promets et jure devant Dieu solennellement, que je serai fidèle à Sa Majesté Britannique le Roy George Second, que je ne prendrai point les armes contre lui, et que je ne donnerai aucun avertissement à ses ennemis, qui lui puisse en aucune manière nuire.'[197] One might have thought the conquest already consummated; if it had not been for the requirement not to furnish information to the French, one might have supposed that Canada had already been ceded to Great Britain. In Quebec, relations between victors and vanquished, though by no means idyllic, were generally good. It did happen that the body of an English soldier who had been mutilated and killed was found in a ditch,[198] and Murray resorted to punitive expeditions to keep the people in line.[199] But these were normal incidents in a zone occupied by an invading army and contiguous to unoccupied territory. It is nonetheless surprising to see how easily the people of the Quebec government appear to have 'reconciled themselves' to the occupying army.[200] A number of individuals returning behind the French lines declared themselves 'quite satisfied with their good treatment at the hands of the English.'[201] On occasion cordial relationships developed between British soldiers and the local inhabitants.[202] British officers in authority were correct in their dealings with Canadians, and their attitude, though doubtless dictated by reasons of policy,[203] had its effect.

It would be a mistake, however, to attribute to this one cause the rapid and easy pacification of a whole district whose population four or five months earlier had been offering fierce resistance to the invaders. What had happened since then? What had happened was that twice in the course of 13 September the Canadians had seen French battalions turn and run before the enemy. The first flight, from the field of battle, might have been redeemed by a vigorous counter-attack; but the second retreat, which began at ten o'clock at night after mature consideration on the part of the commanding officers, was fatal. This time military units ran as one man, so terrified that the soldiers in retreat 'did not dare to pause or blow their noses',[204] even though they were not pursued. Their panic-stricken flight was not forgotten and had far-reaching consequences. When, in mid-November, Murray put the question, 'What can you expect from a weak army, hopelessly crushed and beaten?',[205] he was without knowing it echoing the thoughts of the people of Quebec. No later than 15 September François Daine, the civil and criminal lieutenant-general, Jean-Claude Panet, the king's attorney, Jean Tachet, the merchants' syndic, and twenty-two other 'bourgeois and citizens' of the capital presented a petition to Ramezay requesting him to initiate negotiations for surrender without delay. They represented to him that they had fought to the limit of their strength 'until that fatal day' of 13

September, suffered bombardment for two months, supported privations, vigils, 'fatiguing service'. They had been sustained by the hope of victory and covered by an army. The army had disappeared and the only course open to them was surrender: 'Even if three-quarters of their blood were shed, that would not prevent the last quarter [of the people] from falling under the yoke of the enemy.'[206] After the sudden collapse of military resistance, the people's resistance also collapsed, the more rapidly since it had already been undermined by two separate factors. The first of these was the nature of the defence organized by Montcalm: the policy of passivity that left the besieger free and gave him all the time he wanted to mount his batteries, manoeuvre as if on a parade ground, establish his different camps; a policy that would turn the war into a war of attrition—a type of warfare in which the morale of a people is much more susceptible to deterioration than is that of a professional army such as Wolfe's.

But there was more, infinitely more, than that; the complex nature of the defeat was revealed in the moment of crisis. Here the remark of an eyewitness of the rout of 13 September is particularly revealing: 'Most of the Canadians of the Quebec district took advantage of the disorder to return home, caring little to which master they would belong henceforth.'[207] Too many Frenchmen considered themselves the 'masters' of the Canadians. To come under the yoke of a foreign power was terrifying, but was it such a great misfortune to exchange one servitude for another? The people of the Quebec government were now living in country occupied by the English; they 'were satisfied' with the conduct of the British garrison towards them. Could it be that the enemy troops felt a certain natural sympathy for them? We must not be misled into thinking that the English had established the 'country of Love' in the government of Quebec. Let us rather remember the attitude of the French army towards those same people. During the whole campaign Canadians had seen spread out before them the painful and disconcerting spectacle of undisciplined, drunken French soldiers, hungry for loot, giving themselves up to 'the most unbridled license'. The troopers had taken possession of private property and ravaged the country for several leagues around the places where they were stationed, under the conniving eye of Montcalm, who remained unmoved by the 'jeremiads' of the 'dear Canadians'.[208] 'Nothing,' wrote a contemporary, 'could equal the damage caused by the troops in every part of the countryside where the army has been encamped.' It was even said that on one occasion when an alarm was sounded the general was informed 'that he would have 500 fewer soldiers with which to meet the oncoming enemy' if he did not hasten to call his men back from 'the depths of Charlebourg . . . where they were busy looting right in the houses.'[209] This scandalous conduct was flaunted so shamelessly that it was noticed even by the English. France sent soldiers to Canada, said Wolfe in one of his proclamations, and what good did they do? The answer followed: 'They made [Canadians] feel more bitterly the weight of a hand that oppresses instead of helping them.'[210] A damning charge!

And that was still not all. Even without minimizing their psychological effect, the misdeeds of the French soldiery could be regarded as a passing ill, destined to disappear eventually with the return of more normal conditions. But it was not only by the fact that they were no longer exposed to the force of their arms that Canadians felt themselves drawn towards the English. Messages such as the one that appeared in Murray's declaration of November 1759 struck home: 'We earnestly entreat you to have recourse to a free, wise, generous people, ready to offer you help, to free you from a harsh despotism and to share with you the benefits of a just, moderate, and equitable government.'[211] The 'despotism' referred to by the British military commander in Quebec was not embodied in political institutions; it was much more closely related to what is the essential element in any colonial establishment, the economic structure. Lévis, writing almost at the same time as Murray, made the observation that if France lost Canada, it would be 'very difficult' for her to win the country back in another war. There were many reasons for this, but in his opinion one was paramount: 'The Canadians, judging by what we see of them in Quebec, will not take long to get used to the English government because of the opportunities they will have for trade.'[212] The attitude to which Lévis referred was not entirely new. In the eyes of some Canadians a British régime would be a lesser evil than the state of oppression identified with the Great Society, whose monopoly reached into every sector of the country's economy. 'They write from Quebec,' noted Montcalm in the autumn of 1758, 'that a large number of families are escaping to France. I say escaping, because they are fleeing from an enemy a thousand times more dangerous than the English.'[213] The comparison should be noted. A memorandum drawn up by Bougainville early in 1759 reported rumours current in the colony. 'It was said' that the English would allow 'freedom of religion', that they would supply traders with trading goods at lower prices than those demanded by the Compagnie des Indes, and that they would pay workmen 'generously'. These ideas, as the young officer pointed out, were spreading. They were being expressed 'by some persons above the common people.' Many Canadians were attracted by them, the townspeople especially.[214]

Bigot was furious at the sight of the capital's small merchants clinging for protection to the occupying authorities: 'every individual in Quebec is busy advancing his own affairs; they have little thought for the interests of the king or of the colony.' The commissary-general, Cadet, sent men to Quebec to carry out a mission in which an earlier team had failed, but the intendant foresaw that no good would come of their efforts: 'I think that when they get there they will be bewitched by the English, like the others.'[215] It was the small tradesmen in Quebec, not the big businessmen, that fluttered about Murray. The latter stayed with the Canadian government, on which they held enormous credits, in Montreal, now the provisional capital of the country. The men who had been ousted by the all-powerful Franco-Canadian financial aristocracy, the unlucky competitors who for ten years had had to be satisfied with a modest rank in the feudal state set up in the business world by Bigot and his entourage—these were the vassals who paid faithful homage to the new suzerain and who crawled under the table in search of the crumbs to be picked up there. 'All the French in Quebec,' observed the intendant again, 'seek to pay court in order to procure advantages for themselves. I know that because the merchants tell me so themselves.'[216] The first social class to lose its vitality, the first to disintegrate, was the class of small tradesmen.

Was that American perhaps right, then, who in the autumn of 1759 judged 13 September an unhappy day for Montcalm and his troops, 'but happy for Quebec and its inhabitants' since it made it possible for them to 'enjoy the liberty to which they have hitherto been strangers'?[217] Here we touch on the most elusive misunderstanding in the history of Canada. The last years of the French régime were painful, its last hours dreadful. The face of France reflected in her government and in many of her representatives in the colony was repulsive. That was true. But in spite of that, so long as France was present in America, Canada existed as a country—even though the royal government detached itself from it, even though it was ill-treated by the agents of that government. France might play her part badly, but it was not a useless part; she might agree to being replaced, but that did not make her replaceable. Admittedly France's policy was disastrous, but the remedy was not to be found in a still greater disaster—the conquest. An empire, let us repeat, is an organic whole. At that stage of its development the Canadian community was still an element in the French empire. Introduced into the British empire, it would be a foreign body that would have to be either dissolved or expelled. The evolution that began in the last months of 1759 announced that it would be dissolved. And already the nascent misunderstanding allowed it to be supposed that the process would be an unconscious one.

Chapter IX

The Fall of Canada
1760

The campaign of 1759 laid Canada low; it did not kill her. Her towns-people might be uprooted, her economy in danger of collapse, her territory might shrink from the dimensions of an empire to those of a province, but she was still one body. Her political structure—weakened, shaken, damaged as it was—still stood. Though torn by violent and opposing forces, she was still an organized society. She was not ready to give up and fall to pieces; she could gather her strength and rise for one more effort, one last effort, for she still cherished one last hope: that France would save her either by sending her help or by giving her peace. In July 1760, when all hope of help had vanished, the hope of peace still lived on, and each time the wind blew from the northeast the people looked down the St Lawrence for the ship that would bring them news of liberation from war.[1]

Frenchmen in the colony fully realized the gravity of the situation. Marchant de la Houlière, a senior officer who had returned to France after fighting in the defence of Louisbourg, warned Choiseul in mid-December 1759: 'To send no help means . . . the certain loss of that country.' He recognized that ships carrying men and supplies ran the risk of interception by British squadrons, and that for the French navy in its position of inferiority there were 'no small losses', whether in ships, seamen, or armaments. On the other hand, however, if the colony fell into the hands of the English, it would probably never leave them, and its fall 'would entail the ruin of our trade; for today to aspire to have trade without a navy is to build without a foundation, and in this respect Canada is the most valuable country we have.' Possession of Canada guaranteed possession of the North Atlantic fisheries, and as these constituted 'the best school for our seamen', it was essential to 'make one more effort.'[2]

It was all very well to talk of making an effort, but how? If the court did not know what steps to take, it was not for want of advisers. One of these was Massé de Saint-Maurice, an officer in the Berry regiment who had been sent back to France with the garrison after the surrender of Quebec and who was at Versailles in January 1760. Massé, who knew America well, predicted that the British forces would 'undoubtedly' advance on Montreal by the upper country, and that the town would be attacked by three armies, one coming from Lake Ontario, one from Lake Champlain, and one from Quebec. The reduction of Canada was inevitable unless 'prompt help' were sent. The size of the relief force he proposed was kept to a strict minimum, in all 1,000 men. One first division of 500 would disembark on the St John River and proceed from there towards Quebec. Its numbers would be swelled by some 1,000 Acadians who would be recruited along the way. How would all these men be fed during the long march? Massé had anticipated the question and had an answer for it. A large quantity of 'powdered food' had been prepared for the projected invasion of England. It was easy to transport and would supply the expedition. Meanwhile a second division of the same strength would proceed up the St Lawrence with supplies, munitions, and powerful artillery, establish itself a little above Quebec, and concert its action with the first one. The combined operation, which would not be very costly, would perhaps suffice to block Murray in Quebec, while Lévis, with nothing to fear from that direction, would be free to stop the enemy's armies on Lake Ontario and Lake Champlain. A campaign conceived and carried out along these lines would not make conquests but it would save Montreal. Confidence in France, now 'three-quarters lost', would be restored and finally the day of reckoning would be deferred, at least for a year.[3]

François Le Mercier, who was at Versailles at the same time, had been sent to France in November 1759 by Vaudreuil and Lévis. He had brought dispatches from the colony and he had instructions to confer with Berryer in order to bring home to him the gravity of the situation in Canada and persuade him to lend a sympathetic ear to the governor's plea.[4] Le Mercier presented a stark picture of a desperate situation: the British, masters of Quebec, Lake Champlain, and Lake Ontario, 'hemmed in Canada on every side.' Since the capital was occupied, the militiamen from the Quebec government were lost to the Franco-Canadian army. Stocks of provisions were quite inadequate, and it would be a mistake to count on the forthcoming harvest. So many oxen and horses had had to be killed that the farmers would not be able 'to do enough ploughing for a normal sowing.' With three fronts to defend the forces would have to be divided, and that would 'weaken them every-where.' In a word, no situation could be 'comparable to that of the colony.' But in spite of everything the people of Canada looked towards France, convinced that the king would not 'abandon' them.[5] They were counting on a squadron that would leave the mother country in February, early enough in the year to reach the St Lawrence before the enemy and to act in liaison with Lévis who was planning to besiege Quebec. Time was strictly limited and the general would have to 'lay siege to Quebec and capture it in the course of the month of May.' Le Mercier insisted that May would be the critical month, and he explained why that was so. Before that, the spring floods would prevent the invaders from taking any action against Île-aux-Noix, and by the beginning of June the problem of high water in the Richelieu would have ceased to exist. Lévis must therefore be re-established in Quebec in May, ready to strike back at the enemy and stop their advance on the Richelieu. Thus the recapture of the capital was the key to the whole Franco-Canadian strategy. But it constituted a very difficult task, one that could be accomplished only if Canada's leaders were provided with the necessary means and reinforcements. They asked for 4,000 men and large quantities of provisions and armaments, especially heavy artillery. Smaller quantities would be a total loss for France. 'If the court does not send enough help for the siege of Quebec, it is useless to send any and the colony will certainly be lost.'[6]

After studying Le Mercier's memorandum and decoding the governor's dispatches, the staff of the ministry of marine made a rapid calculation: the help Vaudreuil requested would cost at least eight millions.[7] Berryer was aghast at the very thought of such a sum. Le Mercier's proposals were given a cool reception, and when he tried to present people and circumstances in Canada in a different light from the one in which the Montcalm coterie had shown them, Berryer protested violently. Echoes of his tirade reached the ears of Bougainville, whose uncle, the financier d'Arboulin, reported that Berryer had made a 'long nose' at Le Mercier.[8] There was another reason for the secretary of state's outburst. In his memorandum Le Mercier had dwelt at some length on the 'misfortunes' from which Canadians suffered. Among these he included the pain they would feel at 'seeing their whole fortune in paper money that was no longer current'; at the same time he pointed out to the French government that it was in duty bound to restore the colonists' confidence by giving them cause to 'hope for a future for the paper money that constituted all their wealth.'[9] Outwardly the allusion was discreet, but Berryer was quick to seize its full significance. It was directed at the decree of the council of state of 15 October 1759 stopping payment on colonial bills of exchange. Canadians were still ignorant of this decision. News of it did not reach them until the spring; but as Le Mercier foresaw, the news created consternation in the colony.

This famous decree stipulated that drafts registered at the colonial office in Paris at the time of its promulgation would be honoured three months after the signing of peace, at the rate of half a million livres a month and in the order in which they had been issued. As to claims not yet registered, the government would examine them later and if they were valid would begin to settle them by instalments eighteen months after the signing of the treaty. When transmitting the decision of the council to Bigot, the minister instructed the intendant to 'calm the fears' of the Canadian people; he addressed similar recommendations to Vaudreuil and Lévis and even to the bishop, Monseigneur Pontbriand.[10] The precautions taken by Berryer were unusual but by no means superfluous; they are a clear indication that he knew how heavily he was striking the Canadian population. Vaudreuil did his best to reduce the shock by proclaiming that bills of exchange of 1757 and 1758 would be 'promptly' paid three months after the conclusion of peace. Those of 1759 would be paid next, and notes and orders on the treasury 'as soon as circumstances' allowed.[11] Murray must have roared with laughter on reading the proclamation to which his own circular letter of 27 June was a rejoinder. He declared to the inhabitants that this was a clear case of 'bankruptcy' for which peculation on the part of officials in Canada had been largely responsible. The governor and the intendant were making an awkward attempt to gild the pill. If the government of France honoured the bills of exchange of the years 1757 and 1758, it would be at the rate of six millions a year and 'you need not be a great arithmetician to calculate how many years it would take to pay a hundred or a hundred and twenty millions.' As for the rest of the paper money, continued Murray with biting irony, Vaudreuil and Bigot spoke more truly when they promised that it would be honoured 'as soon as circumstances allowed—for circumstances never would allow this to be done.'[12]

Even without British commentary or propaganda, Canadians could not have failed to understand that what was happening was the collapse of their public finances and the ruin of their savings. The colony's credit was based entirely on bills of exchange authorizing the intendant each year to draw on the treasurer-general of the ministry of marine in Paris to defray the costs of administration and of military operations. Bigot's big budgets and France's increasing financial difficulties had for some years forced the Canadian government to resort to expedients—such as issuing drafts with longer and longer terms—that encouraged speculation and inflation, both prejudicial to the purchasing power of the state. The system creaked but did not break down. For a long time now the only money in circulation had been paper money in some form: cards, orders, notes. The value of all this money fell to nothing, since it was guaranteed by bills of exchange and their value in turn was determined by the proportion of bills the mother country honoured or was prepared to honour. Every Canadian felt the effects of the decree, but those hardest hit were the little people. Specially exempted securities in their port-folios made it possible for a few big financiers to ride out the crisis and wait for the term to present their drafts, but the holders who had to realize them earlier were obliged to sell at a considerable discount—if they could negotiate the drafts at all. Many must have learned at the same time of the decree and of its effect on the notes of exchange they had sent to their agents in Paris the previous autumn. One of the latter wrote in March to inform his correspondent in Montreal that since the publication of 'the fatal news' quotations for unregistered paper were so low that 'at 95 per cent discount you couldn't find a buyer for a sou's worth.' Registered drafts—limited to those issued in 1757 and 1758—found buyers, but 'with difficulty' and with a depreciation of 35 to 50 per cent 'depending on the date of payment.'[13] Bills of exchange from Canada, said another businessman, were 'completely discredited.'[14] When the content of the decrees of October became known, London gloated and to the list of failures reported in the press was added that of 'Louis le Petit, of the city of Paris, peace-breaker, dealer, and chapman.'[15] Lévis warned Berryer that in spite of his insistent assurances that the paper money would be redeemed, he had not been able to reassure the Canadians, and he feared they would not display 'the same will' to fight when he undertook to lead them into battle. Lévis was not shocked by such a reaction; he was too intelligent for that. On the contrary, he under-stood it: 'The people are in despair; they have sacrificed themselves to save the country and they now face hopeless ruin.'[16] Berryer's successor, too, judged this extraordinary decision with some severity. He considered that it had been made 'without sufficient consideration' of its conse-quences, and that even in France it had provoked confusion and 'dis-astrous discredit'.[17] Its repercussions were infinitely more far-reaching in Canada, the victim of a giant swindle at the hands of the French govern-ment.[18] Painful as it was for individuals, the bankruptcy was still more disastrous for the country, whose financial frame collapsed, never to rise again. After the conquest Canada still possessed its means of production. But as what was left of the Canadian community was without finances—and without financiers—the means of production were naturally placed at the service of those with the resources and the credit required for their exploitation. They would build their own economy on the ruins of the one that had been destroyed.

It would be too much to expect of a government that had declared itself bankrupt that it meet the emergency by organizing a good colonial policy. That was a luxury it could not afford. In December 1759 Berryer requested forty million livres for the different branches of his ministry. He received thirty million—or rather nine, for twenty-one million were earmarked in advance for obligations already contracted, cost of administration, and other expenses that had nothing to do with the navy. It was hardly surprising that Canada's share was only 2,400,000 livres— but it was terrifying if one compared the budgets of the French and British navies. The latter amounted to the equivalent of eighteen million French livres for ordinary expenses and ninety-one million for naval operations.[19]

Vaudreuil and Lévis were counting on a major effort by the mother country. Berryer stopped at what he himself called a 'small operation'. He set a limit of 2,000 casks on the cargoes to be sent by the state to Canada, although it was clear, even after careful consideration, that everything the colonial officials had asked for was essential. Where then were the cuts to be made? The minister gave orders, only to countermand them, or to introduce, as he himself admitted, 'endless changes'. Time passed; halfway through February the ships, which should have left, were not yet loaded. The officials charged with equipping them complained that they could not proceed because they had not received the funds promised by the court. The minister replied that he was helpless since his own offices in Paris were experiencing the same difficulties.[20] As a result of delays and official niggardliness the little convoy for Canada did not leave Bordeaux until 10 April. It comprised five merchantmen and one twenty-eight-gun frigate, the *Machault*, and it carried not 4,000 soldiers but 400. The holds were filled with munitions and food, but the latter included a large proportion of 'rotten' beef and horsemeat.[21]

It could hardly have been called a relief squadron even if it had reached Canada, and it did not arrive at its destination. On 15 May the *Machault* and two other ships were in the Gulf of St Lawrence, where the frigate captured a British ship. From letters found on board the prize, the commander of the expedition learned that a British squadron was ahead of him, sailing up the river towards Quebec. Not wishing to offer his ship as a target for an adversary incomparably more powerful than he, he changed course and after capturing five more prizes, dropped anchor in the Baie des Chaleurs. He then sent a messenger overland to Quebec with news of the convoy and letters for Vaudreuil from the court. The governor sent the messenger back with instructions to Giraudais to remain on the Restigouche and 'at the first news of peace' to push forward the Acadian posts as far as possible. His idea was to hold at least a fragment of Acadia for France. It was a good plan but it failed lamentably, for the English, hearing that French ships had been seen in Nova

Scotian waters, hunted them down and destroyed them. Giraudais himself escaped in a small Acadian schooner, landed in the Spanish port of Santander early in September, and delivered Vaudreuil's dispatches in Versailles. It was a fine adventure but the mission had failed—failed, said Lévis and Bigot, because the little fleet had set out from France 'too late'.[22] If it had sailed in February, sighed Malartic, 'we would have recaptured Quebec and held Canada.'[23]

To hold Canada was no more than a faint hope, but Lévis came within an ace of achieving the recapture of Quebec. Early in the winter he was ready, with Vaudreuil, to take advantage of the slightest favourable circumstance—such as an epidemic or unrest in Murray's garrison—to capture the capital by assault. In February, in the course of an unsuccessful attempt to obtain provisions from certain parishes in the Quebec government, the two leaders discovered that the British defence was firm at every point and decided perforce to set aside their projected offensive for the time being and await the opening of navigation. By mid-April their preparations were complete. Success was by no means assured; in fact it appeared most 'problematical', but the attempt had to be made. The governor regarded it as the 'only choice' if they wished to prolong their resistance, and thus be in a position to receive help when it came from Bordeaux and to oppose British advances 'by Lake Champlain and Lake Ontario.'[24] During the preceding months Bigot had done his best to build up a reserve of food, and Lévis had reorganized the armed forces, both regulars and militia. Montcalm had allowed discipline to become relaxed, but Lévis reminded his colonels that 'the strength of the infantry resides in order and discipline' and required them to pay strict attention to 'these two points, unfortunately too much neglected by our troops.' He also forbade ill-treatment of militiamen 'whether by word or otherwise', and he reserved to himself the examination of cases involving ill-treatment and the punishment of offenders. Although arms were in short supply—the militiamen, who had no bayonets, were instructed to fasten their knives to the barrels of their rifles—he regrouped the elements that made up his army and had them well in hand. On 17 April he had under his command 7,260 men, including 3,000 Canadians, grouped in five brigades of two battalions each, the Montreal militia battalion, a cavalry corps, and a band of some 300 Indians. On 30 April he was ready to set his army in motion.[25]

Four days earlier Vaudreuil had addressed an appeal to his compatriots. He was sending 'a very powerful army . . . to lay siege to Quebec.' Lévis, who was in command of the army, loved Canadians 'and inspired their confidence.' Murray had threatened the people in his proclamations; he had harassed them with many 'vexations', and 'without any legitimate right or reason' had shown himself 'harsh and cruel towards them.' The unhappy condition of the colonists, 'their attachment to their country', and their zeal to serve—these all intensified the governor's long-standing desire 'to recapture Quebec and thereby release Canadians from the tyranny they had suffered only too long.' He encouraged them with words of hope: 'The time of triumph is near . . . the moment is at hand when we shall receive powerful aid from France.' Canadians must make the final supreme effort. The time had come for the brave people of Canada to show themselves forth, 'to attempt all, to risk all, for the preservation of [their] religion and the salvation of [their] country.' In order to gain the collaboration of the people in the occupied zone, the governor enlisted the help of the clergy. He begged the priests, for the sake of the love they bore their country, to use their influence and their ascendancy over the minds of their parishioners to convince them that 'their religion, their honour, and their own interest required them one and all to join the army with arms and baggage.'[26] The appeal had its effect. In the last week in May the inhabitants of Beauport were required to provide corvées for Murray. They were the first to be punished for their 'effrontery' in helping the Franco-Canadians during the siege. Murray also published a manifesto offering pardon to colonists who had taken up arms, on condition that they 'mend their past conduct.'[27] Obviously Vaudreuil's appeal had been heard, but by whom? By the common people. Some members of the bourgeois class, even in Montreal, took precautions in view of the possibility of defeat. A Frenchman, observing early in March that auctions were daily occurrences in the town, concluded that 'many people feared for the colony.'[28] The persons who were so anxious to prepare for possible departure from the country were certainly not workmen or peasants.

Lévis's army set out by water from Montreal on 20 April. It was ill-equipped and insufficiently provisioned, but well led. The general's plan was to land at Sillery and throw his army between Quebec and the 1,500 men stationed in advance posts at Lorette and Sainte-Foy.[29] However the British commander had had wind of Lévis's plan as soon as the embarkation of troops began, and he did not allow himself to be caught by surprise.[30] On 21 April he withdrew his men from the advance posts and ordered the people of Quebec to leave the town. The men ground their teeth and the women protested that this was an infraction of the terms of surrender and that the English were 'faithless folk'.[31] On 24 April the Franco-Canadian expedition reached Pointe-aux-Trembles and the second battle of Quebec began. Lévis first outflanked the contingent that tried to stop him at Cap Rouge. He then advanced slowly towards the town and for the next three days evaded the traps that Murray set for him. Murray could have shut himself up in his fortress and allowed the enemy to lay siege to it. But that was not what he wanted; he wanted to scatter the attacking army immediately. Frightened by their superior numbers—he thought they had 10,000 combatants[32]—he was determined to defeat them piecemeal before they could combine forces for a concerted attack. He was in a delicate situation. In October 1759 he had had under his command 9,000 men, of whom 3,000 were unfit for service.[33] The number of sick increased during the ensuing months; early in January the hospitals were full and there were two or three burials every day.[34] The ranks were still further thinned by a month of severe winter weather, and by the end of February fever, dysentery, and scurvy had reduced the garrison to 4,800 able-bodied men.[35] The *New York Mercury* of 10 March assured its readers that the troops in Quebec were 'in good health',[36] but of 6,959 men on the roster a fortnight later only 3,513 were fit to bear arms.[37] Murray declared that between the preceding autumn and 24 April his regiments had lost 1,000 men and that another 2,000 men were too ill to go into battle.[38] These were round numbers and they were exaggerated; but the fact remains that between 18 September 1759 and 24 April 1760 the Quebec army had lost almost 700 men.[39] On 28 April Murray had only 3,900 combatants, including officers and 129 artillerymen, to send into battle.[40]

The large number of artillerymen is an indication of the sort of battle Murray intended to fight. He deployed his troops and his twenty-two guns on the Sainte-Foy heights along an oblique line running to the edge of the 'thin woods' at Sillery. His design was quite evidently to compensate for inferior numbers with superior fire power and a better position: his cannon would pound the columns of the Franco-Canadian regiments and spread panic among the militia. But Lévis, who saw through his game, withdrew first his left and then his right towards the woods. Mistaking his withdrawal for flight, Murray gave up his advantageous position on the heights and allowed himself to be lured down to marshy ground where his heavy artillery could not operate. Just as he thought his men were on the point of crushing Lévis's left, a bayonet charge stopped them short, while at the other end of the line a French brigade led by Lévis turned the British left and caught it on the flank. To avoid being surrounded the regiments on the left withdrew and the whole British line broke and followed them. A short time before, Lévis had dispatched to another brigade, the Queen's, the order to move in behind the enemy's left, but the order miscarried and the Queen's massed behind the French left at the other end of the line. If it had not been for this error, the impetuous British general might have been surrounded and his army destroyed. If that had come about, Quebec would have fallen that very day. But the men who had won the battle were worn out by the marches and countermarches that had brought them victory, and although they pursued the fleeing British troops they did not succeed in entering the city. With the battle, however, the Franco-Canadian force won an important advantage. Although they were in a position of great danger during the early part of the engagement, their losses were limited to 193 officers and men killed and 640 wounded, while on the British side 259 men were killed and 829 wounded. Most of the British casualties resulted from the bayonet charge.[41] One witness testified that Lévis's generalship was 'admired by his army', and Vaudreuil added his tribute of praise to that of the soldiers: that 'brilliant' day was entirely Lévis's work and the victory due to 'his intrepid courage and military sense.'[42] Lévis's success was worthy of their admiration, but Canada needed more than success in one battle. She needed Quebec, and on the day of the battle Lévis wrote to inform the governor that he would lay siege to the town immediately with the modest forces at his command; he anticipated that 'others would arrive.'[43]

Murray's defeat burst like a bombshell on the British world. The officer who brought the news to Halifax added his own pessimistic estimate of the situation: the British army had suffered such heavy losses and was so demoralized that the city could not have held out very long and must have surrendered.[44] Murray's own message to his commander-in-chief was hardly more reassuring: the most he could hope for was 'not to be reduced to the last extremity' before the arrival of the fleet that he expected 'any day'. A copy of the letter forwarded to Pitt aroused the latter's fears of a 'fatal castastrophe'. The minister knew how 'uncertain' navigation was in the Gulf of St Lawrence. He reflected that the river was already open and navigation assured between Montreal and Quebec, while floating ice in the gulf made communication between Halifax and Quebec 'very precarious'. In his opinion England had now no more than a fragile hold on Canada.[45] And what might not happen if things went ill? In spite of her triumphs England was beginning to show signs of war-weariness. There was talk of peace; bases of negotiations were being considered. The prime minister was almost alone in his determination to continue hostilities to the total defeat of France, and he had to use all his wiles to avoid charges of war fanaticism. He felt his work threatened. If the Canadians recovered Quebec, it was not at all certain that Britain would agree to launch another grand-scale offensive against the town. The tide of pacifism threatened to become irresistible, and a treaty signed in such circumstances would not efface Canada from the map of America.[46] Sooner or later it would all have to be done over again, with this difference that France, forewarned, might perhaps in the interval succeed in rebuilding her empire. When on 17 June news of Lévis's victory was published in London it provoked a reaction that was immediately reflected in a drop in the value of state bonds on the stock exchange;[47] the city was threatened with panic. 'Who the deuce was thinking of Quebec?' wrote Horace Walpole. 'America was like a book one has read and done with, but here we are on a sudden reading our book backwards.'[48]

It was not without reason that Britain was alarmed. In order to arrive at a reasonable understanding of the facts we are studying, we must disregard the faded flowers of rhetoric cultivated by those historians who have seen the victory merely as Canada's revenge, a victory with no future—moving, but vain, splendid precisely because it was fruitless— a victory to cleanse the white cockade of France, stained by the defeat and death of Montcalm. When the political and military leaders of the colony planned and prepared their offensive against Quebec, they made a sober estimate of their chances of success. When the expedition left Montreal it was less with the hope of capturing the capital by assualt than with the idea of 'confining' the British garrison, preventing the troops from building supplementary defences around the fort, waiting for the arrival of aid from France 'in order to be able to continue the siege.'[49] Lévis was a realist: as we know, he was counting not so much on his own 'weak resources' as upon the 'other' help that was to come. He had planned his operations to synchronize with the arrival of the reinforcements and equipment that Le Mercier had gone to solicit from the court. His artillery was inadequate, and what little powder he had was of poor quality. The approaches to the town bristled with 'unbeliev-able difficulties'. The men working on entrenchments 'walked on bare rock; they had to carry the earth in bags from a great distance.'[50] In order to provide against the possibility that his guns might burst, Lévis had to limit each piece to twenty shots a day. If in the face of such difficulties he did succeed in doing considerable damage to the walls, it was because he concentrated almost all his fire on the Glacière bastion, whose weakness both he and his engineers knew well.[51] Murray was seriously worried, but Lévis himself cherished no illusions. On 15 May he wrote to Vaudreuil that he was doing all that was 'morally' possible. 'The time has come,' he continued, 'for this to end one way or another; there is a strong breeze from the northeast; so I think it will not be long . . . If we are forunate enough to have aid reach us we shall soon take Quebec.'[52]

At nine o'clock the next evening the end had come; he had no choice but to raise the siege. The outcome had been predictable since 9 May when the British frigate *Lowestoft* had sailed into the harbour. 'The gladness of the [British] troops that day was not to be expressed; both officers and soldiers mounted the parapets in the face of the enemy and huzzaed with their hats in the air for almost an hour.'[53] They were saved! But what was one frigate? One swallow does not make a sum-mer, and Lévis persisted in his unpromising resistance. He would perhaps have beaten an immediate retreat if he had known the news that Captain Deane of the *Lowestoft* had for Murray. The naval division to which the frigate was attached had left England in March, under the command of Captain Robert Swanton, with orders to reinforce Lord Colville's squadron. Colville's ships had left Halifax harbour, where they had spent the winter, on 22 April, and could soon be expected in Quebec. Swanton, forestalling them, appeared on 20 May, and 'in the twinkling of an eye' disabled the two French frigates, *Pomone* and *Atalante*, that had come down with Lévis from Montreal. Two days later, when Colville arrived, Lévis had already withdrawn. The English were masters of the St Lawrence and the *Machault* was in the Baie des Chaleurs. Canada would receive no aid from France; the game was lost.[54]

With British frigates stationed at Cap Rouge, an officer reported 'every face in the garrison brightened up to a degree *à peine reconnaissable.*' At the same time, still writing in French, he confessed to a great sense of relief: 'Entre nous soit dit, nous sommes heureux d'en avoir été quittes pour la peur.'[55] Canadians and old-country Frenchmen on the other hand were consumed with the bitterness of hopes deceived. Lévis had so reduced Murray's strength that the little fleet dispatched 'too late' from Bordeaux 'might perhaps have sufficed to recapture Quebec or at least to prevent the English from extending further their conquests for that year.'[56] Desandrouins recorded a bit of a later conversation with the English engineer Holland:

'Ah! one ship of the line,' I cried, 'and the fortress was ours.'
'You are quite right,' he answered.[57]

Vaudreuil assured the minister of war that 'the sight of a single French flag would have brought about the surrender of Quebec',[58] and his opinion was shared by those about him.[59] Lévis, the only senior officer in Canada who could dare not to mince his words, spoke to Berryer in plain language: 'One frigate, if it had arrived before the English fleet, would have achieved the surrender of Quebec.' He elaborated his statement some months later: 'It was one more misfortune in the series of misfortunes to which this colony had been doomed by some inexplicable fatality, that this year the aid sent by France did not arrive at the critical moment. . . . I think I can affirm that Quebec would have been recaptured.'[60] Bougainville's opinion was that the 'fatality' was Berryer himself, whom he accused of having 'sold a part of what remained of our navy, probably to be rid of the whole business as quickly as possible.'[61] The Canadian campaign of 1760 failed in France, while in London news of the raising of the siege of Quebec was saluted with volleys of gunfire 'from the Tower and in the Park.'[62]

Observers well placed to judge the situation saw the end approaching.

'Unless peace is signed,' wrote Bourlamaque, 'the last moment has come.' The morale of the army and of the country was more seriously impaired by the shock of Lévis's retreat than by the defeat and flight of the army on 13 September. At one time it became impossible to maintain army discipline: the troopers adopted habits of drunkenness and 'thieving', and the militiamen's one thought was to get away.[63] Vaudreuil considered that desertion from companies in the Quebec district was 'excusable'. Who knew whether Murray might not direct his reprisals against the militiamen? They were 'greatly to be pitied.'[64] The governor knew that he had thrown the whole remaining strength of the colony into the Quebec offensive. He had staked all his resources on that one play, and in April he reported to Berryer that the country was stripped bare.[65] Even after he had lost he was not ready to surrender. At the end of May he again addressed his compatriots, and his message was once more a message of confidence and encouragement. He was pleased with them: in this early stage of the campaign they had shown forth their valour and 'their attachment to their country', and they must not be discouraged. Even though French arms had suffered reverses in America, in Europe they had beaten the English and the Prussians, and Louis XV was in Holland at the head of an army of 200,000 men. The British garrisons at Saint-Frédéric, Niagara, and Chouaguen were still 'afflicted with illness', and the strength of the regulars left in New England had 'fallen almost to nothing.' Although Murray had tried to discredit French bills of exchange and paper money, 'British merchants [were] eager to have them.' In short, Canadians need not envy the fate of their enemies. The dawn was just about to break on better days. Canada was 'reaching the end of her suffering and misery.' In August at the latest they would have 'news of peace, provisions, and generally everything else' they needed.[66]

These promises were Vaudreuil's attempt to counter advances that Murray had made to Canadians. They could now, so ran Murray's circular, 'look into their hearts' and reflect on the 'folly' into which they had been led by 'deceitful appearances'. He could mete out punishment, but knowing 'the wiles' employed by their leaders to make them 'fall into the trap', he was disposed to 'forget their past faults'— provided they showed themselves worthy of pardon. 'In short, the most generous people in the world holds out its arms to you a second time.' The British offered 'unfailing aid' while France was unwilling 'to give them any help.' And why should England mistreat them? It would not be in the king's interest to 'reign over a province emptied of its people.' It was the intention of this good sovereign to treat the people well, to maintain 'the religion they cherish and the priests who exercise it.' (The last words were a special invitation addressed to the clergy.) It was also the sovereign's intention to confirm 'communities and individuals in possession of their property, their laws and their customs'— all this on one condition, that the people lay down their arms, submit 'with good grace', and give no help to the French.[67] It was clever propaganda, but it did not stifle all resistance, and Murray had to resort to terror to achieve his aims.

He could speak in a loud voice, because he was strongest. At the very moment when he issued his proclamation a messenger left Albany with a letter from Amherst to Brigadier Whitmore, who commanded the troops in Cape Breton, to embark two regiments of regulars for Quebec.[68] With these reinforcements Murray would be able to launch an offensive, and for the past two months the commander-in-chief had been proclaiming his intention to carry on the 'vigorous campaign' for which preparations were already well forward early in March. He admitted that the 'fortune of arms is inconstant', but he was confident that 'the remains of Canada must fall.'[69] Dismayed for a moment by Lévis's victory, he became more optimistic than ever with confirmation of the rumour that the siege of Quebec had been raised. He rubbed his hands in the joy of anticipation. 'I can't help flattering myself that the conquest of all Canada is certain.'[70]

He had worked out a plan of his own, since Pitt had merely instructed him to 'proceed to the vigorous attack of Montreal . . . in such manner as [he should] judge most proper.'[71] Amherst's plan was to surround the enemy. Given the British superiority in men and equipment, the only risk was that the French troops might move towards the midwest and down towards Louisiana. There had been talk of a retreat to Louisiana in Montcalm's circle ever since 1758, and Bougainville made the suggestion to the court at the end of that year: 'The French are worthy to emulate a Greek action and the retreat of the 10,000 [was] among the greatest of the feats that have immortalized Greece.' At the same time an official of the ministry of marine drew up a memorandum recommending the 'transmigration' of the population of Canada to the Mississippi valley.[72] The second of these ideas smacks decidedly of adventure fiction, but the first could be realized, although with great difficulty. Late in 1760 it was reported that Rigaud, the governor of Montreal, and some other French gentlemen had eluded the invaders: 'It is thought they are on the way to the Mississippi by way of the Uttawawa [sic].'[73] When this dispatch was published, Rigaud was already in France, and no military group succeeded in escaping from the English. The British troops took the precaution of guarding all the gates by which an army might have left Montreal. Thanks to the support of Colville's fleet, Murray was master not only of Quebec but of the river. The

Richelieu offered no possibility as an escape route because it communicated with New York, and in any case a British expeditionary force was preparing to move down the valley. There remained the upper St Lawrence route to the lakes; it could lead on to the isolated posts in the Illinois country in upper Louisiana. The British commander-in-chief would follow this route in the opposite direction when he moved down towards Montreal at the head of the main army of invasion. Amherst's was the main army, but not the only one; for as he advanced down the St Lawrence towards the objective, Murray would move up the river, and Brigadier Haviland would advance on Montreal by way of the Richelieu. While the preceding campaign had been conducted as a pincers movement, this one had the characteristics of a vice. It cannot be denied that Amherst displayed great skill in the conception and execution of the combined operation,[74] but it must also be recognized that he was aided in his task by the penury of Franco-Canadian military resources and the exhausted and demoralized condition of the troops.

In contrast, the invading army was abundantly rich in resources. It counted in all more than 18,000 men: 11,000 including 5,600 regulars in Amherst's army, 3,400 with 1,500 regulars in Haviland's, and in Murray's 3,800, all regulars, with a 'prodigious' artillery support of 105 guns. The great size of these forces, as a French officer justly observed, made it impossible for the Franco-Canadian staff to adopt any fixed plan.[75] The major accomplishment of the British commander-in-chief—and it was no mean one—was perhaps to have assembled such a large number of men under the colours. As a general rule the provincial governments were in no hurry to recruit the contingents they were asked to provide. This was not evidence of ill will on their part, but rather of prudence. The British Americans, like the people of Canada, were convinced that peace was imminent in Europe. They hesitated to assume expense for recruiting regiments that would not be needed if a truce were signed, and their hesitation inevitably resulted in delay.[76] This explains why the armies commanded by Amherst and Haviland and made up of regulars and provincials came into action fairly late in the season. Murray, who did not have to wait for colonials, could act quickly. There were also a few colonies that were unwilling to make any further effort; Virginia was one of them. At the end of 1759 Virginia declared itself unable to maintain more than 400 men under arms. The following spring the governor was authorized to raise 761 men, but on condition that 300 serve only in the province.[77] In December 1759 Pennsylvania disbanded all her troops, with the exception of 150 men. The provincial assembly agreed later to appropriate a sum sufficient to pay 2,700 soldiers, but the procedure followed by the house on this occasion was such that Governor Hamilton wondered whether 'as an honest man' he could sign the bill presented for his approval.[78] The members of the Maryland assembly did not even run that risk. When they voted appropriations for the maintenance of 1,000 men, they did so in the certainty that the bill would be thrown out by the legislative council, which had previously rejected five similar ones.[79] The southern colonies in general behaved as if the war were already over. Pitt, scandalized by such conduct, dispatched to Maryland, Virginia, and the Carolinas a circular letter 'particularly adapted to the want of zeal they have shown on former occasions.'[80] The northern colonies, in contrast to the south, showed up well. This was particularly true of Massachusetts, which undertook to raise 7,500 men, and Connecticut, which promised 5,000. Rhode Island provided 1,000 combatants, New Hampshire 800,[81] New York 2,680. Enthusiasm was stimulated in New York especially by the objective of the high command: 'to make an irruption into Canada in order to reduce Montreal and all the other posts belonging to the French.'[82] There was a colony that realized the value of New France; and even if she had forgotten it, the splendidly profitable dealings of her traders in Niagara in the spring of 1760 would have been an agreeable reminder.[83]

With his forces disposed according to his plan, Amherst held the victory in his hand. It was not he but Murray, however, who played the greatest part in its achievement. Murray, in the opinion of the commander-in-chief, was particularly favoured: he had only to proceed from Quebec to Montreal by the 'easiest' of the three invasion routes.[84] Amherst forgot to add that, although there were in fact fewer natural obstacles along this route, it went through country inhabited by a population that had not yet disarmed. Moreover, Quebec had been through a siege and the force commanded by its military governor was not as strong as it appeared. At the end of May, Murray could count on no more than 2,800 combatants—reinforcements from Louisbourg had not yet arrived—and the troops had suffered so severely from a rigorous winter that some of them had had to be sent to rest on the Island of Orleans. There could be no question of marching overland: the forest was much too close to the road and the regiments would be cut to pieces before they reached their destination. They would go by water and would thus be both safer and freer to manoeuvre. Since he could choose his landing places, Murray could force the Franco-Canadian units, which would otherwise be isolated, to fall back upon Montreal where they would find themselves caught between two fires. On 14 July he took the first step in the execution of this plan by issuing sailing orders to his fleet composed of four warships, nine floating batteries, forty transports, and twenty-six bateaux.[85]

Without deigning to stop, the fleet sailed past the posts at Deschambault, Jacques-Cartier, and Pointe-aux-Trembles, where Lévis had left 1,500 men under the command of Dumas. A few cannon shots were fired at the ships as they passed but the balls did little damage. Observing that the houses were empty, Murray concluded that the farmers must have joined their militia companies and the families taken refuge in the woods. He also observed a detachment of soldiers on the shore following him like a shadow. On 18 July the fleet anchored at Lotbinière.[86] Murray landed his troops two days later after giving the people time to read the proclamation that had been posted on the church doors. He had picked this occasion to strike a spectacular attitude. The time and the place were well chosen. Part of the male population of two parishes—134 men—had come to take the oath of 'neutrality', and Murray invited them to reflect on certain 'arguments'. Was it possible to fight without ships, artillery, ammunition, or provisions? 'At whose mercy' were the farmers' houses, their crops, everything they possessed in this world? Who would protect them from destruction? Let Canadians then consider their own interest! At that moment, observing a priest in the group, he turned to address him: 'The clergy are the source of all the mischiefs that have befallen the poor Canadians whom they keep in ignorance and excite to wickedness and their own ruin. . . . *Preach the gospel* which alone is your province; adhere to your duty and do not presume, directly or indirectly, to meddle with military matters or the quarrel between the two *crowns*.'[87] The situation having thus been made clear to the inhabitants, the conqueror continued on his way.

Not all the country people were as docile as those of Lotbinière. When the fleet reached Batiscan the men rushed into the water musket in hand and, advancing in the face of a barrage of balls to within range of the ships, kept up their fire for half an hour.[88] A short distance above Trois-Rivières the scene was repeated, this time with a sensational variation. Lord Rollo, who had reached Quebec with the Louisbourg regiments two weeks after Murray's departure, had followed his chief up the river, making use of delays caused by spells of calm or contrary winds to pacify the parishes on the north shore. On 17 August, during one of these pauses, a priest appeared on the shore and asked if Lord Rollo was on his ship. This was a worthy ecclesiastic who had dined with his lordship the previous evening. His lordship, who was on board, greeted the priest very civilly, and the latter raised his hat in reply. At this signal the deck was raked with a volley of fire from the shore. Canadians and Indians 'like a parcel of water dogs ran almost up to their waists in the river' to fire from closer range. As the ship moved off with all speed, the English counted their wounded—some ten soldiers and sailors—and were at a loss to account for 'the base treachery' of this 'reverend Judas'.[89]

The two shores of the river presented to the eyes of the invading troops a smiling countryside not yet blackened by the fires later to be set by their torches. One British officer was surprised to find fewer signs of destitution than he had expected. Had he not found 'excellent wheaten bread' in the houses into which he had gone?[90] The houses themselves were empty, for their occupants fled at the approach of the enemy. Lévis shuddered to see Murray's steady advance: not with fear—there was nothing he would have liked more than an engagement that would have allowed him to retard the enemy's advance—but because he saw Murray's game—to push him back against a wall, at the same time avoiding an encounter and using fear as an instrument to break the resistance of the people. On 23 July, Murray issued a proclamation that was savage in its violence. He warned Canadians that the end was approaching: 'You are still for a moment masters of your fate. Once that moment has passed bloody vengeance will punish any who dare to have recourse to arms. Ravaged lands and burned houses will be the least of their misfortunes.'[91]

On 7 August Lévis took his bearings. The first of the British troops had now reached Trois-Rivières. Dumas was following them along the shore and preparing to defend the town. But the British regiments did not halt there. Their plan, as Lévis correctly reasoned, was 'to come to Montreal or Sorel in order to facilitate their junction with M. Amherst.' What could be done about it? Again Lévis gave the succinct answer: 'We have no means of stopping them.' They would refuse to fight before the three armies had effected their junction. Meanwhile, in spite of a number of isolated exploits, Canadian resistance was faltering. The enemy's fleet struck terror into the hearts of the habitants; they feared 'their homes might be burned.'[92]

Their fears were by no means groundless. On 21 August, as his fleet was anchored off Sorel, Murray sent another message to the Canadian population. Its tone was sinister: 'You persist in your obstinacy and force me, in spite of my humanity, to carry out the threats I have made. The time has come for this to begin. I warn you that henceforth I shall treat severely Canadians taken with arms in their hands and I shall burn all villages that I find abandoned.'[93] The time had come to begin, and the commander did not repeat his warning. He ordered Rollo to land a regiment that same night half a mile below Sorel and an infantry detachment one league away from them. The two companies were to march towards one another, 'burning everything before them.' In his report to Pitt, Murray regretted 'the cruel necessity' that forced him to bring suffering to 'so many unfortunates', but his fine sentiments did nothing to alleviate the hard lot of the victims. The next day the general, noting in his diary that a group of people from Sorel had come with a priest to surrender their arms, added the laconic comment: 'Effects of the fire.'[94] The same day Bourlamaque reported to Lévis: 'It is costing us 100 deserters from the militia.' And that was only a beginning.[95]

The morale of the people had not been good at any time since the retreat from Quebec. While some of the militia stood bravely and answered the British cannon with their rifles, others wanted only to go home. It was useless for Vaudreuil to talk to them of French victories in Europe; they could see too plainly that in America the French cause was irretrievably lost. Canadians could no longer believe in France. Refusal of payment on bills of exchange had shown that nothing more could be expected of her—nothing but peremptory orders to accept further sacrifices. Drastic requisitioning of provisions aggravated the situation. Cadet admitted that it had 'completely stripped' the farmers, and in mid-July Lévis confirmed his statement: 'We have been obliged to demand almost all their remaining animals, leaving them only a few cows for their own subsistence.'[96] Military service was also required of them. This would have seemed normal in normal times, but extraordinary measures by means of which military leaders hoped to arrest a general deterioration in morale added to the hardships of army life. On 15 August Lévis recommended to Bourlamaque that the first militiaman guilty of desertion should suffer the death penalty,[97] and a week later Bourlamaque went through the parishes with armed soldiers to hunt down deserters.[98] He even followed the example set by Murray at Sorel, but although he burned houses belonging to Canadians who had surrendered their arms to the English, he had little hope that these harsh measures would be effective. Disheartened by the numbers of defeatists, he reported to Lévis his bitter conviction that 'every house would have to be destroyed.'[99]

By the last week in August Franco-Canadian resistance was crumbling everywhere. Bad news came in from Île-aux-Galops in the upper St Lawrence, and from Île-aux-Noix at the head of the Richelieu. Amherst's flotilla had left Oswego on 10 August and reached Fort Lévis ten days later. His batteries opened fire on 23 August; and on 25 August, after being pounded with projectiles for two days, the fort surrendered.[100] The rest of that phase of the campaign was plain sailing for Amherst, for although the waters of the river were rough he met no further resistance from the enemy. Meanwhile Haviland was proceeding in the same deliberate fashion to carry out his plan to force a passage down the Richelieu. On 14 August his fleet appeared in sight of Île-aux-Noix—five warships, two floating batteries of twenty-four-inch guns, and six rafts carrying twelve-inch guns. On 16 August troops were disembarked; and for three days, while siege batteries were being mounted, the French entrenchments were bombarded steadily by naval artillery.[101] Bougainville had neither the men nor the equipment to withstand a siege. Successive reinforcements added 1,000 men to his original strength of 450,[102] but, he reported, there was not one among the recruits who 'could lay a gun . . . or fire a bomb.' There was no shelter on the island, 'not a corner that was not ploughed up by bombs and cannon-balls',[103] and supplies of ammunition were pitifully meagre. The defenders had to resign themselves to being pounded by the enemy's fire 'almost without answering it', since they had to reserve what little ammunition they had for the time when they would have to repulse 'an attack in full force.'[104] The English had thought that at the approach of their army Bougainville would evacuate the post, blow up its fortifications, and fall back on Montreal.[105] But the young colonel stood firm in spite of Haviland's incessant artillery 'serenade', of which the deepest notes were provided by the booming of 'a great devil of a battery only a rifle shot away from us.'[106] He withdrew to Saint-Jean on 27 August only when the whole of his 'little navy' had been captured and the fort was in danger of being surrounded by a flanking movement. The next day the British troops landed on the island.[107] In the night of 29-30 August they advanced 'in force' on Saint-Jean, where they found that the French had abandoned the fort and set it on fire. The day after the arrival of Haviland's army at Saint-Jean, Murray landed at Varennes and Amherst reached Île-au-Chat, twenty-four miles below Fort Lévis, now renamed William Augustus.[108] The vice was tightening.

By the end of the first week in September it was fast. From Varennes, where he was awaiting the arrival of Amherst, Murray sent detachments of troops to accept the submission of the neighbouring parishes. He also occupied Boucherville, and then Longueuil. His operations and those of Haviland, who captured Chambly and La Prairie, forced the French troops to retreat to the island of Montreal and St Helen's Island, where Vaudreuil stationed 500 men. Almost all the militiamen had deserted and the regulars followed their example whenever they could. On 1 September Roquemaure wrote from La Prairie that his troops were completely riddled by desertion. 'The general cry is for surrender,' wrote another officer.[109] Even his fellow officers were infected with the contagion of defeatism. From Longueuil, Bourlamaque reported that deserters from the regulars were hiding in the woods—when they did not go over to the enemy. 'Soon,' he observed with bitter irony, 'Canadians will be regarded as models of dependability.' Three days after making this observation he noted that desertions were snowballing and that they were aggravated by 'thieving'. Discipline had ceased to exist; to enforce it 'one would have to flog every trooper.'[110] Vaudreuil, so Murray averred, had given him to understand that he was ready to initiate *pourparlers* when Amherst was still three days away from Montreal.[111] This appears to have been an empty boast, but at eight o'clock in the evening of 6 September, the day Amherst's troops landed at Lachine, Vaudreuil called a council of senior land and marine officers. Bigot read an outline of proposed terms of capitulation that were unanimously approved. The officers agreed with Vaudreuil 'that the general interest of the colony demanded that resistance should not be pressed to the utmost extremity', especially since such a course 'would only postpone the loss of the country for a couple of days.'[112]

On 7 September Murray's troops landed at Pointe-aux-Trembles to be met by country people, men and women, with pitchers of milk or water for the soldiers and 'many courteous expressions of concern that they had not better liquor for the officers.'[113] Bougainville had already had a conference with Amherst, who had agreed to almost all the terms proposed by Vaudreuil. On one point, however, he remained adamant. Vaudreuil had requested that the French troops be granted 'the honours of war', but Amherst demanded that they 'lay down their arms.' He explained to Pitt that he wished to 'dishonour' the enemy in reprisal for 'the cruel and barbarous war' they had waged when they thought they had the upper hand.[114] When Vaudreuil renewed his request for consideration he received a short answer: 'no change' would be made in the conditions. 'Your excellency,' added Amherst, 'will be good enough to decide immediately and to forward his answer to me, whether, yes or no, he wishes to accept or to refuse them.'[115] Vaudreuil had to submit. The discussion was closed—with Amherst but not with Lévis, who protested vehemently: such a condition was an insult to 'the honour of the king's arms' and negotiations should be broken off forthwith. The governor replied with a written order: Lévis must submit to the will of the victor 'since the interest of the colony does not permit us to refuse the conditions proposed by the English general, proposals that are to the advantage of the country.'[116]

Contemporaries judged the convention signed by Vaudreuil and Amherst on 8 September 1760 'very favourable to the colonists and all those who have some fortune in the country', its conditions 'most favourable for the principal persons in the colony, all of whose property is protected.'[117] The court professed noble indignation, and Berryer upbraided Vaudreuil. Even 'assuming the obligation to surrender', he should have rejected the 'dishonourable conditions' offered by Amherst and adopted tactics of 'attack or defence' in order to wrest concessions from the English.[118] One official of the ministry of marine went further. He was astonished that Montreal had opened its gates to the enemy 'without having fired a single shot.' He doubted 'the honour of the colony's leaders.' After all, Amherst's troops must be in a state of exhaustion; they had 'come over the Niagara Falls' and 'the least resistance' would have reduced them to 'the last extremity.'[119] The judgement of public opinion was quite different from that of the court. The loss of Canada provoked 'more sorrow than surprise'; it was to be expected. The troops and the 'brave Canadians lacked for everything, and they could only be praised for having capitulated on the terms granted to them.'[120] Vaudreuil presented his own defence in a letter to Berryer: was not the harshness of the terms relating to the troops 'balanced in a way by those protecting the interests of the colony and its people'?[121] Lévis had already written to support the governor. Vaudreuil, he declared, 'had until the very last moment brought to bear every resource of which human wisdom and experience are capable.'[122]

It is difficult to avoid the impression that the dismay and disappointment of the French government were due in large part to the fact that they seem finally to have believed the false news published by the *Gazette de France* during the month of September. The *Gazette* had first published a dispatch from London, according to which Lévis was preparing to march with four or five thousand regulars and six thousand militiamen against Amherst, credited with a fighting force of 10,500. Then it had announced that a revolt of the 'Chiriquois' prevented the British commander-in-chief from leaving Fort Saint-Frédéric, while Murray, 'who had advanced as far as the Richelieu', had been beaten by Repentigny with a detachment of marines and Canadians. Finally the *Gazette* had claimed that a certain 'Minville senior', a shipowner from Bayonne, after capturing in the St Lawrence fourteen enemy ships 'loaded with munitions for Quebec', had unloaded and burned them 'a little above the Baie des Chaleurs' and had transported their cargoes to Montreal. The same article reported that the Canadian crop was an abundant one and that the French in America could maintain their position against the English 'for a long time.'[123] Hopes inflated by stories such as these could not fail to have a great fall, as they did when what had really happened in Canada became known.

And yet one factor, its officially provisional character, made it difficult to appreciate the full gravity of the surrender concluded at Montreal. One article provided that 'everything [should] return to its former state' if news of peace between the two mother countries should arrive and if the terms of the treaty restored the colony to France. This situation could arise, although other articles were designed to regulate certain arrangements in case Britain came out of the peace conference in possession of the country.[124] All hope was not yet dead. In 1761 a Canadian merchant who was then in France had a boat built in Nantes in preparation for carrying on trade in Canada after the storm had passed. He was quite confident of returning to Canada. 'There is much talk here,' he wrote, 'that it will be restored to us. The public news is that peace is imminent. God grant it.'[125] In September 1760 one French

officer was already considering reforms that should be introduced into
the colony when France was re-established there. He thought it essential
to destroy 'even the shadow of the self-interest that was the one primary
cause of the loss of the country.'[126] In 1762 Bourlamaque wrote a remarkable memorandum in which he discussed at length modifications
that would improve the country's administration when England restored it to France. Choiseul thanked him for a document 'containing
valuable reflections.'[127] When this persistent hope finally faded one hard
fact stood out in harsh relief. Even if the capitulation had been ten
times more 'honourable' for the French troops and a hundred times
more 'favourable' for the Canadians, its terms were nonetheless the
death sentence of a society; not in their stipulations—these were after
all of secondary importance—but because they confirmed a fact already
established: the terrible fact of defeat.

The real victors understood this quite well. The real victors were the
British Americans, and they realized at once the immense repercussions
that would follow from this event. They saw in it the annihilation of
that other American society, the enemy that for a century had disputed
their supremacy in the New World. The severity with which God had
treated the people of Canada, said a Massachusetts pastor, was 'righteous'
and yet 'awful'. Their towns and villages were destroyed, their army
disbanded, their leaders gone. As they lost their public posts and employment that had assured them of a high standard of living, leading
citizens were forced to depart, to leave their homes and their friends.
As for the 'rest of the people', they saw themselves 'taken from under
their former king and government and subjected to a new king, new
laws, and a new government.' In a word, the Canadians were 'broken'
as a people. No doubt, reflected this American, the change would
'in the conclusion' be to the advantage of Canadians, 'yet for the present
we must conclude that it is not joyous, but very grievous to many of
them.'[128] His vocabulary, that of his age, and his oratorical style were
inadequate for the expression of extremely complex social facts, but
what admirable lucidity, what sure penetration were displayed in Appleton's analysis of the situation! Every essential element was noted: the
disruption of Canadian society provoked by the collapse of its political
and social framework, and by the immediate departure of the upper
class that up to that time had provided direction and material equipment; the anticipation of assimilation to the British world, a phenomenon
that would be preceded by a 'grievous' period of servitude and homeless-
ness.

The work of arms being accomplished, said another pastor, the
occasion now presented itself for a 'good and great enterprise', the task

of 'propagating our religion and liberty, civil government and gospel order among our new fellow subjects. . . . Such a conquest, following upon this which we are now celebrating, will make it doubly glorious . . . though [it is] in itself perhaps not inferior to any of the kind this day to be found in the British annals.'[129] Benjamin Franklin, the foremost American thinker of the age, estimated that it would take fifty years to achieve a spiritual conquest whose success could be assured by a colonization policy presenting no special difficulties. He did not count on immigration from the British Isles, nor did he consider that it was needed. Relying on the vitality of the American people, he predicted that within ten years the overflow from the British colonies would have provided Canada with twice as many English as, in 1760, it had French inhabitants. The French population would be weakened by the loss of a good number of colonists who would prefer to emigrate to France if they were allowed to sell their property, and 'the rest in that thin-settled country [would] in less than half a century, from the crowds of English settling round and among them, be blended and incorporated with our people both in language and manners.'[130] In other words, from given demographic conditions certain results would follow: the giant blocks lying on the site where Canada had stood would be used in the construction of a new edifice that would be British certainly but not English, since America was rich enough in human resources to become a colonizing power herself.

Of capital importance was the fact that ability to forecast the effects of the conquest of Canada on the destiny—one is tempted to say the manifest destiny—of British America was not limited to Benjamin Franklin and a handful of other enlightened minds; the American people as a whole seemed to sense that it had reached a decisive moment in its history. The *Philadelphia Gazette* hailed the fall of Montreal as 'the most important event, as we apprehend, that has ever happened in favour of the British.' The war had been 'the means of national advantages to us beyond what our most sanguine hopes could flatter us with . . . Instead of being deprived of our natural rights . . . we have trampled our enemies under our feet and risen upon their ruins.'[131] To assimilate a defeated nation is precisely to increase with its substance, to grow out of its ruins. The *Boston News-Letter* shouted for joy: 'The great day is now come, a day . . . made forever illustrious . . . by the fall of the American Carthage.' People kept repeating the news to one another, reminding themselves that it was true: the reduction of Canada was now an accomplished fact. A false rumour indicative of the wishful thinking of certain newsmongers purported to be a summary of conditions of surrender imposed on Montreal and the colony: 'The inhabitants of the city prisoners of war, to be sent to France: the peasants to remain on their lands as neutrals, not to trade with the Indians on pain of death.'[132]

Victory is heady wine. Even in Philadelphia, the peaceful city of brotherly love, guns were fired and bells were rung 'on account of the glorious news of the reduction of Montreal.'[133] Patrician Boston depicted the British triumph in a series of allegorical tableaux in heroic classical style: 'From an illuminated scenery at the balcony of the courthouse were exhibited the following designs: . . . in the middle Britannia sitting; on the left hand Fortitude, on the right Minerva; behind Neptune and Mars in attendance . . . Before Britannia a female figure representing France, prostrate, her sword broken, and subjecting a map of Canada at the feet of Britannia. Behind France . . . Cruelty, Deceit, Craft, and Envy, blasted by a flash of lightning from Jupiter, who sits above with the scales of justice suspended by one hand, and in the other his thunderbolt.'[134] In New York salutes were fired by the guns of Fort George and of ships in the harbour, while the people of Albany 'continued their demonstration of joy for three days without interruption.'[135] A 'Cordial Address' presented to Amherst expressed the enthusiasm and gratitude of the 'mayoralty, aldermen, and commonalty of the ancient City of New York' and at the same time revealed their inmost thoughts on the meaning of the victory. It offered 'most grateful thanks' to the general, not for adding another jewel to the British crown but for 'annexing the extensive country of Canada to his majesty's dominions in America.' The acquisition, 'inestimable in itself', was 'pregnant with the most important consequences', and 'millions yet unborn' would 'reap the happy fruits' of Amherst's victory.[136]

In comparison with those of her colonies, Britain's manifestations of joy seem sober, but that does not mean that there were no celebrations to mark the surrender of Canada. On 5 October salvoes of gunfire announced the news in London and gave the signal for three days of rejoicing. Bonfires in the capital and throughout the kingdom gave vent to British pride and satisfaction and also, as the European press realized, to a sense of relief from anxiety. 'The British empire in that part of the world,' commented the *Mercure de La Haye*, 'by acquiring a vast extent of territory, is assured henceforth of absolute tranquillity.'[137] In his first message to Parliament, George III reflected 'with pleasure on the successes with which the British arms [had] been prospered', and enumerated three great advantages resulting from British victories: they were a fatal blow to the enemy, they assured Britain's supremacy at sea, and they would procure 'most solid benefits' to British commerce, that great source of British wealth.[138] It was a far cry, however, from such expressions of satisfaction to the chorus of joy that swelled from American throats. The Reverend Thomas Foxcroft of Boston, looking back over the past, recalled the many vain attempts to effect what was now 'so happily accomplished. Long has the conquest of Canada been the object of our attention and the matter of our prayers . . . and now at length we see the happy day of its accomplishment.'[139]

In a sermon preached during a service of thanksgiving, the Reverend Nathaniel Appleton of Cambridge acknowledged 'the great and marvellous works of God' for British America. Casting his eye over the Atlantic seaboard from Georgia to Nova Scotia, he admired its provinces with their population of a million souls or more, its many towns, imposing fortresses, delightful estates, fertile countryside. He too looked back over his country's past and marvelled that 'all this [had been] done in the space of one hundred and thirty or forty years.' Did not these achievements authorize the most ambitious prophecies? Who could say what 'great and marvellous things' God reserved for the future? The communities already established were called to create a much greater and more powerful people. The time was approaching when that part of the world would be the joy and pride of the universe.[140] Appleton was endowed with the foresight of prophetic enthusiasm, or rather with the perspicacity of well-directed thought. At that unique moment in her history, when the elements of imminent expansion had been fused by a victory, it was not difficult for an intelligent observer to foresee the future greatness of British America. The colonies had already achieved a remarkable degree of development, they commanded the fabulous resources of a continent, and the competitor that up to that time they had met at every point was now eliminated.

What Americans glimpsed in the intoxication of victory, Europeans discerned by the cold light of reason, and it was not long before some of the latter began to worry about the enormous capacity of the New World for power. America, they thought, might even wrest from Europe its position of leadership—or at least confront a European mother country with the threat of an affirmation of independence. James Murray was one European in whom this particular apprehension manifested itself very early. Malartic recorded in his diary a private conversation that he had with Murray early in June 1760. According to his account the general broached the subject with a question:

'Do you think we are going to restore Canada to you?'
'I am not sufficiently versed in political matters to be able to say.'
'If we are wise, we won't keep it. New England needs a curb. If we allow you to hold this country she will be kept busy champing that bit.'[141]

The idea that this might happen spread quickly and within two or three years inspired a large number of pamphlets charged with emotion. A message from the general assembly of New York to the president of his majesty's council shows that it was already in the air at the end of October 1760. Canada, urged the assembly, must not be restored to France: 'The surrender of this most important conquest, which in the possession of the crown must prove to Britain the source of immense riches, to so perfidious a people would only expose us to the keener revenge of a defeated enemy.' The people's representatives clinched their argument by conjuring up scenes of pillage and bloodshed.[142]

The lines were drawn. A great debate was about to begin.

Part Five

THE GREAT DEBATE

Chapter X

Canada or Guadeloupe

After conquering Canada, would Great Britain allow British America to annex it? These were the terms in which the question was posed on the morrow of the capitulation of Montreal. We have already noted the declaration of the New York assembly, in whose eyes the French colony became automatically a dependency of the British American provinces, and its protest against the possibility of restitution of the conquered colony to its former mother country. New York's attitude rose from fear that the rebirth of French Canada might jeopardize the security of the colonial communities—and eventually, one may add, their enormous possibilities for future expansion. On the English side a parallel fear was beginning to be expressed; the question was being asked whether excessive security for the colonies would not prove fatal to the empire. Would not America, once freed of the French threat, cease to feel the need of English protection? If the mother country gave her a huge slice of the continent, would she not use the gift to achieve a degree of power disproportionate to her colonial status? To win for herself a place among the nations?

These were the themes of the great debate in which the British world became engaged when it became conscious of the far-reaching consequences of its victories. Following the general rule in such cases, the long argument—sometimes learned, sometimes skilful, always inspired by hard-headed self-interest, often crudely materialistic but informed at times with broad views and keen insight—was not long confined within the limits of the problem that gave rise to it. The discussion ranged far and embraced a variety of topics: the links uniting communities of British origin and the divisions arising from their various aspirations, the economic bases and the cultural foundations of the empire, war aims and the significance of the conquest of Canada. Exchanges of view were polarized around two conceptions of empire. The first, narrowly mercantilist and authoritarian in tendency, represented a tradition in which it is possible to recognize one of the primary causes of the schism by which the British world was to be torn within a generation. The second, which appears to be distinctly ahead of its time and to be still feeling its way towards a doctrine, proceeded not from the subordination of the colony's interests to those of the mother country but from the subordination of the interests of both colony and mother country to their common good. It regarded growth in one part of the empire not as a danger for the other parts but as a gain for the whole. Those who supported the first theory opposed the elimination of the French colony. Those defending the second did not recognize the need to 'curb' American expansionism.

The discussion opened with a comparison between Canada and Guadeloupe. The English had taken possession of the island early in May 1759, and one body of opinion, understandably, wanted to see it incorporated permanently into the empire. The colony was a great sugar producer. Its production was greater, so it was affirmed, than that of any British establishment in the West Indies except Jamaica, and economists predicted that Guadeloupe's sugar crop would literally be transmuted into gold; for since Britain's former possessions in the West Indies already supplied her needs, all the sugar produced in Guadeloupe would be available for export. The least optimistic estimates placed the eventual profit from its sale at 300,000 pounds a year. However, the war was not yet over. France still held Menorca and might refuse to give it up without compensation; it might then be impossible to conclude a peace without restoring Guadeloupe to France. On the other hand it was not difficult to predict, even before the end of the campaign of 1760, that the whole of Canada would be occupied by the British. So when the time came to treat finally with the enemy and to agree on concessions to be made, should Britain sacrifice Canada—or Guadeloupe?

On this point opinions were divided. The general conviction was that the small West Indian island would bring in better returns than Canada's vast northern territory. In practical terms, Canada had only one great natural resource, furs, and profits from the fur trade, even in the best years, were less than 140,000 pounds. For pragmatic minds, imbued with the spirit of mercantilism that had created the power of their 'trading nation', it was simply a question of choosing between 300,000 pounds and 140,000. But this short-sighted reasoning was repudiated by the author of a *Letter to the People of England*. 'I must give my voice entirely,' he asserted, 'for those who would rather give up Guadeloupe, with every other acquisition we have made, or may make, in the West Indies, than part with one single foot of Canada.'[1]

The person who placed the unproductive northern colony above a delightful West Indian island bounteous in tropical produce must have detected some special value in Canada, a value that lay outside the sphere of economics. What was it that weighed heavier in the balance than Guadeloupe's sugar? It was all North America, and here the author presented the argument that had already been advanced by the New York assembly: the security of Britain's establishments in North America. His argument, however, followed a somewhat different form: by restoring Canada to France, Britain would expose herself to the risk of another imperialist war. It might be objected that if France embarked on such a war she was beaten in advance. But France had been doomed to defeat in 1754. That truth was later proven by the facts, when she was utterly defeated in the New World. She had taken up arms on that occasion because she had thought, mistakenly, that her hopes of victory were justified. Did anyone think that if she had known she could not measure up to her rival in America she would have adopted a policy of aggression in Acadia and in the Ohio valley?[2] Obviously not, and what had happened once could happen again. Some advisers advanced the opinion that the risk could be averted by confining Canada within frontiers that would make any aggression on her part impossible; no one, even among the partisans of the restitution of Canada to France, would agree to a reconstitution of a New France that included Acadia, Lake Champlain, the Great Lakes, and the Ohio. 'It is much to be doubted,' answered the author, 'whether, if this were practicable, the French would not be as willing to desist entirely from the demand as to be effectually restrained within those bounds to which it is absolutely necessary for us to confine them.'[3] His conclusion was dictated by a clear consciousness of the fundamental objectives of the War of the Conquest.

This reasoning was further developed by another observer of the political scene—perhaps John Douglas, the future bishop of Salisbury.[4] A similar solution, said this author, had already been tried and had not been a success. The Treaty of Utrecht had given the English Acadia and all the disputed territory west and south of the St Lawrence. It had settled the future of America as finally as any treaty could. Canada was to be allowed to survive alongside the British communities, generously provided with space, resources, and native alliances, and henceforth secure from attack and free to trade in every part of the continent—a Canada cut off from her subsidiaries and entirely dependent upon subsistence farming. These conditions would have resulted from the international convention of 1713 if it had been observed. France had violated the treaty and the instances in which she had done so had 'produced the present war.' But although 'Gallic faith' was proverbially bad, the reason for France's disregard of 'the most solemn treaties' could be found 'without supposing that nation more perfidious than others.' When the interests of a nation are in conflict with its obligations, the latter take second place and a state feels bound by its promises only in so far as neighbouring states are strong enough to force it to respect them. In the light of these considerations it was easy to understand what had happened in America. The French had felt the need to extend behind the British provinces, with the double objective of preventing the British from winning over the native tribes and establishing communications for themselves between the St Lawrence and the Mississippi—between Canada and Louisiana. Since the St Lawrence was blocked with ice for half the year, the French also needed a second route of communication between Canada and the Atlantic, and that was the reason for an Acadian policy that ignored the stipulations of the Treaty of Utrecht.[5]

In 1755 Great Britain felt she could no longer tolerate such actions. Conscious at last of the 'infinite importance' of her colonies, she altered the course of her policy and went to war for them. 'And thus England which for half a century had been wasting its millions and lavishing its blood to obtain a barrier in Flanders which [its allies] could not defend or rather did not think it worth while to keep, began the present war, a war truly NATIONAL.'[6] A task undertaken in the interest of the colonies was because of this fact a national war; the reasoning, typical of one whole school of British thought, should be noted. Having thus revealed his profound sympathy with the main current of American thought, the author did not need to say in so many words that he was opposed to the restoration of Canada to France. He did so, however, and gave the reasons for his stand. He did not think Canada had any great value in itself and he was convinced—who would not be?—that France was not attached to the country for its own sake. But suppose it were restored to her. Who could then be sure that she would not make use of it as a base of operations for carving out another great domain for herself, and at the expense of the British provinces? If the Treaty of Utrecht had not prevented the French from encroaching on territories from which it was designed to exclude them, why would another treaty be any more effective? Once re-established on the St Lawrence, they would be under constant temptation to reach out towards Lake Champlain, then towards Lake Ontario, then . . . 'In a word you must keep Canada, otherways you lay the foundation of another war.' If France wanted to recover her colony, it must be for some ulterior reason. Its climate was harsh, it was difficult of access, profits from trade did not suffice to defray expenses. France would have abandoned it long ago if she had not hoped to use it as a starting-point for capturing the whole centre of the continent right down to the mouth of the Mississippi. 'If we do not exclude them *absolutely* and *entirely* from that country we shall soon find we have done nothing.'[7]

Had the English then fought and loaded themselves with debts for the benefit of the American colonists? The author had foreseen the objection and had an answer for it. He agreed that Britain's burden of debt was 'immense': at the end of the war it would be considerably more than a hundred million pounds. But experience proved that the country was not in danger of bankruptcy: 'As our expenses have increased we have found, contrary to the predictions of gloomy politicians, that our abilities to bear them have increased also.'[8] As for benefits to colonials, the point to be emphasized, insisted the author once again, was the 'immense importance' for England of her colonies on the North American mainland. Their population, more than a million customers for British products, assured an outlet for manufactured goods from the old country, and provided an opportunity for 'innumerable ships' to be employed in colonial trade and in the transport of important American products— rice, tobacco, fish—to all the markets of the world. Canada, since it presented an obstacle to the progress of Britain's flourishing establishments, had effectively prevented British shipping and British industry and commerce from developing as they might otherwise have done. To make it possible for Canada to recover would therefore harm England quite as much as her American colonies. Confirmation of the conquest must therefore be 'the *sine qua non* of the peace.'[9] It was certainly to be preferred to any advantage that Britain might gain in Europe, and here the author advised his compatriots not to follow the example of France, 'a sinking monarchy, nay a monarchy already sunk', whose present plight was the direct result of too deep an engagement in German affairs. 'Perhaps,' he reflected, 'it might be an enquiry worthy of another *Montesquieu* to assign the causes of the rise and fall of the French monarchy.'[10] In his opinion—one obviously shared by others—England should disengage herself in Europe now that she had achieved her aim, the conquest of Canada, in America.

The ideas expressed by Douglas, if he was the author of the *Letter*, did not remain unchallenged, but were promptly contested in a pamphlet[11] attributed at the time to Charles Townshend.[12] It seems more probable, however, that it was written by William Burke.[13] The author, a partisan of the abandonment of Canada, reasoned in this way: a victorious power negotiating a treaty has two ends in view, to attain the objectives it pursued when the war began and to obtain a 'reasonable' indemnity for the charges imposed upon it by the war. A nation that demanded more than that could be taxed with ambition. Having laid down these principles the journalist then asked whether Britain, when she decided to resort to arms, had in mind 'the possession of Canada properly so called.' It was not difficult for him to find the answer to his question: no. Assuming that in the very early phase of the disturbances by which America had been torn a realistic assessment of Britain's power had induced France to recognize the just claims of her rival—that is, if she had abandoned all claims to Acadia or Nova Scotia, demolished the forts she had built in the territory of New York (on Lake Champlain and Lake Ontario), and withdrawn from the Ohio—the war would have ceased automatically, since there would have been no cause for it, and Canada would not have changed hands.[14] In other words, during the period between 1754 and 1756 Britain was not fighting a war of conquest but defending colonies against an aggressive neighbour. She had now successfully accomplished that task. What more could she desire?

It was not Britain that wanted more, affirmed the author, but her American provinces, and they were wrong. 'If our American colonies should be so absurd and ungrateful [as] to tell us, after all the blood and treasure expended in their cause, that we do nothing if we do not make conquests for them, they must be taught a lesson of greater moderation.' They made this demand on the pretext of the fear inspired by Canada: a singular pretext indeed! 'If, with a superiority of at least ten to one, with a vast and advantageous barrier, with the proper precautions to strengthen it, under the protection of a great naval power, they cannot think themselves secure, they must blame their own cowardice or ignorance and not the measures of their mother country; who is bound to provide for their happiness and security and not for their vain ambition or groundless fear.' Every society must recognize the possibility of having hostile foreign neighbours. 'The idea of securing yourself only by having no other nation near you is, I admit, an idea of American extraction. It is the genuine policy of savages.'[15] The conquest of Canada was an American idea, the policy of conquest an American policy. This fact, easily demonstrable, could have been expressed in less violent language, but strong words have at least one advantage: they reveal the gulf that separated American opinion from one body of English opinion.

It would be an error, however, to exaggerate this divergence of views. Neither in England nor in America was there any question of restoring New France. The subject under discussion was Canada. The Americans wanted to annex Canada, while one English group preferred to give it back to France in order to acquire something else. Our author belonged to the latter school of thought. The territory he proposed to restore to France under the name of Canada was, as he said, worthless. With the British in possession of the Ohio region, the communication route through the Great Lakes, and especially Niagara, the key post of the whole system, the colony was cut off from its trading territory in the west—the richest in the whole continent—and hence of no further importance economically. Thus there was no need for England to burden herself with 'total possession' of the country; in order to drain into the British empire a great part of the fur trade that 'in the eyes of a commercial nation' constituted Canada's only interest, it sufficed to reduce the country to its true limits.[16] In other words, the American policy would have killed the defeated country with one blow; the policy favoured by some English thinkers would have allowed it to survive, a country without a future. Whether the one or the other plan triumphed, the St Lawrence community could never develop at a rate comparable to that of the neighbouring colonies.

Why then engage in a debate that threatened to degenerate into a quarrel? Because, in the opinion of this author and those who shared his ideas, the acquisition of Canada would procure no immediate gain to the mother country and would benefit only British America, which could do without it. England, for whom the conflict had been chiefly 'an American war',[17] was entitled to compensation. And where would she find it? In Guadeloupe. Profits from that island were already far greater than those from Canada, and under a good British administration they would soon be doubled. France had shut England out from the European sugar markets, but if Guadeloupe changed hands that situation would be reversed. Moreover France's position was much stronger in the West Indies than on the continent of America. The French islands were a much greater threat to the British islands than Canada to the mainland colonies. Proof of this could be found in British naval losses in the Caribbean. For reasons both of economy and strategy England, if she considered her own interests, should choose Guadeloupe rather than Canada.[18]

Another more serious factor would guide her choice in the same direction. The West Indian planter was not really at home in the colonies: he sent his children to be educated in the mother country and he himself retired to England to enjoy the fortune he had made in the islands. If he had ambitions it was in the old country that he sought to satisfy them, and a number of planters held seats in Parliament. England's tropical outposts must preserve their dependents' links with England. Conversely, when did a mainland colonial ever end his days and spend his fortune in the mother country? The industries already established in the northern provinces would eventually suffice for all their needs. New England was even exporting hats. The colonies had established their own 'colleges and academies' for the education of their youth. Their population and industrial plant were increasing rapidly, and the necessity for union with England, with whom they had 'no actual intercourse by a reciprocation of wants', would 'continually diminish.' As American settlements sprang up in the interior, as their centre of gravity moved away from the sea and they lived more and more on their own labour, Americans would be less preoccupied with the mother country: they would not know her as well, they would attach less importance to knowing her. These would be the consequences of British expansion in the New World, unless Canada remained to curb that expansion. Moreover, this evolution was no mere figment of the imagination conjured up by the author; it was dictated by geography, and he invited his readers to reflect upon the consequences of encouraging the development of 'a numerous, hardy, independent people, possessed of a strong country communicating little or not at all with England.' Had the English nation assumed the enormous expenses of the war only to fail now to secure the fruits of war for its posterity? In seizing more territory in North America she would run the risk of losing what she already held. 'A neighbour that keeps us in some awe is not always the worst of neighbours,' he averred, and that was so true in the present case that England would do well not to covet Canada even if she could hold it without giving up Guadeloupe. 'There is a balance of power in America as well as in Europe which will not be forgotten.' It would be disastrous to disturb that balance.[19]

With the publication of this remarkable composition, two schools had expressed their opinion. That section of British opinion that was attracted by the idea of incorporating Canada into the British empire could, without over-simplification, be designated the American school: first because British Americans appeared to be unanimous in favouring the acquisition of the French colony, and secondly because those Britons who shared their opinion did so less as Englishmen than as members of an empire whose American possessions constituted its most important element—after the mother country, of course. It is only to distinguish it from this first school that it may be convenient to call the second the English school. It did not speak for Great Britain as a whole: opinion was more divided in the mother country than in the American provinces, where it was virtually unanimous. But the partisans of restitution perceived in the interests of the colonies elements prejudicial to the interests of the mother country, and naturally they opposed the former and favoured the latter. When lines are thus clearly drawn, one may legitimately speak of an American and an English school.

It was to be expected that at this point in the controversy an American would take up the argument, and circumstances selected Benjamin Franklin for the task. Franklin, who was in England at the time, wrote his pamphlet before the fall of Montreal. It was unsigned, but the publicity with which it was greeted in the American press ensured that the name of the author would be widely known.[20] From Dr Franklin, a learned man and a subtle reasoner, an intensely American and intensely British patriot, one could expect skilful logic supported by thought-provoking facts, and also sudden bursts of eloquence. He was too shrewd a journalist to present himself in Great Britain as the spokesman for American interests only, and the title of his pamphlet began with these words: *The Interest of Great Britain considered . . .*[21] Was his choice of words dictated by policy? Most certainly, but also by conviction. Here was a man deeply imbued with the sense of empire. He did not ask whether the interests of Britain were superior to those of America; he knew that the interests at stake were indivisible. Convinced that the fortune of British America must contribute to the prosperity and power of the mother country, he refused to admit that the fortune of the mother country could derive from restrictions imposed upon the power and prosperity of British America.

An error 'too common' in Britain, said Franklin, was the idea advanced by the English school that the mother country was sacrificing her blood and her wealth 'in the cause of the colonies', that she was 'making conquests for them.' No, England was fighting for herself as well as for her colonies. Americans did undoubtedly yearn for victory, but in what capacity? As British subjects: 'The inhabitants [of the colonies] are, in common with the other subjects of Great Britain, anxious for the glory of her crown, the extent of her power and commerce, the welfare and future repose of the whole British people.'[22] He agreed that the addition of Canada to the empire would result in 'fantastic' expansion of the American population. According to his forecast, British America in 1860 would have a larger population than that of the mother country in 1760. But far from being alarmed at such a prospect, Britain should rejoice. As the population of America increased, British trade would flourish and with it the power of the British navy. For the human body and the body politic do not follow the same rules of growth. When it has attained a certain stature the human body ceases to grow; the body politic, on the other hand, may pass through long static periods that, by reason of a particular conjunction of circumstances, may be followed by periods of growth expanding its dimensions tenfold. In nature the stature of the mother is equalled sooner or later by that of the child, who grows while the mother remains at the same point, but how different is the case of a mother country and her colonies! Here 'the growth of the children tends to increase the growth of the mother, and so the difference and superiority is longer preserved.'[23]

The author professed not to know what constituted an empire, but to be familiar with the state of mind of British America. The opposing school feared the American provinces might unite against the mother country. The provinces unite? Franklin could not refrain from laughing

[304]

at the very idea. He had tried to persuade them to adopt a 'project of union' in 1754. His proposal had been rejected and he had not forgotten his failure to persuade his compatriots on that occasion. If, he asked, the colonies had not agreed to unite against a ruthless enemy, was it reasonable to suppose they would now agree to unite 'against their own nation which protects and encourages them, with which they have . . . ties of blood, interest, and affection, and which . . . they all love much more than they love one another?' No, such a union was not merely 'improbable', it was 'impossible';[24] impossible unless—the threat was scarcely veiled—unless the mother country were to adopt a hostile attitude towards her children in the New World, and she would be manifesting hostility towards them if she were to restore Canada to France in order that the French colony might 'curb' their progress.

It is important to understand Franklin's thought. A great colonial, he was convinced, and rightly so, that population is the vital element in any colonization: upon its success depend the vitality of the colonial establishments and that of the empire from which they spring. British America was being peopled at a more rapid rate proportionally than England because, as we should say today, the growth of population in America was 'free', whereas in England it was 'restricted'.[25] The presence of Canada prevented it from being entirely free, however. The projection of Canada known as New France barred British America from extending towards the interior of the continent and feeding upon the resources of that fabulously rich hinterland. With Canada eliminated, the growth of the colonies would be unrestricted and the population index would rise sharply, to the great advantage of the British world. Reactionary thinkers in England wanted to 'check' the growth of the American societies that otherwise might 'increase infinitely from all causes.' Franklin was furious, with the cold fury of reflection. How was the 'checking' operation to which thinkers of the English school referred to be effected? 'We have already seen in what manner the French and their Indians *check the growth of our colonies.* 'Tis a modest word, this, *check*, for massacring men, women, and children.' He appealed to the conscience of the mother country: 'But if Canada is restored on this principle, will not Britain be guilty of all the blood to be shed, all the murders to be committed in order to check this dreaded growth of our own people?' When this fine reasoning became known to them, Americans would be able to judge the value of the mother country's feelings towards them. 'Will they have reason to consider themselves any longer as subjects and children when they find their cruel enemies hallooed upon them by the country from whence they sprung, the government that owes them protection as it requires their obedience?' Such conduct on the part of the mother country would be the best means of detaching America from England and even driving her into the arms of France. The last phrase had a prophetic ring, but the author's tone was one of bitter irony. England should not go to all this trouble in order to thwart the growth of her colonies; it would suffice for Parliament to decree a second massacre of the innocents, this time in the New World.[26]

The practical thinkers denounced by Franklin were also those that preferred Guadeloupe to Canada, and in this case he had two arguments to oppose to theirs. In advancing the first he met them on their own ground: economics. He argued in effect that the value of Guadeloupe was determined by the value of the region in which it was situated. Formerly imperial powers drew much greater profits from tropical colonies than from colonial settlements in temperate climates. At that time the value of an establishment was measured by the quantity of exotic products supplied by it to the mother country. But with the expansion of white populations overseas, trade between the colony and the mother country had become the prime factor. The worth of a colony to the mother country depended upon the manufactured products it bought rather than upon the raw materials it sold. In that respect the West Indian market had remained stationary, while the North American markets were constantly expanding. The movement was of recent origin, but it was evolving rapidly. In 1744 the North American provinces imported from England goods to the value of 640,000 pounds, while those entering the West Indies were valued at 800,000 pounds. But in the period between 1744 and the end of 1748 the trend began to veer in the other direction: the value of goods sold to the mainland colonies exceeded by 123,000 pounds that of orders from England for the West Indian markets. The gap between the values of imports to the West Indies and to the mainland widened constantly between 1754 and 1758. In 1754 exports to North America brought in a million and a quarter pounds sterling, those to the West Indies 678,675 pounds; in 1758 the difference between imports into the two groups of colonies was slightly less than a million pounds; for the period between 1754 and 1758 it was almost 3,650,000 pounds. Two other curves demonstrated where the buyers of the future would be found. Between 1748 and 1758 the value of English exports to the islands had increased by 400,000 pounds, that of cargoes for North American ports by 4,000,000 pounds. After considering these facts, concluded Franklin, there was no need to ask if Great Britain would be better inspired in favouring her continental colonies rather than her island factories. The American press immediately seized upon the eloquent figures quoted in his letter.[27]

This, however, was only one of the two arguments advanced by Franklin to prove Canada's superiority in comparison with Guadeloupe. Returning to his first theme, he emphasized the fact that Canada had a very small population, while Guadeloupe was thickly peopled with planters of French origin. The latter was settled, the former still entirely open to colonization. A country in which one nation has set up permanent settlements, he argued, is not a profitable possession for a state different in language, customs, and religion. In such a case the costs of occupation may well be greater than the profits from exploitation.[28] These comments from an intelligent observer give us an idea of what Canada was in 1760: a ruin undoubtedly, but the ruin of a meagrely populated colony. The case against the deficiencies of French colonial policy in America could not be better stated. France had failed because she had been parsimonious in her investment of human resources, and now the colonies of a rival empire—Franklin, it will be remembered, did not ask colonists of England—were offering to undertake a settlement project.

Franklin's famous essay contained the essential of American thought. While more expert spokesmen for the English school were preparing their answers, various journalists published commentaries on British policy. One praised Pitt, 'the delight and ornament of his country', whose memory would be celebrated by future generations 'with admiration and gratitude', and recommended that a place be made for Canada in the empire.[29] The recommendation should not, however, be interpreted as an expression of fidelity either to a party or to a statesman. Another, although he ranged himself among the adversaries of Pitt (that Don Quixote whom the English people had followed like a servile Sancho Panza), also wanted Canada.[30] He criticized the former prime minister —he was writing after Pitt's defeat—for having allowed himself to be won over to a policy of large-scale intervention in Europe: 'I must be of opinion that [Britain] can never have a call upon her for the same ruinous connections with [Europe] that she has at present.'[31] He blamed Pitt for having multiplied the nation's debts beyond all reason: 'all the emoluments that possibly can accrue to us from our conquests are insufficient to indemnify us for the sixth part of the annual interest of the money they cost us.'[32] It was therefore imperative not to relinquish the most important of those conquests. England had been justified in declaring war: 'the French encroached upon our back establishments; they erected a chain of forts that bade fair . . . either to thrust us from all our possessions upon the continent of America or to render them insignificant to their mother country.'[33] The security of the colonies had been the prime cause of hostilities, and the acquisition of Canada 'an accidental rather than the primary object of the present war.' As the conflict evolved Canada had become the means of securing the safety of the American provinces, and it was therefore essential for Britain to hold that country.[34] As for Guadeloupe, its acquisition must be regarded as 'extraneous to

[307]

the original necessary principle upon which the war began', and the island must be restored to France. Those who upheld the contrary opinion were merely a 'set of men in this island who find their interest in discouraging the planters of our own islands.'[35] Once Canada was won and Guadeloupe restored to France, peace should be concluded forthwith, for the English people in general were heartily tired of the war. 'None clamour for the continuance of war,' concluded the author, 'but those who gain by it and who, like the coasters in Cornwall and Shetland, subsist upon storms and shipwrecks.'[36] One may wonder why this polemical essay was immediately translated into French. Perhaps the subtle statesmen of Versailles were glad to hear an English voice calling for an end to hostilities, expressing war weariness, offering to restore Guadeloupe and demanding only Canada; perhaps they wanted the French public to hear it also.

Franklin's opponents were rather slow in publishing their replies, but the first of these was both intelligent and vigorous. Its author introduced himself as an English gentleman in Guadeloupe and presented his reflections in the form of five letters to a friend in London.[37] He cherished few illusions, and he knew what it was that gave Britain her predominant position in Europe and the world. Whereas others attributed the greatness of their country to the innate qualities of its inhabitants, he was not vain enough to accept an explanation that explained nothing, and he recognized frankly that England owed 'all her liberty, wealth, and happiness' in great measure 'to her being an island disengaged from the dangers and quarrels of her neighbours.'[38] Her liberty: by that we must understand her political régime and her independence, a political régime born of experiments in revolution that could not have been carried out by a continental power obliged to secure its integrity, an independence reinforced by an excellent political régime but secured in the first place by a protective girdle of water. Only an island could afford to plough the seas, as Britain did, with a great armada of floating fortresses. The island kingdom needed their protection, and since it required only a modest land army it could devote its resources to the creation of a great navy. Canadians, whose economy was shattered by defeat, might have found food for thought in the comment with which, almost casually, the author threw into relief the relation existing between the strength of a group of people and the vitality of its economy: 'If a nation have neither trades, manufactures, shipping, nor commerce, it can never be formidable to its neighbours, though that nation should understand both the theory and practice of agriculture and vegetation better than any people on earth yet does.'[39] The opposite view had been expressed some two years before by a French economist and had apparently surprised the journalist who reviewed the work in which it was presented: 'The author asserts . . . that there is no true power in a state but what arises from agriculture . . . that of all politic states that will ever be the most powerful whose lands are the most fertile; that the grandeur of nations is a superb edifice built upon dirty acres.'[40]

Franklin's opponent had fixed ideas on the respective values of Canada and Guadeloupe; he wanted none of Canada, his choice was Guadeloupe. He deplored the influence of 'private views' on the debate in which he was engaged, and cited as an example an adversary who had already denounced the 'set of men' who favoured the choice of Guadeloupe. He too pointed an accusing finger at the group of influential personalities to whom he attributed the movement in favour of restoring Guadeloupe to France. Incredible as this might seem, they were the big West Indian planters and their allies, the financiers and shipowners of London, Bristol, and Liverpool; all these businessmen were apprehensive lest the introduction of another sugar island into the empire flood the English market and bring down the price of sugar appreciably. Such fears should be dismissed; they were inspired by ignorance, and even if they had been justified they should not be allowed to overshadow the national interest.[41]

The same considerations militated in favour of the return of Canada to France: in the first place the colony had no economic value, for 'what does a few hats signify?' In the second place it was not true that its possession was essential to the security of British America; if that were so Louisiana too would have to be conquered.[42] But these were not the arguments to which the author gave his special attention. His main argument sought to prove that the addition of Canada to the American colonies presented a serious danger for the colonies themselves. Guadeloupe sugar would be a tonic for the empire's commercial organism, while the addition of Canadian territory would weaken its political structure. British America was a young giant. Its area was ten times that of the mother country, and its soil in most regions richer than the soil of England. And what a wealth of resources! The variety of its climates was matched by the rich diversity of its products. An infinite number of waterways provided its economy with excellent communication routes. It had all the raw materials with which to build a great navy: inexhaustible quantities of wood, iron, hemp. 'Such a country, at such a distance, could never remain long subject to Britain.' The last years had added to the strength of the country by giving its inhabitants an opportunity to learn the art of war, and now they were full of the spirit of independence: 'They are always grumbling and complaining about Britain, even while they have the French to dread. What may they not be expected to do if the French is no longer a check upon them?' The Imperial government would be reduced to the costly expedient of 'a numerous standing army' in the colonies 'to overawe them', and even this expedient would soon prove to be as ineffectual as it was costly. For what would happen to these garrisons? The soldiers would become accustomed to living in America and at the end of their period of service would acquire property there, marry, and become Americans. The cure would merely hasten the progress of the disease; the watchdogs would become members of the family from which they were protecting the mother country. These predictions did not result from a gift of prophecy; one had only to consider the logical consequences of the 'popular madness and political enthusiasm' inspiring demands for possession of Canada. Let France keep her colony. 'Nothing can secure Britain so much against the revolting of North America as the French keeping some footing there to be a check upon [British colonials] . . . but if we were to acquire all Canada, we should soon find North America itself too powerful and too populous to be long governed by us at this distance.'[43]

Having spoken of 'political enthusiasm', the 'gentleman in Guadaloupe' cited as an example an article in the *Gentleman's Magazine* of May 1761. The author of the article, completely won over by the American idea, affirmed that 'though America should increase to a hundred million of souls, there would be no danger still; they would depend upon and be subservient to seven or eight million' European Britons. What an absurd suggestion! The error was compounded by the assertion that America's increase in population would be achieved without any corresponding loss to that of the mother country. How then explain the fact that the population of the mother country was not growing as fast as that of her American establishments? And it must not be forgotten that the population of the colonies was improving in quality as well as in quantity: North America was 'advancing with hasty strides towards maturity.' She was beginning to cultivate the arts and the sciences and she had entered the field of trade and industry. How could it be otherwise, when her people enjoyed 'the same laws, liberties and genius' as native Britons? And 'the more she increases in these [domains] the less she must want from Britain', while on the other hand 'the more she rises above a certain pitch, her utility and advantage to Britain must proportionately decrease.' The time was perhaps not very far distant when Americans might refuse to send their tobacco to English ports, when they might realize that they would gain more by selling it themselves in the markets of the world. If such a situation should arise, what steps would the British government take to bring her subjects to heel?[44]

The discovery of America hastened the evolutionary process that early in the sixteenth century began to tranform Europe. British trade, whose importance as a factor in this general movement had increased and which was the base of the industrial and maritime expansion of British power,

was now more flourishing than ever and more active than that of any
other nation. At the same time, three-quarters of that trade was now
carried on with the West Indies and North America. Attracted by new
horizons, commercial interests had allowed their activities to slow down
in certain quarters, notably in the Levant and in Spain; foreigners had
quietly taken up their succession there while Englishmen, who had been
most active in exploiting the opportunities offered by America, concentrated their attention on that country. But they would have a sad awakening if, after neglecting and thus losing their traditional outlets, they found
themselves deprived of their American markets also. And let no one
think the threat was imaginary. It was real and imminent and could not
be parried so long as the public infatuation with continental America persisted. England's colonies there had developed to the point where they
were no longer profitable to the mother country. Although British America 'was just emerging out of infancy', she was producing more goods
than her normal outlets could absorb. Her population doubled every
twenty years, and in every sphere its progress was proportionate to its
growth. The country was already producing a surplus of agricultural
products, and in any case it had developed beyond the point where its
population could be employed exclusively in farming; the next inevitable
step was industrialization. Meanwhile American trade had gained an
important footing in the West Indian market and British trade was beginning to feel the effects of competition there. This trade offensive, in
conjunction with increasing industrialization, would eventually shut out
the old country from the West Indian markets, thus creating a situation
tantamount to the elimination of Great Britain from the New World.
However, the present situation offered an opportunity to ward off the
danger born of the widening disproportion between the tropical and
continental elements in the British American empire: to hold Guadeloupe was to reinforce the former, to cede Canada was to confine the
latter within reasonable bounds. Guadeloupe would offer a new outlet
for northern agriculture and thus distract the larger colonies from the
temptation to industrialize, while at the same time the presence of a
rival, Canada, just across their border would oblige them to seek and to
deserve the protection of the mother country.[45]

The author repudiated in advance the accusation of anti-colonialism,
although he was evidently opposed to colonies that prospered too well.
He agreed that colonies had their advantages. They contributed to the
wealth and dignity of a state, and to its influence on other nations—but
only when their founders followed the dictates of reason, good policy,
and experience. To 'settle colonies in new countries' appeared to him 'to
be no more than creating of a new people to trade with the mother
country, under all the disadvantages to them and all the advantages to

[311]

herself that she pleases to impose upon this new child or vassal.' The usefulness of a colony would then be increased if it required comparatively few immigrants, if its products differed from those of the mother country, and if the mother country took care to maintain a certain margin between its own growth and that of its overseas establishments, thus ensuring that the empire would be guided by its head and not its members. A nation would be mad to settle territories ten times larger than her own, with a similar climate, and with soil fertile enough to yield more abundant harvests of better quality—unless, that is, 'the principal view were to transfer the mother country there, to make the new colonies the mistress of the world and the poor old mother . . . her slave.'[46] This author's concept of empire, though logically consistent, runs counter to history: history moves forward, while his arguments are too firmly rooted to move with it. Two possibilities presented themselves: England could be mistress of an empire or the mother of nations. The author would have preferred a somewhat less vigorous empire, one that did not hold the threat of a nation about to be born. He would have liked time to stand still at that fine hour for England—but he did not propose that the clock should be turned back. He agreed with his adversaries in opposing the restoration of New France. The Canada he would give back to France would be a small country so completely divested of its trading territory that most of its trade would fall into the hands of the British Americans.[47]

Up to this point the author had argued against general ideas; he now attacked ideas as they were expressed in Franklin's pamphlet. Franklin had pleaded for the acquisition of New France 'in the interest of Great Britain.' He had argued that the possession of the American continent would make the English 'the greatest people in the world', and had painted a glowing picture of an England gorged with wealth and of American provinces, freed from the cramping presence of a rival, providing millions of customers for the mother country. His promises, retorted the author of *Reasons for Keeping Guadaloupe*, recalled the words of the tempter: 'Ye shall be as gods.' 'I hope,' he protested, 'we shall be wiser than grasp this gilded snake and be bit to death.' It should be realized that the brilliant advantages, of which North America enjoyed more than any other country in the world, were the very thing that threatened the mother country. If it was true that in a hundred years the population of America would be four times that of England, then it could not be denied that America would be a danger. England could confine the Negroes of Guadeloupe within the limits of an agricultural economy, but she would never succeed in keeping a mass of Americans at that level; whatever Franklin might say on the subject, America would inevitably develop industries and compete with Britain for world markets. Moreover, only the most guileless prophet could suppose that American trading operations would be confined to the empire. It was a well-known fact that even while the country was at war, Americans had trafficked with the French West Indies and carried on exchanges harmful to the common cause not only with foreign neutrals but with the enemy. By the same token the author wondered whether Franklin was not an apostle of American independence.[48] Towards the end of the essay he taunted him openly: if his adversary was as young as his reasoning seemed to suggest, he would perhaps live to see his dreams of independence realized.[49]

Franklin's 'sophisms and subterfuges' were denounced in another pamphlet published about the same time.[50] The 'unprejudiced observer' who was its author bent all his effort towards discrediting Canada. A note acknowledged La Hontan's books as the source of much of his information. The dreadful climate of the country had always been an obstacle to colonization. France had made every effort to establish settlements there, but although advantages of every kind were offered to desirable colonists, none were willing to risk the adventure, and she had finally to resign herself to peopling her colony with her own undesirables: prostitutes and men condemned to the galleys for 'atrocious' crimes. This 'refuse' of French society was naturally almost completely sterile, a fact that explained why Canada's immense territory was populated by fewer than 100,000 inhabitants—inhabitants whose only patrimony was 'the united good qualities of a whore and a thief.'[51] Their manner of living denoted 'the extremest indigence and poverty.' The standard of living even of the 'principal inhabitants' was far inferior to that of the 'ordinary people' in the British colonies. And this was readily understandable. Because of the harshness of its climate and the inadequacy of its population, the country had not been brought under cultivation. It had no roads. In summer travellers paddled canoes 'like so many savages', and in winter they drove in sledges 'like so many Laplanders.'[52]

It was inconceivable that the victor should attach any importance to the possession of such a colony. It had always cost its mother country more than it paid her in benefits. But should England perhaps consider holding it for motives of security? No, since only the 'unexampled' negligence of the English had allowed it to encroach on the territory of its neighbours, and thus constitute a threat to the British provinces. Before Canada had spread out towards the lakes and allied itself with the western tribes it had not been powerful enough to arouse the slightest apprehension, and reduced to its proper dimensions it was neither to be feared nor desired. By holding Acadia and linking the western frontier of British America to the territory of the Hudson's Bay Company, the English would 'entirely surround all Canada' and from these commanding situations could strike directly at the heart of the country if it ever became troublesome. The safety of British America would be assured, and the mother country would not be 'encumbered with the cold, barren, uncomfortable and uninviting country of Canada.' Louisiana, which did not 'want attractiveness', would be a more desirable addition to the empire than Canada. Not only would a British Louisiana procure peace for the American settlements, its resources could be developed and would serve to enrich the British community as a whole. The colony already produced tobacco, indigo, and cotton. The mulberry trees that grew there in abundance gave promise of a flourishing silk industry, and tea might likewise be cultivated since Louisiana was 'nearly in the same latitude as Pekin in China.' Its geographical position had still another advantage: convenient communication with the West Indies. On reflection, Louisiana was to be preferred to Canada on every count. The possessor of the Mississippi valley commanded the vast spaces beyond the Appalachians. The port of New Orleans would serve all that hinterland. As the pressure of overpopulation built up in the east, new colonies would be created in the heart of the continent, and western pioneers who would otherwise be condemned to economic isolation would have access through New Orleans to the Caribbean and the Atlantic. Still more important, the opening of these immense spaces to agriculture would retard the evolution of British America towards industrialization. It was important that the pace of this movement should be slowed down, since progress towards industrialization was inevitably linked with progress towards independence. Let England then demand that France cede Louisiana! Once that condition was accepted, she would gain rather than lose by restoring to France a Canada stripped of its dependencies and reduced 'to the state it was in at the treaty of Utrecht.'[53]

At the same time England should take possession of any sugar islands she could get her hands on. By so doing she might seem to show a shocking lack of moderation in her demands, but that thought should not cause any uneasiness. To limit herself, as the author of one pamphlet proposed, to attaining objectives defined at the beginning of the war and to be satisfied with an indemnity based on the expenses incurred during the conflict—these ideas reflected a 'modern doctrine' justified neither by history nor by reason. If this doctrine were put into practice, all the profits of war would be reaped by the aggressors. The ancients had followed a more reasonable practice: among them 'it was the custom for the victors to proportion their demands according to their successes.'[54] Victorious Great Britain, following in their footsteps, was free to keep what she wanted: a well-balanced empire, suitably provided with northern establishments and tropical plantations. Up to that time the primary resource of the North American colonies had been agriculture, and more West Indian islands would give them more markets for their agricultural products. The 'spirit of manufacturing' was already stirring in the colonies. The restoration of Canada and the annexation of Guadeloupe would favour an incipient movement of industrialism and industrialism would weaken the link between the colonies and the mother country. Britain had then two motives for adding to her possessions in the West Indies, the one just outlined and the desire to build up the British sugar trade from which she would naturally expect to derive substantial profits.[55]

Franklin had advised the mother country against holding Guadeloupe and warned that it would be impossible to assimilate the island's solid French population. The same argument, retorted his adversary, could be applied to Canada, where the inhabitants, under an English government, were 'liable to be reduced to the utmost insignificance and poverty.'[56] The English writer had misunderstood Franklin, who had foreseen the gradual disappearance of Canadians from Canada, but there was little difference between the complete disappearance of the Canadian population and its survival as a poverty-stricken remnant. It is enough to record these two opinions and to observe that they are in agreement. Though forecasts, they should not be regarded as prophecies but rather as what they are: reflections born of a knowledge of what constitutes the structure of societies.

It is now possible to define the main difference between the two currents of British opinion on Canada. Those who opposed the restoration of Canada to France wanted to avoid repetition of the events that had marked the half-century following the Treaty of Utrecht. What did France want in 1755, asked the author of another pamphlet, a European war? By no means. All she wanted was to conquer at least a part of the British settlements in North America. Canada was her base of operations and by restoring that colony, Britain would be exposing herself to the risk of another war. But, it was argued, in adding Canada to the British empire in America she would be exposing herself to the more serious risk of a conflict between the mother country and her colonies. The American school of thought rejected this reasoning out of hand. Such apprehensions betrayed a complete misunderstanding of the filial relationship binding her loyal provinces to the mother country. Were not the inhabitants of these provinces Englishmen or descendants of Englishmen? Did they not also enjoy British liberty? Was their trade not linked with that of Britain? Were their forts not defended by British troops and their shores by the British navy? In such conditions the threat of separation was very remote indeed.[57] This conception of the empire was to survive the approaching schism and would be that of the future.

Certain other observers, leaving these grand considerations of policy in the background, expressed the traditional and conservative view of the mercantilists. For them England was a 'commercial nation' and the empire a business that must be made to prosper. For Henry McCulloh, a member of this group, the decision as to whether Britain should hold Canada or give it up depended on the economic value of the country. What was its value to France? In the first place an annual trade estimated at 420,000 pounds sterling, of which two-thirds came from the fur trade and the rest from naval construction and agricultural products. In the second place, possession of Canada helped to consolidate France's hold on the fisheries of Cape Breton and the Gaspé country, worth perhaps 400,000 pounds. Navigation and transport operations associated with these activities would add some 220,000 pounds, and McCulloh estimated the gross annual contribution of Canada to the French economy at a million pounds sterling. On the other hand the sums spent by the French government for the maintenance of the colony were 'immense', and could not be justified by the profits of Canadian trade alone. But France had two powerful motives for loosening her purse strings. She was thinking of her navy—the fisheries and North American trade employed 9,000 sailors and provided a great school for seamen—and she was planning to expand her empire: possession of Canada made it possible for her to establish herself on the Mississippi and in the midwest, and perhaps eventually 'to open some ports on the western ocean.'[58] But the midwest belonged to England and the British navy did not need the St Lawrence, so Britain had less to gain from occupying Canada than had France. Her best interests would lie in holding most of the conquests she had made in all parts of the world, not in sacrificing others in order to hold this one colony. In North America it would be enough for her to re-establish the stable situation provided for by the Treaty of Utrecht. It gave her 'the whole province of Acadia' as well as 'the lands which of right then belonged to the Five Indian Nations, which included the five Great Lakes and the territories thereunto belonging.' With the exception of the fisheries 'the remainder of Canada . . . is not an object of any great moment to this Kingdom'—or, he might have added, to any kingdom. McCulloh anticipated one objection to his argument: far from settling the American question, the Treaty of Utrecht had created a situation that had given rise to the last war. But he was ready with his answer: the war had been provoked not by the insufficiencies of the treaty but by England's failure 'to form a system in American affairs' that would have ensured its strict observance. Let this be a lesson to her to create such a system![59]

Fighters in the American camp agreed that Canada, shorn of the western territories upon which its economy was based, had little importance in itself. One glance at the map showed that the nation commanding Lake Ontario—attributed to Great Britain by the Treaty of Utrecht—also commanded most of America's furs. The fur trade alone made Canadians rich, or at least made it possible for them to buy manufactured goods from their mother country. Cut off from their fur-trading empire they would have nothing to export to France, and France for her part would have a completely unprofitable colony. In other words, what made it possible for Canada to survive and for the mother country to reap some benefit from her colony was the exploitation of a back country rich in fur to which Lake Ontario was the key, and Lake Ontario did not now belong to France. But, said a spokesman for the American school of thought, it did not follow that this worthless colony should be restored to its former owners. If France was content to take back Canada without Lake Ontario, this would be proof she was meditating some dark design. She could not want Canada for its own sake; if she desired to repossess the country it was reasonable to suppose it was in order to forward some policy prejudicial to British America. And there was also the question of the Indians. During the war the Indians had massacred some 4,000 Americans and laid waste a strip of country 600 miles long and 100 miles wide at the back of the British provinces. They would never have been in a position to inflict such losses if Canada had not supplied them with an abundance of war materials. These considerations could lead to only one conclusion; anyone endowed with good sense and some spirit of impartiality must admit that 'unless we hold Canada, we hold nothing.'[60]

At the point at which we have arrived, this revealing discussion was not yet ended, but events were about to give it a decisive direction. An element in French society was preparing to express its ideas in its turn, but the decision about to be made by the British government would have even greater import. What policy would the ministry adopt?

In the course of the debate, well-founded arguments had been advanced by both sides. As we have pointed out on more than one occasion, the divergence between the two schools of thought was less wide than might at first be supposed. Both ruled out the reconstitution of New France, and this was a point of supreme importance for the future of Canada. Unanimous agreement on this question when opinions differed on so many others indicates clearly that one era in American history was ended.

At the same time the spirited debate revealed the fact that the British empire was at the crossroads. Those who, with Franklin, thought that the interests of England would be served by the development of the American colonies were certainly right. But their opponents were not wrong who foresaw the day when those same colonies would rise against the mother country they had ceased to need as a guardian and protector. What the former sensed was that, whatever happened, the British world

[317]

was too closely integrated ever to cease to form one whole. The latter, short-sighted and arrogant, did not perceive that the empire was already groping for a formula. That Franklin, whose colonialist arguments were more valid than those of his opponents, was destined to become one of the architects of the American revolution is not an 'irony of history'. History does not indulge in irony. It is simply an indication that the empire would not find its formula until too late and that it *could* not find it until too late.

Finally this exchange of views reveals the importance of Canada. The British world was hardly less embarrassed by a Canada in ruins than by the ambitious edifice it had been. Vibrations set up by its fall would hasten the disruption of the forces to which it had itself succumbed.

Chapter XI

From One Empire
to Another

In the spring of 1761 the maritime and colonial war was entering its
eighth year, the European war its sixth, and a certain fatigue was beginning to make itself felt in many quarters. For almost two years there
had been talk of assembling a congress of the belligerent powers, but it
had been inspired by a vague desire to initiate *pourparlers* rather than by
the will for peace. Now, however, the time seemed ripe for more serious
negotiations, and France and England exchanged plenipotentiaries.
François de Bussy was sent to London and Hans Stanley to Paris, but
the true arbiters of Europe's fate continued to be Choiseul and Pitt. The
former sincerely desired the war to end, but at the same time he was
ready to play his trump card, an alliance with Spain, in case negotiations
broke down. The latter, with his customary rigid arrogance, declared in
advance his opposition to any treaty that did not promise England both
Canada and the Newfoundland fisheries.[1] It was easy to foresee a rupture
of negotiations if the British cabinet as a whole held the same views as
Pitt. But the government was divided: some ministers considered that
even though France might agree to give up Canada, she would never
abandon her right to the fisheries, for that would mean sacrificing any
hope of surviving as a naval power.[2] The Duke of Bedford and Lord
Hardwicke even maintained that France should be allowed to repossess
Canada, the former because he thought that would be the best means of
assuring the submission and fidelity of British America, the latter because
he feared the United Kingdom might, like Spain, weaken itself with the
burden of too many colonies.[3] It was not possible, however, for Choiseul
to exploit this divergence of views. Pitt was still powerful enough to win
one last victory over his colleagues; the military triumphs of the last
years had made him the idol of the populace and the mere threat that

he might withdraw into his tent sufficed to muzzle any opposition to his superb intransigence.

If Pitt had wanted only Canada, the government of Louis xv would have been glad to satisfy him. Stanley reports an amusing and significant scene that took place before his eyes on 17 June in Choiseul's office. Negotiations were being carried on with infinite caution and were proceeding at a snail's pace. Finally the French minister, losing patience with the elaborate fencing match, seized a pen and in two minutes wrote down his proposals: France would restore Menorca in exchange for Guadeloupe, Marie-Galante, and Gorée; she would also give up Canada, but she would keep her fishing rights on the American coasts, and since her fishermen would need harbours and drying stations, she would repossess Île-Royale, but would destroy her military establishments there; finally, she would restore the German places captured from Britain's allies. The proposals, as Stanley remarked, covered barely a dozen lines. They were written on 'a little leaf, in size and shape [more] like a *billet doux* for a lady (a correspondence in which he [Choiseul] is much versed), than the memorial for a peace between two great nations.'[4]

The same proposals were developed at greater length and in heavily diplomatic style in a document dispatched from Versailles to the British court on 15 July 1761. The first article confirmed Choiseul's earlier note: 'The King cedes and guarantees to the King of England without restriction Canada as it was possessed, or deemed to be possessed, by France.'[5] The English answer was dated 29 July, and its tone was peremptory. Great Britain demanded all Canada, Cape Breton, and all the islands in the gulf and the river St Lawrence, 'with the fishing rights inseparably attached to the possession of the said coasts and of the channels and straits communicating with them.'[6] In reply to this document, written in the tone of a formal demand, France presented an ultimatum dated 5 August: she reiterated her agreement to give up Canada, and at the same time claimed the 'immemorial right' of her subjects to fish in Newfoundland waters, a right, she added, that would be illusory if her fishermen did not have at their disposal a harbour and drying grounds. For that reason she desired to hold either Cape Breton, or Île-Saint-Jean, 'or any other unfortified port in the gulf or within reach of the gulf.'[7] While repeating that it had not ceased to insist upon 'the complete and absolute cession' of Canada and Cape Breton, the English government agreed on 1 September to reopen the gulf of St Lawrence to French fishermen and to grant them the right to dry their fish 'on a specified part of the coasts of Newfoundland' and to shelter in the port of the little island of Saint-Pierre. But no fortification could be built on Saint-Pierre, only fishing boats would make use of its harbour, an English commissioner would be stationed there, and the commander of the Newfoundland fleet would inspect the island from time to time in order to ensure that the French did not violate the treaty.[8] Saint-Pierre, answered Choiseul, was too small to meet all the needs of the French fishermen, who must also be permitted to moor at Miquelon. France also agreed to the presence of an English agent at Saint-Pierre, and in fact rejected only one of the conditions that Pitt meant to impose upon her: the right of inspection by the admiral on the Newfoundland station. The minister protested that the condition was 'contrary to the dignity of the nation'; it had been introduced into the proposed terms with the single object of 'making an unwarranted claim for English superiority.'[9] This minor difference could have been resolved without difficulty, but Pitt used it as a pretext for an abrupt rupture of negotiations.[10] His real design had always been to exclude France from Newfoundland in order to strike a death blow at her navy. And France—who was still strong enough to do so—refused to bow to demands that would have entailed the disappearance of her ships from the seas.

For months Choiseul kept repeating that he was prepared to cede Canada. On that point he offered no shadow of resistance, but he insisted upon saving the fisheries. These were the two cardinal points of his American policy, and his attitude appears to have been substantially that of the merchants and shipowners. Early in July the chamber of commerce of Saint-Malo had begun to give its attention to the diplomatic conversations, whose serious import was strongly suggested by the prolonged presence of Stanley in Paris. Saint-Malo had suffered severely from the war, and the chamber of commerce, in the hope of obtaining some compensation when the time came to negotiate peace terms, resolved to make representations to the court. In a letter addressed to Choiseul and Berryer, they pointed out that the treaty must not be concluded without first requiring the English to compensate for the losses inflicted by their acts of piracy on French shipping between June 1755 and the date when war was declared. They were still more urgent, however, in their appeal to the two ministers to protect the interests of the fisheries, a 'branch of trade more precious to the state than all the gold of Peru, for gold cannot create a single sailor and it creates several thousand sailors every year.' No fisheries, said the chamber, no sailors, and 'no sailors no navy, no real power.'[11]

A few months later the French government published a memorandum, accompanied by relevant documents, on the negotiations that had been interrupted by Pitt.[12] It was quite clear that if agreement had been reached it would have been the end of Canada and of Canadian trade. La Rochelle was one of the principal ports engaged in that trade, and the documents were a cause of grave concern to its business community. The chamber of commerce decided to associate itself with other chambers of commerce in the kingdom to create a movement of opinion in favour of the restoration to France of her former American colony. The first group to which it wrote was the chamber of commerce in Marseille. The members of the chamber of La Rochelle could not express the 'feeling' they suffered at the 'sacrifice' the king was considering in order to obtain peace for his peoples. They were preparing to present to the duc and the comte de Choiseul a memorandum pointing out 'the infinite importance' of Canada, the loss its cession would inflict on industry, agriculture, and fisheries, and the harm it was sure to do to marine activity. Without the shipping of the northern colonies, they affirmed, the navy would die, trade would cease, and all France's other colonies would fall. In their opinion it was better to continue the war than to lose Canada, and they invited the citizens of Marseille to make their own representations in the same cause.[13] A month later they reported the favourable reception their memorandum had received at court. The duc de Choiseul had answered with congratulations, and even with 'applause'.[14]

Spurred on by this encouraging news, the citizens of Marseille decided to make representations to the minister in their turn, but they clothed their observations in a prudent verbosity of expression. As their colleagues had obtained good results with that formula, they spoke of the 'sacrifice' of Canada to which the king had resigned himself, and added that the fact that he had agreed to such a course showed how cruelly his heart was wrung at the sight of his subjects bowed down with the sufferings of war. If they took the liberty of submitting their reflections to Choiseul, it was less 'to instruct the most enlightened of ministers' than to 'stimulate themselves' to their utmost efforts on behalf of 'a colony so necessary and useful' as Canada. Unfortunately the minister considered that those excitable Marseillais were stimulating themselves rather too much, and snubbed them for their pains. He considered it improper for them to enter into 'a sort of association with other chambers without first being authorized to do so.' He advised them sharply to act in future with 'more reflection and reserve.' But what had they said that had so provoked the minister? They had reminded him of the advantages 'in regard to manufactures and navigation' provided by Canada, and had remarked that the loss of the country would entail the loss of its inhabitants, 'good subjects who would remain under English rule.' They had made a rapid survey of the import and export trade resulting directly from possession of the colony, and had observed that it would be difficult for French fishermen to continue to fish on the Newfoundland banks if they were obliged to give up their stations on the St Lawrence. Finally —and this was perhaps the crime of which they were guilty—they had mentioned the serious difficulties created for shipowners, merchants, and bankers having business relations with Canada by the suspension of payment on bills of exchange. Once launched on that subject, they had even asked when the bills would be 'fully' honoured.[15]

The chamber of commerce of Nantes, careful to avoid such breaches of tact, merely agreed in its answer to La Rochelle that abandonment of the colony would 'doubtless' prove harmful to French trade. At the same time it confessed itself hesitant to make direct representations to the authorities on this subject, for fear of 'displeasing and even offending the minister.' In its letter to Choiseul it praised the persistence with which, in the course of the negotiations, he had pressed for recognition of France's right to the slave trade, freedom to fish off the shores of Newfoundland, and reparation for prizes captured by the English before the declaration of war. As to Canada, which Choiseul had agreed to cede in exchange for some of these advantages, it expressed the modest hope that future successes of the king's arms might one day force the English to accept peace and restore to France 'a colony so useful to the state.'[16]

The citizens of Saint-Malo were even more reluctant to act than those of Nantes. They apologized for not following the example of their compatriots in La Rochelle, and pleaded in excuse that although they were stirred 'by the same patriotic zeal' as the latter, they were not endowed with 'the same talents'. Fundamentally, as they admitted in another letter, their interests were different: they could not speak pertinently of Canada since they knew little of Canadian trade and took no part in it. That did not mean, however, that they would refrain altogether from intervening in the matter. As we know, they had already taken the initiative, while negotiations were still being carried on, in calling the attention of the court to the fisheries, and they now urged the citizens of La Rochelle to make representations to the court concerning 'the abuse on the part of inhabitants of the colonies of the privilege of freedom from pursuit for payment of debts and from seizure and sale of property.'[17] On that point the fate of Canada was for them a matter of grave concern. O shades of Jacques Cartier!

The chamber of commerce of Le Havre shared these preoccupations. They would have liked the coastal cities 'to enter into an agreement . . . and to request all at about the same time' that defaulting debtors in the American colonies be liable to court action, 'as in France', and subject to seizure of their business assets. They had very little interest in Canada, and when solicited by La Rochelle, they answered that having always confined themselves to commercial matters they had observed and would continue to observe a policy of silence 'on political affairs.' When, much later, they decided to write to Choiseul, they congratulated him on his 'firmness' in demanding the restitution of ships captured by the enemy in the months preceding the declaration of war. When they referred to Canada, it was to denounce the beaver monopoly, granted to the Compagnie des Indes, and to affirm that 'if it had not been for its monopoly on that precious fur, there would have been no war in that colony.' This was presumably not a 'political' consideration, but the line was finely drawn. Other proposals were that the Compagnie des Indes should cease to enjoy the monopoly of the slave trade, and that West Indian planters should be forbidden to refine their own product and be obliged to export their raw sugar to France.[18]

The mayor and aldermen of Granville, a port on the west coast of the Cotentin peninsula that sent its fishing fleets to Newfoundland, confessed themselves 'not well informed on Canadian matters.' Rather than comment 'superficially' on them, they preferred to deal with the fishing industry they knew so well, and they repeated the familiar refrain that the fisheries constituted a 'nursery of seamen.' If the king were forced to give up Canada, they would propose that he obtain in exchange the whole south coast of Newfoundland. They were also solicitous for the West Indies—West Indians consumed 'a great deal of cod-fish.'[19]

The Dunkirk chamber of commerce agreed to collaborate with the chamber of La Rochelle; it proposed to support the latter in a memorandum to the court 'on the immense wealth derived from the cod fisheries', and with this end in view it made careful inquiries in some of the other ports where fishing was a major activity: Saint-Malo, Honfleur, Pernef. Its aim was not to save Canada—that was the least of its concerns—but to 'make the ministers aware of the great importance of our fisheries, in order to procure the greatest possible encouragement for them and to ensure that that branch of industry be well known and receive advantageous treatment at the peace.'[20]

The Bayonne chamber, when in turn it was called upon for support, felt it could not refuse this service to a sister chamber. Accordingly it instructed its representative in Paris to put in a good word with the court for Canada, a colony with which La Rochelle 'carried on its principal trade.' At the same time the members asked their agent to declare their agreement with the protest of Nantes against the action of the government in permitting foreigners to sell slaves in the West Indies. Their collaboration was limited, however, to expressions of sympathy. If, they wrote to their anxious compatriots in La Rochelle, the ministers gave way on the question of Canada, it was not because they undervalued the colony, but rather because they felt powerless to recover it. Recognizing the ministers' 'helplessness' in the matter, they feared that further representations might be 'ill received'. As for themselves, since 'each place concerned itself with the principal objects of its commerce', they were reserving their attention for the fisheries, and in conjunction with the shipowners of Saint-Jean-de-Luz were working on a memorandum 'on that interesting subject.'[21]

The Montpellier chamber, like that of Bayonne, took care not to commit itself in a cause that was of so little concern to its members. It thanked the chamber of La Rochelle politely for 'its zeal for the welfare of commerce', and expressed its readiness to 'work towards the same ends' by 'urgent solicitation' of the ministers. It had only one reflection of its own to add: if Canada were abandoned, the little clothmakers of Languedoc would be threatened with ruin.[22]

Bordeaux was the home town of the intendant, Bigot, and of Lamaletie, Latuilière, Roussens, the Gradis, and the Desclaux, all shipowners, merchants, and bankers with important business interests in Canada. The 'sacrifice' of Canada touched these citizens of Bordeaux to the bottom of their cash boxes. Voltaire, an intellectual whose purse was filled from other sources, professed to prefer peace to Canada; the members of the Guyenne chamber of commerce placed Canada above peace, and they did not hide their preference. To justify the regrettable necessity for such an order of priorities, they set before Choiseul a list of the advantages assured to France by the possession of her far-distant colony. Every year sixty ships sailed from the mother country to Canada with cargoes of wines, brandy, cloth, trimmings, silks, 'and generally all sorts of luxury goods.' They represented a capital of ten million livres and a profit of two million. The return cargoes were made up of furs, products from the fisheries, and bills of exchange covering the expenses of the king's service in the colony. Some of the ships engaged in the Canadian trade made the voyage by way of the West Indies, picking up sugar syrup and rum for Quebec on the way out and discharging wood from the St Lawrence valley on the homeward voyage. This triangular trade demonstrated the importance for 'the interests of the islands' of retaining the northern colonies. So much had been accomplished before the war, with an advantageous peace much more could be done. The possibilities offered by Canada had not been fully exploited: they had scarcely been touched. Vast profits could be made from the cultivation and sale of Canadian tobacco, wood, and hemp. And the members of the Bordeaux chamber, like their colleagues in the sister ports, emphasized the importance of fishing operations 'in Canadian waters'. If France wanted to assure the future of her fishing industry, occupation of Saint-Pierre and Miquelon was no substitute for possession of the St Lawrence and 'the cession of Canada would certainly entail [the loss of] the cod fisheries.' Finally, the people of France, who were deeply attached to the West Indian colonies, should remember that possession of Canada was a guarantee of security for the islands. What was to prevent New England, once she was freed from any danger on the mainland, from turning ambitious eyes towards the Caribbean? To sum up this situation in one word, Canada was in-dispensable to France. The internal economy of the mother country cried out for development of the colony's resources: 'Agriculture, manu-factures, the whole mass of French industry' demanded it. Moreover, care for other interests that she intended to maintain in the New World commanded her re-establishment in Canada. From there she could im-pose respect upon an intransigent power that made war 'for gain', a power convinced that possession of wealth would make her pre-eminent and that she would find 'in expansion of her trade the source of that wealth.' In other words, to surrender any element of strength was to add by that much to the strength of the enemy and to doom herself to giving up everything sooner or later. That was why it was better to fight on than to buy at such a price a peace that could only be temporary and that would prepare the ground for 'a still more fatal war.'[23] Bordeaux's letter to Choiseul is one of the best statements of the Canadian case made at that time. No other chamber of commerce presented such weighty argu-ments in defence of the colony.

The Bordeaux letter is quoted whenever an attempt is made to estab-lish the fact that 'France' was moved with regret for the separation of Canada from the mother country. As if the businessmen of Bordeaux were France! Let us review the story briefly. In La Rochelle the chamber of commerce took note of the Franco-British conversations of 1761, and observed that the court had let slip no opportunity of offering to allow England to hold Canada. Its members were disturbed; they protested; and in order to give more weight to their representations to the minister, they tried to induce nine other chambers of commerce to take action. Two of these, the chambers of Marseille and Bordeaux, supported the move. But what of the other seven? Nantes declined to express an opin-ion, Le Havre talked of other matters, Montpellier was concerned for its cloth. Bayonne, Saint-Malo, Dunkirk, and Granville all expressed platonic sympathy for the idea presented by La Rochelle, but each of the four took up the specific cause of its own fishermen. All agreed auto-matically with Choiseul, who had always been much more determined in his efforts to protect French interests in Newfoundland than in his claims to possession of Canada. One can see how absurd it would be to set the court on one side and the business world on the other and to conclude that the latter wanted to hold Canada while the former was willing to give it up.[24]

After the publication of the notes exchanged in 1761 between France and England, the British adversaries of the restoration of Canada could breathe more freely. Their government was on their side. Early in Sep-tember an article in the *St James Chronicle* recalled the objectives that had been decided upon when the nation went to war: to support the colonies and to prevent the ruin of American trade. This was all Britain had asked, but as the war had developed it had given her much more: a large slice of America had been added to the empire as it existed in 1755. Thus the mother country was rewarded for its sacrifices. The expansion of the empire in the New World, judging by the astonishing increase in power, trade, and wealth that England had enjoyed as that continent's lands were brought progressively under cultivation, presaged new heights of prestige and prosperity for the nation.[25] Three months later the same journal observed that Canada must not be omitted from the North American picture. Returns from that country might seem modest in comparison with those from Guadeloupe and Martinique, but the reason for such paltry results lay in France's failure to exploit the resources of the colony. Canada, judged by the volume of its products, was still almost an undeveloped country.[26] It was true that the time was past when the value of colonies was estimated on the rather narrow basis of their products. It was now realized that their value lay not only in what they produced, but in what they consumed. Seen from that angle, the expansion of the American domain seemed even more promising. The expansion in territory could not fail to be followed by an increase in population, and England would be assured of markets so important that in two or three generations she would sell more to America than to all the rest of the world combined.[27]

The English people could congratulate themselves on their good fortune, but that did not mean that they were unanimous in approval of Pitt's American policy. In 1761 one journalist dismissed as 'absurd, contradictory, impolitic' the *pourparlers* that had been carried on in Paris, with Stanley representing the government. In the opinion of this writer, Pitt—who was soon to make the boast that he had never envisaged any other than a war of conquest[28]—and with him his whole cabinet, had given proof of incredible timidity. 'The British ministry ought by all means to have insisted on France ceding *all* North America to Great Britain.' The cession of Canada did not suffice to guarantee the security of the American colonies, since it left the enemy in possession of Louisiana, whence they could launch as many attacks as they had previously been able to organize from their northern colony. Unless the peace terms fixed the western frontiers of the British establishments on the Mississippi, Britain would have fought in vain and the threat to the territorial integrity of her colonies would be as great as it had been in 1754. Wherein lay the value of Canada in the eyes of Frenchmen? In the fact that it communicated with Louisiana. Alone, Canada counted for little in strategic considerations and still less in economic matters. Louisiana was worth 'forty times as much', with its fine climate and well-watered soil, its cotton, rice, indigo, building wood. The minister had committed a gross blunder in allowing himself to be fascinated by Canada and in refusing to see the great importance of Louisiana.[29]

That had not been his only error. He had been equally blind in abandoning to France a share in the Newfoundland fisheries and the island of Saint-Pierre; for Saint-Pierre was 'as well situated as Cape Breton' and, if the enemy ever became established there, might become another Île-Royale. Before the war the fisheries had been immensely valuable. If France were excluded from them, they would bring in two million pounds more a year to Britain's coffers.[30] Sugar was another of the 'principal' branches of the enemy's maritime trade, although before the Treaty of Utrecht, Britain had sold sugar to France. Subsequently, thanks to the development of her Guadeloupe plantations, France had conquered the European sugar markets one after the other, ousting her rival and earning for herself an annual profit equivalent to a million pounds sterling. And now the prime minister was preparing to give back to France her rich West Indian establishments. What could he be thinking of? He was in a position to dictate the terms of peace. Why did he not take advantage of the opportunity to ruin French trade 'by cutting off its sources'?[31] To keep Guadeloupe, to remain sole masters of the Newfoundland fisheries, to capture all North America—these objectives, in the opinion of this extremist, should constitute the triple ambition of the people of England.

At the opposite pole of opinion we find another malcontent. His criticisms were inspired by the feeling that the British government, in its discussions with the French court, had been too greedy for territorial expansion and not sufficiently anxious to secure solid economic advantages. This writer, imbued with the mercantilist tradition, was inclined to cry down all colonies except those that exported tropical products. In his view the West Indian establishments were more valuable than those of the mainland and, on the continent, the southern provinces more valuable than those in the north. England would have been better inspired to set her sights on Florida and Louisiana rather than on Canada, a country too cold to produce anything but furs and too badly situated to have any part in the West Indian trade, which had in any case become a New England monopoly.[32]

If, the author went on, the British negotiator had preferred Canada to more profitable colonies, it was because he had relegated to the background economic advantages that were there for all to see, and preferred gains of a different nature. It was a popular idea that the vast spaces in the interior of the continent on both sides of the Ohio would one day feed British trade with an abundance of useful goods. Doubtless it was that mirage that had misled the minister, who was quite mistaken about the value of that country. Separated from the great traffic routes by distance and by the mountains that intervened between it and the Atlantic coast, it had nothing to offer to British trade except articles whose bulk aggravated the problem of transport. England's good suppliers and good customers were not the colonists in the western settlements, but those in the communities along the coast and on the rivers that flowed into the Atlantic. What did the Ohio country produce? Furs. When the furs were exhausted, its inhabitants would have nothing to export to Great Britain in exchange for the manufactured goods it would always need. When that time came they must either establish manufactures themselves or revert to the condition of savages. But it was not in the interest of the mother country to possess industrialized colonies. It was argued that even if the Ohio did not at that time produce anything but furs, the time would come when it would export all sorts of food products. Some people even envisaged the possibility of manufacturing silk. That was perhaps possible, although it seemed highly improbable and the fact still remained that to overlook establishments already productive in order to acquire the Ohio country was to sacrifice the real to the possible, the certain to the uncertain. And how unreasonable to saddle oneself with Canada in order to get possession of the Ohio! 'These Ohio countries never composed any part of Canada.'[33]

Canada would be of no use to England; she already had colonies along fifteen hundred miles of the coast of America, colonies of which several extended six hundred miles into the interior, which covered an area equal to that of France, Spain, and Italy combined, and which could support a population of thirty million—'possibly as many subjects as our prudence ought to desire, because they are as many as our strength will enable us to govern.' This reflection led the author to challenge Franklin's claim that until Britain possessed Canada, there could be no security for British America. Not only was this assertion not proven, said our author, but Franklin himself had come very close to disproving it. One of his great arguments was that tangible evidence of the Canadian threat could be seen in the ravages caused by Indian raids, although the Indian raids had not prevented a constant increase in the population and development of the colonies. Moreover, still according to Franklin, the progress realized by American trade between 1755 and 1758 had been greater than that of any three-year period previous to 1755, and yet that was the period of the bloodiest raids.[34]

In fact, averred the journalist, possession of Canada was not essential for the security of British America. The war had 'broken' the French and given England Acadia and all the Ohio country. The British had thereby achieved 'irresistible superiority', while the French, beaten and powerless, were 'confined within the real bounds of Canada.'[35] In short, this observer implied, once New France was dismembered, Canada was no longer to be feared. If he had stopped there, his argument could have been defended, but by trying to prove too much, he damaged his own case. He went on to say that Canada had never been a threat to British America: 'It was not the *danger* of our colonies, but the encroachments on our rights, rights which, however remote or inconsiderable, it would not have suited the dignity of our crown tamely to have seen invaded.'[36] A contemporary retorted sensibly that the terrible war that had cost so much in wealth and in human lives could not be attributed to so futile a motive; the truth was that systematic French encroachment had caused grave damage to British possessions in America and destroyed much of their value for the mother country.[37]

The general argument of the pamphlet led to the following conclusion: if for reasons beyond the grasp of the ordinary understanding England persisted in gaining possession of Canada, she should at least realize the price she was going to pay for it. In order to get this colony, she seemed ready to hand over both the Newfoundland and St Lawrence fisheries to France, although either of these fishing grounds was more profitable than Canada. Clearly in such a bargain the French had nothing to lose and the English nothing to gain. But even more astounding was the fact that in order to stay in Canada, Great Britain was inclined to restore Guadeloupe to the enemy. That was too much! Not only was Guadeloupe more valuable than the St Lawrence settlements, it brought in higher profits than any territory on the American continent. If there was one rich populous province, one that had a really good press in the mother country, it was Pennsylvania—and Pennsylvania was less profitable to Great Britain than Guadeloupe. During the first year of British occupation Guadeloupe had imported British goods to the value of 238,000 pounds; one could imagine how the figure would increase in normal conditions. In 1752, a normal year, Pennsylvania had absorbed 201,666 pounds' worth of British products.[38] Would England exchange that province for Canada? When peace terms were being negotiated, England should first seek to recover her losses. The expenses of the war had been enormous and it would be only reasonable for her to hope that her conquests might help to lighten her heavy burden of debt.[39]

All the author's reasoning was based on one fundamental idea: that Canada presented no grave danger to British America. Unless that idea was a sound one the doctrine based upon it could not stand, and an adversary, realizing it, launched an attack on this vulnerable point in the pamphlet we have just summarized. France, he asserted, had never had any considerable power in America outside Canada. Her other establishments had drawn 'their existence, their supplies and their support' from Canada. From Canada had come the troops that had defeated

Braddock and those that had attacked Johnson in 1755; Wolfe and Murray had fought in Canada. Threats to the British provinces 'all had their source in Canada.' It followed that only the definitive conquest of Canada could destroy such threats. Certainly Louisiana, almost empty of inhabitants and always neglected by the mother country, offered no threat to Britain's possessions. Moreover it was easy to exaggerate the unproductiveness of Canada and of the mainland in general, and to overestimate returns from Guadeloupe. The authority of the statistics introduced into the debate by Franklin in 1760 could not be challenged: they established a clearly discernible tendency in British trade to make rapid progress in North America and to remain stationary in the West Indies.[40] To hold Canada was to assure the future of Britain's most important group of colonies.

It might perhaps be argued that the colonies were already too powerful, that they were beginning to compete with the mother country in European markets, and it was true that American trade with Great Britain and other nations was growing daily. Americans exported articles that the English did not offer for sale, because they did not produce them or preferred to keep them for themselves or because it was more profitable for them to sell them in some other part of the world. So far so good. But what if an American exporter appeared in a market where an English exporter was already doing business? In such a case the latter, if he was wise, would consider himself lucky to have as competitor 'a fellow subject and not a foreign rival.'[41] In other words, Americans had as much right as old-country Britons to enrich the British world: economically the empire was one. It was also one politically, in the sense that the rights of the colonies and those of the mother country constituted a 'common cause'. The idea was expressed about the same time by still another author, who proposed to develop the following proposition: 'That the English American colonies are part of the commonwealth, and well entitled to the rights, liberties, and benefits of it.'[42] The idea of empire would travel far on the road thus opened to it.

If, thanks to her empire, England occupied a favourable position among the great nations, it was not only, nor especially, because her possessions brought raw materials to feed her trade; it was really because the New World, producing men, gave her the strength in numbers that she had formerly lacked, and without which she would have remained a third- or fourth-rate power among the nations of Europe.[43] Since possession of Canada would give further impetus to the growth of British America, Britain must resolve to capture Canada. Once that aim was achieved, she must make peace, the sooner the better.[44] To continue hostilities in order to pile up conquests and annihilate France and Spain would be to give way to unreasonable, and in the long run disastrous,

[331]

ambition. Misfortune for other nations did not guarantee England's prosperity, and it would be folly to reduce good customers to conditions of pauperism. Britons must remember that their market was the world.[45]

While this dialogue was in progress the international situation continued to evolve and negotiations were resumed. Towards the end of the summer of 1762 the Duke of Bedford arrived in Paris in great pomp, and on 3 November he set his signature to the preliminaries of peace.[46] In the same month an *Enquiry into the Merits* of the proposed treaty appeared in London. It was full of praise for the terms as they were reported. England had entered the war to achieve security for her colonies, and she had gained her point: the cession of Canada relieved her distant provinces of any threat of danger. British America was now assured of absolute peace and at the same time had gained all the territory at the back of the provinces as far as the Mississippi. The United Kingdom had been engaged for years not in one but in two wars, one maritime and the other continental, one 'successful' and the other 'destructive'. By the preliminary agreement the war in Europe was brought to a satisfactory conclusion and the colonial conflict was crowned with glorious victory. Britain's empire in North America was enriched by the acquisition of Canada, a part of Louisiana, and the Newfoundland and St Lawrence fisheries, while France retained only the island of Saint-Pierre. Miquelon would also be ceded, but these islands were too tiny to be worth settling. 'The whole treaty then taken together,' concluded the author, 'gives us every commercial advantage we ever claimed and secures to us every commercial object which our enemies ever wished to deprive us of. Our American empire will be enlarged beyond our most sanguine expectations.' And that was only the first step. Britain's triumphs stemmed less from military might than from an organized economy, the source of the strength before which her enemies had been forced to bow. Vigorous trade, flourishing colonies—these were the components of the 'superiority' that had been evident even before the outbreak of war and of which her conquests were the fruits. By practising the arts of peace she had developed the power that had enabled her to win the war. With a broader colonial base and assurance of still more active and profitable trade, the empire would increase rapidly in size and importance. Its wealth would grow in proportion to its size and importance, and its importance in proportion to its wealth. The British nation had reached a summit from which it could glimpse still greater heights.[47]

With the publication of the preliminary articles of peace[48] and their acceptance by Parliament, it was evident that Canada would become a part of the British empire and that any attempt to move public opinion in favour of Guadeloupe would be futile. Discussion of the respective

[332]

merits of the two colonies was now purely academic, but that does not mean that the articles agreed to by the colonial powers passed without comment. The preliminary agreement and the Treaty of Paris by which it was ratified (10 February 1763) were studied carefully by more than one observer of the political scene. The views expressed in one of the essays inspired by the event—on the role of economic activity in a great modern state and on that of colonies in the growth of a world power— are worth examining, if only to glean some idea of the character of the empire in which Canada would be incorporated.

Trade, said the author of these *Thoughts on Trade* . . . , and by that he meant maritime trade, was the mainstay of British independence. The neighbour of a nation strong in numbers and power, England would soon have lost her political and social institutions ('our religion and our liberties') if naval strength had not compensated for her numerical weakness. In order to increase her security, she must bend her efforts towards reducing the difference in numbers between her population and that of France, while at the same time she must be watchful to maintain her superiority at sea. The population of Britain would increase only as the nation's economy was organized to provide a larger number of subjects with the means of earning a living. Thus the value of any economic activity must be measured not in terms of profits but by the number of hands it employed. A community strong enough numerically to have no fear of neighbouring groups might conceivably be satisfied with an internal trade capable of absorbing all its members; but a state like Great Britain, requiring a great fleet for its defence, also required overseas trade in order to maintain its navy. Such trade might be carried on either with foreign countries or with colonies.[49] The latter possibility was much more to be desired than the former, for the mother country and her dependencies, 'however divided by distance . . . would still be as one nation; the intervening ocean should be only as a large river dividing between two counties.'[50]

Here is an idea to be remembered: the mother country and her colonies constitute one whole, and the ocean, instead of appearing as a formidable factor of division between the elements of the empire, should be likened to the line of demarcation between the small administrative units of one country. This was the concept of a mind open to the realities of colonial evolution. Although one is tempted to see in it the image of the future, it was in reality that of the present, as opposed to the idea, already outstripped by events, of colonies stabilized in the mode of an outworn mercantilist philosophy. Compared with this broad, perceptive view, those expressed by Choiseul in 1765 seem narrow and antiquated. Choiseul, after defining the aims of colonization, had drawn the following conclusions from his reasoning on the subject: 'The first is that it would

[333]

be an error to consider our colonies simply as provinces of France separated by the sea from the mother country. They differ from provinces as the means differ from the end; they are nothing more than trading establishments. The second consequence is that the more colonies differ from the mother country, the closer they come to perfection as colonies. The third principle inherent in the purpose of colonies is that they must be maintained at the highest possible degree of prosperity and subject to the strictest prohibition in favour of the mother country.'[51] This summary of his convictions reveals quite clearly Choiseul's reasons for surrendering Canada. By contrast, England's action in that critical juncture was that of a great nation. Disregarding the superstitions cherished by some branches of public opinion, she adopted the policy proposed by her boldest thinkers and chose to go forward with them rather than remain anchored in strong but outmoded positions.

In France, Choiseul's narrow colonial views prevailed not only at court but in intellectual circles. Even after casting off their anti-colonial prejudices and accepting the idea of France as a world power, many French men of letters retained extremely narrow views on the empire itself. There is a vast difference, as Gabriel Esquer has pointed out, between the Montesquieu of the *Lettres persanes* (1721), in whose opinion 'the usual effect of colonies is to weaken the country from which the colonists are drawn without peopling the one to which they are sent', and the Montesquieu of *L'Esprit des Lois* (1748), but even the Montesquieu of 1748 saw only one advantage in colonies: they placed the mother country in a position 'to carry on trade under better conditions than with neighbouring peoples.'[52] Enlightened opinion, slow to recognize the fact that colonies had a certain value, was unable to see in them anything more than an opportunity for easy and profitable 'trade'. A symptom of this attitude is the esteem in which the productive West Indian colonies were held even by the doctrinaires of anti-colonialism. The West Indies had brought wealth and happiness to the states that has sent colonists to them. 'Happiness,' wrote the abbé Raynal, 'generally results from luxuries, and increases as these become more varied and widespread. The islands have procured this advantage for their possessors, that they have obtained from those fertile regions attractive products of which the consumption is a source of enjoyment.' Moreover, improvement in the nation's well-being, resulting from an increase in 'commodities' and a more intensified trade, was reflected in international relations: 'These colonies have raised the nations that founded them to positions of influence in the political sphere.'[53] The thinking even of France's most advanced intellectuals was out of date on this point. Unlike the British journalists who set a higher value on Canada than on Guadeloupe, they did not understand that a people of French origin on the North American continent was worth more to its mother nation than all the sugar of the islands. They were much less discerning and less sound in their reasoning than a statesman like La Galissonière who, fifteen years before the Treaty of Paris, had realized that Canada was valuable because it produced men, 'a fortune more to be prized by a great king than sugar or indigo, nay than all the gold of the Indies.'[54] Choiseul thought as the intellectuals did. Unless France recovered her West Indian plantations, he would not sign the treaty, but he abandoned the idea of populating Canada.

To return to the *Thoughts on Trade*, its author considered it highly desirable that colonies should enter the trade stream on which the nation was being borne along, and even that they should compete with the mother country in foreign markets, for such a conflict of private interests was by no means harmful to the general interest. No doubt the colonial merchants did, in these circumstances, force Britain's exporters to accept lower profits, but far from spoiling the market they actually protected it by excluding foreigners who might become dangerous rivals. Moreover, the money gained by colonial merchants in these operations was not lost to British finance; it would circulate in the empire and sooner or later fall into 'the lap' of Great Britain.[55] It was no more harmful for the American colonies to trade with the French West Indies than for England to have commercial relations with France, and the advantages they derived from trading with the islands would make it possible for the American provinces to increase their exchanges with the mother country.[56]

The West Indies, continued the author, had often been compared with the British settlements on the continent. The latter were infinitely more profitable as customers than the West Indies, where Britain always bought more than she sold. The deficit trade would have been a serious handicap if it had not been compensated by a favourable trade balance with the North American colonies, who bought from the mother country much more than they sold to her and who in turn sought to bridge the gap with profits realized on sales in foreign markets. Englishmen who marvelled to see the big island planters making a great show of their wealth and spending fortunes in London would have been less impressed if they had reflected that the money they saw flowing so freely was really their own money. Continental Americans could have cut an equally magnificent figure if their exports had exceeded their imports.[57]

The growth of the North American communities should not be discouraged; rather it should be stimulated. Their assets were in every respect excellent. In the first place the colonies occupied an enormous territory extending from the thirtieth to the forty-sixth parallel. They could grow European crops as successfully as the countries of Europe: hemp and flax as well as Russia; fruits, oil, and wine as well as France, Spain, Portugal,

[335]

Italy or Madeira; cotton could be grown in Georgia. It was just a matter of developing all these resources and to that end encouraging a greater variety of production than had thus far been practised. The development could not be expected to take place spontaneously, for it presupposed a period of transition and some difficulties of adjustment. A tobacco planter could equally well cultivate grapes or olives, but it was not simply from habit that he persisted in raising a crop that was less profitable every year. He was sure of placing his tobacco in England, and since he could not count on a similar market for oil and wine he did not produce them. Such an example helped one to appreciate the beneficial effects of the premiums paid by the Society for the Encouragement of Arts, Manufactures, and Commerce to promote new ventures in new directions. The rewards encouraged originality and provided help for the colonist who did not yet have a stable market for his product. Such practices, if generalized, would help to ensure that the soil of America would give the most profitable returns.[58] Throughout his remarks the author emphasized the part played by citizens of the mother country in the promotion of a colonial economy.

His *Thoughts*, the author went on to explain, must not be mistaken for a sermon. In presenting the case for a richer America he was not preaching philanthropy, for the more prosperous America was the stronger she would be, and the stronger she was the more effective would be the support she could give the old country. In the war just ended the colonies had not remained inactive: they had collaborated in the capture of Louisbourg and in that of Havana, and they had played a still more important part in the conquest of Canada. Here he expressed an idea that was to be taken up again on the eve of the War of Independence and that lies at the root of what an American historian has called 'the American national tradition':[59] 'Without their men either in the provincial or government American regiments we could not have made the figure we have done in the war.'[60] Considering the wealth of the provinces, especially the northern provinces, in human resources, 'we may reasonably conclude that in the space of fifteen years we may raise out of our continental colonies an army of more than 20,000 men (especially if they have no enemy at their back) which may be employed in case of rupture with France against her West Indian Islands.'[61] In fifteen years —the author was not a very good prophet, at least in respect to his time schedule. But the recruiting operation he saw as a possibility for the eighteenth century would be carried out in the twentieth, and on an enormous scale.

The American colonies could play a still more useful role by absorbing the mother country's surplus population. We must not allow ourselves to suppose that there is any contradiction between the idea already advanced by the author—that England must increase her military forces in order to resist pressure from France's superior numbers—and anxiety for the mother country's surplus population. It was an age when demographic phenomena were being subjected to scientific study. Research into such questions was especially active in England, and was farther advanced there than in the other countries of Europe. Our author cites one important conclusion resulting from the research that had been carried on: the mass of world population was increasing faster than were the means of subsistence to be drawn from the earth. Leaving aside the wider implications of the theory, he confined his discussion to the case of Great Britain. He noted that his country needed men, but that she produced more men than she could support, more than she could provide with the work that was their means of livelihood. He rejoiced that her surplus population could find its way to North America rather than to Europe, where it might make an appreciable contribution to the population of France. Thanks to her colonies, England could benefit from the surplus of births: it would supply subjects to maintain British security and prosperity in the New World. Such an outlet was a godsend, especially at a time (1763) when a reduction in the number of industrial workers was imminent, and when the return to a peace economy would deprive thousands of workers of their means of livelihood.[62]

The importance of North America could best be measured by imagining it occupied by the French. In that case the French would profit from the prosperous business relations with the British colonies that England now enjoyed, and by reason of their possession of North America they would be masters of the Caribbean. 'They would be in the highroad to Universal monarchy and our very independency would be endangered. The preservation of the continental colonies we may deem, as things are now circumstanced, essential to our continuing a free people.' In these views the author was not alone.[63]

It followed from this reasoning that the government had been right in demanding the surrender of Canada, possession of which was essential to the peace that British America needed. Those persons were in error who thought that Canada, 'reduced to its true dimensions', would be harmless. To be sure, peace terms that carved off all the outer territories of New France would put an end to the encroachments from which the provinces had suffered, but not to Canadians, the authors of these violations of territory. The writer therefore proposed more radical terms for the future treaty, terms whose object was not merely to counteract the effects of the grievance but to remove its cause. Canadians as such would cease to exist from the day they became British subjects.[64] In these stark terms he expressed his measure of Canada's defeat.

Once the Canadians became British subjects, it was only natural that they should contribute by their work to the prosperity of the empire into which the fortunes of war had brought them. The annual value of Canada's trade was probably more than 100,000 pounds. This was a small sum, but Canada was 'an improvable estate which, if properly managed [would] turn to a most excellent account.' The St Lawrence and its tributaries would constitute an excellent network of inland waterways. (Actually the river was to become the nervous system of British Canada.) But the economy of the new colony, in order to be viable, must be adapted to that of the empire. To achieve this end, radical changes would have to be made. Communication between Quebec and the Caribbean islands would cease altogether, and trade relations with the West Indies would be maintained by the other British colonies, which were better situated and better equipped to develop them. Moreover 'the Canadians must apply themselves to those branches of trade in which our other colonies will not interfere with them': these might include naval stores, pitch, tar, turpentine, iron, copper, hemp. They could sell the products of mines, forests, and agriculture 'without danger of rivalship.' The markets of Cape Breton and the islands, which had formerly provided outlets for their products, were now closed to Canadians. Since they were limited to the small internal market, it followed that only a very small part of the population could profitably engage in the sale of agricultural products; but in the circumstances they had 'no choice'.[65] In other words the conquest, or rather the transfer of Canada from the French to the British empire, would be accompanied by a veritable revolution in the country's economy. The Canadian community, remnants of a defeated people torn from its administrative frame, without leaders and without resources, was in no position to direct the revolution: it could only suffer it, and accept the fate of peoples subjected to revolutions.

With the approach of peace, England saw a glittering prospect opening up before her. She had played well and had won a game that could very easily have been lost, and for that she should give thanks. '[We should be] thankful to almighty God,' proclaimed our author, 'that our case is not what we feared a few years ago in 1757, nor what we have deserved, nor that of our enemies.'[66]

If it was right for England to thank God for having been spared the fate of defeated France, it would have been even more natural for British America to congratulate herself on having escaped the fate of defeated Canada. For the victors, as we have already noted, realized full well the extent of the cataclysm that swept away New France. The men who took part in the great debate we have been studying understood, when they reflected upon it, the extreme gravity of the blow that had struck down the Canadian community. Even those who favoured restoring Canada to France would have surrendered a shrunken, impoverished Canada, a country of restricted horizons whose people would not have had room enough to breathe. The others, those whose idea prevailed, had not the least doubt that the conquest, carried to its natural consummation, would within a comparatively brief period of time result in the complete disappearance of the people of Canada as an organized human group. To take some territory and leave some—even to take a great deal and leave very little—declared one political writer, was to limit the effects of Canadian presence in America; consummation of the conquest implied elimination of that presence. His reasoning should be noted; it shows both what the conquest was and what the conquerors wanted it to be.

The king's council, deliberating in Versailles in December 1758 on conditions in Canada, foresaw what would be the fate of Canadians in the case of defeat: they would be subject to the law of the victor. It is worth noting again here that when they intervened, the chambers of commerce of France talked only of trade, fisheries, credit, and navigation. Only one, the Marseille chamber, referred to the fate of the Canadians who would fall under English rule, and it was the only chamber that was rebuked by the court. What exactly did it mean to be subject to the law of the victor? In the context of the war it could mean only this: to leave the North American field free for the British; in a word (always the same word), to disappear. When the British world took possession of Canada it could not, even if it had desired to do so, serve both its own interest and that of the Canadian community. The two were irreconcilable. Britain had not rent the seamless coat of New France in order to fashion a garment for Canada. The discussions we have followed show quite clearly that that was not their intention.

These discussions also reveal that England decided to hold Canada only after careful reflection. She could not be unaware of the risk involved in introducing Canada into the empire. If only one voice had been raised to warn her of the power of the stimulant the conquest would inject into the American provinces, one would merely wonder at the prophet's gift of foresight and observe that his prediction had been lost in the confusion of practical considerations. But the men who foresaw the results of the destruction of Canada—and they were more than a few —were practical, hard-headed thinkers steeped in the realistic tradition of the mercantilist school. The destruction of the Canadian body politic would prepare a place among the nations for British America. It would either add impetus to the organic transformation taking place in the empire or hasten the empire's disruption. The warning was repeated often enough for England to take heed, and yet she continued on her course.

Why did she do so? Partly, no doubt, because the momentum she had acquired could not be checked; because she convinced herself that everything would come out right in the end; because she was determined not to repeat the experience of 1713; because she thought it prudent to take away France's largest colony; but especially, it would seem, because she had undertaken the war in order to defend her American empire, and repeated setbacks suffered in the first phase of the conflict had proved the necessity for defeating Canada in order to realize that objective. If by taking Canada she was running the risk of upsetting the balance, of favouring the American colonies at the expense of the empire, it was equally true that by allowing Canada to live she ran the risk of compromising the future of the whole British world by permitting a French world to develop beside it. Even conceding that if a French Canada had been allowed to survive it would never have been strong enough to uproot British America, its presence would still have been an obstacle in the latter's path towards the fulfilment of its destiny. History had demonstrated in the half-century following the Treaty of Utrecht that North America could not be divided between two genuinely foreign powers.

Those Britons who allowed themselves to be dazzled by the prospect of immediate gain would have preferred to hold Guadeloupe, whose wealth was immediately negotiable, rather than Canada with its still undeveloped resources. Others were frightened by a possibility soon to become a reality. Their advice was to limit the growth of the American colonies, to leave Britain's aggressive competitor in possession of the neighbouring colony, and by these means to slow down the march of British America towards independence, its logical goal. Rejecting the advice of spokesmen for both these schools of thought, choosing rather to invest in the future, Britain adopted a policy designed to maintain and enhance her position as a great power, a policy that brought rich rewards.

Conclusion

As we complete our study of a troubled period in Canada's history, it would be an error to suppose that at the end of the chapter we can simply turn the page and go on with the story. With the end of the War of the Conquest a book is closed. The story does not continue: a new one begins. An evolution is halted, to resume, with a change of direction, as a different evolution. The turning-point can be easily defined, marked as it is by statements so explicit that one wonders how historians, even while taking note of them, have attached so little importance to them. Thus, fifteen years after the capitulation of Montreal, the spiritual head of the Canadian people, Monseigneur Briand, wrote to one of his flock: 'They say of me, as they say of you, that I am English. . . . It is true, I am English, as you and they [the Canadians] are bound to be. They have sworn an oath, and all laws, human, natural and divine, command them to be English. But neither I, nor you, nor they must adopt the religion of England. That is what they, poor souls, do not understand: they are under English rule, in civil matters.' Thirty years after the Treaty of Paris a political leader in the province of Quebec, Chartier de Lotbinière, defended the constitutional status of the French language with the following argument: the use of French in Quebec must be 'agreeable' to the king, 'since it reminds him of the glory of his empire and gives the strongest proof that the peoples of this vast continent are attached to their prince, that they are loyal subjects, and that they are English at heart even before they can pronounce a single word of English.' These were the words of two, among many, Canadian spokesmen. One grouped his compatriots with English Catholics; to the other they were French-speaking Englishmen. Here we have a strong combination of realism and illusion. These two representative minds had grasped the fact that something very serious had happened to Canadians, that they were no longer the same since they had been brought under British 'rule' and into the British empire. They had been transformed by the transformation of the country in which they continued to live. But two or three soundings would reveal that these changes were deeper than their leaders supposed. A people that had been shaped by trade and had lived by trade much more than by agriculture, a people for whom the land had so little 'charm'—to use Talon's word—that before the end of the French régime the exodus from the country had had to be restricted by law, Canadians now retreated to the country and when they came back to the towns came back as immigrants. After having lived under a military-style government, furnished officers and soldiers for the whole of New France and even for the mother country, and acquired the reputation of 'fighters', this group of men—so divided on other issues—more than once revealed itself unanimous on one point: the refusal to bear arms. The Canadian community, which for a century and a half had produced teams of planners who translated their plans into action—explorers, diplomats, businessmen, soldiers, men capable of organizing and directing the administration, development, and defence of vast and varied territories—now had the greatest difficulty in providing even for its own internal organization. In very truth Canadians had changed.

The bishop and the political leader declared that 'natural, divine, and human laws' had made Englishmen of them, that they had become English 'at heart', but in making such statements they were deluding themselves. The fact was that an English society had closed around the Canadians without absorbing them; it had been created against them and it developed without them. Generations of Canadians succeeded one another in a British empire, a British continent, a British state. The political institutions and the economic conditions in which they lived out their lives were British; the social framework built around and above them could not be other than foreign to them. And since their own society had been shaken to the roots and its growth arrested, they were now no more than the residue of a society, lacking the direction and the means without which they could neither conceive nor put into practice the political and economic policies that were a necessity for them. The consolation they sought could not give them what they had lost. Their condition was not the result of choice: they had had no choice. It was the direct result of the conquest that had disrupted their society, destroyed their political structure, and so thoroughly sapped their inner resources of moral energy that it was consummated in them.

We have been slow to understand the true character of the conflict that two centuries ago brought about the downfall of Canada. There are two main reasons for this. In the first place we had forged an image of the French régime at once dazzling, edifying, and incomplete. It was an age when Canadian society had reached a point of full and, still more important, normal development. Inspired by nostalgia, vanity, and literature, we liked to see it as a great age in history, the creation of extraordinary men in exceptional circumstances. As we saw it, Canadians of that day would have had just cause to thank heaven their society was not like other human societies, where the spirit is incarnate in matter and where quality does not exist distinct from quantity. We tended to see ourselves in terms of the spirit and of abstract quality. Looking at history from that point of view, how could one attach any importance to the collapse in the years following 1760 of the material foundations of Canadian society? The 'Canadian miracle' would go on forever.

In the second place we were slow to measure the repercussions of the defeat, because while we continued to relate the events of the war that preceded it, we did not try to define the causes of that war, to see it in the perspective of the world conflict of which it was an episode, still less to discover the motives of those destined by the fortunes of war to be the victors. It was enough for us, or so it seemed, to know that they were wicked: and it must be admitted that historians provided little help for the common reader. French sources were examined by French and Canadian historians, British collections by American and English. Parkman, that gifted writer and great pioneer in the field, differed from the others in that his documentation was less one-sided. But he used his documents and his great talents chiefly to paint pictures rich in contrast and local colour. Historians in general wrote either from the French or the English point of view. As for Canadians, we tried to behave as if it were possible to probe the meaning of the conquest without inquiring into the objectives of those who achieved it. We did not ask whether they knew what they were doing. As far as we were concerned, they might have been fighting for nothing, for the pleasure of fighting. They, however, had seen more clearly into the future than we have seen into their thoughts. Franklin detected more surely than any of our scholars the consequences of the break-up of Canada. We might also cite the American who in 1760 saw the vanquished as a people 'broken' in the war. He was no prophet but an intelligent man capable of noting correctly a fact he had observed.

To tax the author of this volume with pessimism would be tantamount to a confession of lack of attention on the part of the reader. The seismograph registering an earthquake may be exact or incorrect in its recording; it would never occur to anyone to consider it optimistic or pessimistic according as it registered a quake of greater or lesser violence. The utility of a historical study is to be judged not by the emotions it inspires in the reader, nor by the relief it may provide for his anxieties, but by the light it sheds on the subject of his study. Embellishments are a source of dullness even in fiction, and it should be agreed that they are quite out of place in scientific works. The author who undertakes a piece of historical research hoping to uncover reasons for thrills of pride would show better taste and better judgement by seeking stimulus for his emotions elsewhere. We have reached the end of our study, and we must state in all honesty the conclusion to which we have been led. If, as an excellent English methodologist has said, history is a hypothesis permitting the explanation of present situations by those that preceded them, attentive examination of the systematic and decisive fashion in which the Canadian people was 'broken' must make it possible for us to see in its true light the crisis—so clearly visible—in Canadian society, and to realize that it was not merely the result of a certain conjuncture of circumstances but involved the very structure of that society. The framework of the Canadian community, destroyed in the crisis, was never properly rebuilt.

I am aware that this is a disturbing conclusion, and I confess that if it did not disturb it would be because it had not been understood. It would be curious reasoning, however, that judged a conclusion false because it was harsh, and dangerous because it had been proven. If history were only a game, it would be easy to revel in learned research without relating past facts to the present. But then one would have to find another name for a discipline that performed that function; one would have to create a science that could measure the pressure of the past on the present and determine the nature of that pressure. One would have to invent history, and the first requisite for the newly invented discipline would be scientific detachment. Marc Bloch reports the astonished question of a French officer dismayed by the defeat of 1940: 'Has history deceived us?' He could ask the question because the historical tradition of his group had not prepared him for the possibility of catastrophe, and because of the still more painful fact that it had not even made it possible for him and the society of which he was a member to make any effective effort to ward off the disaster. It was not history that had deceived him but the tradition that passed for history.

One of the functions of history—the most important in my opinion—is precisely to correct systematically the tradition in accordance with which the life of any human group is ordered. It is the business of history to explain the present by showing how it came into being. If history refuses this task, society will allow its attention to be diverted to false problems, because they are the ones that are easier to solve, or—and this amounts to the same thing—it will succumb to the absurd temptation of regarding the gravest problems as old ones solved long since. History, said Lucien Febvre, 'is a means of organizing the past so that it may not be too heavy a burden for the shoulders of men.' Men need history, since without it they might be crushed under the weight of the past. But it goes without saying that if history is for them an absolute need, they need absolutely true history. Their eyes must be opened to reality, no matter how disquieting it may be, so that they may prepare to avoid the dangers it presents.

Notes

Collections of documents to which frequent reference is made are indicated by the following codes:

A&WI	Board of Trade, America and West Indies
AC	Archives des Colonies
B	Depêches envoyées par le ministère de la Marine
C 11A	Correspondance générale, Canada
C 11B	Correspondance générale, Île-Royale
C 11E	Volume 10: *Rivalités des colonies anglaises et des colonies françaises*
F 3	Collection Moreau de Saint-Méry
AE	Ministère des Affaires Étrangères
AG	Archives de la Guerre
AM	Archives de la Marine
BM, Add. MSS	British Museum, Additional Manuscripts
BTNS	Board of Trade, Nova Scotia
NYCD	*Documents Relative to the Colonial History of the State of New York*. E.B. O'Callaghan, ed. 11 vols, Albany, 1853-87.
PAC	Public Archives of Canada
PRO, co 5	Public Record Office, Colonial Office, series 5
RAPQ	*Rapport de l'Archiviste de la province de Québec*

CHAPTER I

[1] 'Mémoire sur les Colonies françoises et angloises de l'Amerique Septentrionale', 1739, *AC*, c 11A, 72:228.

[2] *Lettres d'un François à un Hollandois, au sujet des Differends survenus entre la France & la Grande-Bretagne Touchant leurs Possessions respectives dans l'Amérique Septentrionale* (1755), 4 f., 23 f., 50, 99, 105, 169.

[3] 'Lettre du Roi à M. de Bompar', 21 juillet 1756, *AC*, B 103:28.

[4] 'Relation abregée des hostilités françoises Sur l'Ohio dans l'Amerique Septentrionale en 1754', *AE*, Mémoires et documents, Amérique, 10:150.

[5] *Maryland Gazette*, 13 February 1755.

[6] *The London Magazine or Gentleman's Monthly Intelligencer* (September 1757), 421. Hereafter: *London Magazine*.

[7] John Entick, *The General History of the Late War: Containing it's Rise, Progress, and Event, in Europe, Asia, Africa, and America* (5 vols, London, 1763-4), 3:227. Hereafter: Entick.

[8] 'A Review of the Military Operations in North America, from the Commencement of the French Hostilities on the Frontiers of Virginia in 1753, to the Surrender of Oswego on the 14th of August, 1756; in a Letter to a Nobleman', 20 September 1756, *Collections of the Massachusetts Historical Society for the year 1800-1801* (series 1, vol. 7):75. Hereafter: 'Review of Military Operations'.

[9] *Mémoires des commissaires du Roi et de ceux de Sa Majesté Britannique* (8 vols, Paris, 1756-7).

[10] Guy Frégault, *François Bigot, administrateur français* (2 vols, Montreal, 1948), 2:161.

[11] *Sentiments Relating to the Late Negociation* (London, 1761), 23.

[12] *Mercure historique et politique de La Haye*, 140 (1756):24 f. Hereafter: *Mercure de La Haye*.

[13] Ibid., 148 (1760):5.

[14] Amherst to Whitmore, 28 August 1758, *PRO*, co 5, 53:223 f.

[15] *An Answer to the Letter to two great Men. Containing remarks and observations on that piece, and vindicating the character of a Noble Lord from Inactivity* (London, 1760), 12.

[16] Bougainville à madame Hérault, [septembre] 1757, René de Kerallain, *Les Français au Canada: la jeunesse de Bougainville et la guerre de Sept ans* (Paris, 1896), 90.

[17] *Answer to the Letter to two great Men*, 7.

[18] See Herbert Butterfield, *The Origins of Modern Science* (London, 1950), and Paul Hazard, *La Crise de la conscience européenne: 1680-1715* (3 vols, Paris, 1935).

[19] Quoted by E.-G. Léonard, 'La Question sociale dans l'armée française au xviiie siècle', *Annales: Economies, Sociétés, Civilisations*, 3 (1948):144.

[20] A.L. Burt considers that under the military régime (1760-4) the administration of the country was 'more Canadian in character than it had been during the French régime.' One chapter of his *Short History of Canada for Americans* (Minneapolis, 1944) is presented under the heading 'Liberty to be Themselves'. This curiously retrograde conception of Canadian history harks all the way back to Parkman. See *The Old Régime in Canada* (Boston, 1889), 400 f.

[21] *Maryland Gazette*, 20 February 1755.

[22] Quoted by Alexis de Tocqueville, *Histoire philosophique du règne de Louis XV* (2 vols, Paris, 1846), 2:385 f.

[23] An article from the *Monitor* reproduced in the *London Magazine* (December 1755), 609.

[24] *New York Gazette*, 1 November 1756.

[25] *Pennsylvania Gazette*, 29 August 1754.

[26] *New York Gazette*, 8 November 1756.

[27] 'Discussion Sommaire sur Les anciennes Limites De L'Acadie Et Sur les Stipulations Du traité d'Utrecht qui y sont relatives', *AE*, Mémoires et documents, Amérique, 10:206v.

[28] *Maryland Gazette*, 2 October 1755.

[29] *A Scheme to Drive the French Out of All the Continent of America* (London, 1754), 22.

[30] Ibid., 7.

[31] *New York Gazette*, 4 August 1755.

[32] *New York Mercury*, 18 August 1755: reproduced in *Boston News-Letter*, 29 August 1755.

[33] *New York Mercury*, 27 June 1757.

[34] *New York Gazette*, 26 May 1755.

[35] *New York Mercury*, 22 May 1758.

[36] *Mercure de La Haye*, 139 (novembre 1755):566.

[37] Ibid., 140 (mars 1756):343.

[38] Ibid., 139 (décembre 1755):696.

[39] *New York Gazette*, 23 February 1756.

[40] *Boston News-Letter*, 10 January 1760.

[41] *London Magazine* (January 1755), 33 f.

[42] Ibid. (July 1757), 329 f.

[43] Ibid. (December 1756), 599.

[44] *Pennsylvania Journal*, 18 May 1757.

[45] *London Magazine* (1758), 582. The biography appears in three instalments, (October) 511-13, (November) 582-4, and (December) 617-19.

[46] Horace Walpole, *Memoirs of the Reign of George II* (3 vols, London, 1847), 3:217. See also 2:176, and for Walpole's version of the disgrace of the Cardinal de Bernis, 3:157 f. In a letter to Montagu, 11 October 1759, Walpole gives the following translation of the verses quoted:

> *O France, still your fate may lay at ——'s door;*
> *You was saved by a maid, are undone by a whore.*

Quoted by G. F. C. Stanley, *New France: the Last Phase, 1745-1760* (Toronto, 1968), 271.

[47] [Adèle Cimon], *Les Ursulines de Québec, depuis leur établissement jusqu'à nos jours* (4 vols, Quebec, 1863-6), 2:278.

[48] A.-L. Leymarie, ed. 'Lettres de Mère Marie-André Duplessis de Sainte-Hélène', *Nova Francia*, 4 (1929):57.

[49] Ibid., 113, letter of 8 November 1756.

[50] Samuel Checkley, *The Duty of God's People when engaged in War. A Sermon Preached at the North-Church of Christ in Boston, Sept. 21* (Boston, 1755), 5, 24, 28.

[51] *New York Gazette*, 8 December 1755.

[52] A. G. Doughty, ed., *An Historical Journal of the Campaigns in North America for the Years 1757, 1758, 1759, and 1760, by Captain John Knox* (3 vols, Toronto, 1914-16), 2:239 f., note. Hereafter: Knox, *Journal*.

[53] William Adams, *A Discourse Delivered at New-London, October 23d. A.D. 1760* (New London, 1760), 8, 15.

[54] Nathaniel Appleton, *A Sermon Preached October 9. Being a Day of public Thanksgiving* (Boston, 1760), 25 f.

[55] Hayes Baker-Crothers, *Virginia and the French and Indian War* (Chicago, 1928), 25-8, 73 f.

[56] Lawrence H. Gipson, *Zones of International Friction: North America, South of the Great Lakes Region, 1748-1754* (New York, 1939), 228 f. Hereafter: Gipson, 4.

[57] Ibid., 247.

[58] Ibid., 258-65.

[59] 'Sommation faite par ordre de Mr de Contrecoeur', 16 avril 1754, Fernand Grenier, ed., *Papiers Contrecoeur et autres documents concernant le conflit anglo-français sur l'Ohio de 1745 à 1756* (Quebec, 1952), 117. Hereafter: *Papiers Contrecoeur*. On this collection see *Canadian Historical Review*, 34 (1953):298.

[60] Rouillé à Mirepoix, 13 février 1755, *AE*, Correspondance politique, Angleterre, 438:141v.

[61] Newcastle to Albemarle, 5 September 1754, in T. C. Pease, ed., *Anglo-French Boundary Disputes in the West, 1749-1763* (Springfield, 1936), 50 f.

[62] *State of the British and French Colonies in North America, With Respect to Number of People, Forces, Forts, Indians, Trade and other Advantages . . . With a Proper Expedient Proposed for Preventing Future Disputes. In Two Letters to a Friend* (London, 1755), 11, 14. The first letter, from which these extracts are taken, is dated 10 December 1754.

[63] Ibid., 4 f.

[64] Guy Frégault, *Iberville, le Conquérant* (Montreal, 1944), chap. VI.

[65] See the figures given in *AE*, Mémoires et documents, Amérique, 10:54, and 'Etat de l'Argent payé et des Depenses faites . . . depuis le 1er Novembre 1751. Jusqu'au 31. Decembre 1752', ibid., 49v.-51.

[66] Lawrence H. Gipson, *Zones of International Friction: The Great Lakes Frontier, Canada, the West Indies, India, 1748-1754* (New York, 1942), 179 f. Hereafter: Gipson, 5.

[67] Max Savelle, *The Diplomatic History of the Canadian Boundary 1749-1763* (New Haven, 1940), 148.

[68] Lawrence to Shirley, 5 November 1754, *BTNS*, 15:H 278. See also Lawrence to Governors of British America, 11 August 1755, ibid., H 312.

[69] Shirley to Robinson, 24 March 1755, *NYCD*, 6:942, 944 f.

[70] Harold U. Faulkner, *American Economic History* (New York and London, 1943), 68.

[71] See the interesting study by W. T. Baxter, *The House of Hancock* (Cambridge, Mass., 1945).

[72] 'Additional Instructions to Lieutenant Colonel Moncton', 29 January 1755, *The Northcliffe Collection* (Ottawa, 1926), 27. See also chap. V, note 51 of this volume, and Virginia Harrington, *The New York Merchant on the Eve of the Revolution* (New York, 1935), 211, note 17. On the Apthorps, ibid., 218 f.

[73] Jean Lunn, 'The Illegal Fur Trade out of New-France, 1713-1760', Canadian Historical Association, *Report* (Toronto, 1939), 66.

[74] Peter Wraxall, 'Some Thoughts upon the British Indian Interest in North America' (9 January 1756), *NYCD*, 7:16. See Harrington, op. cit., 232-4, 309 f.

[75] Lawrence H. Gipson, *The Great War for the Empire: The Years of Defeat, 1754-1757* (New York, 1946), 144. Hereafter: Gipson, 6.

[76] 'Review of Military Operations', 85.

[77] A. Pound and R. E. Day, *Johnson of the Mohawks. A Biography of Sir*

William Johnson, Irish Immigrant, Mohawk War Chief, American Soldier, Empire Builder (New York, 1930), 465.

78 Stanley M. Pargellis, *Lord Loudoun in North America* (New Haven and London, 1933), 96.

79 Burnet to Newcastle, 9 May 1727, *NYCD*, 5:820; Burnet to Board of Trade, 9 May 1727, ibid., 818 f.; id., 29 June 1727, ibid., 821 f.

80 See Guy Frégault, *La Civilisation de la Nouvelle-France* (Montreal, 1944), 55-8.

81 Savelle, op. cit., 149.

82 Wraxall, loc. cit.

83 See Frégault, *Francois Bigot*, 1:365.

84 See Guy Frégault, *Le Grand Marquis: Pierre de Rigaud de Vaudreuil et la Louisiane* (Montreal, 1952), 361, note 22.

85 A detailed description, under the heading 'Itinéraire', 1757, is to be found in *AC*, c 11A, 102:332v.

86 Pound and Day, op. cit., 108 f.

87 W. N. P. Dailey, 'Sir William Johnson, Baronet', *Chronicles of Oklahoma*, 22 (1944):165.

88 Frégault, *Le Grand Marquis*, 378.

89 Savelle, op. cit., 154 f.

90 John C. Miller, *Origins of the American Revolution* (Boston, 1943), 55 f.; Harrington, op. cit., 37 f.

91 Joseph Dorfman, *The Economic Mind in American Civilization, 1606-1865* (2 vols, New York, 1946), 1:111, 114 f.

92 *A Miscellaneous Essay Concerning the Courses pursued by Great Britain In the Affairs of her Colonies: with some Observations on the Great Importance of our Settlements in America, and The Trade thereof* (London, 1755), 19.

93 Quoted by Dorfman, op. cit., 1:116.

94 'Mémoire', *AC*, c 11E, 10:262.

95 See Léon Gérin, *Aux sources de notre histoire* (Montreal, 1946), 143-54. On the social history of Canada, see Guy Frégault, *La Société canadienne sous le régime francais* (Ottawa, 1954).

96 Mémoire de Jean Talon à Colbert, 10 novembre 1670, *RAPQ* (1930-1), 126; 'Mémoire de M. de La Chesnaye sur le Canada, 1676', *Collection de manuscrits contenant lettres, mémoires et autres documents historiques relatifs à l'histoire de la Nouvelle-France* (4 vols, Quebec, 1883-5), 1:252. Hereafter: *Coll. de MSS.*

97 See the studies by Jean Delanglez, *Frontenac and the Jesuits* (Chicago, 1939), *Some La Salle Journeys* (Chicago, 1938), and especially *Louis Jolliet, vie et voyages* (Montreal, 1950), 227-9, 288-97. See also Guy Frégault, Michel Brunet, and Marcel Trudel, eds, *Histoire du Canada par les textes* (Montreal, 1952), 47-9.

98 Frégault, *La Civilisation de la Nouvelle-France*, 17 f.; Frégault, Brunet, and Trudel, op. cit., 60-2.

99 'Mémoire de M. Dupuy, intendant de la Nouvelle-France, sur les troubles arrivés à Québec en 1727 et 1728', *RAPQ* (1920-1), 98-100.

100 Frégault, *Le Grand Marquis*, 380.

101 Bigot à Rouillé, 26 octobre 1752, *AC*, c 11A, 90:270.

[102] Except as otherwise indicated, the following paragraphs are based on facts of which detailed analyses are given in Frégault, *Francois Bigot*, chaps VIII to XII, and in Frégault, *Le Grand Marquis*, chap. VII, section 3.

[103] Rouillé à Du Quesne, 31 mai 1754, *AC*, B 99:204.

[104] Machault à Du Quesne, 17 février 1755, *AC*, B 101:144. (Dispatch in code.)

[105] *Lettres d'un Francois à un Hollandois*, 6.

[106] H.-R. Casgrain, ed., *Collection des manuscrits du maréchal de Lévis* (12 vols, Montreal and Quebec, 1889-95). Vol. 7: *Journal du marquis de Montcalm durant ses campagnes au Canada de 1756 à 1760* (Quebec, 1895), 461 f. Hereafter: Casgrain, 7 (Montcalm, *Journal*).

[107] *New York Mercury*, 5 January 1756.

[108] Quoted in Gabriel, *Le Maréchal de camp Desandrouins 1729-1792. Guerre du Canada 1756-1760. Guerre de l'Indépendance américaine 1780-1782* (Verdun, 1887), 129.

[109] Quoted in Frégault, *Francois Bigot*, 2:217.

[110] 'Mémoire', *AC*, C 11E, 10:262.

[111] 'Mémoire', *AC*, C 11A, 104:687.

[112] 'Nombre, Noms et qualité des accusés', *PAC*, Affaire du Canada, 1:7 f.; *Jugement rendu souverainement et en dernier ressort dans l'Affaire du Canada* (Paris, 1763). On the Affaire du Canada, see Frégault, *François Bigot*, chap. XVII.

[113] Casgrain, 7 (Montcalm, *Journal*):461.

[114] Berryer à Vaudreuil et à Bigot, 8 janvier 1759, *AC*, F 3, 15:235.

[115] 'Journal', 24 avril 1757, *RAPQ* (1923-4), 260.

CHAPTER II

[1] *NYCD*, 6:550.

[2] 'An Account of the Number of White Inhabitants in His Majesty's Colonies in North America', 29 August 1755, *A&WI*, vol. 605.

[3] Frégault, *La Civilisation de la Nouvelle-France*, 39.

[4] Montcalm à Bourlamaque, 11 mars 1758, H.-R. Casgrain, ed., *Lettres de M. de Bourlamaque au chevalier de Lévis* (Quebec, 1891), 289. Hereafter: Casgrain, 5 (Bourlamaque, *Lettres*).

[5] *Maryland Gazette*, 4 September 1755, article reprinted from *London Magazine*, May 1755. See also *State of the British and French Colonies*, 15, 139.

[6] *Maryland Gazette*, 4 September 1755.

[7] *Boston News-Letter*, 13 February 1755; *State of the British and French Colonies*, 16.

[8] *New York Mercury*, 20 January 1755.

[9] Ibid., 16 December 1754, supplement.

[10] *State of the British and French Colonies*, 19, 57.

[11] Ibid., 58

[12] Ibid.

[13] Ibid., 53.

[14] Frégault, *François Bigot*, 2:65-7.

[15] Quoted by E.I. McCormac, *Colonial Opposition to Imperial Authority during the French and Indian War* (Berkeley, 1911), 6. See Herbert L. Osgood, *The American Colonies in the Eighteenth Century* (4 vols, New York, 1924), 4:336.

[16] *New York Mercury*, 26 August 1754.

[17] James De Lancey to Lords of Trade, 8 October 1754, *NYCD*, 6:909.

[18] *New York Mercury*, 25 March 1754.

[19] Sharpe to Amherst, 25 February 1760, *PRO*, co 5, 57:413; id., 10 April 1760, *PRO*, co 5, 58:139 f.

[20] Quoted by George L. Beer, *British Colonial Policy, 1754-1765* (New York, 1922), 19.

[21] *Pennsylvania Gazette*, 9 May 1754.

[22] On the congress of 1754, read Gipson, 5:113-66.

[23] Lords of Trade to Robinson, 9 August 1754, and to the king, 9 August 1754, *A&WI*, vol. 604; 'The Draught of a Plan or Project for a General Concert, to be entered into by His Majesty's several Colonies upon the Continent of North America', ibid.

[24] Gipson, 5:140, note 81.

[25] *Pennsylvania Gazette*, 5 September 1754.

[26] He exaggerates: in 1757 France had perhaps twenty million inhabitants, the United Kingdom about eight or nine million. Richard Waddington, *La Guerre de Sept ans. Histoire diplomatique et militaire* (5 vols, Paris, 1899-1914), 1:218 f. On the other hand the population of Canada was about six per cent of that of British America.

[27] *Maryland Gazette*, 26 December 1754.

[28] Letter of 15 December 1754, *NYCD*, 6:926.

[29] McCormac, op cit., 92.

[30] Pargellis, *Lord Loudoun in North America*, 254.

[31] 'A Message from the Governor to the Assembly, 11 January 1755', *Maryland Gazette*, 6 March 1755.

[32] Shirley to Robinson, 4 February 1755, *NYCD*, 6:939.

[33] Paul H. Giddens, 'The French and Indian War in Maryland 1753 to 1756', *Maryland Historical Magazine*, 30 (1935), 299.

[34] Shirley to Robinson, 24 March 1755, *NYCD*, 6:943.

[35] *Maryland Gazette*, 26 June 1755.

[36] Ibid., 3 July 1755.

[37] Giddens, op. cit., 304 f.

[38] W. H. Browne, ed., *Correspondence of Governor Horatio Sharpe* (3 vols, Baltimore, 1888-1911), 1:242 f. Hereafter: *Sharpe Correspondence*.

[39] *Maryland Gazette*, 15 August 1755.

[40] Giddens, op. cit., 290.

[41] Sharpe to the Lords of Trade, 8 February 1756, *Sharpe Correspondence*, 1:353.

[42] Sharpe to his brothers, 25 November 1755, ibid., 1:310 f.

[43] Osgood, op. cit., 4:336; Pargellis, *Lord Loudoun in North America*, 222; McCormac, op. cit., 34 f.

[44] Morris to Robinson, 28 August 1755, *Minutes of the Provincial Council of Pennsylvania, from the Organization to the Termination of the Proprietary*

Government (1683-1775) (10 vols, Philadelphia, 1851-2: *Pennsylvania Colonial Records,* vols 1-10), 6:599. Hereafter: *Pennsylvania Colonial Records.*

45 *Maryland Gazette,* 4 September 1755.

46 McCormac, op. cit., 49.

47 Morris to Thomas Penn, 22 November 1755, *Pennsylvania Colonial Records,* 6:740 f.

48 Lawrence to Halifax, 9 December 1755, Stanley M. Pargellis, ed., *Military Affairs in North America 1748-1765. Selected Documents from the Cumberland Papers in Windsor Castle* (New York and London, 1936), 155 f.

49 Johnson to De Lancey, 30 July 1755, James Sullivan, ed., *The Papers of Sir William Johnson* (3 vols, Albany, 1921-2), 1:794 f. (hereafter: *Johnson Papers);* Johnson to Pownall, 4 September 1755, ibid., 2:9, etc.

50 *New York Mercury,* 23 February 1756, supplement.

51 The essay, *Analysis Number II,* was published by Lawrence H. Gipson in his splendid study, *Lewis Evans* (Philadelphia, 1939), 177-218.

52 See *New York Mercury,* 5 January and 2 February 1756.

53 Halifax to Charles Hardy, 31 March 1756, *PRO,* co 5, 52:86.

54 *New York Gazette,* 6 September 1756.

55 *Boston Gazette,* 13 September 1756.

56 *New York Gazette,* 13 September 1756.

57 *London Magazine* (1756), 631.

58 *New York Gazette,* 29 November 1756.

59 Quoted by Dan E. Clark, 'News and Opinions Concerning America in English Newspapers, 1754-1763', *Pacific Historical Review,* 10 (1941):79.

60 William Smith to Secker, 1 November 1756, *NYCD,* 7:165.

61 Hardy to Board of Trade, 22 December 1756, ibid., 206; Board of Trade to Hardy, 10 March 1757, ibid., 221.

62 Quoted by Hubert Hall, 'Chatham's Colonial Policy', *American Historical Review,* 5 (1899-1900):661 ff.

63 *New York Gazette,* 27 September 1756.

64 *Pennsylvania Journal,* 13 October 1757.

65 Sharpe to Calvert, 14 September 1756, *Sharpe Correspondence,* 1:483.

66 McCormac, op. cit., 69.

67 Sharpe to Calvert, 5 October 1756, *Sharpe Correspondence,* 1:491.

68 *New York Gazette,* 3 May 1756.

69 Denny to Pitt, 9 April 1757, *PRO,* co 5, 18:75.

70 Loudoun to Pitt, 17 June 1757, *PRO,* co 5, 48:404.

71 *New York Mercury,* 10 April 1758.

72 Message of 15 March 1758, *PRO,* co 5, 18:767.

73 De Lancey to Pitt, 17 March 1758, *NYCD,* 7:343.

74 *New York Gazette,* 27 March 1758.

75 Hugh Mercer to Bouquet, 21 March 1759, *BM, Add. MSS,* 21644:114.

76 Fauquier to Stanwix, 24 November 1759, *PRO,* co 5, 57:617.

77 Hall, 'Chatham's Colonial Policy', 667.

78 On smuggling in wartime see Beer, op. cit.; Lawrence H. Gipson, *The Great War for the Empire: The Culmination 1760-1763* (New York, 1954), 78-82 (hereafter: Gipson, 8); Harrington, *The New York Merchant,* 261-7.

[79] Hamilton to Pitt, 1 November 1760, Gertrude S. Kimball, ed., *Correspondence of William Pitt When Secretary of State with Colonial Governors and Military and Naval Commanders in America* (2 vols, New York, 1906), 2:351 f. Hereafter: *Pitt Correspondence.*

[80] Dinwiddie to Robinson, 20 January 1755, *PRO*, CO 5, 15:285-8; Hardy to Lords of Trade, 10 May 1756, *NYCD*, 7:81.

[81] *Maryland Gazette*, 11 September 1755.

[82] *New York Gazette*, 12 April 1756.

[83] Gipson, 8:81 f.; Harrington, op cit., 273 f.

[84] Hardy to Lords of Trade, 19 June 1756, *NYCD*, 7:117.

[85] Id., 10 May 1756, *NYCD*, 7:81.

[86] Id., 13 October 1756, *NYCD*, 7:163.

[87] Quoted by W. T. Selley, *England in the Eighteenth Century* (London, 1949), 105. Cf. Pargellis, *Lord Loudoun in North America*, 261.

[88] 'Mémoire pour Guillaume Estèbe', *PAC*, Affaire du Canada, 3:320.

[89] Hall, 'Chatham's Colonial Policy', 662 f.

[90] Miller, *Origins of the American Revolution*, 39-41.

[91] Loudoun to Pitt, 25 April 1757, *PRO*, CO 5, 48:259 f.

[92] *Pennsylvania Gazette*, 2 October 1755.

[93] E. B. Greene, 'New York and the Old Empire', *Quarterly Journal of the New York State Historical Association*, 8 (1926):126.

[94] *Pennsylvania Journal*, 6 October 1757.

[95] Miller, op. cit., 47 f.

[96] Hardy to Halifax, 7 May 1756, Pargellis, *Military Affairs in North America*, 173.

[97] Pargellis, *Lord Loudoun in North America*, 90 f.

[98] Franklin to Sir Edward Fawkener, 27 July 1756, Pargellis, *Military Affairs in North America*, 185.

[99] Pargellis, *Lord Loudoun in North America*, 186.

[100] 'The Sackville Papers', A. G. Doughty and G. W. Parmelee, eds, *The Siege of Quebec and the Battle of the Plains of Abraham* (6 vols, Quebec, 1901), 6:84.

[101] Thomas Mante, *The History of the Late War in America* (London, 1772), 21 f.

[102] Ephraim Williams to Israel Williams, 2 August 1755, Massachusetts Historical Society (Boston), Israel Williams Papers, 1:163.

[103] *London Magazine* (September 1755), 403 f.; Morris to Shirley, July 1755, *Pennsylvania Colonial Records*, 6:496.

[104] *London Magazine* (1756, supplement), 631.

[105] *An Impartial History of the Late Glorious War* (London, 1769), 11.

[106] Entick, 1:148.

[107] *New York Gazette*, 10 April 1758.

[108] *Boston News-Letter*, 23 March 1758.

[109] See Stanley M. Pargellis's brilliant article, 'Braddock's Defeat', *American Historical Review*, 41 (1936):253-69.

[110] Letter of 18 July 1755, John C. Fitzpatrick, ed., *The Writings of George Washington from the Original Manuscript Sources* (39 vols, Washington, 1931-44), 1:149.

[111] Dinwiddie to Washington, 26 July 1755, R.A. Brock, ed., *The Official Records of Robert Dinwiddie, Lieutenant-Governor of Virginia* (2 vols, Richmond, 1883-4), 2:122. Hereafter: *Records of Dinwiddie*.

[112] Letter of 3 August 1755, *Johnson Papers*, 1:826 f.

[113] *Boston News-Letter*, 21 August 1755.

[114] Clark, 'News and Opinions', 76 f.

[115] Walpole, *Memoirs of the Reign of George II*, 2:29.

[116] *New York Gazette*, 25 August 1755.

[117] *Boston News-Letter*, 14 August 1755.

[118] Ibid., 21 August 1755.

[119] Hall, 'Chatham's Colonial Policy', 663.

[120] *New York Gazette*, 27 February 1758.

[121] Entick, 2:3 f.; Mante, op. cit., 40.

[122] 'Review of Military Operations', 68.

[123] Quoted by Kate Hotblack, *Chatham's Colonial Policy* (London, 1917), 175; see *Maryland Gazette*, 22 May 1755.

[124] Quoted by Gerald S. Graham, *Empire of the North Atlantic. The Maritime Struggle for North America* (Toronto, 1950), 143.

[125] *Boston News-Letter*, 22 May 1755.

[126] *London Magazine* (July 1756), 330.

[127] *Maryland Gazette*, 10 July 1755.

[128] *New York Gazette*, 19 January 1756.

[129] *Maryland Gazette*, 10 July 1755.

[130] *Boston News-Letter*, 28 December 1758.

[131] Frégault, *Le Grand Marquis*, 123, 324-6.

[132] Id., *La Civilisation de la Nouvelle-France*, 269 f.

[133] Casgrain, 7 (Montcalm, *Journal*):420.

[134] Montcalm à Lévis, 17 août 1756, H.-R. Casgrain, ed., *Lettres du marquis de Montcalm au chevalier de Lévis* (Quebec, 1894), 35. Hereafter: Casgrain, 6 (Montcalm, *Lettres*).

[135] Lettre du 12 juin 1756, *Coll. de MSS*, 4:31.

[136] Machault à Dieskau, 25 mars 1755, *AC*, B 101:150; 'Instruction pour M. le marquis de Vaudreuil concernant les troupes de terre', 1er avril 1755, ibid., 157; Machault à Montcalm, 14 mars 1756, *AC*, B 103:135; 'Mémoire du Roy pour servir d'instruction au Sr Mis de Moncalm Marechal de camp', 14 mars 1756, ibid., 136.

[137] Machault à Vaudreuil, 12 mai 1757, *AC*, B 105:18; 'Canada', 1757, *AC*, C 11A, 102:261.

[138] Le Mercier à Machault, 30 octobre 1756, *AC*, C 11A, 101:292v.

[139] Montcalm au ministre de la Guerre, 3 novembre 1756, *AG*, liasse 3417, no 294.

[140] August 1758. Quoted by Gabriel, *Le Maréchal de camp Desandrouins*, 207.

[141] De Blau à Bougainville, 15 août 1759, Kerallain, *Les Français au Canada: la jeunesse de Bougainville*, 134.

[142] Doreil à Paulmy, 31 juillet 1758, *RAPQ* (1944-5), 152.

[143] Pontleroy à Massiac, 1er décembre 1758, *AC*, C 11A, 103:491.

[144] Frégault, *François Bigot*, 2:119, note 82.

[145] Vaudreuil à Machault, 16 janvier 1756, *AC*, c 11A, 101:3v.

[146] Moras à Montcalm, 27 mai 1757, *AC*, в 105:25-6.

[147] 'Extrait d'un Journal tenu à l'armée que commandoit feu Mr de Montcalm', *AC*, c 11A, 104:277; Bigot à Lévis, 8 septembre 1759, H.-R. Casgrain, ed., *Lettres de l'intendant Bigot au chevalier de Lévis* (Quebec, 1895), 56 (hereafter: Casgrain, 9 (Bigot, *Lettres*)); Querdisien à Berryer, 22 septembre 1759, *AC*, c 11A, 104:523-7; 'Proclamation de James Wolfe', 27 juin 1759, H.-R. Casgrain, ed., *Lettres et pièces militaires, instructions, ordres, mémoires, plans de campagne et de défense 1756-1760* (Quebec, 1891), 273-6 (hereafter: Casgrain, 4 (*Lettres et pièces militaires*)).

[148] *Mercure de La Haye*, 145 (1758):28 f.

[149] Journal de Bougainville, *RAPQ* (1923-4), 371. See Bigot à Berryer, 15 avril 1759, *AC*, c 11A, 104:159.

[150] See Lawrence H. Gipson, *The Great War for the Empire: The Victorious Years, 1758-1760* (New York, 1949), 381-4, 388 f. Hereafter: Gipson, 7.

[151] Casgrain, 7 (Montcalm, *Journal*):419.

[152] Montcalm au ministre de la Guerre, 18 septembre 1757, *AG*, 3457: no 141.

[153] Montcalm à Berryer, 12 avril 1759, *Coll. de MSS*, 4:224-7; 'Fautes essentielles qui ont accéléré la perte du Canada', Bibliothèque de l'Arsenal, Archives de la Bastille, 12143:263.

[154] 'Mémoire sur le Traitement des officiers en Amerique', 1756, *AG*, 3417: no 292.

[155] Lévis à Argenson, 26 octobre 1756, H.-R. Casgrain, ed., *Lettres du chevalier de Lévis concernant la guerre du Canada (1756-1760)* (Montreal, 1889), 101. Hereafter: Casgrain, 2 (Lévis, *Lettres*).

[156] Montcalm à Lévis, 13 janvier 1758, Casgrain, 6 (Montcalm, *Lettres*), 115.

[157] Vaudreuil à Berryer, 20 novembre 1758, *AC*, c 11A, 103:320.

[158] Machault à Vaudreuil et à Bigot, 15 juillet 1755, *AC*, в 101:135, 136.

[159] Frégault, *La Civilisation de la Nouvelle-France*, 270.

[160] 'Mémoire sur le Canada', janvier 1759, *RAPQ* (1923-4), 23 f.

CHAPTER III

[1] *New York Mercury*, 24 June 1754.

[2] See *New York Mercury*, 18 November 1754.

[3] Walpole, *Memoirs of the Reign of George II*, 1:399 f.

[4] Machault à Du Quesne, 19 août 1754, *AC*, в 99:217. The best study of the Washington-Jumonville question is Marcel Trudel's article, 'L'Affaire Jumonville', *Revue d'histoire de l'Amérique française*, 6 (1952-3):331-73.

[5] *Virginia Gazette*, 19 July 1754; *New York Mercury*, 22 July 1754; *Boston News-Letter*, 1 August 1754; *Pennsylvania Gazette*, 22 August 1754; *Maryland Gazette*, 29 August 1754. See 'Journal de la campagne de M. de Villiers au fort Nécessité', *Papiers Contrecoeur*, 196-202; 'Capitulation du fort Nécessité', 3 juillet 1754, ibid., 202-5.

[6] Frégault, *Le Grand Marquis*, 337.

7 La Galissonière à Maurepas, 22 octobre 1747, *AC*, c 11a, 87:260v.-1.

8 Frégault, *Le Grand Marquis*, 356.

9 'Journal de la Campagne' de Céloron de Blainville, 1749, *AC*, f 3, 13:346v.-7.

10 Frégault, *Le Grand Marquis*, 380 f.

11 Du Quesne à Contrecoeur, 18 octobre 1754, *Papiers Contrecoeur*, 17.

12 Du Quesne à Saint-Pierre, 30 janvier 1754, ibid., 98 f.

13 Stoddart to Johnson, 15 May 1753, *NYCD*, 6:780.

14 'Copie de la lettre du gouverneur de la Virginie à M. de St-Pierre', 30 [31] octobre 1753, *Papiers Contrecoeur*, 77 f.

15 'Copie de la lettre de M. de St-Pierre au gouverneur de la Virginie', 16 décembre 1753, ibid., 84.

16 *Pennsylvania Gazette*, 5 February 1754.

17 Reprinted in *Pennsylvania Gazette*, 19 February 1754.

18 *Maryland Gazette*, 30 January 1755.

19 *Papiers Contrecoeur*, 130 f.

20 *New York Mercury*, 5 August 1754.

21 *Boston News-Letter*, 25 July 1754.

22 *NYCD*, 6:909.

23 *New York Mercury*, 18 November 1754.

24 *NYCD*, 6:911.

25 Ibid., 922 f.

26 *New York Mercury*, 6 January 1755.

27 Letter dated 17 December 1754, *Maryland Gazette*, 1 May 1755.

28 *Maryland Gazette*, 12 December 1754.

29 Message of 12 December 1754, *Pennsylvania Gazette*, 1 May 1755.

30 William K. Boyd, ed., 'Henry McCulloh's "Miscellaneous Representations Relative to Our Concerns in America" 1761', *North Carolina Historical Review*, 2 (1925):484.

31 Savelle, *The Diplomatic History of the Canadian Boundary*, 149 f.

32 Beer, *British Colonial Policy 1754-1765*, 140.

33 *New York Mercury*, supplement, 16 September 1754.

34 Graham, *Empire of the North Atlantic*, 144.

35 Evan Charteris, *William Augustus Duke of Cumberland and the Seven Years' War* (London, 1925), 169.

36 Selley, *England in the Eighteenth Century*, 68.

37 Treaty of Peace and Friendship between the Most Serene and Most Potent Princess Anne, by the Grace of God, Queen of Great Britain, France, and Ireland, and the Most Serene and Most Potent Prince, Lewis the 14th, the Most Christian King, Concluded at Utrecht the 21/11 Day of March/April 1713. (London, 1713)

38 Pargellis, *Lord Loudoun in North America*, 19-22.

39 Quoted by Julian S. Corbett, *England in the Seven Years' War. A Study in Combined Strategy* (2 vols, London, 1907), 1:10.

40 Charteris, op. cit., 118.

41 Reprinted in *Maryland Gazette*, 6 February 1755.

42 *London Magazine* (December 1755), 622.

43 Entick, 1:16.

44 Quoted by Gerald S. Graham, *Canada: A Short History* (London, 1950), 55 f.

45 *An Impartial History of the Late Glorious War*, 2-3.

46 Letter of 16 January 1755, *AE*, Correspondence politique, Angleterre, 438:19.

47 Reprinted in *Boston News-Letter*, 12 December 1754.

48 *AC*, C 11A, 101:363v.

49 Rouillé à Mirepoix, 3 février 1755, *AE*, Correspondence politique, Angleterre.

50 *Maryland Gazette*, 9 January 1755.

51 Ibid., 2 January 1755.

52 Robinson to Governors in North America, 26 October 1754, *A&WI*, 605.

53 'Sketch for the Operations in North America', 16 November 1754, in Pargellis, *Military Affairs in North America*, 45.

54 Instructions to Braddock, 25 November 1754, Article 1, *A&WI*, 604.

55 Pargellis, *Lord Loudoun in North America*, 31 f.

56 Letter from George Burrington, London, 27 March 1755, reprinted in *New York Gazette*, 16 June 1755.

57 *A Scheme to Drive the French Out of All the Continent of America*, 9-17, 19.

58 *State of the British and French Colonies*, 31.

59 Albemarle to Robinson [reporting an interview with Machault], 23 October 1754, T. C. Pease, ed., *Anglo-French Boundary Disputes in the West, 1749-1763*, 56.

60 Reprinted in *Boston News-Letter*, 12 December 1754.

61 Reprinted in *Boston News-Letter*, 5 December 1754, and in *Maryland Gazette*, 12 December 1754.

62 5 October 1754. Reprinted in *Boston News-Letter*, 26 December 1754.

63 *Boston News-Letter*, 23 January 1755.

64 2 November 1754. Reprinted in *Pennsylvania Gazette*, 4 February 1755.

65 Translated in *AC*, C 11A, 105:314.

66 *New York Mercury*, 3 February 1755.

67 *Boston News-Letter*, 24 April 1755. See also *London Magazine* (February 1755), 94.

68 *Mercure de La Haye*, 138 (janvier 1755):3, 94.

69 Ibid., (février 1755):166.

70 'London. Copy of a Letter from a Gentleman in the Country', *Maryland Gazette*, 23 January 1755.

71 *A Miscellaneous Essay Concerning the Courses pursued by Great Britain In the Affairs of her Colonies* (London, 1755), 18 f., 121 f.; *The Wisdom and Policy of the French in the Construction of their Great Offices* (London, 1755), 83 f.

72 *Mercure de La Haye*, 138 (janvier 1755):321 f.

73 Reprinted in *New York Gazette*, 23 June 1755.

74 Reprinted in *Maryland Gazette*, 13 March 1755.

75 4 September. Dispatch in *New York Mercury*, 3 November 1755.

76 London, 22 May 1755, *New York Gazette*, 11 August 1755.

77 Letter from George Burrington, London, 27 March 1755, *New York Gazette*, 16 June 1755.

78 London, 4 December 1755, *New York Gazette,* 22 March 1756.

79 London, October 1755, *Boston News-Letter,* 29 January 1756.

80 'From a late English Paper', *Pennsylvania Gazette,* 17 July 1755.

81 Reprinted in *Boston Gazette,* 30 October 1755.

82 *Mercure de La Haye,* 138 (1755):164.

83 *London Magazine* (March 1755), 142.

84 *New York Mercury,* 31 March 1755.

85 *Virginia Gazette,* 10 October 1755.

86 *London Magazine* (May 1755), 217.

87 Reprinted in *New York Gazette,* 15 September 1755.

88 Machault à Du Quesne, 17 février 1755, *AC,* в 101:144v.

89 'Instruction Particuliere Pour M. de Vaudreuil sur la Conduite qu'il doit tenir avec les Anglois', 1er avril 1755, ibid., 165.

90 *New York Mercury,* 5 May 1755.

91 *Boston News-Letter,* 6 February 1755.

92 *Mercure de France* (mars 1755), 189 f.

93 Robinson to Governors in North America, 23 January 1755, *A&WI,* 605.

94 *Maryland Gazette,* 29 May 1755.

95 Ibid., 15 May 1755. See also the poem published in the *Boston News-Letter,* 5 June 1755.

96 *Mercure de La Haye,* 139 (octobre 1755):464.

97 Report of 15 April 1755, quoted in Albert von Ruville, *William Pitt, Earl of Chatham* (3 vols, London, 1907), 1:355, note 2.

98 Hocquart à ———, 27 janvier 1755, *AM,* в 4, 68:150v.

99 Machault à Du Quesne, 17 mars 1755, *AC,* в 101:145.

100 *Maryland Gazette,* 26 June 1755.

101 'Escadre de M. du Bois de la Mothe chef d'Escadre des armées navalles', *AM,* в 4, 68:116.

102 Corbett, op. cit., 1:67.

103 Gipson, 6:109.

104 Corbett, op. cit., 1:45.

105 Du Bois de La Motte à Machault, 27 juin 1755, *AM,* в 4, 68:127v.-8.

106 Gipson, 6:11 f. On Pichon see John C. Webster, *Thomas Pichon 'The Spy of Beauséjour'* (Halifax, 1937).

107 'Relation du combat de l'*Alcide* pris par monsieur de Boscawen', *Coll. de MSS,* 3:540-2; [Hocquart], 'Relation de ce qui s'est passé à la prise de l'Alcide', *AM,* в 4, 68:158-9; 'Relation No 24,' ibid., 266v.-7; *Mercure de La Haye,* 139 (août 1755):218; *London Magazine* (July 1755), 346; *Mercure de France* (août 1755), 253 f.

108 Frégault, *François Bigot,* 2:115, note 63.

109 *Mercure de La Haye,* 139 (août 1755):165.

110 *Mercure de France* (août 1755), 254.

111 *Mercure de La Haye,* 139 (1755):117, 120.

112 Ibid., 455, 564; *New York Gazette,* 3 November 1755; *London Magazine* (April 1760), 199; *Observations sur le Mémoire de la France . . . Envoyées dans*

les cours de l'Europe, par le ministère Britannique, pour justifier la réponse faite à la réquisition de S.M.T.C. du 21 décembre 1755 (Paris, 1756), 6 f.

113 *Maryland Gazette,* 17 July 1755.

114 Lawrence to Board of Trade and Plantations, 28 June 1755, *BTNS,* 15:H-300.

115 *New York Mercury,* 21 July 1755.

116 Halifax, 26 July, *New York Gazette,* 11 August 1755; *Maryland Gazette,* 28 August 1755; 'Review of Military Operations', 91.

117 *New York Mercury,* 13 October 1755; *Maryland Gazette,* 23 October 1755.

118 Quoted in French in Ruville, op. cit., 1:365, note 1.

119 Corbett, op. cit., 1:58; John Barrow, *The Life of George Lord Anson, Admiral of the Fleet* (London, 1839), 237.

120 Dieskau à Argenson, ler juillet 1755, *AG,* 3404: no 175.

121 London, 7 October 1755, *New York Mercury,* 8 December 1755.

122 London, 31 October 1755, *New York Gazette,* 26 January 1756.

123 Vaudreuil à Puyzieulx, 2 juillet 1755, *AE,* Mémoires et documents, Amérique, 10:162-3.

124 Du Quesne à Machault, 25 juin 1755, H-R. Casgrain, ed., *Extraits des archives des ministères de la Marine et de la Guerre à Paris* (Quebec, 1890), 13-17.

125 Frégault, *François Bigot,* 2:113 f.

126 Du Quesne à Puyzieulx, 3 juillet 1755, *AE,* Mémoires et documents, Amérique, 10:164v.-5.

127 Bigot à Puyzieulx, 4 juillet 1755, ibid., 166.

128 Shirley to Robinson, 24 March 1755, *NYCD,* 6:942 f.; id., 20 June 1755, ibid., 954-7; Johnson to Shirley, 17 March 1755, ibid., 947. See also *London Magazine* (May 1760), 242.

129 Braddock to Napier, 19 April 1755, Pargellis, *Military Affairs in North America,* 83.

130 Braddock to Robinson, 19 April 1755, *PRO,* CO 5, 46:27 f.

131 *New York Mercury,* 2 June 1755.

132 Captain Shirley to Morris, 23 May 1755, *Pennsylvania Colonial Records,* 6:405.

133 Braddock to Morris, 24 May 1755, ibid., 399 f.

134 Dinwiddie to Board of Trade, 23 June 1755, *Records of Dinwiddie,* 2:71.

135 'Relation depuis le depart des trouppes de Quebec jusqu'au 30 du mois de 7bre 1755', *AG,* 3405: no 106.

136 Gipson, 6:79.

137 Contrecoeur à Vaudreuil, 14 juillet 1755, *AC,* F 3, 14:119; Morris to Sharpe, 3 July 1755, *Pennsylvania Colonial Records,* 6:454; A Message from the Governor to the Assembly, 29 June 1755, *Maryland Gazette,* 3 July 1755; ibid., 10 July 1755.

138 'Acte de sépulture de M. de Beaujeu', *Papiers Contrecoeur,* 389 f.

139 'Relation depuis le depart des trouppes', *AG,* 3405: no 106.

140 The account of the engagement is based on the following sources: Contrecoeur à Vaudreuil, 14 juillet 1755, *AC,* F 3, 14:119v.-20; Dumas à Machault, 24 juillet 1756, *AC,* C 11A, 101:322-31; 'Relation du Combat du 9 juillet 1755', Winthrop Sargent, *The History of an Expedition Against Fort Du Quesne in 1755 Under Major-General Edward Braddock* (Philadelphia, 1855), 409 f.; an anonymous

diary, ibid., 386; Dunbar to Napier, 24 July 1755, Pargellis, *Military Affairs in North America*, 111; 'Journal of Proceedings from Willes's Creek to the Monongahela', ibid., 106; 'Review of Military Operations', 92; *Mercure de France* (octobre 1755), 226 f.; Walpole, op. cit., 2:31.

[141] Adam Stephens to John Hunter, 18 July 1755, Charteris, op. cit., 166.

[142] Sargent, op. cit., 238.

[143] 'Liste des officiers, miliciens, soldats et Sauvages de Canada qui ont esté tués et blessés . . .' *AC*, F 3, 14:117.

[144] 'Etat de l'artillerie, Munitions de guerre et autres effets . . . trouvés sur le champ de bataille . . .', ibid., 116. See also Montreuil à Argenson, 5 août 1755, *AG,* 3405: no 7.

[145] Robert à Machault, 23 août 1755, *AM,* B 4, 68:138; Choiseul-Praslin à Machault, 21 septembre 1755, ibid., 185v.

[146] Banyar to Johnson, 1 August 1755, *Johnson Papers,* 1:811.

[147] Vaudreuil à Machault, 10 octobre 1755, *AC,* F 3, 14:189-99. See also Bigot à Machault, 27 août 1755, ibid., 134v.

[148] *Mercure de France* (octobre 1755), 230.

[149] Message of 31 July 1755, *Boston News-Letter,* 14 August 1755. See also *Pennsylvania Colonial Records,* 6:502.

[150] Message of 5 August 1755, *Records of Dinwiddie,* 2:134 f.

[151] *Boston News-Letter,* 21 August 1755.

[152] Dinwiddie to Dunbar, 26 July 1755, *Records of Dinwiddie,* 2:118 f.

[153] 'Order for Colonel Thomas Dunbar', [12 July 1755], *PRO,* CO 5, 46:101.

[154] 'Review of Military Operations', 94; P.H. Giddens, 'The French and Indian War in Maryland', *Maryland Historical Magazine,* 30 (1935):306.

[155] Morris to Shirley, 30 July 1755, *Pennsylvania Colonial Records,* 6:513.

[156] *Pennsylvania Gazette,* 28 August 1755.

[157] Letter of 2 August 1755, Fitzpatrick, *Writings of George Washington,* 1:157.

[158] Contrecoeur à Vaudreuil, 14 juillet 1755, *AC,* F 3, 14:120.

[159] Robert Napier, 'Sketch for Next Year's Campaign in North America', 6 September 1755, Pargellis, *Military Affairs in North America,* 133 f.

[160] Message of 6 August 1755, Frank H. Severance, *An Old Frontier of New France. The Niagara Region and Adjacent Lakes under French Control* (2 vols, New York, 1917), 2:76 f.

[161] De Lancey to Robinson, 7 August 1755, *NYCD,* 6:991 f.

[162] *New York Mercury,* 18 August 1755.

[163] Vaudreuil à Machault, 10 juillet 1755, Casgrain, *Extraits des archives,* 37.

[164] Frégault, *La Civilisation de la Nouvelle-France,* 205 f.

[165] Vaudreuil à Machault, 24 juillet 1755, Casgrain, *Extraits des archives,* 44.

[166] Id., 10 juillet 1755, ibid., 37.

[167] Id., 24 juillet 1755, ibid., 45-50; Dieskau à Argenson, 1er juillet 1755, *AG,* 3404: no 175.

[168] Id., 5 août 1755, *AC,* F 3, 14:130v.-1.

[169] Bigot à Machault, 27 août 1755, *AC,* F 3, 14:135v.-6; 'Relation de l'action qui s'est passée le 8 Septembre 1755', ibid., 183; Bréard à Machault, 13 août 1755, Casgrain, *Extraits des archives,* 128; 'Relation depuis Le départ des trouppes . . .',

AG, 3405: no 106; 'Memoire pour servir d'Instruction à Monsieur le Baron de Dieskau', *AC,* F 3, 14:162.

[170] Bigot à Machault, 5 septembre 1755, *AC,* F 3, 14:141.

[171] Council of war, 23 August 1755, *NYCD,* 6:1001; see Wraxall to Fox, 27 septembre 1755, Pargellis, *Military Affairs in North America,* 137.

[172] Banyar to Johnson, 6 August 1755, *Johnson Papers,* 1:833 f.

[173] Id., 15 August 1755, ibid., 847.

[174] Ephraim Williams to Israel Williams, Massachusetts Historical Society, Israel Williams Papers, 1:173.

[175] *Maryland Gazette,* 28 August 1755.

[176] On the site of the fort, see Harry Gordon to Napier, 22 June 1756, Pargellis, *Military Affairs in North America,* 179; on Lydius, see 'Review of Military Operations', 97.

[177] Council of war, 23 August 1755, *NYCD,* 6:1001.

[178] Johnson to Lords of Trade, 3 September 1755, ibid., 997; Wraxall to Fox, 27 September 1755, Pargellis, *Military Affairs in North America,* 138; 'Traduction d'un Journal anglois', *AC,* F 3, 14:249.

[179] The account of the three engagements of 8 September 1755 is based on the following sources: Dieskau à Machault, 14 septembre 1755, *AC,* F 3, 14:144-6; Vaudreuil à Machault, 8 juin 1756, ibid., 241-5; id., 25 septembre 1755, ibid., 150-4; Montreuil à Argenson, 14 octobre 1755, *AG,* 3405: no 125; 'Relation depuis Le depart des trouppes . . .', ibid., no 106; 'Dialogue Entre le Maréchal de Saxe Et Le Baron de Dieskau aux Champs Elysées', *AG,* 3404: no 54; 'Relation de l'action qui s'est passée le 8 septembre 1755 au Lac St Sacrement', 4 octobre 1755, *AC,* F 3, 14:183-8; 'Traduction d'un Journal anglois', *AC,* F 3, 14:250; Johnson to the Governors of North America, 9 September 1755, *Boston News-Letter,* 18 September 1755; *New York Gazette,* 15 September 1755, special number; 'Review of Military Operations', 107 f.; Johnson to Hardy, 16 September 1755, *NYCD,* 6:1013 f.; Pownall to Lords of Trade, 20 September 1755, ibid., 1008; Wraxall to De Lancey, 10 September 1755, ibid., 1003 f.; Wraxall to Fox, 27 September 1755, Pargellis, *Military Affairs in North America,* 138-40; *Maryland Gazette,* 16 October 1755.

[180] Montreuil à Argenson, 14 octobre 1755, *AG,* 3405: no 125.

[181] Vaudreuil à Machault, 25 septembre 1755, *AC,* F 3, 14:149v., 152, 156v.

[182] [Cimon], *Les Ursulines de Québec,* 2:281-3.

[183] Pargellis, *Military Affairs in North America,* 140.

[184] *AC,* F 3, 14:145v.

[185] Ibid., 155, 188; *AG,* 3405: no 120; 'Liste des Officiers et Soldats . . . tués ou blessés dans le combat . . . 8 7bre 1755', *AC,* F 3, 14:205.

[186] *Boston News-Letter,* 18 September 1755; *New York Gazette,* 6 October 1755; *Maryland Gazette,* 9 October 1755; *Pennsylvania Gazette,* 16 October 1755; *NYCD,* 6:1006 f.

[187] 'Review of Military Operations', 114 f. See also *New York Gazette,* 19 September 1755, special number.

[188] 'Traduction d'un Journal anglois', *AC,* F 3, 14:251; see also *Virginia Gazette,* 17 October 1755.

[189] Walpole, op. cit., 2:46.

190 Hardy to Halifax, 27 November 1755, Pargellis, *Military Affairs in North America,* 149 f.

191 *AC,* F 3, 14:251.

192 *New York Gazette,* 27 October 1755.

193 'Review of Military Operations', 114.

194 Shirley to Johnson, *Johnson Papers,* 2:62.

195 Vaudreuil à Machault, 25 septembre 1755, *AC,* F 3, 14:157v.; Bigot à Machault, 4 octobre 1755, ibid., 178v.

196 *PRO,* CO 5, 46:94.

197 *New York Mercury,* 14 August 1755, reprinted in *Boston News-Letter,* 21 August 1755.

198 *Maryland Gazette,* 11 September 1755.

199 Ibid., 9 October 1755.

200 Bigot à Machault, 5 septembre 1755, *AC,* F 3, 14:140v.-1.

201 Vaudreuil à Machault, 25 septembre 1755, ibid., 158-9.

202 Shirley to Sharpe, 9 September 1755, *Sharpe Correspondence,* 1:280.

203 Shirley to Johnson, 12 September 1755, *Johnson Papers,* 2:34.

204 'Review of Military Operations', 120-2.

205 *New York Gazette,* 3 November 1755.

206 'Proceedings of the Council of War', *Sharpe Correspondence,* 1:315-20. See also 'Review of Military Operations', 132 f.

207 Johnson to Orme, *Johnson Papers,* 2:53.

208 *New York Gazette,* 29 December 1755.

209 Frégault, *Le Grand Marquis,* 332.

210 Vaudreuil à Moras, 16 février 1756 [1758], *AC,* F 3, 14:222-3.

211 *New York Mercury,* 22 December 1755.

CHAPTER IV

1 Ruville, *William Pitt,* 1:366; Pierre Muret, *La Prépondérance anglaise 1715-1763* (Paris, 1942), 490.

2 *New York Mercury,* 27 November 1755.

3 *Boston News-Letter,* 22 January 1756.

4 *Mercure de La Haye,* 139 (1755):534 f.

5 Ibid., 140 (1756):403.

6 *An Impartial History of the Late Glorious War,* 17.

7 Quoted in Barrow, *Lord Anson,* 241.

8 *Mercure de France* (février 1756), 226 f.

9 *London Magazine* (January 1756), 46.

10 Muret, *La Prépondérance anglaise,* 491.

11 Graham, *Empire of the North Atlantic,* 153. Cf. A.T. Mahan, *The Influence of Sea Power upon History 1660-1783* (Boston, 1894), 291. The author of *Sentiments Relating to the Late Negociation* estimated that France had ninety-two ships of more than fifty guns and forty-seven with from thirty to forty-six guns each (pp. 30-6).

[12] Entick, 2:31-5.

[13] *Mercure de La Haye,* 139 (1755):335.

[14] Entick, 2:35. See the curious 'Plan proposé Par le Sr De La Salle pour S'emparer de Quebec et de Montreal. Avec la lettre de M. le Cte d'affry du 26 mars 1757' *AE,* Mémoires et documents, Amérique, 10:272.

[15] Dispatch of 8 November 1756, *Pennsylvania Journal,* 24 February 1757.

[16] Corbett, *England in the Seven Years' War,* 2:373.

[17] Graham, *Empire of the North Atlantic,* 150 f.

[18] Ruville, op. cit., 2:77 f.

[19] *Mercure de La Haye,* 139 (1755):455.

[20] 'Extract of a private Letter from London . . . dated February 3', *New York Mercury,* 21 April 1755.

[21] *An Impartial History of the Late Glorious War,* 73.

[22] Walpole, *Memoirs of the Reign of George II,* 2:194. On Pitt's oft-quoted remark about 'conquering America on the plains of Germany', see J.A. Williamson, *A Short History of British Expansion* (2 vols, London, 1951), 1:397.

[23] Hotblack, *Chatham's Colonial Policy,* xiii.

[24] *London Magazine* (January 1756), Preface.

[25] Ibid., (March 1756), 146.

[26] *Mercure de La Haye,* 140 (1756):166.

[27] *London Magazine* (March 1756), 152.

[28] Brian Tunstall, *William Pitt Earl of Chatham,* (London, 1938), 154 f.

[29] Ruville, op. cit., 2:76 f.

[30] Ibid., 2:374 f.

[31] *London Magazine* (March 1755), 120.

[32] Charteris, *William Augustus Duke of Cumberland,* 194.

[33] Machault à Vaudreuil, 17 janvier 1756, *AC,* B 103:129; Machault à Vaudreuil et à Bigot, 16 janvier 1756, ibid., 129v.

[34] Selley, *England in the Eighteenth Century,* 94, note 2; Tunstall, op. cit., 252.

[35] London, 21 November 1755, *Boston News-Letter,* 18 March 1756.

[36] Harrington, *The New York Merchant,* 289-91.

[37] Robert Beatson, ed., *Naval and Military Memoirs of Great Britain, from 1727 to 1783* (6 vols, London, 1804), 3:102.

[38] Clark, 'News and Opinions Concerning America in English Newspapers, 1754-1763', *Pacific Historical Review,* 10 (1941):78.

[39] Richard Pares, 'American versus Continental Warfare, 1739-1763', *English Historical Review,* 51 (1936):449 f.

[40] Gipson, 6:185; Bigot à Machault, 12 avril 1756, *AC,* F 3, 14:235v.

[41] *Etat présent de la Pensilvanie, où l'on trouve le détail de ce qui s'y est passé depuis la défaite du Général Braddock jusqu'à la prise d'Oswego* (Paris, 1756), 22-4. This is an abridged translation of William Smith's *A Brief view of the Conduct of Pennsylvania for the year 1755* (London, 1756). For circumstances leading to the translation see *Etat présent,* 4.

[42] Lewis Evans, 'Analysis Number II', 1756, Gipson, *Lewis Evans,* 185.

[43] *New York Gazette,* 20 October 1755.

[44] *Pennsylvania Gazette,* 16 October 1755.

45 *Maryland Gazette,* 9 October 1755.

46 Smith, *Etat présent de la Pensilvanie,* 52 f.

47 *Pennsylvania Gazette,* 25 December 1755; *Boston News-Letter,* 9 January 1756.

48 *New York Mercury,* 29 December 1755; *Boston News-Letter,* 18 March 1756.

49 *Maryland Gazette,* 4 March 1756; *Boston News-Letter,* 8 April 1756; Baker-Crothers, *Virginia and the French and Indian War,* 99 f.

50 *New York Gazette,* 15 March 1756.

51 *Pennsylvania Gazette,* 25 March 1756.

52 *New York Gazette,* 31 May 1756.

53 *Boston News-Letter,* 24 June 1756.

54 *New York Gazette,* 7 June 1756.

55 Vaudreuil à Machault, 8 juin 1756, *AC,* c 11a, 101:22.

56 See Alfred P. James, 'The Nest of Robbers', *Western Pennsylvania Historical Magazine,* 21 (1938):168.

57 Montcalm à Argenson, 12 juin 1756, *AG,* 3417: no 139.

58 'Avec une lettre de M. le Mis de Bonnac du 25 mai 1756. Traduction de l'anglois', *AE,* Mémoires et documents, Amérique, 10:252.

59 'Review of Military Operations', 152.

60 *Virginia Gazette,* 30 April 1756: reprinted in *New York Gazette,* 14 June 1756.

61 Hardy to Halifax, 7 May 1756, Pargellis, *Military Affairs in North America,* 171.

62 *Boston News-Letter,* 15 April 1756.

63 *New York Gazette,* 23 February 1756.

64 Machault à Vaudreuil, 17 janvier 1756, *AC,* b 103:129.

65 Id., 20 février 1756, ibid., 131.

66 Paragellis, *Lord Loudoun in North America,* 60.

67 Ibid., 42.

68 F.W. Seymour, *Lords of the Valley: Sir William Johnson and His Mohawk Brothers* (New York and London, 1930), 129.

69 *New York Mercury,* 26 July 1756.

70 Machault à Vaudreuil et à Bigot, 17 janvier 1756, *AC,* b 103:129v.; 'Ordonnance pour une augmentation de soldats dans les Compagnies du Canada', 14 mars 1756, ibid., 137v.; 'Ordonnance pour l'augmentation de la Compagnie de Canoniers', 14 mars 1756, ibid., 137.

71 *Mercure de la Haye,* 140 (1756):167.

72 Ibid., 276.

73 Frégault, *François Bigot,* 2:119 f.

74 Machault à Vaudreuil, 20 février 1756, *AC,* b 103:131.

75 Machault à Vaudreuil, 15 mars 1756, ibid., 12 *bis;* 'Memoire du Roy pour Servir d'instruction au Sr Mis de Moncalm Marechal de camp', 14 mars 1756, ibid., 7.

76 Argenson à Vaudreuil, 29 février 1756, *AG,* 3417: no 42.

77 Montcalm à sa femme, 16 avril 1757, 'La Correspondance de Montcalm', *Report on the Public Archives for 1929* (Ottawa, 1930), 56.

[78] Ibid., 61.

[79] G.F.G. Stanley, *Canada's Soldiers 1604-1954* (Toronto, 1954), 69 f.

[80] Casgrain, 7 (Montcalm, *Journal*):163; ibid., 181.

[81] Kerallain, *Les Français au Canada: la jeunesse de Bougainville*, 87; Montcalm à Lévis, 16 juillet 1759, Casgrain, 6 (Montcalm, *Lettres*):190. See also Vaudreuil à Argenson, 8 juin 1756, *AG*, 3417: no 132; Vaudreuil à Machault, 7 novembre 1756, *AC*, c 11A, 101:154, etc.

[82] Lévis à Mirepoix, 4 septembre 1757, Casgrain, 2 (Lévis, *Lettres*):155; Montcalm à Bourlamaque, 7 juillet 1759, Casgrain, 5 (Bourlamaque, *Lettres*):336.

[83] Frégault, *François Bigot*, 2:150-2.

[84] Machault à Vaudreuil, 12 avril 1756, *AC*, B 103:24.

[85] Vaudreuil à Machault, 1756, *AC*, c 11A, 101:9 f.

[86] Id., *AC*, c 11A, 102:185 f.

[87] Vaudreuil à Machault, 25 septembre 1755, *AC*, F 3, 14:160v. f.

[88] 'Canada', 4 juin 1756, *AC*, c 11A, 101:373-5. This is a summary of Vaudreuil's letters of 2, 3, 4, 6, 7, and 8 February 1756.

[89] Bigot à Machault, 12 avril 1756, *AC*, F 3, 14:235.

[90] *New York Mercury*, 12 July 1756.

[91] *New York Gazette*, 2 August 1756; *Virginia Gazette*, 27 August 1756.

[92] Wentworth to Fox, 19 July 1756, *PRO*, co 5, 17:536.

[93] Vaudreuil à Machault, 12 août 1756, *AC*, F 3, 14:275-8; Montcalm à Argenson, 12 juin 1756, *AG*, 3417: no 137; id., 26 juin 1756; ibid., no 175; Casgrain, 7 (Montcalm, *Journal*):75-7; Lévis à Argenson, 21 août 1756, *AG*, 3417: no 205; 'Extrait des Nouvelles en Canada 1756', *AC*, c 11A, 101:355.

[94] Casgrain, 7 (Montcalm, *Journal*):77.

[95] Pargellis, *Lord Loudoun in North America*, 94 f.

[96] *PRO*, co 5, 17:691 f.

[97] Montcalm à Argenson, 26 juin 1756, *AG*, 3417: no 174; id., 20 juillet 1756, ibid., no 187.

[98] *PAC,* Lettres de Bourlamaque, 1:13.

[99] Bigot à Machault, 4 octobre 1755, *AC*, F 3, 14:180.

[100] 'Journal de la campagne de M. de Léry', H.-R. Casgrain, ed., *Relations et journaux de différentes expéditions faites durant les années 1755-56-57-58-59-60* (Quebec, 1895), 53-64 (hereafter: Casgrain, 11 (*Relations et journaux*)); Vaudreuil à Machault, 1er juin 1756, P.-G. Roy, ed., *Inventaire des papiers de Léry* (3 vols, Quebec, 1939-40), 2:135-8; Péan à ——, 19 mai 1756, ibid., 134; Bigot à Machault, 12 avril 1756, *AC*, F 3, 14:231-4; 'Envoyé copie aux Ambassadeurs et Ministres du Roy le 29 juin 1756', *AE*, Mémoires et documents, Amérique, 10:256; *New York Gazette*, 19 April 1756; *Journal des campagnes au Canada de 1755 à 1760 par le comte de Maurès de Malartic* (Dijon, 1890), 49; [Cimon], *Les Ursulines de Québec*, 2:291 f.; 'Journal qui m'a été communiqué par M. de Charly', Casgrain, 7 (Montcalm, *Journal*):114-18.

[101] *New York Gazette*, 29 March 1756; ibid., 5 April 1756; *Boston News-Letter*, 22 April 1756.

[102] Vaudreuil à Machault, 15 juin 1756, *AC*, c 11A, 101:29.

[103] Vaudreuil à La Valtrie, 22 avril 1756, Université de Montréal, Collection Baby, dossier La Valtrie.

[104] 'Detail de ce qui s'est passé en Canada depuis le debarquement des troupes de terre ... Jusqu'au 1er mai 1756', *AG*, 3417: no 122.

[105] Hardy to Halifax, 7 May 1756, Pargellis, *Military Affairs in North America*, 176.

[106] Vaudreuil à Machault, 1er août 1756, *AC*, c 11A, 101:72v.-3.

[107] *Boston News-Letter,* 22 April, 6 May, 20 May 1756; Patrick Mackellar, 'A Journal of the Transactions at Oswego from the 16th of May to the 14 of August 1756', Pargellis, *Military Affairs in North America*, 189. See also Pargellis, *Lord Loudoun in North America*, 156 f., and Gipson, 6:201.

[108] Vaudreuil à Machault, 10 juillet 1756, *AC*, F 3, 14:257-9, 261v.-2; 'Journal de l'expédition de M. de Villiers', Casgrain, 11 (*Relations et journaux*):65 f.; Mackellar's journal, Pargellis, *Military Affairs in North America*, 195; *Boston News-Letter*, 8 July 1756.

[109] *New York Gazette*, 28 June 1756.

[110] Harry Gordon to Robert Napier, 22 June 1756, Pargellis, *Military Affairs in North America*, 177.

[111] *New York Mercury*, 26 July 1756. (Dispatch of 2 July from Albany.)

[112] Journal de Villiers, Casgrain, 11 (*Relations et journaux*):68 f.; Vaudreuil à Machault, 10 juillet 1756, *AC*, F 3, 14:259-61; 'Extrait des Nouvelles en Canada 1756', *AC*, c 11A, 101:354; *New York Gazette*, 19 July 1756; *Pennsylvania Gazette*, 29 July 1756; *New York Mercury*, 2 August 1756; Franklin to Fawkener, 27 July 1756, Pargellis, *Military Affairs in North America*, 185; see also ibid., 155 f., 200 f., and Francis Parkman, *Montcalm and Wolfe* (2 vols, Boston, 1888), 1:394-6.

[113] Pargellis, *Lord Loudoun in North America*, 162 f.; William H. Smith, 'The Pelham Papers—Loss of Oswego', *Papers of the American Historical Society*, vol. 4 (Part 4):50.

[114] 'Extrait des Nouvelles en Canada 1756', *AC*, c 11A, 101:353v.-4.

[115] Lettres du 30 juillet et du 2 août 1756, Casgrain, 6 (Montcalm, *Lettres*):28 f. See Vaudreuil à Machault, 1er septembre 1756, *AC*, F 3, 14:297v.-8.

[116] 'Journal & livre d'ordres de Carillon, 1756-1760', *PAC*, Amherst Papers, packet 55.

[117] Desandrouins, 'Recueil et Journal', Gabriel, *Le Maréchal de camp Desandrouins*, 40. See Casgrain, 7 (Montcalm, *Journal*):89-95; Vaudreuil à Machault, 1er septembre 1756, *AC*, F 3, 14:298; 'Relation De La Campagne du Canada Jusqu'au 1er 7bre 1756', *AG*, 3417: no 222.

[118] Desandrouins, 'Recueil et Journal', Gabriel, op. cit., 42-4; Vaudreuil à Machault, 1er septembre 1756, *AC*, F 3, 14:298v.-9; Vaudreuil à Moras, 28 octobre 1756, *AC*, c 11A, 102:125. See also La Rochebeaucour à Fontbrune, 4 août 1756, Casgrain, 6 (Montcalm, *Lettres*):31.

[119] Casgrain, 7 (Montcalm, *Journal*):89.

[120] Ibid., 95. See also Mercer to Craven, 12 août 1756, French translation with Vaudreuil's letter of 1 September, *AC*, F 3, 14:312.

[121] 'Au Conseil de Guerre tenu le 13 d'aoust a Chouaguen', ibid., 310; 'Dans l'assemblée de tous les officiers du fort Ontario', ibid., 314; Casgrain, 7 (Montcalm, *Journal*):96 f.; Pargellis, *Lord Loudoun in North America*, 159.

[122] 'Lettre de M. Desandrouins sur une expedition contre le fort Ontario', 28 août 1756, *AG*, 3417: no 209; *Boston Gazette,* 23 May 1757.

[123] See NOTE appended to this chapter.

[124] Casgrain, 7 (Montcalm, *Journal*):97 f.; Gabriel, op. cit., 58-60; 'Declaration

of some Soldiers belonging to Shirley's Regiment', 21 August 1756, *NYCD*, 7:126; Mackellar's journal, Pargellis, *Military Affairs in North America*, 211-13.

125 'Articles de la capitulation de la prise du fort chouaguen du 14e aoust 1756', *AG*, 3417: no 203.

126 Vaudreuil à Argenson, 30 août 1756, *AG*, 3417: no 214. See statement by Littlehales, Gipson, 6:200, note 129, and *New York Mercury*, 6 September 1756 (also in *Boston News-Letter*, 16 September 1756). Casgrain, 7 (Montcalm, *Journal*):107, reports the number of killed and wounded as 1,742, but this report over-estimated the number of killed by one hundred.

127 Lettre du 28 août 1756, *AG*, 3417: no 209. See La Pause, 'Mémoire et observations sur mon voyage en Canada', *RAPQ* (1931-2):34; Thomas Chapais, *Le Marquis de Montcalm (1712-1759)* (Quebec, 1911), 137 f., note 1.

128 'Liste des batimens qui ont esté pris sur les Anglois dans le port de Chouaguen', *AC*, F 3, 14:325. Statements of supplies of artillery and provisions can be found in *AG*, 3417: no 203, and in *AC*, F 3, 14:309, 324, 326. On the question of pillage, see Montcalm à Argenson, 28 août 1756, *AG*, 3417: no 208 and Vaudreuil à Machault, ler septembre 1756, *AC*, F 3, 14:302v.

129 *AG*, 3417: no 222.

130 Montcalm à Argenson, 28 août 1756, *AG*, 3417: no 208.

131 Bigot à Machault, 3 septembre 1756, *AC*, F 3, 14:316v.

132 Vaudreuil à Machault, ibid., 304 f.

133 This was also Franklin's view. See Franklin to Fawkener, 27 July 1756, Pargellis, *Military Affairs in North America*, 185.

134 Vaudreuil à Argenson 30 août 1756, *AG*, 3417: no 214.

135 'Note détachée de Bougainville', quoted in Kerallain, *Les Français au Canada: la jeunesse de Bougainville*, 48. See also a quotation from Desandrouins in Gabriel, op. cit., 34.

136 Vaudreuil à Lévis, 18 août 1756, H.-R. Casgrain, ed., *Lettres du marquis de Vaudreuil au chevalier de Lévis* (Quebec, 1895), 30 f. Hereafter: Casgrain, 8 (Vaudreuil, *Lettres*).

137 Id., 22 août 1756, ibid., 32.

138 Lévis à Vaudreuil, 7 septembre 1756, Casgrain, 2 (Lévis, *Lettres*):88.

139 Vaudreuil à Lévis, 13 septembre 1756, Casgrain, 8 (Vaudreuil, *Lettres*):37 f. Bigot à Machault, 3 septembre 1756, *AC*, F 3, 14:319v.; Montcalm à Argenson, 22 septembre 1756, *AG*, 3417: no 240.

140 Casgrain, 7 (Montcalm, *Journal*):78; *Boston News-Letter*, 7 October 1756; Montcalm à Argenson, ler novembre 1756, *AG*, 3417: no 287; Johnson to Board of Trade, 10 November 1756, *NYCD*, 7:170.

141 Casgrain, 7 (Montcalm, *Journal*):79-81; Lévis à Belle-Isle, 9 octobre 1756, Casgrain, 2 (Lévis, *Lettres*):96 f.

142 See R.R. Palmer, 'Frederick the Great, Guibert, Bülow: From Dynastic to National War', in E.M. Earle *et al.*, eds, *Makers of Modern Strategy* (Princeton, 1943), 49-74, and more especially 51-7.

143 *Boston News-Letter*, 12 August 1756.

144 *Pennsylvania Gazette*, 13 May, 29 July 1756, etc.

145 Vaudreuil à Machault, 19 septembre 1756, *AC*, F 3, 14:344v.-5; Casgrain, 7 (Montcalm, *Journal*):111; Sharpe to Lyttleton, 23 August 1756, *Sharpe Correspondence*, 1:470; *New York Gazette*, 23 August 1756; *Boston News-Letter*, 2

September 1756; *London Magazine* (November 1756), 563; Smith, *Etat présent de la Pensilvanie*, 100-6.

[146] Horatio Sharpe to John Sharpe, 15 September 1756, *Sharpe Correspondence*, 1:485.

[147] *Boston News-Letter*, 21 October 1756.

[148] *New York Gazette*, 6 June 1756.

[149] Dinwiddie to Loudoun, 14 January 1757, *Records of Dinwiddie*, 2:584; Casgrain, 7 (Montcalm, *Journal*):111.

[150] Vaudreuil à Machault, 8 août 1756, *AC*, c 11A, 101:88v.-94.

[151] Id., 19 septembre 1756, *AC*, F 3, 14:341-50; Montcalm à Argenson, 26 septembre 1756, *AG*, 3417: no 243; id., 24 avril 1757, *AG*, 3457: no 56.

[152] Vaudreuil à Moras, 18 avril 1757, *AC*, F 3, 15:17v.-18.

[153] Id., 19 avril 1757, *AC*, c 11A, 102:9v.

[154] 'Précis des Evenemens de la Campagne de 1756 en la nouvelle france envoyé Le 28 aoust de laditte année', *AG*, 3417: no 209 *bis*. See also Casgrain, 7 (Montcalm, *Journal*):110.

[155] Walpole, op. cit., 2:248, cited by Gipson, 6:200.

[156] Entick, 1:482 f.

[157] *Mercure de France* (décembre 1756), 220-3; *Mercure de La Haye*, 141 (1756): 576-85; Entick, 2:8.

[158] 'Copie d'une Lettre écrite de Montreal le 18 Aoust 1756 à S.-Domingue', *PRO*, co 5, 48:103.

[159] Casgrain, 7 (Montcalm, *Journal*):108 f.

[160] [Cimon], *Les Ursulines de Québec*, 2:290 f.

[161] Journal de Bougainville, *RAPQ* (1923-4), 242.

[162] Pargellis, *Lord Loudoun in North America*, 164 f. See John R. Alden, *General Gage in America* (Baton Rouge, 1948), 37; *Boston News-Letter*, 16 September 1756.

[163] Hardy to Board of Trade, 5 September 1756, *NYCD*, 7:124; Johnson to Board of Trade, 10 September 1756, ibid., 128; Mante, *History of the Late War*, 79 f.

[164] Loudoun to Cumberland, 29 August 1756, Pargellis, *Military Affairs in North America*, 233.

[165] 'Review of Military Operations', 159-63. See *New York Gazette*, 13 September 1756.

[166] *New York Gazette*, 6 December 1756.

[167] Casgrain, 7 (Montcalm, *Journal*):114.

[168] *New York Gazette*, 27 September 1757.

[169] Marcel Trudel, *Le Séminaire de Québec sous le régime militaire, 1759-1764* (Quebec, 1954), 3.

[170] Lévis à Belle-Isle, 9 octobre 1756, Casgrain, 2 (Lévis, *Lettres*):97.

CHAPTER V

[1] 'Copy [in French] of the last Paragraph of a Letter from A Merchant at Quebec, to his Correspondent at Cape Françoise [*sic*] 20th August 1756. Taken from on board the Prize Snow Spring time', *PRO*, co 5, 48:101.

[2] See for example *Boston Gazette*, 1 November 1756.

[3] *London Magazine* (August 1756), 397.

[4] Charteris, *William Augustus Duke of Cumberland*, 237.

[5] *London Magazine* (October 1756), 507.

[6] *Pennsylvania Journal*, 10 February 1757.

[7] *Boston Gazette*, 21 November 1757.

[8] *Pennsylvania Journal*, 24 March 1757.

[9] *London Magazine* (August 1757), 410.

[10] Entick, 3:33; see also *Boston News-Letter*, 15 September 1757.

[11] *London Magazine* (April 1757), 202.

[12] Montcalm au ministre de la Guerre, 24 avril 1757, *AG*, 3457: no 60; 'Liste des differens batimens Anglois qui ont été conduits a Louisbourg par les Corsaires . . . à compter du mois d'Aoust 1756 . . . jusqu'au 24 8bre 1757', *AM*, B 4, 76: 90v.-1.

[13] *Mercure de La Haye*, 145 (novembre 1758):540.

[14] 'The Instructions from the City of London to its Representatives in Parliament', *London Magazine* (November 1756), 543.

[15] See Selley, *England in the Eighteenth Century*, 79.

[16] *Pennsylvania Journal*, 10 February 1757.

[17] Ibid., 17 February 1757.

[18] *Boston Gazette*, 21 February 1757.

[19] *Boston News-Letter*, 17 February 1757.

[20] 'To the King's Most Excellent Majesty', *PRO, CO* 5, 18:2. Published in *Pennsylvania Journal*, 2 June 1757.

[21] *London Magazine* (January 1757), 19.

[22] Ibid. (February 1757), 74.

[23] Ibid. (August 1757), 399.

[24] *Mercure de La Haye*, 142 (janvier 1757):5.

[25] Charteris, op. cit., 205, 267, note.

[26] Loudoun to Fox, 22 November 1756, *PRO, CO* 5, 48:23-7.

[27] Gipson, 6:92; Pargellis, *Lord Loudoun in North America*, 231.

[28] Loudoun to Pitt, 10 March 1757, *PRO, CO* 5, 48:210 f. See also Pargellis, op. cit., 211 and *Military Affairs in North America*, xviii-xix.

[29] Loudoun to Pitt, 3 May 1757, *PRO, CO* 5, 48:369 f.

[30] *New York Gazette*, 2 May 1757.

[31] *Boston Gazette*, 16 May 1757.

[32] See 'Etat Des forces de terre et de mer Destinées a faire la désente et le siege de louisbourg en 1757', *AM*, B 4, 76:25.

[33] Moras à Vaudreuil, 28 février 1757, *AM*, B 4, 76:198-9.

[34] Moras à Vaudreuil et à Bigot, 2 avril 1757, ibid., 200; Moras à Drucourt et à Prévost, 2 avril 1757, ibid., 209; Moras à Vaudreuil, 11 avril 1757, ibid., 203.

[35] See Gipson, 7:102 f.

[36] Bulletin de Brest, 22 juillet 1757, *AC*, C 11A, 102:93.

[37] Vaudreuil à Moras, 20 juillet 1757, ibid., 89.

[38] Waddington, *La Guerre de Sept ans*, 1:253; Graham, *Empire of the North Atlantic*, 165.

[39] *Boston News-Letter*, 4 August 1757; ibid., 29 December 1757; Arthur G. Doughty, ed., *An Historical Journal of the Compaigns in North America for the Years 1757, 1758, 1759, and 1760, by Captain John Knox* (3 vols, Toronto, 1914-16), 1:35. Hereafter: Knox, *Journal*.

[40] Knox, *Journal*, 1:38; [Loudoun], *The Conduct of a Noble Commander in America Impartially Reviewed* (London, 1758), 25-6.

[41] Knox, *Journal*, 1:41.

[42] Montcalm au ministre de la Guerre, *AG*, 3417: no 288.

[43] Vaudreuil à Moras, 13 août 1757, *AC*, c 11A, 102:98v.-9; *Mercure de France* (novembre 1757), 185 f.

[44] 'Relation de la Campagne sur le Lac St Sacrement en Canada pendant l'hyver 1757', *AC*, F 3, 15:25-8.

[45] *Mercure de France* (août 1757), 214.

[46] 'Amérique nouvelles du Canada', 5 juillet 1757, *AE*, Mémoires et documents, Amérique, 10:280v., 282.

[47] Vaudreuil à Moras, 22 avril 1757, *AC*, c 11A, 102:39.

[48] Montcalm au ministre de la Guerre, 24 avril 1757, *AG*, 3457: no 60.

[49] Webb to Loudoun, 5 August 1757, *PRO*, co 5, 48:542 f.

[50] *Pennsylvania Journal*, 11 August 1757.

[51] Sharpe to Denny, 14 August 1757, *Sharpe Correspondence*, 2:73.

[52] Sharpe to Dinwiddie, 16 August 1757, ibid., 74.

[53] Dinwiddie to Lyttleton, 26 August 1757, *Records of Dinwiddie*, 2:690.

[54] Dinwiddie to Sharpe, 26 August 1757, *Sharpe Correspondence*, 2:75.

[55] Loudoun to Holderness, 16 August 1757, *PRO*, co 5, 48:487 f.

[56] Loudoun to Pownall, 18 August 1757, ibid., 561 f.

[57] Loudoun to Webb, 20 August 1757, ibid., 571 f.

[58] Holburne to Holderness, 20 August 1757, ibid., 658.

[59] Webb to Loudoun, 11 August 1757, ibid., 559 f.

[60] Sharpe to Calvert, 5 September 1757, *Sharpe Correspondence*, 2:77 f.

[61] See Chapais, *Le Marquis de Montcalm*, 294 f.

[62] Bigot à Moras, 24 août 1757, *AC*, F 3, 15:59. See also Frégault, *François Bigot*, 2:222 f., note 9.

[63] Vaudreuil à Moras, 16 septembre 1757, *AC*, F 3, 15:82.

[64] Id., 26 et 30 octobre 1757, *AC*, c 11A, 102:113, 145v.

[65] Tunstall, *William Pitt*, 199.

[66] Waddington, op. cit., 1:270.

[67] Corbett, *England in the Seven Years' War*, 1:175. Cf. Osgood, *The American Colonies in the Eighteenth Century*, 4:402.

[68] I.M. Hays, 'A journal Kept during the Siege of Fort William Henry, August, 1757', American Philosophical Society, *Proceedings*, 37 (1898):150.

[69] *New York Mercury*, 22 August 1757.

[70] *New York Gazette*, 22 August 1757.

[71] *Pennsylvania Gazette*, 25 August 1757.

72 *New York Mercury,* 29 August 1757. See also ibid., 24 April 1758.

73 Frégault, *Le Grand Marquis,* 15-17.

74 Loudoun to Holderness, 16 August 1757, *PRO,* CO 5, 48:502 f.

75 Vaudreuil à Moras, 19 avril 1757, *AC,* C 11A, 102:10; id., 12 juillet 1757, ibid., 56v.-7.

76 *Boston News-Letter,* 17 March 1757.

77 Vaudreuil à Moras, 19 avril 1757, *AC,* C 11A, 102:34.

78 'Extract of a Letter from Minisink, in New-Jersey, April 25', *Boston News-Letter,* 26 May 1757.

79 *Boston News-Letter,* 18 August 1757; 'Porté au Roy', octobre 1757, *AC,* C 11A, 102:272.

80 'Extract from a Poem on the Barbarities of the French and their Savage Allies and Proselytes, on the Frontiers of Virginia. By Samuel Davies, A.M.', *New York Gazette,* 9 January 1758.

81 Claude de Bonnault, *Histoire du Canada français* (Paris, 1950), 250; James, 'The Nest of Robbers', *Western Pennsylvania Historical Magazine,* 21 (1938):172; 'The Examination of Monsr. Belestre a French Ensign', 20 June 1757, *NYCD,* 7:282.

82 Montcalm au ministre de la Guerre, 23 mai 1757, *AG,* 3457: no 71; id., 18 septembre 1757, ibid., no 143; Vaudreuil à Moras, 9 septembre 1757, *AC,* C 11A, 102:104.

83 *New York Mercury,* 12 September 1757; *Boston News-Letter,* 6 October 1757; *Boston Gazette,* 10 October 1757; *New York Mercury,* 18 July 1757, etc.

84 Vaudreuil à Moras, 13 février 1758, *AC,* C 11A, 103:17-18v.

85 'Extrait d'une Lettre angloise écritte de la Pensilvanie le 1er novembre 1757', *AC,* C 11A, 102:287v.

86 Vaudreuil à Moras, 22 juillet 1757, *AC,* C 11A, 102:91; id., 9 septembre 1757, ibid., 103; id., 12 septembre 1757, ibid., 105.

87 *Boston News-Letter,* 27 October 1757.

88 Vaudreuil à Moras, 18 avril 1757, *AC,* C 11A, 102:3v.-5.

89 Id., 12 février 1758, *AC,* F 3, 15:91v.

90 Vaudreuil à Moras, 13 février 1758, *AC,* C 11A, 103:20.

91 'Précis de la Campagne de M. de Belestre du 28. 9bre 1757', *AC,* C 11A, 103:443-6; Vaudreuil à Moras, 12 février 1758, *AC,* F 3, 15:86-96; 'Itinéraire partant de L'embouchure de la Riviere de Chouëgen', 1757, *AC,* C 11A, 102:325, 331; J. De Lancey to Board of Trade, 5 January 1758, *NYCD,* 7:341; *Boston Gazette,* 5 December 1757; *Boston News-Letter,* 8 December 1757; ibid., 11 May 1758.

92 *Boston News-Letter,* 1 December 1757.

93 Massiac à Vaudreuil, 24 juin 1758, *AC,* B 107:42.

94 Quoted in Tunstall, op. cit., 199.

95 London, 24 October 1757, *New York Gazette,* 6 February 1758.

96 *New York Gazette,* 31 October 1757.

97 *Mercure de La Haye,* 143 (août 1757):156.

98 Entick, 2:167.

99 *Gazette de France,* 22 (26 mai 1757):257.

100 Gipson, 7:17.

[101] *New York Gazette,* 6 June 1757.

[102] 'To the People of England', *Boston Gazette,* 11 July 1757.

[103] *London Magazine* (1759), appendix, 695.

[104] Article from the *Monitor,* reprinted in *London Magazine* (September 1757), 421, *New York Gazette,* 9 January 1758, etc.

[105] *New York Gazette,* 6 February 1757.

[106] Morris to ——, 9 June 1757, *AM,* B 4, 96:97v.-8. (Letter taken to France on board a prize.)

[107] 'Extrait d'Une Lettre Anglaise ecritte de la Pensilvanie le 1er novembre 1757', *AC,* C 11A, 102:288.

[108] *Boston Gazette,* 22 August 1757.

[109] *London Magazine* (October 1757), 495.

[110] Chesterfield to his son, 7 January 1758, quoted in Ruville, *William Pitt,* 2:168.

[111] 30 July 1757, reprinted in *New York Mercury,* 23 January 1758.

[112] 10 September 1757, reprinted in *Boston Gazette,* 14 November 1757.

[113] Entick, 2:403.

[114] Quoted in Pargellis, *Lord Loudoun in North America,* 338, note 2.

[115] *London Magazine* (December 1757), 622.

[116] Vaudreuil à Moras, 30 octobre 1757, *AC,* C 11A, 102:162.

[117] [Cimon], *Les Ursulines de Québec,* 297-9; Montcalm au ministre de la Guerre, 18 septembre 1757, *AG,* 3457: no 143; see also Frégault, *François Bigot,* 2:226-33.

[118] 'State of Canada, in October 1757, with some thoughts on the Manner of Reducing it', *PAC,* Amherst Papers, packet 57.

[119] *Boston Gazette,* 28 November 1757.

[120] *London Magazine* (December 1757), 592.

[121] Waddington, op. cit., 1:272 f.

[122] James Wolfe to Walter Wolfe, 21 January 1758, Beckles Willson, *The Life and Letters of James Wolfe* (New York, 1909), 351.

CHAPTER VI

[1] Frégault, *François Bigot,* 1:240.

[2] Ibid., 304 f.

[3] *London Magazine* (May 1755), 216; ibid. (July 1759), 355.

[4] *Mercure de France* (octobre 1755), 229.

[5] Shirley to Robinson, 24 March 1755, *NYCD,* 6:944.

[6] For further details, see Frégault, *François Bigot,* 1:353-5 and 2:23-38.

[7] Lawrence to Board of Trade, 15 January 1754, *BTNS,* 15:H-244.

[8] Cornwallis to Duke of Bedford, 23 July 1749, Thomas B. Akins, ed., *Selections from the Public Documents of the Province of Nova Scotia* (Halifax, 1869), 564 (hereafter: Akins); Hopkins to Board of Trade, 23 July 1753, ibid., 199; Lawrence to Board of Trade, 5 December 1753, ibid., 206.

[9] Nova Scotia Council, 21 June 1754, Akins, 211. See also Lawrence to Board of Trade, 1 August 1754, ibid., 214.

[10] Bigot à Rouillé, 18 octobre 1750, *Report Concerning the Canadian Archives for 1905* (2 vols, Ottawa, 1906-9), 2, part 3:380.

[11] La Jonquière et Bigot à Rouillé, 5 octobre 1750, ibid., 379.

[12] Bigot à Puysieulx, 1er août 1750, *AE*, Mémoires et documents, Amérique, 9:278. See also Cornwallis to Board of Trade, 17 October 1749, Akins, 591 f.

[13] La Jonquière à Rouillé, 1er mai 1751, *Report Concerning the Canadian Archives for 1905*, 2, part 3:405.

[14] Cornwallis to Bedford, 11 septembre 1749, Akins, 586.

[15] Gipson, 6:261.

[16] *London Magazine* (April 1749), 183. A French translation of the article is preserved in *AC*, c 11b, 28:233-5.

[17] Gipson, 5:179-81.

[18] Frégault, *François Bigot*, 1:354 f.

[19] Le Loutre à Rouillé, 29 juillet 1749, Henri d'Arles, ed., *Acadie: reconstitution d'un chapitre perdu de l'histoire d'Amérique par Edouard Richard* (3 vols, Quebec and Boston, 1916-21), 2:448 (appendix iv). Hereafter: Arles, *Acadie*.

[20] Le Loutre à Rouillé, 14 octobre 1749, ibid., 453.

[21] Gipson, 5:201.

[22] Lawrence to Board of Trade, 1 August 1754 (postscript of 29 August), *BTNS*, 15:H-256.

[23] L'Isle-Dieu à Pontbriand, 17 avril 1752, *RAPQ* (1935-6), 332.

[24] L'Isle-Dieu à Rouillé, 24 juillet 1752, ibid., 352.

[25] Board of Trade to Lawrence, 4 April 1754, *BTNS*, 36:15.

[26] *London Magazine* (April 1749), p. 184.

[27] Lawrence to Board of Trade, 1 August 1754, *BTNS*, 15:H-256.

[28] Board of Trade to Lawrence, 29 October 1754, *BTNS*, 36:59.

[29] Lawrence to Board of Trade, 1 June 1754, *BTNS*, 15:H-252.

[30] Lawrence to Shirley, 5 November 1754, *BTNS*, 15:H-278. See also Instructions from Lawrence to Monckton, 7 November 1754 and 29 January 1755, *The Northcliffe Collection*, 25-7.

[31] 'Secret Instructions for our Trusty and Wellbeloved Edward Braddock Esqr. Major General of Our Forces', 25 November 1754, *A&WI*, 604.

[32] See note 27 above.

[33] Board of Trade to Robinson, 31 October 1754, *A&WI*, 597:18.

[34] Lawrence to Board of Trade, 12 January 1755, *BTNS*, 15:H-277.

[35] Board of Trade to Lawrence, 7 May 1755, *BTNS*, 36:118.

[36] Shirley to Robinson, 24 March 1755, *NYCD*, 6:942.

[37] Braddock to Napier, 19 April 1755, Pargellis, *Military Affairs in North America*, 81.

[38] Gipson, 6:228-33.

[39] Osgood, *The American Colonies in the Eighteenth Century*, 4:361.

[40] Lawrence to Board of Trade, 28 June 1755, *BTNS*, 15:H-300.

[41] *New York Mercury*, 6 July 1755.

[42] Drucourt à Machault, 10 novembre 1755, *AC*, c 11b, 35:118-19.

[43] Machault à Drucourt, 5 septembre 1755, *AC*, b 101:204; Machault à Vaudreuil, 20 février 1756, *AC*, b 103:2; 'Lettre du Roy à M. de Vaudreuil', 20 février 1756, ibid., 2v.

[44] Vaudreuil à Massiac, 12 juin 1758, *AC*, c 11A, 103:76; see also Casgrain, 7 (*Montcalm, Journal*):314.

[45] Boishébert à Drucourt, 10 octobre 1755, *AC*, c 11B, 35:154.

[46] 'Capitulation du fort de Beauséjour', *AC*, F 3, 14 (supplément):65.

[47] *BTNS*, 15:H-300.

[48] Lawrence to Robinson, 30 November 1755, *PRO*, co 5, 17:46 f.

[49] Lawrence to Board of Trade, 18 July 1755, *BTNS*, 15:H-307; Boishébert à Drucourt, 10 octobre 1755, *AC*, c 11B, 35:152-5.

[50] Minutes of the meeting of 3 July 1755, Akins, 247-55.

[51] Lawrence to Board of Trade, 18 July 1755, *BTNS*, 15:H-307.

[52] Émile Lauvrière, *La Tragédie d'un peuple* (2 vols, Paris, 1924). This is the title of chap. 13.

[53] See note 34 above.

[54] 'Copy of Mr. Chief Justice Belcher's Opinion in Council as to the removal of the French Inhabitants in Nova Scotia dated Halifax 28 July 1755', *A&WI*, 597. For a translation, see Arles, *Acadie*, 2:456-60 (appendix v). The translation was reproduced in Lauvrière, op. cit., without acknowledgment and with the addition of numerous commentaries.

[55] Belcher to Pownall, 24 December 1755, *BTNS*, 16:1-10.

[56] Lauvrière, op. cit., 1:431.

[57] 'At a Council holden at the Governor's house in Halifax on Monday the 28th July 1755', *Report Concerning the Canadian Archives for 1905*, 2, part 3, appendix B:8.

[58] Lawrence to Board of Trade, 18 October 1755, *BTNS*, 15:H-311.

[59] Board of Trade to the King, 26 November 1755, *BTNS*, 36:135.

[60] *BTNS*, 16:I-1.

[61] *BTNS*, 36:273.

[62] Circular from Lawrence to Governors, 11 August 1755, *BTNS*, 15:H-312.

[63] Spencer Phips to Monckton, 20 August 1755, *The Northcliffe Collection*, 37.

[64] *Pennsylvania Colonial Records*, 6:712 f.; message to the Assembly, 24 November 1755, *PRO*, co 5, 17:115.

[65] *Pennsylvania Colonial Records*, 6:730.

[66] Dinwiddie to Fox, 24 November 1755, *PRO*, co 5, 17:I-2.

[67] Id., 9 November 1756, ibid., 733; *Mercure de La Haye*, 141 (juillet 1756):97.

[68] Letter from Board of Trade, 14 April 1756, *A&WI*, 597; Lyttleton to Fox, 16 June 1756, *PRO*, co 5, 17:531 f.

[69] Frégault, *François Bigot*, 2:144, note 164.

[70] Lawrence to Halifax, 9 December 1755, Pargellis, *Military Affairs in North America*, 155.

[71] Lawrence to Board of Trade, 28 April 1756, *BTNS*, 16:I-15.

[72] Circular from Lawrence to Governors, 1 July 1756, *BTNS*, 16:I-24; Lawrence to Board of Trade, 5 August 1756, ibid., I-17; Sharpe to Lawrence, 24 August 1756, *Sharpe Correspondence*, 1:471; Vaudreuil à Machault, 7 août 1756, *AC*, c 11A, 101:85v.-6; id., 6 août 1756, ibid., 81-2.

[73] *Report Concerning the Canadian Archives for 1905*, 2, part 3, appendix B:20.

[74] *New York Gazette*, 1 September 1755; *Maryland Gazette*, 11 September 1755.

75 *Maryland Gazette*, 4 September 1755.

76 *New York Mercury*, 15 September 1755; *Maryland Gazette*, 25 September 1755.

77 *Pennsylvania Gazette*, 13 November and 4 December 1755; *New York Mercury*, 2 February 1756. See also *New York Mercury*, 3 May 1756 and *Pennsylvania Gazette*, 6 May 1756.

78 Appleton, *A Sermon Preached October 9*, 22.

79 *London Magazine* (August 1755), 359.

80 *Mercure de La Haye*, 140 (février 1756):217.

81 'An Impartial and Succinct History of the Origin and Progress of the Present War', *London Magazine* (June 1760), 291.

82 Entick, 1:385.

83 It is difficult to establish an exact figure for the number of Acadians deported in 1755. Lauvrière (op. cit., 1:482-4, 492) states that is was close to 7,000, but the total from the various groups whose numbers he himself established is closer to 6,000. Gipson (6:282) gives 'more than six thousand'.

84 D.C. Harvey, *The French Régime in Prince Edward Island* (New Haven, 1926), 180 f. See also Vaudreuil à Machault, 7 août 1756, *AC*, C 11A, 101:85.

85 Board of Trade to Lawrence, 8 July 1756, *BTNS*, 36:287.

86 *Boston News-Letter*, 5 August 1756; *New York Mercury*, 16 August 1756.

87 Vaudreuil à Machault, 30 octobre 1755, *AC*, C 11A, 100:158; id., 18 octobre 1755, *AC*, F 3, 14:201v.-2. See also Knox, *Journal*, 1:61, note.

88 Vaudreuil à Machault, 6 août 1756, *AC*, C 11A, 101:78-80; 'Porté au Roy Le 15 janv. 1757—Canada', *AC*, C 11A, 102:230.

89 Vaudreuil à Machault, 18 octobre 1755, *AC*, F 3, 14:203-4.

90 Lawrence to Board of Trade, 3 November 1756, *BTNS*, 16:1-22; Board of Trade to Lawrence, 10 March 1757, *BTNS*, 36:300. See also 'Remarks relative to the Convening of an Assembly', August 1758, *BTNS*, 16:1-25.

91 Monckton to Board of Trade, 13 October 1757, *BTNS*, 16:1-42.

92 Knox, *Journal*, 1:99.

93 Ibid., 1:51.

94 Lawrence to Board of Trade, 9 November 1757, *BTNS*, 16:1-46.

95 'A Return of the Number of french Prisoners taken at Cape Sable', 9 November 1759, *BTNS*, 17:K-3.

96 *Boston News-Letter*, 13 April 1758.

97 Board of Trade to Lawrence, 7 February 1758, *BTNS*, 36:323.

98 Villejouin's figure is 4,700, *AC*, C 11B, 38:271.

99 *Boston News-Letter*, 11 January 1759.

100 Villejouin à Massiac, 8 septembre 1758, *AC*, C 11B, 38:271-2.

101 Harvey, op. cit., 190-8. Cf. Lauvrière, op. cit., 2:44-67.

102 Lawrence to Board of Trade, 2 May 1758, *BTNS*, 16:1-69.

103 *BTNS*, 16:1-84; *Boston News-Letter*, 2 November 1758.

104 Lawrence to Board of Trade, 28 December 1758, *BTNS*, 16:1-85.

105 *Boston News-Letter*, 26 October 1758.

106 Knox, *Journal*.

107 Lawrence to Board of Trade, 20 September 1759, *BTNS*, 16:1-93.

[108] Green to Board of Trade, 19 October 1760, *BTNS*, 18:L-12; Belcher to Board of Trade, 26 October 1760, ibid., L-8.

[109] See 'Articles of Capitulation', Montreal, 8 September 1760, Articles 38 and 39, Adam Shortt and Arthur G. Doughty, eds, *Documents Relating to the Constitutional History of Canada* (2 vols, Ottawa, 1918), 1:19. (For English version, see ibid., 33.)

[110] Belcher to Board of Trade, 14 April 1761, *BTNS*, 18:L-43; Belcher to Amherst, 15 April 1761, *A&WI*, 597; Belcher to Board of Trade, 17 April 1761, ibid.

[111] Belcher to Board of Trade, 9 January 1762, *Colonial Correspondence of Nova Scotia*, 1:1.

[112] Akins, 308.

[113] Ibid., 309 f.

[114] Ibid., 311-13.

[115] Ibid., 313.

[116] 'A Proclamation', 11 January 1759, *BTNS*, 16:I-90. Lawrence to Board of Trade, 5 February 1759, ibid., I-89.

[117] Board of Trade to Lawrence, 1 August 1759, *BTNS*, 36:361.

[118] Lawrence to Board of Trade, 20 September 1759, *BTNS*, 16:I-93. See also Lawrence to Board of Trade 10 December 1759, *BTNS*, 17:K-7; Board of Trade to Lawrence, 14 December 1759, *BTNS*, 36:368.

[119] Board of Trade to the King, 20 December 1759, *BTNS*, 36:381.

[120] Memorandum to Lawrence, 3 December 1759, *BTNS*, 17:K-10.

[121] *Boston News-Letter*, 10 July 1760.

[122] Memorandum to Lawrence, 11 December 1759, *BTNS*, 17:K-11.

[123] Belcher to Forster, 18 June 1761, Akins, 319 f.

[124] Lawrence to Board of Trade, 16 June 1760, *BTNS*, 18:L-1.

[125] Letter of 20 September 1761, Akins, 322.

[126] Lawrence to Board of Trade, 11 May 1760, *BTNS*, 17:K-26.

[127] Id., 24 July 1760, ibid., L-5.

[128] Lauvrière, op. cit., 2:19-21.

[129] Amherst to Belcher, 22 March 1761, Akins, 326; id., 28 April 1761, ibid., 328; id. 30 August 1762, ibid., 330.

[130] Belcher to Amherst, 12 August 1762, Akins, 331; Belcher to Bernard, 13 August 1762, *Colonial Correspondence of Nova Scotia*, 1:109.

[131] Minutes of the Nova Scotia Council, 18 October 1762, Akins, 331-4.

[132] 'Extract of the Minutes of the Proceedings of the Lords Commissioners of Trade and Plantations', 3 December 1762, Akins, 337.

[133] Wilmot to Halifax, 22 March 1764, Akins, 345 f.

[134] Id., 29 August 1764, ibid., 349.

[135] Id., 18 December 1764, ibid., 350 f.

[136] *AC*, B 131:272 *bis*.

[137] *State of the British and French Colonies in North America*, 19.

[138] Gipson, 6:284, note 112.

[139] This is Lauvrière's title for chap. 15 of *La Tragédie d'un peuple*.

[140] L.-M. Le Jeune, *Dictionnaire général . . . du Canada* (2 vols, Ottawa, 1931), 2:119.

141 See Lawrence's correspondence with the Board of Trade on the subject of an assembly for Nova Scotia, Akins, 709-29.

142 'Nova Scotia. State of Facts relating to the Complaint of the Freeholders in Nova Scotia', read to the Board of Trade 27 January 1758, *BTNS*, 16:I-50.

143 Letter of 12 April 1759, Adam Shortt, ed., *Documents relating to Canadian Currency, Exchange and Finance during the French Period* (2 vols, Ottawa, 1925-6), 2:894.

144 See Frégault, *François Bigot*, 2:171-83, 193.

145 'Additions to the Freeholders Schedule of Grievances', 1758, *BTNS*, 16:I-51.

146 'Abstract of the Money which is to be Accounted for, For the Expedition of the Bay of Fundi under Colonel Monckton and the removing the French Inhabitants and Carrying on the Works at Fort Cumberland', 9 May 1758, *BTNS*, 16:I-66.

147 Lawrence to Monckton, 31 July 1755, Akins, 268 f.

148 Minutes of the Council, 6 July 1750, ibid., 619 f.

149 Shirley to Lawrence, 6 January 1755, ibid., 399 f.

150 *BTNS*, 68:86.

151 Secretary of the Lords of the Treasury to Board of Trade, 25 March 1760, *BTNS*, 36:228.

CHAPTER VII

1 *Thoughts on Trade in GENERAL, Our West-Indian in Particular, Our Continental Colonies, Canada, Guadaloupe, and the Preliminary Articles of Peace* (London, 1763), 66 f. Hereafter: *Thoughts on Trade in General*.

2 London, July 1758, *New York Gazette*, 16 October 1758.

3 Corbett, *England in the Seven Years' War*, 1:305.

4 Selley, *England in the Eighteenth Century*, 87.

5 *Sentiments Relating to the Late Negociation*, 12.

6 'Tableau des Dépenses faites en Canada depuis 1750, jusques et compris l'année 1760', *AE*, Mémoires et documents, Amérique, 11:97.

7 Gipson, 7:176, 290.

8 Ibid., 312.

9 Pargellis, *Lord Loudoun in North America*, 353.

10 Jonathan Mayhew, *Two Discourses Delivered November 23d. 1758. Being the Day appointed by Authority to be Observed as a Day of Public Thanksgiving* (Boston, 1758), 26 f.

11 William S. Sachs, 'Agricultural Conditions in the Northern Colonies before the Revolution', *Journal of Economic History* (1953), 276 f.

12 Message of December 1758, *PRO*, co 5, 54:53.

13 'On the Present State of Affairs', reprinted in *New York Gazette*, 23 December 1758.

14 *Mercure de France* (avril 1758), 192.

15 *London Magazine* (August 1758), 428.

16 *Gentleman's Magazine* (November 1758), 552.

17 *Pennsylvania Gazette*, 15 February 1759.

18 Tunstall, *William Pitt*, 201 f.

19 *Boston News-Letter*, 23 March 1758.

20 *New York Gazette*, 3 April 1758.

21 Boston, 10 April, *New York Gazette*, 17 April 1758.

22 Gipson, 7:177.

23 Wolfe à Rickson, 7 February 1758, Doughty and Parmelee, *The Siege of Quebec*, 6:25.

24 Corbett, op. cit., 1:307.

25 Ibid., 1:8.

26 Entick, 3:222. On Whitmore see Wolfe to Sackville, 7 February 1758, Willson, *Life and Letters of James Wolfe*, 358.

27 Walpole, *Memoirs of the Reign of George II*, 3:91.

28 Loudoun to Holderness, 17 October 1757, *PRO*, co 5, 490-4.

29 Pargellis, *Military Affairs in North America*, xviii.

30 Loudoun to Pitt, 14 February 1758, *Pitt Correspondence*, 1:192-4.

31 Pargellis, *Military Affairs in North America*, xix.

32 Robertson to Morton, 19 December 1758, ibid., 429-32.

33 Horatio Sharpe to William Sharpe, 27 August 1758, *Sharpe Correspondence*, 2:254. See also *Pennsylvania Gazette*, 6 July 1758.

34 Daine à Moras, 19 mai 1758, *AC*, c 11a, 103:412.

35 [Cimon], *Les Ursulines de Québec*, 2:301-3. See also Casgrain, 7 (Montcalm, *Journal*):356, 362, 366, 373, 451; Daine à Moras, 19 mai 1758, *AC,* c 11a, 103:412.

36 'Mémoire', 15 novembre 1758, *AC*, c 11a, 103:366.

37 See Frégault, *François Bigot*, 2:239-41.

38 [Cimon], *Les Ursulines de Québec*, 2:307 f.; Pierre Pouchot, *Mémoires sur la dernière guerre de l'Amérique septentrionale, entre la France et l'Angleterre* (3 vols, Yverdon, 1781), 1:130.

39 Massiac à Bigot, 7 août 1758, *AC*, b 107:314.

40 'Mémoire', *AC*, c 11a, 104:688 f., 710.

41 Vaudreuil à Machault, 5 août 1755, *AC*, f 3, 14:128.

42 Bigot à Massiac, 21 juillet 1758, *AC*, f 3, 15:110v.

43 See Montcalm au ministre de la Guerre, 1er septembre 1758, ibid., 194.

44 Bigot à Massiac, 21 juillet 1758, *AC*, f 3, 15:110v.-11; see also 'Mémoire' (1758), *AC*, c 11a, 103:317v.

45 Montcalm au ministre de la Guerre, 9 mai 1758, *AG*, 3498: no 80.

46 Vaudreuil à Massiac, 28 juillet 1758, *AC*, f 3, 15:113v.

47 'Relation de ce qui s'est passé en Canada du Commenc^t De la Campagne au 8 Juillet jour de L'affaire des abatis', (1758), *AG*, 3498: no 154.

48 Casgrain, 7 (Montcalm, *Journal*):347 (9 mai 1758).

49 Vaudreuil à Massiac, 10 juin 1758, *AC*, c 11a, 103:103v.

50 Montcalm au ministre de la Guerre, 23 mai 1758, post-scriptum du 12 juin, *AG*, 3498: no 86.

51 Vaudreuil à Massiac, 28 juillet 1758, *AC*, f 3, 15:112v.-13. See also 'Relation de ce qui s'est passé en Canada . . .', *AG*, 3498: no 154.

52 Montcalm à Bourlamaque, 7 mars 1758, Casgrain, 5(Bourlamaque, *Lettres*): 208.

53 Vaudreuil à Berryer, 1er novembre 1758, *AC*, C 11A, 103:262v. See also Moras à Ruis, 16 mars 1758, *AC*, B 108:516.

54 Casgrain, 7 (Montcalm, *Journal*):340 f.

55 Montcalm à Bourlamaque, 16 mars 1758, *PAC*, Lettres de Bourlamaque, 1:229.

56 *Mercure de la Haye*, 144 (mars 1758):381 f.

57 Massiac à Vaudreuil, 7 août 1758, *AC*, B 107:44v.

58 Casgrain, 7 (Montcalm, *Journal*):340.

59 Waddingon, *La Guerre de Sept ans*, 2:336.

60 *Mercure de La Haye*, 144(mars 1758):383; ibid.(avril 1758):513 f.; Osborn to Cleveland, 12 March 1758, *London Magazine* (April 1758), 210, 211; Entick, 3:60; Ruville, *William Pitt*, 177; Waddington, op. cit., 2:334.

61 'Campagne de 1757 et 1758', *AM*, B 4, 80:61; 'Bordereau General des depenses de L'Escadre Commandée par M. le Mⁱˢ Desgouttes', ibid., 95; Prévost à Moras, 4 mai 1758, *AC*, C 11B, 38:219, 223.

62 Ibid., 219-20.

63 La Villéon à Moras, 4 mai 1758, *AM*, B 4, 80:40-1.

64 Louis xv à Beaussier de Lisle, 10 mars 1758, *AM*, B 4, 80:173; Beaussier à Moras, 4 mai 1758, ibid., 176; Beaussier à Massiac, 10 juin 1758, ibid., 180; 'Campagne de 1758. Escadre Commandée par M. Beaussier de lisle', ibid., 185; Kerdisien de Trémais, 'Journal', ibid., 63; *London Magazine* (April 1758), 215; *Mercure de La Haye*, 144 (mai 1758):620; ibid. (juin 1758):768.

65 Du Chaffault à Massiac, 29 juin 1758, *AM*, B 4, 80:211-12; id., 12 août 1758, ibid., 219; Turgot à Berryer, 1er novembre 1758, ibid., 252.

66 Des Gouttes à Moras, 6 mai 1758, *AM*, B 4, 80:67; conseil de guerre, 9 juin 1758, ibid., 134.

67 '1758. Campagne d'Amerique. Breugnon (Cᵗᵉ de)', *AM*, B 4, 80:276 f.; Du Chaffault à Massiac, 12 août 1758, ibid., 219; Kerdisien de Trémais, 'Journal', ibid., 63.

68 'Isle Royale 1758. Blenac et le Cte de Rohan-Montbazon', *AM*, B 4, 80:20; Blénac à Massiac, 28 juin 1758, ibid., 27.

69 'Bordereau General des depenses de L'Escadre Commandée par M. le Mⁱˢ Desgouttes', *AM*, B 4, 80:95; Kerdisien de Trémais, 'Journal', ibid., 63; 'A List of the Different Squadrons . . . Under Commodores de Beaufremont, M. de la Clue, and M. de Beaussier', Beatson, ed., *Naval and Military Memoirs*, 3:202.

70 Knox, *Journal*, 1:257; *Boston News-Letter*, special number, 31 August 1758.

71 Montcalm au ministre de la Guerre, 9 mai 1758, *AG*, 3498: no 80.

72 Lawrence to Pitt, 23 May 1758, *PRO*, CO 5, 53:102. Entick, 3:221 f.; 'A List of Admiral Boscawen's Fleet at the Siege of Louisbourg', Beatson, op. cit., 3:177; 'A Complete Return of the Strength of the Army Against Louisbourg', ibid., 176. See also Barrow, *Lord Anson*, 305.

73 *London Chronicle* (24 August 1758), 183. A translation is preserved in 'Extrait du London Chronicle du 24. Août 1758', *AE*, Mémoires et documents, Amérique, 10:290; Lawrence to Pitt, 9 May 1758, *BTNS*, 16:I-64; Corbett, op. cit., 1:312 f.

74 Wolfe to Sackville, 12 May 1758, Willson, op. cit., 363.

75 Ibid., 365.

76 Amherst to Pitt, 11 June 1758, Knox, *Journal*, 3:1-5.

77 *London Chronicle* (24 August 1758), 183.

[78] Drucourt à ——, 1er octobre 1758, *Mercure de La Haye*, 145 (novembre 1758):519; Drucourt à Praslin, 5 février 1762, *AC*, c 11A, 105:354v.

[79] Conseil de guerre du 9 juin 1758, *AM*, B 4, 80:134-5; ordre de Des Gouttes à Beaussier, 12 juin 1758, ibid., 76; Drucourt à Des Gouttes, 13 juin 1758, ibid., 135v.; Drucourt à Massiac, 12 juin 1758, *AC*, c 11B, 38:27 f.

[80] Corbett, op. cit., 1:321-3, 329-32.

[81] *London Chronicle* (24 August 1758), 183.

[82] Boscawen to Pitt, 28 July 1758, *Pitt Correspondence*, 2:308.

[83] Amherst to Wolfe, 8 August 1758, *PAC*, Amherst Papers, packet 8.

[84] *Boston News-Letter*, special number, 31 August 1758.

[85] Wolfe to Amherst, 8 August 1758, *PAC*, Amherst Papers, packet 8.

[86] 'Resolution between Admiral Boscawen & M. General Amherst', 8 August 1758, *PAC*, Amherst Papers, packet 22.

[87] Massiac à Vaudreuil et à Bigot, 26 août 1758, *AC*, B 107:47 *bis*.

[88] Vaudreuil à Berryer, 4 novembre 1758, *AC*, F 3, 15:215.

[89] Wolfe to Amherst, 1 November 1758, *PRO*, co 5, 53:276 f.

[90] Waddington, op. cit., 2:385; *New York Gazette*, 31 July 1758; Vaudreuil à Massiac, 4 août 1758, *AC*, c 11A, 103:148; 'Relation du 8 juillet 1758', observations de Vaudreuil, ibid., 332 f., 335v. f.; Entick, 3:259.

[91] La Pause, 'Mémoire et réflexions politiques et militaires sur la guerre du Canada depuis 1746 jusqu'à 1760', *RAPQ* (1933-4), 153.

[92] Wolfe to Rickson, 1 December 1758, Doughty and Parmelee, op. cit., 6:27.

[93] Wolfe to his father, 20 May 1758, Willson, op. cit., 365.

[94] Abercromby to Pitt, 12 July 1758, *PRO*, co 5, 50:257; Mante, *The History of the Late War in America*, 144 f.

[95] Abercromby to Pitt, 12 July 1758, *PRO*, co 5, 50:258; *New York Gazette*, 24 July 1758; Entick, 3:257.

[96] Casgrain, 7 (Montcalm, *Journal*):398.

[97] H.-R. Casgrain, ed., *Journal des campagnes du chevalier de Lévis en Canada de 1756 à 1760* (Montreal, 1889), 138. Hereafter: Casgrain, 1 (Lévis, *Journal*). Cf. 'Relation de ce qui s'est passé sur la frontière du Lac St Sacrement depuis le 30 Juin jusqu'au 10 Juillet inclu', *AG*, 3499: no 60.

[98] Vaudreuil à Noailles, 6 août 1758, *AG*, 3499: no 12.

[99] Abercromby to Pitt, 12 July 1758, *PRO*, co 5, 50:258; William Eyre to Napier, 10 July 1758, Pargellis, *Military Affairs in North America*, 420; *Boston News-Letter*, 27 July 1758; Entick, 3:255.

[100] Doreil au ministre de la Guerre, 31 juillet 1758, *RAPQ* (1945-6), 150; Casgrain, 7 (Montcalm, *Journal*):411; lettre de la Mère Marie-André Duplessis de Sainte-Hélène, 20 octobre 1758, *Nova Francia*, 4 (1929):115 f.

[101] Montcalm à Vaudreuil, 9 juillet 1758, *AG*, 3498: no 140; Doreil à Massiac, 28 juillet 1758, *AC*, c 11A, 103:421; Casgrain, 7 (Montcalm, *Journal*):402; *Nova Francia*, 4 (1929):115.

[102] Lévis à Mme de Mirepoix, 28 octobre 1758, Casgrain, 2 (Lévis, *Lettres*):212.

[103] Gabriel, *Le Maréchal de camp Desandrouins*, 193.

[104] Sharpe to Baltimore, 27 August 1758, *Sharpe Correspondence*, 2:256.

[105] William Eyre to Napier, 10 July 1758, Pargellis, *Military Affairs in North America*, 421 f.; James Prevost to Cumberland, 21 August 1758, ibid., 427.

[106] Tulleken to Bouquet, 1 October 1758, *BM, Add. MSS*, 21643:233; *London Magazine* (November 1758), 596; *Boston News-Letter*, 26 October 1758; Bougainville à Crémille, 8 novembre 1758, *AG*, 3499: no 201.

[107] Gipson, 7:238.

[108] *New York Mercury*, 4 September 1758; *New York Gazette*, 2 October 1758; Benjamin Bass, 'A Journal of the Expedition against Fort Frontenac', *New-York History*, 16 (1935):449 ff.; see also Entick, 3:260 f.

[109] Montcalm à Bourlamaque, 10 avril 1758, *PAC*, Lettres de Bourlamaque, 1:269.

[110] Casgrain, 7 (Montcalm, *Journal*):410.

[111] *AC*, F 3, 15:194v.

[112] Vaudreuil à Massiac, 2 septembre 1758, *AC*, C 11A, 103:180-3; id., 30 octobre 1758, ibid., 251.

[113] *New York Gazette*, 4 December 1758.

[114] Wolfe to Rickson, 1 December 1758, R. Wright, *The Life of Major General Wolfe* (London, 1864), 465.

[115] Abercromby to Pitt, 25 November 1758, *PRO*, CO 5, 50:489; *New York Gazette*, 11 September 1758; *New York Mercury*, 25 September 1758; *Boston News-Letter*, 28 September 1758.

[116] Montcalm à Massiac, 1er septembre 1758, *AC*, F 3, 15:194v.

[117] Malartic, *Journal des campagnes au Canada de 1755 à 1760*, 206; see also Lotbinière à Belle-Isle, 11 novembre 1758, *AG*, 3459: no 205.

[118] Waddington, op. cit., 2:387.

[119] Mante, op. cit., 155; Louis K. Koontz, *The Virginia Frontier, 1754-1763* (Baltimore, 1925), 89.

[120] Casgrain, 7 (Montcalm, *Journal*):381 f.

[121] *New York Gazette*, 2 October 1758; *Boston News-Letter*, 12 October 1758; Forbes to Pitt, 20 October 1758, Irene Stewart, ed., *Letters of General John Forbes relating to the Expedition against Fort Duquesne in 1758* (Pittsburgh, 1927), 59. Hereafter: *Letters of General Forbes*.

[122] Montcalm à Bourlamaque, 25 octobre 1758, *PAC*, Lettres de Bourlamaque, 1:365.

[123] *Boston News-Letter*, 2 November 1758.

[124] 'Extrait de 3 Lettres écrites à M. le Mis de Vaudreuil par M. de Ligneris Commandant au fort Duquesne', 18, 20, et 23 octobre 1758, *AC*, F 3, 15:225-230v.; Bigot à Massiac, 22 novembre 1758, ibid., 221-3; Vaudreuil à Massiac, 20 novembre 1758, ibid., 217-20; Forbes to Pitt, 20 October 1758, *PRO*, CO 5, 50:601 f.; *New York Mercury*, 30 October 1758; *Boston News-Letter*, 2 November 1758; ibid., 24 November 1758.

[125] Forbes to Pitt, 20 October 1758, *Letters of General Forbes*, 61.

[126] *BM, Add. MSS*, 21643:247.

[127] James, 'The Nest of Robbers', *Western Pennsylvania Historical Magazine*, 21 (1938):165.

[128] Bouquet to Allen, 25 November 1758, *Letters of General Forbes*, 67 f.

[129] Vaudreuil à Berryer, 20 janvier 1759, *AC*, C 11A, 104:14-15.

[130] Daine à Belle-Isle, 2 décembre 1758, *AG*, 3499: no 217.

[131] *Gazette de France*, 20 janvier 1759, 32; ibid., 27 janvier 1759, 42 f.

[132] *New York Mercury*, 23 December 1758.

[133] *Mercure de La Haye,* 145 (août 1758):240.

[134] Ibid., 145 (septembre 1758):313.

[135] Horatio Sharpe to William Sharpe, 27 August 1758, *Sharpe Correspondence*, 2:253.

[136] *New York Gazette*, 31 July 1758.

[137] Pitt to Abercromby, 18 September 1758, *PAC*, Amherst Papers, packet 22; *Boston News-Letter*, 1 February 1759.

[138] Pitt to Amherst, 18 September 1758, *PAC,* Amherst Papers, packet 22; Pitt to North American Governors, 18 September 1758, ibid., packet 10.

[139] Ligonier to Amherst, 3 September 1758, ibid., packet 11.

[140] Lettre d'Abreu, 3 février 1758, *RAPQ* (1951-3), 432.

[141] Lettre d'Abreu, 26 mai 1758, ibid., 433.

[142] Hester Pitt to William Pitt, 18 August 1758, Ruville, op. cit., 2:214 f.

[143] *New York Gazette*, 27 November 1758.

[144] *Boston News-Letter*, 24 August 1758.

[145] *New York Gazette*, 28 August 1758.

[146] Tunstall, op. cit., 212.

[147] *London Magazine* (August 1758), 384.

[148] Ibid., 428.

[149] Ibid. (September 1758), 480.

[150] Ibid., 447.

[151] Message from Pownall to the Massachusetts Assembly, 30 September 1758, *PRO*, co 5, 18:1015.

[152] London, 20 December 1758, *Boston News-Letter,* 8 March 1759.

[153] Lettre d'Abreu, 31 octobre 1758, *RAPQ* (1951-3), 434.

[154] *PRO*, co 5, 18:1015.

[155] RAPQ (1951-3), 434.

[156] *Boston News-Letter*, 28 December 1758.

[157] Speech of 30 December 1758, ibid., 4 January 1759.

[158] Wentworth to Pitt, 12 November 1758, *PRO*, co 5, 18:1125 f.; 'On the Present State of Affairs', *New York Gazette*, 23 December 1758; message from the Commons to George II, 25 November 1758, *Pennsylvania Journal*, 22 February 1759.

[159] Mayhew, op. cit., 16.

[160] Hotblack, *Chatham's Colonial Policy,* 49 f.

[161] Speech of 4 October 1758, *Boston News-Letter*, 5 October 1758.

[162] London, 20 December 1758, ibid., 8 March 1759.

[163] Lettres d'Abreu, 1er et 8 septembre 1758, *RAPQ* (1951-3), 433.

[164] Casgrain, 7 (Montcalm, *Journal*):468.

[165] Vaudreuil à Massiac, 6 septembre 1758, *Coll. de MSS*, 4:197.

[166] Bigot à Lévis, 5 octobre 1758, Casgrain, 9 (Bigot, *Lettres*):39 f.

[167] *AC*, F 3, 15:194v.

[168] *AC*, c 11A, 103:183v.

[169] Ibid., 184.

[170] Vaudreuil à Berryer, 28 novembre 1758, *AC*, c 11A, 104:130. See also Daine à Belle-Isle, 2 décembre 1758, *AG*, 3499: no 217.

[171] Massiac à Vaudreuil et à Bigot, 26 août 1758, *AC*, B 107:47 *bis*.

[172] Montcalm à Bourlamaque, 11 juin 1758, *PAC*, Lettres de Bourlamaque, 5:195

[173] 'Réflexions générales sur les mesures à prendre pour la défense de cette colonie', 10 septembre 1758, Casgrain, 4 (*Lettres et pièces militaires*):45-51.

[174] Casgrain, 7 (Montcalm, *Journal*):463, 484.

[175] Vaudreuil à Berryer, ler novembre 1758, *AC*, c 11A, 103:260v.

[176] 'Projet sur le Lac Ontario à Communiquer à M. le Mis de Montcalm', juin 1758, *AC*, c 11A, 103:187v.-96.

[177] Vaudreuil à Berryer, ler novembre 1758, *AC*, c 11A, 103:261.

[178] Frégault, *François Bigot*, 2:249 f., 253-7.

[179] *Mercure de France* (octobre 1758), 208.

[180] Montcalm à Bourlamaque, 15 et 18 mai 1759, *PAC*, Lettres de Bourlamaque, 1:467-9, 471-3.

[181] 'Canada', 28 décembre 1758, *AC*, c 11A, 103:452-5.

[182] Frégault, *François Bigot*, 2:254 f.

[183] Belle-Isle à Montcalm [19 février] 1759, *AG*, 3540: no 16.

[184] *AG*, 3540: no 15.

[185] 'Mémoire sur le Canada', 27 décembre 1758, *AC*, c 11A, 103:626-8.

[186] 'Mémoire Concernant les Colonies et relatif a La Paix' par le marquis de Capellis, 11 décembre 1758, *AC*, c 11A, 103:497-8.

[187] Silhouette à —, 8 février 1759, *AC*, c 11A, 104:457-60v.

CHAPTER VIII

[1] 'Journal of a French Officer', Doughty and Parmelee, *The Siege of Quebec*, 4:232 f.

[2] Ruville, *William Pitt*, 2:229.

[3] *Mercure de La Haye*, 146 (janvier 1759):43 f. See also ibid. (mai 1759):532.

[4] Berryer à Vaudreuil, 25 février 1759, *AC*, B 109:389.

[5] Dubois à —, 22 février 1759, *AC*, c 11A, 104:446v.; Berryer à Dubois, 23 mars 1759, *AC*, B 110:102. See also Bernier à Accaron, 8 mai 1759, *AC*, c 11A, 104:351v.

[6] Berryer à Truguet, 13 juillet 1759, *AC*, B 110:212v.

[7] Bougainville à Belle-Isle, 14 mars 1759, *AG*, 3540: no 34.

[8] Berryer à Vaudreuil et à Bigot, 3 février 1759, *AC*, B 109:411-12; '1759, campagne d'amerique (course)', *AM*, B 4, 91:20; Berryer à Vaudreuil et à Bigot, 19 février 1759, ibid., 23; 'Marine', avril 1759, ibid., 25; Juin à Berryer, 16 août 1759, ibid., 30.

[9] Lettre du 3 février 1759, *AC*, B 109:409.

[10] Berryer à Vaudreuil, 16 février 1759, *AC*, B 109:45; *AC*, c 11A, 104:28.

[11] Corbett, *England in the Seven Years' War*, 2:1.

[12] Tunstall, *William Pitt,* 221.

[13] Ibid., 221 f.; Waddington, *La Guerre de Sept ans,* 3:364 f.

[14] *Gazette de France* (21 avril 1759), 194 f.; ibid. (23 juin 1759), 303.

[15] Corbett, op. cit., 2:14.

[16] Tunstall, op. cit., 222.

[17] Corbett, op. cit., 2:19.

[18] *Gentleman's Magazine* (1759), 560, quoted in Knox, *Journal,* 2:29, note 1.

[19] Pitt to Amherst, 29 December 1758, *PAC,* Amherst Papers, packet 10; cf. Pitt to De Lancey, 29 December 1758, ibid.; Amherst to Lawrence, 16 March 1759, Doughty and Parmelee, op. cit., 6:125 f.

[20] Pitt to Amherst, 10 February 1759, *PAC,* Amherst Papers, packet 23.

[21] Id., 10 March 1759, ibid., packet 10.

[22] *New York Mercury,* 23 April 1759.

[23] Address of 2 March 1759, *Boston News-Letter,* 8 March 1759.

[24] 'On the Present Expedition', *Boston News-Letter,* 29 March 1759.

[25] *London Magazine,* 1758, frontispiece.

[26] Ibid., preface, 2; ibid. (January 1759), 38.

[27] 'Expeditions Since the Beginning of the Spanish War, 1739, to the 1st of January, 1759', *London Magazine* (February 1759), 112.

[28] *Mercure de La Haye,* 145 (décembre 1758):661; *Gazette de France* (6 janvier 1759), 7.

[29] *Gazette de France* (24 février 1759), 89.

[30] Ibid. (10 mars 1759), 89. See also *Mercure de La Haye,* 146 (avril 1759):446 f., 459 f.; (mai 1759):564.

[31] Letter of 18 January 1759, *PAC,* Amherst Papers, packet 11; see also Amherst to Pitt, 4 February, *PRO,* co 5, 54:113.

[32] Amherst to Pitt, 18 January 1759, *PRO,* co 5, 54:19 f.

[33] 'Etat des troupes reglées que les Anglois avoient dans L'amerique Septentrionalle En fevrier 1759', *AG,* 3540: no 43.

[34] *Boston News-Letter,* 19 April 1759:; *New York Mercury,* 30 April 1759.

[35] Gipson, 7:290-328.

[36] Montcalm à Lévis, 4 janvier 1759, Casgrain, 6 (Montcalm, *Lettres*):143.

[37] Malartic à Belle-Isle, 9 avril 1759, *AG,* 3540: no 39.

[38] Bernier à Berryer, 15 avril 1759, *AC,* c 11A, 104:349v.

[39] Casgrain, 7 (Montcalm, *Journal*):494 f. (9 février 1759). See also Vaudreuil à Lenormant, 11 avril 1759, *AC,* c 11A, 104:74.

[40] *Mercure de La Haye,* 148 (janvier 1760):61.

[41] Frégault, *François Bigot,* 2:279-82.

[42] Bigot à Berryer, 22 mai 1759, quoted in Malartic, *Journal des campagnes au Canada de 1755 à 1760,* 233, note 3.

[43] Casgrain, 1 (Lévis, *Journal*):179.

[44] '1759. Campagne d'Amerique, Kanon (Jacques)', Knox, *Journal,* 3:359.

[45] Vaudreuil à La Naudière, 23 juillet et 13 août 1759, Université de Montréal, Collection Baby, dossier Vaudreuil.

[46] Casgrain, 1 (Lévis, *Journal*):175 f.

47 Montcalm à Vaudreuil, 27 février 1759, *AC*, F 3, 15:255-7.

48 'Memoire', *AC*, F 3, 15:259-64. Each page of the memorandum contains two columns. The headings of the left and right hand columns are respectively 'Reflections de M. le Marquis de Montcalm' and 'Reponces de M. le Marquis de Vaudreuil'. The 'Reflections' are dated 20 March 1759 and the 'Reponces' 21 March. Printed in Casgrain, 4 *(Lettres et pièces militaires)*:144-52.

49 Vaudreuil, 'Précis du plan des operations Generales de la Campagne de 1759', ler avril 1759, *AC*, C 11A, 104:47-53. Printed in Casgrain, 4:153-62.

50 Vaudreuil à Lenormant, 8 mai 1759, *AC*, C 11A, 104:82.

51 Montcalm à Crémille, 12 avril 1759, *AG*, 3540: no 40; 'Canada', 7 juin 1759, *AC*, C 11A, 104:432.

52 Gipson, 7:382 f.

53 Montcalm à Vaudreuil, 27 février 1759, *AC*, F 3, 15:256.

54 Lévis à Mirepoix, 4 septembre 1757, Casgrain, 2 (Lévis, *Lettres*):143.

55 Gipson, 7:376-8.

56 Casgrain, 7 (Montcalm, *Journal*):550.

57 'Principaux Evenemens De la Campagne 1759. Jusqu'à La prise de Québec', *AG*, 3540: no 85.

58 'Journal' de Foligné, *AC*, C 11A, 104:270v.; see also Vaudreuil à Bourlamaque, 25 juin 1759, *PAC*, Lettres de Bourlamaque, 2:281.

59 See Graham, *Empire of the North Atlantic*, 175, and Mahan, *The Influence of Sea Power upon History*, 294.

60 Wolfe to Sackville, undated, Doughty and Parmelee, op. cit., 6:82.

61 Proclamation of 27 June 1759, Casgrain, 4 *(Lettres et pièces militaires)*:274.

62 Entick, 4:105.

63 'Extract of a Letter from an Officer in Major Genl Wolfe's Army', 10 August 1759, Pargellis, *Military Affairs in North America*, 434. See also 'Journal of Particular Transactions', Doughty and Parmelee, op. cit., 5:184.

64 Murray's journal, 13 November 1759, Knox, *Journal*, 2:273, note 1.

65 'Lettre écrite de la part des Anglois', Casgrain, 4 *(Lettres et pièces militaires)*: 277.

66 See texts quoted in Frégault, *François Bigot*, 2:283 f.; 'Memoire Sur le Canada', *AC*, C 11A, 104:470v.; 'Extrait d'un Journal tenu a L'armée', ibid., 232v.-3.

67 Montcalm à Bougainville, 15 juillet 1759, Doughty and Parmelee, op. cit., 4:4.

68 Wolfe to Holderness, 9 September 1759, ibid., 3:11-13.

69 Sharpe to Baltimore, 4 September 1759, *Sharpe Correspondence*, 2:357.

70 Malartic, *Journal*, 243; Bigot à Berryer, 15 octobre 1759, *AC*, F 3, 15:334v.

71 Daine au ministre de la Guerre, 9 octobre 1759, *AG*, 3540: no 101.

72 [Cimon], *Les Ursulines de Québec*, 2:320 f. Italics in the text. Some writers have singled out a sentence written by another Ursuline, Mère Daneau de Muy: 'Le pays est à bas!', ibid., 317, and by failing to relate it to its context have distorted its import. Mère Daneau had been informed by prisoners—the news was false—that the ships taking Doreil and Bougainville to France had been captured by the English. Like almost everyone else she had supposed that once Montcalm's emissaries had informed the French government of the colony's desparate situation, the mother country would send help to Canada. It was at that moment that she wrote the sentence: 'If the news is true, and we have every

reason to fear it is, our country is lost.' A fervent scholar of Canadian history, after quoting the final clause, adds his own gloss: 'This sentence, sublime in its terseness, means that the language and the religion of the country are doomed!' (P.-G. Roy, *A travers l'histoire des Ursulines de Québec*, 129). The author is letting his imagination run away with him. How did 'the language' get into his flight of rhetoric?

[73] 'Relation du siège de Québec', Doughty and Parmelee, op. cit., 5:307; 'Principaux événemens De la Campagne 1759', *AG*, 3540: no 85.

[74] Knox, *Journal*, 1:378 f.

[75] 'Extrait d'un Journal tenu à L'armée,' *AC*, c 11A, 104:218v.-19; 'Journal of a French Officer', Doughty and Parmelee, op. cit., 4:244; 'Relation du siège de Québec', ibid., 5:308 f.; 'Jugement impartial sur les operations militaires de la campagne de 1759, au Canada', *AC*, c 11A, 104:440 f.; Knox, *Journal*, 1:391 and 418, note 1.

[76] C.V.F. Townshend, *The Military Life of Field-Marshall George First Marquess Townshend, 1724-1807* (London, 1901), 174.

[77] 'Extrait d'un Journal tenu à L'armée', *AC*, c 11A, 104:220-1. See also 'Journal of a French Officer', Doughty and Parmelee, op. cit., 4:245 f.; 'Journal abrégé d'un aide-de-Camp', ibid., 5:287; Henri Têtu, ed., 'Journal' of Récher, *Bulletin des recherches historiques*, 9 (1903):335 f.

[78] Leake to Gist, 5 August 1759, *BM, Add. MSS*, 21644:374.

[79] 'Mémoire sur la défense de Québec', 31 mai 1759, Casgrain, 4 (*Lettres et pièces militaires*):168.

[80] Wolfe to his mother, 31 August 1759, Doughty and Parmelee, op. cit., 6:37.

[81] See Chapais, *Le Marquis de Montcalm*, chap. 1.

[82] Berryer à Vaudreuil, 16 février 1759, *AC*, c 11A, 104:28v. See also Frégault, *François Bigot*, 2:283.

[83] 'Extrait d'un Journal tenu à L'armée', *AC*, c 11A, 104:215; 'Mémoire du Sieur de Ramezay', 1763, *AC*, c 11A, 105:458v.

[84] 'Réflexions sur la campagne prochaine', 29 décembre 1758, *RAPQ* (1923-4), 17.

[85] 'Extrait d'un Journal tenu à L'armée', *AC*, c 11A, 104:249v.-50.

[86] For a facsimile of the original see Knox, *Journal*, 2:108.

[87] Townshend, op. cit., 172; Graham, *Canada: A Short History*, 62.

[88] Têtu, 'Journal' of Récher, 340.

[89] 'Reduced to cinnamon sticks' (i.e., to matchwood). Chapais, op. cit., 15.

[90] *Boston News-Letter*, 13 September 1759.

[91] Malartic, *Journal*, 267.

[92] *Boston News-Letter*, 6 December 1759.

[93] Pontbriand à ——, 5 novembre 1759, *AC*, c 11A, 104:368-9.

[94] Bigot à Lévis, 1er septembre 1759, Casgrain, 9 (Bigot, *Lettres*):53. See also 'Extrait d'un Journal tenu à L'armée', *AC*, c 11A, 104:238v.; 'Journal of Montresor', Doughty and Parmelee, op. cit., 4:329 f., etc.

[95] Gibson to Lawrence, 1 August 1759, ibid., 5:65.

[96] Townshend to his wife, 6 September 1759, Townshend, op. cit., 210.

[97] Monckton, Townshend, and Murray to Wolfe, 29 August 1759, Willson, *The Life and Letters of James Wolfe*, 467 f.; Townshend, op. cit., 204-6.

[98] Pargellis, *Military Affairs in North America*, 187, note 1.

[99] Townshend's 'Journal', Doughty and Parmelee, op. cit., 4:267 f.

[100] 'Journal of Particular Transactions', ibid., 5:184.

[101] 'Extrait d'un Journal tenu à L'armée', *AC*, c 11A, 104:242.

[102] Wolfe to Holderness, 9 September 1759, Doughty and Parmelee, op. cit., 3:13 f.

[103] Townshend, op. cit., 219, note 1.

[104] Wolfe to Burton, 10 September 1759, Doughty and Parmelee, op. cit., 3:17.

[105] Holmes to ——, 18 September 1759, ibid., 4:296.

[106] 'The Fact is we were surprised into a Victory which cost the Conquered very little indeed', Murray to Amherst, 19 May 1760, Knox, *Journal*, 2:439, note.

[107] Gipson, 7:413.

[108] Murray to Townshend, 5 November 1774, *PAC*, Amherst Papers, packet 15.

[109] Knox, *Journal*, 2:105, note; Beatson, *Naval and Military Memoirs*, 3:232; *Boston News-Letter*, 26 October 1759.

[110] Knox, *Journal*, 3:336.

[111] Vaudreuil à Lévis, 13 septembre 1759, Casgrain, 8 (Vaudreuil, *Lettres*):107.

[112] Montcalm à Vaudreuil, 29 juillet 1759, *AC*, F 3, 15:326.

[113] Ibid., 327.

[114] Montcalm à Bougainville, 20 juillet 1759, Doughty and Parmelee, op. cit., 4:9 f.

[115] Malartic, *Journal*, 278.

[116] Montcalm à Bourlamaque, 2 septembre 1759, Casgrain, 5 (Bourlamaque, *Lettres*):348.

[117] Montcalm à Bougainville, 5 septembre 1759, Doughty and Parmelee, op. cit., 4:98.

[118] Id., 10 septembre 1759, ibid., 117.

[119] Knox, *Journal*, 2:92.

[120] Holmes to ——, 18 September 1759, Doughty and Parmelee, op. cit., 4:297.

[121] Casgrain, 7 (Montcalm, *Journal*):610 f.

[122] Knox, *Journal*, 2:99, note 1.

[123] 'Relation du siège de Québec', Doughty and Parmelee, op. cit., 5:322.

[124] 'Journal abrégé d'un aide-de-camp', ibid., 5:298; Vaudreuil à Berryer, 21 septembre 1759, *AC*, c 11A, 104:313v.

[125] Holmes to ——, 18 September 1759, Doughty and Parmelee, op. cit., 4:298; 'Extrait d'un Journal tenu à L'armée', *AC*, c 11A, 104:248; Knox, *Journal*, 2:101.

[126] André Lichtenberger, *Montcalm et la tragédie canadienne* (Paris, 1934), 215 f.

[127] See quotations from Bigot, Vaudreuil, Foligné, Malartic, La Pause, and the 'Extrait d'un Journal tenu à L'armée' in Frégault, *François Bigot*, 2:295-300.

[128] Montreuil au ministre de la Guerre, 22 septembre 1759, *AG*, 3540: no 98. See also 'Journal of a French Officer', Doughty and Parmelee, op. cit., 4:254-6.

[129] See Frégault, *François Bigot*, 2:299.

[130] 'Extrait d'un Journal tenu à L'armée', *AC*, c 11A, 104:247v.

[131] Bigot à Lévis, 9 mai 1760, Casgrain, 9 (Bigot, *Lettres*):92.

[132] Townshend to Pitt, 20 September 1759, *Pitt Correspondence*, 2:166; Knox, *Journal*, 2:99; 'Journal of Particular Transactions', Doughty and Parmelee, op. cit., 5:188; Joannes, 'Mémoire de la campagne de 1759', ibid., 4:226.

[133] Lévis à Belle-Isle, 1er novembre 1759, Casgrain, 2 (Lévis, *Lettres*):244 f.

¹³⁴ Lévis à Bourlamaque, 6 octobre 1759, *PAC*, Lettres de Bourlamaque, 3:155.

¹³⁵ See Waddington, op. cit., 3:311; Ruville, op. cit., 2:268 f., and especially Gipson, 7:418 f. Cf. Chapais, op. cit., 657 f.

¹³⁶ 'Copie du Conseil de Guerre tenu le 13 septembre [1759] chés M. le Marquis de Vaudreuil', *AC,* F 3, 15:324-5; 'Journal of a French Officer', Doughty and Parmelee, op. cit., 4:257; see also Frégault, *François Bigot,* 2:300 f.

¹³⁷ 'Extrait d'un Journal tenu à L'armée', *AC,* C 11A, 104:256.

¹³⁸ Bigot à Berryer, 15 octobre 1759, *AC,* F 3, 15:339.

¹³⁹ Joannes, 'Mémoire de la campagne de 1759', Doughty and Parmelee, op. cit., 4:227-9; Bernetz à Bougainville, 17 septembre 1759, ibid., 131; La Rochebeaucourt à Bougainville, 17 septembre 1759, ibid., 133.

¹⁴⁰ Knox, *Journal,* 2:123.

¹⁴¹ *Mercure de France* (décembre 1759), 202. See also Casgrain, 7 (Montcalm, *Journal*):617.

¹⁴² *Gazette de France* (ler décembre 1759), 605; ibid. (8 décembre 1759), 613.

¹⁴³ Bouquet to Amherst, 13 March 1759, *BM, Add. MSS,* 21634:15.

¹⁴⁴ *Boston News-Letter,* 10 May 1759.

¹⁴⁵ Amherst to Bouquet, 16 March 1759, *BM, Add. MSS,* 21634:20.

¹⁴⁶ *Boston News-Letter,* 16 August 1759.

¹⁴⁷ Horatio Sharpe to William Sharpe, 24 September 1759, *Sharpe Correspondence,* 2:360.

¹⁴⁸ Johnson to Amherst, 25 July 1759, *An Authentic Register of the British Successes* (London, 1760), 80; '*Copie du détail de la défaite des Français près de Niagara et de la reddition du Fort*', 25 juillet 1759, Doughty and Parmelee, op. cit., 4:158 f.; *New York Mercury,* 6 August 1759; *Boston News-Letter,* 16 August 1759.

¹⁴⁹ *Boston News-Letter,* 30 August 1759.

¹⁵⁰ Ibid., 16 August 1759.

¹⁵¹ Casgrain, 1 (Lévis, *Journal*):191 f.; 'Extrait d'un Journal tenu à L'armée', *AC,* C 11A, 104:235.

¹⁵² Lévis à Bourlamaque, 12 août 1759, *PAC,* Lettres de Bourlamaque, 3:95.

¹⁵³ Malartic, *Journal,* 368 f.

¹⁵⁴ Johnson to Board of Trade, 17 May 1759, *NYCD,* 7:736.

¹⁵⁵ De Blau à Bougainville, 10 août 1759, Doughty and Parmelee, op. cit., 4:29.

¹⁵⁶ 'Journal of William Amherst', Knox, *Journal,* 3:38; *Pennsylvania Journal,* 26 July 1759; 'Relation de la campagne de M. le chevalier de La Corne à Chouaguen, en 1759', Casgrain, 11 (*Relations et journaux*):215-18.

¹⁵⁷ Casgrain, 1 (Lévis, *Journal*):192.

¹⁵⁸ Rigaud à Bourlamaque, 2 juillet 1759, *PAC,* Lettres de Bourlamaque, 4:40.

¹⁵⁹ Alden, *General Gage in America,* 49-51; Gage to Amherst, 11 September 1759, *PRO,* CO 5, 57:553: Amherst to Gage, 21 September 1759, ibid., 56:363; Johnson's Journal, in Knox, *Journal,* 3:226.

¹⁶⁰ Vaudreuil à Bourlamaque, ler juin 1759, *PAC,* Lettres de Bourlamaque, 5:63-6; id., 19 juin 1759, ibid., 2:272.

¹⁶¹ 'Extrait d'un Journal tenu à L'armée', *AC,* C 11A, 104:234; Gabriel, *Le Maréchal de camp Desandrouins,* 297.

¹⁶² *Boston News-Letter,* 16 August 1759.

163 Bourlamaque à Lévis, 25 octobre 1759, Casgrain, 5 (Bourlamaque, *Lettres*):68; Bourlamaque à Vaudreuil, 25 octobre 1759, ibid., 70.

164 Ligonier to Amherst, 28 September 1759, *PAC*, Amherst Papers, packet 11; Pitt to Amherst, 29 September 1759, ibid., packet 23.

165 Pownall to Amherst, 11 November 1759, *PRO, CO* 5, 57:89.

166 Amherst to De Lancey, 5 August 1759, *PRO, CO* 5, 56:493 f.

167 De Lancey to Amherst, 17 September 1759, ibid., 563; Amherst to De Lancey, 25 September 1759, ibid., 529.

168 Savelle, *The Diplomatic History of the Canadian Boundary*, 91. See also *Mercure de La Haye*, 147 (juillet 1759):45.

169 Adams, *A Discourse Delivered at New-London, October 23d. A.D. 1760*, 21 f.

170 *London Magazine*, 1759, preface, 1.

171 George to Richard Washington, 20 September 1759, Fitzpatrick, *The Writings of Washington*, 2:337.

172 Samuel Cooper, *A Sermon Preached Before His Excellency Thomas Pownall, Esq.* (Boston, 1759), 46-8.

173 *Boston News-Letter*, 16 August 1759.

174 'My dear confrère, I am of the same opinion as [Voltaire] in Candide that we are fighting for a few acres of snow in that country.' James Abercrombie to Bougainville, 10 September 1759, Doughty and Parmelee, op. cit., 4:120.

175 Alexander Galitzin to Catherine II, 8 October 1759, ibid., 4:150.

176 *London Magazine* (October 1759), 569; *Mercure de La Haye*, 147 (novembre 1759):554, 585 f.

177 *London Magazine* (October 1759), 570.

178 *Boston News-Letter*, 14 February 1760.

179 Walpole, *Memoirs of the Reign of George II*, 3:229 f.

180 Reprinted in *London Magazine* (October 1759), 517.

181 Ibid., 568.

182 Ibid. (November 1759), 579.

183 *Boston News-Letter*, 18 October 1759.

184 *New York Mercury*, 29 October 1759.

185 Cooper, op. cit., 39.

186 Corbett, op. cit., 2:72.

187 'Remarks upon the Present Situation of Canada By Major Grant, November 1759', *PRO, CO* 5, 57:137 f.

188 Amherst to Pitt, 16 December 1759, Knox, *Journal*, 3:77.

189 Lévis à Belle-Isle, 1er novembre 1759, Casgrain, 2 (Lévis, *Lettres*):247 f.

190 Casgrain, 1 (Lévis, *Journal*):229 (27 octobre 1759).

191 Vaudreuil à Lévis, 16 octobre 1759, Casgrain, 8 (Vaudreuil, *Lettres*):127.

192 Beauclair à Lévis, 23 octobre 1759, H.-R. Casgrain, ed., *Lettres de divers particuliers au chevalier de Lévis* (Quebec, 1895), 190. Hereafter: Casgrain, 10 (*Lettres de divers particuliers*).

193 Proclamation of 27 June 1759, Casgrain, 4 (*Lettres et pièces militaires*):275 f.

194 Frégault, *Le Grand Marquis*, 432.

195 M. Perrault à son frère, 15 février 1761, Université de Montréal, Collection Baby, dossier Perrault.

196 *Boston News-Letter,* 26 October 1759.

197 'I promise and swear solemnly before God, that I will be loyal to His Britannick Majesty, King George the Second, that I will not take up arms against him, and that I will give no information to his enemies that might harm him in any way.' 'Form of Oath Administered to the Canadiens Subdued by His Britannick Majesty's Troops in the River St. Lawrence 1759', *PRO,* CO 5, 57:533.

198 Knox, *Journal,* 2:248.

199 Ibid., 279 f.

200 Casgrain, 1 (Lévis, *Journal*):225.

201 Malartic, *Journal,* 292.

202 Knox, *Journal,* 2:147.

203 Ibid., 120.

204 La Pause, 'Mémoire et réflexions politiques et militaires sur la guerre du Canada', *RAPQ* (1933-4):157.

205 Proclamation of 14 November 1759, Casgrain, 4 *(Lettres et pièces militaires)*: 281.

206 Facsimile in *RAPQ* (1922-3):272.

207 Casgrain, 7 (Montcalm, *Journal*):615 f.

208 See quotations in Frégault, *François Bigot,* 2:260 f.

209 'Extrait d'un Journal tenu à L'armée', *AC,* C 11A, 104:257.

210 Proclamation of 27 June 1759, Casgrain, 4 *(Lettres et pièces militaires)*:276.

211 Proclamation of 14 November 1759, ibid., 281.

212 Lévis à Belle-Isle, 1er novembre 1759, Casgrain, 2 (Lévis, *Lettres*):248.

213 Casgrain, 7 (Montcalm, *Journal*):465.

214 'Memoire Sur le Canada', *AC,* C 11A, 104:470v.-1.

215 Bigot à Lévis, 10 octobre 1759, Casgrain, 9 (Bigot, *Lettres*):68.

216 Id., 13 octobre 1759, ibid., 69.

217 *Boston News-Letter,* 26 October 1759.

CHAPTER IX

1 Bernier à Crémille, 12 septembre 1760, *AG,* 3574: no 102.

2 'Affaires Presentes du Canada ⸺ avec la lettre de M. de la Houliere a M. le Duc de Choiseul du 13 Xbre 1759', *AE,* Mémoires et documents, Amérique, 10:326.

3 Massé de Saint-Maurice à Maurepas, 3 janvier 1760, *AC,* C 11A, 105:232 f.; 'Memoire de M. Massé de St Maurice pour contribuer a la deffense de la partie du Canada qui reste encore à la france', ibid., 234-7.

4 Vaudreuil à Belle-Isle, 9 novembre 1759, *AG,* 3540: no 107; Lévis à [Accaron], 12 novembre 1759, *AC,* C 11A, 104:122.

5 Le Mercier, 'Précis de la situation de la france dans l'Amérique Septentrionale', 7 janvier 1760, *AC,* C 11A, 105:257 f.

6 'Mémoire Relatif à la Situation du Canada, en se réduisant à l'indispensable pour conserver au Roy cette Colonie jusqu'au Printems 1761', *AC,* C 11A, 105:267-9.

7 'Campagne d'Amerique. Kanon (Jacques) Lieut. de frégate', décembre 1759, *AM,* B 4, 91; printed in Knox, *Journal,* 3:359.

[8] Bougainville à Bourlamaque, 13 juin 1760, *PAC*, Lettres de Bourlamaque, 3:301; Berryer à Le Mercier, 22 février 1760, *AC*, B 112:62.

[9] *AC*, C 11A, 105:257v., 268v.

[10] Frégault, *François Bigot*, 2:318 f.

[11] Circulaire de Vaudreuil et Bigot, 15 juin 1760, Shortt, *Documents relating to Canadian Currency, Exchange and Finance during the French Period* (2 vols, Ottawa, 1925), 2:940.

[12] 'Circular Letter to the Captains of Militia', 27 June 1760, ibid., 942-4.

[13] Mounier à Ducharme, 1er mars 1760, *AC*, C 11A, 105:126.

[14] Perrault à son frère, 12 décembre 1760, Collection Baby, dossier Perrault.

[15] Walpole, *Memoirs of the Reign of George II*, 3:224.

[16] Lévis à Berryer, 28 juin 1760, Casgrain, 2 (Lévis, *Lettres*):362.

[17] Lettre du 29 octobre 1761 au contrôleur général, *AC*, B 113:242.

[18] Frégault, *François Bigot*, 2:323.

[19] Pares, 'American versus Continental Warfare, 1739-1763', *The English Historical Review*, 51 (1936):451.

[20] Berryer à Rostan, 15 février 1760, *AC*, B 112:53.

[21] Id., 5 décembre 1760, ibid., 283.

[22] 'Journal de la Campagne du S. Giraudais Sur le N[avi]re le Machault', *AM*, B 4, 98:9 f.; Vaudreuil à Berryer, 24 juin 1760, *AC*, C 11A, 105:71v.-2; *Boston News-Letter*, 31 July 1760; Knox, *Journal*, 2:634 f.; Bigot à Berryer, 30 juin 1760, *Coll. de MSS*, 4:271; Casgrain, 1 (Lévis, *Journal*):288.

[23] Malartic, *Journal*, 335.

[24] 'Relation de l'expédition de Québec aux ordres de M. le Chevalier de Lévis', Casgrain, 11 (*Relations et journaux*):221-3; instructions de Vaudreuil à Lévis, 16 avril 1760, Casgrain, 4 (*Lettres et pièces militaires*):213-17; 'Relation des affaires du Canada depuis Le 1er Xbre 1759', *AG*, 3540: no 122; Bernier, 'Evenemens du Canada depuis Le Mois d'Octobre 1759 Jusqu'au mois de Septembre 1760', *AG*, 3574: no 112.

[25] Casgrain, 1 (Lévis, *Journal*):243-58; *AG*, 3540: no 122; Casgrain, 11 (*Relations et journaux*):224; 'Relation de ce qui s'est passé en Canada depuis le 1er Xbre 1759 jusqu'au 1er Juin 1760', *PAC*, Lettres de Bourlamaque, 5:329.

[26] Circulaire de Vaudreuil, 16 avril 1760, *AC*, C 11A, 105:8 f.; circulaire aux curés du gouvernement de Québec, 16 avril 1760, ibid., 10 f.

[27] 'Murray's journal', 23 and 26 May 1760, Knox, *Journal*, 3:306.

[28] Malartic, *Journal*, 309.

[29] Casgrain, 11 (*Relations et journaux*):225.

[30] *Boston News-Letter*, 17 July 1760.

[31] Quoted in French in Knox, *Journal*, 2:379, 382.

[32] Murray to Pitt, 25 May 1760, *Pitt Correspondence*, 2:292.

[33] Murray, 'Monthly Return', 24 October 1759, Knox, *Journal*, 2:247, note 3.

[34] Ibid., 2:318.

[35] Ibid., 2:337, 352.

[36] *New York Mercury*, 10 March 1760.

[37] Roll of 24 March 1760, Knox, *Journal*, 2:364, note 2.

[38] Murray to Pitt, 25 May 1760, *Pitt Correspondence*, 2:291 f.

39 Knox, *Journal*, 2:451, note 1.

40 Ibid., 2:397, note 1.

41 Casgrain, 1 (Lévis, *Journal*):263-9; 'Relation de l'expédition de Québec', Casgrain, 11 *(Relations et journaux)*:230-4; *PAC*, Lettres de Bourlamaque, 5:335-8; Knox, *Journal*, 2:394, 397, note 1; *AG*, 3540: no 122; Vaudreuil à Berryer, 3 mai 1760, *AC*, c 11A, 105:13-15; Têtu, 'Journal' of Récher, *Bulletin des recherches historiques*, 9 (1903):143; Bernier, 'Evenemens du Canada', *AG*, 3574: no 105; Lévis à Vaudreuil, 28 avril 1760, Casgrain, 2 (Lévis, *Lettres*):292 f.

42 *AG*, 3540: no 122; Vaudreuil au ministre de la Guerre, 29 juin 1760, *AG*, 3574: no 67.

43 Lettre du 28 avril 1760, Casgrain, 2 (Lévis, *Lettres*):294.

44 Lawrence to Pitt, 11 May 1760, *Pitt Correspondence*, 2:284.

45 Pitt to Amherst, 20 June 1760, *PAC*, Amherst Papers, packet 24.

46 Ruville, *William Pitt*, 2:282, 298. See also Pares, 'American versus Continental Warfare, 1739-63'; *Gazette de France* (10 mai 1760), 225.

47 *Gazette de France* (28 juin 1760), 310, 312.

48 Quoted by Corbett, *England in the Seven Years' War*, 2:108.

49 'Relation de L'expedition de quebec', *AC*, c 11A, 105:27v.

50 Ibid., 25v.

51 Casgrain, 1 (Lévis, *Journal*):274, 276, 279; Casgrain, 11 *(Relations et journaux)*:240 f.; 'Murray's journal', Knox, *Journal*, 2:421, note 2.

52 Casgrain, 2 (Lévis, *Lettres*):307.

53 Knox, *Journal*, 2:415; Casgrain, 1 (Lévis, *Journal*):277 f.

54 Colville to Pitt, 24 May 1760, *Pitt Correspondence*, 2:290; 'Relation de L'expedition de quebec', *AC*, c 11A, 105:26v.; Barrow, *The Life of George Lord Anson*, 369 f.

55 J. Desbruyères to Townshend, 19 May 1760, Townshend, *The Military Life of Townshend*, 282.

56 'Evenemens du Canada', *AC*, c 11A, 104:262v.

57 Gabriel, *Le Maréchal de camp Desandrouins*, 326.

58 Lettre du 29 juin 1760, *AG*, 3574: no 67.

59 'Relation de L'expedition de quebec', *AC*, c 11A, 105:27v.; Casgrain, 11 *(Relations et journaux)*:261. See also Bigot's letter to Bougainville in Kerallain, *Les Français au Canada: la jeunesse de Bougainville*, 171, note 2.

60 Lévis à Berryer, 28 juin et 25 novembre 1760, Casgrain, 2 (Lévis, *Lettres*):362, 389.

61 Bougainville, 'Journal', *RAPQ* (1923-4), 392.

62 *Mercure de La Haye*, 149 (juillet 1760):84.

63 Bourlamaque à Bougainville, 23 mai 1760, Kerallain, op. cit., 169-71.

64 Vaudreuil à Lévis, 19 mai 1760, Casgrain, 8 (Vaudreuil, *Lettres*):195.

65 Vaudreuil à Berryer, 23 avril 1760, *AC*, F 3, 16:26v.

66 Circulaire du 30 mai 1760, *AC*, c 11A, 87:363-7. (Copy in *PAC*.)

67 'Manifeste du General Murray', 20 mai 1760, *AC*, c 11A, 105:64.

68 Amherst to Whitmore, 19 May 1760, *PRO*, co 5, 58:277.

69 Amherst to Ligonier, 8 March 1760, *PAC*, Amherst Papers, packet 11.

[70] Id., 21 June 1760, ibid.

[71] Pitt to Amherst, 7 January 1760, ibid., packet 24.

[72] Lionel Groulx, 'D'une transmigration des Canadiens en Louisiane vers 1760', *Revue d'histoire de l'Amérique française*, 8 (1954-5):97-125.

[73] *Mercure de La Haye*, 149 (décembre 1760):684 f.

[74] Corbett, op. cit., 2:106, 117; Tunstall, *William Pitt*, 270; Pargellis, *Military Affairs in North America*, xx; Mante, *The History of the Late War in America*, 307 f.; *New York Mercury*, 25 August 1760.

[75] Beatson, *Naval and Military Memoirs*, 3:263 f.; Knox, *Journal*, 3:91; Bernier à Crémille, 12 septembre 1760, *AG*, 3574: no 102.

[76] Amherst to Whitmore, 18 May 1760, *PRO*, co 5, 58:274; Pitt to Amherst, 14 June 1760, *PAC*, Amherst Papers, packet 24.

[77] Fauquier to Amherst, 25 November 1759, *PRO*, co 5, 57:211; id., 5 April 1760, ibid., 58:161.

[78] Hamilton to Amherst, 10 December 1759, ibid., 57:195; id., 2 March 1760, ibid., 409.

[79] Sharpe to Amherst, 10 April 1760, ibid., 58:139 f.

[80] Pitt to Amherst, 17 December 1760, *PAC*, Amherst Papers, packet 34.

[81] Pownall to Amherst, 22 January 1760, *PRO*, co 5, 57:583; *Boston News-Letter*, 31 January 1760; Fitch to Amherst, 20 December 1759, *PRO*, co 5, 57:251 f.; Hopkins to Amherst, 7 January 1760, ibid., 582; id., 11 March 1760, ibid., 58:81; Wentworth to Amherst, 18 January 1760, ibid., 57:579.

[82] Resolution of the Assembly of New York, 14 March 1760, *PRO*, co 5, 58:99.

[83] *New York Mercury*, 19 May 1760.

[84] Amherst to Ligonier, 26 August 1760, *PAC*, Amherst Papers, packet 11.

[85] 'Murray's journal', Knox, *Journal*, 3:306-8; Beatson, op. cit., 3:263.

[86] 'Murray's journal', Knox, *Journal*, 3:308-11; 'Relation de la suite de la campagne de 1760', Casgrain, 11 *(Relations et journaux)*:248 f.

[87] Knox, *Journal*, 2:474.

[88] Ibid., 478 f.

[89] Ibid., 500.

[90] Ibid., 496 f.

[91] Casgrain, 4 *(Lettres et pièces militaires)*:284 f.

[92] Lévis à Belle-Isle, 7 août 1760, Casgrain, 2 (Lévis, *Lettres*): 374 f.

[93] Casgrain, 4 *(Lettres et pièces militaires)*:285.

[94] Murray to Pitt, 24 August 1760, *Virginia Gazette*, 16 January 1761; 'Murray's journal', Knox, *Journal*, 3:324 f.; see also ibid., 2:503 f.

[95] Lettre à Lévis, Casgrain, 5 (Bourlamaque, *Lettres*):101.

[96] Lévis à Belle-Isle, 14 juillet 1760, Casgrain, 2 (Lévis, *Lettres*):371. See also Frégault, *François Bigot*, 2:310 f.

[97] Lévis à Bourlamaque, 15 août 1760, *PAC*, Lettres de Bourlamaque, 3:347.

[98] Bourlamaque à Lévis, 22 août 1760, Casgrain, 5 (Bourlamaque, *Lettres*):102.

[99] Id., 23 août 1760, ibid., 105.

[100] Knox, *Journal*, 2:539; Amherst to Pitt, 26 August 1760, ibid., 3:89; 'The Capitulation of Fort Lévis', ibid., 257; Bernier à Crémille, 12 septembre 1760, *AG*, 3574: no 102.

101 'Relation de la suite de la campagne de 1760', Casgrain, 11 (Relations et journaux):253.

102 Ibid., 248 f.; Casgrain, 1 (Lévis, Journal):291; 'Etat des troupes qui se trouvent à l'Ile-aux-Noix', Casgrain, 10 (Lettres de divers particuliers):147.

103 Bougainville à Lévis, 21 août 1760, Casgrain, 10 (Lettres de divers particuliers): 144 f.

104 Casgrain, 11 (Relations et journaux):253.

105 Boston News-Letter, 10 July 1760.

106 Bougainville à Lévis, 22 [et 24?] août 1760, Casgrain, 10 (Lettres de divers particuliers):146, 142.

107 Casgrain, 1 (Lévis, Journal):299; Casgrain, 11 (Relations et journaux):254; 'The Campaign of Canada . . . 1760', Coll. de MSS, 4:258; Boston News-Letter, 11 September 1760; Bernier à Crémille, 12 septembre 1760, AG, 3574: no 102.

108 Casgrain 1, (Lévis, Journal):300; 'Murray's journal,' Knox, Journal, 3:329; Amherst to Pitt, 8 September 1760, ibid., 3:92.

109 Roquemaure à Lévis, ler septembre 1760, Casgrain, 10 (Lettres de divers particuliers):133; De Laas à Lévis, 30 août 1760, ibid., 166.

110 Bourlamaque à Lévis, 30 août 1760, Casgrain, 5 (Bourlamaque, Lettres):119; id., 2 septembre 1760, ibid., 124; 'Murray's journal', Knox, Journal, 3:330.

111 Murray to Pitt, 7 October 1760, ibid., 3:255 f.

112 Ibid., 2:558, note 1; procès-verbal du conseil de guerre du 6 septembre 1760, AC, F 3, 16:127-30; Casgrain, 1 (Lévis, Journal):303 f.

113 Knox, Journal, 2:521.

114 Amherst to Ligonier, 8 September 1760, PAC, Amherst Papers, packet 11.

115 Amherst à Vaudreuil, 7 septembre 1760, AC, C 11A, 105:155.

116 Lévis, 'Mémoire à M. le marquis de Vaudreuil', 8 septembre 1760, Casgrain, 1 (Lévis, Journal):306 f.; 'Réponse de M. le marquis de Vaudreuil', ibid., 307 f. See also Bernier à Crémille, 12 septembre 1760, AG, 3574: no 102.

117 Bernier à Accaron, 25 septembre 1760, AC, C 11A, 105:202; 'Reddition de Montreal et de tout le Canada aux anglois', 16 octobre 1760, AM, B 4, 98:5.

118 Berryer à Vaudreuil, 5 décembre 1760, AC, B 112:280.

119 'Reddition de Montreal . . .', AM, B 4, 98:5.

120 Mercure de La Haye, 149 (novembre 1760):539 f.

121 Vaudreuil à Berryer, 10 décembre 1760, AC, C 11A, 105:173 f.

122 Lévis à Berryer, 27 novembre 1760, ibid., 183.

123 Gazette de France (6 septembre 1760), 430; (20 septembre), 456; (27 septembre), 465.

124 'Articles of capitulation, Montreal', Shortt and Doughty, Documents relating to the Constitutional History of Canada 1759-1791, 1: 5-24, articles 13, 30, 36, 48.

125 M. Perrault à son frère, 15 février 1761, Collection Baby, dossier Perrault.

126 Bernier à Crémille, 12 septembre 1760, AG, 3574: no 102.

127 Choiseul à Bourlamaque, 18 août 1762, PAC, Lettres de Bourlamaque, 5:123; the memorandum is printed in Bulletin des recherches historiques, 25 (1919):257-76, 289-305, and 26 (1920):193-209, 225-40.

128 Appleton, A Sermon Preached October 9, 29.

129 Thomas Foxcroft, Grateful Reflexions on the signal Appearances of Divine

Providence for Great Britain and its Colonies in America, which diffuse a general Joy. A Sermon Preached in the Old Church in Boston, October 9. 1760 (Boston, 1760), 30 f.

[130] *The Interest of Great Britain considered With Regard to her Colonies, And the Acquisitions of Canada and Guadaloupe. To which are Added, Observations concerning the Increase of Mankind, Peopling of Countries, &c.* (London, 1760), 45 f.

[131] *Pennsylvania Gazette,* 25 September 1760.

[132] *Boston News-Letter,* 18 September 1760.

[133] *Pennsylvania Gazette,* 25 September 1760.

[134] *Boston News-Letter,* 2 October 1760.

[135] *New York Mercury,* 22 September 1760.

[136] 'The Cordial Address of the Mayor Aldermen & Commonalty of the antient City of New York in Common Council Convened', 1760, *PAC,* Amherst Papers, packet 17.

[137] *Mercure de La Haye,* 149 (octobre 1760):458. See also ibid., (novembre 1760):545.

[138] Ibid., (décembre 1760):659-61.

[139] Foxcroft, op. cit., 30.

[140] Appleton, op. cit., 17 f., 36.

[141] Malartic, *Journal,* 331.

[142] *New York Mercury,* 10 November 1760.

CHAPTER X

[1] *A Letter to the People of England, on the Necessity of putting an Immediate End to the War; and the Means of obtaining an Advantageous Peace* (London, 1760), 45-7.

[2] Ibid., 43.

[3] Ibid., 48.

[4] Beer, *British Colonial Policy, 1754-1765,* 143.

[5] *A Letter Addressed to Two Great Men, on the Prospect of Peace; And on the Terms necessary to be insisted upon in the Negociation* (London, 1760), 9, 12-16.

[6] Ibid., 17.

[7] Ibid., 30 f. Italics in the text.

[8] Ibid., 43.

[9] Ibid., 34.

[10] Ibid., 38.

[11] *Remarks on the Letter Addressed to Two Great Men. In a Letter to the Author of that Piece* (London, 1760).

[12] *Sentiments Relating to the Late Negociation,* 12, note.

[13] Beer, op. cit., 143 f.

[14] *Remarks on the Letter Addressed to Two Great Men,* 11 f.

[15] Ibid., 16.

[16] Ibid., 23 f.

17 Ibid., 34.

18 Ibid., 17-25.

19 Ibid., 28-31.

20 *Boston News-Letter,* 18 September 1760.

21 *The Interest of Great Britain considered With Regard to her Colonies, And the Acquisitions of Canada and Guadaloupe. To Which are Added, Observations concerning the Increase of Mankind, Peopling of Countries, &c.* (London, 1760).

22 Ibid., 16.

23 Ibid., 23-5.

24 Ibid., 39.

25 On the question of free, as distinct from restricted, population growth, consult Charles Morazé, *Essai sur la civilisation d'Occident* (Paris, 1950), 72-97.

26 *The Interest of Great Britain considered,* 43 f.

27 *Boston News-Letter,* 7 August 1760.

28 *The Interest of Great Britain considered,* 45 f.

29 *An Answer to the Letter to two great Men,* 12, 14 f., 21.

30 *A Letter to the Right Hon. the Earl of Bute on a late important resignation and its probable consequences* (London, 1761), 56. A French translation based on the third edition was published under the following title: *Lettre au comte de Bute, à l'occasion de la retraite de M. Pitt, & sur ce qui peut en résulter par rapport à la Paix* (London, 1761).

31 Ibid., 54.

32 Ibid., 17.

33 Ibid., 5.

34 Ibid., 26.

35 Ibid., 30.

36 Ibid., 61.

37 *Reasons for Keeping Guadaloupe at a Peace, Preferable to CANADA, explained in five letters, from a Gentleman in Guadaloupe to his Friend in London* (London, 1761).

38 Ibid., 32.

39 Ibid., 46.

40 *New York Gazette,* 18 September 1758.

41 *Reasons for Keeping Guadaloupe,* 3, 8, 13.

42 Ibid., 5.

43 Ibid., 6-8.

44 Ibid., 9-12, 20.

45 Ibid., 27-30.

46 Ibid., 48 f.

47 Ibid., 19 f.

48 Ibid., 51-3, 58.

49 Ibid., 60.

50 *A Letter to a Great M——r, on the Prospect of Peace . . . By an unprejudiced Observer* (London, 1761), 2. The 'Great Minister' was Pitt, ibid., 148.

51 Ibid., 16 f., 21, 44.

[52] Ibid., 19 f.

[53] Ibid., 37 f., 72-8.

[54] Ibid., 79, 104 f.

[55] Ibid., 82, 86.

[56] Ibid., 122.

[57] *A Candid Answer, To a Pamphlet Called Reasons for Keeping Guadaloupe at a Peace, preferable to Canada, explained in Five Letters from a Gentleman in Guadaloupe, to his Friend in London* (London, 1761), 3-8.

[58] W.A. Shaw, ed., *Miscellaneous Representations relative to Our Concerns in America Submitted to the Earl of Bute,* by Henry McCulloh (1761) (London, 1905), 1-3.

[59] Ibid., 6, 9-11.

[60] *The Importance of Canada Considered in Two Letters to a Noble Lord* (London, 1761), 1-19, passim.

CHAPTER XI

[1] Gipson, 8:204-6, 208, 211, 218.

[2] Ibid., 219 f.

[3] Pease, *Anglo-French Boundary Disputes in the West,* Introduction, cxiii-cxiv. See also *Thoughts on a Question of Importance proposed to the Public, Whether it is probable that the Immense Extent of Territory acquired by this Nation at the late Peace, will operate towards the PROSPERITY OR THE RUIN OF THE ISLAND OF GREAT BRITAIN?* (London, 1765), 12.

[4] Tunstall, *William Pitt,* 292.

[5] *Mémoire historique Sur la négociation de la France & de l'Angleterre, depuis le 26 Mars 1761 jusqu'au 20 Septembre de la même année, avec les Pièces justificatives* (Paris, 1761), 83. (An official publication of the French government.)

[6] Ibid., 110.

[7] Ibid., 120-2.

[8] Ibid., 151-60.

[9] Ibid., 174, 182.

[10] Ibid., 184-7.

[11] Lettre du 8 juillet 1761, 'Les Chambres de commerce de France et la cession du Canada', *RAPQ* (1924-5), 201 f.

[12] See note 5 above.

[13] La Chambre de commerce d'Aunis à celle de Marseille, 10 novembre 1761, *RAPQ* (1924-5), 202 f.

[14] Id., 13 décembre 1761, ibid., 204.

[15] Lettre de la Chambre de commerce de Marseille, 21 décembre 1761, ibid., 205 f.; Choiseul à la Chambre de Marseille, 4 janvier 1762, ibid., 206 f.

[16] La Chambre de commerce de Nantes à celle d'Aunis, 16 novembre 1761, ibid., 207; la Chambre de Nantes à Choiseul, 19 novembre 1761, ibid., 213; la Chambre de Nantes au maire de Granville, 26 novembre 1761, ibid., 214.

[17] La Chambre de commerce de Saint-Malo à celle d'Aunis, 27 novembre et 27 décembre 1761, ibid., 208 f.

18 La Chambre de commerce du Havre à celle de Saint-Malo, 14 février 1762, ibid., 209 f.; la même à celle d'Aunis [n.d.], ibid., 222; la même à Choiseul, 14 novembre 1762, ibid., 210 f.

19 Le maire et les échevins de Granville à la Chambre de Nantes, 20 novembre 1761, ibid., 212 f.

20 Ibid., 216 f.

21 Ibid., 218-22.

22 'Chambre de commerce de Montpellier: assemblée du 18 décembre 1761, ibid., 227 f.

23 La Chambre de commerce de Guyenne à Choiseul, 22 décembre 1761, ibid., 223-5.

24 'These documents prove that if the Court abandoned us, this was not true of the Chambers of Commerce in France . . . It seems that our historians and writers have believed too readily that France felt no regret at being separated from her colony', ibid., 200.

25 *AC*, c 11A, 105:314, translated from *St James Chronicle*, 7 September 1761.

26 Ibid., 326 f., translated from *St James Chronicle*, 9 December 1761.

27 John Rutherford, 'The Importance of the Colonies to Great Britain', William K. Boyd, ed., *North Carolina Historical Review*, 2 (1925):371.

28 Gipson, 8:308 f., 312 f.

29 *Sentiments Relating to the Late Negociation*, 1-11.

30 Ibid., 15.

31 Ibid., 18 f.

32 *An Examination of the Commercial Principles of the Late Negociation between Great Britain and France in MDCCLXI. In which the System of that Negociation with Regard to our Colonies and Commerce is considered* (London, 1762), 67.

33 Ibid., 68-71.

34 Ibid., 72-5.

35 Ibid., 85.

36 Ibid., 77.

37 *Thoughts on Trade in General*, 40, 43.

38 *An Examination of the Commercial Principles*, 86 f., 98 f.

39 Ibid., 93 f.

40 *The Comparative Importance of our acquisitions from France in America. With remarks on a pamphlet entitled An Examination of the Commercial Principles of the Late Negociations in 1761* (London, 1762), 22-8.

41 Ibid., 42.

42 *Coloniae Anglicanae Illustratae: or the Acquest of Dominion, and the Plantation of Colonies Made by the English in America, With Rights of the Colonists, Examined, stated, and illustrated* (London, 1762), 2, 4.

43 *The Comparative Importance of our acquisitions*, 42 f.

44 Ibid., 17.

45 Ibid., 6, 9 f.

46 Gipson, 8:304-6.

47 *An Enquiry into the Merits of the Supposed Preliminaries of Peace, signed on the 3rd. inst.* (London, 1762), passim.

[48] *Preliminary Articles of Peace, Between His Britannick Majesty, the Most Christian King, and the Catholick King. Signed at Fontainebleau, the 3d Day of November, 1762.* Published by Authority (London, 1762).

[49] *Thoughts on Trade in General,* 4-7.

[50] Ibid., 10.

[51] Quoted by A. Duchêne, *La Politique coloniale de la France; le ministère des Colonies depuis Richelieu* (Paris, 1928), 101 f.

[52] In an excellent introduction to a selection of extracts from Raynal: *L'Anticolonialisme au XVIIIe siècle: Histoire philosophique et politique des établissements et du commerce des Européens dans les deux Indes* (Paris, 1951), 27 f.

[53] Ibid., 265.

[54] Quoted in Frégault, *François Bigot,* 1:304.

[55] *Thoughts on Trade in General,* 13.

[56] Ibid., 18.

[57] Ibid., 14, 19, 21. His reasoning was sound: see Harold U. Faulkner, *American Economic History,* 79-84.

[58] *Thoughts on Trade in General,* 22 f.

[59] Gipson, 6:3-19.

[60] *Thoughts on Trade in General,* 24.

[61] Ibid., 25.

[62] Ibid., 35 f.

[63] Ibid., 37. See also Mante, *History of the Late War,* 344 f.

[64] *Thoughts on Trade in General,* 38, 43-5.

[65] Ibid., 52-6.

[66] Ibid., 85.

Bibliography

I. MANUSCRIPTS

All the documents listed in this section, with the exception of those in sub-section J ('Other Collections'), can be found either in the manuscript division of the Library of Congress or in the Public Archives of Canada.

A. Archives des Colonies (AC)

Series B—Dispatches from the minister of marine to officials in the ports of France and in the colonies. We have examined volumes 101-13, 115, and 117, covering the years 1755-63. Copies in the Public Archives of Canada; original pagination.

Series C 11A—Correspondance générale, Canada. Volumes 100-5 contain letters to the minister of marine written by military, civil, and religious officials in Canada between 1755 and 1763. A few of the letters in volume 105 date from the years between 1765 and 1769. A number of important documents have been transferred from this series to the Moreau de Saint-Méry collection (see below). The following items in volume 104 are of fundamental importance: 'Extrait d'un Journal tenu à L'armée que Commandoit feu mr de Montcalm Lieutenant General' (folios 213-59), 'Journal Des faits arrivés à l'armée De quebec Capital dans l'amerique Septentrional pendant la Campagne de l'année 1759. par M. de foligné' (265-94), and 'Jugement Impartial Sur les operations Militaires De la campagne en Canada 1759' (301-4). Photostats in the Library of Congress. Microfilm in the Public Archives of Canada.

Series C 11B—Correspondance générale, Île-Royale. This series is the equivalent for Cape Breton of the preceding one for Canada. We have examined volumes 35-8, covering the years 1755-8.

Series C 11E—Volume 10 (1689-1764) contains material on 'rivalries between English and French colonies', including the journal of Washington's mission to the Ohio in 1753, an account of the capture of Fort Bull, and several other interesting documents.

Series D 2—Volume 2, *Officiers civils et militaires. Registre des Formules. 1731-1761,* contains official papers concerning Vaudreuil, Montcalm, Rigaud, Dumas, Le Mercier, Jacau, Vergor, Pontleroy, Lotbinière, etc. Volume 4, *Officiers militaires. Colonies. 1747-1763,* contains records of service for Vaudreuil, Rigaud, and Du Quesne.

[400]

Collection F 3—Collection Moreau de Saint-Méry. This important collection, assembled under the direction of Médéric-Louis-Elie Moreau de Saint-Méry (1750-1819), includes a large number of documents relating to the history of Canada. Many of the documents are copies of originals in series B and C 11A; others—and this is particularly true of the period studied in the present work—have been removed from the series to which they belonged. We have consulted volumes 13 (1741-9), 14 (1750-6), 15 (1757-9), and 16 (1760-91), as well as the 'Supplements' to volumes 14 and 15. Copies in the Public Archives of Canada; original pagination.

B. Ministère des Affaires Étrangères *(AE)*

Mémoires et documents, Amérique—Although it deals essentially with the diplomatic aspects of the War of the Conquest, this series includes a good number of documents relating to actual hostilities, to French and English colonial policy, and to the situation in New France and in British America. Several items in volume 9 concern French and British claims in the Acadian region (1749-52). Volume 10 (1753-71), more important for our study, provides a wealth of information on Franco-Canadian policy in the Ohio valley, on the sea war, on events in Nova Scotia, and on military plans and campaigns between 1754 and 1760. Volume 11 (1713-71) includes a table of 'Dépenses faites en Canada depuis 1750, jusques et compris l'année 1760'. Volume 21 contains a plan for the 'transmigration' of Canadian groups to Louisiana. La Galissonière's memoranda on French colonies in North America (1497-1759) are preserved in volume 24.

Correspondance politique, Angleterre—Volumes 101 and 438, in particular, contain documents relating to matters touched upon in the present study.

C. Ministère de la Guerre *(AG)*

Archives anciennes—It is essential for anyone wishing to follow military and political events in New France between 1755 and 1760 to examine the historical archives of the ministry of war. They include the dispatches and orders sent from the war office to the 'troupes de terre' serving in Canada, and letters and reports from officers commanding infantry units to their superiors in the mother country. Whereas the series *AC,* C 11A gives a general idea of the Canadian point of view on military policy in the colony, the archives of the ministry of war reflect the French point of view. We have utilized the following volumes: 3404 (1755), 3405 (1755), 3417 (1756), 3457 (1757), 3498 (1758), 3499 (1758), 3540 (1759), 3574 (1760). We should have liked to see volume 3628, which contains, according to J.-E. Roy (*Rapport sur les archives de France relatives à l'histoire du Canada,* Ottawa, 1911), memoranda on the navy and the colonies, notably a document on the government of the colonies 'with marginal notes by the duc de Choiseul', but as this volume has not been copied for the Canadian Archives we were unable to consult it.

D. Archives de la Marine *(AM)*

Series B 2—Documents concerning armaments and troops destined for America. Volumes to be examined are: 349-50, 352-3, 356, 358-9, 362, covering the years 1755-60. Unfortunately almost none of this material has been copied for the Canadian Archives. The gap is partially filled by copies from the following series.

[401]

Series B 4—This series contains documents relating to the sea war. The most interesting items are letters, reports, and journals of officers attached to maritime expeditions. We were able to consult the following volumes: 67-8, 73, 76, 80, 91, 95-6, 98. These volumes are essential for any study of the movements of French squadrons between 1754 and 1760, and they also contain important information on the naval strategy of France.

Series C 7—Files of officers in the navy and the colonial service. Each file includes a *curriculum vitae* and most of them also contain documents relating to the salient facts of the life of the person concerned. It is unfortunate that more of these files have not been copied for the Public Archives of Canada. We have found useful material in files 89 (Drucourt), 161 (La Jonquière de Taffanel), and 216 (Montcalm).

Series G—It would be desirable to be able to consult volume 38. According to J.-E. Roy (*Rapport sur les archives de France relatives à l'histoire du Canada*, 246), it contains an 'état alphabétique pour servir à la liste générale des officiers de la Marine, 1755'. This volume is not in the Canadian Archives.

E. Archives Nationales *(AN)*

Series K—Monuments historiques. Carton 1232, no. 50 contains 102 pages of copies of 'Lettres interressantes de M. le Mis de Vaudreuil au Ministre Pendant le Cours de 1759'. These dispatches were collected in 1762 by the commission appointed by the Châtelet to investigate the Canada Affair.

F. Public Archives of Canada *(PAC)*

Series A—Nova Scotia Correspondence 1603-1840. This collection includes documents originally marked *A&WI* (America and West Indies), *BTNS* (Board of Trade, Nova Scotia), Col. Corr. N.S. (Colonial Correspondence, Nova Scotia), etc. Our references are to the original designations. The volumes containing material bearing directly on questions studied in this book are nos 55-65, 67, and 68. They cover the period 1754-62 and correspond to *A&WI*, volume 597, *BTNS* volumes 15-18 and 36, and Col. Corr. N.S., volume 1.

Amherst Papers—This interesting collection includes the dispatches written and received by General Jeffrey Amherst and many other documents preserved by him. We have examined packets 8, 10-13, 15, 17, 19, 22, 24-8. Packet 15 contains some very curious letters from Murray to Townshend and Amherst on the subject of Wolfe. He considered that Wolfe's reputation did him more than justice.

Lettres de Bourlamaque—François-Charles de Bourlamaque, who was sent to Canada with the 'troupes de terre' in 1756, ranked third, immediately after Montcalm and Lévis, among the staff officers. He was second-in-command under Lévis. This collection of original documents is made up of the letters he received and the memoranda he drafted. They fill six volumes with a total of 900 pages. An excellent analytical and descriptive inventory is published in the *Report of the Public Archives for 1923* (Ottawa, 1926), appendix C.

G. Bibliothèque Nationale *(BN)*

Mss fr.—Fonds français. There is a great deal to be gleaned from this extensive collection. Volumes 10764, 11248, 11340, and especially 11342 contain letters, reports, and memoranda with useful information on New France, the navy, and colonial finances at the time of the War of the Conquest.

H. Public Record Office *(PRO)*

Series CO 5—Colonial Office, America and West Indies. Volumes 16-18 contain dispatches from colonial governors to the secretary of state (1755-60); the interest of these items is increased by the supporting documents that often accompany them. This is also true of volumes 46-59, which contain letters from the commanders-in-chief—Braddock, Shirley, Loudoun, Abercromby, and Amherst—and from other superior officers attached to military and naval units serving in America; these volumes also contain important correspondance with provincial administrators, intercepted letters, dispaches from Canada and Europe, messages from legislative assemblies and other public bodies. The series is of prime importance for the study of the period. The pagination is that of the copies in the Library of Congress.

J. Other Collections

Massachusetts Historical Society (Boston)—Many documents in the archives of this society date from the period studied in this volume. The 'Israel Williams Papers', two thick volumes of original documents (1728-80), were especially useful.

Université de Montréal—The Baby collection is made up of original documents classified partly according to their content and partly under the names of the families concerned. A descriptive analysis would facilitate consultation of the documents.

II. PERIODICALS: 1754-63

To manuscript sources must be added contemporary periodicals. Newspapers and reviews print official 'relations' and reports from commanders of expeditions, as well as news items from all parts of the world, letters from their correspondents, extracts from other periodicals, and commentaries on the war and the political situation. A study of the British American press is essential for anyone desiring to follow the movement of American opinion or to be informed on the ideas that appeared in the British press, for the colonial weeklies quoted and discussed articles in European periodicals dealing with American affairs. They also reported a host of incidents to which only brief allusion is made in archival documents, or of which no mention is made. The newspapers are naturally full of propaganda, but even the propaganda is significant. We have examined the following newspapers in the Library of Congress, and the New York and Boston Public Libraries:

> *The Boston Gazette or Country Journal*
> *The Boston Weekly News-Letter*
> *The Maryland Gazette*
> *The New York Gazette or Weekly Post-Boy*
> *The New York Mercury*
> *The Pennsylvania Gazette*
> *The Pennsylvania Journal and Weekly Advertiser*
> *The Virginia Gazette*

We have also examined four European periodicals in the collections of the Library of Congress:

Gazette de France
Mercure de France
Mercure historique et politique de La Haye
London Magazine or Gentleman's Monthly Intelligencer

III. CONTEMPORARY PUBLICATIONS AND COMMENTARIES

To the periodicals must be added chronicles, commentaries, propaganda pamphlets and those inspired by some aspect of the War of the Conquest. As many of these publications are anonymous, we have listed in chronological order those we have utilized:

The Conduct of the French With Regard to Nova Scotia, Virginia and other Parts of the Continent of North America. From its First Settlement to the present Time . . . In a Letter to a Member of Parliament. London and Dublin, 1754.

A Scheme to Drive the French Out of All the Continent of America. London, 1754.

Lettres d'un François à un Hollandois, au sujet des Differends survenus entre la France & la Grande-Bretagne Touchant leurs Possessions respectives dans l'Amérique Septentrionale. [s. 1.], 1755.

A Miscellaneous Essay Concerning the Courses pursued by Great Britain In the Affairs of her Colonies: with some Observations on the Great Importance of our Settlements in America, and The Trade thereof. London, 1755.

State of the British and French Colonies in North America, With Respect to Number of People, Forces, Forts, Indians, Trade and other Advantages . . . With a Proper Expedient Proposed for Preventing Future Disputes. In Two Letters to a Friend. London, 1755.

The Wisdom and Policy of the French in the Construction of their Great Offices, So as best to answer the Purposes of extending their Trade and Commerce, and enlarging their Foreign Settlements. London, 1755.

Barton, Thomas. *Unanimity and Public Spirit. A Sermon Preached at Carlisle, And some other Episcopal Churches in the Counties of* YORK *and* CUMBERLAND, *soon after General* BRADDOCK's *Defeat.* Philadelphia, 1755.

Burr, Aaron. *A Discourse Delivered At New-Ark, in New-Jersey, January 1, 1755. Being a Day set apart for solemn Fasting and Prayer, on account of the late encroachments of the French, and their Designs against the British Colonies in America.* New York, 1755.

Checkley, Samuel. *The Duty of God's People when engaged in War. A Sermon Preached at the North-Church of Christ in Boston, Sept. 21. To Captain Thomas Stoddard, and his Company; On Occasion of their going against the Enemy.* Boston, 1755.

Dwight, Nathaniel. *The Journal of Captain Nathaniel Dwight of Belchertown, Mass., during the Crown Point Expedition, 1755.* New York, 1902.

Malartic. *Journal des campagnes au Canada de 1755 à 1760 par le comte de Maurès de Malartic.* Dijon, 1890.

The Importance of God's Presence with an Army going against the Enemy and the Grounds on which it may be expected. Boston, 1756.

Observations sur le Mémoire de la France . . . Envoyées dans les cours de l'Europe, par le ministère Britannique, pour justifier la réponse faite à la réquisition de S. M. T. C. du 21 décembre 1755. Paris, 1756. Photostat in the library of Harvard University.

Remarks on the French Memorials concerning the Limits of Acadia, Printed at the Royal Printing-house at Paris, and distributed by the French Ministers at all the Foreign Courts of Europe. London, 1756.

'A Review of Military Operations in North America, from the Commencement of the French hostilities on the frontiers of Virginia in 1753, to the Surrender of Oswego, on the 14th of August, 1756; in a Letter to a Nobleman', *Collections of the Massachusetts Historical Society for the year 1800-1801,* series 1, vol. 7:67-163.

Smith, William. *A Brief view of the Conduct of Pennsylvania for the year 1755.* London, 1756. *Etat présent de la Pensilvanie, où l'on trouve le détail de ce qui s'y est passé depuis la défaite du Général Braddock jusqu'à la prise d'Oswego, avec une Carte particuliére de cette Colonie.* Paris, 1756. (An abridged translation.)

Proposals for Uniting the English Colonies on the Continent of America so as to enable them to act with Force and Vigour against their Enemies. London, 1757.

Hays, I.M. *A journal Kept during the Siege of Fort William Henry, August, 1757.* (Reprinted from the *Proceedings* of the American Philosophical Society, 37 (1898):143-50).

Bass, Benjamin. 'A Journal of the Expedition against Fort Frontenac in 1758'. *New York History,* 16 (1935):449-52.

[Loudoun, John Campbell, Earl of.] *The Conduct of a Noble Commander in America Impartially Reviewed with The genuine Causes of the Discontents at New York and Hallifax und The True Occasion of the Delays in that Important Expedition including A regular Account of all the Proceedings and Incidents in the Order of Time wherein they happened.* London, 1758.

Mayhew, Jonathan. *Two Discourses Delivered November 23d. 1758. Being the Day appointed by Authority to be Observed as a Day of public Thangsgiving: Relating, more Especially, to the Success of His Majesty's Arms, And those of the King of Prussia, the last Year.* Boston, [1758].

Rea, Caleb. *The Journal of Dr. Caleb Rea, written during the Expedition against Ticonderoga in 1758.* F.M. Ray, ed. Salem, Mass., 1881.

Y[oung], A. *The Theatre of the Present War in America: with Candid Reflections on the great Importance of the War in that Part of the World.* London, 1758.

Cooper, Samuel. *A Sermon Preached before His Excellency Thomas Pownall, Esq., Captain-General and Governor in Chief, The Honourable His Majesty's Council and House of Representatives Of the Province of the Massachusetts-Bay in New-England, October 16th, 1759. Upon Occasion of the Success of His Majesty's Arms in the Reduction of Quebec.* Boston, [1759].

An Authentic Register of the British Successes; being a Collection of all the Extraordinary And somme of the Ordinary Gazettes from the Taking of Louisbourgh, July 26, 1758, by the Honourable Admiral Boscawen and Gen. Amhurst, to the Defeat of the French Fleet under M. Conflans, Nov. 21, 1759, By Sir Edward Hawke. To which is added, A Particular Account of M. Thurot's Defeat, By Captain John Elliott. London, 1760.

Eloge historique de Monsieur le Marquis de Montcalm. Extrait du *Mercure de France* de 1760. Quebec, 1855.

A Letter Addressed to Two Great Men, on the Prospect of Peace; And on the Terms necessary to be insisted upon in the Negociation. London, 1760.

An Answer to the Letter to two great Men. Containing remarks and observations on that piece, and vindicating the character of a Noble Lord from Inactivity. London, 1760.

Remarks on the Letter Addressed to Two Great Men. In a Letter to the Author of that Piece. London, 1760.

A Letter to the People of England, on the Necessity of putting an Immediate End to the War; and the Means of obtaining an Advantageous Peace. London, 1760. *A Refutation of the Letter to an Hon*ble *Brigadier-General, Commander of His Majesty's Forces in Canada.* London, 1760.

Adams, William. *A Discourse Delivered at New-London, October 23d. A.D. 1760. On the Thanksgiving (Ordered by Authority) For the Success of the British Arms in the Reduction of MONTREAL, and the Conquest of all CANADA.* New London, 1760.

Appleton, Nathaniel. *A Sermon Preached October 9. Being A Day of public Thanksgiving, Occasioned by the Surrender of Montreal, and All Canada, September 8th 1760. To His Britannic Majesty. Effected by the British and Provincial Troops under the Command of General Amherst.* Boston, 1760.

Foxcroft, Thomas. *Grateful Reflexions on the signal Appearances of Divine Providence for Great Britain and its Colonies in America, which diffuse a general Joy. A Sermon Preached in the Old Church in Boston, October 9. 1760.* Boston, 1760.

[Franklin, Benjamin]. *The Interest of Great Britain considered With Regard to her Colonies, And the Acquisitions of Canada and Guadaloupe. To which are Added, Observations concerning the Increase of Mankind, Peopling of Countries, &c.* London, 1760.

A Candid Answer, To a Pamphlet called Reasons for Keeping Guadaloupe at a Peace, preferable to Canada, explained in Five Letters from a Gentleman in Guadaloupe, to his Friend in London. In a Letter to the Author. London, 1761.

The Importance of Canada Considered in Two Letters to a Noble Lord. London, 1761.

A Letter to a Great M------r, on the Prospect of Peace; Wherein the Demolition of the Fortifications of Louisbourg Is shewn to be absurd; The Importance of Canada fully refuted; . . . Containing REMARKS on some preceding Pamphlets that have treated the Subject, and a succinct View of the Whole Terms that ought to be insisted on from France at a Future Negociation. By an unprejudiced Observer. London, 1761.

A letter to the Right Hon. the Earl of Bute on a late important resignation and its probable consequences. London, 1761. *Lettre au comte de Bute, à l'occasion de la retraite de M. Pitt, & sur ce qui peut en résulter par rapport à la Paix. Traduction de l'Anglois sur la troisiéme Edition.* London, 1761.

Mémoire historique Sur la négociation de la France & de l'Angleterre, depuis le 26 Mars 1761 jusqu'au 20 Septembre de la même année, avec les Pièces justificatives. Paris, 1761. Marginal notes by the Duke of 'Brunsvic' are transcribed in the Canadian Archives copy.

Reasons for Keeping Guadaloupe at a Peace, Preferable to CANADA, explained in five Letters, from a Gentleman in Guadaloupe to his Friend in London. London, 1761.

Remarks Upon the Historical Memorial published by the Court of France, in a Letter to the Earl Temple. By a Member of Parliament. London, 1761.

Sentiments Relating to the Late Negociation. London, 1761.

McCulloh, Henry. *Miscellaneous Representations relative to Our Concerns in America.* 1761. William A. Shaw, ed. London, [1905]. Also: William K. Boyd, ed., 'Henry McCulloh's "Miscellaneous Representations Relative to Our Concerns in America" 1761', *The North Carolina Historical Review,* 2 (1925):475-88.

Rutherford, John. 'The Importance of the Colonies to Great Britain, Etc., 1761.' *The North Carolina Historical Review,* 2 (1925): 351-76.

Coloniae Anglicanae Illustratae: or the Acquest of Dominion, and the Plantation of Colonies Made by the English in America, With Rights of the Colonists, Examined, stated, and illustrated. London, 1762.

The Comparative Importance of our acquisitions from France in America. With remarks on a pamphlet entitled An Examination of the Commercial Principles of the Late Negociations in 1761. London, 1762.

An Enquiry into the Merits of the Supposed Preliminaries of Peace, signed on the 3rd. inst. London, 1762.

An Examination of the Commercial Principles of the Late Negociation between Great Britain and France in MDCCLXI. In which the System of that Negociation with Regard to our Colonies and Commerce is considered. London, 1762.

Preliminary Articles of Peace, Between His Britannick Majesty, the Most Christian King, and the Catholick King. Signed at Fontainebleau, the 3d Day of November, 1762. Published by Authority. London, 1762.

Bourlamaque, François-Charles de. 'Un Mémoire sur le Canada', *Bulletin des recherches historiques,* 25 (1919):257-76, 289-305; 26 (1920):193-209, 225-40.

Thoughts on Trade in GENERAL, Our West-Indian in Particular, Our Continental Colonies, Canada, Guadaloupe, and the Preliminary Articles of Peace. Addressed to the Community. London, 1763.

Entick, John. *The General History of the Late War: Containing it's Rise, Progress, and Event, in Europe, Asia, Africa, and America.* 5 vols, London, 1763-4.

Thoughts on a Question of Importance proposed to the Public, Whether it is probable that the Immense Extent of Territory acquired by this Nation at the late Peace, will operate towards the PROSPERITY OR THE RUIN OF THE ISLAND OF GREAT BRITAIN? London, 1765.

An Impartial History of the Late Glorious War, from it's Commencement to it's Conclusion; Containing an Exact Account of the Battles and Sea Engagements, Together with Other Remarkable Transactions, in Europe, Asia, Africa, and America. London, 1769.

Mante, Thomas. *The History of the Late War in America, and the Islands of the West Indies, including the Campaigns of MDCCLXIII and MDCCLXIV Against His Majesty's Indian Enemies.* London, 1772.

Pouchot, Pierre. *Mémoires sur la dernière guerre de l'Amérique septentrionale, entre la France et l'Angleterre. Suivis d'Observations, dont plusieurs sont relatives au théâtre actuel de la guerre, & de nouveaux détails sur les moeurs & les usages des Sauvages, avec des cartes topographiques.* 3 vols, Yverdon, 1781.

Walpole, Horace. *Memoirs of the Reign of George II.* Lord Holland, ed., 3 vols, London, 1847.

IV. COLLECTIONS OF DOCUMENTS

Akins, Thomas B., ed. *Selections from the Public Documents of the Province of Nova Scotia.* Halifax, 1869.

Bates, Albert C., ed. *The Fitch Papers; Correspondence and Documents During Thomas Fitch's Governorship of the Colony of Connecticut, 1754-1766.* Hartford, Conn., 1918. Vol. 17 of the *Collections* of the Connecticut Historical Society.

Beatson, Robert, ed. *Naval and Military Memoirs of Great Britain, from 1727 to 1783.* 6 vols, London, 1804.

Brock, R.A., ed. *The Official Records of Robert Dinwiddie, Lieutenant-Governor of Virginia, 1751-1758.* 2 vols, Richmond, 1883-4. Vols 3 and 4 of the *Collections* (new series) of the Virginia Historical Society.

Browne, William Hand, ed. *Correspondence of Governor Horatio Sharpe.* 3 vols, Baltimore, 1888-1911. Vols 6, 9 and 11 of the *Maryland Archives.*

Casgrain, Henri-Raymond, ed. *Collection des manuscrits du maréchal de Lévis.* 12 vols, Montreal and Quebec, 1889-95.
1. *Journal des campagnes du chevalier de Lévis en Canada de 1756 à 1760.* Montreal, 1889.
2. *Lettres du chevalier de Lévis concernant la guerre du Canada (1756-1760).* Montreal, 1889.
3. *Lettres de la cour de Versailles au baron de Dieskau, au marquis de Montcalm et au chevalier de Lévis.* Quebec, 1890.
4. *Lettres et pièces militaires, instructions, ordres, mémoires, plans de campagne et de défense 1756-1760.* Quebec, 1891.
5. *Lettres de M. de Bourlamaque au chevalier de Lévis.* Quebec, 1891.
6. *Lettres du marquis de Montcalm au chevalier de Lévis.* Quebec, 1894.
7. *Journal du marquis de Montcalm durant ses campagnes au Canada de 1756 à 1760.* Quebec, 1895.
8. *Lettres du marquis de Vaudreuil au chevalier de Lévis.* Quebec, 1895.
9. *Lettres de l'intendant Bigot au chevalier de Lévis.* Quebec, 1895.
10. *Lettres de divers particuliers au chevalier de Lévis.* Quebec, 1895.
11. *Relations et journaux de différentes expéditions faites durant les années 1755-56-57-58-59-60.* Quebec, 1895.
12. *Table analytique de la collection des manuscrits du maréchal de Lévis.* Quebec, 1895.

Casgrain, Henri-Raymond, ed. *Extraits des archives des ministères de la Marine et de la Guerre à Paris. Canada, Correspondance générale: MM. Duquesne et Vaudreuil gouverneurs-généraux. 1755-1760.* Vol. 1, Quebec, 1890. This volume —the only one published—contains material from vol. 100 of the series *AC,* c 11A.

[Cimon, Adèle]. *Les Ursulines de Québec depuis leur établissement jusqu'à nos jours.* 4 vols, Quebec, 1863-6. Important for numerous quotations from early Ursuline records.

Collection de manuscrits contenant lettres, mémoires et autres documents historiques relatifs à l'histoire de la Nouvelle-France, recueillis aux archives de la province de Québec ou copiés à l'étranger. 4 vols, Quebec, 1883-5.

[Courville]. *Mémoires sur le Canada, depuis 1749 jusqu'à 1760. En trois parties; avec cartes et plans lithographiés.* Quebec, 1873. See also A. Fauteux, 'Le S . . . de C . . . enfin démasqué', *Les Cahiers des Dix* (Montreal, 1940), 231-92.

Doughty, Arthur G., ed. *An Historical Journal of the Campaigns in North America for the Years 1757, 1758, 1759, and 1760, by Captain John Knox,* 3 vols, Toronto, 1914-16.

Doughty, Arthur G., and Parmelee, G.W., eds. *The Siege of Quebec and the Battle of the Plains of Abraham,* 6 vols, Quebec, 1901.

Dussieux, L. *Le Canada sous la domination française d'après les archives de la Marine et de la Guerre.* Paris, 1883. Documents, 197-345.

Esquer, Gabriel. *L'Anticolonialisme au XVIIIe siècle. Histoire philosophique et politique des établissements et du commerce des Européens dans les deux Indes* [par l'abbé Raynal]. *Introduction, choix de textes et notes par Gabriel Esquer.* Paris, 1951.

Fitzpatrick, John C., ed. *The Writings of George Washington from the Original Manuscript Sources.* 39 vols, Washington, 1931-44. Vols 1 and 2.

Franquet, Louis. *Voyages et mémoires sur le Canada.* Quebec, 1889.

Frégault, Guy; Brunet, Michel; and Trudel, Marcel, eds. *Histoire du Canada par les textes.* Montreal, 1952.

Gabriel, abbé. *Le Maréchal de camp Desandrouins 1729-1792. Guerre du Canada 1756-1760. Guerre de l'Indépendance américaine 1780-1782.* Verdun, 1887. Numerous quotations from the writings of Jean-Nicolas Desandrouins not available elsewhere.

Gipson, Lawrence Henry, ed. *Lewis Evans To which Is Added Evans' A Brief Account of Pennsylvania Together with Facsimiles of His Geographical, Historical, Political, Philosophical, and Mechanical Essays, Number I and II.* Philadelphia, 1939.

Grenier, Fernand, ed. *Papiers Contrecoeur et autres documents concernant le conflit anglo-français sur l'Ohio de 1745 à 1756.* Quebec, 1952.

Hoyt, Albert H. *Pepperrell Papers, with Sketches of Lieut.-Gen. the Honorable James St. Clair and Admiral Sir Charles Knowles, Bart.* Boston, 1874.

Kimball, Gertrude S., ed. *Correspondence of William Pitt When Secretary of State with Colonial Governors and Military and Naval Commanders in America.* 2 vols, New York, 1906.

Leymarie, A.-L., ed. 'Lettres de Mère Marie-André Duplessis de Sainte-Hélène', *Nova Francia*, 4 (1929).

Minutes of the Provincial Council of Pennsylvania, from the Organization to the Termination of the Proprietary Government (1683-1775) (Pennsylvania Colonial Records, vols 1-10). Philadelphia, 1851-2.

Northcliffe Collection, The. Ottawa, 1926.

O'Callaghan, E.B., ed. *Documents Relative to the Colonial History of the State of New York.* 11 vols, Albany, 1853-87.

Pargellis, Stanley M., ed. *Military Affairs in North America 1748-1765. Selected Documents from the Cumberland Papers in Windsor Castle.* New York and London, 1936.

Pease, Theodore Calvin, ed. *Anglo-French Boundary Disputes in the West, 1749-1763.* Springfield, Ill., 1936. Collections of the Illinois State Historical Library, t. 27.

Rapport de l'Archiviste de la province de Québec [*RAPQ*] *pour 1920-1921.* Quebec, 1921. 'Mémoire de M. Dupuy, intendant de la Nouvelle-France, sur les troubles arrivés à Québec en 1727 et en 1728, après la mort de Mgr de Saint-Vallier, évêque de Québec', 78-105. A. Fauteux, ed., 'Journal du siège de Québec du 10 mai au 18 septembre 1759', 137-241.

RAPQ 1922-1923. Quebec, 1923. Contains photographs of documents relating to the capitulation of Quebec.

RAPQ 1923-1924. Quebec, 1924. 'La Mission de M. de Bougainville en France en 1758-1759', 1-70. Amédée Gosselin, ed., 'Le Journal de M. de Bougainville', 202-393.

RAPQ 1924-1925. Quebec, 1925. 'Mémoire du Canada', 96-198. Claude de Bonnault, ed., 'Les Chambres de commerce de France et la cession du Canada', 199-228: thirty letters and other documents written between 8 July 1761 and 9 November 1762.

RAPQ 1930-1931. Quebec, 1931. 'Mémoire de Jean Talon à Colbert, 10 novembre 1670', 126.

RAPQ 1931-1932. Quebec, 1932. La Pause, 'Mémoire et observations sur mon voyage en Canada' and other documents, 1-125.

RAPQ 1933-1934. Quebec, 1934. 'Les Papiers La Pause', 65-231.

RAPQ 1935-1936. Quebec, 1936. 'Lettres et mémoires de l'abbé de L'Isle-Dieu', 275-410. Continued in *RAPQ 1936-1937,* 331-459, and *RAPQ 1937-1938,* 147-253.

RAPQ 1937-1938. Quebec, 1938. A. Fauteux, ed., 'Relation du siège de Québec (1759)', 1-20.

RAPQ 1938-1939. Quebec, 1939. Joseph Fournerie de Vezon, 'Evénements de la guerre en Canada depuis le 13 7bre 1759 jusqu'au 14 juillet 1760', 1-9.

RAPQ 1945-1946. Quebec, 1946. 'Les Lettres de Doreil', 1-171.

RAPQ 1951-1953. Quebec, 1953. Claude de Bonnault, ed., 'Les Archives d'Espagne et le Canada', 415-46.

Report Concerning the Canadian Archives for 1904. Ottawa, 1905. Appendix G: 'Bigot, Vergor et Villeray'.

Report Concerning the Canadian Archives for 1905. 2 vols, Ottawa, 1906. Appendix N (vol. 2) contains letters on Acadian affairs written by Bigot, La Jonquière, Boishébert, and others.

Report on the Public Archives for 1929. Ottawa, 1930. Appendix A: 'La Correspondence de Montcalm'.

Roy, P.-G., ed. *Inventaire des papiers de Léry conservés aux archives de la province de Québec.* 3 vols, Quebec, 1939-40. Transcripts of documents rather than an inventory.

Sargent, Winthrop. *The History of an Expedition Against Fort Du Quesne in 1755 Under Major-General Edward Braddock, Generalissimo of H.B.M. Forces in America.* Philadelphia, 1855.

Shortt, Adam, ed. *Documents relating to Canadian Currency, Exchange and Finance during the French Period.* 2 vols, Ottawa, 1925-6.

Shortt, Adam, and Doughty, Arthur G., eds. *Documents relating to the Constitutional History of Canada, 1759-1791.* 2 vols, Ottawa, 1918.

Smith, William H. 'The Pelham Papers—Loss of Oswego', *Papers of the American Historical Society,* 4 (Part 4).

Stevens, S.K., Kent, D.H., and Leonard, A.L., eds. *The Papers of Henry Bouquet. The Forbes Expedition.* Vol. 2, Harrisburg, 1951.

Stewart, Irene, ed. *Letters of General John Forbes relating to the Expedition against Fort Duquesne in 1758.* Pittsburgh, 1927.

Sullivan, James, ed. *The Papers of Sir William Johnson.* 3 vols, Albany, 1921-2.

Têtu, Henri, ed. 'M. Jean-Félix Récher, curé de Québec, et son journal, 1757-1760', *Bulletin des recherches historiques,* 9 (1903):97-122, 129-47, 161-74, 289-307, 321-46, 353-73.

V. SPECIAL STUDIES

A complete bibliography of the War of the Conquest would fill a large volume. With the exception of a few general works cited in the text, the following list is limited to specialized studies.

Adair, E.R. 'The Military Reputation of Major-General James Wolfe', The Canadian Historical Association *Report,* 1936 (Toronto, 1936), 7-31.

Alden, John Richard. *General Gage in America.* Baton Rouge, 1948.

Arles, Henri d', ed. *Acadie: reconstitution d'un chapitre perdu de l'histoire d' Amérique, par Edouard Richard.* 3 vols, Quebec and Boston, 1916-21.

Baker-Crothers, Hayes. *Virginia and the French and Indian War.* Chicago, [1928].

Barnes, Viola. *The Dominion of New England: A Study in British Colonial Policy.* New Haven, 1923.

Barrow, John. *The Life of George Lord Anson, Admiral of the Fleet; Vice-Admiral of Great Britain; and First Lord Commissioner of the Admiralty, previous to, and during, the Seven Years' War.* London, 1839.

Baxter, W.T. *The House of Hancock.* Cambridge, Mass., 1945.

Beer, George Louis. *British Colonial Policy, 1754-1765.* New York, 1922.

Bonnault, Claude de. *Histoire du Canada français.* Paris, 1950.

Brebner, John B. *New England's Outpost: Acadia before the Conquest of Canada.* New York, 1927.

Burt, Alfred L. *A Short History of Canada for Americans.* Minneapolis, 1944.

Butterfield, Herbert. *The Origins of Modern Science.* London, 1950.

Casgrain, Henri-Raymond. *Montcalm et Lévis.* Tours, 1898.

Chapais, Thomas. *Le Marquis de Montcalm (1712-1759).* Quebec, 1911.

Chapman, T.J. *The French in the Allegheny Valley.* Cleveland, 1887.

Charteris, Evan. *William Augustus Duke of Cumberland and the Seven Years' War.* London, 1925.

Corbett, Julian S. *England in the Seven Years' War. A Study in Combined Strategy.* 2 vols, London, 1907.

Dorfman, Joseph. *The Economic Mind in American Civilization, 1606-1865.* 2 vols, New York, 1946.

Duchêne, A. *La Politique coloniale de la France; le ministère de la Marine depuis Richelieu.* Paris, 1928.

Earle, E.M., Craig, G.A., and Gilbert, F., eds. *Makers of Modern Strategy. Military Thought from Machiavelli to Hitler.* Princeton, 1943. Chapter III, section 1 (49-74): 'Frederick the Great, Guibert, Bülow; from Dynastic to National War', by R.R. Palmer.

Faulkner, Harold U. *American Economic History.* New York and London, 1943.

Fauteux, Aegidius. *Les Chevaliers de Saint-Louis en Canada.* Montreal, 1940.

Frégault, Guy. *La Civilisation de la Nouvelle-France.* Montreal, 1944.

_____*François Bigot, administrateur français.* 2 vols, Montreal, 1948.

_____*Le Grand Marquis: Pierre de Rigaud de Vaudreuil et la Louisiane.* Montreal, 1952.

_____*La Société canadienne sous le régime français.* Ottawa, 1954.

Gérin, Léon. *Aux sources de notre histoire.* Montreal, 1946.

Gipson, Lawrence Henry. *The British Empire before the American Revolution.*
Vol. 4. *Zones of International Friction: North America, South of the Great Lakes Region, 1748-1754.* New York, 1939.
Vol. 5. *Zones of International Friction: The Great Lakes Frontier, Canada, the West Indies, India, 1748-1754.* New York, 1942.
Vol. 6. *The Great War for the Empire: The Years of Defeat, 1754-1757.* New York, 1946.
Vol. 7. *The Great War for the Empire: The Victorious Years, 1758-1760.* New York, 1949.
Vol. 8. *The Great War for the Empire: The Culmination, 1760-1763.* New York, 1954.

Graham, Gerald S. *Empire of the North Atlantic. The Maritime Struggle for North America.* Toronto, 1950.

_____*Canada: A Short History.* London, 1950.

Harrington, Virginia. *The New York Merchant on the Eve of the Revolution.* New York, 1935.

Harvey, D.C. *The French Régime in Prince Edward Island.* New Haven, 1926.

Hazard, Paul. *La Crise de la conscience européenne: 1680-1715.* 3 vols, Paris, 1934-5.

Hotblack, Kate. *Chatham's Colonial Policy.* London, 1917.

[Kerallain, René de.] *Les Français au Canada: la jeunesse de Bougainville et la guerre de Sept ans.* Paris, 1896.

Koontz, Louis K. *The Virginia Frontier, 1754-1763.* Baltimore, 1925.

Lacour-Gayet, G. *La Marine militaire de la France sous le règne de Louis XV.* Paris, 1910.

Lauvrière, Emile. *La Tragédie d'un peuple: Histoire du peuple acadien de ses origines à nos jours.* 2 vols, Paris, 1924.

Lichtenberger, André. *Montcalm et la tragédie canadienne.* Paris, 1934.

Lunn, Jean. 'The Illegal Fur Trade out of New France, 1713-1760', Canadian Historical Association *Report,* 1939 (Toronto, 1939), 61-76.

McCormac, Eugene I. *Colonial Opposition to Imperial Authority during the French and Indian War.* Berkeley, 1911.

McLennan, J.S. *Louisbourg from its Foundation to its Fall.* London, 1918.

Mahan, A.T. *The Influence of Sea Power upon History 1660-1783.* Boston, 1894.

Martin, Félix. *Le Marquis de Montcalm et les dernières années de la colonie française au Canada.* Paris, 1888.

Miller, John C. *Origins of the American Revolution.* Boston, 1943.

Muret, Pierre. *La Prépondérance anglaise 1715-1763.* Paris, 1942.

Osgood, Herbert L. *The American Colonies in the Eighteenth Century.* 4 vols, New York, 1924.

Pargellis, Stanley M. *Lord Loudoun in North America.* New Haven and London, 1933.

Parkman, Francis. *The Old Régime in Canada.* Boston, 1889.

_____*Montcalm and Wolfe.* 2 vols, Boston, 1888.

Pound, A., and Day, R.E. *Johnson of the Mohawks. A Biography of Sir William Johnson, Irish Immigrant, Mohawk War Chief, American Soldier, Empire Builder.* New York, 1930.

Robitaille, Georges. *Washington et Jumonville, étude critique*. Montreal, 1933.

———*Montcalm et ses historiens, étude critique*. Montreal, 1936.

Roy, J.-J.-E. *Bougainville*. Tours, 1883.

Roy, Pierre-Georges. *La Ville de Québec sous le régime français*. 2 vols, Quebec, 1930.

———*Bigot et sa bande et l'Affaire du Canada*, Lévis, 1950. See also *Revue d'histoire de l'Amérique française*, 3 (1949-50): 609-13.

Ruville, Albert von. *William Pitt, Earl of Chatham*. 3 vols, London, 1907.

Savelle, Max. *The Diplomatic History of the Canadian Boundary 1749-1763*. New Haven, 1940.

Selley, W.T. *England in the Eighteenth Century*. London, 1949.

Severance, Frank H. *An Old Frontier of New France. The Niagara Region and Adjacent Lakes under French Control*. 2 vols, New York, 1917.

Seymour, F.W. *Lords of the Valley: Sir William Johnson and His Mohawk Brothers*. New York and London, 1930.

Stanley, George F.G. *Canada's Soldiers 1604-1954*. Toronto, 1954.

Tocqueville, Alexis de. *Histoire philosophique du règne de Louis XV*. 2 vols, Paris, 1846.

Townshend, C.V.F. *The Military Life of Field-Marshall George First Marquess Townshend, 1724-1807*. London, 1901.

Trudel, Marcel. *Le Séminaire de Québec sous le régime militaire, 1759-1764*. Quebec, 1954.

Tunstall, Brian. *William Pitt Earl of Chatham*. London, 1938.

Waddington, Richard. *La Guerre de Sept ans. Histoire diplomatique et militaire*. 5 vols, Paris, 1899-1914.

Warburton, George. *The Conquest of Canada*. London, 1857.

Webster, John C. *The Forts of Chignecto. A Study of the Eighteenth Century Conflict between France and Great Britain in Acadia*. Sackville, 1930.

Williamson, James A. *A Short History of British Expansion*. 2 vols, London, 1951. Vol. 1: *The Old Colonial Empire*.

Willson, Beckles. *The Life and Letters of James Wolfe*. New York, 1909.

Wood, George A. *William Shirley, Governor of Massachusetts, 1741-1756*. New York, 1920.

Wright, R. *The Life of Major General James Wolfe*. London, 1864.

Wrong, George M. *The Fall of Canada. A Chapter in the History of the Seven Years' War*. Oxford, 1914.

VI. ARTICLES IN PERIODICALS

Andrews, C.M. 'Anglo-French Commercial Rivalry, 1700-1750. The Western Phase', *American Historical Review*, 20 (1914-15):539-56, 761-80.

[Anonyme], 'A propos de M. Rigaud de Vaudreuil,' *Bulletin des recherches historiques*, 45 (1939):53-60.

———'Les Victimes du *Léopard*', ibid., 35 (1929): 615-20.

Bonnault, Claude de. 'Les Français de l'Ohio. Un drame dans la Prairie: l'affaire Jumonville', *Revue d'histoire de l'Amérique française*, 1 (1947-8):501-18.

_____'Le Canada et la conclusion du pacte de famille de 1761', ibid., 7 (1953-4): 341-55.

Clark, Dan E. 'News and Opinions Concerning America in English Newspapers, 1754-1763', The Pacific Historical Review, 10 (1941):75-82.

Clarke, Mary P. 'The Board of Trade at Work', American Historical Review, 17 (1911-12):15-43.

Dailey, W.N.P. 'Sir William Johnson, Baronet', The Chronicles of Oklahoma, 22 (1944):164-76.

Frégault, Guy. 'La Guerre de Sept ans et la civilisation canadienne', Revue d'histoire de l'Amérique française, 7 (1953-4):183-206.

Giddens, Paul H. 'The French and Indian War in Maryland 1753 to 1756', Maryland Historical Magazine, 30 (1935):281-310.

Gipson, Lawrence Henry. 'Connecticut Taxation and Parliamentary Aid', American Historical Review, 36 (1931):721-39.

_____'A French Project for Victory Short of a Declaration of War, 1755', Canadian Historical Review, 26 (1945):361-71.

Grant, W.L. 'Canada versus Guadeloupe. An Episode of the Seven Years' War', American Historical Review, 17 (1912):735-43.

Greene, E.B. 'New York and the Old Empire', The Quarterly Journal of the New York State Historical Association, 8 (1926):121-32.

Groulx, Lionel. 'D'une transmigration des Canadiens en Louisiane vers 1760', Revue d'histoire de l'Amérique française, 8 (1954-5):97-125.

Hall, Hubert. 'Chatham's Colonial Policy', American Historical Review, 5 (1899-1900):659-75.

Hitsman, J. Mackay. 'The Assault Landing at Louisbourg, 1758', Canadian Historical Review, 35 (1954):314-30.

James, Alfred P. 'Fort Ligonier. Additional Light from Unpublished Documents', Western Pennsylvania Historical Magazine, 17 (1934):259-85.

_____'The Nest of Robbers', ibid., 21 (1938):165-78.

Léonard, Emile-G. 'La Question sociale dans l'armée française au xviiie siècle', Annales: Economies, Sociétés, Civilisations, 3 (1948):135-49.

Pares, Richard. 'American versus Continental Warfare, 1739-1763', The English Historical Review, 51 (1936):429-65.

Pargellis, Stanley M. 'Braddock's Defeat', American Historical Review, 41 (1936): 253-69.

Sachs, William S. 'Agricultural Conditions in the Northern Colonies before the Revolution', The Journal of Economic History, 13 (1953):274-90.

Schlebecker, John. 'Braddock's Defeat', The Ohio State Archaeological and Historical Quarterly, 58 (1949):171-84.

Trudel, Marcel. 'L'Affaire Jumonville', Revue d'histoire de l'Amérique française, 6 (1952-3):331-73.

Index